The Learned and Lived Law

Legal History Library

VOLUME 70

The titles published in this series are listed at *brill.com/lhl*

Charles Donahue, 1979
PHOTOGRAPHED BY JOHN CHAPIN

The Learned and Lived Law

Essays in Honor of Charles Donahue

Edited by

Elizabeth Papp Kamali, Saskia Lettmaier and Nikitas E. Hatzimihail

BRILL | NIJHOFF

LEIDEN | BOSTON

Cover illustration: Harvard Law School Library MS 12, Magna Carta cum statutis, c. 1325. A marginal drawing of a widow illustrates the first chapter of the Statute of Merton (1235), concerning dower.

Library of Congress Cataloging-in-Publication Data

Names: Donahue, Charles, Jr., 1941- honouree. | Kamali, Elizabeth Papp, 1975- editor. | Lettmaier, Saskia, editor. | Hatzimihail, Nikitas E., editor.
Title: The learned and lived law : essays in honor of Charles Donahue / edited by Elizabeth Papp Kamali, Saskia Lettmaier, and Nikitas E. Hatzimihail.
Description: Leiden ; Boston : Brill/Nijhoff, 2025. | Series: Legal history library; vol.70 | Includes bibliographical references and index.
Identifiers: LCCN 2024034530 (print) | LCCN 2024034531 (ebook) | ISBN 9789004707948 (hardback) | ISBN 9789004710696 (ebook)
Subjects: LCSH: Roman law. | Law, Medieval. | Conflict of laws (Roman law) | Property (Roman law) | Marriage (Roman law) | Donahue, Charles, Jr., 1941-
Classification: LCC KJA147 L439 2025 (print) | LCC KJA147 (ebook) | DDC 340.5/4–dc23/eng/20240731
LC record available at https://lccn.loc.gov/2024034530
LC ebook record available at https://lccn.loc.gov/2024034531

Typeface for the Latin, Greek, and Cyrillic scripts: "Brill". See and download: brill.com/brill-typeface.

ISSN 1874-1793
ISBN 978-90-04-70794-8 (hardback)
ISBN 978-90-04-71069-6 (e-book)
DOI 10.1163/9789004710696

This book is printed on acid-free paper and produced in a sustainable manner.

Contents

List of Figures and Tables XI
Notes on Contributors XIII

Introduction 1
Elizabeth Papp Kamali and Saskia Lettmaier

PART 1
Roman Law

1 Towards a Taxonomy of Witnesses in Roman Law 21
James R. Townshend

2 "*Si Bononiensis*": Glossators and the Conflict of Laws 63
Nikitas E. Hatzimihail

3 Roman Property, Corporate Personhood, and the Politics of Natural Law in Medieval and Early Renaissance Italy: Venice, Baldus, and the *res communes omnium* 87
Charles Bartlett

4 Abandonment, *animus* and *animalia ferae naturae* in Hugo Grotius' *De iure belli ac pacis* 116
Daniel Jacobs

5 "For the Sake of Mental Health and Mutual Peace": The *Transactio*-Agreement in Early Modern Law and Theology 140
Wim Decock

PART 2
Women, Marriage, and the Law

6 Consent in Medieval English Marriage and Misconduct 161
Elizabeth Papp Kamali

7 Written Law and Practice: Realities for Women in Bas Languedoc in the Eleventh and Twelfth Centuries 192
Elizabeth Haluska-Rausch

8 Sex with Nuns in Medieval France 215
Sara McDougall

9 *Oikos* and *Oikonomika:* The Early Modern Family as a Matrix of Modern Economics 241
John Witte Jr.

10 Legal and Factual Uncertainty in a Seventeenth-Century French Marriage Case 261
Saskia Lettmaier

11 Marriage Law between East and West: Charles Maigrot's *Dissertatio de Matrimonio Sinarum* 283
Stuart M. McManus

PART 3
Medieval and Early Modern Law

12 Getting Ahead in a Twelfth-Century City: The Ambitious Monks of Saint-Clément, Metz 311
Samantha Kahn Herrick

13 The Papal Constitution *Execrabilis* (1317) and Clerical Justices in the English Royal Courts 334
Ryan Rowberry

14 Dangerous Dreams: *Le Songe du Vergier* and the Expulsion of Jews from Fourteenth-Century France 370
Rowan Dorin

15 Suicide in Early Modern Italy 394
Elizabeth W. Mellyn

16 The "Desire of Deeds": On Cherishing Medieval English Charters 424
Carol Symes

PART 4
American Legal History

17 Lawyers and Their Book Collections: Notes from the Eighteenth Century 451
Sally E. Hadden

18 The American Importation of the Comparative Accusatorial/Inquisitorial Divide: Francis Lieber's Failed Transplant and Its Early Twentieth-Century Resurgence 475
Amalia D. Kessler

PART 5
Literature and Legal Theory

19 Faust: Goethe's Guide to Legal Progress 501
Anton Chaevitch

20 Wesley Hohfeld's Modernist Imagination 524
Bharath Palle

APPENDIX
Reflections from Former Students

Appendix 1 When Giants Roamed: A Reflection 547
Thomas S. Burns
Appendix 2 *De magistro eruditissimo et beneficentissimo*: A Reflection 551
Mary Elizabeth Basile Chopas
Appendix 3 The Teachings of Charles Donahue on the Middle Ages from the Perspective of a Student of Mexican Legal History: A Reflection 553
William Suárez-Potts
Appendix 4 Chi Squares, Chant, and Charlie: A Reflection 558
Claire Valente

Bibliography 560
Index 575

Figures and Tables

Figures

16.1a Deposition by Robert Spurway of Tiverton (Devon), testifying to the "desire of deeds," HSC Deeds 117. 425

16.1b–16.1c Dorsal inscription (and detail) by Thomas Worth the younger: "Herein so sign[ifi]e that T Worthe wold not [seal to] a partition for any thing without a deliverance of all deeds of his owne descent." 428

16.2a–16.2b Manumission of Robert Hobekyn (measuring 7.5 × 18 cm.), dated to the 55th year of Henry IV (1270–1271), HSC deeds 8. 430

16.3 Reconstructed folding of the manumission (Figure 16.2), showing its actual size. 431

16.4a–16.4b Undated *inspeximus* of Henry Abbe, made in the 18th year of Edward I (1289–1290), testifying to an earlier undated charter made by his grandfather, William le Abbe, granting a furlong of land to Robert de Hobekyn, HSC Deeds 10. The dark stains, similar to those marking the original manumission (Figure 16.2), may indicate that they were kept together. 432

16.5 Letters patent (measuring 37 × 44 cm.) to John Norys and others, with the great seal of Henry IV (12 cm. circumference); the "H" of the king's name is left unilluminated, HSC Deeds 744. 439

16.6a–16.6b "This charter is the best charter of all the other charters in the monastery"—note (detail) appended to a charter from Dunster Priory (Somerset), HSC Deeds 124. 440

16.7a–16.7b "I wille that Pegg & Robert Barker make / a lauful astate to John Wilne & Margaret his | wife of Þe place & to þe here[s] of Marg[ar]et," HSC deeds 439. 441

16.8 Certificate by Sir John Brode, curate of Minster (Cornwall), testifying that the people of Wooston told "me with oon vois" that they had "never herd it callid or knowen in court or out of court by the name of Wolneston a name feyned & new altered as ferre as any of ham can remember," HSC Deeds 118. Compare the hand to that of the deposition in Figure 16.1. 442

16.9 Letter from Charles Worth to John Worth III, dated March 26, 1800, HSC Deeds 64. The recipient has endorsed this last "deed" in the Worth family archive, "my poor uncle Charles's last letter." 444

Tables

13.1 Patrons and benefices of Gilbert Rothbury. 349
13.2 Patrons and benefices of Hervey de Stanton. 354
13.3 Patrons and benefices of John Bacun. 358

Notes on Contributors

Charles Bartlett
received his Ph.D. in Ancient History from Harvard University and held postdoctoral positions at Duke University and Harvard before joining the faculty at the University of Miami. Professor Donahue was an advisor of his dissertation, which examined the development of Roman property law in antiquity; he undertook this study in order to better appreciate the nuances of Roman law's later history. His research focuses on the formation of political, legal, and economic institutions and ideas, the history of the corporation, and the importance of Roman law to the history of political economy.

Anton Chaevitch
is an associate at Three Crowns. He holds a Ph.D. from Harvard University in Germanic Languages and Literatures and a J.D. from Columbia Law School. His research focuses on international arbitration, legal progress, and interactions between law and literature.

Wim Decock
is Professor of Roman law, legal history and comparative law at the Universities of Louvain-la-Neuve and Liège in Belgium. His research concentrates on the interconnection between juridical, economic and religious thought in the European legal tradition, with a focus on the early modern period. In 2011 he was a Visiting Researcher at the Harvard Law School, which offered him the chance to take classes with Charlie Donahue.

Rowan Dorin
is Associate Professor of History at Stanford University, where his teaching and research focus on the history of Europe and the Mediterranean in the Middle Ages. As a sophomore at Harvard College, he performed dismally on the final exam for Charlie Donahue's Continental legal history course, but Charlie encouraged him to keep studying legal history nonetheless. In addition to a recent monograph, *No Return: Jews, Christian Usurers, and the Spread of Mass Expulsion in Medieval Europe* (2023), Dorin has published articles on Jewish-Christian relations, canon law, digital humanities, and the circulation of people, goods, and manuscripts in the medieval world.

Sally E. Hadden
received her Ph.D. from Harvard University and J.D. from Harvard Law School. She has published *Slave Patrols: Law and Violence in Virginia and the Carolinas* (2001), *Signposts: New Directions in Southern Legal History* (2013, with Patricia Minter) and *A Companion to American Legal History* (2013, with Alfred Brophy). Hadden's research focuses upon eighteenth-century legal history. She is currently finishing a study of lawyers in colonial America, has commenced a book on the early Supreme Court (with Maeva Marcus), and leads a digitization project of early Massachusetts court records on behalf of the Ames Foundation. She studied Roman law and medieval English legal history with Charlie and works with him on Ames Foundation projects. Hadden is a professor in the Western Michigan University Department of History.

Elizabeth Haluska-Rausch
is an independent scholar in Austin, Texas, previously serving as Head of Special Collections for Tarlton Law Library, University of Texas School of Law and Curator of Special Collections, Bridwell Library, Southern Methodist University. She is the author of several articles, book chapters, and exhibition catalogues including "Transformations in the Powers of Wives and Widows in Medieval Montpellier, 985–1213," *The Experience of Power in Medieval Europe 900–1300* (2005); and *The Elizabeth Perkins Prothro Bible Collection at Bridwell Library, 1996–2006* (2006). Professor Donahue served as the second reader on her dissertation in the Department of History, Harvard University, 1998.

Nikitas E. Hatzimihail
is Professor of Private Law, Comparative Law, and Legal History at the University of Cyprus. He studied law at Athens and Harvard and previously worked at Oklahoma and U.L.B. Charlie was his doctoral (S.J.D.) co-supervisor. His dissertation obtained the Addison-Brown commencement prize and eventually gave birth to a lengthy book, *Preclassical Conflict of Laws* (Cambridge University Press, 2021). Much of the time lapse was caused by his undertaking significant administrative responsibilities in a new law school, against Charlie's better advice. In addition to the history of private international law and commercial law, Hatzimihail has published widely (including over a dozen books authored or edited) on matters of contract and commercial law, civil litigation, and private international law doctrine.

Samantha Kahn Herrick
is Associate Professor of History at Syracuse University. Her research focuses on medieval hagiography. She is the author of *Imagining the Sacred*

Past: Hagiography and Power in Early Normandy (2007) and edited *Hagiography and the History of Latin Christendom, 500–1500* (2020). She is currently writing a book examining why many medieval communities envisaged their founding bishops as disciples of Jesus and the Apostles, and how these legends evolved, circulated, and intertwined from about 750–1350. She has held fellowships at the Institute for Research in the Humanities at the University of Wisconsin, Madison, and the Institute for Advanced Study in Princeton. As a member of her dissertation committee, Charlie offered generous and invaluable guidance and support. She also had the privilege and fun of being his Teaching Fellow.

Daniel Jacobs
received his Ph.D. in History from Harvard University in May 2023, with a dissertation on private property and the idea of *ius* in late medieval law and theology. As a graduate student, he studied medieval law in lectures and seminars with Charlie Donahue, and served as a Teaching Fellow for Professor Donahue in several courses. He has a B.A. in Classical Studies from the University of Chicago and an MPhil in Political Thought and Intellectual History from the University of Cambridge.

Elizabeth Papp Kamali
is the Austin Wakeman Scott Professor of Law at Harvard Law School, where she teaches criminal law and English legal history. Her research focuses on the medieval English common law and the history of felony law, with a particular interest in the early criminal trial jury. She took classes with Charlie as a freshman and sophomore at Harvard College; this inspired her to major in History and, with Charlie's guidance and encouragement, to write a senior thesis using Harvard's collection of manor court rolls. She took further coursework with Charlie as a law student, including first-year Property and seminars in legal history, and Charlie co-chaired (with Tom Green) her dissertation committee.

Amalia D. Kessler
is the Lewis Talbot and Nadine Hearn Shelton Professor of International Legal Studies at Stanford Law School. Her research explores law, markets, and dispute resolution in France and the United States. Her current book project is "Arbitration and the Quest for Modern American Democracy: Struggles over Industrialization, Immigration, and State-Building, 1900–1950" (under contract, Yale University Press). She is the author of *Inventing American Exceptionalism: The Origins of American Adversarial Legal Culture, 1800–1877* (2017) and *A Revolution in Commerce: The Parisian Merchant Court and the Rise of Commercial Society in Eighteenth-Century France* (2007). Charlie offered her

invaluable guidance and support as she was deciding whether to pursue both law and history and began her academic career.

Saskia Lettmaier
is a jurist trained in Anglo-American and German law. She holds two German law degrees as well as a B.A. degree in jurisprudence from Oxford University and LL.M. and S.J.D. degrees from Harvard Law School. She is currently a professor of Private Law and Global Legal History with a focus on the Common Law at the University of Hamburg (Germany) and also serves as a judge at the Higher Regional Court of Schleswig. She is the author of *Broken Engagements: The Action for Breach of Promise of Marriage and the Feminine Ideal, 1800–1940* (Oxford, 2010) as well as *Spouses, Church, and State: Marriage Law in England and Protestant Germany from the Reformation until the Close of the Nineteenth Century* (Mohr Siebeck, forthcoming). Charlie was the supervisor of both her LL.M. paper and her S.J.D. thesis.

Sara McDougall
is Professor of History at John Jay College of the City University of New York and on the faculty of the CUNY Graduate Center. She is the author of two books and several articles on topics related to gender, justice, family, and crime in the Middle Ages. She is also a frequent co-editor of several collections including the first of Charlie's festschrifts. She is currently writing a biography of a priest's mistress and assault survivor based on trial records from late medieval Dijon. Recent fellowships and visiting professorships include the Cullman Center for Scholars and Writers of the New York Public Library, Paris II Panthéon-Assas, Oxford University, and the University of Michigan Institute for the Humanities. She met Charlie while working on her dissertation and never dreamed she'd be so lucky as to have Charlie as co-author as well as friend and mentor.

Stuart M. McManus
received his Ph.D. from Harvard University, where he studied civil law with Charles Donahue with whom he also co-authored a philological note on "barbarian" marriage law. McManus is currently an Associate Professor in the Department of History at the Chinese University of Hong Kong and an affiliated scholar of the Center for Comparative and Transnational Law. He is a humanist and legal historian working on law, slavery and empire in world history from a global and multi-ethnic perspective. He also has interests in the history of classical scholarship and Chinese humanities. He is the author of *Empire of Eloquence* (2021), on the global history of renaissance humanism (based on primary research in 13 countries in Latin America, Europe and Asia)

and is currently finishing a book on the global history of slave law. In 2024, he received the Dan David Prize (the largest historical prize in the world).

Elizabeth W. Mellyn
is an Associate Professor of History at the University of New Hampshire where she teaches a range of courses in early modern European history as well as the global history of medicine, disease, and mental illness. Her publications include *Mad Tuscans and their Families: A History of Mental Disorder in Early Modern Italy* (2014). She is currently at work on a history of Santa Dorotea, Florence's first hospital devoted to the care of the severely mentally ill, and co-editing the Renaissance volume in the Bloomsbury Cultural History of Madness series (2025).

Bharath Palle
is a law clerk at Patterson Belknap LLP. He completed his doctorate in legal history under Charlie's supervision at Harvard Law School in 2022. His research interests are at the intersection of intellectual history, analytic legal philosophy, and critical theory. He worked as a litigator for several years in Chennai, India, before pursuing his graduate studies. He is presently completing a book manuscript tentatively titled, *The Struggle for a Modern Legal Science*, which examines the intellectual roots of modern property theory in the United States.

Ryan Rowberry
is the Janice C. Griffith Professor of Law at the Georgia State University College of Law in Atlanta, Georgia, USA. His research includes examining legal issues involving cultural and historic resources as well as investigating the lives of royal justices in medieval England. He took multiple legal history classes from Charlie at Harvard Law School, and under Charlie's supervision conducted extensive archival work at the UK National Archives on medieval justices during the reign of Edward I. When teaching English Legal History at GSU Law, he continues to imitate Charlie by often repeating the phrase, 'jiggery-pokery' when relevant.

Carol Symes
is a Professor of History at the University of Illinois, Urbana-Champaign. While pursuing the Ph.D. at Harvard in the 1990s, she was the Curator of Medieval Deeds and Charters in the Law Library's Historical and Special Collections and, more importantly, a grateful student of Charlie Donahue. Her first book, *A Common Stage: Theatre and Public Life in Medieval Arras*, was honored with numerous prizes and catalyzed the field of medieval media studies. She has

also published widely on the medieval transmission of ancient dramatic texts; the role of medievalism in modern nationalist projects and historiographies; and the material, embodied, and negotiated processes of writing across an array of medieval genres. Since 2014, she has been the founding executive editor of *The Medieval Globe*, the first academic journal to promote and model methods for studying the interconnectivity of the medieval world.

James R. Townshend
is an Assistant Professor in the Department of Classical Studies at Loyola University Chicago. He received his undergraduate degrees in Classical Studies and Law from the University of Auckland in New Zealand before moving to Harvard to complete a Ph.D. in Classical Philology. It was during that time that he worked with Professor Donahue on a year-long module on Roman Law. His teaching and research embrace Greek and Roman languages and literature, including their reception, and classical Roman Law.

John Witte
is Woodruff University Professor, McDonald Distinguished Professor, and Director of the Center for the Study of Law and Religion at Emory University. A specialist in legal history, human rights, religious freedom, marriage law, and law and religion, he has published 350 articles, 18 journal symposia, and 45 books. Recent book titles include *The Western Case for Monogamy over Polygamy* (Cambridge, 2018), *Church, State, and Family* (Cambridge, 2019); *Faith, Freedom, and Family* (Mohr Siebeck, 2021); *The Blessings of Liberty* (Cambridge, 2021); and *Religion and the American Constitutional Experiment*, 5th ed. (Oxford, 2022).

Introduction

Elizabeth Papp Kamali and Saskia Lettmaier

This Festschrift was first conceived as a gift from Charles Donahue's students to mark the occasion of his 80th birthday, which had the misfortune of falling during a global pandemic that shuttered libraries and consequently slowed the progress of the various authors who have, nonetheless, persevered in seeing through their tributes to a beloved professor and mentor. If all goes well, the volume will mark the third anniversary of Charlie's 80th birthday.

During his decades as a law professor at the University of Michigan Law School and the Harvard Law School, Charlie has enriched the lives of countless law students, graduate students, and undergraduates, many of whom had their first taste of law at the bountiful table of Charlie's classes on the legal and constitutional history of England and Continental Europe. All students were always welcome to enroll, regardless of their prior exposure to law. For some, including the two of us, a class with Charlie illuminated—in the usual sense of that term and in the manuscript tradition of supplementing text with gold leaf and rubrication—a future path of study and even a career. Charlie imparts to his students a keen understanding of legal history that is incomplete without the adornment of linguistic, cultural, economic, theological, and other historical contexts, which are never left to the margins, like the glosses of a canon law manuscript, but interwoven with law in order to make sense of the whole. As may be appropriate for a Festschrift conceived in the age of COVID-19, one might say that each of the contributors to this volume caught the proverbial plague—namely, a love for legal history—in Charlie's classroom, sometimes while contemplating the impact of the Black Death on the unfolding of fourteenth-century law; they found Charlie's passion for the historical study of law to be, in fact, infectious. They discovered a vocation and a methodological path forward, one reinforced by close readings of primary source texts. What did the author of Æthelberht's Code (c. 603) mean when referring to the *friwif locbore*—was it about keys or coiffure? Why did the law of covenant become a dead end, making way for the ascendancy of trespass? What might we learn from the decorated Gothic style of cathedral architecture while trying to make sense of fourteenth-century statute-making? And was Christopher Robin right in the end when he declared, "King John was not a good man—he

 | DOI:10.1163/9789004710696_002

had his little ways"?[1] The literary often found its way into Charlie's lectures, from the account of the Battle of Brunanburh (937) recorded by the Anglo-Saxon chronicler, to Sellar and Yeatman's *1066 and All That* (1930). Elizabeth even recalls that Charlie's first-year property exam in 2004 contained an issue spotter—dealing with matters ranging from copyright to cave ownership—that opened with Samuel Taylor Coleridge's poem *Kubla Khan*. Like the subject of that poem, we might say that Charlie's students "on honey-dew hath fed / And drunk the milk of Paradise."[2] (Although Charlie would no doubt resist such a florid characterization of the content of his teaching.)

It is hard to acknowledge Charles Donahue's contribution to the fields of English and Continental European legal history without appearing to overuse the superlative. It is also hard not to fill many pages. In this introduction, we will therefore limit ourselves to describing a few key components of his contribution. Charlie greatly enlarged and enhanced the concerns and methods of legal historiography and the stock of legal-historical knowledge that we have today, particularly regarding the medieval period. Having received his legal education at Yale, a stronghold of legal realism both then and now, Charlie has always been less interested in abstract statements of what the law supposedly is than in how the law is applied to real-life situations. And he was convinced that in order to find out about the latter, one had to study actual cases.[3] Hence, from the beginning of his career, Charlie conducted pioneering archival research on medieval court records, in particular the records of the ecclesiastical courts. And his labor was not limited to excavation. What he did with his hard-won sources was equally innovative.

Charlie's method as a legal historian—whether applied to a medieval court record or to any other kind of primary source—combines careful close reading of the original text or texts with deep contextualization, telling comparison, and intelligent interpretation. Watching him at each of these steps is a master class in legal historiography. Saskia remembers that when she was his doctoral student, Charlie once asked her to read and write up a small passage on Pufendorf's *Ius Naturae*. She duly did. In response, Charlie prepared his

1 This quote from A. A. Milne's *Winnie the Pooh* (first pub. London: Methuen, 1926) featured in Charlie's classroom lecture on Magna Carta (on file with author).

2 From "Kubla Khan," in *The Poetical Works of S. T. Coleridge*, vol. 1 (London: W. Pickering, 1835), 269.

3 Charles Donahue Jr., "*Methodus ad facilem historiarum cognitionem:* Autobiographical and Methodological Reflections," in *Texts and Contexts in Legal History: Essays in Honor of Charles Donahue*, ed. John Witte Jr., Sara McDougall, and Anna di Robilant (Berkeley: The Robbins Collection, 2016), 10.

own (four-page, single spaced) reaction paper on the same text for her benefit, which left her amazed at the wealth of details, assumptions, and allusions that she had missed and that he had extracted from this small text. When it comes to contextualizing his legal sources, Charlie casts the net very wide, taking into account all elements—legal-doctrinal, intellectual, economic, political, religious, social, even individual human factors—that might elucidate what seems puzzling about a document, event, or development. In figuring out which of these contextual elements are likely to have mattered or mattered the most, Charlie often makes shrewdly framed synchronic comparisons between legal systems that present "remarkable similiarities" in their social, economic, and governmental contexts, arguing that where "much is the same, … it is easier to identify those differences that are likely to have made a difference."[4] A great deal of his historical work is comparative in the most exacting sense of that term, a juxtaposition of two or more legal systems in all of their aspects—their rules and doctrines, the history in which these rules and doctrines are embedded, and their institutional and social context. Finally, unlike many historians who do not venture beyond what can be proven strictly by the historical evidence (which is often not much, given that historical sources have a tendency to be incomplete, and frustratingly so), Charlie does not shy away from offering carefully argued hypotheses that might fill in the gaps or explain the inconsistencies that he has uncovered in his sources. Nor is he afraid to combine his scrupulously faithful readings of primary sources with speculative contextual pondering on great, even fundamental questions. His list of publications includes titles like "What Difference Does It Make If Marriage Is a Sacrament? An Historical Approach," "English and French Marriage Cases: Might the Differences Be Explained by Differences in the Property Systems?" and "What Causes Fundamental Legal Ideas?"[5]

Over the years, Charlie has thus amassed a remarkable body of legal-historical scholarship (comprising ten freestanding publications and more than one hundred articles and book contributions with a wide geographical,

4 Charles Donahue Jr., "Comparative Legal History in North America," *Tijdschrift voor Rechtsgeschiedenis* 65 (1997): 12.

5 Charles Donahue Jr., "What Difference Does It Make If Marriage Is a Sacrament? A Historical Approach," in *Jurisprudence of Marriage and Other Intimate Relationships*, ed. Scott FitzGibbon, Lynne D. Wardle, and A. Scott Loveless (Buffalo: William S. Hein & Co., Inc., 2010), 15–35; "English and French Marriage Cases: Might the Differences Be Explained by Differences in the Property Systems?" in *Marriage, Property, and Succession*, ed. Lloyd Bonfield (Berlin: Duncker & Humblot, 1992), 339–66; "What Causes Fundamental Legal Ideas? Marital Property in England and France in the Thirteenth Century," *Michigan Law Review* 78 (1979): 59–88.

temporal, and thematic range, covering Roman law, the law of merchants, canon law, constitutional law, the history of courts, procedure, the legal profession, property law, and marriage law, among others)[6] that in their practice-oriented, contextualizing, comparative, and interpretative dimensions represent innovative, enlightening, and very hard-to-emulate departures in legal historiography. Add to that Charlie's enviable talent for addressing even arcane and technical subjects in a uniquely accessible and readable style (some of those familiar with it even describe it as instantly recognizable), and you have a body of work that deserves to be read and re-read by generations to come.

But Charlie's contribution to the concerns, methods, and substance of legal historiography, however substantial, is only a part of the story. Equally important is his role in recruiting and nurturing (future) legal historians. Charlie's concern for "younger folk" is already apparent from the fact that he has devoted a considerable portion of his valuable research time to editing or helping to edit manuscripts and to compiling bibliographies—which are often boring and thankless tasks for the one who does them, but greatly benefit future examiners of the subject—and that he is in the process of making available forty years' worth of marriage cases culled from English and Continental archives on his faculty webpage.

As a professor at Michigan and later at Harvard, Charlie taught memorable classes, seminars, and reading groups on Roman law, English and Continental legal history, the history of marriage law, and canon law, which often inspired his auditors to work with him more closely. Those who approached him for supervision, whether it be of a paper or of a dissertation, found that the man himself was as accessible and down-to-earth as his style of writing. Almost always to be found at his Langdell and later his Hauser office (even on Sundays, after Mass at St. Paul's), Charlie was as unfailingly patient and attentive in listening to supervisees' struggles and concerns as he was generous with his time and knowledge. He carefully read and provided in-depth, written feedback on many a half-baked work in progress, setting a standard for "supervisory excellence" that is very hard to match. Aspiring legal historians who were not lucky enough to be taught or supervised by Charlie might encounter him at legal history conferences, where he is famous for his rigorous, yet benign and egalitarian, style of questioning (with usually one question for each panelist).

The volume we offer here is a second Festschrift for Charlie Donahue, the first having been published in 2016 and entitled *Texts and Contexts in Legal History: Essays in Honor of Charles Donahue*. This first Festschrift, while

6 For a complete list, see the bibliography appended to this volume.

including some essays by former students, was authored chiefly by Charlie's colleagues and peers. What we had in mind in creating a second Festschrift was to focus entirely on students, broadly defined: those whom Charlie mentored and supervised and who benefited from his knowledge, generosity, and friendship in pursuing academic and non-academic careers alike both here and abroad. Accordingly, every contributor to this volume is proud to call Charlie teacher and mentor, whether as principal doctoral supervisor, a second reader, a dissertation co-chair, or simply an unforgettable and powerfully influential *magister* in a class or two on legal history. Many of the authors represented in this volume have followed in Charlie's footsteps and become independent scholars or university professors of law, legal history, or history themselves. Some are on the brink of starting academic careers. Others yet have opted to go into practice. All of them share a debt of gratitude to a professor who brought the learned law to life.

While this volume is organized around major disciplinary categories—Roman Law; Women, Marriage, and the Law; Medieval and Early Modern Law; American Legal History; and Literature and Legal Theory—in this introduction we would like to highlight some of the overarching themes that surface in this diverse collection of essays and that reflect the cross-cutting currents in Charlie's own scholarship.

1 The Status of Women within Premodern Legal Systems

Charlie is perhaps best known as a historian of the (canon) law of marriage, particularly in medieval England and what he has aptly called the Franco-Belgian region. In his page-turning magnum opus *Law, Marriage, and Society in the Later Middle Ages* as well as a wide range of articles and book contributions, he has illuminated the doctrinal and practical past of the law of marriage like no other historian and, in doing so, has called particular attention to the status of women within medieval law.[7]

---

7 See, e.g., his earliest writings on this topic in the 1970s, such as Charles Donahue Jr., "The Policy of Alexander the Third's Consent Theory of Marriage," in *Proceedings of the Fourth International Congress of Medieval Canon Law*, ed. Stephan Kuttner (Città del Vaticano: Biblioteca Apostolica Vaticana, 1976), 251–81; his *magnum opus*, *Law, Marriage, and Society in the Later Middle Ages: Arguments About Marriage in Five Courts* (New York: Cambridge University Press, 2007); and his expansive more recent work, such as "The Legal Background: European Marriage Law from the Sixteenth to the Nineteenth Century," in *Marriage in Europe 1400–1800*, ed. Silvana Seidel Menchi (Toronto: Toronto University Press, 2016), 33–60. See also "The Dating of Alexander the Third's Marriage Decretals: Dauvillier Revisited after Fifty

Reflecting Charlie's long-standing study of marriage law and its implications for the lives of women, several of the essays included here examine the position of women within premodern legal systems. In her chapter on a classic "Charlie topic," marital consent, Elizabeth Papp Kamali links the consent doctrine of marriage, officially adopted for the Church by Pope Alexander III, with her own abiding interest in the subjective *mens rea* requirements for criminal responsibility in medieval England. After setting out the role of consent in both the medieval English laws of marriage formation and felony adjudication, she explores how marital and criminal consent interacted when a husband and wife stood accused of committing a crime together. Her essay shows that the dynamics of a particular marital relationship (although not her status as a married woman *per se*) could protect a wife from liability if her husband overbore her will, vitiating her consent to the criminal act in question. It also highlights the evidentiary difficulties associated with legal rules that center upon consent and explores how church courts and criminal juries grappled

Years," *Zeitschrift der Savigny-Stiftung für Rechtsgeschichte* 99 (1982): 70–124; "'Clandestine' Marriage in the Later Middle Ages: A Reply," *Law and History Review* 10 (1992): 315–22; "Women Plaintiffs in Marriage Cases in the Court of York in the Later Middle Ages: What Can We Learn From the Numbers?" in *Wife and Widow in Medieval England*, ed. Sue Sheridan Walker (Ann Arbor: University of Michigan Press, 1993), 183–213; "Was There a Change in Marriage Law in the Late Middle Ages?" *Rivista internazionale di diritto commune* 6 (1995): 49–80; "Bassianus, That Is to Say, Bazianus?—Bazianus and Johannes Bassianus on Marriage," *Rivista internazionale di diritto commune* 14 (2003): 41–82; "Johannes Faventinus on Marriage (With an Appendix Revisiting the Question of the Dating of Alexander III's Marriage Decretals)," in *Medieval Church Law and the Origins of the Western Legal Tradition: A Tribute to Kenneth Pennington*, ed. Wolfgang P. Müller and Mary E. Sommar (Washington, DC: Catholic University of America Press, 2006), 179–97; "The Western Canon Law of Marriage: A Doctrinal Introduction," in *The Islamic Marriage Contract: Case Studies in Islamic Family Law*, ed. Asifa Quraishi and Frank E. Vogel (Cambridge, MA: Harvard University Press, 2008), 46–56; "Law, Marriage, and Society in the Later Middle Ages: A Look at the English and 'Franco-Belgian' Regions," in *Proceedings of the Thirteenth International Congress of Medieval Canon Law (Esztergom-Budapest, August 3–9, 2008)*, ed. Peter Erdö and Sz. Anzelm Szuromi (Città del Vaticano: Biblioteca Apostolica Vaticana, 2010), 17–39; "Comparative Approaches to Marriage in the Later Middle Ages," in *Regional Variations in Matrimonial Law and Custom in Europe, 1150–1600*, ed. Mia Korpiola (Leiden: Brill, 2011), 289–316; "Diritto, matrimonio e società nel tardo medioevo: Considerazioni sull'area inglese e area 'franco-belga,'" *Rivista storica italiana* 123 (2011): 1129–79; "The Mysterious Canonist Bazianus on Marriage," in *Law as Profession and Practice in Medieval Europe: Essays in Honor of James Brundage*, ed. Kenneth Pennington and Melodie Harris Eichbauer (Farnham, Surrey: Ashgate, 2011), 263–92; "The Role of the Humanists and the Second Scholastic in the Development of European Marriage Law from the Sixteenth to the Nineteenth Centuries," in *Law and Religion: The Legal Teachings of the Protestant and Catholic Reformations*, ed. Jordan Ballor, Wim Decock, Michael Germann, and Laurent Waelkens (Göttingen: Vandenhoeck & Ruprecht, 2014), 45–62.

with these evidentiary challenges in sorting the married from the unmarried and the guilty from the innocent.

Elizabeth Haluska-Rausch similarly explores the status of women, albeit with a focus on aristocratic women in Bas Languedoc in the eleventh and twelfth centuries and the issue of marital property, another interest of our honorand.[8] Bas Languedoc formed part of the French *pays du droit écrit*, where Roman law never disappeared completely and where legal, including customary, rules were largely written down. Haluska-Rausch demonstrates that between roughly 1000 and 1200, there was an increasing divide between written law and practice regarding dotal property, inheritance, and guardianship among the land-holding aristocracy. Although the applicable laws did not change over the 200-year-period she surveys, the most powerful members of society had stopped observing those rules when the period closed. By the dawn of the thirteenth century, aristocratic women were unlikely to receive dowries in land or interests in their husbands' immovable estates, were basically excluded from the management of the family's land, and eventually even ceased to be the preferred guardians of their children. The chapter demonstrates the complex interplay between law and society, with the needs of the latter sometimes vitiating the efficacy of the former.

2 Marital Households and the Law

Broadening our focus from the marital unit to the larger familial household, several contributions highlight the ways in which theological and legal ideas interacted to shape the lived experience of premodern persons. For example, Elizabeth Mellyn's contribution on suicide in early modern Italy illuminates the interplay between the learned law—of the ecclesiastical and Roman varieties—and the lived experience of families confronted with severe mental illness. Although suicide remained both a mortal sin and a serious crime throughout the period of Mellyn's analysis (1300–1750), emphasis was placed by jurists like Prospero Farinacci (1544–1618) on the broad discretion of judges and magistrates faced with a case of self-murder. Moving beyond the law, Mellyn situates changing societal attitudes toward mental illness as due in part to the development of mental hospitals, which offered families by the

8 For our honorand's work on marital property, see, e.g., Charles Donahue Jr., "Lyndwood's Gloss *propriarum uxorum*: Marital Property and the *ius commune* in Fifteenth Century England," in *Europaïsches Rechtsdenken in Geschichte und Gegenwart: Festschrift für Helmut Coing*, ed. Norbert Horn, Klaus Luig, and Alfred Söllner (München: C.H. Beck, 1982), 1:19–37.

seventeenth century the possibility of sending their loved ones to a safekeeping institution, when earlier generations would have seen a similarly ill family member more likely facing a different institution altogether—a criminal court, sometimes in a post-mortem trial.

Though on one level a reflection on legal practice and what historians can learn from studying the contents of past lawyers' bookshelves, Sally Hadden's piece on lawyers and their book collections in eighteenth-century America also sheds light on the post-mortem disposition of property by lawyers' families, most often widows, with the assistance of professional booksellers with broad networks of potential buyers. The chapter is a fitting tribute to Charlie's undeniable bibliophilia (anyone who has ever attempted the feat of stepping into his office knows that there is hardly a square foot that is not covered in books). Using newspaper advertisements by bookdealers, executors, auctioneers, and others, Hadden reconstructs the types and titles of law books eighteenth-century colonial lawyers accessed, used in practice, or even purchased for their own law libraries. Her article reveals that the earliest colonial book advertisements listed legal guidebooks and manuals that might be used by nearly anyone. For legal practitioners, who needed more sophisticated treatments to assist their clients, law reports, treatises, and abridgments were available as well. Those unable or unwilling to afford the hefty price tag of new law books might purchase second-hand copies at estate auctions and used book sales at a fraction of the original cost. This resale market, often fueled by relatives clearing the office shelves of deceased family members, became particularly important during the War for Independence, as private libraries were looted or moved and supply from overseas became even more uncertain.

Families were thus at the heart of the book trade economy, satisfying the "desire of books" of those setting up a new legal practice. Families are also at the heart of Carol Symes's contribution to this volume, an exploration of the "desire of deeds" she found inscribed on the record of a dispute between two men over a family archive of deeds and other paper and parchment records. Symes stepped into the role of Curator of Medieval Deeds and Charters at the Harvard Law School Library during her doctoral studies, often working closely with our honorand, himself a library and archive enthusiast,[9] as she

9 For examples of Charlie's scholarship dealing with manuscripts, books, libraries, and archives, see Charles Donahue Jr., "Some Thoughts on Michigan's Copy of the Argentoratene Gratian," *Law Quadrangle Notes* 17 (1972): 8–11; "Church Court Records on the Continent and in England," in *Englische und kontinentale Rechtsgeschichte: ein Forschungsprojekt*, ed. Helmut Coing and Knut Wolfgang Nörr (Berlin: Duncker & Humblot, 1985), 63–71; "Introduction" to *Henry Fielding, An Institute of the Pleas of the Crown: An Exhibition of the*

catalogued the Law Library's extensive collection. Attuned to the materiality of the deeds and other legal records, including such treasures as the careworn parchment fragment attesting that Robert de Hobekyn had been made a free man in the late thirteenth century, Symes explores the meanings documents held for families who would continue to cherish such parchment heirlooms centuries after the events that they inscribed. Symes's essay relates directly to one of our honorand's many contributions to the greater world of legal history: his stewardship of the Harvard Law School Library's manuscript collection, including his work with the Ames Foundation to assist the Library in digitizing its medieval and early modern manuscripts and producing comprehensive meta data to make the materials more easily navigable by researchers.

Also at the intersection of family and property law (another "Charlie topic"), John Witte's chapter studies the constructive role of the early modern Protestant family in shaping the values of modern economics. As is well known, Max Weber (1864–1920) traced the emergence of modern capitalism to new Protestant teachings on vocation, predestination, and asceticism. Building on Weber's thesis, Witte argues that the Protestant household in fact functioned as a key stepping stone between Protestant ethics and modern economics, and that it was in the Protestant household that many of the basic habits needed for modern economic life were first instilled and cultivated. He provides case studies of the household manuals of four key Protestant writers to illustrate that—to the extent that Protestantism helped shape the spirit of early modern capitalism, which remains controversial—it did so first of all by rationalizing and routinizing the household and teaching its members the importance of vocation, discipline, and hard work.

Hyde Collection at the Houghton Library, 1987, ed. Hugh Amory (Cambridge, MA: Houghton Library, 1987); "Institutional History from Archival History: The Court of Canterbury Rolls," in *The Weightier Matters of the Law: Essays in Law and Religion, A Tribute to Harold J. Berman*, ed. John Witte Jr. and Frank S. Alexander (Atlanta, GA: Scholars Press, 1988), 33–55; "Reflections on the Editing of Medieval Church Court Records," in *Iuris Historia*: *Liber Amicorum Gero Dolazalek*, ed. Vincenzo Colli and Emanuele Conte (Berkeley, CA: The Robbins Collection, 2008), 345–53; "Another Way of Doing Manuscript Catalogues?" in *English Legal History and its Sources: Essays in Honour of Sir John Baker*, ed. David Ibbetson, Neil Jones, and Nigel Ramsay (Cambridge: Cambridge University Press, 2019), 282–99.

3 History of International Law

Issues of economy have shaped Charlie's most significant contributions to the field of international law, namely his work on the *Lex Mercatoria*.[10] In his contribution, Nikitas Hatzimihail investigates an under-developed area of the history of international law, namely the contribution of the glossators of the early and high Middle Ages to the history of conflict of laws. Historians tracing the history of conflict of laws have tended to commence their discussion in earnest with the commentators of the later Middle Ages, failing to account for the significant contributions made by Accursius (1185–1263) and earlier glossators in interpreting the key texts on the issue. Hatzimihail provides an introduction to the key passages of the *Corpus Iuris Civilis*, particularly the first title of Justinian's Code, *Cunctos populos*, before taking his readers on an intellectual journey through the writings of Master Aldricus in the mid to late twelfth century, Carolus de Tocco in the late twelfth to early thirteenth century, and finally the famous Bolognese professor Accursius, whose *Glossa ordinaria* would ultimately overshadow what came before. Hatzimihail situates Accursius and the other glossators in the broader context of political thought and, in doing so, highlights how conflicts doctrine developed in response to the pressing needs, whether in commerce or in social life, of the high Middle Ages.

Similarly exploring an issue of international law within the field of Roman law, Charles Bartlett's essay examines Baldus de Ubaldis's (1327–1400) discussion of a claim made by Venetian jurists as to the source of Venice's sovereignty, namely, the fact of it having been built on the sea, a classic form of *res communes omnium*, or things common to all. In his analysis, Bartlett draws upon the treatment of "things common to all" in Justinian's *Institutes*, and as elaborated in a curious passage of the *Digest* (D.1.8) on the construction of a fishing hut by the sea. He demonstrates how a concept drawn from the private law of ownership—that the hut builder owned the ground beneath the hut as long as the structure stood—was transformed into a principle constitutive

10 See, e.g., Mary Elizabeth Basile, Jane Fair Bestor, Daniel R. Coquillette, and Charles Donahue Jr., eds., *Lex Mercatoria and Legal Pluralism: A Late Thirteenth-Century Treatise and its Afterlife* (Cambridge, MA: The Ames Foundation, 1998). See also Charles Donahue Jr., "Equity in the Courts of Merchants," *Tijdschrift voor Rechtsgeschiedenis* 72 (2004): 1–35; "Medieval and Early Modern *Lex mercatoria*: An Attempt at the *probatio diabolica*," *Chicago Journal of International Law* 5 (2004): 21–36; "Benvenuto Stracca's *De mercatura*: Was There a *Lex mercatoria* in Sixteenth Century Italy?" in *From* lex mercatoria *to Commercial Law*, ed. Vito Piergiovanni (Berlin: Duncker & Humblot, 2005), 69–120.

of a public-law notion of sovereignty based in part on corporate rather than individual personhood.

4 History of Private Law

Just as the Venetians crossed the line between private law and public law in their arguments for sovereignty, so the honorand did not confine his research to one side of this divide. Alongside his work on the history of public international law stands significant scholarship emphasizing private-law doctrine, whether property, tort, or family law,[11] as is true of two of the essays contained herein. Daniel Jacobs's discursus on *Digest* 41.1.44 helps elucidate the treatment of occupancy by natural lawyer Hugo Grotius (1583–1645) centuries later. Jacobs begins with the infamous fox-hunting case of *Pierson v. Post* (1805), indelibly stamped on the memories of all those who studied Continental European legal history with Charlie, Jacobs included, not to mention the hundreds, if not thousands, of law students who will recall Charlie's grand entrance, stuffed fox tucked under his arm, into the first-year property classroom on the first day of the term. Seeking to understand the roots of the argument posed by Post's attorney, Cadwallader David Colden, i.e., that one might communicate one's intentions to take possession of a wild animal without manucaption, Jacobs turns to what he refers to as the case of the pig in the wolf's jaws from D.41.1.44, then to Hugo Grotius's novel doctrine of lost and abandoned property, articulated in his *De iure Belli ac Pacis* in 1625, and finally to John Locke's (1632–1704) labor theory of appropriation. The journey reveals the deep-rootedness of Locke's labor theory in not only Roman but also biblical law traditions, the latter by way of Grotius and perhaps John Selden (1584–1654). Moreover, the chapter addresses a topic dear to Charlie's heart, as demonstrated by his own scholarship on the occupation of wild animals.[12]

---

11 See, e.g., Charles Donahue Jr., "The Case of the Man Who Fell Into the Tiber: The Roman Law of Marriage at the Time of the Glossators," *American Journal of Legal History* 22 (1978): 1–53; "The Future of the Concept of Property Predicted from its Past," in *Property*, Nomos 22, ed. J. Roland Pennock and John W. Chapman (New York: New York University Press, 1980), 28–68 (dealing in part with Roman property law). For a broader treatment of private law in the history of western legal systems, see Charles Donahue Jr., "Private Law Without the State and During its Formation," *American Journal of Comparative Law* 56 (2008): 541–66, reprinted in *Beyond the State: Rethinking Private Law*, ed. Nils Jansen and Ralf Michaels (Tübingen: Mohr Siebeck, 2008), 121–43.

12 See, e.g., Charles Donahue Jr., "Noodt, Titius, and the Natural Law School: The Occupation of Wild Animals and the Intersection of Property and Tort," in *Satura Roberto Feenstra*, ed. J. A. Ankum, J. E. Spruit, and F. B. J. Wubbe (Fribourg [CH]: Presses Universitaires de

Wim Decock, similarly focusing on private law, elucidates the merging of secular and legal traditions in order to understand debates within the influential School of Salamanca on settlement agreements (*transactiones*) and their relationship to arbitration agreements (*compromissa*) and amicable settlements (*amicabiles compositiones*). *Transactiones* were agreements designed to help parties settle conflicts extracurially through a mutual give-and-take. While these settlement agreements had long been of interest, renewed attention was paid to them by moral theologians and canon lawyers in the early modern Iberian empire, including Antonio de Padilla y Meneses (d. 1580), Luis de Molina (1535–1600), Pedro de Oñate (1568–1646), and Pedro Murillo Velarde (1696–1753). Discussions of *transactio*-agreements attempted to understand their Roman legal origins comprehensively, even when some aspects of Roman law had since been superseded; to take one example, canon law and Spanish law viewed even naked pacts as binding, a clear departure from Roman law. Decock illustrates how such theologians and canonists might have seen themselves drawing upon Roman legal techniques in the service of peace and reconciliation in the law's shadow at a time when jurisdiction shifted from ecclesiastical to temporal authorities. This emphasis on a canon law tradition centered on settlement and reconciliation rather than a winner-take-all approach will sound familiar to those who took Charlie's course on the legal and constitutional history of medieval England.

5 History of Legal Procedure

With regard to the history of legal procedure,[13] James Townshend builds upon the honorand's work on the history of witnessing,[14] but with a focus on classical Roman law rather than the church courts. Townshend undertakes a systematic analysis of the meaning and use of witnesses in Roman law, from the

Fribourg, 1985), 609–29; "*Animalia Ferae Naturae*: Rome, Bologna, Leyden, Oxford and Queen's County, N.Y.," in *Studies in Roman Law in Memory of A. Arthur Schiller*, ed. Roger S. Bagnall and William V. Harris (Leiden: E. J. Brill, 1986), 39–63.

13 For Charlie's work in this field, see, e.g., Charles Donahue Jr., "Procedure in the Courts of the *Ius commune*," in *The History of Courts and Procedure in Medieval Canon Law*, ed. Wilfried Hartmann and Kenneth Pennington (Washington, DC: Catholic University of America Press, 2016), 74–124.

14 See, e.g., Charles Donahue Jr., "Proof by Witnesses in the Church Courts of Medieval England: An Imperfect Reception of the Learned Law," in *On the Laws and Customs of England: Essays in Honor of Samuel E. Thorne*, ed. Morris S. Arnold, Thomas A. Green, Sally Scully, and Stephen White (Chapel Hill: North Carolina University Press), 127–58.

Twelve Tables (fifth century BCE) through Justinian's *Institutes* (sixth century CE), helping fill a glaring gap in English-language scholarship in the field. Acknowledging that legal texts such as the *Digest* say relatively little about witnesses, Townshend draws upon a wide range of other kinds of evidence to answer fundamental questions about who witnesses were, what they did, and how their role changed over time. He focuses on their judicial and transactional roles, their status as both partisan players and neutral parties, and their qualifications. Townshend also endeavors to make sense of the differential treatment of women, minors, adult men *in potestate*, and other categories of persons in the development of rules around who might serve as a witness and in what context. Townshend sees his essay as a first step toward a broader project that would delve even further into philology, epigraphy, and social anthropology to produce a thoroughgoing taxonomy of witnesses in Roman law.

Similarly attuned to the history of legal procedure, Amalia Kessler's contribution focuses upon one particular text—Francis Lieber's (1798–1872) *On Civil Liberty and Self-Government* (1853)—that circulated among American readers and yet failed to "take," such that the accusatorial-inquisitorial divide would only enter the American legal lexicon in the early twentieth century by other means. Despite this fact, Lieber was remarkably prescient in equating accusatorialism with Anglo-American and, more specifically, American procedure. By comparison, nineteenth-century American procedural debates were framed around the distinction between the English common law and the Roman-canon civil law, rather than the accusatorial-inquisitorial divide, possibly due to the fact that the former distinction related more neatly to civil procedure, the focus of American debates, and the latter to criminal procedure. What finally cleared the way for the embrace of the accusatorial-inquisitorial terminology in the early twentieth century was a growing interest among elite American lawyers in German legal science and the tendency of Progressive-era reformers, spurred by a desire to develop new administrative agencies, to look to Europe for inspiration and, in doing so, to introduce the language of accusatorial and inquisitorial procedure into American legal discourse. Kessler's essay ends on a reflective note as she observes that comparative uses of the accusatorial-inquisitorial framework could theoretically promote a reformist agenda today, assuming the presence of the necessary political will.

Taking the history of legal procedure in literary directions, Anton Chaevitch offers a reading of Goethe's (1749–1832) *Faust* as a story of legal progress from a formal and closed legal system to one that is border-unconscious or *gränzunbewußt*. His essay focuses on three distinctly legal aspects of the play, which have so far largely escaped scholarly attention: the absence of clear evidence that Gretchen actually committed the infanticide of which she is convicted;

the contrast between Faust's and Helena's adjudication of Lynceus's fate; and the omission of the text of the written pact between Faust and Mephistopheles. According to Chaevitch, Goethe is here criticizing closed and excessively formal legal systems, which adhere inflexibly to canonical cultural narratives and the written words of a code, statute, or contract. In their place, he is substituting a new vision of a border-transgressing, progressive legal system—one that is exemplified by Helena in *Faust* and by modern systems of international arbitration today—in which alternative narratives (in particular the accused's own) are listened to and validated. Under this system, Gretchen would not be condemned because of a cultural assumption that it is invariably the mother who kills a child, but only on clear and convincing evidence; and the written text of a contract for a man's soul could be omitted because it would not be enforceable anyway.

6 Micro-History and Close Readings of Legal Texts

In thinking about approaches to history, Charlie has emphasized the combination of big data approaches, such as the incredible data gathering underpinning his book *Law, Marriage, and Society*, as well as the close reading of texts, a skill that he imparted to his students. Demonstrating the value to be gleaned from a close reading, Saskia Lettmaier focuses on a single court case from seventeenth-century France. The case, reported by *ancien régime* jurist Gayot de Pitaval (1673–1743), involved an attack on the validity of a marriage of twenty-four years' duration after the death of the wife. It was brought by the wife's half-brother and, at its most basic, revolved around who (the potential husband or the half-brother) would inherit the dead woman's estate. The judgment, which was rendered by a secular court (rather than an ecclesiastical one) because of the claim's essentially proprietary nature, declared the marriage to be invalid, without, however, providing reasons. Relying chiefly on the parties' arguments, which Pitaval reproduced in full, Lettmaier peers behind the inscrutable judgment, hypothesizing about the factual and legal assumptions that may have influenced the court.

Similarly engaged in a close reading of a legal text related to marriage law, Stuart McManus examines an unpublished manuscript entitled *Dissertatio de Matrimonio Sinarum* by Charles Maigrot (1652–1730), a Paris Foreign Missions Society priest. McManus provides the first in-depth analysis of this bilingual (Latin and Chinese) treatise, applying two methods of studying historical sources at which Charlie excelled: philologically attentive close reading and contextual interpretation. Maigrot's *dissertatio* covers the laws on Chinese marriage, impediments, marriage rites, and the validity of Chinese marriages, especially for Christian converts. According to McManus, it offers a mostly accurate, albeit not flawless statement of the laws, customs and rituals related to marriage in China. Some of these were hard to stomach from a Christian point of view, like the ready availability of divorce and the permissibility of concubines. However, the chief value of the treatise does not lie in what it tells us about Chinese marriage. As McManus points out, Maigrot's work is also a fascinating example of comparative law *avant la lettre*, as its author, a Catholic missionary priest, tried to come up with a comparative framework for assimilating differences and understanding how Christian marriage might be transposed to the Chinese context.

Because many good things come in threes, a third essay—this one unrelated to marriage law—similarly employs the Donahue approach. In analyzing the fourteenth-century jurist Evrart de Trémaugon's (d. 1386) *Somnium viridarii* and its vernacular reworking, *Le Songe du Vergier*, Rowan Dorin finds therein a legal discourse on the permissibility of Jewish expulsion. Commissioned by Charles V (r. 1364–80), the *Somnium viridarii* or "Dream of the Orchard" employed the familiar dialogic genre—in this instance a conversation between a cleric and a knight—to affirm the sovereignty of Evrart's sponsor, the French Crown, against ecclesiastical (especially papal) rivalry. Evrart's later vernacular reworking of the treatise expanded on themes, including royal policies toward France's Jewish community. The *Somnium* and *Songe du Vergier* drew upon legal texts, most notably Justinian's *Codex* and Gratian's *Decretum*, in arguing for a new path, one which diverged markedly from the church's prevailing teachings regarding the presumptive right of Jews to live within Christian society. Dorin reveals the role that law, legal reasoning, and rhetoric played in justifying and possibly even aiding the expulsion of medieval France's Jewish community.

7 Religious Life and the Life of the Law

A final theme we have identified in this collection of essays is the intersection of law and religion,[15] more specifically of legal history and the lives of nuns and clerics. For example, Sara McDougall's contribution asks what happened when medieval French nuns, who were generally prized for their chastity, were suspected of having sex or, worse still, got pregnant. Her essay draws on a wide

15 For Charlie's work in this area, see, e.g., Charles Donahue Jr., "The Interaction of Law and Religion in the Middle Ages," *Mercer Law Review* 31 (1980): 466–76; "A Crisis of Law? Reflections on the Church and the Law over the Centuries," *The Jurist* 65 (2005): 1–30.

range of primary sources including court records, law codes, hospital records, stories, and images. McDougall admits that these sources are few and tantalizingly incomplete, making it difficult to know how ecclesiastical authorities, and especially religious superiors within convents, handled nuns' sexual indiscretions. However, she argues that the sources provide little evidence for the regular infliction of harsh punishment on sexually active nuns and, on the contrary, offer a good deal of evidence for the reintegration (indeed sometimes even promotion) of the mothers and care for their children. Her essay largely tells a story of redemption for nuns accused of sexual acts and offers a new understanding of the place of female religious in medieval Christian society, thereby illuminating the close intersection between law and society, a steady theme in our honorand's scholarship.[16]

In her study of urban expansion in twelfth-century Metz, Samantha Kahn Herrick unearths the diverse tactics through which the Benedictine monks of Saint-Clément sought to capitalize upon the new opportunities created by urbanization. Although the monks' abbey was situated outside Metz, their links to the city were manifold and interconnected, enabling them to exploit resources of the natural, spiritual, legal, and commercial varieties. To reinforce their influence within Metz, the monks resorted to litigation and intimidation as well as the careful crafting of hagiographic narratives designed to bolster the reputation of the abbey's patron saint and Metz's founding bishop. Like her mentor, Charlie Donahue, Herrick deploys a broad range of primary source materials—from papal bulls to chronicles and saints' lives to charters—in elucidating the active role of a suburban Benedictine abbey in Metz's rapid urbanization.

Also exploring issues of center and periphery, Ryan Rowberry's essay tests the efficacy of Pope John XXII's (r. 1316–34) bull *Execrabilis* (1317), which required clerics to hold no more than one ecclesiastical benefice involving the cure of souls. Rowberry focuses his analysis on three clerical justices in the English royal courts, each of whom were pluralists—holders of multiple benefices gifted by ecclesiastical patrons—at the time *Execrabilis* was issued. Crafting benefice portfolios for each of the justices, Rowberry demonstrates that each forfeited substantial revenues in the wake of *Execrabilis*. Perhaps of even greater significance than the loss of income was the severing of previously intimate ties with ecclesiastical patrons who might earlier have taken advantage of their close connections to royal justices. This, in turn, contributed

16 See, e.g., Charles Donahue Jr., "The Canon Law on the Formation of Marriage and Social Practice in the Later Middle Ages," *Journal of Family History* 8 (1983): 144–58.

to the laicization of the common-law judiciary, a process that would reach completion less than two decades after the issuance of this papal bull.

8 Legal Theory

We close our tour de Festschrift with a note on an essay that deals with a subject matter possibly most familiar to the first-year law students who had the good fortune to study property law with Charlie. As if the Rule Against Perpetuities and the petty assizes were not complicated enough, Charlie introduced his students to the conceptual work of Wesley Hohfeld (1879–1918), with his categorization of jural opposites (e.g., right and no-right) and jural correlatives (e.g., right and duty). While students may not have appreciated it at the time of initial introduction, Hohfeld's mapping of legal concepts no doubt informed their ability to make crisp distinctions and even inspired some of Charlie's more academically minded students down particular research paths. Bharath Palle situates Hohfeld's legal theory in its broader cultural—especially intellectual—context, thus filling a lacuna in the existing analysis of Hohfeld's work.[17] In an innovative move, he reads Hohfeld alongside a pivotal text in literary modernism: Hugo von Hofmannsthal's (1874–1929) *The Lord Chandos Letter*. This juxtaposition reveals that, like Hohfeld, literary modernists rejected the notion that the world of ordinary language can straightforwardly capture the world of experience and that they, too, grappled with developing an entirely new vocabulary and set of conceptual resources. Palle argues that Hohfeld's abiding concern with the inadequacy of ordinary legal terms to represent a complex social reality and his efforts to elaborate a more precise and scientific system of logical concepts mark Hohfeld as a distinctly modernist figure. Apart from helping our understanding of Hohfeld and his work, Palle's contribution also suggests that intellectual histories of legal theory that fail to take into account the broader context of the period's intellectual developments might be unduly narrow.

This returns us to our honorand and his own approach to legal history. In a 2009 contribution to a Festschrift for his colleague, Morton Horwitz, Charlie posed the question: "Whither legal history?"[18] His essay was partly about the

---

17 For a recent collected volume on Hohfeld, see *Wesley Hohfeld a Century Later: Edited Work, Select Personal Papers, and Original Commentaries*, ed. Shyamkrishna Balganesh, Ted M. Sichelman, and Henry E. Smith (Cambridge: Cambridge University Press, 2022).

18 Charles Donahue Jr., "Whither Legal History," in *Transformations in American Legal History: Essays in Honor of Professor Morton J. Horwitz*, ed. Daniel W. Hamilton and Alfred L. Brophy (Cambridge: Harvard Law School, 2009), 327–43.

fate of legal and constitutional history in college and law school curricula, and partly about the varying justifications for and approaches toward writing legal history. In summarizing one of his arguments, Charlie wrote:

> pure external and pure internal legal history as recently defined are likely to be bad history, or, at least, incomplete history. Those who start with a political or social movement and discover that it had legal ramifications need to immerse themselves in legal sources that show how those ramifications were worked out. Those who start with a particular piece of legal discourse or change in legal discourse need to look outside the confines of the legal system to see both whether it is being pushed by developments within the realm of general ideas, politics, or the broader society, and what effect it may have had on general ideas, politics, or the broader society.[19]

In various ways, the contributions to this Festschrift have straddled the divide between internal and external legal history and between the learned law and the law as lived by those individuals subject to, and in some instances complacent toward or defiant of, its strictures. We hope these chapters will be judged "good history" by our dear mentor.

Acknowledgments

We would like to thank Petra Stiglmayer, Alessandra Giliberto, Wendel Scholma, and Peter Buschman for shepherding the volume through Brill's editorial processes. We are also most grateful to our multi-talented copy editor, Patricia Crotty, who worked with grace under time pressure in the final stages of manuscript preparation. For the cover art, from a manuscript used by our honorand in teaching, we thank Sarah Wharton and Historical & Special Collections at the Harvard Law School Library.

19 Donahue, "Whither Legal History," 337.

PART 1

Roman Law

CHAPTER 1

Towards a Taxonomy of Witnesses in Roman Law

James R. Townshend

1 Introduction

In December 1949, Fritz Pringsheim opened his lecture to the *Institut de Droit Romain* at the University of Paris by remarking that no history of the witness had yet been written, and even as he spoke one would not know how to write one.[1] Pringsheim's wariness was directed at a history of witnesses writ large across all systems. Still, an account of witnesses within a given system was more feasible, as his own sketch for Ancient Greek and Roman witnesses indicates. Such a study of witnesses in Roman law is necessitated by two factors. First, witnesses are everywhere in Roman law, from the Twelve Tables of the fifth century BCE to the *Corpus Iuris Civilis* compiled under Justinian in the sixth century CE.[2] Witnessing was, quite literally, an everyday occurrence for Romans. In his letters, Pliny the Younger (61/62–ca. 112 CE) numbered being a witness among the tasks that seem pointless (*inania*) if one thinks about their daily (*cotidie*) repetition (Plin. *Ep.* 1.9.2–3). Witnessing was considered a sufficiently important social duty (*officium*) that the second-century CE jurist Venuleius believed local magistrates should take care to make themselves and others available as witnesses and signatories to anyone who wanted them (*D.* 22.5.22).[3] We even see the statesman and orator Cicero (106–43 BCE) doing just this in 50 BCE when he was governor of Cilicia (Cic. *Att.* 7.2.3).[4] The second

1 Fritz Pringsheim, "Le témoignage dans la Grèce et Rome archaïque," *Revue Internationale des Droits de l'Antiquité* 6 (1951): 161.

2 In this chapter, I employ the following abbreviations: *C.* = the *Code* of Justinian; *D.* = the *Digest* of Justinian; *Inst.* = the *Institutes* of Justinian; *Inst.*Gai. = Gaius's *Institutes*; *FIRA* = *Fontes Iuris Romani Antejustiniani*; *PS* = the *Sententiae* of Paul (*FIRA* 2.317–417); *Epit. Ulp.* = the *Epitome Regularum Ulpiani* (*FIRA* 2.259–301); *CTh.* = *Codex Theodosianus*; *TPSulp.* = *Tabulae Pompeianae Sulpiciorum* (edited by Camodeca); *TH*^{2} = *Tabulae Herculanensis* (edited by Camodeca). All other abbreviations for classical works follow the conventions of the fourth edition of the *Oxford Classical Dictionary*.

3 On witnessing as a kind of *officium*, see also Jane F. Gardner, *Being A Roman Citizen* (London: Routledge, 1993), 118.

4 Cicero writes to his friend Atticus that he, along with his brother Quintus, Quintus's son, and his praetorian entourage (*cohors*), witnessed the will of Manius Curius. Both Atticus and Cicero received small bequests in that will.

 | DOI:10.1163/9789004710696_003

factor necessitating such a study is that despite this ubiquity and importance, the Romans themselves have not left a full account of witnesses. The most detailed discussion comes at *Digest* 22.5, which carries the promising title "On Witnesses" (*De Testibus*). Unfortunately, the scope of this title is limited: it focuses primarily on witness capacity and credibility in court, with some brief comments about witnesses for wills. There is, therefore, a real need for a comprehensive study of witnesses in classical Roman law.

The Latin word for "witness" is *testis*. There are other Latin words which mean "witness" in certain contexts, but *testis* is the principal word by the classical period of Roman law and the word overwhelmingly used by the jurists.[5] This is also clear from the compounds and derivatives associated with witnessing, which are all formed on *testis* instead of other words.[6] Although the exact etymological descent of *testis* is somewhat contested, it is generally agreed that a *testis* is a "third" person.[7] The *testis*, then, is not simply an observer in some other individual's business. The *testis* must, at least originally and etymologically, be present at the interaction of two other parties. This observation only takes us so far: it provides a starting point, not an end point. The analysis that follows will, therefore, have some regard for development over time, but "presence" remains an abiding feature of witnessing.

Yet it is not enough to be present. Witnesses are ultimately called upon to speak to or vouch for what they experienced through that presence. That brings into consideration their reliability or, in Latin, their *fides*. To put it somewhat simplistically, for the Romans *fides* expresses the extent to which others can expect a person to stand behind their own words and actions—the extent

---

5 To be clear, understanding those other words in context may help to understand Roman witnesses more generally, but due to the restrictions of space, I cannot offer a full etymological survey and analysis of all such words. That will have to wait for the longer treatment.

6 See Alfred Ernout and Antoine Meillet, *Dictionnaire Étymologique de la Langue Latine: Histoire des Mots*. Rev. 4th ed. (Paris: Klincksiek, 1985), s.v. *testis*.

7 See e.g., Helmut Rix, "Review of Martino, Paolo *Arbiter* …," *Indogermanische Forschungen* 95 (1990): 283; Joshua T. Katz, "*Testimonia Ritus Italici* …," *Harvard Studies in Classical Philology* 98 (1998): 184, with citations. Émile Benveniste, *Vocabulaire des Institutions Indo-Européennes* (Paris: Les Éditions de Minuit, 1969), 2.277; Felix Solmsen, "Beiträge zur geschichte der lateinischen sprache," *Zeitschrift für vergleichende Sprachforschung auf dem Gebiete der Indogermanischen Sprachen* 37, no. 1 (1904): 19, who sees the word as a compound of "third" and "stand"; cf. George Redard, "Latin *testis* 'témoin = troisième'?," in *Recherches de Linguistique: hommages à Maurice Leroy*, ed. J. Bingen, A. Coupez, F. Mawet (Bruxelles: Editions de l'Université de Bruxelles, 1980), 163–172, who rejects the connection with "third" or "three," preferring instead a meaning of French *assistant* or English "bystander," though he offers no etymological descent.

to which they can rely on that person.[8] It was so fundamental to Roman social relations that the Twelve Tables prescribed that if a *patronus* committed *fraus* (harm, wrongdoing, fraud) against his *cliens* and thus violated the demands of *fides*, he was to be *sacer* (XII 8.21 *FIRA* 1.62): accursed, his life forfeit to the gods.[9] According to Cicero, *fides* is the very foundation of justice, the steadfastness and truth of words and pacts (Cic. *Off.* 1.23). Witnesses were inextricably bound by the same ties of *fides*. This manifests, for example, in the oath witnesses swore before testifying in court and is reflected in sanctions for refusing to testify and giving false testimony.[10] Moreover, *fides* and presence work together symbiotically. As the first-century CE rhetorician Quintilian notes, written testimony of an absent witness is much easier (*simplicior*) to impeach than the "great battle" (*ingens dimicatio*) of challenging a witness who is present in court (Quint. *Inst. Or.* 5.7.1–4). *Fides* is, therefore, the characteristic quality needed of the witness, and the witness's presence activates that *fides*.[11]

This chapter is divided into two main parts. In the first part, I will consider what witnesses do, that is, I will consider their functions. This functional analysis will examine two key ways that scholars have attempted to describe witnesses. The first is a distinction based on context, which can be briefly stated here as judicial or evidentiary as opposed to instrumental or transactional. The second is a question of partisanship: whether the witness should be understood as a neutral party or a committed supporter and whether that understanding may have changed over time. These two lines of analysis are, as I will show, related. In both cases, however, the need for the presence of a witness possessing *fides* is clear. In the second part, I examine who witnesses are. Specifically, I explore the qualifications of witnesses: who gets to be a witness

8 The bibliography on *fides* is extensive: see e.g., Gérard Freyburger, *Fides: Étude sémantique et religieuse depuis les origines jusqu'à l'époque augustéenne* (Paris: Les Belles Lettres, 1986), 218–222 for witnesses; Roberto Fiori, "*Fides et bona fides*: Hiérarchie sociale et catégories juridiques," *Revue historique de droit français et étranger* 86, no. 4 (2008): 465–473; Remus Valsan, "*Fides, bona fides*, and *bonus vir*: Relations of Trust and Confidence in Roman Antiquity," *Journal of Law, Religion and State* 5, no. 1 (2017): 48–85.

9 On *fides* in the patron-client relationship, see e.g., Freyburger, *Fides*, 149–160; Valsan, "*Fides, bona fides*, and *bonus vir*," 69.

10 For witness oaths in court, see e.g., Cic. *Rosc. Am.* 101; *QRosc.* 44–46; *Arch.* 8; *Flacc.* 8; *Font.* 29; Liv. 26.3.5–6; Sen. *Dial.* 4.29.3; *C.* 4.20.5 (rescript of Diocletian and Maximian, 286 CE). For refusal to testify, see XII 8.22 *FIRA* 1.62, discussed briefly in this chapter. False testimony carried the death penalty under the Twelve Tables (XII 8.23 *FIRA* 1.62; Gell. *NA* 20.1.53). See also Freyburger, *Fides*, 221; Roberto Fiori, "La gerarchia come criterio di verità …," in *QUID EST VERITAS?* …, ed. Cosimo Cascione and Carla Masi Doria (Napoli: Satura Editrice, 2013), 223–224.

11 See also *D.* 22.5.2–3 (Modestinus and Callistratus).

and—more importantly—why. The rules here are well documented, but their development has not been as thoroughly explored. I will sketch some preliminary lines of inquiry about this development. It may seem counterintuitive to consider the "who" after the "what." However, the question of who can be a witness is in large part informed by what witnesses do, and thus is placed second. For reasons of space, I can necessarily only trace here the broader outlines of a comprehensive study in preparation for a later, fuller treatment: a storyboard rather than a feature film. Still, I hope to make some specific individual observations that will facilitate a more detailed understanding of witnesses in classical Roman law.

2 What Witnesses Do: Functions and Roles

The key to the role of witnesses is their presence: one cannot be a witness without being in some way present at and in the moment. The question then becomes: in what capacity is the witness present? What function(s) does the witness perform? The semantic range of *testis* in Latin maps almost exactly onto the English "witness," so the functional contexts in which the two words appear also overlap. On the one hand, there are those who come to a judicial context in order to say what they have seen or heard. In modern scholarship these have been called "judicial witnesses" (*témoins judiciaires, Prozeßzeugen*), though "evidentiary witnesses" (*témoins probatoires*) may be preferable since Roman witnesses may appear in court without necessarily testifying. On the other hand, there are "instrumental" or "transactional witnesses" (*témoins instrumentaires, Geschäftszeugen*). These are third parties present at transactions—that is, at the moment of the creation of legal obligations between two other persons—where that very presence is necessary for the transaction to be legally valid.

The second major question about the role of witnesses is whether they act as neutral third parties who uphold the structures and morals of society in general or as partisan supporters of the specific (potential) litigants. This question of neutrality is in part tied to the voluntary nature of witnessing in Roman law. This voluntary aspect can be seen in a provision of the Twelve Tables which speaks of "whoever allows himself to act as a witness" (*qui se sierit testarier*, XII 8.22 *FIRA* 1.62).[12] Some five hundred years later, Quintilian can declare that

12 See also Henri Lévy-Bruhl, *Le témoignage instrumentaire en droit romain.* (Doctoral thesis, Arthur Rousseau, Paris, 1910), 19–21 and 52–54, who discusses evidence for the language used by instrumental witnesses when accepting the role.

there are two kinds of judicial witnesses: "voluntary and those to whom in public trials it is customary to give statutory notice" (Quint. *Inst. Or.* 5.7.9).[13] Only prosecution witnesses in public (i.e., criminal) trials were subject to such a notice (*denuntiatio*). This indicates that "voluntary" witnessing was the norm in the first century CE (as it likely had been up to that point). That remained so until the emergence of the *cognitio*-system which gave the presiding official the power to compel witnesses to appear. Despite this general lack of compulsion, witnesses in Roman law still performed their role at the request of another party.[14] In some instances, such a request was formalized in ritual, but in other cases there seems to have been no particular mechanism.[15] That is true whether the witness was instrumental or judicial. Yet the very fact of a request means that the "neutrality" of a witness who chooses to comply is open to question. Evidence on the partisan-vs-neutral question points in both directions.[16] It is a fair hypothesis that the need for witness neutrality develops rather than being present from the start. That development also entails a shift in the nature—or, better, direction—of the witnesses' *fides*: it would no longer be only the parties themselves who would rely on it but the community as a whole.

There is an impulse in the scholarship to keep instrumental and judicial witnesses distinct.[17] Thus, for example, Henri Lévy-Bruhl focuses on instrumental

13 On this passage and *testes denuntiati*, see Charles Guérin, *La voix de la vérité: Témoin et témoignage dans les tribunaux romains du Ier siècle avant J.-C.* (Paris: Belles Lettres, 2015), 108–114; Giovanni Pugliese, "La Preuve dans le Procès Romain de l'Époque Classique," in *La Preuve. Première Partie: Antiquité.* Recueils de la Société Jean Bodin 16 (Bruxelles: Éditions de la librairie encyclopédique, 1964), 314–315.

14 So, too, Max Kaser, "*Testimonium*," in *Realencyclopädie der classischen Altertumswissenschaft*, ed August Friedrich von Pauly and Georg Wissowa, 2nd series, vol. V A.1 (Stuttgart: Metzler, 1890–1980), 1024.63–68.

15 The mechanism(s) of summoning witnesses are, for reasons of space, beyond the scope of this chapter and must be left to the fuller treatment.

16 For explanations of witnesses as partisan supporters, see e.g., Pringsheim, "Le témoignage," 162; Umberto Vincenti, "*Duo Genera Sunt Testium*": *Contributo allo Studio della Prova Testimoniale nel Processo Romano.* (Padova: CEDAM, 1989), 6–7; Pugliese, "La Preuve," 312–313. As neutral parties: Guérin, *La voix de la verité*, 25, 30–33, 75–76; see e.g., *PS* 5.15.1 (*FIRA* 2.402).

17 See e.g., Pugliese, "La Preuve," 282 n. 1 and 311–312. There are exceptions: Gerardo Broggini, "La Prova nel Processo Romano Arcaico," *Ius* 11, no. 3 (1960): 372–373; Geoffrey MacCormack, "Witnesses in the Law of the Twelve Tables," *Bullettino dell'Istituto di Diritto Romano* 15 (1973): 230–231; Michel Humbert, "*Intestabilis*," in *Fides Humanitas Ius: Studii in Onore di Luigi Labruna IV*, ed Cosimo Cascione and Carla Masi Doria (Napoli: Editoriale Scientifica, 2007), 2544 n. 3; Fiori, "La gerarchia," 221.

witnesses to the near exclusion of judicial witnesses.[18] In contrast, Charles Guérin's exploration of the place of witnesses in the courts of the late republic introduces instrumental witnesses only to set them aside.[19] Despite gestures at the possible connection between the two roles, the result is discussions of "witnesses" that diverge in fundamental ways from each other.[20] Instrumental witnesses are considered principally for their civic roles and thus as extensions of the community, for which neutrality would seem crucial. Judicial witnesses are assessed within the theoretical framework of proof and persuasion, where their partisan nature can become more apparent. This dichotomy admittedly maps onto the nature of the ancient sources for each function. Up until about 100 CE judicial witnesses tend to be discussed by writers of rhetorical handbooks—people like Cicero and Quintilian.[21] They discuss witnesses in the courtroom context of questioning and cross-examination without any interest in the legal rules of evidence. The jurists, in contrast, have little to say about judicial witnesses until the late second century CE when changes in the judicial process (viz. the increasing shift away from the formulary procedure towards *cognitiones*) seem to make questions of proof and witness reliability more "legal" and rule-bound.[22] The matter of instrumental witnesses, on the contrary, is always a "legal" question because their presence or absence has legal consequences. That makes it a juristic focus from the beginning.

These categories can be useful for the analysis of discrete instances of witnessing. Importantly, however, these categories are not Roman categories, even if on rare occasions the Romans seem to treat these functions as separate.[23]

18 Lévy-Bruhl, *Le témoignage instrumentaire*, 7–8. He does concede at times that as the law develops, the two roles can become connected—the instrumental leading to the evidentiary—but this is for him a development of the classical period. See also Broggini, "La Prova," 372–373.

19 Guérin, *La voix de la verité*, 30–34.

20 In Guérin's case, it is arguably more than a "gesture": he suggests that the judicial witness descends in part from the instrumental witness, a connection that for Lévy-Bruhl is more incidental than genetic.

21 See e.g., Cic. *Part. Or.* 48–51 and 117–118; Quint. *Inst. Or.* 5.7.

22 See esp. the works cited at *D.* 22.5.

23 See, for example, the story of Taracia (discussed below with text at nn. 165–166). There, the sources distinguish the right to give testimony (*ius testimonii dicendi*) from the right to be an instrumental witness (being *testabilis*). This distinction likely reflects the fact that at the time when the tradition about Taracia developed, the roles of judicial and instrumental witnesses were, in the case of women, separable and distinct. Women could testify in court but could not act as instrumental witnesses: see briefly the discussion in section three; more fully in James Townshend, "*Mulier Testabilis*: Women as Witnesses in Roman Law," in *Female Agency in the Ancient Mediterranean*, ed. Greg Gilles, Karolina Frank, Christine Plastow, and Lewis Webb. (Liverpool: Liverpool University Press, 2024).

Neither the rhetorical writers nor the jurists ever explicitly speak of "judicial" or "instrumental" witnesses. They simply talk about "witnesses."[24] The modern bright line between the two categories deliberately ignores the terminological overlap. Moreover, when the two categories are too rigidly defined, a problematic gap develops. If judicial witnesses are *only* those that testify in court and instrumental witnesses are *only* those whose presence validates an act, then there are "witnesses" to whom neither category is necessarily applicable. This would include persons designated as witnesses who are present at transactions but whose presence is not strictly necessary to make the transaction valid. Conversely if the boundaries become too porous, the categories break down. Geoffrey MacCormack has articulated the central question well: "Does the function of the witnesses whose cooperation is necessary for the completion of a legal act or procedure differ *in some fundamental way* from the function of witnesses whose role is confined to the giving of evidence *apud iudicem*?"[25]

Significantly, from at least the time of the Twelve Tables, the Romans themselves acknowledged the overlap.[26] The archetype of the instrumental witness in Roman law is the witness to an act "by bronze and scale" (*per aes et libram*). Such acts include the *mancipatio*, a conveyancing ritual used to transfer ownership of certain kinds of property (*res mancipi*: see *Inst.*Gai. 2.14a and 22), as well as its manifold derivative acts: the mancipatory will (discussed below), releases from certain kinds of debt, and various acts affecting personal status (adoptions, emancipations, *coemptio* of a bride).[27] In all these cases, there must be at least five male witnesses, each of age and of Roman citizen status, as well as a sixth person sharing these characteristics to act as the scales-holder (*libripens*).[28] The absence of these persons renders the act

---

24 See also Lévy-Bruhl, *Le témoignage instrumentaire*, 3, who in his foreword remarks that the absence of any comprehensive study of *témoignage instrumentaire* was explained, if not justified, by the failure of the ancient Roman jurists to construct a theory of such witnessing.

25 MacCormack, "Witnesses in the Law," 227 (emphasis added); see also pages 229–230.

26 See also MacCormack, "Witnesses in the Law," 231; Humbert, "*Intestabilis*," 2544 n. 3. Cf. Kaser, "*Testimonium*," 1021.44–65, who sees them as necessarily evidentiary in a time before extensive writing and then retained due to the conservatism of Roman law; Pugliese, "La Preuve," 311–312.

27 See *Inst.*Gai. 1.113, 119, 132, 2.104–108, 119, 3.173–174. In the interests of space, I will not discuss in detail all juridical acts which scholars have argued require instrumental witnesses: see e.g., Kaser, "*Testimonium*," 1026.27–50; Broggini, "La Prova," 372–373; Arnaldo Biscardi, "'*Testes Estote*' Contribution à L'étude du Témoignage en Droit Romain," *Revue historique de droit français et étranger* 49, no. 3 (1971): 403–404; MacCormack, "Witnesses in the Law," 225–227.

28 For more on these "qualifying" characteristics, see section three below.

void. It is a reasonable inference that originally the witnesses to the *mancipatio* served a validating function: as representatives of the community they affirmed that the transferor in fact owned the property in question and that ownership was now transferred to the other person. That would also suggest a neutral, non-partisan role.[29] Aulus Gellius, writing in the second century CE, preserves a provision of the Twelve Tables, a portion of which has been cited above: "Whoever allows himself to act as a witness or is a scales-holder, if he should not speak his testimony, let him be *improbus* and *intestabilis*" (Gell. *NA* 15.13.11; XII 8.22 *FIRA* 1.62).[30] The inclusion of the *libripens* here means that this provision embraces within its scope acts *per aes et libram* and thus specifically includes "instrumental" witnesses.[31] I will discuss in section three what being "*improbus* and *intestabilis*" might entail—at a minimum it disqualifies the person from acting as a witness. The key point here is that by the middle of the fifth century BCE the role of an "instrumental" witness was understood by the Romans to entail the potential and obligatory role of "judicial" witness.[32] Further, the performance of both roles demanded the witness's presence.

29 We may compare the role of the magistrate in the *in iure cessio* for analogous transactions.

30 The word I have translated as "speak" (*fariatur*, the consensus reading of the manuscripts) is generally agreed to be corrupt. It seems, however, that the verb should be connected with "speaking" (*fari*): see e.g., Ernout and Meillet, *Dictionnaire Étymologique*, s.v. *farior*; Leofranc Holford-Strevens, *Gelliana: A Textual Companion to the Noctes Atticae of Aulus Gellius* (Oxford: Oxford University Press, 2020), 138.

31 The phrase *libripensve fuerit* also confirms that the provision imagines after-the-fact testimony rather than a refusal to be a witness in the moment: so too Lévy-Bruhl, *Le témoignage instrumentaire*, 39 with n. 7. Some have advocated for omitting *libripensve fuerit* from the provision as a reflection of later developments: Franz Wieacker, "Zwölftafelprobleme," *Revue Internationale des Droits de l'Antiquité*. Series 3. 3 (1956): 464–465; Humbert, "*Intestabilis*," 2543 n. 1. The reasoning, however, is somewhat circular. Cf. MacCormack, "Witnesses in the Law," 232, who supports deleting the phrase because its inclusion would seem to limit the provision *only* to transactions *per aes et libram* and not other instances of "witnessing." This is incorrect. The disjunctive *-ve* means that *libripens* is not a *necessary* but simply a *possible* counterpart to the other witnesses. Max Kaser and Karl Hackl, *Das Römische Zivilprozessrecht*. 2nd ed. Handbuch der Altertumswissenschaft 10.3.4. (München: C. H. Beck, 1996), 119 n. 36 acknowledge the implication of the inclusion of *libripens* in the provision, but hold open the possibility that it applies to witnesses in other contexts.

32 Cf. Humbert, "*Intestabilis*," for whom these instrumental witnesses are never *merely* potential sources of evidence but active collaborators in the legal act. I leave for another time the question of whether this provision applies to judicial witnesses: see e.g., Lévy-Bruhl, *Le témoignage instrumentaire*, 39 n. 7 and MacCormack, "Witnesses in the Law," 233–234, arguing that judicial witnesses are strictly not caught by the clause because they have not incurred an obligation to give evidence on a later day.

This early development is, I suggest, closely tied to the replacement of violent self-help with a state-controlled legal system. In this regard, we can consider the role of *superstites* in the so-called *manuum consertio*, a process connected with the archaic *legis actio sacramento in rem*.[33] Our primary sources are Cicero and Gellius, though only Cicero mentions *superstites*.[34] Gellius reports that the Twelve Tables included an explicit provision about "engaging hands in court" (*in iure manum conserere*) in order to claim ownership of a piece of property (Gell. *NA*. 20.10.8; XII 6.6a *FIRA* 1.45).[35] Gradually, Roman territory became so big that the praetor could not travel to every district in order to hear cases. Thus, the Romans developed the *ex iure manuum consertio*, notwithstanding the fact that it was strictly contrary to the Twelve Tables (Gell. *NA* 20.10.9). In court before the praetor, the two parties would both summon each other to the property that was the subject of the dispute "to engage by hand according to law" (*ex iure manu consertum*).[36] As part of that exchange of summonses, the praetor would add the following statement: "With each of their *superstites* present, I proclaim the route; go by the route" (Cic. *Mur*. 26). This indicates that the *superstites* had to be present in court when the parties each made their claims.[37] More than mere presence, however, the praetor's language indicates that these *superstites* were not random bystanders but accompanied each of the parties to court. The *superstites* are *sui utrique* and so "belong" in a sense to each party. This implies a more partisan "supporter"

33 The phrase *manuum consertio* is not itself ancient: the sources use the supine-phrase *ex iure manu consertum*.

34 Cic. *Mur*. 26 (the only instance of *superstes* in Cicero with this meaning); Gell. *NA* 20.10.7–9. Also relevant is Festus 394.37L, 396.2–4L, and 516.31–33L. It seems that *Inst.* Gai. 4.17 might have offered further confirmation of what we find in Cicero and Gellius. Unfortunately, the page in which Gaius sets out the ritual acts and words is missing from the manuscript (that he did include them is recoverable from the Antinoite fragments). Gaius's *Institutes* do nevertheless confirm the reason for the ritual (apparent from Gellius but noticeably absent from Cicero's disdainful summary): the property under dispute must be physically present in the court, so the parties must bring back a representative and symbolic piece of it.

35 On the textual issues, see Holford-Strevens, *Gelliana*, 164.

36 See Johannes Platschek, "*Ex iure manum conserere*: Zur symbolischen Gewalt im frühen römischen Eigentumsprozess," *Tijdschrift voor Rechtsgeschiedenis* 74 (2006): 245–260, for the argument that Gellius wrongly understands *ex iure* to mean "outside of the court" rather than "according to law." It is not clear from Cicero's brief presentation whether the defendant also asserts a claim to the land, e.g., Henri Lévy-Bruhl, "La '*manuum consertio*'," *IVRA: rivista internazionale di diritto romano e antico* 4 (1953): 166, or simply offers a counter summons, e.g., Alan Watson, *Rome of the XII Tables: Persons and Property* (Princeton: Princeton University Press, 1975), 125–127.

37 So too Lévy-Bruhl, *Le témoignage instrumentaire*, 13; Biscardi, "*Testes Estote*," 398.

role: these *superstites* appear as extensions of those parties rather than separate (or "third") entities.[38]

Given that the phrase *manum conserere* suggests an original trial by combat, it would not be surprising for each party to bring some "muscle" to back their claims.[39] For this reason I have to this point avoided calling them "witnesses."[40] That, however, is how the classical sources present them. The second-century CE lexicographer Pompeius Festus is explicit: *superstites* means "witnesses who are present" (Festus 394.37L).[41] The direct equation *superstites* = *testes* reflects the emergence of the state-controlled legal system by the time of the Twelve Tables. Any violence in the *manuum consertio* will have been ritualized within the state-controlled system so that the outcome is determined by legal process rather than force. This is apparent also from the explicit provision in the Twelve Tables about "engaging hands *in* court" (XII 6.6a *FIRA* 1.45). Here, the violence of *manuum consertio* has been reduced to the symbolic grasping of the property.[42] Any violence, such as it is, has been brought under the direct control of the state. Hence also the praetor's explicit intervention: "Both of you release [the property]" (*Inst.*Gai. 4.16). The role of the *superstites* will thus have shifted at a very early stage in Roman legal history from supporters of the claimants to observers of the ritual act—witnesses.[43] It is debatable whether they are

38 See also Lévy-Bruhl, *Le témoignage instrumentaire*, 13–14; "La '*manuum consertio*'," 167; Henri Lévy-Bruhl, "Les témoins de la *litis contestatio*," *Annales de la Faculté de Droit d'Istanbul* 3 (1955): 7; Biscardi, "*Testes Estote*," 398. *Pace* Elizabeth A. Meyer, *Legitimacy and Law in the Roman World: Tabulae in Roman Belief and Practice* (Cambridge: Cambridge University Press, 2004), 118, who, following Alan Watson, *International Law in Archaic Rome: War and Religion* (Baltimore: Johns Hopkins University Press, 1993), 10–19, argues (1) that *testes* are initially judges of the rightness of an act and (2) drawing on Festus 394.37L, that *testes* and *superstites* are simple synonyms (an assertion not made by Watson).

39 On the violence implicit in *manum conserere*, see Platschek, "*Ex Iure Manum Conserere*," 250 with citations. But see Lévy-Bruhl, "La '*manuum consertio*'," 165, who suggests that the commonly found meaning of the phrase as a synonym for *pugnare* is a subsequent development, citing an earlier edition of Ernout and Meillet, *Dictionnaire Étymologique*, s.v. *sero* II.

40 Cf. Lévy-Bruhl, *Le témoignage instrumentaire*, 82–83, who thinks these *superstites* should be excluded from the classification of *témoins instrumentaires*, as he defines it.

41 Festus epitomizes the Augustan-period lexicographer Verrius Flaccus. See also Paul. Fest. 395.7L; Isid. *Etym.* 18.15.8. Despite being cited by some scholars, Serv. *Ad Aen.* 3.339 is not germane.

42 For the symbolic grasping of the property, see Gell. *NA*. 20.10.7–8 and *Inst.*Gai. 4.16–17. Gaius notes that the *festuca-vindicta* represented a spear (*quasi hastae loco*); Platschek, "*Ex Iure Manum Conserere*," esp. 251–252, on the change in the "violence."

43 See Festus 396.2–4L, who states that the proof that *superstites* are *testes* is "the fact that with *superstites* present, those between whom there is a disagreement are ordered to take

validators of the act who assure in the moment that the parties are properly carrying out the *manuum consertio* (whether in or away from court) or (potential) sources of testimony about the property and the parties' claims.[44] Most likely, they are both. In performing both roles, however, the societal demands of *fides* require a level of neutrality, since it is the court rather than the individual who must rely on the witnesses' statements. The court needs to be able to trust the witnesses. And because the *manuum consertio* was in place at the time of the Twelve Tables, this need for neutrality must have developed early in the Roman legal system.

A similar early shift can be seen in the role of witnesses to the *litis contestatio*, the final moment of the *in iure* proceedings, which marked the transition to the trial *apud iudicem*. According to the excerpts of Festus compiled by Paul the Deacon in the eighth century CE, "two or more opponents are said to '*contestari litem*' because when a court case has been instituted it is customary for each party to say '*testes estote*'" (Paul. Fest. 50L).[45] At whom is the imperative *estote* directed? Lévy-Bruhl has observed that this moment is too important to rely on chance bystanders in the forum; therefore, the witnesses are likely summoned in advance by each of the litigants.[46] This observation gains an added point if, as Gellius suggests (Gell. *NA*. 20.10.9), in the very early period the magistrate traveled beyond the city to hear claims, in which case there would be no forum bystanders to call upon. These witnesses thus appear similar to the *superstites* of the *manuum consertio*.

The details of the *litis contestatio* and the utterance "*testes estote*" are admittedly a matter of conjecture.[47] Alan Watson has argued that in the archaic

---

up their claims." This explains why the comic playwright Plautus, writing some 250 years after the Twelve Tables, can use the word to denote someone who is present and thus can hear the speaker (Plaut. *Truc.* 387; *Art.* fr. 1.1 quoted at Festus 396.5–7L).

44 A small difficulty: Gellius and Gaius do not mention witnesses at all; Festus refers specifically to the same moment in court described by Cicero. There is no evidence for the role of witnesses beyond that specific moment. We know for certain only that the *superstites* accompanied the parties to court, so any reconstruction of the witnesses' role *away from court* is admittedly speculative. See e.g., Lévy-Bruhl, "La '*manuum consertio*'," 167, who argues for performance away from the court (although we may then wonder why, per *Inst.*Gai. 4.17, a representative piece had to be brought back).

45 See also Paul. Fest. 34L; Biscardi, "*Testes Estote*," 386–387. Cf. Broggini, "La Prova," 377, who suggests that *superstites* was probably the technical designation for all witnesses to archaic *in iure* procedural acts.

46 Lévy-Bruhl, *Le témoignage instrumentaire*, 18–19 and "Les témoins de la *litis contestatio*." See also Biscardi, "*Testes Estote*," 397 and 404–405, who calls them *advocati*.

47 Lévy-Bruhl, *Le témoignage instrumentaire*, 15–16 and Biscardi, "*Testes Estote*," 410 both suggest that surviving accounts of the *litis contestatio* derive from after the *lex Aebutia* (late

period *testis* means "judge" rather than "witness" so that "*testes estote*" constitutes the appointment of the judges.[48] I am not convinced. The fact that the phrase is plural and that each party gives the command militates against such an interpretation. So too does the discussion of judge selection for the *legis actio sacramento in personam* provided by the second-century CE jurist Gaius (*Inst.*Gai. 4.15).[49] Max Kaser and Karl Hackl, on the other hand, place the call for witnesses before the oaths required by the *legis actio sacramento*, in order that the witnesses might later testify that the proper language and actions took place.[50] I find this generally persuasive but wish to offer a supplemental suggestion about the development of this role, particularly beyond the *legis actio sacramento*.

The *litis contestatio* is necessarily a feature of the state-controlled system that replaces violent self-help. The parties' declarations "*testes estote*" articulate the moment when partisan supporters (i.e., *superstites*) are transformed into neutral third parties (i.e., *testes*).[51] The role of those accompanying each of the parties shifts from supporting the specific oppositional claims to witnessing and affirming a shared set of circumstances in court. Moreover, this functional shift may help explain why the witnesses are mentioned only in the lexicographical sources and not the juristic sources, especially if we accept that the sources reflect more closely the realities of the formulary process.[52] Presuming

second century BCE) and reflect the circumstances of the formulary procedure rather than the *legis actiones*.

48 Watson, *International Law in Archaic Rome*, 13–16.

49 Gaius's discussion of the appointment of judges for the action *in rem* is missing from the manuscripts. There is no reason, however, to think that it differed materially from the action *in personam* on this point.

50 Kaser and Hackl, *Das Römische Zivilprozessrecht*, 76, arguing in n. 40 that *ordinato iudicio* at Paul. Fest. 50L refers not to the appointment of the judge but to the establishment of the issue for trial. For Kaser and Hackl, the use of witnesses is evidence of the oral nature of early process. See also Broggini, "La Prova," 373 n. 98; MacCormack, "Witnesses in the Law," 230–231, who suggests that it is reasonable to suppose that the witnesses to *litis contestatio* serve an evidentiary function. Cf. Lévy Bruhl, "Les témoins de la *litis contestatio*," 8–9; Biscardi, "*Testes Estote*," 405.

51 *Pace* Biscardi, "*Testes Estote*," 405, who sees this as the moment that these summoned individuals become *sui testes* who give weight to the declarations of the party they support; also Lévy-Bruhl, "Les témoins de la *litis contestatio*," 6, though at 8, he suggests that they are also "*accessoirement probatoire*[s]" since they may affect the mindset of the opponent or the judge.

52 The other explanation for the nature of the sources is more banal, albeit not mutually exclusive. By the time the *Digest* is compiled, both the *legis actiones* and the formulary procedure have been replaced by the *cognitiones*. Consequently, what is now called the *litis contestatio* is fundamentally different from the moment previously described as such under the earlier systems.

they still play a role at all, the witnesses will have become an empty formality. The presumption that they were still present rests on the following: (1) the general conservatism of Roman law;[53] (2) the use of the present tense *dicere solet* in the lexicographical explanation; and (3) the explicit presence of witnesses in other *contestationes*, even in the post-classical period.[54] Their presence, however, is no longer felt to have any instrumental effect since it is now the magistrate who gives legal force to the proceedings. Once the formulary procedure replaced the *legis actiones*, the specific question to be decided by the judge (i.e., the formula) was written down rather than announced orally. That means there was no evidentiary need for witnesses about the nature of the trial proceedings—except, perhaps, as sealers of the wax tablets (*tabulae*) on which the formula was written.[55] In either case, they stand as neutral guarantors of the process rather than partisan supporters of the litigants. In that capacity, their *fides* is owed to the whole community rather than the individual parties.

The overlap of instrumental and judicial functions and the developing need for neutrality are observable in other examples of self-help remedies. For instance, the Twelve Tables allowed a thief to be lawfully killed during the day if the thief (1) was apprehended in the act and (2) defended himself with a weapon, but only after the victim summoned witnesses by shouting (XII 8.13 *FIRA* 1.58).[56] This is the so-called *endoploratio*.[57] Cicero explains that the victim should cry out so that others may hear and assemble, and he remarks upon the leniency (*clementia*) towards criminals of the law which did not permit the

53 See e.g., the continued use well into the imperial period of the *mancipatio* formalities, the witnessing of which Ulpian refers to as a *contestatio* (*D.* 28.1.20.8).

54 See e.g., *CTh.* 12.6.2.1, a rescript of Constantine dated July 19, 325 CE, which specifies *inter alia* that a person can pay their taxes at any time during the year and that if payment is refused, they should make an attestation after calling witnesses (*testibus adhibitis contestationem debebit proponere*).

55 See e.g., *TPSulp.* 31 (the formulas for an *actio de sponsione* and *actio certae creditae pecuniae*). Other magistrate orders were sealed, see e.g., *TH*² A3, a praetorian grant of *bonorum possessio* recorded and sealed by witnesses. For more on witnesses and sealing, see text below beginning at n. 72.

56 See also M. H. Crawford, ed., *Roman Statutes*. 2 vols. BICS Supplement 64 (London: Institute of Classical Studies, 1996), 2.609–613, who additionally touches on the killing of a thief caught in the act at night which did not require witnesses.

57 On *endoploratio*, see also Franz Wieacker, "*Endoplorare*: Diebstahlsverfolgung und Gerüft im altrömischen Recht," *Festschrift für Leopold Wenger: zu seinem 70. Geburtstag dargebracht von Freunden, Fachgenossen und Schülern* (München: C. H. Beck, 1944), 129–179. By the late republic and certainly the early empire, the use of this rule had evolved, it seems, into one of self-defense for homicide rather than self-help against a thief.

armed defense of one's own life at home without witnesses (Cic. *Tull.* 50).[58] Cicero indicates that these other people would assemble in order to act as witnesses: they are summoned to give publicity both to the apprehension of the thief and to the theft itself. It is open to argument whether they are meant to judge the validity of the killing in the moment or whether they are meant to testify about it later (e.g., in a homicide trial)—or even whether they initially joined the fight as partisan supporters.[59] Indeed, they may have performed all these functions at different stages in the law's development.[60] Most importantly for my point, the sources do not specify or draw any distinction. The witnesses are simply required.

This early functional overlap can be seen also in the rules for *furtum conceptum*. From the time of the Twelve Tables this delict resulted when stolen property was found during searches that required the presence of witnesses (*Inst.*Gai. 3.186 and 191).[61] The search was the start, not the end of the process,

58 This is, I suggest, how we should understand Gaius's use of the verb *testificari* with shouting (*D.* 9.2.4.1). The standard English edition of the *Digest* translates *testificari* here as "provide evidence"—but to whom? The victim does not shout "to provide evidence" but rather as a kind of summons, thus rendering *testificari* closer to "invoke witnesses" or "call for witnesses." For this meaning, cf. OLD s.v. *testificor* §2. Cf. Wieacker, "*Endoplorare*," 146–147.

59 Pringsheim, "Le témoignage," 169 suggests that initially they were supporters who aided in the fight, then became validators of the act whose statements would bind a judge, and finally morphed into material witnesses; Wieacker, "*Endoplorare*," esp. 151–162, sees very early development from helpers to judges of sorts to testifiers; Biscardi, "*Testes Estote*," 403–404 sees them as validators; MacCormack, "Witnesses in the Law," 226 asserts that they are meant to testify, but may have become involved in the fracas.

60 This would be especially true if Cicero's phrase *sine testibus et arbitris* reflects an original differentiation of roles (e.g., *testes* as testifiers, *arbitri* as validators: cf. Wieacker, "*Endoplorare*," 162). There is, however, no strong reason to believe that Cicero replicates the language of the Twelve Tables, since the phrase belongs to his explanation of the law's purpose rather than the law itself. Still, some hold that the doublet *testes et arbitri* is archaic: see e.g., Biscardi, "*Testes Estote*," 404; Broggini, "La Prova," 366–367 and 376–377, who also assumes that witnesses to searches *lance et licio*, to *manus iniectio*, and to *obvagulatio* were also "*testes atque arbitri*," though they are not described as such anywhere. In one fourth-century CE text, witnesses to a deed of gift are called *arbitri* (Vat. Fr. 249.6 [FIRA 2.514–515] = *CTh.* 8.12.1.2). No editors of the Twelve Tables have included the phrase in their restorations of the relevant sections.

61 Also Gell. NA 11.18.9 and 16.10.8; see e.g., Francis de Zulueta, *The Institutes of Gaius*, 2 vols. (Oxford: Clarendon Press, 1946–53), 2.201–203 for a survey of older interpretations of these rules. I leave aside the relationship between the two different kinds of searches mentioned by Gaius (including the *lance et licio*). While Gaius does not specify anything about the witnesses beyond their presence, the early sixth-century *Lex Romana Burgundiorum* required three freeborn witnesses (*cum tribus ingenuis testibus*, LRB 12.1).

so the witnesses' role was preliminary to state-controlled judicial proceedings. This is evident from the account of Gaius, who discusses the consequent actions and penalties as set out in the Twelve Tables. It is reasonable, therefore, to infer that the witnesses would later be called to testify about the search and what was found. It is also possible that originally the witnesses aided in the search. In a time before a strong state-controlled legal system, self-help remedies might still require a degree of community sanction that manifests as witnesses. Once the state system emerges as the dominant legal actor, the role of "witnesses" changes. They no longer validate the action taken in the moment (whether killing or search) but instead attest to its validity later in court by confirming the attendant circumstances.[62] It is possible then to see the provisions of XII 8.22 (*FIRA* 1.62) about failing to testify as applying to these witnesses as well: in agreeing to be witnesses, they bind themselves to appear in court later. Thus the slide from instrumental to judicial functions—or perhaps better, the blurring of the two functions—happens very early in the Roman system, as does the emergence of a need for neutrality.

The conception of such witnesses as potential sources of evidence rather than validators of an act takes root in the Roman legal system. This is apparent from the provisions of the first-century Augustan law on adultery, the *lex Iulia de adulteriis*, which contemplate circumstances comparable to those of the *endoploratio*. The jurist Ulpian, writing in the early third century CE, explains that the law provided that a husband who caught an adulterer with his wife (*in uxore*) could, if unwilling or unable to kill him, choose to detain him for up to twenty hours for the purposes of witnessing the matter (*D.* 48.5.26.1). Ulpian is explicit that the words *testandae eius rei gratia* are included in order to allow for witnesses who will testify that the accused adulterer was caught by the plaintiff in the act (*D.* 48.5.26.5). The Augustan rule is therefore clearly envisaged as a step preliminary to judicial proceedings.

An interesting case of the interrelationship of these validating and evidentiary functions is the conflation of the role of *testis* with that of *signator* "sealer," particularly for wills. Originally, wills were made orally before the assembled citizenry, either in a civilian context (*calatis comitiis*) or in a military context (*in procinctu*); these archaic forms were then superseded by the mancipatory will (*testamentum per aes et libram*).[63] The mancipatory will was an *ad hoc* adaptation of the original *mancipatio* (discussed above). According to Gaius, it was first developed to address the threat of sudden death (*Inst.*Gai. 2.102).[64] It

62 Cf. Broggini, "La Prova," 376–377.

63 *Inst.*Gai. 2.101–104; Gell. *NA* 15.27.3.

64 Cf. e.g., Cic. *Clu.* 37, where Avilius pretends to be sick and wants to make a will.

also involved the mancipation of the whole *familia* (the estate and household) rather than a specific piece of property. These factors suggest a slightly different role for the witnesses than in an ordinary *mancipatio*. A witness might in the moment deny that the testator has capacity to make the will or might declare that the *familiae emptor* or heir is ineligible. It is less clear that witnesses might object to the mancipation of the abstract *familia* as they might to the transfer of an individual and identified piece of property. Still, persons present at the testamentary *mancipatio* might later be called upon to testify about the formalities, per the Twelve Tables, should a civil law heir-upon-intestacy attempt to claim the estate. The role of the witnesses therefore is no more about affirming the validity of the act in the moment than it concerns attesting to it afterwards. While their presence makes the act valid, that validity only matters if it is later called into question, so their function is equally evidentiary.

When we look at references to wills in the works of Cicero, the witnesses are friends, acquaintances, and colleagues in the main—or whoever was available, though a testator might also prevail upon persons of high(er) social status and prestige or potential allies, if they were amenable.[65] This is consistent with Gaius's suggestion that the *testamentum per aes et libram* was developed for urgent situations that might, therefore, require witnesses immediately to hand (*Inst.*Gai. 2.102). The jurists call such witnesses *rogati* ("invited" or "solicited").[66] Gaius indicates that they were ritually asked for their testimony as part of the *nuncupatio* (*Inst.*Gai. 2.104).[67] Ulpian explains that the rule is that

65 General "availability": Cic. *Att.* 7.2.3 (he and his entourage are just passing through on their return to Rome from his province), Suet. *Tib.* 76, *D.* 22.5.22 (Venuleius); social "betters" and allies: Cic. *Att.* 14.3.2, *Att.* 14.14.5, and *Mil.* 48 (with Clodius!), Val. Max. 7.7.2, Suet. *Claud.* 44.1, Plin. *Ep.* 1.9.2–3. Invitations and the sealing as a kind of social event: Cic. *Att.* 12.18a.2, Plin. *Ep.* 2.20.10–11. For an (admittedly fragmentary) example of an invitation, see *P. Mich.* 466. On wills generally, see Edward Champlin, *Final Judgments: Duty and Emotion in Roman Wills, 200 B.C.–A.D. 250* (Berkeley: University of California Press, 1991), 75–81.

66 See e.g., *D.* 22.5.11 (Pomponius) and *D.* 28.1.21.2 (Ulpian); *CTh.* 4.4.7.2; *P.Berol.* Inv. 7124 (= *ChLA* X 412), with the discussion of Francesca Terranova, "Sull'*antestatus* negli atti *per aes et libram*," *IVRIS ANTIQVI HISTORIA: An International Journal on Ancient Law* 2 (2010), 134–136, though I am not persuaded by her assertion that since the mancipatory clause itself is a remnant rather than a record of the *mancipatio*, only one of the witnesses needs to have been recorded as "called." It is worth nothing that *adhibere* is the standard term for using someone as a witness, whereas *perhibere* (especially with *testimonium*) is about performing witness functions; *rogatus* is used only for wills and not for other mancipatory acts.

67 Most scholars presume that some sort of ritual assent was then given in response, which would trigger the consequent obligation to testify under the Twelve Tables: see e.g., Lévy-Bruhl, *Le témoignage instrumentaire*, 132–133; Biscardi, "*Testes Estote*," 405, drawing analogy with the *stipulatio*; Kaser and Hackl, *Das Römische Zivilprozessrecht*, 70 n. 40.

witnesses to a will should be invited (*rogati*) for that specific purpose, but witnesses present for another purpose can still serve as witnesses (*testimonium perhibere*), provided that they are informed beforehand that they will be witnessing a will (*D.* 28.1.21.2).[68] Such looseness could, however, be exploited. Cicero reports how Avilius impersonates Asuvius in order to forge the latter's will, while Oppianicus gathers persons to seal the will who would be familiar with neither man and therefore unable to detect the fraud (Cic. *Clu.* 37). As Edward Champlin has noted, there is a certain distance between the testator and the witnesses.[69] This supports the idea that in the classical period the witnesses do not have a stake in the legal act: they are in this case (meant to be) neutral.[70]

Initially the mancipatory will was entirely oral.[71] By the late republic, however, it was standard for the contents of the mancipatory will to be written in *tabulae*.[72] The wax tablets containing these written wills were sealed. The *lex Cornelia de falsis* on forgery (80/79 BCE) made tampering with these seals a crime.[73] At some point before 70 BCE, the praetor declared in his edict that he would grant *bonorum possessio* of the estate according to the terms of a written document (*secundum tabulas*) so long as the tablets were sealed "with no less

---

68 But see also the remark that for establishing the fact of an event even an unsolicited witness counts (*D.* 22.5.11 [Pomponius]).

69 Champlin, *Final Judgments*, 78–81, noting witnesses tend not to receive from the wills they have sealed.

70 See also text below at nn. 133–134.

71 The remark in the *Institutes* of Justinian that, unlike for the praetorian will, "in civil law the seals of witnesses were not required" (*Inst.* 2.10.2) reflects the original oral nature of Roman wills (i.e., there was nothing for witnesses to seal), as does Ulpian's comment that the testator may name the heir either by writing or by nuncupation (*D.* 28.1.21pr); cf. Suetonius's account of the poet Horace's will (Suet. *Vita Hor.* 48). See also de Zulueta, *Institutes of Gaius*, 2.87–90; Pasquale Voci, "Linee storiche del diritto ereditario romano I. Dalle origini ai Severi," *Aufstieg und Niedergang der römischen Welt* II, Band 14 (1982): 403; Otto Karlowa, *Römische Rechtsgeschichte*, 2 vols. (Leipzig: Veit and Co, 1885–1892), 2.855; Alan Watson, *The Law of Succession in the Later Roman Republic* (Oxford: Clarendon Press, 1971), 11–12, suggesting also that the mancipatory will was contemplated by the Twelve Tables, though he seems to amend this position subsequently (e.g., Watson, *Rome of the XII Tables*, 60–61).

72 This practice is, I suggest, linked closely to the development of the "heir." Originally, the *familiae emptor* took full ownership of the estate and there was no "heir" (see *Inst.* Gai. 2.103). Both the institution of an heir and the practice of setting the will down in writing in *tabulae* facilitate composing a will in advance of the moment of death. See also Watson, *Rome of the XII Tables*, 60–61; Voci, "Linee storiche," 403.

73 See *PS* 4.7.1 and 5.25.1 (*FIRA* 2.376 and 410); Meyer, *Legitimacy and Law*, 165.

a number of seals than required by the statute" (Cic. 2 *Verr.* 1.117).[74] By the time of Gaius, that number is seven (*Inst.*Gai. 2.119 and 147). This corresponds to the five witnesses plus the *libripens* and the *familiae emptor* all present at the *mancipatio*.[75] The number seven is also reflected in contemporary practice as preserved in the documentary record.[76] There is no reason to think the number was not also seven in the late republic.[77] The seals on the *tabulae* must belong to someone, and it is a natural inference that from the start they belong to the witnesses and that these later provisions reflect that practice. By the second century CE, sealers and witnesses are considered the same thing.[78]

74 The exact identity, nature, and scope of the *lex* to which Cicero refers at Cic. 2 *Verr.* 1.117 have been a subject of debate. I will not rehearse that debate here: see e.g., Watson, *Law of Succession*, 14–15 with citations, who addresses and dismisses arguments doubting the existence of such a statute. Karlowa, *Römische Rechtsgeschichte*, 2.856–857; Meyer, *Legitimacy and Law*, 165, nn. 127–128.

75 The edict as consolidated by the jurist Julian for the Emperor Hadrian (ca. 131 CE) seems to have specified the seals of seven Roman citizen witnesses: Lenel *EP* 25, §149; *D.* 37.11.7 (Julian); *Epit. Ulp.* 23.6 and 28.6 (*FIRA* 2.289 and 298). See also Terranova, "Sull'*antestatus*," 143, who suggests that the role of the *familiae emptor* likely comes to be considered as another witness after the introduction of *bonorum possessio secundum tabulas*. Certainly, after the development of the institution of the heir, the role of *familiae emptor* becomes ritually formalistic (cf. Karlowa, *Römische Rechtsgeschichte*, 2.855–856).

76 See e.g., the will of Antonius Silvanus, dated March 27, 142 CE (*FIRA* 3.129–132, no. 47), the will of Gaius Longinus Castor, dated February 21, 197 CE (*FIRA* 3.146–153, no. 50), and the fragmentary papyrus (copy?) will of an unknown testator from 91 CE (*ChLA* IX.399). Several documents among the Bloomberg Tablets from London dating to the late first century CE (accessible at https://romaninscriptionsofbritain.org/tablondbloomberg) feature witness lists, though none is sufficiently intact to identify the nature of the document (*Tab.Lond.Bloomberg*, WT 63–68: Roger Tomlin, *Roman London's First Voices: Writing Tablets from the Bloomberg Excavations, 2010–14*. MOLA Monograph 72. (London: Museum of London Archaeology, 2016), 202–215). Cf. Lévy-Bruhl, *Le témoignage instrumentaire*, 154–155.

77 Cf. Lévy-Bruhl, *Le témoignage instrumentaire*, 127–132; Watson, *Law of Succession*, 17–18. The number may only/initially have been five or six (depending on whether the *libripens* is considered a witness), but there is no evidence that the statutory number was ever changed. If it were changed, a possibility might be the so-called *lex Iulia vicesimaria* of Augustus (5/6 CE), which introduced a five percent tax on testamentary inheritances to help fund military pensions.

78 *D.* 28.1.27 (Celsus) dismissing as foolish any doubt that one who writes and seals a will is also a witness; *D.* 28.1.30 (Paul) where the *witnesses* mark their own *seals*; *PS* 5.25.6 (*FIRA* 2.411) on the *SC Neronianum*; *D.* 28.1.22.4 (Ulpian) where *testes* have to sign *and* seal a will. See also Meyer, *Legitimacy and Law*, 133–134 and 159–164, suggesting that this conflation of *testis* and *signator* happens first with testamentary witnesses-sealers in the late republic given the importance of *fides* for the mancipatory will.

On the one hand, this is an evidentiary extension of the witnesses' role at the *mancipatio*.[79] The sealing does not make the *tabulae* a "valid" will under the law.[80] The will's validity still rests on the proper performance of the *mancipatio* (including the presence of the witnesses).[81] After all, *bonorum possessio* is granted *in the absence of* a valid will, and even then only in specific cases of invalidity.[82] On the other hand, sealing is a validating function for the document itself. The seals attest to the authenticity of the document. It also relies on the presence of the witnesses/sealers, since sealing must be done in person, and it invests the document with the *fides* of the witnesses.[83] We may note in this context two rules. First, that according to the first-century CE jurist Labeo, the praetor could compel witnesses (*testes*) to appear in court to authenticate their seals (*D.* 43.5.3.9 [Ulpian]).[84] The second rule is preserved by the early third-century CE jurist Paul: the witnesses—or at least a majority of them—had to be present when the will was opened to acknowledge their seals (*PS* 4.6.1 [*FIRA* 2.375–376]; see also Lenel *EP* 26, §167).[85]

The incorporation of the seals into both statute and the praetorian edict demonstrates the evidentiary value of those seals.[86] The seals validate the document and show that it is genuine. This creates a sufficiently strong (albeit rebuttable) presumption that the person named as heir in the *tabulae* would have and should have been the heir, but for the lack of proper formalities. That person will receive *bonorum possessio* unless and until a person with a civil law claim-upon-intestacy can show that the will was invalid. In the mid-second century CE, the emperor Antoninus Pius held that the person who receives *bonorum possessio* according to the terms of an improperly executed will should be given an *exceptio doli mali* against a civil law heir-upon-intestacy

79 So too Maria Nowak, *Wills in the Roman Empire: A Documentary Approach*. Journal of Juristic Papyrology Supplement 23 (Warsaw: University of Warsaw, 2015), 37; Kaser, "*Testimonium*," 1021.44–65; Lévy-Bruhl, *Le témoignage instrumentaire*, 133–134. A similar phenomenon is discernible with other transactions relying on the *mancipatio* (see e.g., *TPSulp.* 43 and 44; *TH*² 59–62; *FIRA* 3.287–301, nos. 88–94).

80 Hence a will could still be entirely oral, even in the empire, though scholars disagree as to the frequency of this: see Nowak, *Wills in the Roman Empire*, 20 n. 3 for citations.

81 By the second century CE, however, the *mancipatio* may not have been performed so much as recorded: see Terranova, "Sull'*antestatus*," 133; Nowak, *Wills in the Roman Empire*, 21–25.

82 See e.g., Cic. *Top.* 18; *Inst.*Gai. 2.147; *D.* 37.11.1.8 (Ulpian).

83 See also Meyer, *Legitimacy and Law*, 133–134.

84 This was under the interdict *de tabulis exhibendis*, which pertained to production of testamentary documents. See also Lenel *EP* 43 §232.

85 The rule is generally believed to go back to the so-called *lex Iulia vicesimaria* cited at n. 77 above.

86 So too Meyer, *Legitimacy and Law*, 165.

and would therefore retain the inheritance (*Inst.*Gai. 2.120). From that point on we can begin to think of the seals as validating the written document not just as a true record of the testator's intent but as the will itself. Thus emerges the so-called "praetorian will" which is sealed by seven witnesses without *mancipatio* and for which the evidentiary function and the validating function of sealing by the witnesses are one and the same.[87]

A similar effect is observable in the use of "witnesses" on documents for other legal acts which—at least according to the jurists—had no need of witnesses to be effective.[88] In these instances, there is a shift from the use of witnesses as validating documentary records of transactions to validating the transactions themselves. Pre-classical evidence for such transactions is necessarily scanty, first because little evidence survives from before the first century BCE and second because the use of writing in Roman legal practice is a later development. It is clear, however, that in the classical period, such witnesses serve an indispensable evidentiary function.[89] Cicero suggests that a *stipulatio*—a binding contract made orally by the formal request for a promise and the formal making of that promise (see *Inst.*Gai. 3.92–93)—might be

---

87 *Inst.* 2.10.2. Precisely when the "praetorian will" becomes standalone is difficult to determine. It is unknown to Gaius in the second century CE. A fragment of Ulpian's *Disputations* asserts that a will unsealed by the testator but then resealed with the seals of seven witnesses will be valid (*valebit*) in both civil and praetorian law (*D.* 28.1.23). The reference to the *ius civile* has been suspected of interpolation, but there still remains the assertion that the seven seals make the will valid in praetorian law. We may compare a *constitutio* of Gordian from 242 CE that *bonorum possessio* under the praetorian edict cannot be claimed unless the *tabulae* are sealed by seven witnesses, but that if the will were made not in writing but orally and it can be proved that seven witnesses were present when it was made, it will appear valid under the *ius civile* and possession will be granted according to the *nuncupatio* (*C.* 6.11.2). For summary discussion and citations, see Nowak, *Wills in the Roman Empire*, 34–41.

88 Cf. Meyer, *Legitimacy and Law*, 117–119, who suggests that Gaius omits the "presence and probable recitation of *tabulae*" from the ritual formalities of the *stipulatio* as well as the need for witnesses, while recording them for other transactions, because in his day they had ceased to be used. On the need for *tabulae*, this is unconvincing since Gaius goes on to state explicitly in regard to obligations *consensu* that they require no formalities of words or writing (*Inst.*Gai. 3.136) in contrast to the other kinds of contract (see also Cic. *Parad.* 3.21 for *depositum nullo teste*). We may also note the complaints of Seneca the Younger at Sen. *Ben.* 3.15, discussed just below. Moreover, the evidentiary desirability of writing down the *stipulatio* does not make writing a necessary formality of the contract. First, the ancientness of the *stipulatio* tells against the need for writing (compare the mancipatory will); second, the way such undertakings are recorded (especially the use of the perfect tense) arguably demonstrates that the *tabulae* are precisely evidentiary rather than formal: see e.g., *TPSulp.* 50–59. The need for witnesses is less certain.

89 See also Kaser, "*Testimonium*," 1027.64–1028.14.

made in the presence of witnesses and written down (Cic. *Rosc. Com.* 13–14 and 38).[90] A wooden tablet from London dated to the first century CE records a fragmentary *cautio* acknowledging a loan (*Tab.Lond.Bloomberg* WT 55). While the names themselves are lost, the extant text indicates that the acknowledgment was made "in the presence (*coram*) of those who are written above in their own hand."[91]

This trend is reflected even in juristic writing. The jurist Paul draws an equivalence between a written instrument and the role of witnesses, namely, to provide evidence of a *cautio* (*D.* 13.6.17.3). Such witnesses are *not yet* judicial witnesses: they are not testifying. Rather, we can see how the Roman conception of witnesses to a transaction clearly embraces a potential testimonial function. At the same time, the witnesses are also not transactional inasmuch as the *cautio* would technically be valid without them. Yet the practical reliance on writing and sealing begins to generate slippage so that (just as with wills) the writing comes not only to be evidence of the act but even to create a presumption that the underlying act took place.[92] When properly signed and sealed by witnesses, therefore, the documents go beyond merely providing evidence that the act in fact happened to establishing the act *de iure*.[93]

In the early empire, the philosopher and imperial advisor Seneca the Younger (ca. 4 BCE–65 CE) complains about precisely this increased reliance on witnessed and sealed documents. He laments that in his own day *fides* is so lacking that not only are good faith contracts of sale-and-purchase (*emptio venditio*) reduced to the *stricti iuris stipulatio*, but the agreements are also guarded by seals; in any transaction witnesses are summoned on both sides, debts are noted in multiple record books, and an individual is not satisfied with the (oral) question-answer format of the *stipulatio* unless it is reinforced by hand, i.e., signed and sealed (Sen. *Ben.* 3.15). Seneca describes a "belt-and-suspenders" approach to ensuring that no one should be able to avoid their obligations. Witnesses, writing, and sealing all contribute to creating not the obligation itself but an inescapable record of it.[94] What I want to focus on here

---

90 These passages show only that witnesses *might* be present, not that they *should/must be* present (*pace* Meyer, *Legitimacy and Law*, 118 n. 110).

91 Cf. *Tab.Lond.Bloomberg* WT 56, 61, and 62, where the texts are less extant, but some traces of the witness names remain: see Tomlin, *Roman London's First Voices*, 178–183 and 194–201.

92 See e.g., *D.* 45.1.134.2 (Paul); *D.* 45.1.30 (Ulpian).

93 But see *D.* 22.4.5 (Callistratus) that the absence of a written and sealed instrument will not invalidate a transaction.

94 Compare the practice of having military *diplomata* (technically copies of the official inscription in Rome) witnessed by seven witnesses.

is Seneca's reference to *fides*. *Fides* is a necessary precondition for commerce. Therefore, if *fides* is lacking between parties to a transaction, it must be supplemented by witnesses and their seals. Witnesses are, therefore, a source of *fides* and so must possess it themselves.[95] *Fides* defines the role of a witness whether that role is evidentiary or validating. In fact, it is the importance of *fides* to both functions that unites those functions together in the person of the witness.

The witnesses' *fides* is also bound up with the idea of neutrality, as the example of *testationes* demonstrates. *Testationes* are statements made and recorded before witnesses who then seal the record, and while there is some scholarly debate about the need for writing, the very name suggests that witnesses are integral to the act.[96] Cicero reports two such *testationes* in his speech for Publius Quinctius (81 BCE). In the first example, Cicero remarks that the other litigant, Sextus Naevius, simply sent for his friends (*amici*) and close acquaintances (*necessarii*) to gather as witnesses for a *testatio sistendi*, an affidavit that Quinctius failed to appear at an agreed upon time and place (Cic. *Quinct.* 25).[97] The document was then signed and sealed by "noble men" (*hominum nobilium*). Importantly, Naevius is not acting in good faith: there was no agreement to meet at that specific time and place and Quinctius was out of town (Cic. *Quinct.* 23). Naevius unscrupulously relies on this document, signed by "friends" of high status, to seek and obtain an order from the praetor (Cic. *Quinct.* 25).[98] The implication is that the praetor (wrongly) relies on the validity of the *testatio* and thus the *fides* of the witnesses. Later, Cicero recalls that Alfenus summons several "good men" (*viros bonos*) in order to make a *testatio* that (1) he enjoys a relationship with both Naevius and Quinctius and (2) he, Alfenus, will defend any legal action brought by Naevius against Quinctius (Cic. *Quinct.* 66–67). These "good men" then sign and seal the document. The point is clear: unlike Naevius who simply relies on "friends" (regardless of their

---

95 The Senecan irony is, of course, that the witnesses of the first century CE have no more *fides* than those seeking to rely on them.

96 For physical remains of *testationes*, see *TPSulp.* 16–21, the last in particular preserving six names of the seven *signatores*. The Pompeian documents, like the Ciceronian passage, include the specific time and place at which the *testatio* was made. A similar process was used for *vadimonia*, promises to appear at a particular time and place in order to conduct judicial proceedings: see *TPSulp.* 1–15, though only the last retains its (fragmentary) list of *signatores*, and *TH*[2] 6 (with *signatores* mostly intact). The sealers are all free adult men: Giuseppe Camodeca, *Tabulae Pompeianae Sulpiciorum* (*TPSulp.*)*: Edizione critica dell'archivio puteolano dei Sulpicii* (Roma: Edizione Quasar, 1999), 1.36–37. On *testationes*, see also Meyer, *Legitimacy and Law*, 132–133; Lévy-Bruhl, *Le témoignage instrumentaire*, 88–94 and 103–104 (skeptical of the need for writing).

97 Cf. Cic. 2 *Verr.* 5.102.

98 On the quality of Naevius's witnesses, see also Cic. *Quinct.* 75.

social standing), Alfenus gathers "good men," that is, men of outstanding *fides* and probity. Their character—and therefore the quality of their evidence—is above reproach. Allowing, then, for Ciceronian polemic, it is apparent that by the late republic, witnesses to such juridical acts are expected not to be partisan but must instead neutrally stand for and vouch for the truth, especially where those acts will be relied upon in court.

As the classical period of Roman law faded, written proofs became more and more important, evidentiary witnesses less and less so. The late antique *Sententiae Pauli* state directly that witnesses cannot be examined contrary to written evidence when there has been nothing said about the trustworthiness (*fides*) of the documents (*PS* 5.15.4 [*FIRA* 2.403]). And a rescript of the emperor Severus Alexander in 224 CE held that claims of free birth must be made with documentary evidence since witnesses are insufficient proof in such cases (*C.* 4.20.2).[99] The evidentiary function of witnesses slides back towards validation, though in a different manner from how it began. Witnesses now validate the documents that will serve as proof rather than the transactions themselves. But the question of the individual witnesses' integrity—their *fides*—still remains. This, then, leads to the second part of this study: a consideration of who can and should be a witness.

3 Who Witnesses Are: (Dis)Qualifications

Who can be a witness and in what circumstances?[100] As I noted at the outset, the rules here are generally clear from the sources. What is less apparent is the underlying rationale for each (dis)qualification. While space prevents full discussion, I offer here some account of the rules and why the Romans allowed some to act as witnesses and excluded others. Here, the division into instrumental and judicial witnesses becomes pertinent since in very broad terms the qualifications for being a judicial witness were much less stringent than those for instrumental witnesses, at least in the classical period.[101]

99 See also *C.* 4.20.1, an undated Greek text stating that unwritten testimony is no good against written testimony.

100 Qualifying characteristics at the time of the transaction are at issue: *D.* 28.1.22.1 (Ulpian).

101 See Guérin, *La voix de la verité*, 32–33 and 94–95 for the suggestion that initially judicial witnesses were restricted to the same qualifications as instrumental witnesses (male, of age, Roman citizen), especially in *iudicia privata*; Pugliese, "La Preuve," 315–316.

Free status is the first major criterion. Enslaved persons (*servi*) could not be witnesses to legal transactions or processes (*D.* 28.1.20.7 [Ulpian]).[102] This exclusion is closely tied to the fact that enslaved persons lacked fundamental legal personality and agency in Roman law. Although Roman law recognized the humanity of enslaved persons in some instances,[103] they were not legally their own persons but the property—and in a very real sense an extension—of the master/owner (*dominus*). This explains, for example, the long-standing noxal liability of the *dominus* for any delict committed by the *servus* (see *Inst.*Gai. 4.75–79; *D.* 9.4.1 [Gaius]). It also meant that if an enslaved person acquired any property, it legally belonged to the *dominus* (*Inst.*Gai. 1.52 and 2.87).[104] Their legal agency was also limited. Enslaved persons could undertake no legal obligations of their own and could not be sued. Originally their actions did not even bind the *dominus*. Later, as it became increasingly common to conduct business through enslaved persons, several causes of action developed in the praetorian edict that further recognized the legal bond between *dominus* and *servus*. These arose especially when the actions of the enslaved person were authorized by or undertaken with the knowledge of the *dominus*. These so-called *actiones adiecticiae qualitatis* allowed a party to sue the *dominus* to recover for obligations undertaken by the enslaved person, though in some cases the liability of the *dominus* was limited (see *Inst.*Gai. 4.69–74). The action was brought against the *dominus*, not the enslaved person, precisely because those engaging in business with the enslaved person placed greater stock in the *fides* of the *dominus* than the *servus* (*Inst.*Gai. 4.70).

The reference to *fides* is noteworthy. *Servi* were not expected to have *fides*.[105] They were, therefore, unsuitable for witnessing. Furthermore, the lack of personal agency and legal identity would make enslaved persons inappropriate candidates for instrumental witnessing. If they lack the agency to complete legal transactions for themselves and are not expected to bear legal responsibility for their actions, they must also lack the necessary personal qualities to

---

102 Indirect evidence also at Plaut. *Curc.* 620–627: the soldier Therapontigonus objects to Curculio's being a witness for *in ius vocatio* by alleging that he is enslaved (*servom antestari? Curc.* 625). This suggests that the import of *licet* in the question "*licet antestari*" is not just one of willingness but also legal capacity.

103 For example, some protections against maltreatment developed in the imperial period: see e.g., *D.* 1.6.2 (Ulpian); *D.* 40.8.2 (Modestinus); *D.* 48.8.11.1–2 (Modestinus).

104 Both noxal liability and the rule about acquisition of property apply to free persons in the *potestas* of the *dominus* (most particularly, sons and grandsons).

105 Thus, for example, Valerius Maximus can include an entire title on *De Fide Servorum* precisely because the examples he records are *more* praiseworthy insofar as they are *less* expected (Val. Max. 6.8pr.).

give validity to the legal transactions of others—a rationale observable also in the cases of women and minors. Finally, since the enslaved person is not at law their own person but an extension of the *dominus*, it would be the *dominus* rather than the *servus* who would act as an instrumental witness, and this would undermine the fundamental requirement that witnesses be present so that they can speak to what they have seen and heard.[106]

The presumptive lack of *fides* of enslaved persons also affects the rules about judicial witnessing. The testimony of enslaved persons was not considered of the highest probative value and was only to be believed, according to the third-century CE jurist Modestinus, when there was no other proof to elicit the truth (*D.* 22.5.7). And (in)famously, for the judicial testimony of enslaved persons to be accepted, it had to be given under torture (e.g., *D.* 22.3.7 [Paul]; *D.* 22.5.21.2 [Arcadius Charisius]; *PS* 5.16 [*FIRA* 2.403–404]).[107] Cicero states that the underlying principle was that the necessity to speak generated by the pain of torture creates greater "credibility," i.e., *fides* (see Cic. *Top.* 74). To be clear, however, the Romans themselves recognized that testimony produced under torture was not always reliable (see e.g., Cic. *Part. Or.* 50; Quint. *Inst. Or.* 5.4.1–2; *D.* 48.18.1.23–24 [Ulpian]). Such evidence was permissible in both private and criminal cases, though the sources suggest it was significantly more common in criminal trials; and it was especially appropriate when it concerned the enslaved person's own actions or status (see *D.* 22.5.1.1 [Arcadius Charisius] and *D.* 48.18.9 [Marcian]).[108] The major exception is in cases against the *dominus*: an enslaved person cannot testify against the *dominus* even under torture. This was an enduring rule. Cicero attributes it to the *mos maiorum* (Cic. *Reg. Deiot.* 3; *Part. Or.* 118), and it is reiterated during the empire and then by Justinian's compilers (see *PS* 1.12.3 and 5.16.4–8 [*FIRA* 2.330 and 403–404];

106 Compare Ulpian's statement at *D.* 45.1pr. that in order to make a *stipulatio*, both parties must be present to both speak and hear the request and promise. Therefore, if a person who cannot speak or hear wishes to make a *stipulatio*, they must do so through an enslaved person who is present (*per servum praesentem*). The use of the word *praesens* indicates that the *dominus* and the *servus* must both be in attendance for the *stipulatio* to be valid.

107 On evidentiary torture of enslaved persons, see also Alan Watson, *Roman Slave Law* (Baltimore: Johns Hopkins University Press, 1987), 84–89; William Warwick Buckland, *The Roman Law of Slavery: The Condition of the Slave in Private Law from Augustus to Justinian* (Cambridge: Cambridge University Press, 1908), 86–91. In the imperial period, such evidence should not be a first resort and there were instances when torture should not be used: *D.* 48.18.1 (Ulpian) and *D.* 48.18.9 (Marcian).

108 For private law cases, see e.g., *D.* 27.3.1.3 (Ulpian) on the *actio tutelae*; *PS* 5.16.1 (*FIRA* 2.403) and *C.* 9.41.15 (a rescript of Diocletian and Maximian dated to 294 CE) on contract cases. Criminal cases are covered in *D.* 48.18.

D. 48.18.2 [Ulpian] and *D.* 48.18.9.1 [Marcian]).[109] Alan Watson has suggested that given the prevalence of enslaved persons in the conduct of commercial transactions, any incapacity to obtain testimony from an enslaved person against the *dominus* potentially forces the other party to ensure sufficiency of evidence for the scope and nature of the transaction.[110] Perhaps. But the Roman distaste for enslaved testimony would provide incentive for other forms of proof generally. Such evidentiary pressures are perhaps apparent in and explain the increasing use of written records of transactions (discussed above).

When we consider free persons, social status was an important criterion when selecting witnesses as the higher a person's social status, the higher the presumptive level of *fides*.[111] We see this in the late republic in the works of Cicero.[112] I also noted in the introduction the frustration of Pliny the Younger at the daily obligation of having to be a witness. Pliny belonged to the highest echelons of Roman imperial society: he served as suffect consul in 100 CE and governor of Bithynia-Pontus ca. 110–112 CE, and he was on close terms with the emperor Trajan. He was, therefore, an attractive candidate as a witness. By late antiquity, this preference for witnesses of higher social status had hardened into a legal rule. In 334 CE the emperor Constantine held that witnesses of higher social standing (*honestiores*) should be considered of greater *fides* (*CTh.* 11.39.3 = *C.* 4.20.9). This affirmed a rule that emerged in the third century CE (see *D.* 22.5.3pr. and 2 [Callistratus]). Low social status was not disqualifying, especially amongst members of the same class. The documentary remains

109 Cf. *D.* 48.18.18.5–8 (Paul), where the rule appears limited to capital (i.e., criminal) cases. Cicero suggests that evidence under torture *in caput domini* is admissible in trials for *incestus* (sexual crimes violating natural and divine law) and *coniuratio* (likely treason): Cic. *Mil.* 59; *Part. Or.* 118. In the imperial period, exceptions seem to have existed for trials for adultery under the Augustan *lex Iulia de adulteriis* and for treason (*maiestas*), as well as census fraud (*D.* 48.5.28.6 [Ulpian]; *D.* 48.18.5 [Marcian]; *D.* 48.18.17pr. [Papinian]; *C.* 9.8.6.1 [Paul], *C.* 9.8.6.4 [Marcian], and *C.* 9.41.1pr. [rescript of Septimius Severus and Caracalla dated to 196 CE]). In such cases, the enslaved person usually became the property of the state: see Peter A. Brunt, "Evidence given under Torture in the Principate," *Zeitschrift der Savigny-Stiftung für Rechtsgeschichte. Romanistische Abteilung* 97, no. 1 (1980): 256–259; Vincenti, "*Duo genera sunt testium*," 86–89.

110 Watson, *Roman Slave Law*, 86. He also suggests that because the *dominus* could always produce the *servus* for torture to support his own case, this would incentivize care and honesty in the enslaved person.

111 On the relationship between social standing and *fides*, see also Freyburger, *Fides*, 219–221; Fiori, *Fides et bona fides*, 469–471 and "La gerarchia come criterio di verità," esp. 242–249; Valsan, "*Fides, bona fides*, and *bonus vir*," 55–56.

112 See the discussion above at nn. 65 and 97–98.

from Pompeii and Herculaneum, for example, reveal freedmen acting as witnesses. It did, however, affect the level of *fides* attributed to an individual. By the early third century CE, and perhaps even by the reign of Marcus Aurelius (161–180 CE), lower status witnesses (*humiliores*) were subject to torture just as enslaved persons.[113]

By default, a male Roman citizen of age could be both instrumental and judicial witness.[114] Women, on the other hand, could give testimony in court but seem to have been barred from acting as instrumental witnesses.[115] The jurists Paul and Ulpian both note that a conviction for adultery under the *lex Iulia de adulteriis* will disqualify a woman from giving testimony in court, but it therefore follows that women have a right to be judicial witnesses: you cannot take away what is not there![116] As I have argued elsewhere, women's capacity for judicial testimony seems to develop in the later republic alongside two other developments. The first is a more general increase in the role of women in public life, although not directly in the formal political processes at Rome. The second is a shift in judicial procedure away from the highly formalized *legis actiones* to the more flexible formulary process. Both developments create greater space for women in the courts as witnesses and parties.

Ulpian notes in the passage just mentioned that despite their more general testimonial competence, women cannot give testimony on wills. This must follow from their incapacity to act as instrumental witnesses when wills were made.[117] We can see a further application of this rule against women acting as instrumental witnesses in Paul's remark that whether an intersex person

---

113 See briefly Brunt, "Evidence given under Torture," 259–265.

114 The evidence of the fourth-century *Epitome Regularum Ulpiani* suggests a loosening of the "citizen" requirement since Junian Latins are said to be eligible to act as witnesses to *mancipatio* and wills (*Epit. Ulp.* 19.3–4 and 20.8 [*FIRA* 2.280 and 283]). Junian Latins were a category of formerly enslaved persons created by an Augustan-era *lex Iunia* (before 4 CE). A *servus* became a Junian Latin when the formalities of manumission had been improperly performed, but they still had the possibility of becoming full citizens under the provisions of the *lex Aelia Sentia* of 4 CE (a process which required seven Roman citizen witnesses): see *Inst.*Gai. 1.22–35; *TH*^{2} 89 and 5. We may contrast *Epit. Ulp.* 28.6 (*FIRA* 2.298) where *bonorum possessio* will still be granted for a will otherwise deficient under the *ius civile* so long as it is sealed by no fewer than seven Roman citizen witnesses with no reference to Junian Latins.

115 See Townshend, "*Mulier Testabilis*," for detailed discussion of women as witnesses in Roman Law.

116 *D.* 22.5.18 (Paul) and 28.1.20.6 (Ulpian). It is noteworthy that women are also absent from the list of persons disqualified from testifying under the *lex Iulia de vi* (*D.* 22.5.3.5 [Callistratus]).

117 See *Epit. Ulp.* 20.7 (*FIRA* 2.283).

(*hermaphroditus*) is able to witness a will depends on their sexual development, i.e., whether they are sufficiently "male" (*D.* 22.5.15.1 = *PS* 3.4a.15 [*FIRA* 2.359]). This exclusion of women from acting as instrumental witnesses appears tied to long-standing Roman ideas about the appropriateness of women participating in public life and particularly acting on behalf of others. These prejudices and the rules that reinforced them remained in place even after women began to play a more active role in the Roman commercial and political world and without any real regard for women's actual abilities. We can compare Paul's observation that as a matter of custom (*moribus*) women and enslaved persons could not be appointed judges in trials not because they lack judgment (*iudicium*), but because it was accepted (*receptum est*) that they should not administer public duties (*D.* 5.1.12.2).[118] This acknowledgement of women's capacity for judgment must explain at least in part the fact that women could be judicial witnesses whereas minors could not.[119]

The Romans held that minors lacked judgment and so were not legally capable of handling their own affairs, let alone those of other persons.[120] This is a manifestation of Roman law's protective attitude towards children.[121] Though it was likely long-standing custom, a prohibition against minors acting as instrumental witnesses had been articulated by no later than the first century BCE: the late antique grammarian Priscian preserves the dictum of Aelius that a minor (*impubes*) cannot be a scales-holder or be called as a witness (Prisc. *Inst.* 8.16 = Keil *Gramm. Lat.* 2.382).[122] This lack of judgment also kept minors away from court—certainly from criminal cases and likely from private suits as well. Ulpian remarks that *pupilli* (i.e., those still under the guardianship rules of *tutela*) cannot be summoned to give testimony (*D.* 22.5.19), while an excerpt

118 See also Gardner, *Being A Roman Citizen*, 118.

119 Juristic acknowledgment of women's capacity for rational decision-making is perhaps most famously expressed in Gaius's dismissal of the traditional rationale for women's continued subjection to *tutela*—namely, women's "lightness of mind" (*levitas animi*)—which he rejects as seeming "more specious than true" (*Inst.* Gai. 1.190).

120 For minors' lack of judgment, see e.g., *Inst.* Gai. 1.144 and 189–190 as basis for *tutela impuberis*; for why minors cannot make a will, see *Epit. Ulp.* 20.12 (*FIRA* 2.283).

121 See Thomas A. J. McGinn, "Roman Children and the Law," in *The Oxford Handbook of Childhood and Education in the Classical World*, ed. Judith Evans Grubbs and Tim Parkin (Oxford: Oxford University Press, 2013), 341–362, for a summary treatment of children under Roman law.

122 This Aelius is likely Aelius Gallus (first century BCE), whose *De Significatione Verborum* (in at least two books) dealt with legal terms (see Festus 224L and 336L). As noted by Terranova, "Sull'*antestatus*," 122, this is the only non-judicial text to use *antestari* in the context of an act *per aes et libram* rather than *in ius vocatio*. For the disqualification of minors, see also *Epit. Ulp.* 20.7 (*FIRA* 2.283), using *pupillus* ("ward") rather than *impubes*.

from the second book of Venuleius's work *De Iudiciis Publicis* applies the exclusion to those under twenty-five years of age (*D.* 22.5.20).[123] This exclusion of minors from giving testimony was also incorporated explicitly into statute. The third-century CE jurist Callistratus notes that the first-century *lex Iulia de vi* included minors in its catalogue of persons disqualified from being witnesses in prosecutions under that law (*D.* 22.5.3.5). Callistratus goes on to list the various rationales for the exclusions including "instability of their judgment" (*propter lubricum consilii sui*), which must apply to minors.[124]

Other characteristics could disqualify a person in certain circumstances. Disabilities, for example. According to the fourth-century CE *Epitome Regularum Ulpiani*, persons who cannot speak, who cannot hear, and who have a mental illness are all disqualified from witnessing or being *libripens* for a will (*Epit. Ulp.* 20.7 [*FIRA* 2.283]). The inability to speak would prevent the witness from assenting to the role or subsequently communicating what had happened. A deaf witness would be unable to hear the required words. Persons with mental illness were considered unable to comprehend the nature of the activities they were witnessing or form the requisite intent, although they became competent during any periods of lucidity (*D.* 28.1.5 [Ulpian]).[125] While Ulpian does not make the reasoning explicit in his discussion of witnesses, he provides analogous rationales when he explains that these same groups lack the right to make a will of their own (*Epit. Ulp.* 20.13 [*FIRA* 2.283–284]).[126]

Family relationships could be disqualifying. Fathers and sons were not suitable witnesses for each other (*D.* 22.5.9 [Paul]). This seems to be a general principle applicable to both judicial and transactional contexts.[127] Close family or social ties could also be grounds for refusing a summons to testify in court.[128]

---

123 Ulpian's phrasing (*pupillis testimonium denuntiari potest*) may indicate that the prohibition was specifically against the prosecution calling the ward of a defendant. Venuleius is more general.

124 The other two rationales relate to respect for persons (applicable to patron-freedperson relations) and bad reputation (convicted criminals and those engaged in activities bringing *infamia*).

125 Compare the list of those excluded by the praetorian edict from making application to the praetor at *D.* 3.1.1.3 (Ulpian), those who cannot act as arbiters or judges at *D.* 4.8.9.1 (Ulpian) and *D.* 5.1.122 (Paul), and those who cannot be appointed as a tutor at *D.* 26.1.17 (Paul). There is also some overlap with those subject to *curatio* (see e.g., *D.* 26.5.8.3 [Ulpian]). See also Lévy-Bruhl, *Le témoignage instrumentaire*, 38–39.

126 We may also compare the jurist Paul's remarks that a blind person is still able to make a will since they are able both to know the identity of the witnesses and to hear them fulfilling their function (*PS* 3.4a.4 [*FIRA* 2.358]).

127 See also Guérin, *La voix de la verité*, 98.

128 See e.g., Paul and Gaius on the first-century *lex Iulia iudiciorum publicorum*: *D.* 22.5.4–5; *PS* 5.15.2–3 (*FIRA* 2.402–403).

Such rules rest on two bases. The first is that such persons would by default fail to meet the criterion of neutrality expected of such witnesses.[129] The second is that testifying could lead to tensions (if not ruptures) in the fabric of the family. Somewhat different reasons underlie similar disqualifications for instrumental witnesses. Persons in close *potestas* relationships with either the testator or *familiae emptor* could not be witnesses or the *libripens* for wills (*Inst.*Gai. 2.105–107; *D.* 28.1.20pr–1 [Ulpian]).[130] Ulpian elsewhere notes that this rule about persons *in potestate* applies to all transactions in which property is transferred (*D.* 20.1.20.3). There is a logic to such prohibitions. In a very real way, a man still in the *potestas* of his father was not a separate person (e.g., any property acquired by the *filius familias* would technically belong to the *pater*).[131] Consequently, to have a son-in-power of a testator or *familiae emptor* act as witness would be tantamount to the person being his own witness, which was not allowed.[132]

Interestingly, from the republic through to the late second century CE the heir instituted in the will could be a witness, even if it was likely uncommon. Gaius thought it inadvisable (*Inst.*Gai. 2.108).[133] Gaius's account of wills reveals that originally the *familiae emptor* took immediate ownership of the estate, essentially replacing an heir (*Inst.*Gai. 2.103). As the form of the will develops and it becomes standard to institute an heir, the *familiae emptor* becomes a placeholder role, but the heir must not have been felt to have an interest in the actual transaction as it happened. Plainly this is not the case, and Gaius's discomfort shows an awareness of this. At any rate, the rule had changed by the

129 See e.g., *PS* 5.15.1–3 (*FIRA* 2.402–403).

130 The rule is maintained by Justinian (*Inst.* 2.10.9). In the classical period, Gaius (*Inst.*Gai. 2.106) and Ulpian (*D.* 28.1.20.2, citing Marcellus) disagree about whether a father and a brother in the same *potestas* can be used as a witness to a will for a *peculium castrense* (Justinian says "no": *Inst.* 2.10.9).

131 See *Inst.*Gai. 2.87; *Epit. Ulp.* 19.18–19 (*FIRA* 2.281–282).

132 See e.g., *D.* 22.5.10 (Pomponius): *nullus idoneus testis in re sua intellegitur*. Pomponius's pronouncement is aimed at judicial witnesses, but it applies equally and logically to instrumental witnessing since the *testis* is, by definition, a third party; see also Lévy-Bruhl, *Le témoignage instrumentaire*, 119–120. A *pater* and *filius familias* or two sons both in the *potestas* of the same *pater* could act as witness to the same transaction (*D.* 22.5.17 [Ulpian]; *Epit. Ulp.* 20.6 [*FIRA* 2.283]).

133 For specific instances, see Cic. *Mil.* 48 where Cicero remarks that both he and Clodius were named as *heredes* in and acted as witnesses for the will of the architect Cyrus; at Cic. *Att.* 7.2.3 Cicero confides to Atticus that they will both receive shares from Manius Curius's will, which Cicero himself witnessed: Champlin, *Final Judgments*, 80–81.

early third century CE: Ulpian states directly that one who is instituted as heir in a will cannot be a witness to the same will (*D.* 28.1.20pr).[134]

Other than the disqualification of minors, fathers, and sons, the classical period sees no customary restrictions on judicial testimony. Indeed, the late third-century CE jurist Arcadius Charisius remarks that witnesses can be called in both criminal cases and private suits so long as their testimony is not barred and they are not excused by some statute (*D.* 22.5.1.1).[135] We have already seen a particular statutory disqualification for women in the provisions of the *lex Iulia de adulteriis*. This disqualification may also have applied to men. Papinian, one of the most prominent jurists of the early third century CE, alludes to a debate about whether a person condemned for adultery can be a witness to a will. Here he can only be referring to men since women could not witness wills. He remarks that quite rightly such a person will be barred from "the office of witnessing" (*testimonii officio*); therefore, any will witnessed by that person will be invalid under both civil and praetorian law (*D.* 22.5.14). According to Papinian's interpretation *testimonii officium* embraces instrumental witnessing, but the implication of the passage is that others have held that it applies (only) to some other kind of witnessing, namely, judicial witnessing.

A similar exclusion from judicial witnessing followed a conviction for *repetundae*, unjust enrichment during one's term administering a province and thus a charge applicable only to men of the highest social order.[136] The first-century CE jurist Cassius Longinus held that one so convicted cannot be a judge or give testimony (*testimonium dicere*) since the *lex Iulia repetendarum* forbids this (*D.* 1.9.2 [Marcellus]).[137] By the early third century CE, however, there was some disagreement about the scope of the provision. Ulpian held that a convicted person may still witness a will since it prohibited being a witness *in court* (*in iudicium, D.* 28.1.20.5).[138] Paul, however, asserts that a person convicted of *repetundae* cannot be a witness to a will or give testimony (*D.*

134 The disqualification of the heir was maintained by Justinian, noting explicitly that this had not always been the case (*Inst.* 2.10.10): see also Lévy-Bruhl, *Le témoignage instrumentaire*, 122–125. The rule did not apply to legatees or persons appointed as tutors, who could be witnesses.

135 Such excuses were usually based on kinship or close social relations: see e.g., *D.* 22.5.4–5 (Paul and Gaius).

136 Cf. also line 3 of the *lex Latina Tabulae Bantinae*, though fragmentary: briefly Crawford, *Roman Statutes*, 1.193–208, esp. 205–206.

137 Crawford, *Roman Statutes*, 2.770 connects this provision to the late second-century BCE *lex repetendarum* of Gaius Gracchus, though the earlier law does not mention witnessing.

138 But see Lévy-Bruhl, *Le témoignage instrumentaire*, 117–118 with citations, for the argument that the word *non* has dropped out of Ulpian's text.

22.5.15 = *PS* 3.4a.14 [*FIRA* 2.359]). Here, Paul uses *testamentum* and *testimonium* in parallel to cover both instrumental and judicial witnessing.

A more general statutory bar was for a person to be *intestabilis*. As already noted in section two, the Twelve Tables declared that any person who acted as a witness or a *libripens* and then did not give testimony would be "*improbus* and *intestabilis*" (XII 8.22 *FIRA* 1.62).[139] The provision seems to have had a long life. The historian Sallust alludes to it in the first century BCE (Sall. *Iug.* 67.3); the fourth-century CE scholiast Servius quotes it in a note on the *Aeneid* (Serv. *Aen.* 4.386); and the language is reproduced in the *Institutes* of Justinian in the sixth century CE (*Inst.* 2.10.6). Despite, or perhaps due to, this longevity, there is disagreement in the sources and the scholarship about the effect of being declared *intestabilis*. A preliminary matter is whether *improbus* and *intestabilis* should be taken together as a single unit or whether each denotes different consequences.[140] It may be that *improbus* marks the social stigma while *intestabilis* expresses the legal disqualification.[141] Alternatively, it has been suggested that *improbus* marks an individual as unsuitable to be a witness while *intestabilis* renders that person unable to call witnesses.[142] Whether or not the terms were distinguishable initially, it does seem that the classical jurists felt only *intestabilis* had legal force.[143] This is apparent from the fact that only *intestabilis* is

139 In the interests of space, I omit any discussion of the relationship between this provision and the rule on *obvagulatio* (XII 2.3 *FIRA* 1.31).

140 So too Lévy-Bruhl, *Le témoignage instrumentaire*, 40–41, surveying previous views before declaring that the distinction is immaterial to determining the general effect of the provision in the Twelve Tables.

141 Wieacker, "Zwölftafelprobleme," 464–465 sees *improbus* as simply "unsuitable" (*untauglich*), but is agnostic about the full force of *intestabilis* (n. 19); Gardner, *Being A Roman Citizen,* 217 n. 18 suggests that "No particular legal significance can be attached to the former word"; Crawford, *Roman Statutes,* 2.691 translates *improbus* as "unacceptable," to which *intestabilis* then gives "precision"; Humbert, "*Intestabilis*," 2557–2558 with n. 20, strongly opposes such a distinction, though he also suggests that *intestabilis* renders the consequences in more concrete terms.

142 See e.g., Kaser, "*Testimonium*," 1026.1–18; MacCormack, "Witnesses in the Law," 234; Kaser and Hackl, *Das Römische Zivilprozessrecht*, 119.

143 See also Liv. 10.9.5–6, where the *lex Valeria de provocatione* of 300/299 BCE forbade the beating or execution of a citizen who appealed; if the magistrate nevertheless carried out the beating/execution, the law declared it "improperly done" (*improbe factum*). The historian Livy (59 BCE–17 CE) remarks that this seemed a sufficient restraint for persons in that day due to their sense of shame (*pudor*), even if it would be ineffective in his own time. This indicates that Livy saw the declaration as a social rather than legal consequence. But see Humbert, "*Intestabilis*," 2557 n. 20 for a forceful statement that Livy has interpreted the *lex Valeria* incorrectly and that *improbus* in both that law and the Twelve Tables marks the act or person as excluded from the world of law and without ritual purity.

discussed as a penalty in statutory provisions for other wrongs, notably for defamatory publication.[144] It is worth stressing here that being *intestabilis* is a specifically statutory condition imposed by law and it carries distinctly negative connotations.[145] While it disqualifies the individual from certain acts (to be discussed below), it would be incorrect to class all equivalent incapacities as "being *intestabilis*" if they do not result from the statutory designation.[146]

For some scholars, the *intestabilis* provision of the Twelve Tables not only disqualified a person from being a witness (what has been termed "active" intestability), it barred them from making use of witnesses (or "passive" intestability).[147] This would prevent an individual from many activities in the legal sphere.[148] An *intestabilis* person would not be able to participate in any form of the *mancipatio*. A person's ability to participate in judicial proceedings would be drastically curtailed since the *litis contestatio* requires the calling of witnesses—and that is presuming an *intestabilis* plaintiff were able to get a defendant to court without the need for physical force, since the use of force also required witnesses. And what proof could they rely on at trial? This interpretation relies in particular on the evidence of the comic playwright Plautus (*fl.* early second century BCE), whose texts are closest in time to the Twelve Tables. In Plautus's works, the word *intestabilis* occurs twice: *Curculio* 30 and *Miles Gloriosus* 1417.[149] In both cases, Plautus uses puns on *testis* as both "witness"

144 The account of Ulpian suggests that this provision was included in the *lex Cornelia de iniuriis* and covered any defamatory *written* material; it was later extended by *senatus consultum* to any epigram or defamatory verse without writing (*D.* 47.10.5.9–10); see also *D.* 22.5.21pr. (Arcadius Charisius) and *D.* 28.1.18.1 (Ulpian). Cf. Lévy-Bruhl, *Le témoignage instrumentaire*, 111–114.

145 The word comes to be used most often in non-legal contexts as a synonym for *improbus* or *detestabilis* or *infamis*: see *TLL* 2.7.1.38–2.20 (Kornhardt); *OLD* s.v. *intestabilis* §2. Due to the restrictions of space, I will not discuss here the potential legal connections between being *intestabilis, sacer*, and *infamis*.

146 See e.g., Humbert, "*Intestabilis*," who vacillates between focusing on the word *intestabilis* and defining the concept of "intestability."

147 See e.g., Lévy-Bruhl, *Le témoignage instrumentaire*, 39–43; Broggini, "La Prova," 378; Humbert, "*Intestabilis*," esp. 2546–2549, arguing that to be *intestabilis* disqualifies a person from participating in any way in any act that requires witnesses, since one must be able to be the principal in a transaction in order to also participate as a third party.

148 On the implications, see e.g., Lévy-Bruhl, *Le témoignage instrumentaire*, 42–43; Gardner, *Being A Roman Citizen*, 118–121; Humbert, "*Intestabilis*," 2544.

149 The pun in the *Miles Gloriosus* is amplified in the line before by the inclusion of another similar word, *intestatus*, which here also suggests "without testicles" or "unmanned" and makes the threat of castration immediate. The most common meaning of this word—found also in the Twelve Tables (XII 5.4 *FIRA* 1.38)—is "intestate" or "without a will," but it can also mean "without witnesses": see *TLL* 7.2.1.29–4.81 (Kornhardt); *OLD* s.v. *intestatus*. The word *intestatus* also appears at Plaut. *Curc.* 622, on which see John Crook, "Intestacy

and "testicle" to insinuate that being *intestabilis* means being castrated. In neither case, however, does the anatomical punchline require a complete one-to-one relationship between not having testicles and not having witnesses. It is also worth remembering that at this point in the developmental history of Roman law, only men could be witnesses. For a man to lose the "witnesses" of his manhood would potentially disqualify him from being a witness—that is, to be castrated would render a man doubly *intestabilis*: both "without testicles" and (therefore) "unable to be a witness."[150] Plautus is, in the end, a comic playwright, so we should be wary of taking the evidence from his plays too dogmatically. The most we can say is that Plautus expects his audience to recognize the phonic interplay and connection of witnesses and testicles.

The meaning of the word *intestabilis* in the archaic period may be irrecoverable.[151] The classical period is a different story.[152] Ulpian holds that being *intestabilis* means being able neither to make a will nor to be witness to a will (*D.* 28.1.18.1). Scholars disagree about whether Ulpian limits the disqualification to wills specifically or whether it applies to witnessing more generally.[153] Michel Humbert has argued that Ulpian's position is indicative of both the original principle and the state of the law in his own time, namely, that witnesses must enjoy a reciprocal capacity to that of the testator.[154] For Humbert, the "active testability" of the witness (i.e., capacity to *be* a witness) corresponds to the testator's "passive testability" (i.e., capacity to *rely on* witnesses) that is part of the testator's *testamenti factio* (capacity to make a will), and the loss of

in Roman Society," *Proceedings of the Cambridge Philological Society* 19 (1973): 41, suggesting that it means *intestabilis*, which he takes as "so infamous as not to be permitted to give testimony in the Courts."

150 The sources are not explicit on *spadones* as witnesses: Lévy-Bruhl, *Le témoignage instrumentaire*, 39 with n. 3.

151 Cf. Crawford, *Roman Statutes*, 2.691, who states that it cannot be known whether passive intestability is original to the Twelve Tables or a result of juristic interpretation.

152 Cf. Lévy-Bruhl, *Le témoignage instrumentaire*, 109–116, who suggests that *intestabilis* in the classical period is quite different, applying only to those convicted for a *carmen famosum* since the witnesses to *mancipatio* had diminished into mere means of proof no longer under an obligation.

153 Gardner, *Being A Roman Citizen*, 118 understands Ulpian as referring very specifically to wills and sees his interpretation of *intestabilis* as a development in the law. So too seemingly Crawford, *Roman Statutes*, 2.691, who calls Ulpian's position "idiosyncratic."

154 On the reciprocity of *testamenti factio* (i.e., the testator must be able to make a will *with* the specific individuals acting as witnesses), see also *Epit. Ulp.* 20.2 (*FIRA* 2.282); Hugo Krüger, "*Testamenti Factio*," *Zeitschrift der Savigny-Stiftung für Rechtsgeschichte. Romanistische Abteilung* 53, no. 1 (1933): 505–508.

one entails the loss of the other.[155] This is superficially compelling since most of the categories of ineligible witnesses are also unable to make a will. But three categories remain which contradict the "logic" of Humbert's formulation: women, Junian Latins, and adult men still *in potestate*.

Since at least the second century BCE, Roman women were able to make a will.[156] Despite this ability, they could not be witnesses to wills. Conversely, according to the *Epitome Regularum Ulpiani*, a Junian Latin was barred by statute from making a will (*Epit. Ulp.* 20.14 [*FIRA* 2.284]), but could nevertheless be a witness, *libripens*, or *familiae emptor* since there was *testamenti factio* with him (*Epit. Ulp.* 20.8 [*FIRA* 2.283]).[157] It is possible to explain the anomalous position of women and Junian Latins by reference to the incremental development of the law and the idea that discrete (dis)abilities are established without regard to fundamental principles. Put another way, women may just be an "exception" and the position of Junian Latins may just be a recent development reflecting the changed nature of witnesses from active participants to mere spectators and *signatores*.[158] But this cannot explain the third category, adult men *in potestate*.[159] Like Junian Latins, these men are unable to make a will but can be witnesses, so long as they are not in the *potestas* of the testator or the *familiae emptor*.[160] Nor is there any evidence that their capacity to act as witnesses is somehow recent. A letter of Cicero to Atticus from 50 BCE shows a father and son both witnessing the same will (Cic. *Att.* 7.2.3), a situation which the classical jurists found perfectly acceptable.[161] We would have to posit a rule

---

155 Humbert, "*Intestabilis*," 2550–2557, arguing also that this principle is reflected in the sixth-century CE provision of Justinian's *Institutes* (*Inst.* 2.10.6) and distinguishing those instances where a person has been disqualified from being a witness without being designated *intestabilis* (e.g., *D.* 22.5.14–15 [Papinian and Paul]). See also Lévy-Bruhl, *Le témoignage instrumentaire*, 106–108; Gardner, *Being A Roman Citizen,* 118 on Justinian's *Institutes.*

156 Vestal Virgins were an exception. The Roman tradition assigned to them the right to make a will from the very creation of that priesthood by Numa Pompilius in the regal period: see Plut. *Num.* 10.3; Gell. *NA.* 1.12.9–10.

157 On the legal status of Junian Latins, see above n. 114.

158 See Humbert, "*Intestabilis*," 2550 and 2554 for women, 2555 n. 17 for Junian Latins. To suggest that developments around Junian Latins are "recent" may be misleading. Junian Latins as a legal category had existed since the reign of Augustus. And as already noted in section two, the conflation of the two roles of *testis* and *signator* begins in the Republic and is complete by the second century CE, well before the *Epitome* is compiled.

159 Humbert in fact says nothing about this group.

160 See above at n. 130.

161 The will belongs to Manius Curius, details above at n. 4. For the late classical period, see *D.* 22.5.17 (Ulpian); *Epit. Ulp.* 20.6 (*FIRA* 2.283). Cf. Lévy-Bruhl, *Le témoignage instrumentaire*, 44–45, arguing that there is no evidence that this rule is "ancient."

(for which there is no evidence) that originally a witness to a will had to be a *pater familias* (i.e., a *sui iuris* man). In actuality, our sources indicate the opposite since the earliest wills (both *comitiis calatis* and *in procinctu*) were made in public before the assembled citizenry where distinctions between *patres* and *filii familias* had no application.[162] Thus Humbert's argument about the underlying principle fails to convince and brings us no closer to confirming the force of *intestabilis*.

Ulpian is not necessarily an outlier in his interpretation of *intestabilis*. Less than a century earlier, Gaius had stated that when an individual was declared *intestabilis* by law, the individual's testimony cannot be used (*D.* 28.1.26).[163] Gaius adds that some go further and believe that the individual cannot call witnesses either. Importantly this is only the opinion of some (*ut quidam putant*), not a definite rule, and there is evidence that Gaius's more restricted position reflects the more common understanding of the term in the classical period—that being *intestabilis* was limited to the incapacity to *be* a witness rather than an inability to *call* witnesses.[164] Aulus Gellius, a contemporary of Gaius, reports a story about a Vestal Virgin named Gaia Taracia, which he most likely found in the work of the first-century BCE historian Valerius Antias.[165] Taracia was rewarded for her beneficence to Rome with a set of honors bestowed by a *lex Horatia*, among which were the right to give testimony (*ius testimonii dicendi*) and that she alone of women would be *testabilis* (Gell. *NA*. 7.7.1–4). Gellius's phrasing indicates that he understands these as two distinct honors: being *testabilis* is not, therefore, the same as having the *ius testimonii dicendi*. Nor does being *testabilis* refer to a Vestal Virgin's right to make a will since that was already established.

This is the only instance of *testabilis* in extant Latin, but Gellius remarks that the word's opposite (*contrarium*) is found in the Twelve Tables, citing precisely XII 8.22 (*FIRA* 1.62). The logic of the story presumes that prior to being declared *testabilis* by the statute, Taracia must have been under the same legal incapacity as that expressed by the word *intestabilis*. Taracia's position as a Vestal Virgin gave her the right to make a will and, therefore, the right to

162 See e.g., Gell. *NA* 2.2, esp. 9 and 13.

163 Note also that Arcadius Charisius confirms that one condemned for a *carmen famosum* becomes *intestabilis* at the beginning of a passage discussing testimony in court (*D.* 22.5.21). Humbert, "*Intestabilis*," 2553 n. 14, asserts that Gaius is discussing the provision of the late republican *lex Cornelia de iniuriis* rather than the Twelve Tables.

164 See also Lévy-Bruhl, *Le témoignage instrumentaire*, 115–116, remarking that the uncertainty indicates the infrequency of the penalty; Gardner, *Being A Roman Citizen*, 118.

165 See Townshend, "*Mulier Testabilis*," for full discussion of this passage.

call witnesses. It follows, then, that her previous incapacity—her "intestability"—cannot have been an inability to call witnesses and thus make a will. Rather, as I have argued elsewhere, the implication is that Taracia—alone of all women—is granted the privilege to act as an instrumental witness to legal transactions, especially those acts *per aes et libram*.[166] The *lex Horatia* empowers her to be both a judicial and an instrumental witness at a time when women could be neither. Gellius's account certainly reveals what *he* believes *intestabilis* to mean in the mid-second century CE: an inability to *act* as a witness. There is also enough to conclude that this is how the word was understood in the first century BCE. If we presume that Taracia's story and the *lex Horatia* are created entirely by Valerius Antias, the meaning of *testabilis* (and therefore the import of the privilege) would still depend on the meaning of *intestabilis* as a back-formation of the earlier word.

This classical meaning is further confirmed by Pomponius Porphyrio, a third-century CE scholiast of the Augustan poet Horace (65–8 BCE). Porphyrio observes in his note on Hor. *Sat.* 2.3.181 that in olden times they used to call *intestabiles* those whom they refused to be admitted as witnesses to a will, to wit, those whose testimony was bad and detestable.[167] This, I suggest, is the natural inference to be drawn from the Twelve Tables. The condition "if he should not speak his testimony" (*ni testimonium †fariatur†*) imagines a situation where a witness does not testify about the transaction or event. In other words, it punishes a failure to act as a judicial witness—a failure to be present—when that presence is a necessary corollary of being a witness in another context. Such a failure renders the individual unsuitable and incapable of being a witness in the future because that failure is a breach of *fides*. That quality of trust and honesty is so fundamental to a system where a person's word is their bond and (in the archaic period) written records are a rarity, thus requiring the need for the confirmation of witnesses. The need for *fides* is especially relevant if, as seems likely, the witnesses explicitly consent to their role.[168] Any person who cannot be trusted or relied upon should not be a witness.

---

166 Cf. Humbert, "*Intestabilis*," 2549–2550, who argues that this right was enjoyed by all Vestal Virgins since they all could make wills.

167 Compare the fifth-century Pseudo-Acronian note on the same line ("They are called *intestabiles* whose testimony has no value," Ps. Acro on Hor. *Sat.* 2.3.181) and Isidore's gloss that an *intestabilis* is one "whose testimony has no value and what he says is of no effect and to be rejected" (Isid. *Etym.* 10.135L).

168 See e.g., *Inst.*Gai. 2.104, which gives the formal language calling for witnesses during the *mancipatio*, and PS 3.4a.4 (*FIRA* 2.358), which strongly implies a spoken affirmation by the witnesses. A similar assent-formula has been posited for the *litis contestatio*: Lévy-Bruhl, *Le témoignage instrumentaire*, 19–20; Biscardi, "*Testes Estote*," 405. For reasons of space,

4 Envoi

This chapter has sought to introduce some key concepts and questions about witnesses in Roman law and to lay out the groundwork for a fuller, more comprehensive account. I have not sought to be exhaustive. I have chosen to focus on how the different aspects of witnessing became blurred even at a very early stage in the developmental history of the law—presuming they were ever distinct to start. In so focusing, I have highlighted the consistent importance of two factors: the need for witnesses to be present, and the need for witnesses to possess *fides*. The lack of either element fundamentally undermines a person's capacity to be a witness. This focus does mean I have omitted discussion of a number of questions. These include why the number of witnesses for a given transaction might be so, how those witnesses are chosen or summoned, what the specific obligations of a witness may be once the role is undertaken, and how the failure to perform the role of witness properly might be sanctioned. I have also avoided speculation about the genesis of the role of witnesses and detailed reconstruction of the acts which they attended. For as the honorand of this volume once said to me, we just don't know what witnesses did in the earliest days of Roman law. Needless to say, a full historical account of witnessing in Roman law will grapple with such questions and will do so in a truly interdisciplinary way, drawing on legal studies, philology, epigraphy, and social anthropology. Only when all these tools are properly brought to bear can we truly move towards a taxonomy of witnesses in Roman law.

Acknowledgments

I offer this chapter in full admiration and partial imitation of this volume's honorand who himself contributed a piece on witnesses in the church courts of medieval England in just such a collection (Donahue, "Proof by Witnesses"). I can only hope that this piece in some small way achieves and reflects Charlie's encyclopedic grasp of the source materials that so often impressed me during my time working with him. My thanks to Charles Bartlett, the editors, and the reviewers for their suggestions and feedback. All translations are my own.

I have not discussed the *licet antestari?—licet* formula and its implications for witnesses consenting to their role.

Bibliography

Arangio-Ruiz, Vincentus, ed. *Fontes Iuris Romani Antejustiniani Pars Tertia: Negotia*. 2nd ed. Florence: Barbèra, 1972 [*FIRA* 3].

Baviera, Johannes, and J. Furlani, eds. *Fontes Iuris Romani Antejustiniani Pars Altera: Auctores; Libri Syro-Romani Interpretationem A C. Ferrini Confectam*. 2nd ed. Florence: Barbèra, 1968. [*FIRA* 2].

Benveniste, Émile. *Le Vocabulaire des Institutions Indo-Européennes*. 2 vols. Paris: Les Éditions de Minuit, 1969.

Birks, Peter, and Grant McLeod, eds. *Justinian's Institutes, with the Latin text of Paul Krueger*. Ithaca: Cornell University Press, 1987.

Biscardi, Arnaldo. 1971. "'*Testes Estote*' Contribution à L'étude du Témoignage en Droit Romain." *Revue historique de droit français et étranger* 49, no. 3 (1971): 386–411.

Broggini, Gerardo. "La Prova nel Processo Romano Arcaico." *Ius* 11, no. 3 (1960): 348–385 (= Broggini, Gerardo. *Coniectanea: Studi di Diritto Romano*, 133–186. Milan: Giuffrè, 1966).

Brunt, Peter A. "Evidence given under Torture in the Principate." *Zeitschrift der Savigny-Stiftung für Rechtsgeschichte. Romanistische Abteilung* 97, no. 1 (1980): 256–265.

Buckland, William Warwick. *The Roman Law of Slavery: The Condition of the Slave in Private Law from Augustus to Justinian*. Cambridge: Cambridge University Press, 1908.

Camodeca, Giuseppe. *Tabulae Herculanensis: Edizione e Commento*. Roma: Edizione Quasar, 2017. [TH^2].

Camodeca, Giuseppe. *Tabulae Pompeianae Sulpiciorum (TPSulp.): Edizione critica dell'archivio puteolano dei Sulpicii*. 2 vols. Roma: Edizione Quasar, 1999. [*TPSulp.*].

Champlin, Edward. *Final Judgments: Duty and Emotion in Roman Wills, 200 B.C.–A.D. 250*. Berkeley: University of California Press, 1991.

Crawford, M. H., ed. *Roman Statutes*. 2 vols. BICS Supplement 64. London: Institute of Classical Studies, 1996.

Crook, John. "Intestacy in Roman Society." *Proceedings of the Cambridge Philological Society* 19 (1973): 38–44.

de Zulueta, Francis. *The Institutes of Gaius*. 2 vols. Oxford: Clarendon Press, 1946–53.

Donahue, Charles. "Proof by Witnesses in the Church Courts of Medieval England: An Imperfect Reception of the Learned Law." In *On the Laws and Customs of England: Essays in Honor of Samuel E. Thorne*, edited by Morris S. Arnold, Thomas A. Green, Sally A. Scully, and Stephen D. White, 127–158. Chapel Hill: University of North Carolina Press, 1981.

Ernout, Alfred, and Antoine Meillet. *Dictionnaire Étymologique de la Langue Latine: Histoire des Mots*. Rev. 4th ed. Paris: Klincksiek, 1985.

Fiori, Roberto. "*Fides et bona fides*: Hiérarchie sociale et categories juridiques." *Revue historique de droit français et étranger* 86, no. 4 (2008): 465–481.

Fiori, Roberto. "La gerarchia come criterio di verità: *boni* e *mali* nel processo romano arcaico." In *QUID EST VERITAS? Un Seminario su Verità e Forme Giuridiche*, edited by Cosimo Cascione and Carla Masi Doria, 169–249. Napoli: Satura Editrice, 2013.

Frier, Bruce W., ed. *The Codex of Justinian*. 3 vols. Cambridge: Cambridge University Press, 2016.

Freyburger, Gérard. *Fides: Étude sémantique et religieuse depuis les origines jusqu'à l'époque augustéenne*. Paris: Les Belles Lettres, 1986.

Gardner, Jane F. *Being A Roman Citizen*. London: Routledge, 1993.

Glare, P. G. W., ed. *Oxford Latin Dictionary*. 2nd ed. Oxford: Oxford University Press, 2012. [*OLD*].

Guérin, Charles. *La voix de la vérité: Témoin et témoignage dans les tribunaux romains du Ier siècle avant J.-C.* Paris: Belles Lettres, 2015.

Holford-Strevens, Leofranc. *Gelliana: A Textual Companion to the Noctes Atticae of Aulus Gellius*. Oxford: Oxford University Press, 2020.

Humbert, Michel. "*Intestabilis*." In *Fides Humanitas Ius: Studii in Onore di Luigi Labruna IV*, edited by Cosimo Cascione and Carla Masi Doria, 2543–2558. Napoli: Editoriale Scientifica, 2007.

Karlowa, Otto. *Römische Rechtsgeschichte*. 2 vols. Leipzig: Veit and Co, 1885–1892.

Kaser, Max. "*Testimonium*." In *Realencyclopädie der classischen Altertumswissenschaft*, edited by August Friedrich von Pauly and Georg Wissowa, 2nd series, vol. V A.1, 1021–1062. Stuttgart: Metzler, 1890–1980.

Kaser, Max, and Karl Hackl. *Das Römische Zivilprozessrecht*. 2nd ed. Handbuch der Altertumswissenschaft 10.3.4. München: C. H. Beck, 1996.

Katz, Joshua T. "*Testimonia Ritus Italici*: Male Genitalia, Solemn Declarations, and a New Latin Sound Law." *Harvard Studies in Classical Philology* 98 (1998): 183–217.

Keil, Henricus, ed. *Grammatici Latini*. 8 vols. Leipzig: Teubner, 1855–1923.

Krüger, Hugo. "*Testamenti Factio*." *Zeitschrift der Savigny-Stiftung für Rechtsgeschichte. Romanistische Abteilung* 53, no. 1 (1933): 505–508.

Lenel, Otto. *Das Edictum Perpetuum*. 3rd ed. Aalen: Scientia Verlag, 1974. [Lenel *EP*].

Lévy-Bruhl, Henri. "La '*manuum consertio*'." *IVRA: rivista internazionale di diritto romano e antico* 4 (1953): 163–173.

Lévy-Bruhl, Henri. *Le témoignage instrumentaire en droit romain*. Doctoral thesis, Arthur Rousseau, Paris, 1910.

Lévy-Bruhl, Henri. "Les témoins de la *litis contestatio*." *Annales de la Faculté de Droit d'Istanbul* 3 (1955): 1–10.

MacCormack, Geoffrey. "Witnesses in the Law of the Twelve Tables." *Bullettino dell'Istituto di Diritto Romano* 15 (1973): 225–243.

McGinn, Thomas A. J. "Roman Children and the Law." In *The Oxford Handbook of Childhood and Education in the Classical World*, edited by Judith Evans Grubbs and Tim Parkin, 341–362. Oxford: Oxford University Press, 2013.

Meyer, Elizabeth A. *Legitimacy and Law in the Roman World: Tabulae in Roman Belief and Practice*. Cambridge: Cambridge University Press, 2004.

Mommsen, Theodor, Paul Krueger, and Alan Watson, eds. *The Digest of Justinian*. 4 vols. Philadelphia: University of Pennsylvania Press, 1985. (Revised English translation, 1998).

Mommsen, Theodor, and Paul M. Meyer, eds. *Theodosiani libri xvi cum Constitutionibus Sirmondianis: et Leges novellae ad Theodosianum pertinentes*. Berlin: Weidmann, 1904.

Nowak, Maria. *Wills in the Roman Empire: A Documentary Approach*. Journal of Juristic Papyrology Supplement 23. Warsaw: University of Warsaw, 2015.

Platschek, Johannes. "*Ex iure manum conserere*: Zur symbolischen Gewalt im frühen römischen Eigentumsprozess." *Tijdschrift voor Rechtsgeschiedenis* 74 (2006): 245–260.

Pringsheim, Fritz. "Le témoignage dans la Grèce et Rome archaïque." *Revue Internationale des Droits de l'Antiquité* 6 (1951): 161–175.

Pugliese, Giovanni. "La Preuve dans le Procès Romain de l'Époque Classique." In *La Preuve. Première Partie: Antiquité*. Recueils de la Société Jean Bodin 16, 277–348. Bruxelles: Éditions de la librairie encyclopédique, 1964.

Redard, Georges. "Latin *testis* 'témoin = troisième'?" In *Recherches de Linguistique: hommages à Maurice Leroy*, edited by J. Bingen, A. Coupez, and F. Mawet, 163–172. Bruxelles: Editions de l'Université de Bruxelles, 1980.

Riccobono, Salvator, ed. *Fontes Iuris Romani Antejustiniani Pars Prima: Leges*. 2nd ed. Florence: Barbèra, 1968. [*FIRA* 1].

Rix, Helmut. "Review of Martino, Paolo *Arbiter* (Roma: Consiglio Nazionale delle Ricerche e Dipartimento di Studi Glotto-antropologici dell'Università 'La Sapienza,' 1986)." *Indogermanische Forschungen* 95 (1990): 281–283.

Solmsen, Felix. "Beiträge zur geschichte der lateinischen sprache." *Zeitschrift für vergleichende Sprachforschung auf dem Gebiete der Indogermanischen Sprachen* 37, no. 1 (1904): 1–26.

Terranova, Francesca. "Sull'*antestatus* negli atti *per aes et libram*." *IVRIS ANTIQVI HISTORIA: An International Journal On Ancient Law* 2 (2010): 103–146.

Thesaurus linguae Latinae. Berlin (formerly Leipzig): De Gruyter (formerly Teubner), 1900–. [*TLL*].

Tomlin, Roger S. O. *Roman London's First Voices: Writing Tablets from the Bloomberg Excavations, 2010–14*. MOLA Monograph 72. London: Museum of London Archaeology, 2016.

Townshend, James R. "*Mulier Testabilis*: Women as Witnesses in Roman Law." In *Female Agency in the Ancient Mediterranean*, edited by Greg Gilles, Karolina Frank, Christine Plastow, and Lewis Webb. Liverpool: Liverpool University Press, 2024.

Valsan, Remus. "*Fides*, *bona fides*, and *bonus vir*: Relations of Trust and Confidence in Roman Antiquity." *Journal of Law, Religion and State* 5, no. 1 (2017): 48–85.

Vincenti, Umberto. *"Duo Genera Sunt Testium": Contributo allo Studio della Prova Testimoniale nel Processo Romano*. Padova: CEDAM, 1989.

Voci, Pasquale. "Linee storiche del diritto ereditario romano I. Dalle origini ai Severi." *Aufstieg und Niedergang der römischen Welt* II, Band 14 (1982): 392–448.

Watson, Alan. *International Law in Archaic Rome: War and Religion*. Baltimore: Johns Hopkins University Press, 1993.

Watson, Alan. *The Law of Succession in the Later Roman Republic*. Oxford: Clarendon Press, 1971.

Watson, Alan. *Roman Slave Law*. Baltimore: Johns Hopkins University Press, 1987.

Watson, Alan. *Rome of the XII Tables: Persons and Property*. Princeton: Princeton University Press, 1975.

Wieacker, Franz. "*Endoplorare*: Diebstahlsverfolgung und Gerüft im altrömischen Recht." In *Festschrift für Leopold Wenger: zu seinem 70. Geburtstag dargebracht von Freunden, Fachgenossen und Schülern*, 129–179. München: C. H. Beck, 1944.

Wieacker, Franz. "Zwölftafelprobleme." *Revue Internationale des Droits de l'Antiquité*. Series 3. 3 (1956): 459–492.

CHAPTER 2

"*Si Bononiensis*": Glossators and the Conflict of Laws

Nikitas E. Hatzimihail

> Argumentum quod si Bononiensis conveniatur Mutinae non debet iudicari secundum Statuta Mutinae quibus non subest, cum dicat: quos nostrae clementiae.
>
> Accursius ad C.1.1.1 v° *quos*

1 Introduction

"What happened in Bologna?" This was the first question Charles Donahue ever asked me in our tutorial meetings, in preparation for my S.J.D. comprehensive exams. Charlie had in mind, of course, the academic revolution that took place there, in the High Middle Ages, leading to the revival in the Western study of Roman law and the birth of the learned-law tradition we have come to refer to as *ius commune*. Among other things, this intellectual Renaissance is connected to the doctrinal beginnings of my own legal field, the conflict of laws or private international law. It is quite a separate discussion as to whether we can really speak of medieval "conflict of laws"—or indeed, what we could mean when using such terms and concepts.[1] My own doctoral project, co-supervised by Charlie, came to include the study of a canonical text from the Late Middle Ages. That text, by the illustrious Bartolus da Sassoferrato (1314–1357), is itself an extended commentary on a gloss by Accursius (c. 1182–c. 1260), from a century earlier.[2]

The gloss "*si Bononiensis*" has often been seen as a foundational moment in the historical consciousness of private international law.[3] Yet glossators have not received their due attention in the history of private international law. The

1 See Nikitas E. Hatzimihail, *Preclassical Conflict of Laws* (Cambridge: Cambridge University Press, 2021).

2 Bartolus ad C. 1.1.1, 5b–12a, Basel 1562, nu. 13–57.

3 See Hatzimihail, *Preclassical Conflict of Laws*, 110–124.

 DOI:10.1163/9789004710696_004

first histories of this emerging legal discipline, written in the late nineteenth century, began with the commentators or their *ultramontani* teachers.[4] It was Karl Neumeyer, in the beginning of the twentieth century, who brought into focus the latter part of the early Middle Ages and the high Middle Ages and directed our attention to several important texts, including notably the ones discussed in this chapter.[5] Neumeyer evidently influenced the most important works of conflicts historiography, including those by Max Gutzwiller and E. M. Meijers.[6] Today, a glossator's name often glosses (pun intended) historical narratives in conflict-of-laws works; such references, however, tend to be ornamental, their value lying in what they tell us about the historical consciousness of modern private international lawyers, rather than the doctrinal evolution of the field itself.

In my contribution in honor of our teacher, I have chosen to go back to Bologna and the glossators.[7] As stated, I owe to Charlie my first exposure to this period. In fact, I even owe to him the translations of the four texts discussed in this chapter. Moreover, this goes back to our long discussion that actually draws on an argument by Samuel Thorne, Charlie's predecessor as Paul Freund Professor at Harvard Law School, who had questioned the relevance of medieval texts for contemporary conflict of laws.[8] Thorne had found Medieval "conflict of laws" rules strikingly similar to English rules about statutory interpretation and concluded that conflict of laws properly speaking appears with the Dutch school, and territorial sovereignty, in the sixteenth century.[9] My doctoral work, which was originally not intended to veer beyond the nineteenth century, thus became a twin struggle—on the one hand, against medievalists who viewed my field too narrowly (and were probably appalled by the way history was treated in doctrinal texts); on the other hand, against the anachronistic

4 François Laurent, *Droit civil international*, vol. 1 (Bruxelles: Bruylant-Christophe & Cie., Éditeurs, 1880), 273 ff.; Armand Lainé, *Introduction au droit international privé*, 2 vols. (Paris: Librairie Cotillon, 1888–1892).

5 Karl Neumeyer, *Die gemeinrechtliche Entwickelung des internationalen Privat- und Strafrechts bis Bartolus*, vol. 1 (Munich: J. Schweitzer, 1901), and especially vol. 2 (Munich: J. Schweitzer, 1916).

6 Max Gutzwiller, "Le développement historique du droit international privé," *Recueil des cours* 29 (1929): 287–400; E.-M. Meijers, "L'histoire des principes fondamentaux du droit international privé à partir du Moyen Age," *Recueil des cours* 49 (1934): 543–686.

7 My contribution draws significantly from an article addressed to an audience of doctrinal private international lawyers: Nikitas Hatzimihail, "On the Doctrinal Beginnings of the Conflict of Laws," *Yearbook of Private International Law* 21 (2019/2020): 101–133.

8 Samuel E. Thorne, "Sovereignty and the Conflict of Laws," in Università degli Studi di Perugia, *Bartolo Da Sassoferrato: Studi E Documenti Per Il VI Centenario* (Milan: Giuffrè, 1962), 673–89.

9 Thorne, "Sovereignty and the Conflict of Laws," 673–84.

invocations of "history" in my doctrinal field, especially with regard to its early history.[10] It is as part of this ongoing struggle that I have selected these specific texts: all but one of them are obscure to legal historians, but these are the ones we have and, notably, the ones that have staked claims as discursive ancestors in private international law.

Inevitably, the star in this chapter is Accursius, a seminal figure in legal history whose gloss became the starting point for the subsequent, more famous conflicts treatments. But this is the story of three Bologna jurists—Aldricus (active 1154–1177), Carolus (mid-twelfth century–post 1215), and Accursius—representing three succeeding generations of scholarship, and indeed three stages in the intellectual evolution of the school. The same holds true of their respective texts, which vie for pride of place as the first doctrinal contribution to the conflict of laws. Aldricus lived at the time of the first peak of high medieval legal scholarship but before the consolidation of masters' colleges produced the medieval university and the doctrinal literature with which we are familiar. In the time of Carolus, doctrinal discussion was especially prolific and vibrant, culminating in efforts of systematization and consolidation by the time of Accursius. This was also a transformative time both for political theory and the formation of the Italian polities, which became the focus also of the subsequent, better known, generations of medieval jurists.

2 Context

Ius civile scholarship is presented, in legal history, in terms of two schools: the glossators who flourished in the twelfth and thirteenth centuries (i.e., the high Middle Ages) and the commentators who flourished especially in the fourteenth but also dominated the fifteenth century (i.e., the late Middle Ages). These schools are connected by the late thirteenth-century postglossators who taught in the universities of southern France (hence *ultramontani*).[11] The school of glossators took its name from the *glossae*, explanatory notes made

10 This twin struggle involved the study of historical narratives in Hatzimihail, *Preclassical Conflict of Laws*, esp. 47–136.

11 See especially Randall Lesaffer, *European Legal History: A Cultural and Political Perspective*, trans. Jan Arriens (Cambridge: Cambridge University Press, 2009), 25–29; O. F. Robinson, T. D. Fergus, and W. M. Gordon, *European Legal History: Sources and Institutions*, 3rd ed. (Oxford: Oxford Univeristy Press, 2000), 42 et seq., 59 et seq.; Franz Wieacker, *A History of Private Law in Europe*, trans. Tony Weir (Oxford: Clarendon Press, 1995), 28 et seq., 55 et seq.; Francesco Calasso, *Medio Evo del diritto*, vol. 1 (Milano: Guiffrè, 1954), 511 et seq., 563 et seq. Friedrich Carl von Savigny, *Geschichte des Römischen Rechts im Mittelalter*,

on the margins of the authoritative main text.[12] The period of the glossators culminated in the consolidation of glosses (*apparatus*) by Accursius, around 1220–1250, which became known as the Standard Gloss (*Glossa ordinaria*).[13]

3 Political Theory

As a rule, glossators were heavily invested in the revival of the Roman imperial idea and in the elevated position of imperial Roman law. They were more reluctant to acknowledge deviations from the scope of local law than their successors, the *ultramontani* French jurists of the late thirteenth century and the commentators of the fourteenth (and fifteenth) century, who insisted on the legal power of Roman law but could no longer harbor illusions of an actual political restoration of imperial power.

Medieval jurists were faced with the revived imperial Roman law (the "common law," *ius commune*), on the one hand, and local norms derogating from that common law, on the other. Such local law consisted of customs and statutes. Many customs *de facto* preceded the effective revival of Roman law, but *de jure* Roman law had preceded them, and any legal authority they would possess was supposed to emanate from Roman law. Older customary law had given way to written codifications, first by private initiative and eventually given official sanction or form. For example, the customs of Bologna were reportedly first written down *in curia Bulgari*, i.e., at the initiative of Bulgarus (d. 1166), one of the leading twelfth-century glossators, perhaps as he exercised some adjudicative function.[14]

In fact, when Emperor Henry V in 1116 granted to the *concives* of Bologna the privilege of imperial protection and of pursuing their own customs (*consuetudines*) in matters of commerce, that privilege did not comprise public rights.[15]

2nd ed. (Heidelberg: J. C. B. Mohr, 1834–1851) still remains a vital reference, especially for biographical information.

12 See, e.g., Manlio Bellomo, *The Common Legal Past of Europe*, trans. Lydia Cochrane (Washington, DC: The Catholic University of America Press, 1995), 129 et seq.

13 The traditional view held that a first edition of the Glossa (minus the *Institutes*), was published by 1228. It is now believed that the Glossa was constantly revised over a broader time frame, such as 1220–1250. See, e.g., Robert Charles Figueira, "Glossa Ordinaria: Roman Law," in Christopher Kleinhenz, ed., *Medieval Italy: An Encyclopaedia*, vol. 1 (New York: Routledge, 2003), 437–39.

14 Bellomo, *Common Legal Past*, 84.

15 Giorgio Tamba, "Civic Institutions (12th–early 15th centuries)," in Sarah H. Blanshei, ed., *A Companion to Medieval and Rennaissance Bologna* (Leiden: Brill, 2017), 211.

Indeed, at the Diet of Roncaglia (1158) the famous Four Doctors, including Bulgarus, declared that the Emperor maintained power in matters such as taxation and appointment of magistrates.[16] But a century later, in 1265, when the time came to update the statutes of Bologna, 265 volumes had to be examined.[17] It is telling that, whereas glossators called statuta "written custom," by the mid-fourteenth century Baldus called custom a "tacit statute" (tacitum statutum).[18]

4 Legal Literature

Research into medieval conflicts doctrine draws primarily from two groups of literary sources: systematic works and discussion of individual cases.[19] Sources from the first group are found inside systematic doctrinal expositions of Roman law, organised around the individual passages of the *Corpus Iuris*, especially the *Code* and the *Digest*. Most of our earliest texts come from these sources, which span the entire period from 1200 to 1600. It is these texts that have traditionally been discussed in the literature. In the case of glossators, such texts tend to have the size of a paragraph or even be limited to a single sentence, whereas commentators produced booklet-size treatments. In either case, the fact that these texts form part of systematic works does not mean that they themselves are exhaustive or comprehensive, or even that they do not contradict other passages by the same author in the same work. Medieval doctrinal writing was a multi-generational endeavour: such systematic works developed gradually and, especially at first, in the shadow of a rich oral tradition.[20]

16 Kenneth Pennington, *The Prince and the Law, 1200–1600: Sovereignty and Rights in the Western Legal Tradition* (Berkeley: University of California Press, 1993), 8 et seq.

17 Philip Jones, *The Italian City-State: From Commune to Signoria* (Oxford: Clarendon Press, 1997), 373.

18 Joseph Canning, *The Political Thought of Baldus de Ubaldis* (Cambridge: Cambridge University Press, 1987), 102 n. 31.

19 This account is by definition incomplete. It moreover cannot do justice to the many literary forms in which the glossators' prolific inventiveness appears to have been expressed but do not have an immediate relation with our subject. See, e.g., Robinson et al., *European Legal History*, 52–56.

20 In the words of Bellomo, *Common Legal Past*, 129–30: "If over the years some professors and a good many students had not noted down their *glossae* on parchment as a way of documenting and remembering the *lecturae*, we would know little or nothing of that world of ideas, beliefs and values today. Thanks to them, we can manage to know something—on the condition that we keep in mind that the *glossae* were only an extremely feeble projection of a much fuller investment of both individual and collective reflection, and that we remember that they are a fragmentary and highly reductive expression of the oral

Some of the late medieval conflicts treatments that made their way into systematic works originally came in the form of a *repetitio*—an evening lecture, delivered separately from the standardised morning lectures on the curriculum, where the professor would analyse in depth a textual fragment.[21] On the contrary, we have no examples of a standalone short treatise (*tractatus*) dedicated to our subject.[22]

The second group of sources consists of material involving concrete cases, notably *quaestiones* and *consilia*. In a *quaestio*, a genre developed and used to great effect by the glossators, a problem was raised and discussed, often with a position and a counter-position presented. In many older *quaestiones*, the master's own answer is laconically stated with a simple yes or no.[23] Such *quaestiones*—which may or may not have arisen out of actual cases—were often put together in collections including the texts and ideas of several authors. Many of them found their way to systematic works. The *consilium* was a legal opinion, concerning an individual case, rendered, at the instigation of the court or a party to the case, by a jurist who was concerned less with bringing up for discussion both sides of the argument and more with providing support for the solution he proposed.[24] Glossators evidently wrote *consilia* (indeed we cannot know when a *quaestio* was a purely academic one or inspired from an actual case or even consultation given by its author) but it was the subsequent school of commentators who developed this genre.[25]

activities that revolved around a central nucleus of the few certain, authoritative, and sacred texts."

21 Lesaffer, *European Legal History*, 252; Bellomo, *Common Legal Past*, 137–39.

22 Robinson et al., *European Legal History*, 53, 64–65.

23 Bellomo, *Common Legal Past*, 139–43.

24 Robinson et al., *European Legal History*, 55, 66–67; Bellomo, *Common Legal Past*, 211–15.

25 Such *consilia* circulated more broadly in the age of the printed book, when it became easier, and more affordable, to assemble the entire work (*omnia opera*) especially of famous jurists. Not unlike the present, some medieval scholars did their best work in commissioned legal opinions. Baldus, for example, who wrote a landmark systematic treatment, second only to Bartolus's among medieval jurists, was especially prolific as an author of *consilia*. A subsequent Bartolist, Alexander Tartagnus, became known primarily because of his *consilia*, through which Bartolan doctrines on conflicts survived, albeit in caricatured form, to the nineteenth century. These *consilia* were, among others, republished with commentaries by Dumoulin, himself the author of the most famous *consilium* in the history of private international law.

5 Legal Bases

As medieval jurists moved from ad hoc to more systematic works, treatments of legal subjects were anchored to specific passages of the *Corpus Iuris Civilis*. The principal one, for our purposes, has been the first title of Justinian's *Code*, known by its first words, *Cunctos populos*, but better known as the Edict of Thessalonica.[26] With this 380 AD edict, Theodosius I and his co-emperors reaffirmed Nicene Christianity as the official religion of the Empire and laid the foundation for the suppression of all Christian heresies and polytheistic religions:

> *Emperors Gratian, Valentinian, and Theodosius Augusti to the People of Constantinople*: We desire that all people (*cunctos populos*) who are governed by the moderation of Our Clemency shall practice that religion which was handed down by the divine Apostle Peter to the Romans, as shown by the religion introduced by him and transmitted down to this day—the religion which, it is clear, is now followed by the Pontiff Damasus and by Peter, Bishop of Alexandria, a man of apostolic sanctity; that is, according to apostolic learning and the teaching of the evangelists, we shall believe in one deity of the Father and the Son and the Holy Spirit, in equal majesty and in a pious Trinity. 1. We order all who obey this law to embrace the name of Catholic Christians, and all others, whom We deem mad and insane, to suffer the infamy of heretical doctrine; they shall be stricken, first, by divine vengeance and, second, also by the vengeance of Our wrath, which We shall take in accordance with the judgment of Heaven.[27]

---

26 C. 1.1 (De summa trinitate et de fide catholica et ut nemo de ea publice contendere audeat).

27 C. 1.1.1, as translated in Bruce Frier, ed., *The Codex of Justinian* (Cambridge: Cambridge University Press, 2016), 14: "Imppp. Gratianus Valentianus et Theodosius AAA. ad populum urbis Constantinopolitanae. Cunctos populos, quos clementiae nostrae regit temperamentum, in tali volumus religione versari, quam divinum Petrum apostulum tradidisse Romanis religio usque ad nunc ab ipso insinuata declarat quamque pontificem Damasum sequi claret et Petrum Alexandriae episcopum virum apostolicae sanctitatis, hoc est ut secundum apostolicam disciplinam evangelicamque doctrinam patris et filii et spiritus sancti unam deitatem sub pari maiestate et sub pia trinitate credamus. 1. Hanc legem sequentes christianorum catholicorum nomen iubemus amplecti, reliquos vero dementes vesanosque iudicantes haeretici dogmatis infamiam sustinere, divina primum vindicta, post etiam motus nostri, quem ex caelesti arbitrio sumpserimus, ultione plectendos."

Medieval scholars glossed the passage with comments on subjects for which they regarded it as constituting authority, including, as might be expected, the definition and consequences of heresy, insanity, and infamy; legal aspects of religion (e.g., usury); and the meaning of certain words such as the pronoun *qui* (who) and the verb *volere* (will/desire).[28] They also added glosses on the "matter of statutes," as reframed much later than our texts by Baldus.[29]

The other main contender has been a passage in the first book of the *Digest*, known as *l. de quibus*, which states the following:

> What ought to be held in those cases (*de quibus causis*) where we have no applicable written law, is the practice established by customs and usage (*quod moribus et consuetudine inductum est*). And if this is in some way deficient, we should hold to what is most nearly analogical to and entailed by such a practice. If even this is obscure, then we ought to apply law as it is in use in the City of Rome. 1. Age-encrusted custom is not undeservedly cherished as having almost statutory force, and this is the kind of law which is said to be established by use and wont. For given that statutes themselves are binding upon us for no other reason than that they have been accepted by the judgment of the populace, certainly it is fitting that what the populace has approved without any writing shall be binding upon everyone. What does it matter whether the people declares its will by voting or by the very substance of its actions? Accordingly, it is absolutely right to accept the point that statutes may be repealed not only by vote of the legislature but also by the silent agreement of everyone expressed through desuetude.[30]

The *Institutes* contain a sibling passage to l. de quibus, known as *ex non scripto*, which states: "Law comes into being without writing (*ex non scripto ius venit*) when a rule is approved by use (*usus*). Long-standing custom (*mores*) founded on the consent of those who follow it is just like legislation."[31]

Another passage in the *Code* (C. 8.52: *Quae sit longa consuetudo*) provided authority for the status of long-held customs (*longa consuetudo*) but also a reservation that they cannot overcome reason or law, whereas C. 8.48.1, which

28 See, e.g., Bartolus ad C.1.1.1, nus. 1–12.

29 Baldus ad C. 1.1.1, nu 49 ("Nunc venio ad materiam statutorum").

30 D.1.3.32 (Julian, *Digest*, Book 84). Translation from Alan Watson, *The Digest of Justinian*, vol. 1 (Philadelphia: University of Pennsylvania Press, 1985), 13.

31 Translation from Paul Kreuger, ed., *Justinian's Institutes*, trans. Peter Birks and Grant McLeod (Ithaca, NY: Cornell University Press, 1987), 39.

stated that a father born elsewhere is able to emancipate his son if munipical law conferred such power upon the local magistrates, could and was used to provide support for the validity of local statutes.[32]

Finally, the first title from the fifth book of the *Digest*, entitled "Actions: Where a Man Should Sue and be Sued," was invoked on occasion. Its first passage reads as follows: "If people submit themselves and agree to someone's jurisdiction, any judge who is in charge of a seat of judgment or has other jurisdiction has jurisdiction over those agreeing."[33]

6 Aldricus

Relatively little is known about Master (*Magister*) Aldricus: his work has survived in the texts of others, but there is clear evidence that he was alive between 1154 and 1177 and probably taught in Bologna.[34] He was thus a contemporary of the famous Four Doctors—Martinus, Bulgarus, Jacobus, and Hugo—whom we saw above taking a pro-imperial legal stance but also better known as the main pupils of Irnerius, the man who recomposed and established an authoritative version of the entire *Corpus Iuris Civilis* and thus laid the foundations for the textual authority on which all subsequent medieval scholarship relied.[35] We saw above that Bulgarus is associated with the writing down of Bolognese customary law: he is also regarded as having advocated "a more rigorous method for analysis of the formal logic of Justinian law," in contrast to Martinus, who explored the equitable possibilities of the *ius commune*.[36] This would mean that Aldricus lived in an environment where not just the hierarchy but the *content* of the sources of law themselves was still a work in progress.

All this should illuminate the passage for which he has found a place in the history of the conflict of laws.

> It is asked: if men of different provinces which have different customs litigate before one and the same judge (*iudex*), which of them [the customs]

32 Both of these texts were used by Azo and Accursius, as noted by Meijers, "L'histoire des principes fondamentaux," 593 n. 1.

33 D 5.1.1 (Ulpian, Edict, bk. 2). Translation from Watson, *Digest of Justinian*, 164.

34 Hermann Lange, *Römisches Recht im Mittelalter*, vol. 1 (Munich: Beck, 1997), 202–4; Savigny, *Geschichte des Römischen Rechts*, 4:231–36, noting that what we have from Aldricus consists of subsequent authors referring to his oral lectures.

35 Wieacker, *History of Private Law*, 28, 40; Savigny, *Geschichte des Römischen Rechts*, 4:9 et seq.

36 Bellomo, *Common Legal Past*, 167.

> ought the judge who undertakes to judge the case follow? I reply that [custom] which seems stronger and more useful (*potior et utilior*). For he ought to judge according to what has seemed better to him. According to Aldricus.[37]

We must first consider the text itself. This passage is found in a collection of "Disputes among the masters" (*dissensiones dominorum*).[38] These collections presented conflicting interpretations of legal questions by various glossators, between those insisting on strict law and those advocating a more equitable approach.[39] In this case, our passage comes at the end of a discussion on whether a custom could prevail over or abrogate a law (*An consuetudo legem vincat vel abrogare possit*). The passage takes the form of a *quaestio*, but we cannot know if it referred to an actual case. We cannot in fact even know how the passage relates to the broader argument originally provided by Aldricus. We can draw inferences in considering the entire text, but caution must be exercised.

With this in mind, we shall consider the argument—and the norm—advanced. It must be noted that our text does not specify if the forum (the "one and same judge") is found in the province of one of the parties, or in a third province. In this regard, the text is markedly different than all the subsequent ones we will examine, where not only the forum, but also its connection to both litigants is clearly defined.

There is more than one way to read the text.

The first one is to think in terms of a "domestic" case. In the early Middle Ages, the *iudex* tended to simply mean the one who judges, not necessarily a trained jurist.[40] A *iudex* in the Kingdom of Lombardy presided over a judicial territory including several smaller court districts (*schulteis*).[41] The solution that Aldricus gives compels the judge to exercise his judgment by choosing

37 Codex Chisiani collectio §46 (*An consuetudo legem vincat vel abrogare possi*), in fine: "Sed quaeritur, si äomines diversarum provinciarum, quae diversas habent consuetudines, sub uno eodemque iudice litigant, utrum earum iudex qui iudicandum suscepit sequi debeat? Respondeo eam, quae potior et utilior videtur; debet enim iudicare secundum quod melius ei visum fuerit. Secundum Aldricum."

38 Codex Chisianus collectio, §46, in Gustavus Haenel, *Dissensiones dominorum sive controversiae veterum iuris romani interpretum qui glossatores vocantur* (Leipzig: Scientia Verlag Aalen, 1834), 151–53.

39 Robinson, *European Legal History*, 55.

40 Bellomo, *Common Legal Past*, 45.

41 Katherine Fischer Drew, *The Lombard Laws* (Philadelphia: University of Pennsylvania Press, 1973), 25.

between the competing customs as alleged by the parties and thus deciding the case himself, instead of relying upon compurgation or judicial duel—the ancient method of judicial proof under Lombard law, which had been waning for centuries. This would be in the spirit of the procedural reform movement, which had started in ecclesiastical courts. It would also lead to the ascertainment and writing down of customary law, in the spirit of Bulgarus and in the light of eleventh-century efforts, such as the *Lombarda*, to organise systematically early medieval Lombard legislation.[42]

But it is also possible, and indeed desirable, to examine the text from a conflict-of-laws perspective. It must be apparent that I do not share the enthusiasm of some modern authors, who regard Aldricus as offering us an early example of a multilateral or a better-law approach.[43] An important reason for such misreading is that the passage is read as synchronous to the subsequent medieval texts, all the while appearing very different from them. Glossators, such as Carolus and Accursius, and commentators, such as Bartolus, primarily addressed questions of conflicts between the *ius commune* and the local custom or statute. Once the power of a city to issue a statute governing the conduct of its own "subjects" in its own territory had been established, the next question concerned the power of the city to govern the same conduct by "non-subjects" in its own territory, and then by its subjects outside its territory. This is the reason why medieval jurists have tended to be regarded as unilateralists in conflicts literature.

Aldricus himself addresses a horizontal conflict—one between different customs of different territories. He thus avoids any consideration of the role of the *ius commune*—he could have offered the same answer before a provincial imperial court in the Late Antiquity. He even uses the political vocabulary of Late Antiquity, in speaking of "provinces" rather than referring to cities. He also avoids any consideration of political power (and jurisdiction). In fact, his actual solution confirms this. Rather than employing formal criteria, such as the custom prevailing in his own province, the judge should use his own judgment to select that custom which seems to him *stronger* and *more useful*. What meaning is ascribed by Aldricus to each of these two attributes is unclear. Yet their combined use makes evident where Aldricus lies in the debate between "strict law" and an equitable approach.

42 Robinson et al., *European Legal History*, 23.

43 See, e.g., Gutzwiller, "Le développement historique du droit," 301 (Aldricus "at the forefront of those distinguished by an independent and novel conception of the problem of application of laws"). For an overview of the position of Aldricus in the genealogy of especially modern conflict of laws, see Hatzimihail, *Preclassical Conflict of Laws*, 122–124.

A third, intermediate, approach would be for us not to think in purely abstract terms, which has predominantly been the case in our historical literature. We should instead consider the kind of problems with which each text is concerned. Given that our glossators' texts offer us little help by themselves, we must infer from what we know through general legal and social history. There we can discern an expansion of the material scope of local norms, as we move from the transactional *consuetudines* of the early twelfth century to elaborate systems of *statuta* regulating especially patrimonial aspects of family and succession, by the fourteenth century.[44]

This expansion is evident, for example, in Bartolus, writing in the mid-fourteenth century. His conflicts treatment, appearing as a commentary on the Accursian gloss, contains nine sections, the first five concerned with the scope of city law within the city's territory; the last four with its extraterritorial effects. But once we look more closely, we shall see that it is only the final eight, concerned primarily with questions of capacity, status, and succession, as well as penal laws, which address the question in terms of defining the personal, territorial, and material scope of derogation of such city statutes from the *ius commune*, Roman law.[45] Contracts are dealt with in the treatment's very first section.[46] That section looks very different from the other eight, both as to how the question is posed and as to the wording of Bartolus's solutions, which indeed look like multilateral choice-of-law rules from the classical or modern period. Even the distinctions Bartolus employs, in that first section, have affinities to our own classical and modern schemes: "matters arising out of the nature of the contract itself at the time it was made" are governed by the law of place where the contract was concluded, whereas "matters arising ex post facto due to neglect or delay" are governed by the place of performance.[47] Bartolus devotes some effort to distinguishing conceptually between the place of the trial and the place of contractual performance, almost a century after Jacobus Balduinus (1175–1235), who had reputedly first drawn a distinction between matters concerning the manner of conducting the case (*ad ordinatoria litis*)

44 For an overview of potential issues, see, e.g., Thomas Kuehn, "Property of Spouses in Renaissance Florence," in *Family Law and Society in Europe from the Middle Ages to the Contemporary Era*, edited by Maria Gigliola di Renzo Villata (Cham: Springer, 2016), 109–33; Julius Kirshner, "Materials for a Gilded Cage: Nondotal Assets in Florence, 1300–1500," in *Marriage, Dowry, and Citizenship In Late Medieval and Renaissance Europe*, edited by Julius Kirshner (Toronto: University of Toronto Press, 2015), 74–93.

45 Bartolus ad C.1.1.1, nus. 20–51.

46 Bartolus ad C.1.1.1, nus. 13–19.

47 Bartolus ad C.1.1.1, nus. 13–19.

and matters concerning the decision itself (*ad litis decisionem*), in which it was not necessary for the law of the judge to apply.[48]

Let us also consider, in this regard, an anonymous gloss, probably authored in Paris in the generation following Aldricus.[49] The gloss is as follows:

> Let us suppose that it is the custom in the city of Paris that if someone contracts marriage with some woman, the marriage having been dissolved by the death of the woman, the man ought to have half the goods given on account of the marriage (*donatio propter nuptias*) and it is the custom of the city of Chartres, that if the marriage is dissolved by the death of the woman, the man has nothing. Let us suppose that someone contracts marriage in the city of Paris and afterwards goes to the city of Chartres and stays there properly (*recte*) for a year and more and in that city the woman dies. The man seeks a half of the *donatio propter nuptias*. It is asked whether he can claim [to get it], because the heirs [of the woman] want to have the case decided by the customs of the city of Chartres and not by the custom of Paris. But someone said in reply that he can properly claim.[50]

48 Meijers, "L'histoire des principes fondamentaux," 595 and Neumeyer, *Die gemeinrechtliche Entwickelung*, 2:86–87. This is reported by Jacobus's students, Odofredus and Jacobus de Ravanis in their glosses to D. 5.1.1.

49 E. M. Meijers brought the text to light, as part of his discussion of early customary and court practice, which precedes his discussion of the "Italian theory." See Meijers, "L'histoire des principes fondamentaux," 585. With reference to A. Fliniaux, "Le manuscrit 141 de la Bibliothèque municipale d'Avranches et le problème de l'introduction en France au Moyen-âge de texte des compilations de Justinien," in *Atti del Congresso internazionale di diritto romano (Bologna e Roma, 17–28 Aprile 1934)*, vol. 1 (Pavia: F. Fusi, 1934), 313–327, he concluded that the manuscript was in France before 1200 and the passage was probably authored by someone who taught in Paris (before the Pope abolished law teaching in Paris in 1219).

50 MS 141, Bibliothèque municipale d'Avranches, fol. 248v. "Hic ponitur quedam questio. Ponamus ut est de consuetudine in civitate Parisiensi quod si aliquis contrahat matrimonium cum aliqu[a] muliere, matrimonio soluto per mortem mulieris, vir debet habere medietatem rerum donatarum propter nuptias, et est de consuetudine in civitate Carnotensi, quod si matrimonium dissolvatur per mortem mulieris, quod vir nihil habebat. Ponamus quidam contrahit matrimonium in civitate Parisiensi et postea advenit ad civitatem Carnotensem et ibi moratur recte per annum et amplius et in illa civitate mulier decedit; ille vir petit medietatem donationem propter nuptias. Queritur utrum potest, quia heredes volunt quod illa causa determinatur ex consuetudinibus Carnotensibus et non ex consuetudine Parisiensi. Sed quidam respondens dicebat quod bene potuit petere."

This is a classic case that was to be raised again and again over the next centuries, including in some of the most canonical texts of preclassical and even classical conflict of laws, even as both the subject moved (from contracts to family law), and conflicts doctrine evolved (from being an interpretative method to a legal discipline and thinking in terms of *conflits de systèmes*). The wife dies childless, which means that her blood relatives are her heirs. With the marriage dissolved, the wife's proprietary interests must be restituted to her heirs, which raises the question of whether the husband should be allowed to keep part of the gift bestowed upon him by his wife, by way of contribution to the household needs. Such gifts raised questions because of the Roman law restrictions of gifts between spouses. A conflict is thus triggered between the laws of the place where the marriage was celebrated (and the dowry contract executed), and the place where the couple subsequently made their home (the husband's domicile). What makes this case even more interesting is that here each party seeks application of the custom (and jurisdiction of the courts) of the place of the other party's domicile.

For a contemporary conflicts lawyer, this text makes clearer sense than the ones from Bologna. It also clearly indicates that we are talking about a contractual case—something that may be simply alluded to in our other texts. Yet the anonymous author takes no position here, except to refer to a *responsum* by a jurist who advocated the application of the custom of Paris.[51] It would be tempting to read into our text, especially the *responsum* in the final sentence, a preference for *lex fori* or for the place of contracting—or, alternatively, for the expansive application of the custom of Paris (which moreover was closer to the Germanic ideas of northern French customary law about community of property). It is equally, if not more, likely that there were substantive considerations involved: it is stated that the couple lived "properly" (*recte*) and therefore the contract of marriage was fulfilled, inducing the husband into expenses for which the donation constituted consideration. So would it not be unjust for him not to keep anything? On the other hand, especially given that the couple lived together for a little more than a year, would it not be too generous for the husband to keep half of the *donatio propter nuptias*? And what should we make of the fact that the wife's family only expected to receive half of the donation in case of early dissolution of the marriage? The truth is we do not know the arguments on which the case was decided or even which solution

51 It is unfortunate we cannot know the arguments of the *responsum*, especially because, for many centuries, subsequent scholarship took the opposite position. See, e.g., Bartolus ad C.1.1.1, nu. 19 and discussion in Hatzimihail, *Preclassical Conflict of Laws*, 226–28, 286–87, 294–98.

prevailed. And this may well have been the author's purpose: our text looks more like a *quaestio*, with the facts balanced so as to best invite arguments on both sides, and readers left imagining what these arguments were.

I would argue that this text as well should support the notion that Aldricus had in mind a contractual case and thus better place him in perspective. His approach undoubtedly captured the tensions, inherent in the judicial work of the time, between creative work and formalized decision making. It is also remarkable how many ideas are included in these thirty-seven words. But, in the end, Aldricus did not provide any standards useful to the thousands of lawyers and judges who came to be faced with an increasing number of such cases. His solution moreover does not take into account political power or the hierarchies of jurisdiction. This may explain why we have little evidence of Aldricus's approach having lasting influence on subsequent jurists, including on the Parisian gloss. The single exception of Hugolinus (d. 1233), whose own collection of *quaestiones* was characteristically entitled *Insolubilia*, almost proves the point.[52]

7 Carolus

Carolus de Tocco lived in the late twelfth and early thirteenth century.[53] This was a time of prolific literary production, including the first serious efforts at comprehensive treatments of the *Corpus Iuris* material: Carolus's more famous contemporaries, Hugolinus and especially Azo, are known for their *apparatus*, especially on the *Code*. The late twelfth century also saw the first instances of professors leaving Bologna for other towns attempting to set up universities. Carolus himself taught in Bologna but also spent some time in Piacenza and exercised judicial functions in Salerno. His most celebrated and widely circulated work was his systematic commentary (*apparatus*) on the *Lombarda*.[54] In contrast, little has survived of his glosses and *summae* on the *Corpus Iuris*, but that includes the following gloss on *cunctos populos*:

> Here note that he does not want to bind others than those who are subject to his *imperium*, and there is an argument [in this direction] below [C.3.1.14]. This is, however, contrary to the customs of the cities which

52 Meijers, "L'histoire des principes fondamentaux," 593 n. 1, following Neumeyer and citing Hugolinus ad C.8.52–53.1 v° *controversiarum*.

53 See Savigny, *Geschichte des Römischen Rechts*, 5:174–83.

54 See, e.g., Calasso, *Medio Evo del diritto*, 1:552.

> also want to bind others with their statutes. And there is an argument that if a Modenese litigates against a Bolognese in this city [i.e., Bologna] that the statute not harm the Modenese. But some, however, say the contrary to this, [using the] argument that the Modenese here follows the forum by summoning the Bolognese [to the Bolognese court], and by this act (*unde*) he accepts all the laws of this forum.[55]

This text is markedly different from the previous ones. Unlike Aldricus, Carolus defines the issue in terms of a conflict between the law in place in two different city-states and seems to acknowledge the existence of political and jurisdictional entities. There are elements of a *quaestio* in the way in which Carolus presents both sides of the argument without taking himself a clear position but we also see, for the first time, actual arguments and references to legal authorities.

Moroever, Carolus has anchored the text on *l. cunctos populos,* making an argument by analogy. More precisely, he makes an argument *a maiore ad minus* with allusions to an argument *a contrario*: if, in a matter as vital as religion, imperial Roman law would restrict its application to those under the Emperor's power, it goes without saying that neither would Roman law apply beyond the territory of the Empire, nor could the local laws and customs of cities apply beyond the narrow confines left to them by Roman law, for example over a citizen of another city. The starting point is the argument by analogy from *cunctos populos*, as was suggested above: a polity can only bind those subject to its *imperium*. This is an argument that was to have a long life thereafter. However, unlike the commentators of a century later, Carolus does not elaborate on this point or draw distinctions. Neither is there any reference to a political word such as "citizens" (*cives*), "subjects" (*subditi*), or "foreigners" (*forenses*). He does refer in support to another passage of the *Code* (*rem non*

---

55 Carolus ad C.1.1.1 MS Bibl. nat. 4546 v° *clementiae* fol. 2a. "Hic nota quod alios noluit ligare nisi subditos imperio suo et est argumentum, infra, de iudiciis l. rem. primo responso (C.3.1.14 v° *quum igitur*, etc.). Est autem hoc contra consuetudines civitatum quae etiam alios constringere volunt cum suis statutis. Et est argumentum si litigat Mutinensis contra Bononiensem in hac civitate, quod statutum non noceat Mutinensi. Sed quidam contra hoc autem dicunt, argumento illo quod Mutinensis hic forum sequitur conveniendo Bononiensem, unde omnes leges illius fori recipiat." The text was transcribed by Neumeyer, *Die gemeinrechtliche Entwickelung*, 2:75 (who attributed the manuscript to Rodofredus) and then Meijers, "L'histoire des principes fondamentaux," 594. Neumeyer followed Savigny in attributing the manuscript to Rodofredus. See the contrary argument of Meijers, "L'histoire des principes fondamentaux," 594 n. 1.

novat): this is a *constitutio* of Justinian, which extols legal certainty and orders the judges to apply his law.[56]

At this point the opposing arguments, in favor of the application of Bolognese law, appear. Carolus makes a pragmatic remark: this line of argument runs contrary to the customs of the cities, which want to bind "others" with their statutes. This is an acknowledgment of the existing practice of cities applying "their" law in cases brought before them.[57] Glossators found imperial Roman support for this practice by relying, on the one hand, on the acknowledged force of a custom and, on the other hand, on the *Digest* passage regarding submission to a judge's jurisdiction.[58] It is to that *locus* that Carolus seems to allude in the argument he provides.

It is tempting to think of Carolus as offering a choice-of-law rule. Moreover, Carolus seemingly argues that a civil defendant's *submission* to jurisdiction also constitutes submission to the pertinent customs and statutes of the city. This would tempt many conflicts scholars to regard our text as the first recorded instance of a tacit agreement, or consent, being invoked in order to determine the applicable law: by suing in the courts of Bologna, the Modenese has accepted all the laws of the Bolognese court. One cannot deny the affinities in argumentative patterns with subsequent doctrine, but we must also consider the context. The notion of consent is connected to the doctrine on custom.

An argument based on submission would make sense especially with regard to commercial transactions, where the judge should choose between competing trade usages. But it also pertinent in other contractual disputes. For example, on the issue of prescription: Bartolus offered the case of a Florentine who borrowed money *in curia Romae* with the promise to repay the money in Perugia, where however such actions are barred after ten years.[59] Bartolus reports consensus as to the opinion that the law of Perugia should apply and the action is barred. Earlier jurists however, argued that this is so because Perugia is the place of trial (*locus iudicii*), whereas Bartolus argues that Perugia is the place of performance.[60] Or in the manner of dowry contracts, where it took a few centuries for the argument of presumed intention of the parties to be employed as an argument in favor of the matrimonial domicile, rather than the place of celebration of the marriage (and conclusion of the contract).[61]

---

56 C. 3.1.14.

57 See Meijers, "L'histoire des principes fondamentaux," 594, citing Azo and Accursius (in other glosses).

58 D 5.1.1.

59 Bartolus ad C.1.1.1, nu. 19.

60 Bartolus ad C.1.1.1, nus. 13–9.

61 Carolus Molinaeus, Consilium 53, *Opera Omnia*, vol. 2 (Paris 1681), fol. 953–956b.

Carolus de Tocco was a representative of his age—an age of learned-law exploration of *ius commune* and its relation with the emerging *iura propria*, and of efforts to consolidate three generations' worth of scholarly work. His short text puts together not just opposing answers to the conflict-of-laws question but also opposing approaches: legal hierarchies and political power, jurisdiction and substantive law are contrasted to submission and consent, procedural law, and custom. Carolus acquired a place in our historical consciousness because of the invocation of *l. lex cunctos populos*, but his true legacy appears to be in illustrating the different directions that could be taken.

8 Accursius

We thus come to Accursius (1185–1263), professor at Bologna and author of the Standard Gloss (*Glossa ordinaria, Magna Glossa*, or simply "the Gloss"). Accursius consolidated a lot of pre-existing material and was especially influenced by his master Azo, but also by the latter's rival, Hugolinus. Over time, the work of Accursius overshadowed much of that earlier material.[62] The *Glossa ordinaria* maintained its authoritative status up to the seventeenth century, but Accursius has also invited a lot of hostility and accusations of unoriginality.

There are several glosses of interest to our subject in the Gloss, but they fall outside the scope of this study. Accursius has secured his place in our historical consciousness with the following gloss to *l. cunctos populos*:

> Argument that if a Bolognese (*si Bononiensis*) is sued in Modena he ought not be judged according to the statutes of Modena to which he is not subject, because it says [i.e., the *lex*] 'which [the *imperium*] of our clemency [rules].'[63]

There are three separate questions here. The first one concerns the relation between *si Bononiensis* and Carolus's *si Mutinenis*. The second is about the significance of *si Bononienis* in its own context. The third is about the relation of *si Bononiensis* to subsequent doctrine.

62 J. W. Wessels, *History of the Roman-Dutch Law* (Grahamstown: Africa Book Company, 1908), 116–17, quoting Savigny, *Geschichte des Römischen Rechts*, 5:262 et seq.

63 Accursius ad C.1.1.1 v° *quos*, Lyon 1527, fol. 13: "Argumentum quod si Bononiensis conveniatur Mutinae non debet iudicari secundum Statuta Mutinae quibus non subest, cum dicat: quos nostrae clementiae."

Viewed in isolation, the gloss of Accursius sounds like a response to Carolus. We could even be tempted to perceive the gloss *si Bononiensis*, which only presents one side of the argument, as lacking in comparison with *si Mutinensis*, which presented a fuller discussion, a clear indication that there were arguments on both sides. Likewise, Accursius is here setting unequivocal limits on the city's ability to regulate its own territory, even though we know that Italian cities had in the meantime pushed further with their projects of asserting political and legal power. On the other hand, if we follow Meijers's thesis that the most important development for the birth of conflict-of-laws doctrine was the notion that a forum may not necessarily apply its "own" law, it must be granted that Accursius states this position unequivocally, unlike Carolus.

Carolus had left open the possibility that the claim of a Modenese being sued in Bologna will be adjudicated in accordance with Bolognese statutes. Accursius reverses the facts of the case. This does not appear accidental: given his conclusion, this reversal makes it more palatable to an audience that should include at least as many, if not more, Bolognese as Modenese. The effect of Accursius's position is thus to spare the Bolognese his subjection to Modenese statutes and customs. Nothing is said about the reverse case—and this would remind a modern jurist of unilateralism—but the principle that Accursius states should be regarded as applicable in the reverse case as well.

Meijers presents *si Bononienis* as a mild variation of *si Mutinensis*.[64] Meijers considers the positions Accursius takes in other glosses (including *de quibus*), in which he appears more favorable to the idea of the court applying its own laws to a case and surmises that Accursius originally followed the position of his master Azo, to that effect, with *si Bononiensis* being a relatively late addition (around 1245).[65]

I am not in position to dispute this conclusion and indeed there is no reason to—but this does not mean that Accursius changed his mind. Accursius was certainly very much influenced by Azo, but he also incorporated into his own *apparatus* other material and ideas; he himself lived a long and full life, getting involved in the practice and politics of his time and establishing a dynasty of jurists. We know that the Gloss was written over a long period of time and a work of such scope and ambition was not meant to be without any internal

64 Meijers, "L'histoire des principes fondamentaux," 595 ("cette glosse a été répétée avec quelque variante par Accurse").

65 Meijers, "L'histoire des principes fondamentaux," 595 ("Accurse avait soutenu d'abord, dans son appareil primitive, l'opinion de son maître Azon, qu'on doit suivre toujours la *lex fori*.") and 593 n. 1, where Meijers refers to Azo ad D 5.1.1 and Accursius ad C. 8.52.1, v° *controversiarium*, ad C. 8.48. v° *duumviris*, D. 1.3.32 v° *de quibus*.

contradictions.[66] But it would befit the scholastic spirit to consider whether there is concordance between these diverse glosses. My tentative conclusion would be that such concordance should be found in Accursius: even if he was content with the customary *locus iudicii* to provide the solution in such cases, this would not prejudice his answer to the general question. In his other glosses, Accursius is dealing with concrete legal problems, such as the ones discussed in the preceding sections, which tend to involve "conflicts" between customary norms or usages. For example, the cases Accursius uses in his gloss on *de quibus causis* concern *statuta* altering norms of feudal law.[67] All indications are of a "domestic" case.[68]

On the contrary, *si Bononienis* does not only provide a general rule but also deals with a different kind of problem: a conflict between city statute and the *ius commune*, which is vertical as well as horizontal. Accursius seems concerned, in his gloss, with instances where city legislation is encroaching upon the *ius commune*, especially in matters pertaining to status, succession, and patrimonial aspects of the family. The proliferation of such legislation by the time of Bartolus, a century later, makes this trend especially visible in his work, whose bulk is devoted to such questions: to give an example, alongside the simple, "horizontal" conflict of laws as to dowry we must add questions scattered in that *repetitio* about the effect of statutes prohibiting a husband from instituting his wife as heir, or prohibiting one spouse from leaving a legacy to another.[69] And to them we should add, as the medieval practitioner probably would, statutes altering the legal norms as to who could be heir (notably daughters or illegitimate children), which would thus have a transformative effect upon the same question.

Accursius responded to these emergent questions by stating the classic position expected of a glossator, who stood for imperial power: the city statutes represent a local derogation from the *ius commune* and may therefore only bind their city's own citizens. The argument by analogy from the limitation of imperial power is expressly made in the gloss and then again repeated in the paratitla. Contrary to a modern lawyer's reflective understanding, the Bolognese facing the Modena court could not be subject to Bolognese law: it

66 The traditional view held that a first edition of the Glossa (minus the *Institutes*) was published by 1228. It is now believed that the Gloss was constantly revised over a broader time frame, such as 1220–1250. See, e.g., Figueira, "Glossa Ordinaria: Roman Law," 437–39.

67 Accursius ad D 1.3.32 v° *de quibus causis*, Lyon 1627, fol. 41.

68 Accursius ad D 5.1.1 v° *Si se*, Lyon 1627, fol. 633, is a *casus* involving two Modenese agreeing to litigate in Bologna.

69 Bartolus ad C.1.1.1, nu. 26, 32.

would appear highly unlikely for a thirteenth-century Modena court to apply a particular Bolognese statute. The alternative to the law of Modena is the common Roman law.

The same would be expected of another case not mentioned in the gloss: whether a Bologna statute might regulate the conduct of Bolognese outside the territory of their town. Accursius settles the matter easily and by implication. By the time of Bartolus, however, such an answer would not suffice. It is in responding to that question that Bartolus employs his typology of statutes, which became associated with medieval conflicts doctrine. Bartolus draws at a primary level a distinction between prohibitive and permissive statutes. Within each category, further distinctions are drawn: between statutes regarding a thing or person, and between "favorable" (*favorabilia*) and "burdensome" (*odiosa*) statutes.[70] This is obviously not the place to discuss Bartolus but, on the whole, he seems to have attempted to minimize disruption of the common legal regime and fourteenth-century social life. Bartolus and his contemporaries, however, faced a very different political and legal landscape and approached the role of learned law and the relationship between Roman law and Italian society through another lens.

The very act of inclusion of the gloss in his work would be enough for Accursius to merit a place in our historical consciousness. Azo, his master, does not discuss at all the subject in his own gloss on *l. cunctos populos*.[71] But even Odofredus, his contemporary (possibly a student and to some extent one of the high medieval voices not completely shadowed by Accursius), limits himself to noting that such city statutes do not extend over "scholars" (this includes university students) and clerics—a first step, in the same direction as Accursius, but hardly a general principle.[72]

But we should not limit ourselves to this. Accursian doctrine captures the political and social, as well as legal and jurisdictional, transformation of Italian polities. It is easy to dismiss the gloss as a relic of the *Romidee*, obsolete in its own time. But it must be acknowledged that it gave the impetus for the rich doctrinal discourse of the next century, and beyond. In the long run, it identified the political dimension of what we regard as private law. In its own time, it signifies an awareness that a new way of thinking would be required to manage the legal regulation of emerging social problems.

70 Bartolus ad C.1.1.1, nus. 32–33.

71 Azo ad C 1.1, *Summa*, Venice 1631, fol. 7–9.

72 Odofredus ad C. 1.1.1, nu. 2, *Lectura super Codice*, Lyon 1552, fol. 5rb. "Statuta civitatum non ligant scolares aut clericos."

9 Conclusion

The polities of the high Middle Ages attempted to address the needs of commerce and social life by navigating between tradition and innovation, and the same holds true of learned law in this context. This is reflected in the conceptual evolution that, if carefully examined, is discernible in our principal texts (as well as the other medieval texts discussed in the background). In the medieval theory of sources, with which especially the so-called "Italian school" of conflicts doctrine is intimately connected, custom equalled statute. But, in terms of law and society, it appears that the polities' move from custom to statute entailed a different approach to thinking about the scope of law and the relation between *ius commune* and *iura propria*.

The use of *l. cunctos populos* as the principal anchor of conflicts discussions was strongly contested, if not outright derided, in subsequent eras.[73] We may even quote a late thirteenth-century French jurist, Petrus Bellaperticus (Pierre de Belleperche), remarking that *cunctos populos* may not have raised the same questions if it was found at the end of the book, "but it is the first, and this place vests it with a solemn character."[74] One may argue that *l. de quibus* would at first look like a more appropriate locus to discuss the legal status of customs. But it could be either too restrictive ("no applicable written law") or too permissive (allowing city judges to define too broadly what is not expressly covered by Roman law). In the long run, it possessed the advantage of allowing different types of norms to be treated differently—eventually encouraging the Bartolan typology of distinguishing between "burdensome" and "favorable," "permissive" and "prohibitive" norms. But it provided no general rule, no answer to the question of whether such a custom would extend its effect over all those found within the city's territory—notably foreigners, but also clerics who possessed a distinct legal and jurisdictional regime.[75]

L. cunctos populos could provide some better guidance in that regard, which also happened to fit the imperialist attitude of the leading glossators. The opening phrases of the imperial Edict provided a powerful argument by analogy. More precisely, an argument *a maiore ad minus* with allusions to an argument *a contrario*: if, in a matter as vital as religion, imperial Roman law would restrict its application to those under the Emperor's power, it goes without saying that neither would Roman law apply beyond the territory of the Empire, nor could

73 See Hatzimihail, *Preclassical Conflict of Laws*, 115–22.

74 Lainé, *Introduction au droit international privé*, 1:106 ("la revète d'un caractère solennel").

75 See in this regard Bartolus ad C.1.1.1, nus. 28–31. For a discussion, see Hatzimihail, *Preclassical Conflict of Laws*, 231–3 and 260–1.

the local laws and customs of cities apply beyond the narrow confines left to them by Roman law, for example over a citizen of another city.

Ernst Rabel suggested that "this branch of law ... seems predestined always to lag behind the currents of general jurisprudence."[76] In his turn, S. E. Thorne used a relatively narrow definition of conflict of laws to question the genealogical relevance of medieval scholarship to our field.[77] Neither need be so, however: we cannot understand the conflict of laws without understanding the "general jurisprudence" on which it has been constructed, and with which it has to constantly interact. Yet we must also be mindful of the potential contribution, and even the capacity, of this specialised discourse to help in the understanding of the legal phenomenon.

Bibliography

Bellomo, Manlio. *The Common Legal Past of Europe*. Translated by Lydia Cochrane. Washington, DC: The Catholic University of America Press, 1995.

Calasso, Francesco. *Medio Evo del diritto,* vol. 1. Milano: Guiffrè, 1954.

Canning, Joseph. *The Political Thought of Baldus de Ubaldis*. Cambridge: Cambridge University Press, 1987.

Drew, Katherine Fischer. *The Lombard Laws*. Philadelphia: University of Pennsylvania Press, 1973.

Figueira, Robert Charles. "Glossa Ordinaria: Roman Law." In *Medieval Italy: An Encyclopaedia*, vol. 1, edited by Christopher Kleinhenz. New York: Routledge, 2003.

Frier, Bruce, ed. *The Codex of Justinian*. Cambridge: Cambridge University Press, 2016.

Gutzwiller, Max. "Le développement historique du droit international privé." *Recueil des cours* 29 (1929): 287–400.

Haenel, Gustavus. *Dissensiones dominorum sive controversiae veterum iuris romani interpretum qui glossatores vocantur*. Leipzig: Scientia Verlag Aalen, 1834.

Hatzimihail, Nikitas. "On the Doctrinal Beginnings of the Conflict of Laws." *Yearbook of Private International Law* 21 (2019/2020): 101–133.

Hatzimihail, Nikitas E. *Preclassical Conflict of Laws*. Cambridge: Cambridge University Press, 2021.

Jones, Philip. *The Italian City-State: From Commune to Signoria*. Oxford: Clarendon Press, 1997.

76 Ernst Rabel, *Conflict of Laws: A Comparative Study*, vol. 1 (Ann Arbor: University of Michigan Law School, 1945), 9.

77 Thorne, "Sovereignty," 685 et seq.

Kirshner, Julius. "Materials for a Gilded Cage: Nondotal Assets in Florence, 1300–1500." In *Marriage, Dowry, and Citizenship In Late Medieval and Renaissance Europe*, edited by Julius Kirshner, 74–93. Toronto: University of Toronto Press, 2015.

Krueger, Paul, ed. *Justinian's Institutes*. Translated by Peter Birks and Grant McLeod. Ithaca, NY: Cornell University Press, 1987.

Kuehn, Thomas. "Property of Spouses in Renaissance Florence." In *Family Law and Society in Europe from the Middle Ages to the Contemporary Era*, edited by Maria Gigliola di Renzo Villata, 109–34. Cham: Springer, 2016.

Lainé, Armand. *Introduction au droit international privé*, 2 vols. Paris: Librairie Cotillon, 1888–1892.

Lange, Hermann. *Römisches Recht im Mittelalter*, vol. 1. Munich: Beck, 1997.

Laurent, François. *Droit civil international*, vol. 1. Bruxelles: Bruylant-Christophe & Cie., Éditeurs, 1880.

Lesaffer, Randall. *European Legal History: A Cultural and Political Perspective*. Translated by Jan Arriens. Cambridge: Cambridge University Press, 2009.

Meijers, E.-M. "L'histoire des principes fondamentaux du droit international privé à partir du Moyen Age." *Recueil des cours* 49 (1934): 543–686.

Molineaus (Dumoulin), Carolus. *Omnia quae extant opera*. vols. 1–4. Paris: Apud viduam Gervasii Alliot & Antonium Clement, 1558.

Neumeyer, Karl. *Die gemeinrechtliche Entwickelung des internationalen Privat- und Strafrechts bis Bartolus*, 2 vols. Munich: J. Schweitzer, 1901–1916.

Pennington, Kenneth. *The Prince and the Law, 1200–1600: Sovereignty and Rights in the Western Legal Tradition*. Berkeley: University of California Press, 1993.

Rabel, Ernst. *Conflict of Laws: A Comparative Study*, vol. 1. Ann Arbor: University of Michigan Law School, 1945.

Robinson, O. F., T. D. Fergus, and W. M. Gordon. *European Legal History: Sources and Institutions*. 3rd ed. Oxford: Oxford University Press, 2000.

Savigny, Friedrich Carl von. *Geschichte des Römischen Rechts im Mittelalter*. 2nd ed. Heidelberg: J. C. B. Mohr, 1834–1851.

Tamba, Giorgio. "Civic Institutions (12th–early 15th centuries)." In *A Companion to Medieval and Rennaissance Bologna*, edited by Sarah H. Blanshei. Leiden: Brill, 2017.

Thorne, Samuel E. "Sovereignty and the Conflict of Laws." In Università degli Studi di Perugia, *Bartolo Da Sassoferrato: Studi E Documenti Per Il VI Centenario*, 673–89. Milan: Giuffrè, 1962.

Watson, Alan. *The Digest of Justinian*, vol. 1. Rev. ed. Philadelphia: University of Pennsylvania Press, 1985.

Wessels, J. W. *History of the Roman-Dutch Law*. Grahamstown: Africa Book Company, 1908.

Wieacker, Franz. *A History of Private Law in Europe*. Translated by Tony Weir. Oxford: Clarendon Press, 1995.

CHAPTER 3

Roman Property, Corporate Personhood, and the Politics of Natural Law in Medieval and Early Renaissance Italy: Venice, Baldus, and the *res communes omnium*

Charles Bartlett

> Hac ratione Veneti praetendunt libertatem,
> quia non aedificaverunt in solo alicuius
>
> By this reasoning the Venetians assert their independence:
> that they did not build [their city] on anyone else's territory
>
> BALDUS DE UBALDIS ad D.1.8 (*Rubrica*), nu. 8

Of the categories of things listed at the beginning of the second book of Justinian's *Institutes* (promulgated in 533 CE, hereafter I.), the first is "things common to all."[1] This category, denoted by the phrase *res communes omnium*, includes the air, flowing water, the sea, and the seashore.[2] This is not the only place in the *Corpus Iuris Civilis* where "things common to all" are described vis-à-vis other types of property. At *Digest* (hereafter D.) 1.8.2.pr.–1, the jurist Marcian provides the same list—the air, flowing water, the sea, and the seashore—to populate this category of Roman property. These elemental things or spaces cannot be owned by anyone according, we are told in both instances, to natural law. Natural law is defined at the opening of the first book

1 I.2.1.pr.–10, especially 2.1.1. In addition to the *Institutes*, Justinian commissioned the creation of the *Code* (the first edition of which was completed in 529 and superseded by the second of 534, hereafter C.) and the *Digest* (also promulgated in 533), which collected and arranged the opinions of prominent jurists active from the 2nd century BCE to the 4th century CE. These three works together with the *Novels* (the legislation issued by Justinian after 534 but never officially compiled before his death) constitute the *Corpus Iuris Civilis*.

2 There is a sizeable bibliography on this Roman property category; see Domenico Dursi, Res communes omnium: *Dalle necessità economiche alla disciplina giuridica* (Naples: Jovene, 2017), 1–2. He is surely correct in seeing this category as the creation of late-2nd-century and early-3rd-century jurists, even if previous jurists had discussed questions related to such spaces at length; see p. 19 on Marcian (fl. early 3rd century CE) especially and pp. 139–41.

 | DOI:10.1163/9789004710696_005

of the *Institutes* as "what nature has taught to all animals."[3] The inability to own the air or the sea derives therefore from that most universal source of law.

It is, however, by a means unknown to most other animals that humans can effectively remove from this category of "things common to all" one of the delineated items. Reading on in D.1.8, we find that anyone fishing on the sea is entitled to build a hut in which he can shelter and recover from the day's labor.[4] What follows this rule is another passage from the aforementioned work of Marcian in which he specifies the legal position of the person erecting such a hut by relating a larger principle of initiative and the law's protection:

> [This principle] is carried to the extent that such people who build there are made owners also of the ground [beneath the structure], but only so long as the structure stands: at whatever time it collapses the place reverts to its previous condition as if by the law of *postliminium*, and if another person builds in the same place, the place will become his.[5]

In this short passage, we see that anyone who builds a structure—*aedificium* can be applied to a wider range of buildings, including more substantial ones, than can *casa* of D.1.8.5.1—on the seashore becomes the owner not only of the structure but of the area of the seashore on which the structure stands. Other uses of this area are precluded by the presence of the structure, but Marcian's statement that anyone can acquire ownership, albeit temporary, of what had been a *res communis omnium* in such a manner is remarkable.

This chapter is interested not in the origins of this rule or in instances where it was tested in antiquity. It considers instead the later life of this idea

---

3 I.1.2.pr.: "ius naturale est quod natura omnia animalia docuit" (this definition is also found verbatim at D.1.1.1.3, from Ulpian's *Institutes*, book 1). Interestingly, this definition appears at first to differ from that found at I.2.1.11, which comes immediately after the schematization of property just mentioned. There natural law is equated to the *ius gentium* or "the law of nations." At I.1.2.1, the *ius gentium* is described as the law that binds all peoples and emerges from *naturalis ratio* or "natural reason." It is not a stretch, if we wish to make these passages cohere with one another, to understand the *ius gentium* as the area of natural law that applies to all peoples as distinct from other animals, relying as it does upon the consistent exercise of *ratio*.

4 D.1.8.5.1 (from Gaius's *Quotidian Matters or Aurea*, book 2): "In mare piscantibus liberum est casam in litore ponere, in qua se recipiant."

5 D.1.8.6.pr. (from Marcian's *Institutes*, book 3): "In tantum, ut et soli domini constituantur qui ibi aedificant, sed quamdiu aedificium manet: alioquin aedificio dilapso quasi iure postliminii revertitur locus in pristinam causam, et si alius in eodem loco aedificaverit, eius fiet." *Postliminium* provides for the nullification, once the owner is restored, of illegitimate acts carried out while a piece of land was under the control of someone other than the owner.

by analyzing another case of construction along the seashore, or indeed on the sea, and the ownership of something that had previously belonged to no one. In his commentary on the opening book of the *Digest*, the renowned jurist Baldus de Ubaldis (1327–1400) reports that it is this reasoning—that they built their city on the sea and thus on the territory of no ruler or group of people—by which the Venetians claim their independence.[6] This claim represents a fascinating extension of a private legal rule into the realm of inter-polity relations and assertions of sovereignty in medieval and early Renaissance Italy. Due to the ways in which the Venetians describe their own communal existence—as predating but reified by the construction of their city—this claim also informs upon how professions of political community that are based in a numinous and intentionally ill-defined antiquity may gain purchase in reality, and more generally how Roman property law could be mobilized in political and theoretical circumstances quite different from those in which it took shape.

Before concentrating on these aspects of the Venetians' claim, this chapter first considers two additional passages from the *Digest* that discuss the *res communes omnium*. We examine these in order to show that, in antiquity, this category was not entirely coherent in terms of its conceptualization or the rules governing its operation. The first of these passages also allows us to appreciate a fundamental aspect of the acquisition of ownership through construction as discussed in our ancient sources, namely that it was temporary. We then move to the claim at the core of this study, as preserved by Baldus. We will see how Venetian jurists mobilized an argument grounded in the *ius gentium*—namely that they built their city on a *res communis omnium* and that it therefore belonged to them—to assert their sovereign independence. As we will see, this claim is entirely consistent with Venetians' pursuit of independence, and especially with their utilization of natural law to describe the internal regulation of their city in that pursuit. In making this claim based in the property category of *res communes omnium*, Venetian jurists transposed their collective society into what had been the place of an individual person in this rule of private law as described in the *Corpus Iuris Civilis*. I argue that the Venetians' reputation for harmonious and effective self-governance, and indeed the unusual

---

6 Baldus ad D.1.8 (*Rubrica*), nu. 8. There are many editions of Baldus's commentary on the *Digest*; one that is easily accessible electronically is Baldus de Ubaldis, *In Primam Digesti Veteris Partem Commentaria* (Venice: Giunti, 1577), in which these remarks are found on 45v. Electronic versions of 16th-century editions of Baldus's other works published by this press, rendered *apud Iuntas* in Latin, are also easily accessible. For information on Baldus's life and career, see Joseph Canning, *The Political Thought of Baldus de Ubaldis* (Cambridge: Cambridge University Press, 1987), 1–16.

topographical character of their city, facilitated the advancement of the notion of corporate personhood.

The next section explores juristic comparisons between Venice and Genoa. Attempts were made to describe the latter as a corporate entity for the purpose of utilizing rules of private law, but with less success. The details of these attempts suggest the importance of features of the built and natural environment in the development of arguments of corporate personhood, as well as of the details of polities' conception and administration. We see also that juristic juxtapositions of the constitutions and governance of Venice and Genoa deepen our understanding of what we might call, anachronistically, comparative constitutionalism in the medieval and Renaissance world. We then invoke briefly the better-known comparison between Venice and Florence, made increasingly from the 14th century by political theorists, historians, and politicians. The relatively short treatment of this latter comparison underscores my assertion that many of the themes of juristic discussion accord with those of political debate—especially the focus on internal concord, the benefits of a mixed constitution, and the co-existence of several senses of liberty—and here I argue for the necessity of incorporating juristic sources into the analysis of Renaissance political theorization. The conclusion recalls a more famous event in the history of the development of notions of corporate personhood to show the purchase of this formulation from the 13th and 14th centuries, namely Pope Innocent IV's *persona ficta*.

This chapter traces how, in making claims about the status of their city, Venetian jurists attempted to translate private legal rules, categories, and sensibilities to inter-polity and public-law conversations. It demonstrates that their arguments were not only intelligible to but also consistent with those made by jurists of other polities, and indeed that they were at times successful. I argue that medieval and Renaissance jurists' discussions of the sovereign status of different polities are integral to our understanding of the development of corporate personhood, especially in regard to the utilization in that development of ideas rooted in natural law and to the imagery crafted. These juristic discussions are also crucial to our appreciation of the mobilization of natural law, moderated through Roman legal categories, in inter-polity negotiations. Such conversations stress that a political community's internal concord and adherence in its conception and governance to natural-law principles should have bearing on its sovereign independence vis-à-vis other polities.[7]

---

7 It is a particular pleasure to explore this topic in a volume dedicated to Charles Donahue, Jr. I first met Charlie when I approached him to ask about the possibility of an independent study in Roman law during my third year of graduate school. In what was the first of many

We turn now to two additional passages from the *Digest* that further illuminate the nature of the *res communes omnium* in antiquity. D.41.1.14 expands upon the question of the acquisition of ownership of land along the seashore through the building of a structure in that space. This passage, written by Neratius Priscus, suffect consul in 97 CE and legal advisor to the Emperor Hadrian, begins by stating the rule found in D.1.8.6 that whatever any person builds on the seashore becomes the property of the person who builds it.[8] The later jurist Marcian, the author of D.1.8.6 quoted above, would not repeat all of what Neratius goes on to say. Neratius continues that upon the collapse or removal of the building, the condition of the underlying ground must be inspected to determine whether the site remains the property of the person who built there or whether it reverts to public ownership. He prefers the latter course, but only if the original form of the seashore can be regained.[9] We might wish for clarification as to how the temporary owner who has altered the form of the seashore was expected to make amends, as such alteration surely could not result in the straightforward acquisition of that land by the owner on a permanent basis, but we are left to wonder, not least because Marcian would provide no subsequent clarification.[10]

---

demonstrations of his generosity, he agreed to the independent study for the following year, despite the fact that he would be on sabbatical. I will never forget our inquiry that year, in which I learned innumerable details about the legal system that the Romans developed, as well as how to ask questions that ensured I did not miss the forest for the trees. Charlie became and remains an inspiration, not least for his productivity. Among his many publications is "*Animalia Ferae Naturae*: Rome, Bologna, Leyden, Oxford and Queen's County, N.Y.," in *Studies in Roman Law in Memory of A. Arthur Schiller*, ed. Roger S. Bagnall and William V. Harris (Leiden: Brill, 1986), 39–63, in which he examines the life after antiquity of I.2.1.12–13. This text, which follows the first cited in this chapter and to which I refer below, treats the means by which wild animals become the property of someone pursuing them. Charlie's occupation of the subsequent history of this text, which winds through legal, theoretical, and societal contexts vastly different from one another—and of course from Justinian's and from that of the *Res cottidianae* (the immediate source of I.2.1.12–13 is a passage from the *Res cottidianae sive Aurea*, which the *Digest* ascribes to Gaius but which is generally thought to be post-classical; cf. Donahue, "*Animalia Ferae Naturae*," 43–44)—is a model of historical scholarship. His piece begins fittingly with a discussion of legal education, and I thank him for providing the foundation of mine.

8 D.41.1.14.pr. (from Neratius's *Parchments*, book 5): "Quod in litore quis aedificaverit, eius erit."

9 D.41.1.14.1: "Illud videndum est, sublato aedificio, quod in litore positum erat, cuius condicionis is locus sit, hoc est utrum maneat eius cuius fuit aedificium, an rursus in pristinam causam reccidit perindeque publicus sit, ac si numquam in eo aedificatum fuisset. Quod propius est, ut existimari debeat, si modo recipit pristinam litoris speciem."

10 Dursi has argued that jurists from Neratius through to Marcian never intended that permanent ownership be granted to people building in this way; see especially Res communes omnium, 65–75. While his reasoning is persuasive, the fact that phrases such as

This is not the only aspect of D.41.1.14 that prompts as many questions about this legal category as it answers. Neratius explains the acquisition of temporary ownership of the seashore by means of a comparison that, at first glance, seems odd. He describes the seashore as different from the public property of a polity and instead akin to that which nature has provided and which has not yet become the property of anyone. This reasoning leads him to assert that the seashore is rather like fish and wild animals that, once caught, become the property of whoever has gained control of them.[11] In making this argument, Neratius references the seminal characteristic of the group of things that is discussed immediately after the schematization of property in Justinian's *Institutes*, that is, at I.2.1.11–18. There we read that wild animals, birds, and fish that are not the property of anyone become the property of whoever catches them, for the reason that whatever previously belonged to no one comes to belong to the first person who seizes it, according to "natural reason."[12] Neratius's extension of this characteristic to the seashore appears strained in several respects, namely that there seems not to be, in the case of a wild animal, an analog to the construction, which functions both as the means of effecting the seizure and the primary object of the person building; and that, as stated at I.2.1.12, it does not matter whether one captures this wild animal on his own property or on another's. The aspects of this comparison that make D.41.1.14 fascinating in and of itself are not the focus of this chapter. These elements do, however, serve to demonstrate that the conceptual foundations of this category of property were by no means settled when this and other juristic texts of the classical period—which were incorporated into the *Digest* because they were still judged in the 6th century to provide crucial information on the *res communes*—were written.

Before moving to early Renaissance Venice, let us consider a second additional passage from the *Digest* that demonstrates that the operation of this

eius erit at D.41.1.14.pr. can certainly be translated as "he will own"—and that there are other such phrases found in D.41.1, namely *eius esse* (D.41.1.30.3 and D.41.1.56.1) and *meum fit* (D.41.1.30.4), that can be understood to specify ownership—ensures that this matter will continue to be debated.

11 D.41.1.14.pr.: "Nam litora publica non ita sunt, ut ea, quae in patrimonio sunt populi, sed ut ea, quae primum a natura prodita sunt et in nullius adhuc dominium pervenerunt: nec dissimilis condicio eorum est atque piscium et ferarum, quae simul atque adprehensae sunt, sine dubio eius, in cuius potestatem pervenerunt, dominii fiunt."

12 I.2.1.12: "quod enim ante nullius est id naturali ratione occupanti conceditur." This usage of *naturalis ratio* further reinforces the notion that this *ratio* is the means by which *natura* instructs mankind. For a discussion of the later history of this passage, see Donahue, "*Animalia Ferae Naturae*," as discussed above.

property category in practice was also somewhat incoherent in antiquity. D.41.1.50, excerpted from a text by the 2nd-century jurist Pomponius, relates the details of the process whereby permission to build on the seashore was obtained.[13] Here we read that a person intending to build had to receive a decree from the urban praetor at Rome; this was in the case of a larger, sturdier structure rather than a makeshift fisherman's hut. The granting of a decree would have followed a hearing wherein the praetor learned of and weighed objections from those opposed to the potential construction. We read also that when someone tried to build contrary to the interests of others—and, although the text is not perfectly clear, we can be relatively certain that construction without a decree is meant—that person could be physically prevented from doing so. Pomponius explains that such physical prevention would be enough to preclude the construction, because there exists no civil action whereby the person intending to build can assert his right at law to do so. Other jurists of the later 2nd and early 3rd centuries would further specify the details of this adjudication, with the result that the process of resolving competing claims on such spaces came largely, but not entirely, to resemble other areas of Roman legal administration.[14] There remained an ill-defined place in this process, however, for private, almost extra-legal initiative aimed at preventing construction. Nor does this passage explain what recourse the public had to reacquire land along the seashore that had been degraded after a structure had been built and had come down. For these reasons, ownership of the seashore and of other *res communes omnium* appears different from, and less settled than, *dominium* elsewhere.

13 D.41.1.50 (from Pomponius's *From Plautius*, book 6): "Quamvis quod in litore publico vel in mari exstruxerimus, nostrum fiat, tamen decretum praetoris adhibendum est, ut id facere liceat: immo etiam manu prohibendus est, si cum incommode ceterorum id faciat: nam civilem eum actionem de faciendo nullam habere non dubito."

14 Those jurists are Scaevola (D.43.8.4), Papinian (D.41.3.45.pr.), Ulpian (D.8.4.13.pr.; 39.1.1.18; 39.2.24.pr.; 43.8.2.8–9; and 43.12.1.17), and Paul (D.18.1.51; 41.1.65.1; and 47.10.14). Mario Fiorentini describes the interdicts and the action on *iniuria*, a more general action by which claims could have been brought, without guaranteed success, by people attempting to build; see his *Fiumi e mari nell'esperienza giuridica romana: profili di tutela processuale e di inquadramento sistematico* (Milan: Giuffrè, 2003), 277–426. Bruce W. Frier is right to characterize Deveney's opinion (Patrick Deveney, "Title, jus publicum, and the Public Trust: An Historical Analysis," *Sea Grant Law Journal* 1 (1976): 23–25) that these instruments had minimal effect as "entirely gratuitous," while stressing the difficulty of enforcing magistrates' decisions. See Bruce W. Frier, "The Roman Origins of the Public Trust Doctrine," *Journal of Roman Archeology* 32 (2019): 646, n. 30. We can add to this the logistical hurdles to attending a hearing, when was one granted.

1 Private Ownership and the Sovereignty of Political Communities: Venice

Throughout the Middle Ages and Renaissance, Venice asserted its uniqueness as a means to pursue its sovereign independence. The events in Venice's political history that testify to this uniqueness and that signified or suggested its de facto or de jure independence vis-à-vis external political entities have been thoroughly examined by scholars, and some of these are briefly recounted below. These events complemented and reflected claims made by Venetians about several salubrious characteristics of their city and the bearing that successful internal governance should have on their independence from other polities. Integral to the claims that beneficial, effective internal governance should lead to sovereign independence were, among other considerations, the position of the doge within the city's mixed constitution and the harmonious relations among its citizens.[15] Crucially, Venetians adduced the supposed faithfulness of the city's legislation to principles of natural law in order to bolster Venice's international reputation and to account for its internal harmony.

The dynamics of this politics of natural law have received less attention from scholars than have the issues of the doge's position and the city's internal civic concord. But the claim of legislative faithfulness to natural-law principles is not the only glimpse we have onto this politics. Venetian jurists also argued that the fact that their city was built on the sea—and therefore on the territory of no ruler or group of people—should result in their independence from any external ruler or group of people, according to natural law. The Venetians thereby resuscitated this rule governing the *res communes omnium*, which as we have seen included not only the seashore but the sea itself, but with a fascinating alteration: whereas the ancient jurists had discussed the dealings of private individuals in connection to the *res communes omnium*, the Venetians now placed their entire community in the position of an interested party in such a case. I argue here that Venetian jurists' discussion of the relevance of the *res communes omnium* is consistent with other Venetian claims about the

---

15 This implicates the much-discussed "myth of Venice." Of the many treatments of aspects of this topic, see the citations in James S. Grubb, "When Myths Lose Power: Four Decades of Venetian Historiography," *Journal of Modern History* 58, no. 1 (1986): 44, n. 2 and Felix Gilbert, "The Venetian Constitution in Florentine Political Thought," in *Florentine Studies: Politics and Society in Renaissance Florence*, ed. Nicolai Rubinstein (London: Faber and Faber, 1968), 466, n. 1. Although concerned with an event after the period of primary interest to this chapter, see Claire Judde de Larivière, *La révolte des boules de neige: Murano face à Venise, 1511* (Paris: Fayard, 2014), among the studies of episodes that complicate this serene picture.

importance of their city's internal characteristics, only with more explicit ramifications for Venice's independence. Further, that the *res communes omnium* are clearly grounded in natural law in the *Corpus Iuris Civilis* allows for deeper appreciation of how this source of law could be deployed within international legal discussions.[16]

This section will first recall the better-known events in Venetian history that reflected and perpetuated Venice's assertion of sovereign independence. We will see that the city's physical characteristics, particularly its remove from even those areas of the Italian peninsula in the vicinity of the lagoons, were crucial to this self-presentation. We will then consider the Venetians' insistence on the faithfulness of the city's regulations to the principles of natural law. This will put us in good stead to analyze the claim at the heart of this study, namely that, according to Venetian jurists, Venice should be independent because it was built on a *res communis omnium*, as described in the *Institutes* and detailed further in the *Digest*. Analyzing Baldus's presentation of this claim in several places across his oeuvre will allow us to see how it fits with the Venetians' larger project of asserting sovereign independence through an emphasis on uniqueness and natural law. This section will conclude by examining the innovation of this claim within the history of Roman law in medieval and Renaissance Italy, with particular attention paid to conceptions of the corporation. We will see that Venetian jurists, against the backdrop of their reputation for effective governance and internal concord, placed their society into the role occupied by one of the individuals in a private-law dispute, as described in several places in the *Corpus Iuris Civilis*. Our focus especially at the end of this section on the supposed concord within the city will prime us to locate this Venetian claim within wider discussions of political institutions and imagery developing at the time, which will be our task in the following section; there we will consider at greater length the constitutional position of the doge.

Although Venice had been incorporated into the Byzantine Empire and briefly that of Charlemagne, already from the second half of the 9th century Venetian rulers had begun to dispense with the formulae acknowledging such

16 Here I do not claim the existence of an international law akin to the collection of norms and systems that emerged centuries later, in regard to which time scholars cease to have reservations about using the term. On different conceptions of international law, see David Armitage, *Foundations of Modern International Thought* (Cambridge: Cambridge University Press, 2013), 151–53. Indispensable is Martti Koskenniemi, *The Gentle Civilizer of Nations: The Rise and Fall of International Law 1870–1960*. (Cambridge: Cambridge University Press, 2008); see especially 1–10.

subjugation.[17] Venice's distinctive position was bolstered by the Golden Bull of 1082, through which the Byzantine emperor granted the city special commercial privileges in return for its help against the Normans; that Venice's help was rewarded rather than expected is telling.[18] Of paramount importance to Venetian claims of theoretical as well as de facto political autonomy were the events of 1177, which feature prominently in the curated presentations of the city's chroniclers and artists.[19] In this year in which Pope Alexander III and Emperor Frederick Barbarossa were at war over territory in Italy, Venice sheltered the Pope as he fled from the Emperor's advance. In the ensuing naval battle, the Venetian fleet played a decisive role, even capturing the Emperor's son, which ensured that peace negotiations would finally take place. At the direction of Doge Sebastiano Ziani (c. 1102–1178; doge 1172–1178), the Pope was conveyed back to Rome with great ceremony, and en route the pontiff bestowed various trappings of sovereignty upon the city's leader; among these were the right to seal documents with lead, a sword, and a ring to symbolize the wedding of Venice and the sea.[20] Most significant of all in terms of the publicity of such political symbolism was the Pope's insistence, over the protestations of the Emperor, that a third umbrella be produced for the doge during an outdoor ceremony, so that the Venetian leader was not obliged to sit in the shadow of either of the theoretically universal rulers. William Bouwsma describes the attendant elevation of the doge to a position "equal" and "parallel" to that of the Emperor and the Pope, which was later depicted in two paintings hung respectively in

17 William J. Bouwsma, *Venice and the Defense of Republican Liberty: Renaissance Values in the Age of the Counter Reformation* (Berkeley: University of California Press, 1968), 54. On these events, see Guido Ruggiero, *The Renaissance in Italy: A Social and Cultural History of the Rinascimento* (Cambridge: Cambridge University Press, 2015), 38–47.

18 On the Golden Bull of 1082, see Peter Frankopan, "Byzantine Trade Privileges to Venice in the Eleventh Century: The Chrysobull of 1092," *Journal of Medieval History* 30 (2004): 135–60, who argues that it should actually be dated to 1092.

19 There exist more than 2,000 Venetian manuscripts that contain chronicles written from the 11th through the 18th centuries. The certainty of their authorship as well as the reliability of these chronicles vary dramatically. See Şerban V. Marin, "Between Authorship and Anonymity. The Case of the Venetian Chronicles," in *The Medieval Chronicle 13*, ed. Erik S. Kooper and Sjoerd Levelt (Leiden: Brill, 2020), 149–81, for a discussion of some general aspects of the chronicles and Ruggiero, *The Renaissance in Italy*, 39 and 41–45 for his description of the chronicle written by Doge Andrea Dandolo (1306–1354; doge 1343–1354), which quite substantially embellishes the details of Venice's involvement in the events of 1177.

20 Bouwsma, *Venice and the Defense of Republican Liberty*, 54; see also John B. Freed, *Frederick Barbarossa: The Prince and the Myth* (New Haven: Yale University Press, 2016), 401–8.

the Hall of the Great Council and in the Hall of the Senate.[21] This positioning vis-à-vis the Emperor can also be seen when Venice did not behave as did other Italian polities upon Emperor Henry VII's entry into Italy in 1310. With several other cities, Venice refused to swear fealty.[22]

The city's singular topography allowed for a degree of detachment from the affairs and impositions of the mainland, and Venice's hesitancy to enter into disputes and conflicts produced for the city a reputation for self-interested disengagement.[23] There was, alongside the episodes in Venice's political history just recounted, the assertion of many of the city's historians and chroniclers that Venice was founded in the 5th century specifically to escape the turbulence of the mainland and by people devoted to liberty.[24] Already in the 11th century, a chronicle circulating under the name of Giovanni Diacono so characterized the city's founders.[25] Guido Ruggiero has described Doge Dandolo's account of Venice's involvement in the war between Pope and Emperor in 1177 as "largely mythic," but he stresses that in the Doge's claim that the Pope found safety in the lagoons is but one more instance in which Venice proved "a haven for the oppressed;" indeed, Dandolo's chronicle, which draws on earlier sources, emphasizes this supposed motif of Venetian history.[26] As Bouwsma notes, this element of Venetian self-fashioning occupied an ever greater role in the city's historiography through the 15th century.[27] It was the surrounding lagoons that provided this refuge and defined the city.

Venice's famous moniker "La Serenissima" derives from the purported absence of internal discord in the city. This image was widely promoted by

---

21 So Bernardo Bembo, "Commonplace Book," *British Museum*, Add. MS. 41,068A, fol. 44r: "Et illa hystoria est picta in aula civitatis Venetiarum. Ed est etiam picta in aula civitatis Senatorum" (*non vidi*, as quoted in Gilbert, "The Venetian Constitution," 467, n. 1); see Bouwsma, *Venice and the Defense of Republican Liberty*, 54 and Freed, *Frederick Barbarossa*, 408–13.

22 On Henry VII's difficulties in Italy, see William M. Bowsky, *Henry VII in Italy: The Conflict of Empire and City-State, 1310–1313* (Westport, Ct: Greenwood Press, 1974).

23 See Bouwsma, *Venice and the Defense of Republican Liberty*, 53–55.

24 See the extended discussions in Gaetano Cozzi, "Cultura politica e religione nella 'pubblica storiografia' veneziana del '500," *Studi veneziani* 5–6 (1963–1964): 215–94, and Franco Gaeta, "Storiografia, coscienza nazionale e politica culturale nella Venezia del Rinascimento," in *Storia della cultura veneta*, vol. 3.1, ed. Girolamo Arnaldi and Manlio Pastore Stocchi (Vicenza: Neri Pozza, 1980–1981), 1–91.

25 See Gina Fasoli, "Nascita di un mito," in *Studi storici in onore di Gioacchino Volpe*, 1 (Florence: Sansoni, 1958), 453–61 for a discussion of this chronicle, as well as Franco Gaeta, "Alcune considerazioni sul mito di Venezia," *Bibliothèque d'Humanisme et Renaissance* 23 (1961): 60–61.

26 Ruggiero, *The Renaissance in Italy*, 41.

27 Bouwsma, *Venice and the Defense of Republican Liberty*, 54.

Venetian diplomats, chroniclers, and others, and to considerable effect. This image is a chief component of the "myth of Venice," the mutually self-reinforcing collection of tenets that supposedly describe the city's unique history and civic culture.[28] When accounting for this alleged internal harmony, Venetians before and during the 14th century adduced, among other explanations, that the city's rules were uniquely faithful to the principles of natural law.[29] James Grubb examines this idea in relation to public law in the city, but others have argued that any consistency with what was understood as natural law derived from the city's reputation as a commercial center and the operation of the *lex mercatoria* in its jurisdiction.[30] Just what is meant by the principles of natural law is not entirely certain: this area of law is famously malleable, as scholars have demonstrated time and again.[31] What is clear, however, is that Venetians understood this claim to have purchase in wider discussions about the rectitude of certain legal systems and their foundations. These wider discussions can justifiably be said to constitute a politics of natural law.

Venetians further engaged this politics through their invocation of the *res communes omnium*, which as we have seen are defined as unique spaces according to natural law. At this point we turn to Baldus, who preserves the claim at the core of this study in several places across his works. In addition to his comment on the opening book of the *Digest* quoted as this chapter's epigraph, Baldus mentions the sovereign status of Venice elsewhere in his commentaries on the *Corpus Iuris Civilis*, in his commentary on the *Liber extra* (hereafter X.), and in his *Consilia*.[32] We can divide his comments on the independence

28 See Grubb, "When Myths Lose Power," 44 for a succinct summation of the aspects of the myth of Venice; although the myth with all the components listed by Grubb was not fully articulated until the 16th century, the city's reputation for internal concord and dedication to liberty had been established for centuries by that time. See also n. 15 above.

29 See Laura Ikins Stern, "Politics and Law in Renaissance Florence and Venice," *American Journal of Legal History* 46, no. 2 (2004): 209–34 for a sustained discussion of the impact of politics on law in Venice.

30 James S. Grubb, *Firstborn of Venice: Vicenza in the Early Renaissance State* (Baltimore: Johns Hopkins University Press, 2019), 10–11; see also Maria Fusaro, "Politics of Justice/Politics of Trade: Foreign Merchants and the Administration of Justice from the Records of Venice's *Giudici del Forestier*," *Mélanges de l'école française de Rome: Italie et Méditerranée modernes et contemporaines* 126, no. 1 (2014): 139–60, and Kenneth Pennington, "*Lex naturalis* and *ius naturale*," *The Jurist* 68 (2008): 569–91.

31 See the citations in Guido Fassò, "Natural Law in Italy in the Past Ten Years," *Natural Law Forum* (1956): 122–34, as well as those in the contributions to George Duke and Robert P. George, eds., *The Cambridge Companion to Natural Law Jurisprudence* (Cambridge: Cambridge University Press, 2017).

32 Dante Fedele, *The Medieval Foundations of International Law: Baldus de Ubaldis (1327–1400), Doctrine and Practice of the* Ius Gentium (Leiden: Brill, 2021), 153–54, n. 458. Fedele

of Venice into three categories. The first category locates the authority of the Venetians' claim in the *ius gentium* and includes specifically that this is a claim made by Venetians. The following quotation is representative of this first type:

> And so act the Venetians, who laid their foundation in the sea, and according to the *ius gentium* polities built on the sea belong to those who built them. ... By this reasoning the Venetians assert their independence: that they did not build [their city] on anyone else's territory.[33]

In a second category of his comments, Baldus presents the claim as valid due to experience rather than law:

> Similarly [if it were an island, Venice] would belong to the Holy Roman Emperor, because all islands belong to the Empire ... and experience itself teaches the opposite of this.[34]

This differentiation between experience and law is significant not only for our interest in the purchase of the property category of *res communes omnium* in the 14th century, but also because it leads Baldus in still other places to claim that, in fact, Venice cannot assert its independence vis-à-vis the Empire. Fedele and others have noted that Baldus is inconsistent in terms of his opinion as to whether the Venetians' claim to independence can be made against the

collects most of these references, although with a few typographical errors that cannot be explained by the publication histories of the texts: while we read *Consilia* 4.455 and 5.411 as two places where Baldus discusses the status of Venice, those citations are in fact *Consilia* 4.445 and 5.410, respectively. To his list we can also add *Consilium* 5.325 and ad C.7.44.1, nu. 5. In addition to their commentaries on the components of the *Corpus Iuris Civilis*, Baldus and other jurists commented on elements of the *Corpus Iuris Canonici*, such as the *Liber extra* (also known more formally as the Decretals of Gregory IX), and offered responses (*consilia*) to specific legal questions.

33 "Et ita Veneti faciunt, qui sunt fundati in mari, et de iure gentium civitates in mari aedificatae sunt ipsorum qui aedificant.... Hac ratione Veneti praetendunt libertatem: quia non aedificaverunt in solo alicuius." Baldus ad D.1.8 (*Rubrica*), nu. 8. Omitted through the ellipsis is only a cross-reference to a later remark in Baldus's commentary on this title of the *Digest*.

34 "Item esset Romani principis, quia omnes insulae sunt imperii ... cuius contrarium ipsa experientia docet." Baldus *Consilia* 5.410, nu. 2. Omitted through the ellipsis are only citations of several sources that Baldus adduces in support of his point that all islands belong to the Empire.

Emperor.[35] The following two quotations—which, respectively, concern the internal governance of the city in particular, the customary aspects of which we are told do not indicate independence, and Venice's sovereign status in general—are representative of this third category:

> But is a people able because of the absence of the Emperor to elect a leader for itself, as the Venetians and the Genoese do? I respond that this is not done according to law, because it is not assented to by their superior ... but from custom, of which the Emperor knows, and which he tolerates, because of the effective governance of these polities.[36]

> It is alleged that the polity of the Venetians, which was built in the sea, is free. This is true, but not however from the jurisdiction of the Empire.[37]

Clearly, the Venetians' claim that their city should be independent and should belong to themselves met with varied success, even across the writings of this one prominent jurist. Nor can we conclude that a simple de jure and de facto distinction explains the inconsistency, as across these passages Baldus uses the same grammatical formulation—namely the genitive case to indicate the person or entity to which the city belongs—to specify ownership of the city by the Venetians (as at ad D.1.8 (*Rubrica*), nu. 8) and, alternatively, by the Emperor (as at ad X.2.24.29, nu. 6). This is to say that in different places in Baldus's work, both the Venetians and the Emperor are placed in the position of de jure owners. Nonetheless, in Baldus's presentations of this claim we see that it was based in the *ius gentium*, which was itself derived from natural law, and in the effective governance of the city, which was explained with reference to the adherence of Venetian legislation to natural law. Thus two considerations primarily internal to the city and rooted in natural law were adduced to assert the propriety of Venetian independence.

The next section will consider further the sovereign status of the city and the success of Venetian jurists' attempts to present their political community

35 Fedele, *The Medieval Foundations of International Law*, 153–54, n. 458 and Ugo Petronio, "Civitas Venetiarum est edificata in mari," in *Studi veneti offerti a Gaetano Cozzi*, ed. Gino Benzoni et al. (Venice: Il Cardo, 1992), 175.

36 "Sed nunquid populus propter absentiam Imperatoris potest eligere sibi Ducem, sicut faciunt Veneti, et Genuenses? Respondeo quod non de iure, quia non est confirmatum a superiore ... sed ex consuetudine, ex quo Imperator scit, et tolerat, propter bonum regimen eorum." Baldus ad C.1.2.16, nu. 3. Once again, all that is omitted through the ellipsis is a citation of an ancient text that Baldus adduces in support of his point.

37 "Allegatur quod civitas Venetorum, quae est aedificata in mari, sit libera. Quod verum est, non tamen a iurisdictione Imperii." Baldus ad D.39.1.1.18, nu. 1.

as a corporate person by referencing how jurists treated other polities; the section will also stress that juristic writing ought to figure more prominently in analyses of medieval and Renaissance political thought. Before concluding this section, let us describe the importance of the city that emerges from Baldus's characterization. In each of Baldus's descriptions of Venice, regardless of the stance taken on the question of independence, the city is portrayed as unusual. In these depictions, Venice comes across as a different sort of space, and one well governed by a singular people renowned for its dedication to liberty and coterminous with its particular space. Baldus repeats the fact of the city's construction on the sea and, as seen just above, refutes the idea that Venice is an island. In the same passage in which we find the argument from experience that Venice is not an island, because otherwise it would belong to the Emperor, Baldus takes pains to demonstrate that topographical definitions of an island also require that Venice not be so categorized.[38] He does not supply a different word to characterize the space, preferring instead to describe it as *civitas Venetorum* or *Venetiarum*, "the polity of the Venetians" or "of Venice."

In terms of the administration of the city and the identification of the Venetians with its physical instantiation, we have seen Baldus's report that the Venetians were allowed to elect their doge because of the city's *bonum regimen* or "effective governance." Elsewhere Baldus makes clear that, alongside having a reputation for beneficial administration, the Venetians were known for their dedication to their independence. He writes in *Consilium* 4.445 that "the Venetians do not recognize a superior from the true and deep-seated [commitment to] liberty of that polity so famous."[39] While the intensity of their commitment to preserving their independence makes them unusual, the idea that Venetians are the only people who could inhabit their polity makes them and their relationship to their physical space unique. This seminal idea comes across clearly in Baldus's *Consilium* 5.410. In listing the reasons why Venice must not be considered an island, he states "[s]imilarly if the polity of the Venetians were an island constructed in the sea, then if the citizens withdrew, it would be ceded to the occupiers, which is a falsehood."[40] This remarkable statement

38 "Modo civitas Venetiarum nullo ex istis modis potest insula appellari" ("In no way according to these [topographical] measures can the polity of Venice be called an island"). Baldus *Consilium* 5.410, nu. 2. Later in the same passage we read that "what is maintained by pilings in a channel cannot be called an island" ("Item non potest dici insula, quae pontonibus sustentatur in alveo"). *Consilium* 5.410, nu. 3.

39 "Veneti non recognoscunt superiorem ex vera, et inveterate civitatis tam inclitae libertate." Baldus *Consilium* 4.445, nu. 1.

40 "Item si civitas Venetorum esset insula in mari facta, ergo civibus recedentibus, concederetur occupantibus, quid falsum est." Baldus *Consilium* 5.410, nu. 2.

indicates that the Venetians are the owners of the city, and that without them the city would cease to exist, as it cannot be taken over by occupiers: this particular space is only conceivable, in Baldus's presentation, as belonging to this particular people.

Such a situation is intelligible thanks to the specification in D.1.8.6—which, as we have seen, Baldus connects explicitly to Venice—that what someone builds on a *res communis omnium* becomes that person's property.[41] The deviation, however, from the rule in the *Digest* is that here Venetian jurists belonging to a political community, which is to say to a corporation, are presenting that corporation as an individual person through their invocation of this rule of private law. Joseph Canning and Kenneth Pennington both detail the terms in which medieval political communities regularly presented themselves as coherent corporate entities.[42] We examine legal constructions of corporate personhood also in the other sections of this chapter, but we note here the importance of the Venetians' reputation for effective self-governance to the feasibility of this self-presentation, as the relative absence of societal turmoil suggests a unity. Crucial as well is the visible manifestation of the people in the city. The claim whose analysis is the core of this study then emerges as the idea that Venetian society is not divided but unified and harmonious, that this people is coterminous with its city and vice versa, and that this unity and its clear identification with a qualitatively different and territorially circumscribed political center allow for the metaphorical transposition of the collective into the place of an individual person. This transposition, through the invocation of a rule of private law for use in inter-polity legal negotiation, should be seen in the context of a contemporary development in notions of corporate personhood. However, as we will see in this chapter's final section, the details of the Venetians' claim allow us to appreciate the importance of territoriality to such changing notions.

---

41 Baldus ad D.1.8 (*Rubrica*), nu. 8; in this comment, Baldus points ahead to D.1.8.6 to explain the Venetians' claim.

42 Canning, *Political Thought*, 180–81 and 185–208 and Kenneth Pennington, *The Prince and the Law, 1200–1600: Sovereignty and Rights in the Western Legal Tradition* (Berkeley: University of California Press, 1993), 202–17, especially 208. However, neither considers the uniqueness of the Venetian case from the standpoint of its topography or its reputation for effective governance, or the transposition of a collective into what had been the place of an individual in a private-law rule. They are of course among the few scholars who have devoted significant study to the political importance of medieval and Renaissance juristic writing.

2 Political Comparisons and the Revival of Ancient Political Thought

Implicit and at times explicit in discussions of Venice is comparison with other polities in northern Italy, especially with other republics. This section begins with the comparison repeated across Baldus's writings and those of other jurists, namely that with Genoa. These two commercially minded, maritime republics were often related to one another in juristic texts due in large part to the apparent similarity of their assertions of jurisdictional and commercial privilege. However, closer inspection reveals several consequential differences between the two polities' respective abilities to mobilize arguments derived from Roman private law. These differing abilities to act as a corporate person, I argue, are the result of variations in the two cities' physical characteristics, the details of their foundations, and their reputations for harmonious administration. In regard to the last of these points, we will see that Baldus and others by no means always maintain that Genoa enjoyed a *bonum regimen*. Following this juxtaposition of Venice and Genoa we will briefly turn to what is perhaps a more familiar comparison, namely that with Florence. This comparison intensified toward the end of the period of interest to this study. We will highlight several enduring themes of this comparison, focusing especially on the cities' mixed constitutions and the internal concord, or lack thereof, enjoyed by each.

The presence or absence of internal strife had bearing on whether or not either polity could be considered the model republic, while the cities' constitutions were of central importance to the debate over what has been called the two senses of Renaissance liberty. Bouwsma declared these two senses to be "independence of the state" from any "earthly superior," and "self-government by citizens."[43] We will see that juristic sources not only contain many of the ideas integral to this debate, but that they indeed deepen our appreciation of Renaissance liberty through their discussion of the Venetians' attempts to act as a corporate person in pursuit of sovereign independence. As has been shown, these attempts rested on a politics of natural law. When considered in the context of the long-standing debates over sovereign independence and internal self-government by citizens, juristic writings encourage us to realize that Renaissance thought permitted the fractalization of arguments in favor of self-government by citizens—which stressed the relevance to such governance

43 Bouwsma, *Venice and the Defense of Republican Liberty*, 12–14. For a recent discussion of the operability of these ideas, see James Hankins, *Virtue Politics: Soulcraft and Statecraft in Renaissance Italy* (Cambridge, MA: Harvard University Press, 2019), 63–102, especially 91 ff. Of particular importance to this question was the Peace of Constance of 1183; see Canning, *Political Thought*, 94 and 115, n. 69.

of conceptions of proper individual constitution and conduct, most famously encapsulated in discussions of *virtù*—in the form of the application of such concerns to a polity presented as a corporate person. We will emphasize that the anatomical metaphor of interest to us was central to theoretical descriptions of how different segments of society interact, and we will see that within such descriptions, ideas revived from antiquity were of seminal importance. Indebtedness to antiquity is yet another element common to the discussions of jurists and to those of theorists and politicians.

Baldus and other medieval and early Renaissance jurists saw several reasons to compare Venice and Genoa. Foremost among these was that the two cities were maritime republics that enjoyed privileges not granted to other polities, especially the election of a doge, as seen above. On the topic of the cities' political systems, Baldus's *Consilium* 5.325 considers this question of the cities' constitutions and treats the ruler of Venice and the ruler of Genoa in exactly the same way vis-à-vis the Empire. Despite this similarity in Baldus's discussion of the Genoese and Venetian doges, he presents the two polities as markedly different in terms of the relation of their respective citizens to the cities' physical environments. The city of Genoa is not rendered indistinguishable from its citizens in anything like the manner analyzed at the end of the previous section. Further, although we read of Genoa's *bonum regimen* at Baldus ad C.1.2.16, nu. 3, the Ligurian city did not enjoy a reputation for harmonious governance to the degree that Venice did. Indeed Baldus's *Consilia* 5.325 and 5.326 were the direct result of the city's asking him to pronounce on the legal issues at play when Doge Antoniotto Adorno was expelled for the second, and not the last, time in 1390.[44] Relatedly, Genoa's legislation was not considered particularly to reflect natural-law principles. And as we might expect, Baldus nowhere says that Genoa was constructed on a *res communis omnium*. The Genoese were less able to mobilize these considerations—harmonious administration, legislation consistent with natural law, and the utilization of the *res communis omnium*—to present their city as a corporate person.

A challenge to this notion that Venice and Genoa were fundamentally distinguished from one another in terms of the degree to which their citizens were capable of acting as a collective in inter-polity legal matters may seem to come from the fact that both cities made a similar claim, and one akin to that of the Venetians regarding the sovereign independence of their city, which is at

44 See Vito Piergiovanni, "Diritto e potere a Genova alla fine del Trecento: a proposito di tre 'consigli' di Baldo degli Ubaldi," in *Norme, scienza e pratica giuridica tra Genova e l'Occidente medievale e moderno*, 2 vols. (Genoa: Società Ligure di Storia Patria, 2012), 1:166–69 for a treatment of these *consilia* and the events that prompted and followed them.

the core of this study. As with the claim of the Venetians in which their corporation inhabits the place of the individual of D.1.8.6.pr., both Venice and Genoa argued that they could exercise control of the seas in their immediate environs through a mechanism used by individuals in antiquity. The mechanism, known as *longi temporis praescriptio*, allowed a person to claim that long-established possession—ten or, in some cases, twenty years—of a piece of land entitled him to continued use of it. In relation to Venice and Genoa, this would mean that their customary pre-eminence in the seas in their immediate vicinities should afford certain privileges. Just what this customary pre-eminence would allow them to assert, however, was far from clear and, crucially, *longi temporis praescriptio* was almost entirely disconnected from the *ius gentium* or any other consideration of natural law.[45]

Although not his primary focus, Robert Fredona demonstrates in an exploration of *longi temporis praescriptio* in relation to the "Gulf of the Venetians" that the transposition of a collective in the 14th century into the place of an individual in ancient Roman texts was accomplished much more effectively by the Venetians.[46] He analyzes the opinion of Angelus de Ubaldis—the younger brother of Baldus and himself a highly respected jurist in the 14th century—regarding the Venetian assertion that they are able to bar the merchants of specific polities from the Adriatic Sea on the basis of their widely known predominance in the area.[47] The relevant *consilium* should be seen in light of what Aldo Mazzacane identified as the tendency of jurists associated with the law school at Padua, a city within the Venetian orbit, to be pressed for legal opinions that favor Venetian positions on particular issues.[48] Lest we think that Angelus's

45 On this mechanism in Roman law, see Max Kaser, *Das römische Privatrecht* (Munich: C.H. Beck, 1959), 2:285–88 and Giovanni Pugliese, *Istituzioni di diritto romano* (Turin: G. Giappichelli, 1998), 339–40.

46 Robert Fredona, "Angelo degli Ubaldi and the Gulf of the Venetians: Custom, Commerce, and the Control of the Sea Before Grotius," in *New Perspectives on the History of Political Economy*, ed. Robert Fredona and Sophus A. Reinert (London: Palgrave Macmillan, 2018), 29–73. Fredona has instead the important goal of detailing Grotius's debts, often unacknowledged, to premodern jurists; see especially 57.

47 Angelus *Consilium* 290; see Fredona, "Angelo degli Ubaldi," 35–39 for information about the publication history of Angelus's *Consilia*. On the life of Angelus, see Carla Frova, "Angelo degli Ubaldi sr. (Perugia, 1327/8–1407)," in *Dizionario biografico dei giuristi italiani* (*XII–XX secolo*), vol. 2, ed. Italo Birocchi et al. (Bologna: Mulino, 2013), 68–71.

48 See Aldo Mazzacane "Lo Stato e il dominio nei giuristi veneti durante il 'secolo della terraferma,'" in *Storia della cultura veneta*, vol. 3.1, ed. Girolamo Arnaldi and Manlio Pastore Stocchi (Vicenza: Neri Pozza, 1980–1981), 576–650, as well as Mario Ascheri, *The Laws of Late Medieval Italy (1000–1500): Foundations for a European Legal System* (Leiden: Brill, 2013). See Fredona, "Angelo degli Ubaldi," 35 for his discussion of this question in relation to Angelus's *consilium*.

conclusion—that the Venetian argument based on *praescriptio* was viable, albeit with certain limitations—was only the opinion of a hired hand, this assertion had been reified by inclusion and revision in two treaties, namely the treaty of 1355 that ended the Third Genoese War and the Treaty of Turin in 1381, which concluded the War of Chioggia.[49] Indeed even Genoese chroniclers and politicians use the phrase "Golfo di Venetia" in a matter-of-fact way from the 13th to the 15th century, and the Adriatic would regularly be so labeled on maps in subsequent centuries.[50] Baldus himself had considered the Genoese argument from *longi temporis praescriptio* and found it lacking.[51] As with the physical layout of the respective cities, the topography of the Adriatic facilitated the Venetian claim much more readily than did the Tyrrhenian Sea suggest the Genoese, where cartographers and jurists differed markedly in their definition of the Gulf of Genoa. We see that not only the built environment of a city but also the intelligibility of the natural areas that were implicated in its corporate personhood claims had bearing on the acceptance of a political community's utilization of the rules of Roman private law.

Crucially, however, Angelus and other jurists could not claim that the Venetians owned the sea in the same way in which they owned their city. It was in fact the category of the *res communes omnium* that made this clear. In overcoming this hurdle, Angelus showed himself to be making a different sort of argumentative move than were the Venetians who asserted ownership over their city. Rather than invoking an established understanding of a rule of Roman private law and inserting the Venetian collective into the place of the singular person discussed by ancient jurists, Angelus proposed a new understanding. Although the *ius gentium* rendered the sea common to all, what that meant, he alleged, was that no one was prohibited from owning it. As even partial owners, the Venetians could argue that they were defending themselves against others who would eject them from their property, and so could themselves bar the Genoese from sailing in the Adriatic.[52] The Genoese were far less successful when they tried to make a similar claim. This argument did not establish unassailable Venetian control of the Adriatic, which as we might expect turned instead on the ability to enforce such a state of affairs. However,

49 Fredona, "Angelo degli Ubaldi," 37–39. For characterizations of these two wars and the histories and chronicles that treat them, see Heinrich Kretschmayr, *Geschichte von Venedig*, vol. 2 (Gotha: Fr. A. Perthes, 1920), 207–15 and 604–5 for the Third Genoese War, and 229–42 and 608–11 for the War of Chioggia.

50 Fredona, "Angelo degli Ubaldi," 41–43.

51 See Canning, *Political Thought*, 100–104.

52 See Fredona, "Angelo degli Ubaldi," 41–42.

the writings of Angelus and other jurists show the depth of the comparison between Venice and Genoa, as well as the stark difference that emerges from that comparison in terms of the viability of notions of corporate personhood connected to the respective polities.

Likely more familiar to students of Italian political history is the comparison between Venice and Florence. This comparison was made across a generically wide range of texts and concerned the internal concord, or lack thereof, and the constitutions of the two polities. As people from elsewhere visited Venice increasingly in the 13th and 14th centuries, fascination with the city grew.[53] Felix Gilbert considered the impression that the city's canals and gondolas, as well as the precious stones visible in the city's cathedrals, made on outsiders.[54] That these visitors also came to the city during the long and relentless trend toward other republics' incorporation into larger political entities or their replacement by other constitutional forms only added to the allure of Venice and its tradition of independence. This context also prompted intensified comparisons with other polities, especially Florence given that republic's prominence. The similarities between the cities did not extend much further. Burckhardt famously described Florence as "the city of incessant movement," and Venice as that of "apparent stagnation and of political secrecy," as rendered in Middlemore's translation.[55] This incessant movement included not only perennial involvement in the wars and negotiations of other polities throughout Italy and beyond, but also and especially internal discord through the competition of factions and segments of society.[56] Gilbert and others have

53 On substantial travel to Venice, see Gilbert, "The Venetian Constitution," 466.

54 Gilbert, "The Venetian Constitution," 466. The prominence of St. Mark within the city's religious landscape will again have been distinctive but intelligible to visitors, as indeed many cities cultivated and projected their close association with a particular patron saint. See Gilbert, "The Venetian Constitution," 464, as well as Hans Conrad Peyer, *Stadt und Stadtpatron im mittelalterlichen Italien* (Zurich: Europa, 1955), for the notion that a city's unique connection to its patron saint would have counseled against attempting to reproduce any other city's societal characteristics therein. Botero thought that the city's canals contributed to its internal concord, as they hindered the ability of the populace to assemble quickly; see *Della ragion di Stato* 5.7. A recent and accessible translation of this text is Giovanni Botero, *The Reason of State*, ed. Robert Bireley (Cambridge: Cambridge University Press, 2017).

55 Jacob Burckhardt, *The Civilization of the Renaissance in Italy*, trans. S.G.C. Middlemore (London: Penguin Classics, 2004), 57–58.

56 On the many histories of Florence from the 13th through 15th century, see Gaetano Cozzi, "Cultura politica e religione nella 'pubblica storiografia' veneziana del '500," *Studi veneziani* 5–6 (1963–1964): 215–94, and Gaeta, "Storiografia, coscienza nazionale e politica culturale."

championed the notion that the constant agitation in Florence was generative of the political theorization for which the city continues to be known.[57] But Gilbert notes too that in consequence of this turbulence, Florence could not easily be considered the model republic within the theoretical discussions in which its citizens were leading lights, and which revived the classical terminology of Greek and Roman political theory.

Venice by contrast could boast of a relative scarcity of internal disruption, whether in comparison with Florence or with other polities, which as we have seen complemented its reputation for devotion to sovereign independence. Such internal concord was thought throughout the medieval period to derive in large part from the reasoned collaboration of the different elements of Venetian society. Sanuto praised the absence of sedition in the city as well as the ability of the patricians to work together; such common purpose and commitment to the city's greatness were superb indicators that Venice would continue to prosper indefinitely.[58] Others noted the many freedoms enjoyed by Venetians, as well as their character. Petrarch famously described the city as rich in material goods but richer still in reputation, and as protected more by the wisdom and intelligence of its citizens than by the sea surrounding it.[59]

Oceans of ink have been spilt in discussion of civic humanism in the Renaissance.[60] Among the many themes that have emerged in this scholarship, two—namely the sustained interest among 14th- and 15th-century writers in the benefits conferred by a mixed constitution, and the complex nature of the meaning of liberty during this time—are particularly relevant to our analysis of the self-fashioning of polities in relation to one another and of the dynamics of corporate personhood. Of seminal importance to the avoidance of internal strife in Venice, it was thought, was the moderate conduct and constitutional legitimacy of the doge. It circulated as the opinion of Thomas Aquinas that

57 Gilbert, "The Venetian Constitution," 467–68; see also Christopher S. Celenza, *The Intellectual World of the Italian Renaissance: Language, Philosophy, and the Search for Meaning* (Cambridge: Cambridge University Press, 2018), 71–93 and Stefano U. Baldassarri, ed., *Coluccio Salutati: Political Writings* (Cambridge, MA: Harvard University Press, 2014), vii–xxiv.

58 See Giuseppe Maranini, *La costituzione di Venezia dopo la serrata del Maggior Consiglio* (Venice: La Nuova Italia, 1931), 14.

59 Petrarch, *Lettere Senili*, 4.3.

60 For helpful bibliographies in recent works, see Hankins, *Virtue Politics*; Celenza, *The Intellectual World of the Italian Renaissance*; and Ruggiero, *The Renaissance in Italy*. See also Mikael Hörnqvist, "The Two Myths of Civic Humanism," in *Renaissance Civic Humanism: Reappraisals and Reflections*, ed. James Hankins (Cambridge: Cambridge University Press, 2000), 105–42, and Hankins, *Virtúe Politics*, 94–102 *inter alia* for discussions of this phrase.

of all the rulers in northern Italy, only the doge had his power curtailed and was non-tyrannical.[61] The monarchic doge shared power with the aristocratic Senate and the democratic Great Council in what was regarded as a particularly successful mixed constitution.[62] A mixture such as this would seem an ideal to more theorists and observers over the course of the 16th century following the translation of the sixth book of Polybius's *Histories* and Machiavelli's arguments for a constitutional structure of this sort, but James Blythe has shown that 14th-century political observers and theorists deployed the ideas related to mixed constitutionalism that they found in medieval Aristotelianism.[63] Further, he demonstrates that the understanding of Venice in particular as having a mixed constitution is itself medieval.[64] An effective constitutional structure also made possible the second sense of Renaissance liberty. In addition to the emphasis on a polity's independence vis-à-vis others that we discussed in the previous section, Denys Hay and others have demonstrated that *libertas* signified also a non-tyrannical regime, and have detailed the importance of this sense to Venetian political thought and self-conception.[65] Here the position of the doge seemed to reflect and perpetuate the domestic freedom enjoyed by Venetians.

As ideas that had been developed from Aristotle's works in the previous centuries were circulating, the long-serving Florentine chancellor Coluccio Salutati (1331–1406) became an important patron of humanistic thought; this accelerated a revival of ancient political terminology from the late 14th century.[66] Gilbert has shown that this patronage occurred in the context of deep

61 Thomas Aquinas, *De Regimine Principum* 4.8; this section was written not by Aquinas but by Ptolemy of Lucca. For the popularity of this opinion among Venetians, see Gilbert, "The Venetian Constitution," 467, where Bernardo Bembo's restatement of the opinion found in *De Regimine Principum* is adduced: "Omnes principes Italiae sunt tiranni Duce Venetiarum excepto, qui habet regimen temperatum. Verbi sunt Sancti Thome" (Bernardo Bembo, "Commonplace Book," fol. 45r.). On this text, see Holly Hamilton Bleakley, "The Art of Ruling in Aquinas' *De Regimine Principum*," *History of Political Thought* 20, no. 4 (1999): 575–602.

62 On the flexibility of the term "mixed constitution" in the 14th century, see James M. Blythe, *Ideal Government and the Mixed Constitution in the Middle Ages* (Princeton: Princeton University Press, 1992), 161.

63 Blythe, *Ideal Government and the Mixed Constitution*, 161–64, 203–40, and 278–300. For the life of these ideas during the 16th century, see J.G.A. Pocock, *The Machiavellian Moment: Florentine Political Thought and the Atlantic Republican Tradition* (Princeton: Princeton University Press, 2003), 83–271.

64 Blythe, *Ideal Government and the Mixed Constitution*, 278–300, especially 278, 286–287, 295.

65 Denys Hay, *The Italian Renaissance in Its Historical Background* (Cambridge: Cambridge University Press, 1977), 119–23 and Gilbert, "The Venetian Constitution," 466–67; see also Hörnqvist, "The Two Myths of Civic Humanism," 105–12.

66 Celenza, *The Intellectual World of the Italian Renaissance*, 44–70.

Florentine interest in the Venetian constitution, and of increasing Venetian commitment to securing humanistic engagement with and praise of Venetian civic society, above all in classical political terms.[67] The patrician Francesco Barbaro (1390–1454) became the patron of George of Trebizond (1395–c. 1484), the Greek scholar whom he brought to Venice from Crete in 1417. George of Trebizond would express to Barbaro his opinion that "clearly your ancestors, who laid the foundations of your republic, collected everything from the *Laws* of Plato by which a republic is able to be good and long-lasting."[68] Plato's *Laws*, which George of Trebizond invoked in relation to Venice's internal governance and which he had just translated into Latin, contains the famous analogy of the body politic, which is discussed over much of the text. While this metaphor was known through Aristotle's use of it, particularly at *Politics* 1.2 (1253a), George of Trebizond's translation increased its relevance.[69] When juxtaposed with the texts that often feature in analyses of Renaissance political thought, we see the compatibility of juristic conceptions of corporate personhood with their metaphors and central concerns. Most convincingly developed in connection to Venice, these conceptions drew upon the political community's internal liberty and concord, which was consistently maintained in accounts of the city and understood as a benefit of its particular mixed constitution, and emphasized as well the importance of the city's built environment and natural surroundings. By rendering the Venetians unified and physically coterminous with their city, Baldus's refraction, especially for his inconsistency as to the implications of such imagery and the arguments seen for Venetian sovereignty, deepens the complexity and excitement of Renaissance political thought.

---

67 See especially Gilbert, "The Venetian Constitution," 467–68, including 468, n. 1.

68 "Leges quoque Platonis, ex quibus aperte intellexi, Majores vestros, qui Reipublicae vestrae fundamenta jecerunt, ex his certe libris omnia, quibus Respublica diu felix esse possit, collegisse." George of Trebizond to Francesco Barbaro, December 5, 1451, in M.A. Quirini, ed. *Francisci Barbari et aliorum ad ipsum Epistolae* (Brescia, 1743), no. 198, p. 290. See also Hankins, *Virtue Politics*, 377–81 for his analysis of the "Platonizing [of] Venice's Constitution."

69 For a description of a widely known medieval Latin translation of the *Politics*, that of William of Moerbeke, see Claire Richter Sherman, *Imaging Aristotle: Verbal and Visual Representation in Fourteenth-Century France* (Berkeley: University of California Press, 1995), 25. See also 1–35 for a discussion of Nicole Oresme and his French translation *Politiques* (where this passage is found on p. 49). See also Blythe, *Ideal Government and the Mixed Constitution*, 203–40. For the history of this metaphor in the medieval period, see Anton-Hermann Chroust, "The Corporate Idea and the Body Politic in the Middle Ages," *Review of Politics* 9, no. 4 (1947): 423–52. He does not mention any medieval jurists.

3 Conclusion: Corporate Persons Ecclesiastical and Civil

By way of conclusion, we note that Plato's and Aristotle's uses of the body as an image for a larger corporation were not the only deployments of this metaphor. Pope Innocent IV, in his commentary on the *Liber extra* (published shortly after the First Council of Lyon in 1245), had written that the ecclesiastical college (*collegium*) "was figured as a person in legal matters involving the corporation."[70] This is often considered the origin of the image of corporate personhood in the Roman legal tradition, and the formulation almost immediately had a deep impact.[71] The explosion of creativity in that tradition, an example of which has been the focus of this chapter, was made possible by a revival no less significant than that of ancient political thought and terminology discussed above. Around the year 1100, the *Digest* started to be increasingly widely known in northern Italy and southern France, with consequences hard to overstate.[72] In another example of their characteristic assertion of uniqueness, Venetians claimed that this rediscovery had little if any impact on the laws of their city.[73]

We have seen in this chapter that renewed engagement on the part of Venetian jurists with the *Corpus Iuris Civilis*, as preserved in the writings of one of its foremost interpreters, gave the inhabitants of that city a new lexicon of terms and concepts with which to articulate their aspirations to sovereign independence, especially through the promotion of tenets derived from natural law. In so doing, they advanced a notion of corporate personhood through the innovative transposition of their corporate collective into what had been the place of an individual in the ancient legal texts now at their disposal. We cannot say whether this Venetian claim, which Baldus does not date, was articulated before Innocent's famous formulation. But it is certain that the *res communes omnium*, somewhat unsettled as a property category in antiquity, later

70 "Cum collegium in causa universitatis fingatur una persona." Innocentius P. IV ad X.2.20.57, nu. 5.

71 Amid the many treatments of this topic, see Maximilian Koessler, "The Person in Imagination or Persona Ficta of the Corporation," *Louisiana Law Review* 9, no. 4 (1949): 435–49.

72 The bibliography on this moment and the subsequent centuries is quite large. See the helpful citations in Peter Stein, *Roman Law in European History* (Cambridge: Cambridge University Press, 2005), 38–103. See also Charles M. Radding and Antonio Ciaralli, *The* Corpus Iuris Civilis *in the Middle Ages: Manuscripts and Transmission from the Sixth Century to the Juristic Revival* (Leiden: Brill, 2006), and the references therein.

73 See Stein, *Roman Law in European History*, 72, where the famous question of Venetian wills, which disproves this claim, is discussed.

sparked particularly intriguing juristic ideas. This chapter, in unpacking the world of the Venetians' claim, has endeavored to show that legal texts—and, more specifically, those sub-genres of legal texts that engage with technical questions of private law—are indispensable to our understanding of political thought in the medieval and Renaissance world.

Bibliography

Armitage, David. *Foundations of Modern International Thought*. Cambridge: Cambridge University Press, 2013.

Ascheri, Mario. *The Laws of Late Medieval Italy (1000–1500): Foundations for a European Legal System*. Leiden: Brill, 2013.

Baldassarri, Stefano U., ed. *Coluccio Salutati: Political Writings*. Cambridge, MA: Harvard University Press, 2014.

Bleakley, Holly Hamilton. "The Art of Ruling in Aquinas' *De Regimine Principum*." *History of Political Thought* 20, no. 4 (1999): 575–602.

Blythe, James M. *Ideal Government and the Mixed Constitution in the Middle Ages*. Princeton: Princeton University Press, 1992.

Botero, Giovanni. *The Reason of State*, edited by Robert Bireley. Cambridge: Cambridge University Press, 2017.

Bouwsma, William J. *Venice and the Defense of Republican Liberty: Renaissance Values in the Age of the Counter Reformation*. Berkeley: University of California Press, 1968.

Bowsky, William M. *Henry VII in Italy: The Conflict of Empire and City-State, 1310–1313*. 1960. Reprint, Westport, Ct: Greenwood Press, 1974.

Burckhardt, Jacob. *The Civilization of the Renaissance in Italy*, translated by S.G.C. Middlemore. 1878. Reprint, London: Penguin Classics, 2004.

Canning, Joseph. *The Political Thought of Baldus de Ubaldis*. Cambridge: Cambridge University Press, 1987.

Celenza, Christopher S. *The Intellectual World of the Italian Renaissance: Language, Philosophy, and the Search for Meaning*. Cambridge: Cambridge University Press, 2018.

Chroust, Anton-Hermann. "The Corporate Idea and the Body Politic in the Middle Ages." *Review of Politics* 9, no. 4 (1947): 423–52.

Cozzi, Gaetano. "Cultura politica e religione nella 'pubblica storiografia' veneziana del '500." *Studi veneziani* 5–6 (1963–1964): 215–94.

Deveney, Patrick. "Title, jus publicum, and the Public Trust: An Historical Analysis." *Sea Grant Law Journal* 1 (1976): 13–81.

Donahue, Charles, Jr. "*Animalia Ferae Naturae*: Rome, Bologna, Leyden, Oxford and Queen's County, N.Y." In *Studies in Roman Law in Memory of A. Arthur Schiller*, edited by Roger S. Bagnall and William V. Harris, 39–63. Leiden: Brill, 1986.

Duke, George and Robert P. George, eds. *The Cambridge Companion to Natural Law Jurisprudence*. Cambridge: Cambridge University Press, 2017.

Dursi, Domenico. Res communes omnium: *Dalle necessità economiche alla disciplina giuridica*. Naples: Jovene, 2017.

Fasoli, Gina. "Nascita di un mito." In *Studi storici in onore di Gioacchino Volpe*, 1, 445–79. Florence: Sansoni, 1958.

Fassò, Guido. "Natural Law in Italy in the Past Ten Years." *Natural Law Forum* (1956): 122–34.

Fedele, Dante. *The Medieval Foundations of International Law: Baldus de Ubaldis (1327–1400), Doctrine and Practice of the* Ius Gentium. Leiden: Brill, 2021.

Fiorentini, Mario. *Fiumi e mari nell'esperienza giuridica romana: profili di tutela processuale e di inquadramento sistematico*. Milan: Giuffrè, 2003.

Frankopan, Peter. "Byzantine Trade Privileges to Venice in the Eleventh Century: The Chrysobull of 1092." *Journal of Medieval History* 30 (2004): 135–60.

Fredona, Robert. "Angelo degli Ubaldi and the Gulf of the Venetians: Custom, Commerce, and the Control of the Sea Before Grotius." In *New Perspectives on the History of Political Economy*, edited by Robert Fredona and Sophus A. Reinert, 29–73. London: Palgrave Macmillan, 2018.

Freed, John B. *Frederick Barbarossa: The Prince and the Myth*. New Haven: Yale University Press, 2016.

Frier, Bruce W. "The Roman Origins of the Public Trust Doctrine." *Journal of Roman Archaeology* 32 (2019): 641–47.

Frova, Carla. "Angelo degli Ubaldi sr. (Perugia, 1327/8–1407)." In *Dizionario biografico dei giuristi italiani (XII–XX secolo)*, vol. 2, edited by Italo Birocchi et al., 68–71. Bologna: Mulino, 2013.

Fusaro, Maria. "Politics of Justice/Politics of Trade: Foreign Merchants and the Administration of Justice from the Records of Venice's *Giudici del Forestier*." *Mélanges de l'école française de Rome: Italie et Méditerranée modernes et contemporaines* 126, no. 1 (2014): 139–60.

Gaeta, Franco. "Alcune considerazioni sul mito di Venezia." *Bibliothèque d'Humanisme et Renaissance* 23 (1961): 58–75.

Gaeta, Franco. "Storiografia, coscienza nazionale e politica culturale nella Venezia del Rinascimento." In *Storia della cultura veneta*, vol. 3.1, edited by Girolamo Arnaldi and Manlio Pastore Stocchi, 1–91. Vicenza: Neri Pozza, 1980–1981.

Gilbert, Felix. "The Venetian Constitution in Florentine Political Thought." In *Florentine Studies: Politics and Society in Renaissance Florence*, edited by Nicolai Rubinstein, 463–500. London: Faber and Faber, 1968.

Grubb, James S. "When Myths Lose Power: Four Decades of Venetian Historiography." *Journal of Modern History* 58, no. 1 (1986): 43–94.

Grubb, James S. *Firstborn of Venice: Vicenza in the Early Renaissance State.* Baltimore: Johns Hopkins University Press, 2019.

Hankins, James. *Virtue Politics: Soulcraft and Statecraft in Renaissance Italy.* Cambridge, MA: Harvard University Press, 2019.

Hay, Denys. *The Italian Renaissance in Its Historical Background.* 1961. Reprint, Cambridge: Cambridge University Press, 1977.

Hörnqvist, Mikael. "The Two Myths of Civic Humanism." In *Renaissance Civic Humanism: Reappraisals and Reflections*, edited by James Hankins, 105–42. Cambridge: Cambridge University Press, 2000.

Judde de Larivière, Claire. *La révolte des boules de neige: Murano face à Venise, 1511.* Paris: Fayard, 2014.

Kaser, Max. *Das römische Privatrecht*, vol. 2. Munich: C.H. Beck, 1959.

Koessler, Maximilian. "The Person in Imagination or Persona Ficta of the Corporation." *Louisiana Law Review* 9, no. 4 (1949): 435–49.

Koskenniemi, Martti. *The Gentle Civilizer of Nations: The Rise and Fall of International Law 1870–1960.* 2001. Reprint, Cambridge: Cambridge University Press, 2008.

Kretschmayr, Heinrich. *Geschichte von Venedig*, vol. 2. Gotha: Fr. A. Perthes, 1920.

Maranini, Giuseppe. *La costituzione di Venezia dopo la serrata del Maggior Consiglio.* Venice: La Nuova Italia, 1931.

Marin, Şerban V. "Between Authorship and Anonymity. The Case of the Venetian Chronicles." In *The Medieval Chronicle 13*, edited by Erik S. Kooper and Sjoerd Levelt, 149–81. Leiden: Brill, 2020.

Mazzacane, Aldo. "Lo Stato e il dominio nei giuristi veneti durante il 'secolo della terraferma.'" In *Storia della cultura veneta*, vol. 3.1, edited by Girolamo Arnaldi and Manlio Pastore Stocchi, 576–650. Vicenza: Neri Pozza, 1980–1981.

Pennington, Kenneth. *The Prince and the Law, 1200–1600: Sovereignty and Rights in the Western Legal Tradition.* Berkeley: University of California Press, 1993.

Pennington, Kenneth. "*Lex naturalis* and *ius naturale.*" *The Jurist* 68 (2008): 569–91.

Petronio, Ugo. "Civitas Venetiarum est edificata in mari." In *Studi veneti offerti a Gaetano Cozzi*, edited by Gino Benzoni et al., 171–85. Venice: Il Cardo, 1992.

Peyer, Hans Conrad. *Stadt und Stadtpatron im mittelalterlichen Italien.* Zurich: Europa, 1955.

Piergiovanni, Vito. "Diritto e potere a Genova alla fine del Trecento: a proposito di tre 'consigli' di Baldo degli Ubaldi." In *Norme, scienza e pratica giuridica tra Genova e l'Occidente medievale e moderno*, 2 vols., 1:159–70. Genoa: Società Ligure di Storia Patria, 2012.

Pocock, J.G.A. *The Machiavellian Moment: Florentine Political Thought and the Atlantic Republican Tradition.* 1975. Reprint, Princeton: Princeton University Press, 2003.

Pugliese, Giovanni. *Istituzioni di diritto romano*. 1991. Reprint, Turin: G. Giappichelli, 1998.

Radding, Charles M. and Antonio Ciaralli. *The* Corpus Iuris Civilis *in the Middle Ages: Manuscripts and Transmission from the Sixth Century to the Juristic Revival.* Leiden: Brill, 2006.

Ruggiero, Guido. *The Renaissance in Italy: A Social and Cultural History of the Rinascimento*. Cambridge: Cambridge University Press, 2015.

Sherman, Claire Richter. *Imaging Aristotle: Verbal and Visual Representation in Fourteenth-Century France*. Berkeley: University of California Press, 1995.

Stein, Peter. *Roman Law in European History*. 1999. Reprint, Cambridge: Cambridge University Press, 2005.

Stern, Laura Ikins. "Politics and Law in Renaissance Florence and Venice." *American Journal of Legal History* 46, no. 2 (2004): 209–34.

CHAPTER 4

Abandonment, *animus* and *animalia ferae naturae* in Hugo Grotius' *De iure belli ac pacis*

Daniel Jacobs

1 Introduction

Pierson v. Post, the celebrated case about the capture of a fox argued before the New York Supreme Court in 1805,[1] serves as an appropriate introduction to private property in the United States for two reasons. First, it took place when American law was in its infancy. Second, it deals with the origin of title, the beginning of private property itself. In two articles, and in his course and seminar on continental European legal and constitutional history, this volume's honorand has shown that what is presented to most law students as the beginning of one story is also a later chapter of another.[2] Not only did the debate on *occupatio* reach back to the classical Roman jurists, but, in the 200 years before Jesse Pierson fatally clubbed the fox before Lodowick Post's eyes, that debate underwent a transformation in the writings of the natural law school. Hints of that transformation are detectable in the case report composed by George Caines (1771–1825).[3]

By the time students in Professor Donahue's course on continental legal history reach *Pierson v. Post*, they might well think that Post committed an error fatal to his own case when he argued as if bringing an action for trespass.[4] He

1 3 Cai. R. 175 (N.Y. Supreme Court 1805). On the case record, see Angela Fernandez, "The Lost Record of Pierson v. Post, the Famous Fox Case," *Law and History Review* 27, no. 1 (2009): 149–78. See generally Angela Fernandez, *Pierson v. Post: The Hunt for the Fox: Law and Professionalization in American Legal Culture* (Cambridge: Cambridge University Press, 2018).

2 Donahue, Charles Jr. "*Animalia ferae naturae*: Rome, Bologna, Leyden, Oxford and Queen's County, N.Y.," in *Studies in Roman Law in Memory of A. Arthur Schiller*, ed. Roger Bagnall and William V. Harris (Leiden: E.J. Brill, 1986), 39–63 and "Noodt, Titius, and the natural law school: The occupation of wild animals and the intersection of property and tort," in *Satura Roberto Feenstra: sexagesimum quintum annum aetatis complenti ab alumnis collegis amicis oblata*, ed. J.A. Ankum, J.E. Spruit, and F.B.J. Wubbe (Fribourg, Suisse: Éditions Universitaires, 1985), 609–29.

3 George Caines, *New York Term Reports of Cases Argued and Determined in the Supreme Court of that State*, vol. 3 (New York: Isaac Riley & Co., 1806), 175–82.

4 See Donahue, "Noodt, Titius," 610 and *passim*.

 | DOI:10.1163/9789004710696_006

could have staked his argument on the claim that Pierson interfered tortiously with the hunt, rather than that Post had already gotten possession of the fox. After all, neither side denied that Post was on the verge of catching the fox when Pierson intervened, and Pierson could hardly deny that his actions constituted interference. By claiming possession of a fox over which he never had physical control, Post put himself at odds with most of the authorities cited by the litigants.

Most, but not all. In order to claim possession, Post's attorney, Cadwallader David Colden, made the case that there were ways of acquiring a right in a wild animal other than depriving it of its natural liberty. He argued that manucaption

> is only one of many means to declare the intention of exclusively appropriating that, which was before in a state of nature. Any continued act which does this, is equivalent to occupancy. Pursuit therefore, by a person who starts a wild animal, gives an exclusive right whilst it is followed. It is all the possession the nature of the subject admits; it declares the intention of acquiring dominion, and is as much to be respected as manucaption itself. The contrary idea, requiring actual taking, proceeds, as *Mr. Barbeyrac* observes, in *Puffendorf, B.* 4, c. 6, *S.* 10, on a "false notion of possession."[5]

Colden was invoking the authority of Jean Barbeyrac, the eighteenth-century French commentator on, among others, two of the most influential members of the natural law school, Hugo Grotius (1583–1645) and Samuel Pufendorf (1632–1694). Pufendorf was an admirer of the political philosophy of Thomas Hobbes (1588–1679), according to whose famously bleak portrait of human life outside the sovereign power of the state, "all men have a right to all things." In such a world, the hunter owned their prey only so long as they had physical control of it.[6] Colden argued on the contrary that peaceful communication of one's intentions was possible in a state of nature, and was sufficient to create an actionable right.

5 Caines, 176–77.

6 *Leviathan*, Chapter XIII: "It is consequent to the same condition, that there be no Propriety, no Dominion, no *Mine* and *Thine* distinct; but onely that to be every mans, that he can get; and for so long, as he can keep it." Richard Tuck and Thomas Hobbes, *Hobbes: Leviathan: Revised Student Edition*, Cambridge Texts in the History of Political Thought (Cambridge: Cambridge University Press, 1996), 90.

In this essay, I examine the roots of Colden's argument in the early natural law school. As Professor Donahue has shown, Colden made his case on a Lockean conception of property, in which "mixing one's labor" with a piece of property suffices to acquire ownership. I look into the history of the natural law school to show how alternatives to manucaption were developing even before John Locke (1632–1704) formulated his idiosyncratic theory of private property in the *Second Treatise of Government*.[7] I argue that an important piece of background to Locke's theory was the long-running argument over the role of *animus* or intention in the recovery of lost goods. The argument turned on the answers to three questions. First, do the owner's intention and expectation at the moment they lost possession of the goods determine whether the owner retains ownership? Second, do the finder's intention and expectation at the moment they found the goods determine whether the finder has committed theft? If the answer to either of these questions is yes, how do we determine retroactively what those intentions and expectations were? These questions pit objective standards, like the nature of the animal lost and the fact of its survival, against presumptions of people's intentions.

I begin by examining an intriguing case preserved in Justinian's *Digest* on the loss and capture of pigs (D.41.1.44)—which may be wild, or not. The peculiar difficulties presented by this case tested the Roman jurists' rules about the capture of wild animals and the recovery of lost property. In particular, the jurists struggled to decide what action could be brought against the finder of lost property that had miraculously escaped destruction. I then explain how Hugo Grotius formulated a different doctrine of lost and abandoned property, quite unlike what he found in the *Corpus Iuris Civilis*, in his *De iure belli ac pacis* (first published 1625). Grotius advanced a theory of property that was much more optimistic than that of the Roman jurists about the possibility of clear communication between individuals in nature. I argue that Grotius' treatment of lost property presaged theories of private property like Locke's, in which clear communication and shared moral norms, even in nature, are essential to private ownership.[8] I close with a brief discussion of one of the sources of Grotius' treatment of lost property, *Deuteronomy* 22.1–3, and suggest that it made an important contribution to the rules governing lost property that appeared in the writings of the natural law school.

---

7 See §§27 and 28 of the Second Treatise in John Locke, *Two Treatises of Government*, Peter Laslett, ed., Cambridge Texts in the History of Political Thought (Cambridge: Cambridge University Press, 1960, repr. 1988), 287–89.

8 For this interpretation of Locke's theory of property, see Carol M. Rose, "Possession as the Origin of Property," *The University of Chicago Law Review* 52, no. 1 (1985): 73–88.

2 The Rule Scheme of Justinian's *Institutes*

I would like to begin by reviewing the passages of Justinian's *Institutes* (533 CE) that discuss the capture and loss of wild animals, the loss of other kinds of property, and the abandonment of property. While the *Institutes* treats of these topics in the same title, it draws clear distinctions among them. Since Grotius did not draw these distinctions as clearly, it will be important to know what they are.

The first title of the second book of Justinian's *Institutes* (hereafter JI) treats of both the capture of wild animals and the abandonment of property. It is a long title, and these two topics appear thirty-four sections apart. The rule on the capture (and loss) of wild animals appears at 2.1.12:

> An animal thus caught by you is deemed your property so long as it is completely under your control; but so soon as it has escaped from your control, and recovered its natural liberty, it ceases to be yours, and belongs to the person who subsequently catches it. It is deemed to have recovered its natural liberty when you have lost sight of it, or when, though it is still in your sight, it would be difficult to pursue it.[9]

The difference between this passage and Gaius' *Res cottidianae* (mid-second century CE), preserved at D.41.1.5, is, for my purposes, trivial. Both Gaius and Justinian say that the hunter loses ownership as soon as the animal has escaped the hunter's control and regained its natural liberty, and that it has regained its natural liberty as soon as the hunter has lost sight of it or when pursuit has become difficult.

The escape of an animal is, of course, different from abandoning a piece of property. JI.2.1.46–7 reads:

> Nay, in some cases the will of the owner, though directed only towards an uncertain person, transfers the ownership of the thing, as for instance when praetors and consuls throw money to a crowd: here they know not which specific coin each person will get, yet they make the unknown recipient immediate owner, because it is their will that each shall have what he gets. Accordingly, it is true that if a man takes possession of property abandoned by its previous owner, he at once becomes its owner

9 John Baron Moyle, *The Institutes of Justinian*, 5th ed. (Oxford: Clarendon Press, 1913), quoted at Donahue, "*Animalia ferae naturae*," 42. All translations of the *Institutes* are Moyle's.

> himself: and a thing is said to be abandoned which its owner throws away with the deliberate intention [*ea mente*] that it shall no longer be part of his property, and of which, consequently, he immediately ceases to be owner.[10]

The Sabinians and Proculians had debated this last point, i.e., whether the initial owner ceases to own the property at the moment that they leave it behind or at the moment that another person begins to possess it.[11] Nonetheless, the basic difference between abandoning one's property and losing a wild animal is clear enough. Wild animals cease to be ours the moment they have escaped our control, regardless of our hope or expectation of recovering them. Property of other kinds remains ours even after we have lost it, unless we have deliberately divested ourselves of it for the sake of no longer owning it. In the latter situation, intentionality comes to the fore.

Loss of property other than a wild animal is something else again, and intentionality is once again a key concern. The final section of book two of Justinian's *Institutes*, JI.2.1.48, which follows immediately after the passage on abandonment, reads:

> It is otherwise with things which are thrown overboard during a storm, in order to lighten the ship; in the ownership of these things there is no change, because the reason for which they are thrown overboard is obviously not that the owner does not care to own them any longer, but that he and the ship besides may be more likely to escape the perils of the sea. Consequently any one who picks them up at sea and keeps them, intending to make a profit thereby [*lucrandi animo*], commits a theft; for such things seem to be in much the same position as those which fall out of a carriage in motion unknown to their owners.[12]

---

10 Moyle, *Institutes*, 45. "Hoc amplius interdum et in incertam personam collocata voluntas domini transfert rei proprietatem: ut ecce praetores vel consules, qui missilia iactant in vulgus, ignorant, quid eorum quisque excepturus sit, et tamen, quia volunt quod quisque exceperit eius esse, statim eum dominum efficiunt. 47. Qua ratione verius esse videtur et, si rem pro derelicto a domino habitam occupaverit quis, statim eum dominium effici. pro derelicto autem habetur, quod dominus ea mente abiecerit, ut id rerum suaram esse nollet, ideoque statim dominus esse desinit." The Latin text of the *Institutes* is from Theodor Mommsen and Paul Krueger, eds., *Corpus Iuris Civilis*, 21st ed. (Dublin: Weidmann, 1970).

11 See §102.2 (p. 426), vol. I of Max Kaser, *Das römische Privatrecht*, neubearbeitete Aufl., Handbuch der Altertumswissenschaft 10 (München: Beck, 1971).

12 JI.2.1.48, Moyle, *Institutes*, 45. "Alia causa est earum rerum, quae in tempestate maris levandae navis causa eiciuntur. hae enim dominorum permanent, quia palam est eas non eo animo eici, quo quis eas habere non vult, sed quo magis cum ipsa nave periculum

The last sentence of this passage is of special interest. The classical rule of jettisoned goods seems to have been that the owner retained ownership so long as they kept up the search for them. If the owner's search led them to the finder, and the finder withheld the goods, then the action for theft would lie.[13]

The person who found jettisoned goods some time after the moment of jettison, and refused to return them to the owner upon the owner's request, could be held for theft (D.47.9.1.2–3). Thus, just as the owner could express the intention to retain ownership after the moment of jettison by keeping up the search, so could the finder express the *animus furandi* even after the moment of discovery.[14] This stretched the meaning of *contrectatio*, the "illicit handling" at the heart of the Roman concept of *furtum*, to include the refusal to surrender goods that were not necessarily taken with theftuous intent.[15]

The compilers of Justinian's *Digest* threw these rules into confusion. A long and tortuous passage of the title *De furtis* attributed to the early third-century CE jurist Ulpian (D.47.2.43.10–11) made the question of title dependent on the owner's intention at the moment of jettison, rather than on whether they attempted a search thereafter:

> 10. If someone deliberately discards or jettisons a thing, but not with the intention of abandoning it, and you take the thing, are you liable for theft? That is the question raised by Celsus in the twelfth book of his *Digest*. He says that if you thought that it was abandoned, you will not be so liable; but if you did not think that way, he says that there is room for doubt;

---

maris effugiat: qua de causa si quis eas fluctibus expulsas vel etiam in ipso mari nactus lucrandi animo abstulerit, furtum committit. nec longe discedere videntur ab his, quae de rheda currente, non intellegentibus dominis cadunt."

13 See Herbert Felix Jolowicz, (*Justinian*) *Digest XLVII. 2 "De Furtis"* (Cambridge: Cambridge University Press, 1940), 57–8 n. 11.

14 D.47.9.3pr. The Praetorian Edict gave an action for fourfold the goods' value against anyone who "looted or wrongfully received" goods taken from a fire, building collapse or shipwreck (D.47.9.1pr). The damages were of the same value as those for *furtum manifestum*, but the wrong was not *furtum per se*. See §189 of Otto Lenel, *Das Edictum perpetuum: ein Versuch zu seiner Wiederherstellung*, 2. Neudruck der 3. Aufl. Leipzig 1927. (Aalen: Scientia Verlag, 1974). The translation is from Alan Watson, ed. *The Digest of Justinian*, vol. 4 (Philadelphia: University of Pennsylvania Press, 1998), 282. I have consulted both this edition and the 1985 English-Latin edition: Theodor Mommsen, Paul Krueger, and Alan Watson, eds. *The Digest of Justinian*. 4 vols. (Philadelphia: University of Pennsylvania Press, 1985).

15 For this definition of *contrectatio*, and the difficulties of the concept, see Alan Watson, "The Definition of *Furtum* and the Trichotomy," *Tijdschrift voor rechtsgeschiedenis*, 28, no. 2 (1960), 198 and *passim*.

> still, on the whole, he would say that there is no liability in theft because there cannot be a deliberate appropriation of what another deliberately discards.[16] 11. If a person take what is jettisoned from a ship, is he liable for theft? The issue turns on whether the goods are abandoned or not. If the mind [*animo*] of the jettisoner were such that since he expected that the goods would be lost and thus that whoever found them would appropriate them, a not unreasonable general assumption [*quod plerumque credendum est*], there would be no theft. But if he were not of that mind but of the conviction that if the thing survived, it would still be his, then it could be taken away from the finder. And if the latter had an idea that this was so but took the thing with theftuous intent, he would be liable for theft. If, though, he took it with a view to preserving it for its owner, he would not be liable for theft. Nor would he be if he thought it to have been simply discarded.[17]

As Jolowicz put it in his comment on this passage, and as the long entry in the *Index Interpolationum* suggests, "There is something seriously wrong."[18] According to the classical rule, conjectures about the jettisoner's intention at the moment of jettison, and about the intention of the finder, were beside the point. The owner's search for the goods sufficed to prove that (s)he had not abandoned them, and the finder's refusal to surrender them upon request proved that (s)he had the *animus furandi*. Jolowicz believed this extract to be heavily interpolated, "not due to a systematic scheme, but 'slapdash.'"[19]

---

16 Cf. D.47.2.43.6.

17 10. "Si quis sponte rem iecit vel iactavit, non quasi pro derelicto habiturus, tuque hanc rem tuleris, an furti tenearis, Celsus libro duodecimo digestorum quaerit. et ait: si quidem putasti pro derelicto habitam, non teneris. quod si non putasti, hic dubitari posse ait: et tamen magis defendit non teneri, quia, inquit, res non intervertitur ei, qui eam sponte reiecit. 11. Si iactum ex nave factum alius tulerit, an furti teneatur? quaestio in eo est, an pro derelicto habitum sit. et si quidem derelinquentis animo iactavit, quod plerumque credendum est, cum sciat periturum, qui invenit suum fecit nec furti tenetur. si vero non hoc animo, sed hoc, ut, si salvum fuerit, haberet: ei qui invenit auferendum est, et si scit hoc qui invenit et animo furandi tenet, furti tenetur. enimvero si hoc animo, ut salvum faceret domino, furti non tenetur. quod si putans simpliciter iactatum, furti similiter non tenetur." Translation from Mommsen, Krueger and Watson, *Digest* (1985), vol. 4, 747. For the Latin text of the *Digest*, I have consulted the facing pages of Mommsen, Krueger, and Watson's 1985 edition (vol. 4, 747), as well as Theodor Mommsen and Paul Krueger, eds. *Corpus Iuris Civilis*, 21st ed. (Dublin: Weidmann, 1970).

18 Jolowicz, *De furtis*, 56. *Index Interpolationum* vol.III, coll. 489–90.

19 Jolowicz, *De furtis*, 58. On the compilers' "predilection for *animus*" as opposed to "applying objective legal rules to the facts," see his introduction, lviii.

Nonetheless, as we will see, it may well have influenced Grotius' doctrine of lost and abandoned property.

In summary, Justinian's *Institutes* distinguishes clearly among (1) the loss of a wild animal upon its escape from our physical control, (2) the abandonment of property, and (3) the loss of property other than a wild animal. While one could (and some did) dispute what it meant for pursuit of a wild animal to be difficult, loss of a wild animal was treated differently from both abandonment and loss of other property, in that the hunter's intention had no effect on their title. All that mattered was that the animal had recovered its natural liberty. The classical rules on recovery of abandoned property were similarly objective: the persistence of the jettisoner in their search, and the refusal of the finder to surrender the goods on request, sufficed to express intention. No speculation about their inner workings at the moment of jettison or finding was necessary. The same cannot be said of post-classical ideas that insinuated themselves into the *Digest*.

3 Ulpian on the Pigs in the Wolf's Jaws (D.41.1.44)

Justinian's *Digest* preserved a case, discussed by Ulpian and Pomponius (second century CE), that tested the classical rules by raising the question of what would happen to property that seemed to be as good as destroyed, but miraculously survived. No one could reasonably intend to recover the property after losing it, and yet, the possibility of recovery presented itself. I quote the extract of Ulpian in full:

> The following case is discussed by Pomponius: When wolves were carrying off pigs from my swineherd, a farmer on a neighboring estate, with some strong and powerful dogs which he kept to protect his own herd, pursued the wolves and snatched the pigs away from them [*eripuit*]; that or the dogs tore them away [*extorserunt*]; but when my swineherd claimed the pigs, the question arose whether the pigs had become the property of their rescuer or remained mine; for, in a way, the dogs got them by hunting. He [Pomponius], however, used to ponder whether, since animals caught on land or sea belong to their captors on regaining their natural freedom, so also things captured from a man's property by wild animals of land or sea cease to be his, when the beasts elude his pursuit. Who indeed can say that what a bird, flying by, takes from my threshing-floor or land or snatches from me myself remains mine? If, then, ownership is so lost, the thing will belong to the first taker on

> being freed from the beast's mouth, just as a fish, wild boar, or a bird, which escapes from our power, will become the property of anyone else who seizes it. But he [again Pomponius] thinks that rather is it the case that the thing remains ours so long as it can be recovered; what he writes about birds, fish, and wild animals, however, is true. He also says that what is lost in a shipwreck does not cease forthwith to be ours; indeed, a person who seizes it will be liable for fourfold its value. And it is certainly preferable to say that what is seized by a wolf remains ours so long as it can be retrieved. If, then, it does so remain, I am of the opinion that even the action for theft will lie; for even if the farmer did not give chase with the intent to steal, though he may have had that intent, nevertheless, when he does not restore on request, he appears guilty of detaining and appropriating. Accordingly, I am of the view that he is liable to both the action for theft and that for production; and the pigs, when produced, can be reclaimed from him by a *vindicatio*.[20]

The best way to explain the difficulties of this case, and Ulpian's solution to it, is to consider the position of the neighbor who retook the pigs, or whose dogs retook them for him.[21] As I see it, he has two arguments.

---

20 D.41.1.44, *Ulpianus libro nono decimo ad edictum*. "Pomponius tractat: cum pastori meo lupi porcos eriperent, hos vicinae villae colonus cum robustis canibus et fortibus, quos pecoris sui gratia pascebat, consecutus lupis eripuit aut canes extorserunt: et cum pastor meus peteret porcos, quaerebatur, utrum eius facti sint porci, qui eripuit, an nostri maneant: nam genere quodam venandi id erant nancti. cogitabat tamen, quemadmodum terra marique capta, cum in suam naturalem laxitatem pervenerant, desinerent eorum esse qui ceperunt, ita ex bonis quoque nostris capta a bestiis marinis et terrestribus desinant nostra esse, cum effugerunt bestiae nostram persecutionem. quis denique manere nostrum dicit, quod avis transvolans ex area aut ex agro nostro transtulit aut quod nobis eripuit? si igitur desinit, si fuerit ore bestiae liberatum, occupantis erit, quemadmodum piscis vel aper vel avis, qui potestatem nostram evasit, si ab alio capiatur, ipsius fit. sed putat potius nostrum manere tamdiu, quamdiu reciperari possit: licet in avibus et piscibus et feris verum sit quod scribit. idem ait, etsi naufragio quid amissum sit, non statim nostrum esse desinere: denique quadruplo teneri eum qui rapuit. et sane melius est dicere et quod a lupo eripitur, nostrum manere, quamdiu recipi possit id quod ereptum est. si igitur manet, ego arbitror etiam furti competere actionem: licet enim non animo furandi fuerit colonus persecutus, quamvis et hoc animo potuerit esse, sed et si non hoc animo persecutus sit, tamen cum reposcenti non reddit, supprimere et intercipere videtur. quare et furti et ad exhibendum teneri eum arbitror et vindicari exhibitos ab eo porcos posse." Translation from Mommsen, Krueger, and Watson, *Digest* (1985), vol. 4, 497–98.

21 The use of the the first person in the fragment indicates that the pigs were not, in fact, the property of the swineherd. The speaker is apparently the owner of the pigs, and the

4 The Neighbor's Two Arguments

4.1 *The Wildness of the Pigs*

The first argument available to the neighbor is that the pigs themselves are wild animals that have recovered their natural liberty in—of all places—the wolf's jaws. As wild animals, they belong to the first taker as soon as they recover their natural liberty by *any* means, or lose the *animus revertendi* to a particular place.[22] It is the weaker of the neighbor's two arguments, but it is still a point worth considering. Ulpian calls the pigs in question *porci*, a word best translated as "pigs," as opposed to *apri*, which means "wild boar."[23] A passage on cattle thieves (also attributed to Ulpian) lists *porci* alongside goats and ewes.[24] Unlike *porci*, *apri* were definitely wild. Other uses of the word *aper* in the *Digest* confirm this, though perhaps we need only think of the Uffizi boar.[25]

However, external evidence supports the neighbor's case. In his study of animals in Roman legal texts, Grant McLeod cited three passages, one of them juristic, that attest to the difficulty the Romans had classifying pigs as wild or tame. A passage attributed to Gaius (D.9.2.2.2) notes that it had been asked whether pigs (here, *sues*) should take the name of *pecus*.[26] Gaius reports the jurist Labeo (early first century CE) saying that they should, but it is telling that the question had to be asked at all. McLeod's non-juristic passages show why. In his *Res Rusticae*, Varro (116–27 BCE) called pigs a kind of "wild livestock (*pecudes ferae*)."[27] Pliny (23–79 CE) wrote in his *Naturalis Historia* that "no other kind (*genus*) of animal is so easily crossed with the wild variety. Their offspring used in the past to be called 'hybrids' (*hybridae*) or 'half-wild' (*semiferi*)."[28] As McLeod noted, the passage of Pliny suggests that the ability to cross-breed put *apri* and *porci* in the same *genus*; yet the behavior of pigs, even the tamer variety, did not suggest to the Romans complete domestication. The

swineherd his employee or tenant. For simplicity's sake, I will refer to the pigs as belonging to the swineherd.

22 Cf. D.41.1.5.5.

23 *Thesaurus linguae Latinae* (Berlin: de Gruyter, 2006), s.v. *aper*.

24 D.47.14.1.2. See *Vocabvlarivm ivrisprvdentiae romanae* (Berolini, de Gruyter, 1903–), s.v. *porca, porcus*.

25 David Hughes, "*Furtum Ferarum Bestiarum*," *Irish Jurist* 9, no. 1 (1974): 187 n. 17, with references; see esp. D.9.2.29.6.

26 Grant McLeod, "Wild and Tame Animals and Birds in Roman Law," in Peter Birks, ed. *New Perspectives in the Roman Law of Property* (Oxford: Clarendon Press, 1989): 176. Cf. Hughes, "*Furtum*," 186–87.

27 *Res Rusticae* 2.1.5. Translation given at McLeod, "Wild and Tame," 173.

28 *Naturalis Historia* 8.79.213. Translation given at McLeod, "Wild and Tame," 173.

archaeological evidence indicates that the prevalent pig breed in Italy for most of the Roman period was "wild-boar-like," small and bristled, and, importantly, left to forage in the woods for food.[29] These pigs seem to have been allowed to wander more or less freely. Should they have wandered into a wolf's jaws, perhaps they belonged to the first (human) taker.

4.2 *The Wildness of the Wolf*

The second argument available to the neighbor is that put forward by Pomponius via Ulpian: "Who indeed can say that what a bird, flying by, takes from my threshing-floor or land or snatches from me myself remains mine?" In this case, the wildness of the wolf is the decisive fact.[30] Even if the pigs are not wild by nature, at the moment they entered the wolf's jaws, they fell under its control, and no one will deny that the wolf is a wild and dangerous animal. By this argument, the swineherd's claim to his former chattel goes no further than his power to deprive a hungry wolf of its lunch.

Ulpian made what seems to be a conclusive argument against this (D.10.2.8.2):

> Pomponius also thinks that if any of our livestock is carried off by a wild beast, it is included in the action for dividing an inheritance if it escapes [*evaserit*] from the beast; for, he says, the better view is that anything carried off by a wolf or other wild beast does not cease to be our property so long as it has not been eaten by the beast.[31]

At first glance, this seems to settle the case in the swineherd's favor. However, the neighbor might respond by arguing that the pigs did not merely *evadere* the wolf, but were saved from it, either by the neighbor himself or by his dogs. This might be what Ulpian had in mind when he lingered over the exact means by which the pigs got out of the wolf's jaws: either the neighbor snatched them away (*eripuit*) or the dogs tore them away (*extorserunt*). This was more than mere evasion: it was the active investment of work—at great danger—on

29 Michael MacKinnon, "High on the Hog: Linking Zooarchaeological, Literary, and Artistic Data for Pig Breeds in Roman Italy," *American Journal of Archaeology* 105, no. 4 (2001), 664–65.

30 Cf. Hughes, "*Furtum*," 187.

31 *Ulpianus libro nono decimo ad edictum*. "Sed et si quid de pecoribus nostris a bestia ereptum sit, venire in familiae erciscundae iudicium putat, si feram evaserit: nam magis esse, ut non desinat nostrum esse, inquit quod a lupo eripitur vel alia bestia, tamdiu, quamdiu ab eo non fuerit consumptum." Translation from Mommsen, Krueger, and Watson, *Digest* (1985), vol. 1, 310.

the part of the neighbor and his animals. The choice of verb could also tell us whether the pigs had been destroyed beyond recovery or not: we may entertain greater hope of the survival of pigs "snatched away" by a human being than of those "torn away" by hunting dogs.

5 Ulpian's Decision, and the Question of Theft

Ulpian granted ownership of the pigs to the swineherd based on an analogy to jettisoned goods. *Digest* 41.1.44 does not address the question of the wildness of the pigs, and gives surprisingly short shrift to the argument based on the wildness of the wolf. Ulpian's reasoning seems to be that the objective fact of the pigs' survival is what counts: so long as they survive, they remain the property of the swineherd.[32]

The real puzzle of the case for Ulpian was whether the finder could be held for theft. Ulpian's logic follows that of the classical rule on jettison to the conclusion that the neighbor had indeed committed theft. The neighbor could exhibit theftuous intent by refusing to surrender the pigs, even if he did not think himself to be stealing them at the moment he (or the dogs) took them from the wolf. By refusing to return them to the swineherd upon request, he exhibited the *animus furandi*. This argument, as we have seen, presupposes a very broad notion of *contrectatio*, illicit handling—one that extends far beyond the intention of the taker at the moment of taking.[33] The language with which Ulpian deems the neighbor guilty of theft does not suggest complete confidence: *supprimere et intercipere videtur*, "he appears guilty of detaining and appropriating." Ulpian emphasizes that he is expressing his own view on this (*ego arbitror etiam furti competere actionem*), and does not say how Pomponius answered the question of *furtum*.[34]

In conclusion, the neighbor would have had no choice but to argue against Ulpian's analogy between the wolf and the storm-tossed sea. He would have had to stake his claim to the pigs on the status of the wolf as an *animal ferae naturae*, and a dangerous one at that. Perhaps his case would not have been

32 Cf. Hughes, "*Furtum*" 187, with a similar argument.

33 I regret that I do not have more to say about the medieval jurists here; Accursius' gloss on D.41.1.44, *videtur* takes up the issue of *contrectatio*. I accessed Accursius' gloss online via the digitization at [*Corpus iuris civilis*] … *commentariis Accursii, scholiis Contii, paratitlis Cuiacii … novae accesserunt ad ipsum Accursium Dionysii Gothofredi, I. C. notae, …* (Lugduni: Horatius Cardon, 1604), https://nrs.lib.harvard.edu/urn-3:hls.libr:3491162.

34 Cf. Hughes, "*Furtum*" 186.

hopeless. It is clear that Ulpian and Pomponius had misgivings about the previous owner's claim to property that fell under the power of a wild animal. A pig that a wolf takes in its power might belong to no one—until someone goes to the trouble of taking it away from the wolf. It helped this argument that the pigs may not have been totally domesticated to begin with.

If he could not retain ownership of the pigs, the neighbor might have had better luck arguing against the accusation of theft. He could claim with some justification that he regarded pigs in a wolf's jaws as abandoned by their owner, and, in any case, his accuser would have had to rely on a very broad notion of *contrectatio*.

6 Grotius on Wild Animals, Lost and Abandoned Property

Hugo Grotius' treatment of lost and abandoned property differs from Ulpian's in interesting ways. Though Grotius too was interested in how theft could arise in cases of lost property, I will suggest that his departures from Roman juristic doctrine originated outside of the work of the civilians. Grotius used non-Roman sources to impose a different kind of obligation on the finder of lost property. I will close by suggesting what Grotius' ideas about lost property reveal about the theory of private property in the natural law school.

7 Grotius on Lost Property in a Wild Animal (IBP 2.8.3)

Before seeing how Grotius handled the pig in the wolf's jaws, we ought to note that he had a different understanding of *animalia ferae naturae* than did Ulpian or Justinian. While his position on the initial capture of wild animals basically agrees with that of Justinian's *Institutes*, Grotius' rule on the loss and recovery of wild animals in nature is more complicated:[35]

35 *De iure belli ac pacis* (hereafter, IBP) 2.8.3. "Feras simul atque naturalem libertatem recipiunt, nostras esse desinere aiunt Romani iurisconsulti: atqui in rebus omnibus aliis a possessione quod incipit dominium, non ideo amissa possessione [sic] amittitur; imo ius dat etiam ad repetendam possessionem. Res autem nostras alius a nobis auferat, an ipsae sese, ut servus fugitivus, non multum refert. Quare verius est non per se amitti dominium, eo quod ferae custodiam evaserint, sed ex probabili conjectura, quod ob difficillimam persecutionem eas pro derelictis habere credamur, praesertim cum internosci quae nostrae fuerint ab aliis non possint. Sed haec coniectura per alias coniecturas elidi potest, ut si addita sunt ferae γνωρίσματα, sive crepundia, qualia scimus habuisse cervos quosdam et accipitres, atque inde agnitos et dominis redditos. Requiritur autem corporalis

> The Roman jurists say that wild beasts cease to belong to us at the moment they regain their natural liberty: and in all other things, though ownership begins with possession, it is not lost with the loss of possession; rather, it gives a right to the recovery of possession. Whether another person takes our things away from us, or the things [take away] themselves, as in the case of a fugitive slave, makes little difference. Wherefore it is more truly said that ownership is not lost by the very fact that the beasts escaped our custody, but from the probable conjecture, that we are believed to regard them as abandoned on account of the extreme difficulty of pursuit, especially when those [beasts] which are ours cannot be discerned from others. But this conjecture may be destroyed by other conjectures, as by putting γνωρίσματα [marks] or *crepundia* upon them, as has been often done to stags and hawks, whereby they have been known, and returned to their owners. However, some kind of corporal possession is required for the acquisition of ownership; and therefore it does not suffice to have wounded [the animal], as was rightly decided against Trebatius.

The logic of this passage is very hard to follow. Grotius first distinguishes wild beasts from all other kinds of property, just as the Roman jurists did. As Grotius says, we can retain ownership of most kinds of things even after losing physical control of them. However, contrary to what Grotius says, the Roman jurists differentiated wild animals from all other kinds of property precisely because wild animals do not follow this principle. According to JI.2.1.12, we lose ownership of a wild animal as soon as we lose physical control of it, regardless of whether we hope or expect to get possession back.

Grotius' qualification, that the hunter lost ownership on account of the "probable conjecture that we [the hunter] are believed to regard them as abandoned," is thus a strange departure from Justinian's rule. It suggests that the animal is no longer ours, not because it is beyond our physical reach, but because we so despair of recapturing it that we have lost the will to own it. In Grotius' view, the despondent hunter has not so much lost the animal as abandoned it.

---

quaedam possessio ad dominium apiscendum; atque ideo vulnerasse non sufficit, ut recte contra Trebatium placuit." The Latin text comes from pp. 232–33 of the first edition: Hugo Grotius, *Hugonis Grotii De iure belli ac pacis libri tres. In quibus ius naturæ & gentium: item iuris publici pacecipua explicantur* (Parisiis: Apud Nicolaum Buon, in via Iacobaea, sub signis s. Claudii, & hominis Siluestris, 1625). All English translations of Grotius are mine, but I have sometimes consulted Hugo Grotius, *The Rights of War and Peace*, Natural Law and Enlightenment Classics (Indianapolis: Liberty Fund, 2005).

The hunter can retain ownership merely by giving sufficient signs of their intent to own. Grotius' words for these signs are *indicia*, γνωρίσματα, and *crepundia*. Liddell, Scott, and Jones' *English-Greek Lexicon* translates γνωρίσματα as "marks," "tokens," or "objects by which lost children could be found."[36] *Crepundia* originally referred to rattles given to infants as toys, or, more darkly, rattles given to exposed infants as *insignia* or *indicia*.[37] If the last of these senses is what Grotius had in mind, his use of these words suggests still more strongly that he was thinking of abandonment.

Grotius' early commentators noticed his departure from Justinian's rule, and took him to task for it. In his comment on IBP 2.8.3, Caspar Ziegler (1621–1690) wrote,

> But the reason for the difference [between wild animals and other kinds of property] is clear and perspicuous. For wild animals become ours by losing their natural liberty. Therefore they cease to be ours through the recovery of their natural liberty, and in consequence ownership of them is judged to consist in actual possession. But the other things [that Grotius mentions] do not have this natural liberty [references omitted]. So, because the owner knows that the nature of these animals is wild, he cannot otherwise keep his ownership intact, than by keeping diligent custody of them [...] But if he should lose custody, and the beast should escape, since in this case he knows well that his ownership ceases, the beast not undeservedly belongs to the taker, even in the forum of conscience, even though the taker have notice from bells or some other means that the beast previously belonged to Titius or Seius.[38]

---

36 Henry George Liddell, *A Greek-English Lexicon*, A new ed., rev. and augm. by Henry Stuart Jones (Oxford: Clarendon Press, 1951), s.v. γνωρίσμα.

37 See *Thesaurus Linguae Latinae*, s.v. *crepundia* 1a.

38 "Sed ratio differentiae clara est et perspicua. Ferae enim per amissionem libertatis fiunt nostrae. Ergo et per recuperationem libertatis nostrae esse desinunt, et per consequens dominium earum in actuali possessione consistere censetur. At reliquae res non habent hanc naturalem libertatem, Harprecht *ad* §. 12. *J. de R. D.* Franzk. *d.l.* Quin quia novit dominus feram istorum animalium naturam, non potest aliter dominium suum salvum habere, nisi per diligentem custodiam, et exhinc igitur eius animi esse debet, ut tamdiu dominus esse velit, quamdiu custodit, aut saltem in eo est, ut custodiat. Quod si intermiserit custodiam, et fera elapsa fuerit, quia in hunc eventum dominium suum desinere bene novit, fera non immerito fit noviter occupantis, etiam in foro conscientiae, utcunque hic feram Titii aut Seji antea fuisse ex crepundiis aut aliunde notum habeat." Caspar Ziegler, Johann Reinhold Dulssecker, and Hugo Grotius, *Casparis Ziegleri J.C. ... In Hugonis Grotii De jure belli ac pacis libros quae naturae et gentium ius explicavit notae et animadversiones subitariae* (Argentorati: Jo. Reinh. Dulsseckeri, 1706), https://catalog.hathitrust.org/Record/009334489, 316. My translation. For biographical details on Ziegler,

As Ziegler's comment suggests, Grotius was moving away from the two standards of Justinian, to wit, the wild/domesticated distinction, and the recovery of the animals' natural liberty. In Grotius' view, initial capture of a wild animal created a durable claim of ownership, one that could survive the loss of possession as long as the captor retained the intent to own, and made clear signs to that effect.[39]

8 Grotius on *Digest* 41.1.44 (IBP 2.4.5.1)

Grotius' citation of D.41.1.44 appears in a passage on the power of silence or inaction to express our will. He is arguing that if we make no sign of our intention to recover a piece of property, that in itself is a sign that we no longer consider the thing ours. What he means to prove by way of the pig in the wolf's jaws is hard to say:

> Considered morally, under "things done" fall also things not done, circumstances depending. So, he who, being present and informed, remains silent seems to have consented, unless circumstances show that he was prevented from speaking by fear or some other chance event. So, that thing is judged to be lost the hope of recovering which is all but gone [*cuius recuperandi spes proiicitur*], like pigs taken by a wolf; and, according to Ulpian, those things that we lose in a shipwreck cease to be ours not immediately, but when they cannot be recovered, that is, when it is not possible that anyone should believe it to be the intention [*animum*] of the owner to retain them: when no indications [*indicia*] of such a will remain. For if people were sent out to inquire about the thing, if a reward [μηνύτεον] were promised, it would be judged otherwise.[40]

---

see "Ziegler, Caspar" in *Deutsche Biographische Enzyklopädie Online*, Rudolf Vierhaus, ed. (Berlin, New York: K. G. Saur, 2011), available with a subscription through https://doi.org/10.1515/dbe. See also Pufendorf *De iure naturae et gentium*, 4.6, §12, p. 542 at *Samuelis Pufendorfii de jure naturae et gentium libri octo, cum annotatis Johannis Nicolai Hertii*, j[uris]c[onsul]ti, *editio nova* … (Francofurti ad Moenum: Friderici Knochii et filii, typis Dieterici Caesaris Mulleri, 1716), https://catalog.hathitrust.org/Record/001756466.

39 Raphaëlle Soffe also discusses the difficulties presented by IBP 2.8.3 in her unpublished paper on D.41.1.44 (p. 16).

40 IBP 2.4.5.1, p. 167 of the 1625 edition (*supra*, n. 35). "Sub factis autem moraliter veniunt et non facta, considerata cum debitis circumstantiis. Sic qui sciens et praesens tacet videtur consentire: nisi circumstantiae ostendant, quominus loquatur, metu eum vel alio casu impediri. Sic amissum censetur id cuius recuperandi spes proiicitur, ut porcos a lupo raptos, et quae naufragio amittimus nostra esse desinere ait Ulpianus, non statim, sed ubi

Grotius seems to side with Ulpian and the swineherd on the question of ownership. He implies that the swineherd's search for the pigs constitutes *indicia* of the will to own them, which preclude abandonment. But his reasoning leaves even more of an argument to the neighbor than did Ulpian's. Yes, the swineherd signaled his intention to recover the pigs by seeking them out. But the neighbor could easily contend that "it is not possible that anyone should believe it the intention of the owner to recover them." It would have been a more than reasonable assumption—a probable conjecture—to suppose that the owner of pigs in a wolf's jaws had given up hope.

On the question of theft, Grotius is silent at IBP 2.4.5.1. He avoids entirely the difficulties arising from the notion of *contrectatio*, which gave Ulpian and Pomponius pause. To settle the issue, I have to turn to another chapter of the *De iure belli ac pacis*. I submit that Grotius would have held the neighbor liable for theft, but his reasoning would have seemed very strange to Ulpian, and, ultimately, his reasoning is the important thing. It shows that Grotius was willing to depart from the Roman law of obligations in order to put the liability for theft on surer footing.

IBP 2.10 is entitled, *De obligatione quae ex dominio oritur*, "On the obligation that arises from ownership."[41] In this chapter, Grotius argues that the finder of another's goods should do everything possible to restore them to their owner. Included in this obligation was the duty to announce the discovery of the goods: "He is held to indicate, that another person may recover what is his own."[42] This rule followed from the natural community of goods prior to the establishment of private property: "For if the power of ownership went no further than that things should be returned to their owners upon request, the keeping of property [*custodia*] would be too costly."[43]

The first edition of the *De iure belli ac pacis* cites very few authorities to support this claim. One of them is a passage of Ulpian in the *Digest* that says

recipi non possunt, id est ubi non est cur credatur aliquis animum domini retinere: ubi nulla talis voluntatis indicia exstant. Nam si missi essent qui rem inquirerent, si promissum μηνύτεον, aliud esset iudiciandum."

41 See pp. 253–60 of the 1625 edition.

42 "Indicare tenetur, ut alter recipere suum possit," p. 254 of the 1625 edition.

43 "Nam sicut in rerum communium statu observanda erat aequalitas quaedam, ut huic non minus quam alteri rebus communibus uti liceret; ita introducto dominio haec quasi societas inter dominos contracta est, ut qui rem alienam in sua haberet potestate, eam domino redderet. Nam si dominii ea tantum fuisset vis, ut poscenti domino reddenda res esset, nimis sumtuosa custodia. Neque his consideratut [sic] bona quis an mala fide rei possessionem nactus sit: alia enima obligatio est ex delicto, alia ex re." From p. 254 of the 1625 edition.

that it is customary (*solent plerique*) to announce the discovery of lost goods.[44] Ulpian might have been suggesting that the custom is a morally upright one to which all people should adhere. But even that does not quite say what Grotius wants it to say, namely, that the finder has a legal obligation to announce the discovery. Such a duty made little sense within the context of the Roman law of obligations. It is well known that the Roman jurists did little to develop unjust enrichment as an independent source of obligation.[45] They generally hesitated to recognize an obligation where a contractual or delictual legal relationship between two parties was lacking. An obligation could not arise from a relationship between the finder and the property itself; for Ulpian, there had to be a second party at the opposite end of the chain—the *iuris vinculum*—between her-/himself and the finder.[46] Grotius may not have been as committed to this sense of *obligatio* as Ulpian had been.

9 Another View of Abandonment and Presumption

I have shown that the Roman law of lost property and of wild animals struggled with the question of why the finder of lost property in a wolf's jaws should be liable for theft. I would like to close by showing how Grotius and his contemporaries transmitted a different idea of lost property into the early natural law school.

By imposing on the finder of lost goods a duty to announce their discovery, Grotius incorporated into the law of nature what Ulpian had treated as no more than a moral obligation. This makes good sense in light of his sources. In an article on Grotius' doctrine of unjust enrichment, Robert Feenstra observed

44 D.47.2.43.8. *Ulpianus libro quadragensimo ad Sabinum*: "Proinde videamus, si nescit cuius esset, sic tamen tulit quasi redditurus ei qui desiderasset vel qui ostendisset rem suam, an furti obligetur. et non puto obligari eum. solent plerique etiam hoc facere, ut libellum proponant continentem invenisse se et redditurum ei qui desideraverit: hi ergo ostendunt non furandi animo se fecisse. Quid ergo, si εὕρετρα quae dicunt petat? nec hic videtur furtum facere, etsi non probe petat aliquid." Mommsen, Krueger, and Watson, *Digest* (1985), vol. 4, 747.

45 For this topic in Grotius, see Robert Feenstra, "Grotius' Doctrine of Unjust Enrichment as a Source of Obligation: its Origin and its Influence in Roman-Dutch Law," in *Unjust Enrichment: The Comparative Legal History of the Law of Restitution*, ed. Eltjo J. H. Schrage (Berlin: Duncker & Humblot, 1995), 197–236. See esp. pp. 209–10 for IBP 2.10.

46 Cf. JI.3.13pr: "obligatio est iuris vinculum, quo necessitate adstringimur alicuius solvendae rei secundum nostrae civitatis iura."

that Grotius derived his *obligatio ex dominio* from the later scholastics.[47] Grotius could have reached back even further. Consider Deuteronomy 22.1–3:

> You shall not watch your neighbor's ox or sheep straying away and ignore them; you shall take them back to their owner. [2]If the owner does not reside near you or you do not know who the owner is, you shall bring it to your own house, and it shall remain with you until the owner claims it; then you shall return it. [3]You shall do the same with a neighbor's donkey; you shall do the same with a neighbor's garment; and you shall do the same with anything else that your neighbor loses and you find. You may not withold your help.[48]

This is a reformulation of a similar passage on lost animals in Exodus.[49] It is clearly dealing with domesticated animals. For my purposes, its interest lies in the combination of a negative prohibition with a positive command: not only must the finder not ignore the lost animal, but they are obligated to restore it to its owner. The obligation arises from the finding of the thing itself.

The obligation arising from finding continued to interest natural law theorists. Fifteen years after the first edition of Grotius' *De iure belli ac pacis* appeared, the English scholar, lawyer, and statesman John Selden (1584–1654) published his own study of natural law, entitled *De iure naturali et gentium iuxta disciplinam Ebraeorum*, "On natural law and the law of nations according to the teaching of the Hebrews." In it Selden displayed his mastery of Hebrew and his formidable knowledge of Talmud and rabbinical law. He discussed lost and abandoned property in the fourth chapter of Book Six. His discussion makes no explicit distinction between wild and domesticated animals. However, as he reported, Jewish law did distinguish lost objects whose discovery had to be announced from lost objects that belonged to the first taker. Selden's source for this distinction is the *Mishneh Torah*, or *Code of Jewish Law*, by the Jewish philosopher Moses Maimonides (1135–1204). Selden quoted the following passage of Maimonides' *Code* (in Latin translation):

47 Feenstra, "Unjust Enrichment," 209.

48 Translation from *The New Oxford Annotated Bible: New Revised Standard Version: With the Apocrypha: An Ecumenical Study Bible*, 5th ed. (Oxford: Oxford University Press, 2018), 285–86.

49 The passage of Exodus (23.4–5) reads "enemy's" where Deuteronomy reads "neighbor's." See *New Oxford Annotated Bible*, 116.

> 2. The following rule applies to lost property: As soon as any article with no mark of identification—such as a single nail or a single needle or a coin—is lost and its owner becomes aware that it is lost, it is presumed that the owner has abandoned hope of its recovery, for he cannot identify it to retrieve it, and it therefore belongs to the finder. 3. If, however, any property has a mark of identification, such as a garment or an animal, it is presumed that the owner has not abandoned hope of its recovery, for he expects to retrieve it by stating its identification marks. The finder must therefore advertise it unless he knows that the owner has abandoned hope of its recovery. Thus, if he hears the owner say, "What a misfortune that I've suffered a loss of money," or use a similar expression which indicates that the owner has abandoned hope of its recovery, the lost property in question belongs to the finder. 4. Similarly, if one finds identifiable property in the sea or in a river or in some other location, or in a place where the majority of the inhabitants are heathen, it is presumed that the owner abandoned hope of its recovery the moment it fell, and consequently it belongs to the finder even if he has not heard the owner actually abandon hope of its recovery.[50]

We can make three observations. First, Maimonides distinguished between marked and unmarked objects: signs of the will to own suffice to preserve the right of ownership, even in a lost animal. Grotius too emphasized the marks of ownership over the nature of the animal itself. Second, the power of presumption is strong here. Both the marks on the object (or lack thereof) and the circumstances in which it was found entitle the finder to make a probable conjecture about the hope and expectation of the owner. In the case of unmarked objects, a presumption that the owner despairs of recovery suffices to remove the right of ownership. Third, in the case of marked objects, the obligation of the finder to announce the discovery of lost property provides a neat solution to the problem of the theft of the pigs in the wolf's jaws. It forces the finder to disclaim the *animus furandi* proactively, and to declare the intention to restore the property to its owner. The finder's intentions are made clear immediately after the finding, with no prompting from the owner.

50 Translation from Moses Maimonides, *The Code of Maimonides, Book 11* (*The Book of Torts*), trans. Hyman Klein (New Haven: Yale University Press, 1949), 140. I have also made use of Michael J. Broyde and Michael Hecht, "The Return of Lost Property According to Jewish and Common Law: A Comparison," *Journal of Law and Religion* 12, no. 1 (1995–1996): 225–54.

10 Conclusion

At the beginning of this essay, I posed three questions about the loss of property. First, do the owner's intention and expectation at the moment they lose possession of the goods determine whether they retain ownership? Second, do the finder's intention and expectation at the moment they find the goods determine whether they commit theft? These two questions raised a third: How do we determine retroactively what the intentions and expectations of both owners and finders are? The classical Roman jurists sought objective answers to these questions. In the case of wild animals, the nature of the animal and the captor's physical control over it determined title. In the case of other kinds of property, the owner's continued search for lost goods, and the finder's refusal to hand them over upon request, answered the questions of ownership and theft, respectively.

The pigs in the wolf's jaws tested these objective standards. Even if Ulpian saw to it that the standards held good in his solution to the case, he betrayed some misgivings about them in the effort. On the questions of ownership and theft of the pigs, the neighbor had a better case than Ulpian let on. A confusing passage in the *Digest* suggests that the Justinianic compilers also saw the shortcomings of the objective rules, or at least saw the appeal of an alternative based on presumption.

Grotius was less committed to these rules than was Ulpian. His doctrine of occupancy virtually erased the difference between losing a wild animal in nature and abandoning property. His citation of the pigs in the wolf's jaws is more equivocal than Ulpian's on the issue of ownership. When he settled on a rule to resolve disputes about theft of lost property, he took the rule from outside of the Roman legal tradition altogether. The duty to announce the discovery of lost property has a solid foundation in biblical law, and became an important part of the Jewish law of lost property, but makes little sense within the Roman scheme of obligations. The obligation to announce was neither contractual nor delictual, but, as Ulpian himself suggested, it was clearly a moral duty. Grotius imported that moral duty into the law of nature, as Selden would soon after him, and Pufendorf after Selden.[51]

In summary, Grotius was far more willing to allow hunters, jettisoners, and finders to send clear signals of their intentions, and to suppose that other hunters, etc., could and should correctly interpret those signals. The reliance on presumption and interpretation of *indicia* required shared ideas in nature about

51 See Pufendorf's *De iure naturae et gentium*, 4.6, §12, p. 543.

acquiring and losing property. In this respect, Grotius' treatment of lost and abandoned goods bears a meaningful resemblance to theories of private property in which, to borrow Colden's words, manucaption was only one of "many means to declare the intention of exclusively appropriating that, which was before in a state of nature." It makes sense that Locke's theory of appropriation, grounded as it was in expression of the owner's *animus*, should have pursued a line of thinking that also ran through arguments about lost and abandoned property. The question of *re*capture is, after all, a critical test for the labor theory: If something escapes my grasp after I have made it mine, is it still mine?[52] I submit that Grotius' use of the pigs in the wolf's jaws is one chapter in the prehistory of the labor theory, one of the last chapters before Locke introduced the theory itself into European legal philosophy.

Acknowledgments

This paper began as a series of conversations with Raphaëlle Soffe; reading and discussing her unpublished paper on *Digest* 41.1.44 stimulated my thinking on the subject. Elizabeth Kamali gave thoughtful and detailed feedback on a first draft (which led to substantial revisions), and, together with Saskia Lettmaier and Nikitas Hatzimihail, invited me to contribute to this volume. Tamara Morsel-Eisenberg gave me generous guidance on points of Jewish law. Kenny Yu read a draft and gave me guidance on matters of both substance and form. I am delighted to thank all of the above. I remain solely responsible for any errors contained herein.

Bibliography

Broyde, Michael J., and Michael Hecht. "The Return of Lost Property According to Jewish and Common Law: A Comparison," *Journal of Law and Religion* 12, no. 1 (1995–1996): 225–54.

Caines, George. *New York Term Reports of Cases Argued and Determined in the Supreme Court of that State*, vol. 3. New York: Isaac Riley & Co., 1806.

52 For a similar observation, see John Salter, "Hugo Grotius: Property and Consent," *Political Theory* 29, no. 4 (2001), 545–46.

[*Corpus iuris civilis*] ... *commentariis Accursii, scholiis Contii, paratitlis Cuiacii ... novae accesserunt ad ipsum Accursium Dionysii Gothofredi, I. C. notae,* .... Lugduni: Horatius Cardon, 1604. https://nrs.lib.harvard.edu/urn-3:hls.libr:3491162.

Donahue, Charles Jr. "Noodt, Titius, and the natural law school: The occupation of wild animals and the intersection of property and tort." In *Satura Roberto Feenstra: sexagesimum quintum annum aetatis complenti ab alumnis collegis amicis oblata*, edited by J.A. Ankum, J.E. Spruit, and F.B.J. Wubbe, 609–29. Fribourg: Éditions Universitaires, 1985.

Donahue, Charles Jr. "*Animalia ferae naturae*: Rome, Bologna, Leyden, Oxford and Queen's County, N.Y." In *Studies in Roman Law in Memory of A. Arthur Schiller*, edited by Roger Bagnall and William V. Harris, 39–63. Leiden: Brill, 1986.

Feenstra, Robert. "Grotius' Doctrine of Unjust Enrichment as a Source of Obligation." In *Unjust Enrichment: The Comparative Legal History of the Law of Restitution*, edited by Eltjo J. H. Schrage, 197–236. Berlin: Duncker and Humboldt, 1995.

Fernandez, Angela. *Pierson v. Post: The Hunt for the Fox: Law and Professionalization in American Legal Culture*. Cambridge: Cambridge University Press, 2018.

Fernandez, Angela. "The Lost Record of Pierson v. Post, the Famous Fox Case." *Law and History Review* 27, no. 1 (2009): 149–78. https://doi.org/10.1017/S0738248000001693.

Grotius, Hugo. *Hugonis Grotii De iure belli ac pacis libri tres. In quibus ius naturæ & gentium: item iuris publici paæcipua explicantur*. Parisiis: Apud Nicolaum Buon, in via Iacobaea, sub signis s. Claudii, & hominis Siluestris, 1625.

Grotius, Hugo. *The Rights of War and Peace*. Natural Law and Enlightenment Classics. Indianapolis, Ind.: Liberty Fund, 2005.

Hughes, David. "*Furtum Ferarum Bestiarum*," *Irish Jurist* 9, no.1 (1974): 184–90.

Jolowicz, Herbert Felix. (*Justinian*) *Digest XLVII. 2 "De Furtis."* Cambridge: Cambridge University Press, 1940.

Kaser, Max. *Das römische Privatrecht*. 2., Neubearbeitete Aufl. Handbuch der Altertumswissenschaft 10. Abt., 3. T., 3. Bd. München: Beck, 1971.

Lenel, Otto. *Das Edictum perpetuum: ein Versuch zu seiner Wiederherstellung*. 2. Neudruck der 3. Aufl. Leipzig 1927. Aalen: Scientia Verlag, 1974.

Liddell, Henry George. *A Greek-English Lexicon*. A new edition, revised and augmented by Henry Stuart Jones. Oxford: Clarendon Press, 1951.

Locke, John. *Two Treatises of Government*. Edited by Peter Laslett. Cambridge Texts in the History of Political Thought. Cambridge: Cambridge University Press, 1960, repr. 1988.

MacKinnon, Michael. "High on the Hog: Linking Zooarchaeological, Literary, and Artistic Data for Pig Breeds in Roman Italy." *American Journal of Archaeology* 105, no. 4 (2001): 649–73.

Maimonides, Moses. *The Code of Maimonides, Book 11* (*The Book of Torts*). Translated by Hyman Klein. New Haven: Yale University Press, 1949.

McLeod, Grant. "Wild and Tame Animals and Birds in Roman Law." In *New Perspectives in the Roman Law of Property: Essays for Barry Nicholas*, edited by Peter Birks, 169–76. Oxford: Clarendon Press, 1989.

Mommsen, Theodor, and Paul Krueger, eds. *Corpus Iuris Civilis*. 21st ed. Dublin: Weidmann, 1970.

Mommsen, Theodor, Paul Krueger, and Alan Watson, eds. *The Digest of Justinian*. 4 vols. Philadelphia: University of Pennsylvania Press, 1985. Rev. English translation, 1998.

Moyle, John Baron. *The Institutes of Justinian*. 5th ed. Oxford: Clarendon Press, 1913.

Pufendorf, Samuel. *Samuelis Pufendorfii de jure naturae et gentium libri octo, cum annotatis Johannis Nicolai Hertii, j*[uris]c[onsul]*ti, editio nova* .... Francofurti ad Moenum: Friderici Knochii et filii, typis Dieterici Caesaris Mulleri, 1716. https://catalog.hathitrust.org/Record/001756466.

Rose, Carol M. "Possession as the Origin of Property." *The University of Chicago Law Review* 52, no. 1 (1985): 73–88.

Salter, John. "Hugo Grotius: Property and Consent." *Political Theory* 29, no. 4 (2001): 537–55.

Selden, John, and Johann Heinrich Boecler. *Joannis Seldeni De jure naturali et gentium juxta disciplinam Ebræorum libri septem*. Wittenbergae: apud Godofredum Zimmermannum, 1712. https://catalog.hathitrust.org/Record/009035397.

The New Oxford Annotated Bible: New Revised Standard Version: With the Apocrypha: An Ecumenical Study Bible. 5th ed. Oxford: Oxford University Press, 2018.

Thesaurus linguae Latinae. Berlin: de Gruyter, 2006.

Tuck, Richard, and Thomas Hobbes. *Hobbes: Leviathan: Revised Student Edition*. Cambridge Texts in the History of Political Thought. Cambridge: Cambridge University Press, 1996.

Vocabvlarivm ivrisprvdentiae romanae. Berolini: Typis et impensis G. Reimeri, 1903.

Watson, Alan. "The Definition of *Furtum* and the Trichotomy," *Tijdschrift voor rechtsgeschiedenis*, 28, no. 2 (1960): 197–210.

Watson, Alan, ed. *The Digest of Justinian*. Rev. English ed. Philadelphia: University of Pennsylvania Press, 1998.

Ziegler, Caspar, Johann Reinhold Dulssecker, and Hugo Grotius. *Casparis Ziegleri J.C. .... In Hugonis Grotii De jure belli ac pacis libros quae naturae et gentium ius explicavit notae et animadversiones subitariae*. Argentorati: Jo. Reinh. Dulsseckeri, 1706. https://catalog.hathitrust.org/Record/009334489.

"Ziegler, Caspar." In *Deutsche Biographische Enzyklopädie Online*, edited by Rudolf Vierhaus. Berlin, New York: K. G. Saur, 2011. https://www.degruyter.com/database/dbe/html?lang=en.

CHAPTER 5

"For the Sake of Mental Health and Mutual Peace": The *Transactio*-Agreement in Early Modern Law and Theology

Wim Decock

1 Introduction

Drawing on Roman law and medieval canon law, jurists from the fifteenth through the eighteenth centuries generally considered *transactio* as the agreement by which parties settle their conflict out-of-court by mutually "giving and taking" something with regards to the subject of a dispute or a lawsuit, the outcome of which is uncertain. For example, if parties disagreed about the amount of a damage claim, they could decide to reach a mutual agreement whereby the injured party accepted a certain but potentially lower compensation than he or she could perhaps have obtained in court, while the defendant accepted to pay damages immediately rather than speculating on a dismissal or a lower sentence by the court. Given its huge practical relevance as a consensual means of settling conflicts, it is small wonder that there was a lot of debate on *transactiones* in the early modern civilian tradition. However, the attention paid to the dynamic of settlement agreements by moral theologians and canon lawyers, in particular, is even more striking. Although following in the footsteps of a much older tradition, their renewed interest in the *transactio*-agreement might be revealing of broader developments in law and society in early modern Europe. At a time when jurisdictional power massively shifted from ecclesiastical to temporal authorities and theologians and canonists saw themselves sidelined by jurists who emphasized their autonomy, they might have been tempted to think of themselves, increasingly, as promoters of peace and reconciliation "in the shadow of the law." Settlement agreements offered a privileged way to solve conflicts outside of court, without recourse to a judge appointed by the prince, but, ideally, with the help of expert mediators such as pastors, confessors, and other religious authorities.

The present contribution will draw mostly on some of the most influential works on the topic written by jurists and theologians who lived in the early modern Iberian empire: Antonio de Padilla y Meneses (d. 1580), Luis de Molina (1535–1600), Pedro de Oñate (1568–1646) and Pedro Murillo Velarde

 | DOI:10.1163/9789004710696_007

(1696–1753). While Molina, Oñate, and Murillo Velarde were Jesuits trained in theology and canon law, Padilla y Meneses was a jurist from the University of Salamanca who went on to become judge and president at the Consejo de Órdenes and the Consejo de Indias.[1] His long, autonomous commentary on the title *De transactionibus* in Justinian's *Code* stands out among civilians' treatments of the subject.[2] It impacted Murillo Velarde's views on settlement agreements, which are briefly but clearly laid out in his seminal *Curso de derecho canonico hispano e indiano*.[3] That seminal textbook on the application of canon law in the Indies also bears the mark of Molina's influential views on the topic. With three *disputationes* and a total of twenty-five columns dedicated to *transactiones* in his *De iustitia et iure*, the Jesuit theologian from Cuenca provided a rather detailed account of settlement agreements.[4] But it was the starting point for an even more extended exposition on both settlement and arbitration agreements counting no fewer than 150 pages in the third volume of Oñate's impressive *De contractibus*.[5]

2 *Sedes Materiae* in Roman and Canon Law

Although they offered far more detailed, sophisticated, and systematic treatments of the subject than the original sources, it is important to remember that early modern Spanish lawyers and theologians' understanding of the basic features of the *transactio*-contract did not differ significantly from that of civilians and canonists in earlier times. Like them, they drew on seminal passages from the *Digest*, the *Code* and the *Liber extra* to develop their

1 For biographical notices on Padilla y Meneses, see Ignacio Ezquerra Revilla, "Antonio Padilla y Meneses," in *Felipe II (1527–1598). La configuración de la Monarquía hispana*, ed. Martínez Millán, José Javier de Carlos Morales, and Carlos Javier de Carlos Morales (Vallodolid: Junta de Castilla y León, 1998), 447–448.

2 A digital copy of the first, 1566 Salamanca edition of his *In Titulum de Transactionibus Codicis Commentarius* has been made available online by the Bavarian State Library, see http://mdz-nbn-resolving.de/urn:nbn:de:bvb:12-bsb10146947-5.

3 On Murillo Velarde, a Jesuit active in the Philippines, see the biographical note by Luis Díaz de la Guardia y López, "Datos para una biografía del jurista Pedro Murillo Velarde y Bravo," *Espacio, Tiempo y Forma* 14 (2001): 407–471.

4 For further details on Molina's life and work, see Wim Decock, "Luis de Molina: De iustitia et iure (1593–1609)," in *The Formation and Transmission of Western Legal Culture: 150 Books that Made the Law in the Age of Printing*, ed. Serge Dauchy et al. (Cham: Springer, 2016), 142–144.

5 See E. Fernández, "Oñate, Pedro de," in *Diccionario histórico de la Compañía de Jesús biográfico-temático*, ed. Charles E. O'Neill and Joaquín María Domínguez (Rome/Madrid: Universidad Pontificia Comillas, 2001), vol. 3, 2870–2871.

views. In Justinian's *Digest*, seventeen provisions are dedicated to settlement agreements under the title *De transactionibus* (Dig. 2,15), which directly follows the title *De pactis* (Dig. 2,14). Incidentally, these are the two titles with which the second book of the *Digest*, which treats of various subjects related to the administration of justice, ends. In the *Code*, the title *De transactionibus* (C. 2,4) also follows a treatment entitled *De pactis* (C. 2,3) and is even longer, including forty-three imperial constitutions, often dealing with settlements in matters of succession. In the canon law tradition, too, pacts and settlement agreements were discussed in successive order, as is obvious from the *Liber extra*, where the title *De transactionibus* (X 1,36) immediately follows the title *De pactis* (X 1,35). The inter-connectedness between discussions on pacts and settlements is important, if only because in the canon law tradition the new, consensualist approach to the enforceability of pacts would have a direct impact on the understanding of the enforceability of settlement agreements. *Digest* 2,15 contains a lot of provisions about solemn ways in which to make *transactiones* enforceable, e.g., through adding a so-called *stipulatio acquiliana*. But such discussions lose significance among the canon lawyers and moral theologians, since they consider all pacts, however naked, to be binding (*pacta quantumcumque nuda servanda*).

By the mid-seventeenth century, Oñate maintained rather straightforwardly that the entire Roman doctrine about stipulations and clothed settlement agreements had become obsolete and pointless, at least in the Spanish empire, since both canon law and Spanish law recognized the binding force of a *transactio nuda*.[6] But authors steeped in the tradition of the medieval *ius commune*, including moral theologians such as Oñate, nevertheless spent very long hours explaining the intricacies of the Roman law of settlements and its differences with the canon law. Of special significance in this regard is the voluminous treatise on settlement agreements by Giovanni Battista Caccialupi (c. 1420–1496), a professor of civil law at the University of Siena who went on to teach canon law at Rome.[7] In a treatise of one hundred pages, he outlined all the legal problems related to settlement agreements, which he saw as an essential

6 Pedro de Oñate, *De contractibus*, Rome, 1654, vol. 3 (*De contractibus onerosis*), part. 1, tract. 26, disput. 92, sect. 4, nr. 78, p. 808: "Sed notandum valde hanc stipulationem non requiri iure canonico, ut transactio etiam nuda, et per pactum nudum celebrata pariat actionem et obligationem, ut tenent omnes canonistae; et alias probavimus nec iure nostro regio Hispano (…). Et ideo tota praefata doctrina in terris pontificis et in toto regno Hispano iam utilis non est, sed in aliis, quae adhuc subiacent iuri communi."

7 Giuliana D'Amelio, "Caccialupi, Giovanni Battista," in *Dizionario Biografico degli Italiani*, vol. 15, 1972, available online at https://www.treccani.it/enciclopedia/giovanni-battista-caccialupi_(Dizionario-Biografico)/.

instrument for lawyers wishing to comply with their professional duty to promote peace and concord among litigating parties. In the Holy Roman Empire, where the *ius commune* remained an important source of law in the early modern period, a succinct but influential analysis of the *transactio*-agreement was offered by Matthew Wesenbeck (1531–1586). In his commentary on Justinian's *Digest*, the Antwerp-born *doctor utriusque iuris* who emigrated to Wittenberg because of his Lutheran sympathies made the connection between the discussions on *pacta* and *transactiones* explicit by stating that the settlement agreement was just a species of the generic notion of pact.[8] Adhering to the opinion that bare agreements should be enforceable, Wesenbeck considered that, in his time—and contrary to what was the case in Roman law—*transactiones* should be considered as *contractus*, viz. as binding agreements.

3 Definition of the *Transactio*

Drawing on the afore-mentioned sources, the early modern canon lawyers started their discussions by giving a definition of the *transactio*. An illustrative example can be found in Pedro Murillo Velarde's textbook on canon law. He defined the *transactio* properly as "a non-gratuitous agreement about a dubious and controversial issue, or an uncertain lawsuit which has not yet come to an end" (*un pacto no gratuito acerca de una cosa dudosa y controvertida, o de un pleito incierto y aún no terminado*).[9] Similar definitions can be found in the works of Padilla and Molina. Its core elements—non-gratuity; dubious and controversial nature of the object of the settlement; unfinished character of the lawsuit—reach back to *Digest* 2,15 and *Code* 2,4 and the interpretations of those Roman texts in the work of *ius commune* jurists such as Caccialupi.[10] The non-gratuitous character of the settlement agreement sets it apart from a simple donation or abandonment of right. As an onerous agreement, it requires a commitment to do or give something from both parties. Drawing on Roman law,[11] Padilla y Meneses highlighted that a transaction always presupposes that

8 Matthaeus Wesenbecius, *In pandectas iuris civilis et codicis iustinianei lib. iix commentarii* (Basel, 1579), ad Dig. 2,15, nr. 1–2, pp. 54–55: "Pacti species est transactio (…) At hodie cum obliget, ex cap. 1 de pactis, arbitror transactionem dici contractum posse."

9 Pedro Murillo Velarde, *Curso de derecho canónico hispano e indiano*, ad X 1,36,1, nr. 369. I am using the first volume of the edition published by El Colegio de Michoacán and the Universidad Nacional Autónoma de México in 2004, pp. 435–437.

10 J. B. Caccialupus, *Tractatus de transactionibus*, quest. 1, nr. 1, in *Tractatus et commentaria de transactionibus* (Frankfurt/Oder, 1586), vol. 1, p. 4.

11 Cod. 2,4,38.

something is given or promised by each of the parties, who engage in a kind of mutual "giving and taking."[12] Murillo Velarde, too, emphasized that each party must be given or promised something or allowed to retain something. If not, the settlement is in reality an "amicable agreement" (*amicabilis compositio*), often fostered by a mediator, which can only be considered as a transaction in an improper, wide sense of the word. As will be explained below, the technical difference between a *transactio* in the strict sense and an amicable settlement matters, because spiritual goods cannot form the subject matter of a *transactio* in the proper sense, although they can be the object of an *amicabilis compositio*. A prominent example concerns papal "Bulls of compositio" such as the Bulla Cruciata issued by Pope Gregory XIII in 1573. Molina made it clear that that Bull was rightly called a bull promoting *compositio* and not a *transactio*, since the Pope—as a third party—intervened to provide relief for uncertain debts and no mutual sacrifices were being agreed upon between the debtor and the creditor(s) themselves.[13]

As far as the "dubious" or "uncertain" nature of the object of the settlement is concerned, it is important because otherwise the parties have unjustly received or retained something as part of the bargain. For example, if the plaintiff has received a sum to renounce his action in court, while he actually had no right to sue whatsoever, the transfer of the money happened without a legal title. Conversely, the defendant who has been allowed to retain something when he knew he did not have a claim to anything has also been enriched without legal cause. As a matter of conscience, Murillo Velarde explained, parties have to make restitution in such cases, and in the external court the transaction is considered void. The requirement of uncertainty also explains why the controversy should not yet have been settled definitively by a court sentence. In other words, a "judged thing" (*res judicata*), viz. a judicial sentence that has gained definitive force, is considered an impediment to a lawful settlement out-of-court. A *transactio* requires that the controversy is not yet over, regardless of whether a lawsuit is already pending or—as Justinian's *Code* implied by referring to siblings settling an inheritance case out of mere fear of future litigation[14]—the matter is so disputed that a lawsuit can come of it. Molina even specified that the uncertain nature of the object of the controversy should be evaluated from an entirely subjective point of view, that is from the

12 Padilla y Meneses, *In Titulum de Transactionibus Codicis Commentarius*, ad Cod. 2,4,38, p. 165–168. Similar observations can be found in Wesenbecius, *In pandectas iuris civilis*, ad D. 2,15, nr. 6, p. 57.

13 Luis de Molina, *De iustitia et iure* (Mainz, 1602), tract. 2, disp. 556, col. 1366, lit. c-d.

14 Cod. 2,4,2.

point of view of the disputing parties. Sometimes it could happen that from an objective perspective, a thing was no longer controversial or had been settled by court sentence already, but the parties themselves ignored that. Under such circumstances, the Jesuit theologian held, the uncertainty has to be assessed from the point of view of the parties.[15] Moreover, the doubt among the parties has to be considered at the moment of concluding the *transactio*. Information received subsequent to the conclusion of the settlement is irrelevant to its validity. "No matter the truth," Molina explained, "no matter what would be subsequently revealed by the lapse of time," a transaction includes the "sale and exchange of a dubious right, to the extent that it was doubtful at that moment, against the thing that was given in exchange for it."[16] In conclusion, the notions of objective truth and true knowledge are irrelevant to the justice of a settlement agreement.

Since a *transactio* was considered an agreement (*pactum*) by Roman law but had no specific legal remedies attached to it that were named after it, early modern jurists still classified it theoretically under the category of "innominate contracts."[17] In theory, at least, this had consequences when it came to enforcing a settlement agreement. According to the famous rule in Roman law that naked agreements are not binding but can only give rise to an *exceptio*,[18] one could not sue the other party to the transaction by virtue of the mere settlement agreement itself. However, thanks to the reversal of this rule in early modern canon law and Hispanic law, in particular, as Molina rightly insisted,[19] early modern canon lawyers in the Spanish world could consider settlements as fully binding agreements by virtue of the consent between the parties alone. As a consequence, Murillo Velarde was right to emphasize that a settlement agreement was binding for both parties by virtue of their mutual consent, meaning that it was irrelevant whether form requirements such as those prescribed by the Roman *stipulatio* had been observed or not. Their agreement had the same force as a judicial sentence (*res judicata/cosa juzgada*), with all consequences related to this status when it came to declaring the agreement void. Probably following the German canonist Heinrich Pirhing (1606–1679),

15 Molina, *De iustitia et iure*, tract. 2, disp. 556, col. 1365, lit. a-b.

16 Molina, *De iustitia et iure*, tract. 2, disp. 556, col. 1371, lit. c.

17 Padilla y Meneses, *In Titulum de Transactionibus Codicis Commentarius*, ad Cod. 2,4,28, p. 126, col. 1, nr. 9.

18 Dig. 2,14,7,4.

19 Molina, *De iustitia et iure*, tract. 2, disp. 556, col. 1368, lit. e-col. 1369, lit. c. For further explanation, see Wim Decock, *Theologians and Contract Law. The Moral Transformation of the Ius commune (c. 1500–1650)* (Leiden/Boston: Nijhoff/Brill, 2013), 142–162.

Murillo Velarde further specified that a settlement agreement could have a "real" or a "personal" character, depending on whether it was binding upon the inheritors of the settling parties.[20] A "real" *transactio* followed the goods about which a settlement had been reached, transferring the rights and obligations ensuing from the *transactio* to the rightful heirs of those goods. A "personal" *transactio*, on the other hand, lasted during the lifetime of the settling party only.

4 Differences between *Compromissum* and *Amicabilis Compositio*

Jurists and canonists in the tradition of the *ius commune* understood the *transactio* or settlement agreement to be technically distinct from the *compromissum*. As Juan de Hevia Bolaño (1570–1623) explains in his *Curia filípica*, the *compromissum* involves the appointment of an *arbiter*, a third party charged with settling the dispute, which is not the case in a *transactio*.[21] In the strict sense of the word, the *transactio* was also distinguished from the so-called "amicable settlement" (*amicabilis compositio*), since the latter was characterized by its gratuitous character and often involved a third party, such as a mediator. The technicalities of these distinctions were worked out very carefully by Pedro de Oñate. He discussed the nature of the arbitration agreement (*compromissum*) extensively in a separate chapter of more than one hundred pages that immediately followed his lengthy treatment of settlements. What united both agreements, according to Oñate, was that they both served as contractual modes of conflict resolution, allowing the litigants to settle their disputes out-of-court (*extraiudicialiter*), in a binding fashion, but without recourse to a judge or tribunal in the formal sense of the word.[22] Private modes of dispute settlement were popular in practice, Oñate explained, because they allowed the parties to settle their dispute far away from "the noisy business of the courts" and in a quicker and more cost-efficient fashion. The difference between both forms of private resolution of conflicts is that a *compromissum* involves the appointment of a third party (*arbiter*), who renders a judgment that binds the parties to the *compromissum*. A *transactio*, on the other hand,

20 Murillo Velarde, *Curso de derecho canonico hispano e indiano*, ad X 1,36,1, nr. 369, towards the end. Compare the *Synopsis pirhingiana seu compendiaria canonum doctrina*, ad X 1,36, §1, p. 209.

21 Juan de Hevia Bolaño, *Curia filípica* (Madrid, 1790), tom. 2, lib. 2, cap. 14 (*Compromiso*), nr. 1, p. 432.

22 Oñate, *De contractibus*, vol. 3, part. 1, tract. 27, disput. 93, introd., nr. 1, p. 843.

involves mutual giving and taking between the parties themselves, even if they are assisted by mediators or advisors.

Drawing on well-known doctrinal distinctions elaborated by the civilians and canonists of the *ius commune*,[23] Oñate went on to explain that the power of the third party designated as an arbiter by the *compromissum* could vary according to the will of the litigants.[24] If the parties wanted the third party to judge according to the strict rules of law (*servato iuris ordine*), then they designated an *arbiter*. An arbiter cannot deviate from the laws, even if he is allowed to pay more attention to statutory laws and local customs than to Roman law. Technically speaking, the third party is designated by a different name, namely *arbitrator*, if, by virtue of the *compromissum*, the parties allow him to base his judgment on other considerations than just the law. Typically, this includes resolving the conflict by relying on notions of equity (*ex aequo et bono*), morality, and even friendship. An *arbitrator* enjoys a wide margin of discretion, but, even so, he should not indulge in arbitrary decision-making, let alone proceed according to the whims of his fantasy (*secundum phantasiam*). Following the seminal analysis by Abbas Panormitanus, a late medieval canonist, Oñate lists thirteen differences between *arbitri* and *arbitratores*, one of the most notorious being that a woman can act as an *arbitrator*, but not as an *arbiter*, since she cannot serve as an ordinary judge, who is tied to following the strict order of law, either. Women's major role as *arbitratores*, or rather *arbitratrices*—Oñate uses the female noun—was widely recognized, if only because of the famous example of Eleanor of Aquitaine (1122–1204). The reason why *arbitri* and *arbitratores*, on the one hand, were distinguished from *amicabiles compositores*, on the other, is that the former were deemed capable of delivering a true judgment that was binding by virtue of the arbitration agreement (*compromissio*). The efforts made by the *amicabilis compositor* could only result in advice or propositions.

5 Persons Capable of Entering into a *Transactio*

Since settling a dubious and controversial case out-of-court by virtue of a settlement agreement implies concluding an agreement, it requires legal capacity, and, more specifically, the capacity to alienate (*ius disponendi*) the good

23 Mark Godfrey, "Arbitration in the Ius Commune and Scots Law," *Roman Legal Tradition*, 2 (2004): 122–135; Anne Lefebvre-Teillard, "L'arbitrage de l'histoire," *Archives de philosophie du droit*, 52 (2009): 1–14.

24 Oñate, *De contractibus*, vol. 3, part. 1, tract. 27, disput. 96, sect. 4, p. 925–928.

that is under dispute. Drawing on Roman law rules about the power to alienate, Murillo states that sanity of mind is the principal criterion to evaluate this capacity. As a result, physical impairments such as deaf- and muteness are no impediment to concluding a settlement agreement, but being afflicted with dementia is. If they are represented by a tutor, pupils and minors are allowed to settle, just like a prodigal person represented by his curator, but those tutors and curators need an authorization by a judge if the object of the settlement is an immovable good or any other precious thing. Authorization by their superior is also required from "síndicos" and town administrators wanting to settle regarding immovable or precious goods. Prelates, church administrators, and rectors can settle about goods of moderate value, even if they are immovables, but they need to observe the same solemnities that are required for the alienation of church goods. The possibility of a more direct form of agency exists for prelates, church administrators, and rectors, according to Murillo Velarde, if they have received a "mandato procuratorio libre con la cláusula de haberlo por rato del cabildo," meaning that the entity they are representing automatically ratifies their acts.[25] He even adds that those administrators taking care of the interests of church property can settle about any good, provided that they can retain or recover it or improve its condition, even if that requires paying some money. Simple members of a religious community, however, cannot settle about anything without the consent of their superior.

An issue of particular concern in the Spanish context related to heirs who were charged with transmitting part of the heritage they had received to a fideicommissary, especially in the case of the famous majorat (*mayorazgo*), an inheritance technique used by rich bourgeois and aristocratic families to hand down large family estates from one generation to the next.[26] As a result of the creation of a *mayorazgo*, assets were normally concentrated in the hands of the oldest son and became inalienable in principle. However, by royal permission they could be turned into mortgages, that is, collateral for loans.[27] This practice became widespread in the early modern period, with the authorities granting many authorizations. Consequently, *mayorazgos* also started to become the subject of settlement agreements, despite the fact that this entailed an act

25 Murillo Velarde, *Curso de derecho canónico hispano e indiano*, ad X 1,36,1, nr. 370.

26 Bartolomé Clavero, *Mayorazgo. Propiedad feudal en Castilia, 1369–1836* (Madrid: Siglo XXI de España, 1989).

27 Wolfgang Forster, "Failed Memoria: Rights of Patronage and of Burial in Bankruptcy," in *Dealing with Economic Failure: Between Norm and Practice (15th to the 21st Century)*, ed. Albrecht Cordes and Margrit Schulte Beerbühl (Frankfurt am Main: Peter Lang, 2016), 54–55.

of alienation, urging theologians like Molina to find sophisticated reasons to defend the practice.[28] Vassals, too, were in principle prohibited from concluding a settlement about feudal land or inherited goods. Since they had no power to alienate the goods which they possessed, they needed consent by the feudal lord to reach a settlement. As can be seen in Molina's *De iustitia et iure* and other texts, this issue was also hotly debated. If the interests of the agnatic family members were not put at risk, Molina accepted that a transaction could be concluded between the feudal lord and his vassal.[29] Juan de Solórzano Pereira (1575–1655) adopted a similar line of reasoning in the second volume of his *De indiarum iure,* explaining that *transactiones* about feudal land could be considered valid if not imperiling the interest of the feudal lord or his heirs.[30] He reasoned by analogy to extend this rule to the problem of *transactiones* about *encomiendas* (i.e., grants of power over indigenous people) and *mayorazgos* (i.e., entails typical of Spanish succession law). Solorzano maintained that settlements about *encomiendas* and *mayorazgos* were forbidden if they were harmful to the interests of their lords or their heirs, but could still be allowed by the authority of the prince. Less than a decade later, he repeated his views in the *Política indiana.*[31]

6 Subject Matter of *Transactio*—The Danger of Simony

An issue of paramount concern to early modern canon lawyers was the prohibition on settlements regarding spiritual goods, because it touched upon the central issue of simony, viz. the prohibition to offer a temporal advantage, e.g., money, rights, or homage, to obtain a spiritual favor. For example, if two priests disagree about an ecclesiastical benefice, they cannot settle their dispute through a *transactio,* that is by mutually giving and taking something, on pain of committing the mortal sin of simony. This followed, as a specific application, from the general prohibition on bargaining about spiritual goods laid down in the last canon of the title of the *Liber extra* dealing with agreements (*pacta*) in general, which immediately precedes the title on settlement agreements (*transactiones*).[32] Along with questions of agency and representation,

28 Molina, *De iustitia et iure*, tract. 2, disp. 557, col. 1378–1380.

29 Molina, *De iustitia et iure*, tract. 2, disp. 557, col. 1377, lit. e.

30 Juan de Solórzano Pereira, *De indiarum iure sive de iusta indiarum occidentalium gubernatione*, vol. 2, Madrid, 1639, lib. 2, cap. 14, f. 404, nr. 57.

31 Juan de Solórzano Pereira, *Politica Indiana*, vol. 1 (Madrid, 1776), lib. 3, cap. 15, n. 34, pp. 311–312.

32 X 1,35,8 (canon *Pactiones*).

this was the main topic in the papal decretals dealing with settlement agreements and a standard part of all discussions regarding settlements, especially if benefices were involved.[33] As a sign of the intimate connection between moral theology and canon law in the early modern Spanish world, it is interesting to note that the *correctores romani* added a gloss to the Gregorian edition of the *Corpus Iuris Canonici* (1582) referring to Martín de Azpilcueta (1492–1586) and Domingo de Soto (1494–1560), two leading scholars of the School of Salamanca, for further explanation about the invalidity of agreements about spiritual goods. While not mentioning the *transactio* agreement in particular, Azpilcueta does specify in his *Manual for Confessors* that all agreements in which a spiritual good is esteemed at a price, not just sale contracts, are tainted by the mortal sin of simony.[34] Soto does not go into settlement agreements either, but spends very long pages on the sin of simony in his *On Justice and Right*, giving as an example the sale of a "ius patronatus," understood as the right to propose a candidate for an ecclesiastical benefice.[35]

Next to settlement agreements about benefices, one of the most discussed examples of forbidden *transactiones* concerns marriages. Because of the sacramental nature of the marital bond, the last canon of the title *De transactionibus* in the *Liber extra* makes it very clear that in matrimonial matters judges are not allowed to encourage the litigants to settle.[36] Civil lawyers also adopted this viewpoint, arguing that, on account of its sacramental character, settling about marriage went beyond the power of husband and wife.[37] In the exceptional case that marriages need to be dissolved, a judicial procedure for annulment has to be followed.[38] However, mediation or settlement in a wider sense (*compositio*) is allowed in marriage disputes, as the gloss already recognized.[39] The reason being that, technically speaking, a *compositio* is not defined as an onerous agreement. Hence, it does not involve the "giving and taking" that is proper to *transactiones* in the strict sense of the word. If the

33 X 1,36,4 (canon *Constitutus*), X 1,36,7 (canon *Super eo*), X 1,36,10 (canon *Praeterea*).

34 Martín de Azpilcueta, *Manuel de confessores y penitentes* (Salamanca, 1556), cap. 23 (*De los siete pecados mortales*), tit. *De la symonia*, p. 482, nr. 99.

35 Domingo de Soto, *De iustitia et iure* (Lyons, 1582), lib. 9, q. 7, art. 1, f. 298v.

36 X 1,36,11 (canon *Ex parte tua*).

37 Padilla y Meneses, *In Titulum de Transactionibus Codicis Commentarius*, ad Cod. 2,4,43, p. 210, col. 1, nr. 5.

38 On the continued relevance of these old norms in modern canon law, see Paolo Moneta, "La transazione nel diritto canonico," in *Forme stragiudiziali o straordinarie di risoluzione delle controversie nel diritto commune e nel diritto canonico*, ed. Pedro Bonnet and Luca Loschiavo (Naples: Edizioni Scientifiche Italiane, 2008), 133–152.

39 Gloss *Sacramentum* ad X 1,36,11.

rights and obligations following from the sacred marriage contract are not the subject of bargaining, and the gratuitous character of the settlement is guaranteed, the canon lawyers do not object to attempts at reconciliation by negotiation. Moreover, the gloss applied the same reasoning to *compositiones* regarding spiritual goods.[40] Even if spiritual goods cannot be the subject of onerous agreements such as *transactiones*, they can be negotiated through an amicable settlement (*amicabilis compositio*), since such an agreement does not imply the exchange of any kind of temporal good for a spiritual one. For the same reason, a *permutatio*, that is a pure exchange of two spiritual goods, e.g., of the prebend attached to a particular church with the prebend attached to another ecclesiastical office, does not violate the prohibition on simony, as long as the barter does not imply additional compensation agreements involving the payment of pensions of one party to the other. In the early modern period, this idea became widespread through Soto's treatment of the subject, which was referenced in the Gregorian edition of the *Corpus Iuris Canonici*.[41]

In his textbook on canon law, Murillo Velarde lays down as a rule that settlement agreements can concern any subject, as long as there is no specific prohibition on a particular kind of *transactio*.[42] Apart from the cases discussed in the previous paragraphs, he mentions two further cases of *transactiones* in the field of private law that are prohibited unless the judge authorizes them: settlements about future alimony payments (*manutención*), especially *causa mortis*, and settlements about the inheritance of a living person or the goods inherited through a testamentary bequest. According to Murillo Velarde, the main reason why those agreements are forbidden if uncontrolled by a judge is that they put at risk the testator's will. Furthermore, he draws attention to settlements that imperil the public order and the prosecution of criminal offences. The possibility of settling disputes and lawsuits following from crimes had formed the object of continuous and controversial debates since the medieval *ius commune*.[43] Following an influential provision from Justinian's *Code*,[44] he argues that it is allowed to settle about a capital crime except in the case of adultery. The reason is, according to early modern civil and canon lawyers, that everybody has the right to redeem his blood by any means possible.[45] However,

40 Gloss *Ut si super decimis* ad X 1,36,2.

41 Soto, *De iustitia et iure*, lib. 9, q. 7, art. 2, f. 299r–300r.

42 Murillo Velarde, *Curso de derecho canónico hispano e indiano*, ad X 1,36,1, nr. 371.

43 Raphaël Eckert, "La transaction pénale du XIIe au XVe siècle. Étude de droit savant, de législation et de coutume" (Ph.D. thesis, Université de Strasbourg, 2009).

44 Cod. 2,4,18.

45 Wesenbecius, *In pandectas iuris civilis*, p. 56; E. Pirhing, *Synopsis Pirhingiana seu compendiaria canonum doctrina* (Augsburg/Dillingen, 1695), ad X 1,36, §4, p. 210.

pursuant to the famous principle that "crimes should not be left unpunished,"[46] other public crimes, which do not require blood punishment, cannot be settled, not even in a gratuitous, amicable way through the *amicabilis compositio*. If parties settle about non-blood crimes, Murillo Velarde explains, the settlement is taken as a confession of guilt. But he allows for an exception: if the offender can prove that he settles to avoid vexation (*vejación*) or the expenses of a lawsuit, then the settlement is allowed and not taken as a confession of guilt.[47] Another exception pertains to the crime of falsifying, since it is punished with *infamia*, which is as severe as capital punishment. Therefore, an offender accused of forgery can try to reach a settlement agreement.

7 Force of the Settlement and Remedies

Early modern Spanish law expressly recognizes the executory force of a settlement agreement, provided that it is concluded in the presence of a public notary (*escrivano publico*).[48] Some authors, such as Hevia Bolaño, emphasize this form requirement, but others, such as Murillo Velarde, do not mention it explicitly.[49] Padilla y Meneses points out that the automatic execution of a transaction agreement is daily practice in the Spanish realm on account of royal law. He recalls the requirement of conclusion in the presence of a public notary, but rejects the notion that *transactiones* need to be concluded before an ordinary or delegated judge to obtain executory force.[50] Following an authoritative provision from Roman imperial law,[51] all authors agreed that a valid settlement agreement was considered to have the same force as a judicial sentence (*res judicata/cosa juzgada*). In other words, for the sake of the peace

46 Dig. 9,2,51,2; see also Peter Landau "Ne crimina maneant impunita. Zur Entstehung des öffentlichen Strafanspruchs in der Rechtswissenschaft des 12. Jahrhunderts," in *Der Einfluss der Kanonistik auf die europäische Rechtskultur, vol. 3: Straf- und Strafprozessrecht*, ed. Mathias Schmoeckel and Orazio Condorelli (Cologne: Böhlau, 2012), 23–36.

47 Here, Murillo Velarde's opinion seems to contrast with that of Pirhing, *Synopsis*, ad X 1,36, §4, p. 211, who does not mention the possibility of reversing the presumption of confession.

48 King Philip II, *Recopilación*, Alcalá de Henares, 1581 (= Nueva Recopilación, 1567), part. 1, lib. 4, tit. 21, ley 4, f. 258v; King Carlos II, *Recopilación*, Madrid 1681 (= Recopilación de Leyes de los Reynos de las Indias, 1680), lib. 5, tit. 10, ley 5, f. 169v.

49 Hevia Bolaño, *Curia filípica*, tom. 1, part. 2, par. 3 (*cosa juzgada*), n. 12, p. 107; Murillo Velarde, *Curso de derecho canonico hispano e indiano*, ad X 1,36,1, nr. 371.

50 Padilla y Meneses, *In Titulum de Transactionibus Codicis Commentarius*, ad Cod. 2,4,10, nrs. 7–8, pp. 58–59.

51 Cod. 2,4,20.

in the republic, a *transactio* puts an end to a private dispute in the same, definitive manner as a judicial sentence. As a consequence, it cannot be invalidated easily, unless grave lack of consent to the agreement can be demonstrated. For example, if new documents appear that prove one of the parties wrong, this is not sufficient to invalidate the settlement agreement, at least if the *transactio* has been entered into with good faith.[52] The validity of a *transactio* can only be questioned if one of the parties has fallen victim to duress (*metus*), deceit (*dolus*), or fundamental error (*error substantialis*).[53] According to the general rule that juridical acts can be undone in the same way that they have been established,[54] the parties who concluded the settlement agreement can themselves decide to declare it null by mutual consent, but a settlement cannot be invalidated by the public authorities, e.g., through an imperial rescript.

A much-disputed issue concerned the possibility of attacking a settlement that was considered to be unbalanced and unfair, for instance because one of the parties had "given" far more than it had "taken." This problem tied in with general debates on justice in contractual exchange and the remedy provided for "lesion beyond moiety" (*laesio enormis*).[55] According to a standard interpretation of this remedy, which is based on Justinian's *Code* (C. 4,44,2), a party who has been treated unfairly, because he or she has been damaged for an amount "more than half of the just price" (e.g., merchandise evaluated by experts to be worth roughly 1000 guilders is sold for more than 1500 guilders), has the right to invoke this remedy; at the option of the defendant, the contract can then be invalidated or its price reconsidered. Generally speaking, canon lawyers and moral theologians in the early modern Spanish world requested the strictest observance of rules of justice in exchange, deeming any deviation from the so-called "just price," which was considered to have a certain "latitude" (in the aforementioned case somewhere between 900 and 1100 guilders), illicit and giving rise to a duty of restitution. Famous canonists such as Martín de Azpilcueta urged the civil courts to adopt the canon law principle of commutative justice for the sake of protecting the souls of the citizens. He proposed to extend the remedy against *laesio enormis* or "gross disparity" to any case where the just price had not been observed.[56] The civil courts, however, deemed such

52 Padilla y Meneses, *In Titulum de Transactionibus Codicis Commentarius*, ad Cod. 2,4,19, col. 1, nr. 3, p. 98.

53 Murillo Velarde, *Curso de derecho canonico hispano e indiano*, ad X 1,36,1, nr. 372.

54 Dig. 50,17,35.

55 Decock, *Theologians and Contract Law*, 507–604.

56 Decock, *Theologians and Contract Law*, 544–553.

a strict regulation impractical. At most, they were willing to provide relief for cases of *laesio enormis*, as in the original Roman provision.

Interestingly, many canon lawyers were willing to accept the idea that their more rigorous understanding of the need to observe the principle of justice in exchange did not apply to settlement agreements. Considering that it has the legal force of a definitive judicial sentence, Pedro Murillo Velarde maintained that a settlement could not be avoided on account of any kind of *laesio*, not even if the *laesio* is beyond half of the just price.[57] His opinion was more straightforward than that of a civilian like Wesenbeck.[58] In the interest of maintaining the established peace and putting a definitive end to the dispute, Murillo Velarde and other canonists were willing to accept that application of one of the major principles of contract law was frustrated in the specific case of *transactiones*.[59] Put differently, the canonists preferred at some point to preserve peace rather than fight unfair bargains. In the Spanish context, canonists regularly cited the authority of Gregorio López's (1496–1560) gloss on the *Siete Partidas* to defend this view. As a matter of fact, López explains that not even the most serious forms of lesion (*laesio enormissima*) can lead to questioning the validity of a settlement agreement.[60] Nevertheless, the issue remained controversial. Luis de Molina was unimpressed by López's gloss and remained supportive of the opinion that *laesio enormis* was applicable to *transactiones*, even though he acknowledged that an attempt to avoid a settlement by virtue of the remedy of *laesio enormis* had very little chance, in practice, to succeed.[61] He could rely on the authority of Arias Piñel (1515–1563), a professor of law at Coimbra and Salamanca, a successful legal practitioner and author of an influential commentary on Cod. 4,44,2.[62] After spending long pages examining the quality of a multitude of diverging opinions in this controversial matter, Piñel

57 Murillo Velarde, *Curso de derecho canónico hispano e indiano*, ad X 1,36,1, nr. 372.

58 Wesenbecius, *In pandectas iuris civilis*, p. 58, nr. 8. While showing sympathy for the contrary opinion, Wesenbeck referred to court practice and the "more equitable and human opinion" of Bartolus to defend the view that *transactiones* could be attacked on the grounds of *laesio enormis*.

59 Similar arguments are still used in contemporary canon law, see Moneta, "La transazione nel diritto canonico," 138 and 144.

60 G. López, Gloss *Quanto quier* on Siete Partidas, part. 5, tit. 14, l. 34, Salamanca, 1555, f. 105v–106r.

61 Molina, *De iustitia et iure*, tract. 2, disp. 556, cols. 1372–1373.

62 Wim Decock, "Elegant Scholastic Humanism? Arias Piñel's (1515–1563) Critical Revision of Laesio enormis," in *Reassessing Legal Humanism and its Claims: Petere Fontes?*, ed. John W. Cairns and Paul du Plessis (Edinburgh: Edinburgh University Press, 2013), 137–153.

eventually concluded that the remedy of *laesio enormis* should be available in settlement agreements.[63]

8 Concluding Remarks

Against the background of a Christian belief system that promotes concord, reconciliation, and peace, early modern jurists and theologians were eager to use a legal technique, inherited from Roman law, that could serve as an efficacious tool for consensual, rather than antagonistic forms of conflict management: the *transactio*-agreement. Christians were called upon to end conflicts by settlement rather than endless lawsuits, and even to drop a case rather than try at all costs to win it.[64] "All laws allow *transactiones*," Murillo Velarde insisted at the beginning of his exposition, "because every Christian must try out settlement before taking the case to court."[65] He thought that clergymen were under a particular obligation to foster settlement out-of-court, since it was their duty to bring peace and restore harmony to the litigating parties. But as the prologue to Caccialupi's treatise demonstrates, the exhortation to reconcile litigants out-of-court was addressed equally forcefully to legal professionals themselves. Having previously written a treatise on the professional ethics of lawyers (*De advocatis*), the jurist from San Severino Marche recalled at the beginning of his *Tractatus de transactionibus* that urging his client to try and settle with his adversary before taking him to court was a matter of a lawyer's deontology. Judges, too, were constantly reminded of their duty to encourage reconciliation out-of-court.[66] Padilla y Meneses even thought that they should sometimes do so against the will of the parties.[67] It is small wonder then that, as Carlos Garriga has observed with regards to legal practice in the Spanish Indies, conflict resolution in the early modern period depended more on settlements, informal agreements, and social networks than on supreme courts and judicial institutions.[68] There was a general consensus that *transactio* was

63 A. Piñel, *Ad rubricam et legam 2, Cod. de rescindenda venditione commentarii*, ad l. 2, part. 1 (Rinteln, 1667), p. 214–227.

64 Raoul Naz, "Transaction," in *Dictionnaire de droit canonique*, ed. Raoul Naz (Paris: Librairie Letouzey et Ané, 1965), vol. 7, cols. 1314–1319.

65 Murillo Velarde, *Curso de derecho canónico hispano e indiano*, ad X 1,36,1, nr. 369, in the beginning.

66 Glosses *Ex parte tua* and *Ad componendum* to X 1,36,11.

67 Padilla y Meneses, *In Titulum de Transactionibus Codicis Commentarius*, p. 4, nr. 2.

68 Carlos Garriga Acosta, "Sobre el gobierno de la justicia en Indias (siglos XVI–XVII)," *Revista de Historia del Derecho*, no. 34 (2006): 67–160.

a substantial means to settle disputes, if only because, as Oñate observed,[69] "it extinguishes the flames of lawsuits, takes away the toxic heat of conflict, fosters mental health and brings peace of heart to both parties."

Acknowledgments

This article offers an expanded version of the entry on "Transacciones" in the forthcoming *Diccionario Histórico de Derecho Canónico en Hispanoamérica y Filipinas (s. xvi–xviii)*; see Wim Decock, "Transacciones (Diccionario Histórico de Derecho Canónico en Hispanoamérica y Filipinas)," *Max Planck Institute for Legal History and Legal Theory Research Paper Series*, no. 3 (2021): 1–15, http://dx.doi.org/10.2139/ssrn.3815785.

Bibliography

Azpilcueta, Martín de. *Manuel de confessores y penitentes*. Salamanca, 1556.

Bonnet, Pedro and Luca Loschiavo, eds. *Forme stragiudiziali o straordinarie di risoluzione delle controversie nel diritto commune e nel diritto canonico*. Naples: Edizioni Scientifiche Italiane, 2008.

Caccialupus, J. B. *Tractatus et commentaria de transactionibus*, vol. 1. Frankfurt/Oder, 1586.

Clavero, Bartolomé. *Mayorazgo. Propiedad feudal en Castilia, 1369–1836*. Madrid: Siglo XXI de España, 1989.

D'Amelio, Giuliana. "Caccialupi, Giovanni Battista." In *Dizionario Biografico degli Italiani*, vol. 15, 1972. Last accessed June 5, 2022. https://www.treccani.it/enciclopedia/giovanni-battista-caccialupi_(Dizionario-Biografico)/.

Decock, Wim. *Theologians and Contract Law. The Moral Transformation of the Ius commune (c. 1500–1650)*. Leiden/Boston: Nijhoff/Brill, 2013.

Decock, Wim. "Elegant Scholastic Humanism? Arias Piñel's (1515–1563) Critical Revision of Laesio enormis." In *Reassessing Legal Humanism and its Claims: Petere Fontes?*, edited by John W. Cairns and Paul du Plessis, 137–153. Edinburgh: Edinburgh University Press, 2013.

69 Oñate, *De contractibus*, vol. 3, part. 1, tract. 26, introd., nr. 1, p. 795: "Extinguit enim flammas litium, aufert calorem noxium, confert salutem mentium, utramque pacem cordium."

Decock, Wim. "Luis de Molina: De iustitia et iure (1593–1609)." In *The Formation and Transmission of Western Legal Culture: 150 Books that Made the Law in the Age of Printing*, edited by Serge Dauchy et al., 142–144. Cham: Springer, 2016.

Decock, Wim. "Transacciones (Diccionario Histórico de Derecho Canónico en Hispanoamérica y Filipinas)." *Max Planck Institute for Legal History and Legal Theory Research Paper Series*, no. 3 (2021): 1–15. http://dx.doi.org/10.2139/ssrn.3815785.

De Luca, Luigi. La transazione nel diritto canonico: *contributo alla dottrina canonistica dei contratti*. Rome: Edizioni universitarie, 1942.

Díaz de la Guardia y López, Luis. "Datos para una biografía del jurista Pedro Murillo Velarde y Bravo." *Espacio, Tiempo y Forma* 14 (2001): 407–471.

Ebel, Friedrich. *Berichtung, transactio und Vergleich. Untersuchungen zu Schuldversprechen und Vergleichsvertrag des Zivilrechts*. Tübingen: Mohr, 1978.

Eckert, Raphaël. "La transaction pénale du XIIe au XVe siècle. Étude de droit savant, de législation et de coutume." Ph.D. thesis, Université de Strasbourg, 2009.

Ezquerra Revilla, Ignacio. "Antonio Padilla y Meneses." In *Felipe II (1527–1598). La configuración de la Monarquía hispana*, edited by José Martínez Millán and Carlos Javier de Carlos Morales, 447–448. Vallodolid: Junta de Castilla y León, 1998.

Fernández, E. "Oñate, Pedro de." In *Diccionario histórico de la Compañía de Jesús biográfico-temático*, edited by Charles E. O'Neill and Joaquín María Domínguez, vol. 3, 2870–2871. Rome/Madrid: Universidad Pontificia Comillas, 2001.

Forster, Wolfgang. "Failed Memoria: Rights of Patronage and of Burial in Bankruptcy." In *Dealing with Economic Failure: Between Norm and Practice (15th to the 21st Century)*, edited by Albrecht Cordes and Margrit Schulte Beerbühl, 53–75. Frankfurt am Main: Peter Lang, 2016.

Garriga Acosta, Carlos. "Sobre el gobierno de la justicia en Indias (siglos XVI–XVII)." *Revista de Historia del Derecho*, no. 34 (2006): 67–160.

Godfrey, Mark. "Arbitration in the Ius Commune and Scots Law." *Roman Legal Tradition* 2 (2004): 122–135.

Hermann, Hans-Georg. "§779 BGB." In *Historisch-kritischer Kommentar zum BGB*, vol. 3, Schuldrecht, edited by Joachim Rückert and Frank Schäfer, 2356–2408. Tübingen: Mohr Siebeck, 2013.

Hevia Bolaño, Juan de. *Curia filípica*. Madrid, 1790.

Landau, Peter. "Ne crimina maneant impunita. Zur Entstehung des öffentlichen Strafanspruchs in der Rechtswissenschaft des 12. Jahrhunderts." In *Der Einfluss der Kanonistik auf die europäische Rechtskultur, vol. 3: Straf- und Strafprozessrecht*, edited by Mathias Schmoeckel and Orazio Condorelli, 23–36. Cologne: Böhlau, 2012.

Lefebvre-Teillard, Anne. "L'arbitrage de l'histoire" *Archives de philosophie du droit* 52 (2009) : 1–14.

Molina, Luis de, *De iustitia et iure*. Mainz, 1602.

Moneta, Paolo. "La transazione nel diritto canonico." In *Forme stragiudiziali o straordinarie di risoluzione delle controversie nel diritto commune e nel diritto canonico*, edited by Pedro Bonnet and Luca Loschiavo, 133–152. Naples: Edizioni Scientifiche Italiane, 2008.

Murillo Velarde, Pedro. *Curso de derecho canónico hispano e indiano*, vol. 1. Zamora Michoacán, Mexico: El Colegio de Michoacán, 2004.

Naz, Raoul. "Transaction." In *Dictionnaire de droit canonique*, vol. 7, cols. 1314–1319. Paris: Librairie Letouzey et Ané, 1965.

Oñate, Pedro de. *De contractibus*, vol. 3. Rome, 1654.

Padilla y Meneses, Antonio. *In Titulum de Transactionibus Codicis Commentarius*. Salamanca, 1566. http://mdz-nbn-resolving.de/urn:nbn:de:bvb:12-bsb10146947-5.

Piñel, A. *Ad rubricam et legam 2, Cod. de rescindenda venditione commentarii*. Rinteln, 1667.

Pirhing, E. *Synopsis Pirhingiana seu compendiaria canonum doctrina*. Augsburg/ Dillingen, 1695.

Solórzano Pereira, Juan de. *De indiarum iure sive de iusta indiarum occidentalium gubernatione*, vol. 2. Madrid, 1639.

Solórzano Pereira, Juan de. *Politica Indiana*, vol. 1. Madrid, 1776.

Soto, Domingo de. *De iustitia et iure*. Lyons, 1582.

Tamayo Haya, Silvia. "El contrato de transacción: principales líneas de su evolución histórica." *Anuario de Derecho Civil* 57, no. 3 (2004): 1105–1146.

Wesenbecius, Matthaeus. *In pandectas iuris civilis et codicis iustinianei lib. xii commentarii*. Basel, 1579.

PART 2

Women, Marriage, and the Law

CHAPTER 6

Consent in Medieval English Marriage and Misconduct

Elizabeth Papp Kamali

At the Wiltshire Eyre in 1249, the hundred of Bradford presented to the justices a series of crimes and misadventures, including the accidental deaths of two young men crushed by mill wheels, the violent rape of a woman by a man who confessed the deed later, coin clipping, and several homicides.[1] One incident stands out: a man named Batinus was pursued by the hue and cry from Wiltshire into the neighboring county of Somerset; he was captured and placed in the Somerset county gaol, where he eventually died before facing trial.[2] He appears to have been part of a roving band of criminals involved in battery, robbery, and burglary.[3] Strikingly, he had allegedly engaged local accessories, including a married couple, Agnes and Robert le Folur, who might themselves have had broader criminal connections, judging from the fact that they were accused of various crimes alongside two other women and five other men.[4] Six of those seven alleged associates were acquitted outright, leaving Agnes, Robert, and a woman named Christiana Hobelot to learn their fates from a local jury. The jury initially appears to have declared all three guilty of harboring the thief Batinus, fully aware of his status as an outlaw. However, the jury delved further into the question of Agnes's complicity. While Robert le Folur and Christiana Hobelot would hang for their deeds, Agnes was ultimately acquitted after the jury determined that she was "so subjected to [her husband] that she had to obey" (*ei sic subdita quod necesse habuit parere*).[5] Agnes was spared thanks to the power dynamics of her marriage to Robert and not, as Christiana's fate demonstrates, due simply to her status as a female member of

1 C. A. F. Meekings, ed. and trans., *Crown Pleas of the Wiltshire Eyre, 1249* (Devizes: Wiltshire Archaeological and Natural History Society, 1961), 178–81.

2 Meekings, *Wiltshire Eyre*, 180, no. 146 (discussed in Elizabeth Papp Kamali, *Felony and the Guilty Mind in Medieval England* (Cambridge: Cambridge University Press, 2019), 61). See also Meekings, *Wiltshire Eyre*, 179–80, no. 144. Throughout I will use the Middle English spelling "gaol" rather than "jail."

3 Meekings, *Wiltshire Eyre*, 204, no. 288.

4 *Meekings*, *Wiltshire Eyre*, 180, no. 146.

5 *Meekings*, *Wiltshire Eyre*, 180, no. 146.

 | DOI:10.1163/9789004710696_008

an apparent criminal enterprise. Having consented to bind herself to Robert in marriage at some point in time, Agnes subsequently became incapable (in the eyes of the law) of freely consenting to participation in his crimes due to the degree of control Robert exercised over her. Her marital subjection would save her neck, although she would be left widowed and penniless following Robert's death at the gallows.[6]

Thus, the dynamics of a particular marital relationship might serve as a shield protecting a wife from liability if her husband coerced her to participate. However, marital status alone afforded no excuse for a wife accused of felony. Just as a woman could freely consent to marriage, she could also consent freely to participation in crime, even that of her husband. In general, consent was a central consideration in both the law of marriage and the law of crime in thirteenth- and fourteenth-century England, the twelfth century having been a time in which consent's role in the spheres of marriage and sin had been debated and formalized. This essay will offer a brief overview of the place of consent in medieval English marriage law, relying largely on our honorand's groundbreaking work in this field. It will then focus on the role played by consent within the realm of sin and crime, ultimately tying the issue back into marriage by considering the interplay between consent and criminality when husbands and wives—like Agnes and Robert le Folur—engaged in criminal conduct.

1 Consent in Marriage

Consent was foundational to marriage formation in medieval England. According to the theologian Gratian, writing in the first half of the twelfth century, a marriage came into existence with the exchange of consent, although it was not indissoluble until intercourse.[7] Peter Lombard (c. 1096–1160) took matters a step further: according to him, a couple's exchange of words of present consent resulted in an indissoluble marriage.[8] Toward the end of his pontificate, Pope Alexander III (r. 1159–1181) officially adopted the view that an indissoluble marriage could be formed through two avenues: 1) the free exchange of words of present consent or 2) the free exchange of words of future consent followed by

6 *Meekings, Wiltshire Eyre*, 180, no. 146. While Robert had 10s. worth of chattels, forfeited at the time of his death, Agnes is said to have had nothing.

7 R. H. Helmholz, *Marriage Litigation in Medieval England* (Cambridge: Cambridge University Press, 1974), 26.

8 Helmholz, *Marriage Litigation*, 26.

intercourse.[9] After the Fourth Lateran Council (1215), a series of English synods would clarify and disseminate the church's marriage rules to a broad audience through sermons and the confessional, producing widespread familiarity with the Alexandrine rules.[10] Charles Donahue has argued that Alexander's rules "constitute[d] a conscious, and at least partially successful, attempt to use the canon law to influence the course of social development."[11] The rules were an innovation, not flowing organically from earlier traditions but informed by "a vision of what marriage ought to be" and one "far from the social reality of the time in which Alexander lived."[12] That social reality included control by lords and families alike over marital arrangements.[13] In arriving at his ultimate set of rules, Alexander "carefully stripped away from the prior law all of those elements which could be used by family or lord to control the wills of the marriage parties," such as any requirement of parental consent.[14] The rules broadened the range of relationships, including concubinage and cohabitation, that could be categorized in some circumstances as true marriages.[15]

It was a radical vision.[16] Neither parents nor priest nor anyone else had to consent to the match.[17] The Alexandrine rules emphasized that there were

9 For a brief yet more comprehensive summary of the rules, see Charles Donahue, Jr., "The Canon Law on the Formation of Marriage and Social Practice in the Later Middle Ages," *Journal of Family History* 8:2 (1983): 144.

10 Frederik Pedersen, *Marriage Disputes in Medieval England* (Hambledon: Hambledon Press, 2000), 7.

11 Charles Donahue, Jr., "The Policy of Alexander the Third's Consent Theory of Marriage," in *Proceedings of the Fourth International Congress of Medieval Canon Law*, ed. Stephan Kuttner (Città del Vaticano: Biblioteca Apostolica Vaticana, 1976), 253, 274.

12 Donahue, "Canon Law on the Formation of Marriage," 145. See also James A. Brundage, *Law, Sex, and Christian Society in Medieval Europe* (Chicago: University of Chicago Press, 1987), 332–33. But see Anne J. Duggan, "The Effect of Alexander III's 'Rules on the Formation of Marriage' in Angevin England," *Anglo-Norman Studies* 33 (2011): 2–3 (arguing that Alexander was not involved in "conscious law-making" and in fact "more than once … refused to lay down definitive rules").

13 Donahue, "Policy of Alexander the Third's Consent Theory," 257 (describing the "family, financial, and feudal concerns" at the heart of marriage in twelfth-century England).

14 Donahue, "Policy of Alexander the Third's Consent Theory," 271.

15 James A. Brundage, "Marriage and Sexuality in the Decretals of Pope Alexander III," in *Sex, Law and Marriage in the Middle Ages* (Aldershot: Variorum, 1993), 82.

16 But see Duggan, "Effect of Alexander III's 'Rules,'" 4 (arguing that the emphasis on "the free consent of the parties was no new principle, even though centuries of social convention had all but smothered it in practice, for it had been the traditional teaching of the Church fathers from Augustine and Ambrose onwards") and 13 (arguing that arranged marriages and exercise of lordly rights over marriage both pre- and post-dated the papacy of Alexander III).

17 Helmholz, *Marriage Litigation*, 27.

only two principals involved in the formation of the marriage bond: the man and the woman.[18] Consent was at the core of the sacrament. There were, of course, potential impediments to be considered, most notably the question of whether both parties had reached the age of consent.[19] Consent might also be vitiated or impeded by other conditions, including insanity, impotence, or frigidity, and such fear as would constitute duress.[20] In fact, even a marriage supported by words of present consent and an oath might be dissoluble if it were found that "one of the parties had acted under compulsion strong enough to have moved a 'constant man or woman.'"[21]

Marriages could also take place anywhere, even in "houses, fields, and taverns."[22] No formal ceremony was required, although clandestine marriages were discouraged given the difficulties they could pose, particularly if one party later wished to deny the marriage.[23] While an English theologian like Thomas Chobham (c. 1160—c. 1233/36) might emphasize that no "formal ritual" was necessary, the Canterbury synod of 1213–1214 insisted on "proper public forms for the entry into matrimony."[24] Nonetheless, concern regarding clandestine marriage persisted. In his early fourteenth-century religious poetical treatise *Handlyng Synne*, Robert Mannyng (c. 1275—c. 1338) would urge men not to exchange wedding vows with women "out of holy church's sight"

18 Shannon McSheffrey, *Marriage, Sex, and Civic Culture in Late Medieval London* (Philadelphia: University of Pennsylvania Press, 2011), 21.

19 Charles Donahue, Jr., *Law, Marriage, and Society in the Later Middle Ages: Arguments About Marriage in Five Courts* (Cambridge: Cambridge University Press, 2007), 20–21.

20 Donahue, *Law, Marriage, and Society*, 19–22. On the legal capacity to consent, see also Eliza Buhrer, "Disability and Consent in Medieval Law," *Postmedieval* 10:3 (2019): 346.

21 Richard Helmholz, "Pope Innocent III and the Annulment of Magna Carta," *Journal of Ecclesiastical History* 69:1 (2018): 9 (citing *Decretales Gregorii IX*, Lib. 4, tit. 1, cap. 13–15). On the application of this principle in English cases, see Pedersen, *Marriage Disputes*, 120–33.

22 McSheffrey, *Marriage, Sex, and Civic Culture*, 22. See also Helmholz, *Marriage Litigation*, 29 (adding references to marriages contracted under an ash tree, in bed, in a storehouse, near a hedge, and even on the king's highway).

23 Helmholz, *Marriage Litigation*, 27; Donahue, "Canon Law on the Formation of Marriage," 146. Donahue and Brundage contend that Alexander foresaw and accepted the consequence that his rules would produce more clandestine marriages. Donahue, "Policy of Alexander the Third's Consent Theory," 274; Brundage, *Law, Sex, and Christian Society*, 335–36.

24 Pedersen, *Marriage Disputes*, 7. Chobham himself followed up his statement of the consent theory of marriage with an emphasis on the necessity "of religious and public celebration." Duggan, "Effect of Alexander III's 'Rules,'" 12.

even if friends were willing to bear witness.[25] He would also warn women about men who might "beguile a woman with words" to encourage her to "give her troth but lightly, for no reason but to lie by her [i.e., take her to bed]," but with the effective result of encumbering them both in marriage.[26] Ecclesiastical court records suggest that it could be a sensible course of action to undertake solemnities in a church after contracting marriage solely in the presence of lay persons.[27] Not all couples took such precautions, of course. Marital disputes raised in ecclesiastical courts confirm that betrothals were exchanged in informal settings without any later solemnities. Such was the case with the verbal promises allegedly uttered by Alice Dolling and William Smith—names familiar to students in Charles Donahue's legal history classes—in 1269 in the house of John le Ankere in Winterbourne Stoke, beside the bed that Alice shared with another young woman in the household.[28] The fact that marriages could be contracted anywhere, even by a young woman's bedside, did not mean that all locales were deemed appropriate. Given the important role taverns played in communal life in medieval England, it is perhaps not surprising that they served as more public locales for the exchange of marital promises.[29] In guiding their dioceses in the thirteenth century, some English bishops explicitly cautioned against the exchange of marital vows in taverns, given the potential for alcohol to vitiate consent.[30] To take one example, in the mid-thirteenth century, the bishop of Winchester advised that, because it was necessary to find legitimate consent (*legitimus ... consensus*) in marriage, and given the

25 Robert Mannyng of Brunne, *Handlyng Synne*, ed. Idelle Sullens (Binghamton: Medieval & Renaissance Texts & Studies, 1983), 210, lines 8367–70. "3yf þou a womman trouþe plight / Out of holy cherches sight, / Men oghte nat so for to do / Þogh þat frendes consente þar to."

26 Mannyng, *Handlyng Synne*, 211, lines 8397–8402. "A werse spyce 3yt men holdes, / To bygyle a woman wyþ words, / To 3yue here trouþe but lightly, / For no þyng but to lygge here by. / Wyþ þat gyle þou makst here asente / And bryngst 3ow boþe to cumbremente."

27 See, e.g., the deposition of Roger, a priest, regarding the marriage of his niece Alice to John the Blacksmith c. 1200: Roger reported that a baker named Ralph had asked him whether he intended to attend a marriage between a young man and Roger's niece "who, as [Ralph] said, had already been joined, faith having been given before lay people, but for greater security he wished that this be confirmed before a priest." Norma Adams and Charles Donahue, Jr., *Select Cases from the Ecclesiastical Courts of the Province of Canterbury, c. 1200–1301* (London: Selden Society, 1981), 25 (A.7. Alice c. John the Blacksmith).

28 Donahue, *Law, Marriage, and Society*, 46–47.

29 On the sheer number of taverns and alehouses in medieval England, see Gregory A. Austin, *Alcohol in Western Society from Antiquity to 1800: A Chronological Survey* (Santa Barbara, CA: ABC-Clio Information Services, 1985), 100.

30 Elizabeth Papp Kamali, "The Horrible Sepulture of Mannes Resoun: Intoxication and Medieval English Felony Law," *Rechtsgeschichte—Legal History* 30 (2022): 15 and n. 65.

fact that words spoken by drunk persons or in jest (*ab ebriis vel jocandi animo*) might seem to call into doubt the legitimacy of a person's consent, couples should not contract marriage in taverns or other public drinking places.[31]

Was marital consent constituted by an outward gesture, whether by speech or a physical act, or was it fundamentally a state of heart or mind, merely confirmed by the outward gesture? Consent was typically exchanged through spoken words, described by Shannon McSheffrey, drawing upon J. L. Austin, as "a performative utterance that constituted the contract."[32] In the fifteenth century, those accused of the heresy of Lollardy would be condemned, in part, for the belief that words were superfluous insofar as the marital bond could be formed "*sine aliquo contractu per verba*" but rather through "consent of love" alone, a subversive idea traced by Alastair Minnis to the writings of John Wycliffe (c. 1328–1384) a century earlier.[33] Namely, in Wycliffe's *Trialogus* (1382), the character Phronesis argued for the primacy of internal consent over verbal utterance in the formation of marriage, a clear contradiction of the Alexandrine rules.[34] Thomas Netter (c. 1375–1430) would oppose vehemently this Wycliffite innovation in his *Doctrinale antiquitatum fidei catholicae ecclesiae*, reinforcing the traditional view that external signs, typically spoken words, were required for marriage formation, with a presumption that "external signs express internal consent."[35]

31 F. M. Powicke and C. R. Cheney, eds., *Councils & Synods with Other Documents Relating to the English Church*, vol. 2 (1205–1313), Part 1 (1205–1265) (Oxford: Clarendon, 1964), 411–12. "Capitulum 56. Item, quia in matrimoniis ex deliberato consilio legitimus debet inueniri consensus, nec potest dici legitimus qui ab ebriis uel iocandi animo seu demonstrandi causa fit, precipimus quod nullus uir aut mulier fidem sibi adinuicem dare de contraendo matrimonio per quecumque uerba presumant in tabernis aut in puplicis potacionibus. Si quis contrauenerit, siue uir fuerit uel mulier, trine fastigacionis pene tribus locis publicis subiacebunt. Laici quidem qui talibus contractis consenserint uel auctoritatem prestiterint grauiter puniantur." My thanks to Charles Donahue and Maddy Scannell.

32 McSheffrey, *Marriage, Sex, and Civic Culture*, 22 and n. 18; Helmholz, *Marriage Litigation*, 27. Persons who were mute were capable of consenting through the use of non-verbal gestures. McSheffrey, *Marriage, Sex, and Civic Culture*, 22. But see Buhrer, "Disability and Consent," 346 (noting that those who were deaf and mute (*surdus et mutus*) "lacked the legal capacity to consent, and thus could not make wills, sell or donate land, bring a suit to court, and in most cases marry"). *Bracton* recognized that some authorities held that the mute could consent "by signs and a nod." George E. Woodbine, ed., *Bracton on the Laws and Customs of England*, trans. Samuel E. Thorne (Cambridge: Belknap, 1968) [hereafter "*Bracton*"], vol. 2, 52.

33 Alastair J. Minnis, "'Oonly consent of love is sufficiant for matrimonie': Translating John Wyclif's Word of the Mind," in *Lost in Translation?*, ed. Denis Reveney and Christiania Whitehead (Turnhout: Brepols, 2009), 192–93.

34 Minnis, "Oonly consent of love," 193–94.

35 Minnis, "Oonly consent of love," 194–95.

The dispute highlights the evidentiary difficulties of a rule centered upon consent: without the utterance of words or some other external sign, how might one prove the exchange of consent, particularly if one party to the alleged marriage denied the agreement later? Even if consent were a purely internal matter, not dependent upon external signs, it is understandable that canon law would require external signs for the sake of proof. Even then, proving a valid marriage could be far from a simple enterprise, with courts sometimes having to investigate whether the precise words employed signaled a future promise or a present exchange of consent to marriage.[36] Referring to Alexander's scheme as "no masterpiece of human wisdom," Frederic Maitland would observe: "Of all people in the world, lovers are the least likely to distinguish precisely between the present and future tenses."[37] The matter was further complicated by the two-witness requirement for full proof in the ecclesiastical courts; there might not have always been two witnesses present when parties exchanged words of consent in private and, even if there were, their testimony might differ. Robert Mannyng cautioned against private exchanges of consent in *Handlyng Synne*, advising:

> Therefore I now warn you all,
> Man and woman, for it may befall,
> That you be never so foolhardy
> To give your troth so privily,
> Nor woman's troth for to take
> Nor troth to give for wedding's sake,
> Until holy church has deemed right
> With witnessing of friends' sight.[38]

By placing the couple's consent at the core of the law of marriage, the Alexandrine rules sacrificed the administrability that would have accompanied the formal requirement of other solemnities, such as a priest's officiation or the use of churches as the sole site for sacramental marriage.[39] Even with

---

36 Helmholz, *Marriage Litigation*, 33–40.

37 Donahue, "Policy of Alexander the Third's Consent Theory," 252. He cites F. Pollock and F. W. Maitland, *The History of English Law* (2nd ed., 1968), vol. 2, 368–69.

38 Mannyng, *Handlyng Synne*, 211, lines 8403–10. "Þarfore now y warne ȝow alle, / Man & womman, for þyng may falle, / Þat ȝe be neure so fole hardy / To ȝyue ȝoure trouþe so pryuyly, / Ne wommans trouþe for to take / Ne trouþe ȝyue for weddyng sake, / Tyl holy cherche haue demed ryght / Wyþ lokyng of frendes syght."

39 Some formalities would be introduced at the Council of Trent (1545–1563), which declared that, going forward, marriages not solemnized before a parish priest and two witnesses would be invalid. See Donahue, *Law, Marriage, and Society*, 633–34.

a reliance on outward signs, the church's emphasis on consent came at the cost of evidentiary challenges that courts would have to grapple with when disputes inevitably arose. A similar challenge may be found in the criminal law context, where an emphasis on *mens rea* in determining a person's culpability, rather than simply the act itself, presented challenges of proof to juries tasked with sorting the guilty from the innocent.

2 Consent in Sin

Consent would become foundational to medieval English felony law due to its centrality within the realm of sin. In a strain of thought traceable to the Paris theologian Peter Abelard (c. 1079–1142) but part of a broader twelfth-century intellectual trend, it was the sinner's consent to the wrongful act that produced the state of culpability for which the individual might deserve condemnation and punishment.[40] Admittedly, to the modern ear, this is an odd understanding of consent, focused on a person's internal consent to their own act, as opposed to thinking of consent as a response to a proposal from another person.[41] For Abelard, consent was key to understanding sin, while the sinful act itself was comparatively inconsequential.[42] In defining sin, Abelard distinguished among the act itself, the will to do the act, and consent, this last concept being intertwined with the idea of contempt toward God.[43] In a passage that, for the modern reader, inevitably calls to mind Abelard's infamous affair with Heloise, Abelard states: "So sin is not lusting for a woman but consenting to lust; the consent of the will (*voluntatis consensus*) is damnable, but not the will for intercourse."[44]

40 To situate Abelard in his contemporary theological milieu, see Jean Porter, "Responsibility, Passion, and Sin: A Reassessment of Abelard's Ethics," *The Journal of Religious Ethics* 28:3 (2000): 367–94.

41 My thanks to John Goldberg for highlighting this point.

42 This is not to suggest that Abelard's approach was entirely subjective in emphasis. See Porter, "Responsibility, Passion, and Sin," 379 ("Abelard's emphasis on interiority is not inconsistent with the claim that there are objective moral criteria, according to which some kinds of actions are morally wrong").

43 On the meaning of contempt toward God in Abelard's *Ethics*, see Porter, "Responsibility, Passion, and Sin," 385.

44 D. E. Luscombe, ed. and trans., *Peter Abelard's* Ethics: *An Edition with Introduction* (Oxford: Clarendon, 1971), 15.

For Abelard, the will to sin did not suffice in producing culpability. Will, or *voluntas*, was a desire or struggle that was antecedent to consent.[45] One had to take a further internal step toward accomplishing the sinful act:

> The time when we consent to what is unlawful is in fact when we in no way draw back from its accomplishment and are inwardly ready, if given the chance, to do it. Anyone who is found in this disposition incurs the fullness of guilt; the addition of the performance of the deed adds nothing to increase the sin. On the contrary, before God the man who to the extent of his power endeavours to achieve this is as guilty as the man who as far as he is able does achieve it—just as if, so the blessed Augustine reminds us, he too had also been caught in the act.[46]

Thus, in Abelard's schema, which conceptually anticipates the development of a law of criminal attempt, the person who tries but fails to carry out a sinful act is just as culpable as the person who successfully achieves his or her sinful goal. Culpability resides in the person's affirmative affective disposition toward the completion of the wrongful act.

Later theologians would build upon this idea.[47] Robert Courson (c. 1160/70–1219), who taught at Paris between 1204 and 1210 and composed his influential *Summa* during that time, discussed the interplay of act and intentionality and took a somewhat different path than Abelard.[48] Namely, rather than placing sole emphasis on consent in defining a state of culpability, Courson conceded "that that person who committed actual and mental homicide is more guilty of crime and therefore ought to have greater penance enjoined against him."[49] He then considered the case of the person who acted, but did so without wrongful intent, concluding:

---

45 Luscombe, *Peter Abelard's* Ethics, 13.

46 Luscombe, *Peter Abelard's* Ethics, 15.

47 On the role of consent in twelfth-century theology and its emphasis in confession by the thirteenth century, see D. W. Robertson, Jr. "Cultural Tradition of Handlyng Synne," *Speculum* 22, no. 2 (1947), 170–72.

48 On these details of Courson's biography, see V. L. Kennedy, "Robert Courson on Penance," *Mediaeval Studies* 7:1 (1945): 292. For a survey of past Courson biographies and a comprehensive new one, see also Marcel Dickson and Christiane Dickson, "Le Cardinal Robert de Courson: Sa vie," *Archives d'histoire doctrinale et littéraire du Moyen Age* 9 (1934): 53–142.

49 Kennedy, "Courson on Penance," 312. "Quod concedimus dicentes quod ille qui et actuale et mentale commisit homicidium magis reus est criminis et ideo maior est ei inungenda [sic] penitentia." My thanks to Noah Delwiche.

> However, for that person who does not intend to kill and nevertheless kills, in no way is penance to be enjoined against him for any crime because he incurs no stain in that he had a simple and sincere eye (*oculum simplicem et sincerum*), according to which: if your eye was simple then your whole body will be clear[.][50]

Practically speaking, this internal disposition, Courson's "simple and sincere eye," was not easily ascertained; furthermore, even an unintended homicide brought with it harmful consequences that might merit redress. Therefore, in doling out penance, the church might sometimes assign penance when a person had performed an apparently sinful act but appeared to have done so without mental culpability or, to put it in Abelard's terms, without having crossed the consent threshold of associating one's will and desire with a sin so resolutely as to have demonstrated contempt of God.

Courson provided a vivid example. Namely, he described the situation of a man who, without intending to kill his father and in fact trying to defend his father against the attack of a wild beast, nevertheless accidentally killed the father when interposing himself between the father and the beast. "That person is not guilty of any homicide," observed Courson, "because God does not weigh the deed but the affect; therefore, penance is not enjoined for the crime of homicide."[51] Nevertheless, penance might be assigned. In a preceding *obiectio*, Courson had presented the counter-argument that it was wrong to punish the son who accidentally killed his father: "If therefore you enjoin penance upon him, you punish him undeservingly. But the church punishes thus; therefore, [it does so] unjustly when there is no cause."[52] Responding to this objection in his *solutio*, Courson explained the church's rationale for imposing penance, which reflected a practical compromise between theory

50 Kennedy, "Courson on Penance," 312–13. "Illi autem qui non intendit interficere et tamen interficit, nulla pro aliquo crimine iniungenda est ei penitentia quia nullam maculam incurrit eo quod habuit oculum simplicem et sincerum, iuxta illud: Si oculus tuus simplex fuerit totum corpus tuum lucidum erit[.]" Here, "eye" carries the meaning of interior vision or the mind's eye. See R. K. Ashdowne, D. R. Howlett, and R. E. Latham, eds., *Dictionary of Medieval Latin from British Sources* (Oxford: Oxford University Press, 2018), *s.v.* "oculus." Courson, in referencing the "simple and sincere eye," seems to imagine a situation in which the actor not only lacked intent to kill but also lacked some lesser form of ill intent, such as the intention to inflict a non-fatal wound.

51 Kennedy, "Courson on Penance," 312. "Iste non est reus alicuius homicidii cum deus non pensat factum sed affectum; ergo pro reatu homocidii non est iniungenda pentitentia."

52 Kennedy, "Courson on Penance," 312. "Si ergo ei iniungis penitentiam, indigne punis eum. Sed ecclesia punit tales; ergo iniuste cum non subsit causa."

(i.e., excusing the son entirely from penance due to his lack of *mens rea*) and administrability:

> [I]t is not without reason that the church is in the habit of enjoining penance in such cases [i.e., of accidental homicide], indeed for three reasons: one is the pecuniary penalty that is enjoined for sustenance of the children whom the father leaves behind as well as perhaps for marriageable maidens; another reason is, of course, due to the horror of the deed, such that the punishment of one should invoke fear in others; [and] a third is because the priest should always presume that the person committed such a homicide from some contempt or negligence.[53]

Courson's reference to acting "from some contempt or negligence" (*aliquo contemptu vel negligentia*) resonates with Abelard's understanding of consent as contempt of God (and goes even further in suggesting the possibility of negligence serving as an alternative source of potential culpability); Courson's formulation appears to have been driven by a concern with the difficulties of proving—or disproving—consent to sin or crime. How could one prove a crime had occurred until an act was carried out in the world and, conversely, how could one disprove culpable intent when death or some other injury had been inflicted but the circumstances favored a non-culpable explanation, such as accident?

This grappling with the interplay of consent and act appears in vernacular texts as well, such as the *Speculum Christiani*'s explanation that the fifth commandment against homicide applied equally to all kinds of killings: "In this euery maner slaughtur es vnleful, es for-boden, which es som-tyme to consente, som-tyme of word, som-tyme of dede, and som-tyme of thoght."[54] The *Ayenbite of Inwyt* or *Prick of Conscience*, a mid-fourteenth-century Middle English translation of a late thirteenth-century French text, suggested that some acts done without full consent (in Abelard's sense) might nevertheless be sinful, possibly reflecting the church's cautious approach to doling out penance in doubtful

53 Kennedy, "Courson on Penance," 312–13. "non sine causa solet tali ecclesia iniungere penitentiam, immo triplici de causa; una est pena pecuniaria que iniungenda est ad parvulos sustentandos quos pater reliquit et virgines forte nubiles; alia causa est scilicet propter facinoris horrorem ut pena unius sit metus aliorum; tercia quia sacerdos debet semper presumere quod aliquo contemptu vel negligentia commisit tale homidicium."

54 Gustaf Holmstedt, ed., *Speculum Christiani: A Middle English Religious Treatise of the 14th Century* (London: Oxford University Press, 1933), 24 (discussed in Kamali, *Felony and the Guilty Mind*, 213).

circumstances. Namely, in discussing the tenth commandment against coveting one's neighbor's possessions, the *Ayenbite* equivocates: "if there is any evil arising without will and without consenting to harm others it is not sin. [But] if there is sin, it is light sin."[55] Possibly drawing upon the *Ayenbite* or a similar source, Geoffrey Chaucer (c. 1340–1400), in his *Parson's Tale,* divided ire into two categories: "sodeyn Ire or hastif Ire, withouten avisement [i.e., deliberation] and consentynge of resoun," and ire that "comth of felonie of herte avysed and cast biforn [i.e., deliberate and set beforehand]" and to which "his resoun consenteth."[56] While sudden ire, due to the absence of consent, was a venial sin, slow-burning ire was deadly.[57] Echoes of Abelard appear elsewhere in Chaucer's *Parson's Tale,* which observed, "ther is no deedly synne that it nas [was not] first in mannes thought and after that in his delit, and so forth into consentynge and into dede."[58]

The progression from thought to delight and finally consent and deed reflected a world view in which temptation was both ever-present and potent yet ultimately resistible. From birth, a child embarked upon a pilgrimage through a world of peril and therefore ought to bear in mind the approach of death and the fate of Adam, thrust from paradise due to Satan's wickedness, as a fourteenth-century lullaby soberly reminded:

> Child, thou art a pilgrim born into wickedness,
> Thou wandrest in this false world, thou [must] look before thee;
> Death shall come with a blast out of order well dim,
> To cast down Adam's kin, as he himself hath done before.
> Lullay, lullay, little child, so woe to thee like Adam,
> In the land of paradise through the wickedness of Satan.[59]

---

55 Dan Michel, *Ayenbite of Inwyt or Remorse of Conscience,* vol. 1, ed. Pamela Gradon (London: Oxford University Press, 1965), 11 (discussed in Kamali, *Felony and the Guilty Mind,* 65 and n. 77). "yef þer is / eni kuead arizinge / wyþ-oute wylle / and wyþ-oute grantinge / to harmi oþren: hit ne is no zenne. And yef þer is zenne: hit is liȝt zenne." For the meaning of "grantinge," see Robert E. Lewis et al., eds., *Middle English Dictionary* (Ann Arbor: University of Michigan Press, 1952–2001). Online edition in Frances McSparran et al., eds., *Middle English Compendium* (Ann Arbor: University of Michigan Library, 2000–2018), *s.v.* "grauntinge," defined as "consenting, agreement, yielding to sin." http://quod.lib.umich.edu/m/middle-english-dictionary/.

56 Larry D. Benson, ed., *Riverside Chaucer* (Boston: Houghton Mifflin, 1987), 305 (discussed in Kamali, *Felony and the Guilty Mind,* 139).

57 Benson, *Riverside Chaucer,* 305.

58 Benson, *Riverside Chaucer,* 295 (discussed in Kamali, *Felony and the Guilty Mind,* 207).

59 "Lollai litel child whi wepistow so sore?," in Carleton Brown, ed., *Religious Lyrics of the XIVth Century* (Oxford: Clarendon, 1952), 36, lines 25–30. "Child, þou ert a pilgrim in

Although the church would not deny the influence of the devil on worldly affairs, neither did it permit a person to escape responsibility for sin by claiming the devil's duress. Rather, individuals were understood to have free will, even when the devil might exert great efforts to lead a person toward sin.[60] According to the *Speculum Christiani*, by choosing to sin, a person committed a wrong against God, provoked other persons toward a like path, strangled good conscience, and slayed truth and righteousness.[61] Moreover, in so doing, the person exhibited contempt toward God by prioritizing "their own will and worldly vanity above God and His commandments."[62] One sermon, for example, chided individuals who, in making excuses for their sinful behavior, might refer to their "destiny" or "the star of [their] birth" when in fact they had succumbed to the devil's temptation through "their own foolish consenting" (*foly consenting*), the language here reinforcing an ultimate act of free and deliberate will.[63]

3 Consent in Crime

Given its centrality to medieval English conceptions of sin, it perhaps comes as little surprise that consent was also at the core of crime. Consent pervaded felony law by the thirteenth and fourteenth centuries in a range of subtle ways. After England abandoned trial by ordeal c. 1215 and shifted toward the use of juries to issue felony verdicts in the 1220s, it was understood that a

wikidnis ibor, / þou wandrest in þis fals world, þou loke þe bi-for; / deth ssal com wiþ a blast vte of a wel dim horre, / adam-is kin dun to cast, him silf haþ ido be-for. / Lollai, lollai, litil child, so wo þe worp adam, / in þe lond of paradis þroȝ wikidnes of satan." The phrase "out of horre" can mean "out of order, in a foolish or disorderly fashion, helter-skelter;" with "horre" itself referring literally to the hinge of a door or lock. See *Middle English Dictionary*, s.v. "herre."

60 See Penelope B. R. Doob, *Nebuchadnezzar's Children: Conventions of Madness in Middle English Literature* (New Haven: Yale University Press, 1974), 17, observing that the devil was generally understood to exert power only after a person consented in some way.

61 Holmstedt, *Speculum Christiani*, 52. "It suffisede not oonly to them-selfe to do wronge to god, bot also thei prouokede ofte other men to do wronge to god. Thei haue strangled boldly gude conscience; thei haue slayne wyttyngly verrey treuth and rightfulnes; thei haue exilede fer fro hem holy charite and heleful techynge; thei haue had the correccyon of god and of holychyreche in gret hate; the[i] haue louede her owne wyl and worldly vanyte a-boue god and hys commandmentes."

62 Holmstedt, *Speculum Christiani*, 52.

63 Gloria Cigman, ed., *Lollard Sermons* (Oxford: Oxford University Press, 1989), 159 (cited in Kamali, *Felony and the Guilty Mind*, 64).

defendant had to consent to being tried by a jury. Such "consent" might be secured through the use of *peine forte et dure*, typically involving the placing of weights upon the body of the recalcitrant defendant.[64] Consent was also foundational to the practice of abjuration, insofar as sanctuary seekers had to commit themselves to leaving England's shores by means of a freely willed confession made in the presence of the local coroners and other witnesses. Of course, consent also arose in thinking about the interests of victims, such as the person whose property was taken without their consent or a woman who was forced to engage in nonconsensual sexual activity (as opposed to the idea of *raptus* involving, in some cases, voluntary elopement).[65] However, these are not the manifestations of consent of greatest interest for the purposes of this essay. Rather, consent had a broader significance in medieval English felony law, which defined the bounds of criminal responsibility in terms of a defendant's state of mind in committing an alleged felony. As I have argued elsewhere, felony required more than an *actus reus*; a felonious *mens rea* was also necessary and necessarily involved a freely made, purposeful choice.[66]

This is not to suggest that *mens rea* alone constituted a felony. As criminal law and penitential theory developed in England, a purely Abelardian approach was never adopted. Just as the law of marriage required an outward sign, typically spoken words, to manifest consent, the secular law of felony required, in most instances, some act in addition to a culpable mental state. As will be discussed below, accomplice liability sometimes presented an exception, with its emphasis on what an accomplice was prepared to do if necessary. Practically speaking, judges (and later, juries) could have had an endless docket of crimes to redress had Abelard's understanding been incorporated without qualification into the criminal law, yet without reliable tools for determining whether a

---

64 See, generally, Sara M. Butler, *Pain, Penance, and Protest: Peine Forte et Dure in Medieval England* (Cambridge: Cambridge University Press, 2021).

65 In the medieval English context, *raptus* could refer either to rape (in our modern sense of a severe sexual assault) or abduction, and could occur with or without a woman's consent. See Caroline Dunn, *Stolen Women in Medieval England: Rape, Abduction, and Adultery, 1100–1500* (Cambridge: Cambridge University Press, 2012), 30. Consider, for example, Chapter 13 of the First Statute of Westminster (1275), which stated: "And the king prohibiteth that none do ravish nor take away by force any maiden within age, neither by her own consent, nor without; nor any wife or maiden of full age, nor any other woman, against her will." A transgression was punished with two years in prison. Chapter 34 of the Second Statute of Westminster (1285) introduced the death penalty: "It is provided, that if a man from henceforth do ravish a married woman, maid, or other, where she did not consent neither before nor after, he shall have judgment of life and member." Translations from Dunn, *Stolen Women*, 197.

66 Kamali, *Felony and the Guilty Mind*, 90.

given individual had actually moved internally from desire and struggle to full consent. Once again, concerns with proof appear to have driven the direction of the legal requirements.

Such practicalities guided the work of the men charged with investigating serious crime in medieval England. The emphasis was on gathering facts that, viewed together, might provide enough circumstantial and direct evidence to establish culpability. In cases of homicide, coroners were instructed to inquire into all the circumstantial details, including where the killing transpired and when, who was present, and so forth. Furthermore, the coroner was expected to gather information as to who was guilty of the deed, "and who of aid, or of force, or of commandment, or of consent ("*ou del consentment*"), or of knowingly receiving such felons."[67] Ultimately, these factual inquiries, including into aspects of the *actus reus* of an alleged crime, helped determine whether the accused individual had acted with a sufficiently guilty mind to merit conviction and whether that person had accomplices who had similarly consented to their involvement. As the early thirteenth-century treatise *Bracton* described it:

> Remove will (*voluntatem*) and every act will be indifferent. It is your intent (*affectio*) that differentiates your acts, nor is a crime committed unless an intention to injure (*voluntas nocendi*) exists; it is will and purpose (*voluntas et propositum*) which distinguish *maleficia*.[68]

In its use of the term *propositum*, the treatise signaled something stronger than desire, namely, "a plan, intention, design, resolution, purpose."[69] The person who undertook the criminal act with such a purpose had crossed the consent threshold and entered a state of culpability, unless there was some excusing circumstance, such as necessity (e.g., self-defense) or an inability to consent (e.g., insanity).

The consent of an alleged criminal became much more difficult to ascertain when they were not the sole actor or perhaps did not undertake a physical act at all. In the context of what we today refer to as complicity or accomplice liability, consent was a crucial concept in differentiating the truly complicit individual from the bystander or involuntary agent. Accomplices to crime were characterized by an agreement to assist the principal actor. As the twelfth-century treatise *Leges Henrici Primi* described it:

67 Francis Morgan Nichols, ed. and trans., *Britton*, vol. 1 (Oxford: Clarendon, 1865), 10.
68 *Bracton*, vol. 2, 23 (discussed in Kamali, *Felony and the Guilty Mind*, 86).
69 *Lewis & Short*, s.v. "propositum."

> [N]ot only is the perpetrator (*auctor*) of the crime himself to be punished, but anyone who by giving or receiving or defending (*dando vel recipiendo vel defendendo*) or by accident (*casu*) or by providing advice (*consilio*) has knowledge of it or consents (*conscius fuerit aut … consentaneus*) to it in any respect shall be subject to the same punishment.[70]

We find this borne out in trial records. For example, when Engelram of Barton was accused of being an accessory to homicide at the 1221 Warwickshire Eyre, having allegedly commanded Roger of Wulward to kill Simon of Barton and then having taken Simon's palfrey after the killing, he disclaimed his alleged role in the homicide and denied "the death and the consent and the command, etc." (*et mortem et consensum et preceptum etc.*).[71] He reported, in fact, that Simon's widow had previously accused him, and that he had been acquitted already. To take a second example, although Henry of Dunchirche alone had struck a fatal blow against Thomas fitz Walter c. 1298, two other men were also determined to be responsible for the homicide: Peter of Thirneby, a monk of Pipewell, and Henry Mareschal of Dunchirche, both of whom had accompanied Henry of Dunchirche on that fateful day and had been ready to support him due to a preexisting dispute with Thomas fitz Walter.[72] A law report produced in the aftermath gives a sense of the inquiry that followed:

> It was presented that a man killed another. There were others in the company, but they did not strike the victim. The court asked the jurors whether the others would have assisted their companion if he had been getting the worst of it. The jurors said that they would have. The court therefore held them all equally guilty (*owelement coupables*).[73]

The inquiry aimed not to discern what the men had actually done, but what they stood ready to do if the opportunity presented itself, reminiscent of Abelard's reference to those who stood "inwardly ready, if given the chance," to commit an unlawful act.[74] Similarly, when Robert Bernard, leaving a tavern

70 L. J. Downer, ed. and trans., *Leges Henrici Primi* (Oxford: Clarendon, 1972), 262–63, no. 85.2a (discussed in Kamali, *Felony and the Guilty Mind*, 79).

71 F. W. Maitland, ed. and trans., *Select Pleas of the Crown*, vol. 1 (1200–1225) (London: Selden Society, 1888), 101, no. 158.

72 Donald W. Sutherland, ed. and trans., *The Eyre of Northamptonshire, 3–4 Edward III, A.D. 1329–1330*, vol. 1 (London: Selden Society, 1983), 186.

73 Sutherland, *Northamptonshire Eyre*, vol. 1, 185–86.

74 Luscombe, *Peter Abelard's* Ethics, 15.

at curfew, struck and killed Ralph son of Ralph outside the Bromham church in 1272, the coroner held an inquest to piece together what had occurred. Representatives of one of the villages summoned to provide testimony indicated that Robert Bernard was solely responsible for the death, although three other men had been with Robert at the tavern that evening. The representatives of three other villages, however, testified that the three other men "consented to do any other misdeed and were waiting to do injury to someone else there."[75] All four men were to be arrested. It is not uncommon to find the language of consent employed in allegations of accomplice liability, such as the suspicion reported against Adam Poret, Agnes his wife, Nicholas Sperwe, and John Fole "for consenting to and aiding Nicholas Bugge of Wood Norton" in committing homicide and robbery, as reported at the delivery of Norwich Castle gaol in 1316; Adam and his wife were released on manucaption since the principal had not yet been convicted.[76]

Due to the centrality of consent, alleged accessories to a crime might be treated with leniency if they were perceived not to have consented to the crime. For example, in 1306, William de Hampton and Henry of Woolchurch Haw were acquitted of felony despite the fact that they had made duplicate keys and files that were used to perpetrate a gaol-breaking. The woman who paid for the gaol-breaking equipment was hanged, while William and Henry were spared because the jury determined that they had not acted feloniously or consented to the woman's felony. Nevertheless, because they had acted without thought (*inconsiderate*), presumably failing to inquire why the woman wanted these particular items, they were sent to gaol for a year.[77]

Having received some punishment for supplying burglary tools to a felon, William and Henry were only partially excused for acting thoughtlessly. Individuals claiming to have been insane at the time of an alleged felony received, by comparison, a full excuse, resulting in either an acquittal or, more commonly, a royal pardon. When John son of William stood trial for arson in

75 R. F. Hunnisett, ed. and trans., *Bedfordshire Coroners' Rolls* (Streatley: Bedfordshire Historical Record Society, 1961), 55 (discussed in Kamali, "Horrible Sepulture," 20).

76 Barbara A. Hanawalt, ed. and trans., *Crime in East Anglia in the Fourteenth Century: Norfolk Gaol Delivery Rolls, 1307–1316* (Norwich: Norfolk Record Society, 1976), 112, no. 727.

77 Kamali, *Felony and the Guilty Mind*, 77, citing Ralph B. Pugh, ed., *Calendar of London Trailbaston Trials under Commissions of 1305 and 1306* (London: HMSO, 1975), 122–23, no. 317. This requirement of consent in accomplice liability has modern echoes. See, e.g., Learned Hand's opinion in *United States v. Peoni*, 100 F.2d 401 (2d Cir. 1938), 402 (requiring that an accessory have "a purpose attitude" toward the object crime). My thanks to John Goldberg.

1349, the jury found John not responsible for his acts in light of his illness. The record tells us:

> Jurors from the aforesaid vicinity ... say on their oath that the aforesaid John is a lunatic, vexed by the illness of dementia three or four times per year, and they say that the same John on the day and year aforesaid and for eight days preceding and for eight days following was continually detained by the aforesaid illness, having no awareness or discretion of good or evil or of his own deeds and thus on account of this aforesaid infirmity he burned the aforesaid house and not through felony or any other malice aforethought[.][78]

Found to be *non compos mentis*, John was acquitted. Generally, excuses grounded in insanity described a defendant incapable of exercising meaningful agency in carrying out an apparently felonious act.[79] Just as persons deemed insane could not consent to marriage or to a business contract, they could not engage in felony if found to have been insane at the time of the alleged incident. In the context of land transactions, the treatise *Bracton* observes that a person "can neither consent nor dissent" while in a state of insanity.[80]

What about married women accused of felonious acts, particularly in concert with their husbands? Were they presumptively culpable, or were they more like William and Henry, the thoughtless suppliers of burglary tools, or like the insane individual, incapable of acting feloniously? Somewhere between the unwitting aider and the insane actor lay cases of duress and necessity, most frequently claims of self-defense, which might bear a closer resemblance to the plight of a married woman faced with spousal pressure to engage in crime. To secure a pardon, self-defenders had to demonstrate that they had no possibility of escape and no alternative but to resort to lethal violence to save their own lives.[81] As will be explored below, a married woman might similarly claim,

78 TNA KB27/355, m. 29 (1350), accessible at http://aalt.law.uh.edu/E3/KB27no355/bKB27no355mm1dtoEnd/IMG_8326.htm (incipit "Johanes filius Willelmi") and discussed in Kamali, *Felony and the Guilty Mind*, 59 (with thanks to Robert Palmer).

79 For two more representative examples, see TNA JUST 3/48, m. 20 (1315), accessible at http://aalt.law.uh.edu/AALT7/JUST3/JUST3no48/aJUST3no48fronts/IMG_0047.htm (case of Philip Statheman); and Sutherland, *Northamptonshire Eyre*, vol. 1, 215–16 (case of Robert fitz Adam of Clipston), viewable at TNA JUST 1/635 (1329/30), m. 17, http://aalt.law.uh.edu/AALT4/JUST1/JUST1no635/aJUST1no635fronts/IMG_0698.htm.

80 *Bracton*, vol. 3, 28.

81 On the rules of self-defense, see Thomas Andrew Green, *Verdict According to Conscience: Perspectives on the English Criminal Trial Jury, 1200–1800* (Chicago: University of Chicago Press, 1985), 30.

in some circumstances, to have had no alternative but to participate in her husband's crimes due to the pressures he placed upon her, thereby shedding light on the complex interplay between marital dynamics and consent to crime.

4 Marital Status and Consent to Crime

In her article on peasant families and crime in fourteenth-century England, Barbara Hanawalt quipped, while acknowledging that her research could neither confirm nor deny, that "the family that slays together stays together."[82] Admittedly, crime could strain a marital relationship. In the case that opened this essay, Agnes le Folur was initially said to have been guilty of harboring the thief Batinus, but upon further inquiry, she was acquitted while her husband Robert and another woman, Christiana Hobelot, would hang for the deed. The record attributes Agnes's lack of culpability to the fact that she had no alternative but to obey her husband. Agnes's excuse, however, was not universally available to married women implicated in crimes with their husbands. Rather, marital status gave rise to rebuttable presumptions—that a wife might have had no alternative but to obey her husband, that a husband might have acceded to his wife's criminal behavior.[83] Ideally, further inquiry would shed light upon the intra-marriage dynamics and the decisions made by spouses aware of their partners' misdeeds, thereby aiding the jury in reaching a reasoned verdict.

In some instances, like the case of Agnes le Folur, a married woman who allegedly committed a crime with her husband might avoid the gallows if a jury, though willing to convict the husband, found that the wife had not truly consented but rather had acted against her will, calling to mind the modern doctrine of duress. For example, when Christiana Sprot was accused of killing a merchant in concert with her husband, she was acquitted at the 1249 Wiltshire Eyre, the jury having concluded that "Christiana was not consenting (*non fuit consenciens*) unless against her will (*nisi invita*) by compulsion and

82 Barbara Hanawalt, "The Peasant Family and Crime in Fourteenth-Century England," *The Journal of British Studies* 13, no. 2 (1974): 16. My thanks to Tom Green for the reference. On rural and urban patterns in family cooperation in committing crimes in thirteenth-century England, see James Buchanan Given, *Society and Homicide in Thirteenth-Century England* (Stanford: Stanford University Press, 1977), 176–77.

83 On the use of presumptions in the common law, see generally David J. Seipp, "Presumptions in Early English Common Law," in *The Law of Presumptions: Essays in Comparative Legal History*, ed. R. H. Helmholz and W. David H. Sellar (Berlin: Duncker & Humblot, 2009), 117–36.

fear of her husband (*per compulsionem et timorem viri sui*)."[84] And although, at the delivery of the Norwich Castle gaol in 1309, Geoffrey le Kokener and Catherine his wife were both accused of stealing a sheep in the fields of Worthing, a jury acquitted Catherine, while Geoffrey faced the gallows.[85] In cases of this kind, where the husband was convicted while the wife walked free, the plea roll language sometimes alludes to the wife's inability to oppose her husband. For example, according to the record of the 1257 Yorkshire Eyre, Hawysa, wife of Robert, had been by her husband's side when he had slashed the throat of a woman named Amabilia in her home in the middle of the night. Nevertheless, the court determined that Hawysa, "because she was [Robert's] wife, so betrothed, could not contradict the will of her husband."[86] Similarly, at the 1255 Surrey Eyre, when Alicia, wife of William le Sleghe, was accused of harboring her husband after he was outlawed, a jury determined that Alicia "could not contradict (*contradicere*) him," and that she should therefore be acquitted.[87]

When a rationale for leniency is discernable in the plea rolls, it typically references the wife's subjection to her husband's will. To take an example, at the 1329–1330 Northamptonshire Eyre, Alice and her husband Richard fitz John Byyondethebrok of Wendlyngburgh [possibly Wellingborough, Northants] were convicted together of the theft of ten oxen and cows in several Northamptonshire townships.[88] Richard was to be hanged immediately, while

84 Meekings, *Wiltshire Eyre*, 238, no. 445 (discussed in Kamali, *Felony and the Guilty Mind*, 61). See also Margaret H. Kerr, "Husband and Wife in Criminal Proceedings in Medieval England," in *Women, Marriage, and Family in Medieval Christendom: Essays in Memory of Michael M. Sheehan,* C.S.B., ed. Constance M. Rousseau and Joel Thomas Rosenthal (Kalamazoo: Medieval Institute, 1998), 236. For another example of a wife acquitted of a crime—in this instance, robbery—because she had been forced by her husband to participate, see Hanawalt, "Peasant Family," 13–14 and n. 52.

85 Hanawalt, *Crime in East Anglia*, 32, no. 98. See also Hanawalt, 47, no. 211 (Walter of Pikerel hanged for burglary while his wife Matilda is acquitted); 64, no. 360 (Peter Thur hanged for robbery while his co-accused wife, Alice, is acquitted); 118, no. 771 (Geoffrey of Somerset to be hanged for theft, while his wife Alice was acquitted).

86 TNA JUST 1/1109 (1257), m. 10 (final entry), viewable at http://aalt.law.uh.edu/AALT4/JUST1/JUST1no1109/aJUST1no1109fronts/IMG_8755.htm ("quia ipsa fuit uxor s[ic] desponsata nec potuit contradicere voluntatem viri sui"). My translation presumes the abbreviated "s" to be a "sic." Thanks to Henry Summerson, who shared this citation in a note to a case in *Crown Pleas of the Devon Eyre of 1238* (Torquay: Devonshire Press, 1985), 86–87, no. 524. See also Henry Summerson, "Maitland and the Criminal Law in the Age of *Bracton*," *Proceedings of the British Academy* 89 (1996): 117.

87 TNA JUST 1/872, m. 33d (1255), viewable at http://aalt.law.uh.edu/AALT4/JUST1/JUST1no872/bJUST1no872dorses/IMG_9225.htm (incipit: "Alicia que fuit uxor"). See also Summerson, *Devon Eyre of 1238*, 86–87, no. 524, and "Maitland the Criminal Law," 117.

88 Sutherland, *Northamptonshire Eyre*, vol. 1, 179–80.

Alice received a temporary reprieve due to the fact that she was pregnant. A corresponding law report suggests that the eyre justices might have failed to undertake all the relevant inquiries under the circumstances. "The justices did not inquire," the law report notes, "whether the woman committed the robbery in the company of her husband, nor whether her husband forced her to do it (*ne si ele le fist par cohercion de son baron*), but condemned them to be hanged."[89] This suggests some concern about affording due process to ensure that a wife accused alongside her husband not be wrongfully condemned, particularly if she had been coerced into participating or perhaps had not participated at all. This concern with coercion reflected broader ideas about the malleability of a woman's will, as suggested by this fourteenth-century vernacular poem:

> Women never wrought any wrong
> Unless through men's enticement.
> Men beseech women so powerfully
> And say in fire they might be burned,
> And woo them so long,
> To bring them to their assent.[90]

Nevertheless, women could be convicted of crime, with coercion only realistically serving as an excuse within the context of a marital relationship in which a husband placed undue pressure upon a wife.[91]

When it was the wife who was the principal criminal actor within a marital household, a husband might rebut a presumption that he had consented to his wife's misdeeds. However, the reasons for an excuse differed. Inquiry did not focus on whether the wife had coerced her husband to participate, but rather whether the husband was unaware of his wife's wrongdoing or, once aware of it, had distanced himself from her illegal activities. There does not appear to have been any expectation that the husband turn his wife over to the authorities, just as *Bracton* would indicate that a wife had no obligation

---

89 Sutherland, *Northamptonshire Eyre*, 179. See also Gwen Seabourne, *Women in the Medieval Common Law, c. 1200–1500* (London: Routledge, 2021), 140 and n. 112.

90 "This World's Weal Comes from Women," in *Minor Poems of the Vernon Manuscript*, part 1, ed. Frederick J. Furnivall (London: Kegan Paul, 1892), 706 (discussed in Kamali, *Felony and the Guilty Mind*, 61). "Wimmen wrouȝte neuer so wrong / But þorw Monnes entysement. / Men secheþ wimmen so strong, / And sei in Bale þei mote be brent, / And ligge aboute hem so long, / To bringen hem til heore a-sent".

91 For a refutation of the "exaggerated view of the 'shielding' effect of marriage for women in terms of culpability," see Seabourne, *Women in the Medieval Common Law*, 138.

to report her husband's criminal activity.[92] At the delivery of Newgate gaol in 1305, Catherine, wife of John Aleyn, was hanged and her husband acquitted once the jury determined that the wife had acted "without her husband's knowledge and in his absence" when she received several thieves and "shared in their pelf."[93] Another case in the same context gives a sense of the questions posed to juries when faced with the possibility of a husband's complicity: after finding Agnes Crok guilty of being "a common receiver of thieves and pelf" and a "common thief" in her own right, the jury responded in the negative when asked whether Agnes's husband had consented to those deeds.[94] A law report dated to 1322 describes how a husband, wife, and son were implicated in the theft of several sheepskins and a coat after the items were discovered in their household. While the wife and son were found guilty, the husband was acquitted when it was discovered that he had removed himself from their company and even moved out of the household due to his awareness of their felonious activity.[95] In another case, when Walter Asketel, Catherine his wife, and Catherine's mother Joan were accused together of possessing goods stolen by a convicted thief named Adam of Wroxham, both Walter and his mother-in-law were acquitted while Catherine alone was convicted, her execution delayed after a jury of matrons confirmed that she was pregnant.[96] The record fails to explain why the husband escaped conviction. Likewise, when William Aiswy and Alice his wife were accused together of larceny and burglary at the 1249 Wiltshire Eyre, William was acquitted while Alice was found guilty of petty larcenies and ordered to find pledges for her future good behavior.[97]

Unlike a husband who could remove himself from the household once aware of his wife's criminal behavior, a wife might not so easily extract herself from the marital home. This point comes through obliquely in the late thirteenth-century treatise *Fleta*, which observes that the situation of wives differs from that of concubines and household servants. Unlike a wife, a concubine or servant who learned of a man's criminal behavior was "bound to accuse [the man] or to withdraw from his service: otherwise she will appear

92 *Bracton*, vol. 2, 428.

93 Pugh, *Calendar of London Trailbaston Trials*, 72, no. 107.

94 Pugh, *Calendar of London Trailbaston Trials*, 78, no. 134.

95 David J. Seipp, compiler, *An Index and Paraphrase of Printed Year Book Reports, 1268–1535*, accessible at bu.edu/phpbin/lawyearbooks/search.php, no. 1322.018; Sutherland, *Eyre of Northamptonshire*, vol. 2, 791–92.

96 Hanawalt, *Crime in East Anglia*, 99, no. 623.

97 Meekings, *Wiltshire Eyre*, 174, no. 116.

to consent."[98] By comparison, *Fleta* notes, the "wife of a thief will not be held responsible for her husband's delict, for a penalty should strike those who do the deed."[99] According to *Bracton*, if stolen goods were discovered in a marital household, the default presumption was to find the husband solely liable unless he could find a warrantor to defend his possession.[100] His wife would not be presumptively liable, as the goods would be understood to be within the *potestas* (the treatise here adding a Romanist flair) of the husband alone.[101] The wife's presence in the household did not give rise to a presumption of complicity in her husband's crimes, and even her receipt of stolen goods could be cast in a forgiving light if her husband were willing to warrant that he had delivered the goods to her to sell.[102]

However, the wife could find herself chargeable with theft, too, when the circumstances suggested that she exercised willful control over stolen items. While the husband was the primary source of authority within a marital household, a wife had certain spheres within which she had meaningful clout. According to *Bracton*:

> In certain cases of theft, however, she will be liable, where the stolen property is found under her keys, for a wife ought to have those keys in her care and custody, namely, the keys of her store-room, her chest and her cupboard, and if any stolen property is found locked up under the said keys she and her husband will be guilty.[103]

In some instances, the wife alone might be liable for a theft, as when the stolen goods were discovered in the wife's hands.[104] The husband in that instance,

98 H. G. Richardson and G. O. Sayles, eds. and trans., *Fleta*, vol. 2 (London: Bernard Quaritch, 1955), 92. Nearly identical language appears in *Bracton*, vol. 2, 428–29.

99 *Fleta*, vol. 2, 92.

100 *Bracton*, vol. 2, 428.

101 *Bracton*, vol. 2, 428. See also Kerr, "Husband and Wife," 235.

102 See, e.g., the case of Margaret de Hatfeld, accused of stealing two overcoats. Her husband, John le Saucer, would hang for the deed after clearing Margaret's name. Pugh, *Calendar of London Trailbaston Trials*, 106–07, no. 251.

103 *Bracton*, vol. 2, 428. Teresa Phipps speculates that wives, given their expertise as "household managers," might have committed receipt of stolen goods with some frequency, either instigating such crimes themselves or having been drawn in by their husbands. Teresa Phipps, *Medieval Women and Urban Justice: Commerce, Crime and Community in England, 1300–1500* (Manchester: Manchester University Press, 2020), 135, 164.

104 See *Bracton*, vol. 2, 428. See also *Fleta*, vol. 2, 92: "If stolen property is found, however, under the wife's lock and key she will be held liable jointly with her husband, and she alone will be held liable if the stolen property should perchance be found in her hand."

Bracton observes, would not be liable "unless he expressly consented, as where, when she has vouched him to warranty he has warranted the thing to her."[105] *Fleta* similarly observes: "A husband, to be sure, is in no wise [liable for his wife's thefts], unless he expressly consent thereto or she be warranted by him; and unless one avoid the wrongdoing of the other, evidently the consent of both to the crime may be presumed."[106] *Bracton* continues: "He is presumed to consent unless he expressly dissents, or unless there is a presumption that he is law-abiding, since he had eschewed the company of his wife as much as he could."[107]

While terse records may conceal some details of an investigation or prosecution, courts do not appear to have always inquired into a husband's participation when a married woman was accused of a crime. For example, married women working as alewives might find themselves accused directly of using false measures and would be obliged to find pledges, with no implication that their husbands should have to answer directly for their alleged misbehavior.[108] Similarly, when Margaret, wife of Simon of Barwick, was accused of burglary in Norwich in 1315, she was convicted and sentenced to hang with no apparent inquiry into her husband's knowledge or involvement, although her execution was postponed when she was found to be pregnant.[109]

While a wife might be coerced into felonious behavior, she could also be a full partner in crime with her husband according to the treatises *Bracton* and *Fleta*. *Bracton* observed that wives must not be "discharged in every case," because they might be guilty of "counsel, aid and consent."[110] *Bracton* elaborated: "Since they are partners in crime, they will be partners in punishment. And though she ought to obey her husband she need not be obedient to him in heinous deeds."[111] *Fleta* reached a similar conclusion: "It is possible, too, for

105 *Bracton*, vol. 2, 428.

106 *Fleta*, vol. 2, 92.

107 *Bracton*, vol. 2, 428.

108 G. Herbert Fowler, ed. and trans., "Roll of the Justices in Eyre at Bedford, 1202," in *The Publications of the Bedfordshire Historical Record Society*, vol. 1 (Aspley Guise: Bedfordshire Historical Record Society, 1913), 245–46, nos. 262 and 263 (accusations against Matilda, wife of Hugh, and Clarice, wife of Laurence, son of Walter). On litigation involving married women, see also Phipps, *Medieval Women and Urban*, 56–57, 64–79. And on direct accusations against wives alone in regulatory offenses, see Kerr, "Husband and Wife," 239.

109 Hanawalt, *Crime in East Anglia*, 71, no. 411. See also Hanawalt, 77, no. 454 (Amice, wife of John Henry, convicted for knowingly receiving felons); 108, no. 692 (Beatrice, wife of William Attesee, convicted of burglary and the theft of a sheep and two bushels of barley and sentenced to be hanged).

110 *Bracton*, vol. 2, 428.

111 *Bracton*, vol. 2, 428.

the man to hold and the wife to slay, freely and without coercion (*sponte et non coacta*), and the other way round; and therefore, since they are partners in crime, they should be partners in the penalty, and thus both should be held liable if they are convicted of common consent (*de communi assensu*)."[112] A similar language of partnership, albeit not applied specifically to spouses, can be found in Chaucer's *Parson's Tale*, in which it is stated: "they that eggen or consenten to the synne been parteners of the synne, and of the dampnacioun of the synnere."[113]

To take an example of such a partnership in sinful or criminal acts, John le Gaunter and his wife Agnes together beat a woman named Isabel, who was the widow of Geoffrey le Sachier. Although Isabel initially escaped, John le Gaunter visited her home at night to kill her, fleeing afterwards with Agnes. John was outlawed, and Agnes, having been declared an accomplice to the death by the mayor and alderman of London, was waived, the female form of outlawry.[114] Similarly, at the Northamptonshire Eyre of 1329–1330, it was reported by the hundred of Hamfordshoe that William Wydewesone and his wife Alice had been arrested together for the burglary of the home of Henry Tebbe of Harrowden, including the theft of a tunic of bluet valued at 2s.; both husband and wife had been hanged for the deed upon the judgment of Robert of Granesete, the abbot's seneschal.[115] Likewise, in Norwich in 1316, Alexander of Necton and Margery Bryn his wife were accused of stealing twelve pounds of wax from various churches. Alexander turned king's evidence, agreeing to confess his crime and bring accusations against his accomplices, while Margery was convicted and ordered to be hanged.[116] Similarly, both William of Markaunt and Emma his wife were convicted of stealing a sheet, surcoat, hand towel, and tunic.[117] To take one final example, at the 1249 Wiltshire Eyre, it was reported that Roger de Fonte had trussed up and tried to carry off a sheep belonging to the bishop of Winchester. The bishop's shepherd, Walter, had chased after Roger, and during the ensuing altercation had killed Roger in self-defense.[118] Remarkably, Roger's wife Joan took flight after her husband's death, eventually confessing to her own thievery and abjuring the realm.

---

112 *Fleta*, vol. 2, 92. This might alternatively be translated as "of common assent."

113 Benson, *Riverside Chaucer*, 323. See also *Middle English Dictionary*, s.v. "consenten."

114 Martin Weinbaum, ed. and trans., *The London Eyre of 1276* (London: London Record Society, 1976), 70, no. 250.

115 Sutherland, *Northamptonshire Eyre*, vol. 1, 168.

116 Hanawalt, *Crime in East Anglia*, 98, no. 617.

117 Hanawalt, *Crime in East Anglia*, 106, no. 677.

118 Meekings, *Wiltshire Eyre*, 184, no. 165.

Reminiscent of understandings of consent in the formation of marriage, some persons were incapable of freely choosing to commit a felony, whether due to their status as minors, lunatics, or even married women acting under the duress of their husbands, like Agnes, wife of Robert le Folur, discussed at the start of this essay.[119] At the intersection of crime and marriage, marital status gave rise to presumptions regarding consent, and the presumptions differed for husbands and for wives. A wife might be presumed to have had no alternative but to obey a husband bent on her participation in a crime. A husband aware of his wife's criminal behavior might be presumed to have consented to that behavior, and therefore be found culpable as well, unless he could rebut that presumption. These default "rules" were created by the marital bond, just as coverture gave rise to rules in other areas of law, such as contract.[120] There was no sense, however, that women could not generally consent to crime; even a married woman might be held accountable for a crime committed with her husband if the circumstances warranted it. Moreover, while a married woman could be coerced into felonious behavior by her spouse, she was also understood to have the capacity and responsibility to influence her husband's behavior. A wife, the *Bracton* treatise observed, should not expose her husband's criminality, yet she also had an obligation "to keep him as best she can from felony and wickedness."[121] The late-thirteenth-century treatise *Fleta* drew upon *Bracton* in similarly advising: "A wife, moreover, should neither accuse her husband nor consent to his felony; but she is required to hinder him so far as she is able."[122] The marital bond forged by the exchange of consent produced mutual obligations, yet husband and wife could still be judged separately and, indeed, could hang separately if a court determined that both had consented freely to a felonious deed.

---

119 See, generally, Kamali, *Felony and the Guilty Mind*, 51–70.

120 See, e.g., "Anon. v. Anon," in *The Eyre of Kent, 6 & 7 Edward II, A.D. 1313–1314*, vol. 2, ed. William Craddock Bolland, Frederic William Maitland, and Leveson William Vernon Harcourt (London: Bernard Quaritch, 1912), 48, detailing a husband's response to a writ of debt brought against himself and his wife by an executor. The husband claimed that if any contract had been made, it had been done so "without our consent and against our will," such that he could not be liable. The executor was out of luck, insofar as the wife could now vouch the record if he brought the claim against her solely. Chief Justice Bereford advised: "You should have thought of all that before you lent your money."

121 *Bracton*, vol. 2, 428.

122 *Fleta*, vol. 2, 92.

5 Conclusion

Consent was a pivotal concept in twelfth-century theology and subsequently played a central role in the laws of marriage and felony in medieval England. Although an indissoluble marriage was forged through the exchange of present consent, something more than internal accord was required: consent was typically understood to be manifested through the exchange of spoken words. Should a dispute arise, witnesses would have to be prepared to testify to words or signs clearly indicative of the couple's consent to marriage. Similarly, in the law of felony, an actor's state of mind determined whether or not they were guilty of an alleged crime, such that a person might be convicted by virtue of standing ready to assist should their help be needed. Although culpability was understood to be situated in the felon's heart or mind, investigation centered upon visible facts ascertained through circumstantial inquiry that might shed light on whether a person had truly consented to a felonious deed. Within the marital context, presumptions aided adjudication, and these presumptions differed for husbands and wives. A wife might be found to have acted under the compulsion of her husband, but not vice versa. And a husband might be presumed to be complicit in his wife's felonious behavior unless he physically distanced himself from her, even to the point of departing the marital household, thereby creating a visible sign of his non-consent. Such inquiries into the consent of husband and wife to each other's crimes were in some ways not unlike any other inquiry into accomplice liability. However, the marital bond, itself forged by consent, created unique presumptions that had to be accounted for in the investigation of alleged crimes by husbands and wives. The danger otherwise is that a jury might be too quick to find in the bond of matrimony—and the resulting intimacy of household—evidence of consent not only to marriage but to felony.

Acknowledgments

Thanks are due to Sonia Tycko and the participants in the 2022 Radcliffe Exploratory Seminar on *Historicizing Consent*, as well as to Tom Green, Saskia Lettmaier, Justice Rosalie Silberman Abella, John Goldberg, Henry Smith, and research assistants Noah Delwiche, Yudith Pereira-Lopez, and Maddy Scannell. I am also grateful to the FRIDA staff at the Harvard Law Library, including Alethea Jones, Anna Martin, Sara Newberg, Rachel Parker, and Kaylee Paul. Unless otherwise indicated, translations are my own.

Bibliography

Adams, Norma, and Charles Donahue, Jr. *Select Cases from the Ecclesiastical Courts of the Province of Canterbury, c. 1200–1301*. London: Selden Society, 1981.

Ashdowne, R. K., D. R. Howlett, and R. E. Latham, eds. *Dictionary of Medieval Latin from British Sources*. Oxford: Oxford University Press, 2018.

Austin, Gregory A. *Alcohol in Western Society from Antiquity to 1800: A Chronological Survey*. Santa Barbara, CA: ABC-Clio Information Services, 1985.

Benson, Larry D., ed. *Riverside Chaucer*. Boston: Houghton Mifflin, 1987.

Bolland, William Craddock, Frederic William Maitland, and Leveson William Vernon Harcourt, eds. *The Eyre of Kent, 6 & 7 Edward II, A.D. 1313–1314*, vol. 2. London: Bernard Quaritch, 1912.

Brown, Carleton, ed. *Religious Lyrics of the XIVth Century*. Oxford: Clarendon, 1952.

Brundage, James A. *Law, Sex, and Christian Society in Medieval Europe*. Chicago: University of Chicago Press, 1987.

Brundage, James A. "Marriage and Sexuality in the Decretals of Pope Alexander III." In *Sex, Law and Marriage in the Middle Ages*, 59–83. Aldershot: Variorum, 1993.

Buhrer, Eliza. "Disability and Consent in Medieval Law." *Postmedieval* 10, no. 3 (2019): 344–56.

Butler, Sara M. *Pain, Penance, and Protest: Peine Forte et Dure in Medieval England*. Cambridge: Cambridge University Press, 2021.

Cigman, Gloria, ed. *Lollard Sermons*. Oxford: Oxford University Press, 1989.

Dickson, Marcel, and Christiane Dickson. "Le Cardinal Robert de Courson: Sa vie." *Archives d'histoire doctrinale et littéraire du Moyen Age* 9 (1934): 53–142.

Donahue, Charles, Jr. "The Canon Law on the Formation of Marriage and Social Practice in the Later Middle Ages." *Journal of Family History* 8, no. 2 (1983): 144–58.

Donahue, Charles, Jr. *Law, Marriage, and Society in the Later Middle Ages: Arguments About Marriage in Five Courts*. Cambridge: Cambridge University Press, 2007.

Donahue, Charles, Jr. "The Policy of Alexander the Third's Consent Theory of Marriage." In *Proceedings of the Fourth International Congress of Medieval Canon Law*, edited by Stephan Kuttner, 251–81. Città del Vaticano: Biblioteca Apostolica Vaticana, 1976.

Doob, Penelope B. R. *Nebuchadnezzar's Children: Conventions of Madness in Middle English Literature*. New Haven: Yale University Press, 1974.

Downer, L. J., ed. and trans. *Leges Henrici Primi*. Oxford: Clarendon, 1972.

Duggan, Anne J. "The Effect of Alexander III's 'Rules on the Formation of Marriage' in Angevin England." *Anglo-Norman Studies* 33 (2011): 1–22.

Dunn, Caroline. *Stolen Women in Medieval England: Rape, Abduction, and Adultery, 1100–1500*. Cambridge: Cambridge University Press, 2012.

Fowler, G. Herbert, ed. and trans. "Roll of the Justices in Eyre at Bedford, 1202." In *The Publications of the Bedfordshire Historical Record Society*, vol. 1. Aspley Guise: Bedfordshire Historical Record Society, 1913.

Furnivall, Frederik J., ed. *Minor Poems of the Vernon Manuscript*, part 1. London: Kegan Paul, 1892.

Given, James Buchanan. *Society and Homicide in Thirteenth-Century England.* Stanford: Stanford University Press, 1977.

Green, Thomas Andrew. *Verdict According to Conscience: Perspectives on the English Criminal Trial Jury, 1200–1800*. Chicago: University of Chicago Press, 1985.

Hanawalt, Barbara A., ed. and trans. *Crime in East Anglia in the Fourteenth Century: Norfolk Gaol Delivery Rolls, 1307–1316.* Norwich: Norfolk Record Society, 1976.

Hanawalt, Barbara. "The Peasant Family and Crime in Fourteenth-Century England." *The Journal of British Studies* 13, no. 2 (1974): 1–18.

Helmholz, R. H. *Marriage Litigation in Medieval England.* Cambridge: Cambridge University Press, 1974.

Helmholz, Richard. "Pope Innocent III and the Annulment of Magna Carta," *Journal of Ecclesiastical History* 69, no. 1 (2018): 1–14.

Holmstedt, Gustaf, ed. *Speculum Christiani: A Middle English Religious Treatise of the 14th Century*. London: Oxford University Press, 1933.

Hunnisett, R. F., ed. and trans. *Bedfordshire Coroners' Rolls*. Streatley: Bedfordshire Historical Record Society, 1961.

Kamali, Elizabeth Papp. *Felony and the Guilty Mind in Medieval England.* Cambridge: Cambridge University Press, 2019.

Kamali, Elizabeth Papp. "The Horrible Sepulture of Mannes Resoun: Intoxication and Medieval English Felony Law." *Rechtsgeschichte—Legal History* 30 (2022): 2–26.

Kennedy, V. L. "Robert Courson on Penance." *Mediaeval Studies* 7, no. 1 (1945): 291–336.

Kerr, Margaret H. "Husband and Wife in Criminal Proceedings in Medieval England." In *Women, Marriage, and Family in Medieval Christendom: Essays in Memory of Michael M. Sheehan, C.S.B.*, edited by Constance M. Rousseau and Joel Thomas Rosenthal, 211–51. Kalamazoo: Medieval Institute, 1998.

Lewis, Robert E., et al., eds. *Middle English Dictionary*. Ann Arbor: University of Michigan Press, 1952–2001. Online edition in McSparran, Frances et al., eds. *Middle English Compendium*. Ann Arbor: University of Michigan Library, 2000–2018. http://quod.lib.umich.edu/m/middle-english-dictionary/.

Luscombe, D. E., ed. and trans. *Peter Abelard's* Ethics: *An Edition with Introduction.* Oxford: Clarendon, 1971.

Maitland, F. W., ed. and trans. *Select Pleas of the Crown*, vol. 1. London: Selden Society, 1888.

Mannyng of Brunne, Robert. *Handlyng Synne*. Edited by Idelle Sullens. Binghamton: Medieval & Renaissance Texts & Studies, 1983.

McSheffrey, Shannon. *Marriage, Sex, and Civic Culture in Late Medieval London*. Philadelphia: University of Pennsylvania Press, 2011.

Meekings, C. A. F., ed. and trans. *Crown Pleas of the Wiltshire Eyre, 1249*. Devizes: Wiltshire Archaeological and Natural History Society, 1961.

Michel, Dan. *Ayenbite of Inwyt or Remorse of Conscience*, vol. 1. Edited by Pamela Gradon. London: Oxford University Press, 1965.

Minnis, Alastair J. "'Oonly consent of love is sufficiant for matrimonie': Translating John Wyclif's Word of the Mind." In *Lost in Translation?*, edited by Denis Reveney and Christiania Whitehead, 189–203. Turnhout: Brepols, 2009.

The National Archives (TNA) JUST 1/635, m. 17 (1329/30).

TNA JUST 1/872, m. 33d (1255).

TNA JUST 1/1109, m. 10 (1257).

TNA JUST 3/48, m. 20 (1315).

TNA KB 27/355, m. 29 (1350).

Nichols, Francis Morgan, ed. and trans. *Britton*, vol. 1. Oxford: Clarendon, 1865.

Pedersen, Frederik. *Marital Disputes in Medieval England*. Hambledon: Hambledon Press, 2000.

Phipps, Teresa. *Medieval Women and Urban Justice: Commerce, Crime and Community in England, 1300–1500*. Manchester: Manchester University Press, 2020.

Porter, Jean. "Responsibility, Passion, and Sin: A Reassessment of Abelard's Ethics." *The Journal of Religious Ethics* 28, no. 3 (2000): 367–94.

Powicke, F. M., and C. R. Cheney, eds. *Councils & Synods with Other Documents Relating to the English Church*, vol. 2 (1205–1313), Part I (1205–1265). Oxford: Clarendon, 1964.

Pugh, Ralph B., ed. *Calendar of London Trailbaston Trials under Commissions of 1305 and 1306*. London: HMSO, 1975.

Richardson, H. G., and G. O. Sayles, eds. and trans. *Fleta*, vol. 2. London: Bernard Quaritch, 1955.

Robertson, D. W., Jr. "Cultural Tradition of Handlyng Synne." *Speculum* 22, no. 2 (1947): 162–85.

Seabourne, Gwen. *Women in the Medieval Common Law, c. 1200–1500*. London: Routledge, 2021.

Seipp, David J., compiler. *An Index and Paraphrase of Printed Year Book Reports, 1268–1535*, accessible at https://www.bu.edu/phpbin/lawyearbooks/search.php.

Seipp, David J. "Presumptions in Early English Common Law." In *The Law of Presumptions: Essays in Comparative Legal History*, edited by R. H. Helmholz and W. David H. Sellar, 117–36. Berlin: Duncker & Humblot, 2009.

Summerson, Henry, ed. *Crown Pleas of the Devon Eyre of 1238*. Torquay: Devonshire Press, 1985.

Summerson, Henry. "Maitland and the Criminal Law in the Age of *Bracton*." *Proceedings of the British Academy* 89 (1996): 115–43.

Sutherland, Donald W., ed. and trans. *The Eyre of Northamptonshire, 3–4 Edward III, A.D. 1329–1330*, vols. 1 and 2. London: Selden Society, 1983.

United States v. Peoni, 100 F.2d 401 (2d Cir. 1938).

Weinbaum, Martin, ed. and trans. *The London Eyre of 1276*. London: London Record Society, 1976.

Woodbine, George E., ed. *Bracton on the Laws and Customs of England*, vol. 2. Translated by Samuel E. Thorne. Cambridge: Belknap, 1968.

CHAPTER 7

Written Law and Practice: Realities for Women in Bas Languedoc in the Eleventh and Twelfth Centuries

Elizabeth Haluska-Rausch

Languedoc is a territory in the south of France stretching from the Massif Central and the Cévennes region in the northwest, the river Garonne in the southwest, and the river Rhône in the east. Languedoc, from "*langue d'oc*," the Occitan word for yes, included Haute Languedoc in the west with Toulouse as its traditional center, and Bas Languedoc in the southeast, with Montpellier as its historical capital. Much of the area is now incorporated into the modern administrative region Occitanie. Bas Languedoc corresponds roughly to the historical region of Languedoc-Roussillon, and in the medieval period, the prosperous cities and towns of the coast played an important role in the development of regional legal practice. In this study Montpellier and its environs are the geographical focus.

Medieval Languedoc boasted a vital culture, creatively and intellectually. Unfortunately, a common language and culture did not translate into peaceful co-existence in the eleventh and twelfth centuries. Political relationships were complex, often involving convoluted family ties. Regional leaders continually renegotiated their relationships.[1] By the end of the eleventh century, Languedoc was dominated by the counts of Toulouse and the counts of Barcelona. The twelfth-century hegemony of the counts of Toulouse extended from the Aquitaine to the Mediterranean. By the twelfth century their rivals, the counts of Barcelona, who after 1150 were also the kings of Aragon, held interests on both sides of the Pyrenees.[2] Throughout the twelfth century, Toulouse

1 Frederic Cheyette, *Ermengard of Narbonne and the World of the Troubadours* (Ithaca: Cornell University Press, 2001), esp. 14–35; Joseph R. Strayer, *The Albigensian Crusades* (New York: Dial Press, 1971), 2–10. The inherent weakness of southern alliances was ultimately exploited by the leaders of the Albigensian crusade.

2 Thomas N. Bisson, *The Medieval Crown of Aragon: A Short History* (Oxford: Oxford University Press, 1986), 26–27. The betrothal in 1137 and marriage in 1150 of Ramon Berenguer IV (1131–1162), count of Barcelona, to the heiress of the king of Aragon created the Crown of Aragon and made the counts of Barcelona into count-kings. Bisson, *The Medieval Crown of Aragon*, 27–34.

 | DOI:10.1163/9789004710696_009

and Barcelona competed for Provence, and to the southeast, the rich towns of coastal Bas Languedoc. The viscounts and lords of these Mediterranean communities vacillated between the two great powers. In general, the lords of Montpellier allied with the counts of Barcelona. The Albigensian crusades (1209–1229) ended with the acquisition of Languedoc by the French crown in the thirteenth century and ended the independence of the region.

Languedoc, and Bas Languedoc, were part of the *pays de droit écrit*. The term first appears in the eighteenth century during the dismantling of the *ancien régime*. France was divided in terms of its legal history into two regions: the north, the *pays de droit coutumier* (land of customary law), where customary laws descending from those of the largely Germanic peoples in the area dominated, and the south, the *pays de droit écrit* (land of written law), where Roman law never completely lapsed. The boundary was roughly the river Loire. Regardless of what some modern scholars theorize about the actual preservation of Roman law by the Visigothic inheritors of the region, there is no question that they wrote things down. Written the law may have been, but that did not mean that practice followed a juridical ideal. There was a considerable drift in practice over time. By the early thirteenth century many laws and customary practices were largely ignored by the most powerful members of society in the region, whereas they had been clearly accepted as little as a hundred years earlier. For many women, this resulted in a likelihood of exclusion from interests in land by the thirteenth century and diminished visibility in the written record.[3]

This study consists of four sections. The first briefly introduces the laws known in the region. The second provides an overview of the surviving primary source material. Next a chronology of change illustrates broader changes in the participation of women in the public sphere. The final section compares laws applying to dotal property, inheritance, the administrative powers of wives and widows, and testamentary dispositions and guardianship to the practice of major landholders, and, as possible, the practice of less prominent

3 Space constraints make it impossible to adequately contextualize this examination in the now expansive field of women in medieval society. Older but useful, a broad historiographic overview may be found in Susan Mosher Stuard, ed., *Women in Medieval History and Historiography* (Philadelphia: University of Pennsylvania Press, 1987). An early work of David Herlihy (1930–1991) provides a seminal exploration of the divergence between the public potency of women in southern Europe and their northern neighbors. See David Herlihy, "Land, Family and Women in Continental Europe, 701–1200," *Traditio* 18 (1962): 89–120.

propertied members of society.[4] In each division, demonstrative examples follow an overview of the evolution of practice.

1 Law

Three written legal traditions were familiar in the region—the *Lex Romana Visigothorum* and its successor *Leges Visigothorum*, portions of the *Corpus Juris Civilis* after the eleventh century, and regional customs. Salic law (laws of the Salian Franks) left a faint impression, invoked only occasionally. Although the aristocratic population by the tenth century was a fusion of Visigoths, Gallo-romans, and Franks, the laws of the region seem to have had firmly Visigothic origins until the twelfth century.[5] Some time ago, André Gouron (1931–2009) demonstrated that it was not until the second half of the twelfth century that indisputably Roman terminology began replacing older terms.[6]

Alaric II, King of Toulouse (c. 458/466–507), commissioned the *Lex Romana Visigothorum*, also known as the Breviary of Alaric (506), a legal work that incorporated portions of the Theodosian Code (438), and versions or excerpts of Gaius's *Institutiones* (c. 161), the *Codex Gregorianus* (c. 291), the *Codex Hermogenianus* (c. 293), and others. It was officially replaced by the legal commission of King Recceswinth (r. 649–672), the *Liber iudiciorum* (654), also known as the *Leges Visigothorum* (later the Visigothic Code or *Fuero juzgo*).[7] This version of early codes, or a variation, remained in use in Spain until 1254; in Languedoc it endured until the end of the Albigensian crusades.

The *Corpus Juris Civilis*, a monumental juridical enterprise commissioned by the Emperor Justinian (482–565) between 529 and 534, was an attempt to provide a uniform framework for what had become a confusion of old laws,

4 Women from families with minor properties and women belonging to the nascent bourgeoisie and artisanate are poorly recorded in the period before the Albigensian crusade. Occasional wills survive in the records of ecclesiastical institutions, but it is not until notarial records begin in the mid-thirteenth century that anything substantive could be claimed about practice. What survives from the earlier period is suggestive, but not conclusive.

5 Claudie Duhamel-Amado, *Genèse des linages meridianaux*, 2 vols. (Toulouse: CNRS, 2001, 2007), vol. 1, 28; Duhamel-Amado, "Poids de l'aristocratie d'origine wisgothique dans la genèse de la noblesse septimanienne," *L'Europe héritière de l'Espagne wisigothique (Paris, 14–16 mai, 1990)*: 81–99.

6 André Gouron, "Les étapes de la pénétration du droit romain au XIIe siècle dans ancienne Septimanie," *Annals du Midi* 69 (1957): 103–20.

7 Karl Ubl, ed. *Bibliotheca legum regni Francorum manuscripta*, assisted by Dominik Trump and Daniela Schulz (Cologne, 2012), http://www.leges.uni-koeln.de/en/lex/lex-romana-visigothorum; Karolus Zeumer, ed., *Leges Visigothorum* (Hanover: Hahn, 1902).

new laws, and scholarly interpretations. The result was a four-part work, the *Codex* (imperial *constitutiones*, second century forward), the *Digesta* (juristic writings second and third century), *Institutiones* (a textbook), and the *Novellae* (laws after 534).[8] When the west fell again after Justinian's reign, the *Corpus Juris Civilis* faded as well. However, as noted above, older forms of Roman law—most incorporated into the *Corpus Juris Civilis*—had survived in writing in the region in question. It has now been shown that it is far more likely that the *Corpus Juris Civilis* never disappeared completely in western Europe, even if surviving in a highly attenuated form.[9]

Finally, there are the customs of Montpellier, highly influential in Languedoc and as far west as Rouergue.[10] Although the *pays de droit écrit* was so named, there were customary laws in most cities. As early as the mid-twelfth century Montpellier was a center for legal learning, although the School of Law was not to be incorporated until 1289.[11] That the customs of the prosperous merchant city were recorded and promulgated early is not a surprise. The first reference to the customs of Montpellier is as early as 1134.[12] The first versions of the customs of Montpellier survive in two forms, a fragment dated 1190 in the *Liber instrumentorum memorialium,* and a full set dated 1204, preserved in *Le petit thalamus*. The date 1204 marked the highly contested transition from the late Guillem VIII (d. 1202), seigneur de Montpellier, to his sole legal heir Marie de Montpellier (1182–1213), the only child from the marriage of Guillem VIII and Eudocia Comnena. The *Commune clôture* (the city consulate) obviously saw an opportunity to expand upon—or document more thoroughly—the rights they had demanded in the early 1140s during a three-year insurrection. It seems probable that some version of the customs was recorded at that time, even if no evidence of the physical document survives. The customs as preserved in the 1204 redaction include 122 or 123 articles, depending on the edited version.[13]

8 Paul Krueger and Theodor Mommsen, *Corpus Iuris Civilis* (Berlin: Weidmann, 1889).

9 Charles Radding and Antonio Ciaralli, *The* Corpus Iuris Civilis *in the Middle Ages. Manuscripts and Transmission from the Sixth Century to the Juristic Revival* (Leiden: Brill, 2006).

10 André Gouron, "*Libertas hominum Montispessulani*: Rédaction et diffusion des coutumes de Montpellier," *Annales du Midi* 90 (1978): 289–318.

11 Gouron, "Penetration du droit," 103–4, 108–12.

12 Gouron, "*Libertas*," 296.

13 There are two printed editions. *Thalamus parvus: Le petit thalamus de Montpellier*, ed. F. Pégat, E. Thomas, et al. (Montpellier: Martel, 1840); *Layettes du Trésor des Chartes*, ed. Alexandre Teulet et al., 5 vols. (Paris: Plon, 1863–1909), no. 721, hereafter *LTC*. All further references are to the Pégat edition.

2 Sources

Primary sources are plentiful for the region during the period, but medieval Languedoc was not a region rich in narrative histories, but rather in charters.[14] There are thousands of charters in the municipal and departmental archives of the region, while others survive in the national archives. The charters themselves are mostly unimpressive pieces of parchment, generally smaller than an ordinary piece of office paper, written in Latin in a clear script. Scholars from the seventeenth century forward have edited manuscripts for publication. Among these are the *Histoire générale de Languedoc*, *Gallia Christiana*, publications of the area's archeological societies, and numerous cartularies including episcopal cartularies, cartularies of religious houses, and a few lay cartularies, including that of the Lords of Montpellier (the Guillems), the *Liber instrumentorum memorialium.*[15] This list is hardly comprehensive and continues to change as modern scholars add new editions.[16] In general, documents preserved by ecclesiastical institutions represent the bulk of the surviving material. A few manuscript volumes are decorated, such as *Le Petit thalamus*, but none are lavishly illuminated with the exception of the *Liber feudorum maior*, the cartulary of the Counts of Barcelona, which includes illuminated miniatures.[17]

---

14 Thomas Bisson, "Unheroed Pasts: History and Commemoration in South Frankland before the Albigensian Crusades," *Speculum* 65 (1990): 281–308.

15 Claude Devic and J.-J. Vaissete, *Histoire générale de Languedoc*, 16 vols. (Toulouse: Privat, 1876–1892), hereafter *HL*; *Gallia christiana in provincias ecclesiasticas distributa; qua series et historia archiepiscoporum, episcoporum et abbatum,* 16 vols. (Paris: Ex Typographia Regia, 1744–1877); *Bullaire de l'église de Maguelone*, ed. Jean Rouquette and André Villemagne (Montpellier: Valat, 1911); *Cartulaires des abbayes d'Aniane et de Gellone*, ed. L. Cassan and E. Meynial (Montpellier: Martel, 1898–1900); *Cartulaire de Maguelone,* ed. Jean Rouquette and André Villemagne, 5 vols. (Montpellier: Valat, 1912–1924), hereafter *CM*; *Liber instrumentorum memorialium: Le cartulaire des Guilhems de Montpellier*, ed. Alexandre Germain and Charles Chabaneau (Montpellier: Martel, 1884–1886), hereafter *LIM*.

16 For example: *Le cartulaire du chapitre cathédral Saint-Étienne d'Agde*, ed. Raymonde Foreville (Paris: CNRS, 1995); Joseph Dovetto, *Cartulaire des Trencavel: analyse détaillée des 617 actes, 957–1214* (Carcassonne: Centre de recherches et d'information historiques des conférenciers de la Cité, 1997); Laurent Macé, *Catalogues raimondins. Actes des comtes de Toulouse, ducs de Narbonne et marquis de Provence* (*1112–1229*) (Toulouse: Archives Municipales de Toulouse, 2008).

17 *Le petit thalamus*, Archives Municipales de Montpellier, AA9; see also http://thalamus.huma-num.fr/; *Liber feudorum maior*, Arxiu de la Corona d'Aragó (ACA), Cancelleria reial, registres, 1; see also https://www.mcu.es/archivos/MC/ACA/Miniaturas/miniaturas/llibre02/000.htm.

3 Chronology

There were three fluid periods for the participation of noblewomen in public life in the area.[18] The first stretches from before the year 1000 through around 1120. Before the late eleventh century, full partition of inherited land among sons and daughters was common. During this period brides were endowed with familial land and received in return an undivided interest in all or some portion of her bridegroom's lands, a noble wife was often the administrative partner of her husband, and after his death, a widow usually became responsible for their children and assumed his public duties during the minority of his heirs and sometimes longer, occasionally for as long as another generation. The next period begins in the first decades of the twelfth century and ends in the middle of the century. Dowries among the landed elite were likely to be in moveable goods, and life estates in land were less likely to be carved from a bridegroom's immoveable property. During this transitional period, the administrative responsibilities of wives and widows began to diminish, although it remained relatively common for a widow to retain guardianship of her children. From the last quarter of the twelfth century through the first years of the thirteenth, widows among the landed elite ceased to be the preferred guardians of their children and infrequently assumed responsibility for their husbands' holdings. Noble women held fewer interests in land than they had, proportionally, a century earlier.[19]

18 For more on these transformations see Elizabeth Haluska-Rausch, "Transformations in the Powers of Wives and Widows in Medieval Montpellier, 985–1213," in *The Experience of Power in Medieval Europe 900–1300*, ed. Alan Cooper, Bob Berkhofer and Adam J. Kosto (Aldershot: Ashgate, 2005), 147–62.

19 See also Martin Aurell, "La détérioration de la statut de la femme aristocratique en Provence (xe–xiiie siècles)," *Le Moyen Age* (1985): 5–32; Aurell, *Une famille de la noblesse provençale au Moyen-Âge: Les Porcelet* (Avignon, 1986); Aurell, *Les noces du comte: Mariage et pouvoir en Catalogne (785–1213)* (Paris: Publications de la Sorbonne, 1995); Pierre Bonnassie, *La Catalogne du milieu du Xe à la fin du xie siècle: Croissance et mutations d'une société*, 2 vols. (Toulouse: Association des Publications de l'Université de Toulouse-Le Mirail, 1975–1976); Monique Bourin-Derruau, *Villages médiévaux en Bas-Languedoc: Genèse d'une sociabilité, xe–xive siècle*, 2 vols. (Paris: Harmattan, 1987); Claudie Duhamel-Amado, "Une forme historique de la domination masculine: Femme et mariage dans l'aristocratie languedocienne à la fin du xiie siècle," *Cahiers d'histoire de l'Institut de Recherches Marxistes* 6 (1981): 125–39; Duhamel-Amado, *Genèse des lignages meridionaux*; Duhamel-Amado, "Les Guillems de Montpellier à la fin du xiie siècle, un lignage en péril," *Revue des langues romanes* 89 (1985): 13–28; Duhamel-Amado, "Femmes entre elles: Filles et épouses languedociennes (xie et xiie siècles)," in *Femmes: Mariages—lignages, xiie–xive. Mélanges offerts à Georges Duby* (Brussels: De Boeck, 1992), 125–55; John Mundy,

4 Law and Practice

4.1 *Marriage Prestation*

It is not practical to separate the endowment of children, especially female children, with familial property neatly into inheritance and marriage prestation—propertied families did not make that distinction. Regionally, families mentally conflated the dotation of married children and inheritance, and in law as well. Discussion of testamentary disposition beyond the endowment of daughters appears below.

In Languedoc a transfer of property invariably accompanied marriage, if the individuals were propertied to even a small degree, following both Visigothic and Roman tradition. The exchange reached beyond ensuring the financial well-being of the new couple and was a central feature of the contract.[20] Only one change in marriage prestation over the course of the period can be traced with certainty. After the middle of the twelfth century families substituted dowries in moveable goods for dowries in land.[21] Marriage prestations were reciprocal, echoing Roman tradition, although sometimes it appeared that the main contribution of some influential families was a daughter or son. Gifts from groom to bride varied considerably in form and content, from an undivided interest in some portion of the groom's estate to a few named properties. Although the former seems to have disappeared from general use by the middle of the twelfth century, collections of enumerated properties remained common donations *propter nuptias* throughout the entire period.[22] By the end of the twelfth century the form had become fixed and its terminology took on a definitively Roman cast.[23]

Men and Women at Toulouse in the Age of the Cathars (Toronto: Toronto University Press, 1990); Jean-Pierre Poly, *La Provence et la société féodale, 879–1166* (Paris: Bordas, 1976).

20 Jean Hilaire, "Les régimes matrimoniaux aux XIe et XIIe siècles dans la région de Montpellier," *Recueil de mémoires et travaux publiés par la Société d'Histoire du droit et des institutions des anciens pays de droit écrit* 3 (1955): 15–38.

21 Elizabeth Haluska-Rausch, "Family, Property, and Power: Women in Medieval Montpellier, 985–1213," (Ph.D. diss., Harvard University, 1998), 53.

22 For a detailed analysis of regional marriage contracts see Hilaire, "Les régimes matrimoniaux." The last examples in *LIM* date from 1150 and 1153. *LIM*, nos. 145, 551.

23 Hilaire, "Les régimes matrimoniaux," 18–20, 23. See also Paul Ourliac and Jean-Louis Gazzaniga, *Histoire du droit privé français: De l'an mil au Code civil* (Paris: Albin Michel, 1985), 36–37, 53, 288–304.

4.1.1 Visigothic Law

Several Visigothic laws concerning marriage gifts had a lingering influence. Visigothic law required that the property exchange precede the written contract, in addition to requiring the contract itself. For example, marriage could not be entered into without a dowry. Widows also inherited half their husband's goods for life—a concept which reappeared in the *sponsalitia* (gift from groom to bride) of the coast in the twelfth century.[24]

4.1.2 Roman Revival

The most important legal premise descending from Roman law was that of equal responsibility for marriage prestations on the part of the bride's and the groom's families. The idea seems to have reappeared locally in the twelfth century.[25] Dotal property was reserved for the enjoyment of the wife.[26] Much of the evidence for the reintroduction of Roman law is linguistic and begins around 1130. In the second half of the twelfth century, prestation from the bride's side tended to be called a "dowry" (*dos*), and that from the groom's side a variety of terms, of which *donatio propter nuptias* (a post-Justinian phrase), was probably the most common after 1129.[27]

4.1.3 Customs

The customs of Montpellier from 1204 did not require that marriage prestations be equal in value. Article 96 specifically addresses marriage prestation.[28] Furthermore, the customs prohibited the alienation of a wife's dotal property without the express permission of her natal family.[29]

4.1.4 Practice

Most twelfth-century dowries provided by the Guillems and their neighbors for their daughters took the form of moveable goods. None of the written laws of the area required marriage prestations in immoveables. However, it is clear from the surviving evidence that land was the preference through the eleventh century and into the early part of the twelfth, perhaps because

---

24 *Leges Visigothorum*, 3.1.1, 3.1.6, 4.2.1, 4.2.9, 4.2.14.

25 Hilaire, "Les régimes matrimoniaux," 18–20, 23. See also Ourliac and Gazzaniga, *Histoire du droit privé français*, 36–37, 53, 288–304.

26 Justinian's *Code*, C.5.23.1. Book IV of the *Code* and Book XXIII of the *Digest* include multiple articles on dowries and donations *propter nuptias*. See also *Digest*, D.24.3.

27 Gouron, "Penetration du droit," 109.

28 *Le petit thalamus*, Article 96.

29 *Le petit thalamus*, Article 14 (1205). The numbering reflects the additions made by Peter II in 1205.

of the conceptual conflation of dowry and inheritance. The last magnate of coastal Bas Languedoc to endow a daughter with land was Raimond Trencavel (d. 1167), viscount of Béziers, in 1154.[30] From 1121, the lords of Montpellier tended to endow each daughter similarly, with dowries in money and chattels, although the eldest or first married appears to have received a somewhat more sumptuous provision. The most complete evidence for the contents of endowments of daughters is testamentary. For example, although the eldest daughter of Guillem V (d. 1121) was to receive 7000 sous as a dowry, his two younger daughters were to receive only 5000 sous apiece. The 1146 testament of Guillem VI (d. after 1149) was the first to include a list of household goods with which he intended to endow his daughters in addition to money. His son, Guillem VII, requested similar provisions for four of his daughters in 1172.[31] Dowries also remained relatively static from one generation to the next, which suggests family tradition or local custom may have determined the quantity and quality of a young woman's marriage portion.

Marriage prestations from groom to bride also shifted over time. The marriage contract of Bernard IV, count of Melgueil (d. 1132), and Guillemette, daughter of Guillem V, clearly following the Visigothic preference for a written document, provides an example of an undivided interest in the groom's property.[32] In 1120 he promised his bride half his possessions, possibly reflecting the Roman requirement for prestations of equal value. A typical late twelfth-century example is in the contract of the lord of Anduse and his wife, the lady of Roquefeuil, providing his bride with a life usufruct of the castle of Breissac, and the villa of Valeraugues, again a written contract, and the conveyance of significant immoveable property. The last example in the area of an undivided interest in the groom's property appeared in 1187, with the anomalous *donatio propter nuptias* of ten percent of his goods, which Guillem VIII presented to his second wife.[33] In each case the agreement was written, following Visigothic norms, and reciprocal, following Roman preference. By the 1187 contract, fully reciprocal prestations had fallen almost completely out of use.

30 *HL*, vol. 5, cols. 1171–74.

31 *LIM*, nos, 59, 94, 95, 96 and 99. For more on daughters' marriage prestations see Haluska-Rausch, "Family, Property, and Power," 56, 58–59.

32 *LIM*, no. 94; *CM*, 1, no. 43.

33 Luc d'Achery, *Spicilegium: sive Collectio veterum aliquot scriptorum qui in Galliae bibliothecis delituerant*, ed. Joseph de Barre. 3 vols. (Paris: Apud Montalant, 1723), vol. 3, 457–59, 550.The last examples of enumerated properties in *LIM* date from 1150 and 1153. *LIM*, nos. 145, 551.

The principle of exclusion from testamentary bequests in the region of Montpellier was closely linked to dowries, and ultimately the condition of wives as well as daughters. It appears that as Roman law became better known in Montpellier and much of Bas Languedoc, *dos* was increasingly equated with *hereditas*, and represented a daughter's share of family wealth. This is particularly evident in customs regarding intestate disposition. Intestate equality without male preference and the exclusion of dowered children was perhaps uniquely southern French.[34] The concept of "conjugal patrimony" never took hold, and a woman's dowry remained theoretically separate. A married woman may only have realized control of marriage prestations after her husband's death, when she obtained control of property provided by her birth family, and a life usufruct in some portion—usually half—of her husband's property, both inherited and acquired. After the mid-twelfth century most testaments required that the widow remain unmarried.[35] Visigothic and Roman law, as well as regional customs, supported a woman's right to her dotal goods. Probably the most dramatic flouting of this custom was Peter II, Count of Barcelona and King of Aragon (1178–1213) insisting that his wife Marie de Montpellier provide her patrimony as a dowry for their infant daughter. She capitulated under duress, but her response was dramatic, with a clear message that she thought the demand unjust and inappropriate—she says of his relentless insistence "I have been debased and tormented" (*deducta et cruciata fui*). She had, however, married a king.[36]

Smaller landholders continued to provide dowries at least partially in land throughout the period. Here there is the suggestion that an older customary form of wealth—land—defined the more fluid term—goods. For example, in the middle of the twelfth century a small landholder, Garburgis, divided her immoveable property among her three daughters and her granddaughter, specifically as dowries.[37] In 1214 at the very end of the period, Maria, widow

34 Laurent Mayali, *Droit savant et coutumes: L'exclusion des filles dotées, XIIe–XVe siècles* (Frankfurt am Main: V. Klostermann, 1987), 55–57; Hilaire, "Les régimes matrimoniaux," 33. The customs of Montpellier included a similar provision. See *Le petit thalamus*, Article 13.

35 Hilaire, "Les régimes matrimoniaux," 25–26, 29, 33–34. Hilaire argues that Roman terms were applied to extant practices.

36 *HL*, vol. 8, cols. 533–34; English translation in Elizabeth Haluska-Rausch, "Unwilling Partners: Conflict and Ambition in the Marriage of Peter II of Aragon and Marie de Montpellier," in *Queenship and Political Power in Medieval and Early Modern Spain*, ed. Theresa Earenfight (Aldershot: Ashgate, 2005) 3–20, 11–12. For the marriage agreement see *Spicilegium*, vol. 3, 567.

37 Archives Départmentales de l'Hérault, 59H56, hereafter AD.

of Raimund de Oliveto, retired to the monastery of St. Mary-Magdalene leaving her dowry in land equally to her son and her younger daughter. The older daughter had been previously endowed.[38] The sample is small but suggests that minor landholders may have followed custom more closely than did their superiors.

4.2 *Administrative Responsibilities in Marriage*

It appears to have been relatively common for men from noble families to include their wives in the management of their lands in the early twelfth century, and uncommon for them to do so by the end of the century. In *La Catalogne*, Pierre Bonnassie (1932–2006) argues that the unusual prominence of women in medieval Catalonia found its roots in Visigothic law, which provided women with near equality in terms of property ownership and management. Since Bas Languedoc was in most ways tied more closely to the Counts of Barcelona than the Kings of France, this is significant.[39] However, most living prominent landholders began excluding their wives from administration of their holdings beginning in the early twelfth century. Women who had inherited land outright generally appear to have at least participated in the administration of their own property through the end of the period. None of these shifts had anything to do with the written law as it existed locally.

4.2.1 Visigothic Code

Visigothic law did not specifically address the question of a woman's right to participate in the management of her husband's or joint property, but the expectation was that she could see to her own affairs. The *Leges Visigothorum* permitted a woman to pursue an action in court on her own behalf, for example.[40] Property acquired by dowry or gift remained at the woman's full disposal, with certain exceptions to ensure that the property passed to the children of the marriage at her death.[41]

4.2.2 Roman Revival

Roman law constrained the capacity of women, but the courts routinely upheld their right to act on their own behalf—or their husbands'—in legal matters.[42]

38 AD 59H16.

39 Bonnassie, *La Catalogne,* see esp. 274.

40 *Leges Visigothorum*, 2.3.6.

41 *Leges Visigothorum*, 4.5.2, 5.2.4.

42 For an overview see Jane F. Gardner, *Women in Roman Law and Society* (Bloomington: Indiana University Press, 1986).

The *Digest* is littered with cases of wives and widows selling property, managing their affairs, and participating in the public lives of their adult children.[43] After the first-century Velleian decree, women could not act as sureties in a contract.[44] They could, however, form contracts of their own. Justinian's *Code* permits men absolute authority over the property of their wives, providing there is no malfeasance.[45] There is little evidence of a direct connection from the laws in the rediscovered *Digest* and the legal habits of the region, but the laws of the Roman Empire that had made their way into the Visigothic Code had a long legacy.

4.2.3 Customs

The customs of Montpellier expressly extended to a woman the ability to act as a *fidejussor* in credit agreements, gifts, matters pertaining to her own property, renunciations of privileges, redemption of pledges and mortgages in questions of freedom, dowries, and in the practice of a craft or business, or with the permission of her husband.[46] This provided women with the ability to form contracts, at least on behalf of another and presumably on her own.

4.2.4 Practice

In the area around Montpellier, the exercise of comital and seigneurial power was primarily a male pursuit, but before the middle of the twelfth century, sometimes with the counsel of the office-holder's wife. What is very clear from the surviving documents is that there was no question of female legal capacity. Whether or not legal authority was extended in practice was a personal preference, and the duration of feminine influence varied depending on the family. For example, if the Guillems had ever included their wives in the governing of Montpellier, they had ceased to do so routinely by the early twelfth century. Other powerful couples in and around Montpellier appear to have administered their land jointly part of the time. For example, the earliest surviving documents of the Counts of Melgueil included the count and countess

43 See e.g., D.1.6.4.

44 The Velleian senate decree was enacted c. 46 A.D. Under the terms of the decree, women were generally prohibited from assuming liability for others as a surety or guarantor. D.16.1.2; D.16.1.13.2; C.4.29.15.

45 C.2.17.21.

46 *Le petit thalamus*, Article 39. Kathryn Reyerson, "Women in Business in Medieval Montpellier," *Women and Work in Preindustrial Europe*, ed. Barbara Hanawalt (Bloomington: Indiana University Press, 1986), 117–44, 118. As Reyerson notes, if a woman could form a contract on behalf of another, she could do the same for herself.

in each transaction.[47] Throughout the eleventh century husband and wife co-authored most documents.[48] The involvement of the countesses of Melgueil in the administration of the county began to wane in the next generation. The name of the wife of Raimond II, count of Melgueil (d. 1120), for example, is known only because his son used it as a matronymic.[49] In the dozen or so years Bernard IV (d. 1132) ruled as count, his wife Guillemette did not visibly assist in the feudal affairs of the county.[50]

There are other regional examples. An early case is Bernard-Aton IV, viscount of Béziers (d. 1129) who married Cécile de Provence in 1083. Bernard-Aton IV was a member of the sprawling Trencavel family—viscounts of Béziers, Carcassonne, Razès, Albi, Nîmes, and Agde. He authored charters with his mother more often than his wife until 1097, after which he drew Cécile into the administration of his considerable holdings. As time passed, her name was consistently coupled with his in documents. After his death she continued to assist her sons in the management of the viscounties for another ten years.[51] In general the viscountesses of Béziers were more involved in the governance of their husbands' lands for a longer period than were the wives of other Trencavels. After the early twelfth century most of the viscounts excluded their wives from administrative responsibilities. The third son of Bernard-Aton IV and Cécile, Bernard-Aton V, viscount of Nîmes and Agde (d. 1163) was an exception. He had married Guillemette, daughter of Guillem VII of Montpellier by 1146. He drew his wife into the administration of his property not long after their marriage.[52] It appears that Guillemette joined Bernard-Aton V most often in matters pertaining to his relationship to his vassals; these were also the first responsibilities she relinquished when their son came of age. However, this branch of the family also began excluding their wives in the next generation. The wife of their son, Bernard-Aton VI (d. 1214), was almost invisible. Female capacity remained in the written law, but it had become highly attenuated in practice.

Although several heiresses appear to have largely managed their own affairs early in the twelfth century, by the end of the century there are no examples of heiresses independently managing their lands, even if under both Visigothic and customary law they still had the right to do so.[53] The *Liber instrumentum*

---

47 *LIM*, no. 70.

48 *CM*, vol. 1, no. 6, 10, 11, 12, 13, 14; *LIM*, nos. 57, 58.

49 The count appeared twice as Bernard, son of Marie. *CM*, vol. 1, nos. 55, 56.

50 Guillemette's name appears in only three documents. *CM*, vol. 1, nos. 54, 55, 57.

51 *HL*, vol. 5, cols. 977, 1002, 1015.

52 *LTC*, vol. 1, no. 95. *LIM*, no. 95; AD, 1H4.

53 See Cheyette, *Ermengard of Narbonne*, 14–31.

memorialium preserves evidence of the administrative responsibilities of eight heiresses to major holdings, all related by blood or marriage to the Guillems—Tiburge d'Orange (d. 1150) and her youngest daughter Tiburgette (d. before 1172), Beatrice, countess of Melgueil (d. 1174), Ermessende de Castries (d. 1157), Adalais de Conas, Tiburge and Sybille d'Aumelas, and Marie de Montpellier. The earliest, Tiburge d'Orange, and the latest, Marie de Montpellier, are at opposite ends of the experience. Tiburge d'Orange governed the county of Orange without the assistance of her husband Guillem d'Aumelas. Peter II effectively excluded Marie de Montpellier from decisions concerning her inheritance.

The townspeople of Montpellier retained respect for female capacity, as reflected in the customs of Montpellier. Women were active in the artisanate—Raimonda *de carboneris*, a charcoal maker, left the materials of her craft to her son in 1189, and two tanners, Guillema *rancurella* and Ricarda *rancurella*, a female mercer, Ricarda *merceria*, a fishmonger, Betalla *peisoneria*, and a candlemaker, Raimunda *teisendaria*, all appear in the tax records from 1201. Twelve percent of the names in the tax rolls are indisputably feminine, which meant the women were heads of household or sufficiently independent to incur a tax liability.[54] Where evidence exists, it appears that joint administration of property continued into the thirteenth century for these less prominent levels of society. It appears that the social and economic considerations that encouraged the land-based aristocracy to limit the property-holding of women did not operate in merchant society. Rather than "losing" daughters, daughters were integral to the expansion of a merchant family's interests.[55]

4.3 *Testamentary Dispositions*

Although *dos* and *hereditas* were conflated, testamentary dispositions hold additional evidence of changes in practice over the two centuries in question. Most dramatically, cadet (younger) sons were reduced to contingent beneficiaries to immoveable property in order of birth, and in effect dowered daughters were better off than their brothers. The administrative responsibilities of widows also changed from the near assumption of a dead husband's role, and guardianship—sometimes complete, sometimes shared—of their minor children as late as the mid-twelfth century, to a much-diminished role by the end of the period. This change could be evidence of competing legal systems, or it could have arisen out of necessity—financial or political.

54 *LIM*, nos. 287, 289, 291, 293; Archives Municipales de Montpellier, EE297, hereafter AM.

55 Mayali, *Droit savant et coutumes*, 64, 67, 71.

4.3.1 Visigothic Code

Partition was the norm in Visigothic law. In Book IV of the Visigothic Code a very brief entry requires that brothers and sisters should inherit equally. Elsewhere, the law states that women were entitled to any part of an extended estate on their mother's side, and children were to be preferred in any intestate disposition.[56] The preferred guardian after a death was expressly articulated—father if mother died, mother if father died—as long as she should remain a widow.[57]

4.3.2 Roman Revival

Under Justinian's *Code* children, male and female, had a right to a portion of the familial property. If one son was given preferential treatment in a parental will, it was actionable.[58] A woman had the right to enjoy a usufruct left to her by her husband without interference.[59] It was also possible for a woman to assume guardianship of her children, even under the Velleian decree, but male guardians were actively preferred. A widow could petition for guardianship of her minor children but was required not to remarry.[60] In the case of dotal property a woman had more rights, including the power to choose guardians for her heirs.[61]

4.3.3 Customs

Many articles in *Le petit thalamus* are dedicated to the questions of inheritance, dotal property, and minor children. The following is a small sampling. Article 54 provides that "[a] son wed or daughter married by the will of [his or her] father is known to be emancipated"—an article relevant to both dotal property and testamentary disposition.[62] Article 59 of the 1204 customs of Montpellier provides for equal distribution of property among children in the case of intestacy, with preference to the unmarried children, and specifically rejects "Roman" law.[63] Finally, Article 7 addresses the assignment of guardians.[64]

---

56 *Leges Visigothorum*, 4.2.1, 4.2.2, 4.2.10.

57 *Leges Visigothorum*, 4.2.13, 4.3.3.

58 C.3.28.33. Most of Book III is dedicated to these questions. See also D.5.2.

59 C.3.33.9, 3.33.10, 3.33.12.

60 C.4.29.6, 5.10.1, 5.35.1, 5.35.2, 5.35.3.

61 C.5.23.2, 5.28.4.

62 *Le petit thalamus*, Article 54.

63 *Le petit thalamus*, Article 59. Article 13, discussed above, was similar.

64 *Le petit thalamus*, Article 7 (1205). The term "tutor" appears infrequently. In regional wills the phrase in *protectione et custodia et defensione*, or a similar protection phrase, was far more common. See *LIM*, nos. 94, 95, 97, 99, and 116.

4.3.4 Practice

Three changes in the way local noble families handled land contributed to the exclusion of women from interests in immoveable property by the end of the twelfth century. Two were testamentary. The first was a gradual shift from partition among all or most offspring, to partition among sons alone, to near primogeniture. The second change was a shift in the choice of guardian. Finally, magnates began excluding their wives from administration, as discussed above. None of these transformations are associated with changes in written law. The exclusion of first daughters and then cadet sons from a share of the patrimony were the most important changes over time, and do not appear to have been a product of changes in the law.[65] As noted above, Visigothic law actively promoted equal inheritance among siblings. These were the laws as written and were echoed in the customs of cities in the region. Although a parent supposedly had the right to bequeath property to whomever he or she desired, the reality was that children were preferred to any other claimants, including the siblings of the decedent. Intestate disposition provides a clearer sense of the values of the community than do the testaments of nobles, which frequently reflected the immediate needs and concerns of a single individual.[66] It appears to have been customary to endow both daughters and sons at marriage, effectively "disinheriting" daughters *and* married sons.[67] The customs of Montpellier encouraged parity, but long held practice produced a different reality for certain groups, chiefly the aristocracy. Among the modestly propertied inhabitants of Montpellier and its surroundings, partition of goods and property among all children may have been more often the rule than the exception, and certainly seems to have been the ideal.

As partition disappeared from use among the nobility, wives were similarly excluded from testamentary dispositions and denied full guardianship of the couples' minor children. Into the early twelfth century, it does not seem to have been unusual for partition of an estate to include the widow of the holder, although she ordinarily held her portion only for life. However, the number of wives of magnates who participated in the administration of their husbands' estates after the husband's death appears to have declined over time.[68] Among other things, the trend probably reflected a later tendency for male testators

65 Jean Yver, *Egalité entre héritiers et exclusion des enfants dotés: Essai de géographie coutumière* (Paris: Sirey, 1966), 155, 221.

66 *Le petit thalamus*, Article 59.

67 Yver, *Egalité entre héritiers*, 1–10, 39–40; Mayali, *Droit savant et coutumes*, 55–57.

68 Unfortunately, relatively few examples survive, lending an anecdotal quality to the evidence.

to entrust their property to male friends and relatives rather than their widows. Around Montpellier, most inheritors of great estates named their widows guardians of any minor children and left all or part of their estates in the hands of their widows during the minority of their heir or heirs through the early twelfth century. After the middle of the twelfth century it became uncommon for a woman to assume fully her husband's role, and by the end of the century no examples survive of a high-ranking man naming his widow sole guardian of their children, and few even included their widows among the administrators of their property during the minority of heirs. If a woman's husband left her with control of both children and property, she was placed, temporarily, to assume her spouse's former position. A widow addressing the responsibilities left to her by her husband either identified herself by the feminine form of whatever title or titles had belonged to her dead spouse or as his widow.[69]

Presumably following Visigothic tradition, partition was equal in the early years of the seigneury of Montpellier. In the generation of Guillem III (d. 1068) and Guillem IV there were four sons, Guillem, Pierre, Bernard Guillem (d. 1076), Pons, and a daughter Engelrada. The property was fully partitioned, but most of the family failed to reproduce, which effectively negated any diminution of the patrimony brought about by the practice. Guillem III acted as head of the family until his death, after which his brother Bernard Guillem—known as Guillem IV—became lord of Montpellier. There was a single child in the next generation, Guillem V.[70] The first shift from Visigothic legal tradition, perhaps reinforced by newly reintroduced Roman law, appears in the testament of Guillem V in 1121. Immoveable property was unequally divided, but following local legal practice he left his five unmarried children in the care of their mother, Ermessende. The property of the two younger sons was left in the control of their mother with the provision that as they reached majority she would relinquish the bequests. She retained an annuity and usufruct of a portion of the larger estate for life.[71] Similarly, and with a similar unequal partition of immoveable property, Guillem VI placed his nearly adult children "*in garda et in bailia*" (under protection and tutelage) of his mother, and asked his brother-in-law, Pons de Mataplana, to "hold, govern and defend," his children and their inheritance in 1146.[72] At the end of the period, however, Guillem VIII

69 Ermessende, widow of Guillem V, appeared in documents during the minority of her sons as *uxor quondam Guillemi, domini Montispessulani*, or as *Domina Ermessende*.

70 Ghislaine Fabre and Thierry Lochard, *Montpellier: La ville médiévale* (Paris: Imprimerie Nationale, 1992), 29–30.

71 *LIM*, no. 94.

72 *LIM*, no. 95.

left almost all lands to his eldest son (one of eight children) and placed the responsibility of guardianship with a cousin, Étienne de Servian, and an ally, Bernard d'Anduse, excluding his widow completely in a marked break with the legal traditions in writing at the time.[73]

Without examining the testamentary dispositions in detail of the Trencavels to the south in detail, it is clear that the widows of the Trencavels played an even more conspicuous and public role in the feudal order through the middle of the twelfth century than did the widows of the Guillems, both taking over their husbands' offices as widows, and as guardians of their children.[74] However, by the end of the century, the Trencavels also ceased to award guardianship of minor children to their wives and excluded their wives from the administration of their lands during the minority of their heirs. In 1118 Bernard-Aton IV, viscount of Béziers, intended to leave his wife Cécile to govern his property and his family in his place.[75] His brother Bernard-Aton V, viscount of Nîmes and Agde, left his widow in sole command of his lands, titles, and infant son after his death. In the first testament of Raimond Trencavel in 1154, he designated his wife *seigneuress* and countess of all his lands.[76] However, although the heir of Raimond Trencavel, Roger II, left his young son Raimond Roger in the partial care of his widow, Adelais de Toulouse, in 1194, he did not entrust her with the administration of his lands during their son's minority.[77]

Members of minor aristocratic families, in contrast, continued to name their wives guardians for a longer period, and those testaments of burgesses which survive suggest that they entrusted their widows with their children and property.[78] The customs of Montpellier required that anyone leaving male children of less than fourteen years in age, or female children of less than twelve years in age, name a guardian or guardians. According to the law, this

73 *LIM*, no. 99.

74 For examples see *HL*, vol. 5, cols. 794–95, 840–41, 865–68, 894–96, 957–58, 1171–74, 1299–1302; *HL*, vol. 8, cols. 281–83, 326–28, 579–81, 859–60; *LTC*, vol. 1, nos. 95, 101–3, 112, 119–20, 161, 195–96, 198, 202–4, 206, 211, 217, 224, 226, 228–35, 239, 260, 262.

75 *HL*, vol. 5, cols. 1094, 1098. In his final testament (1129), he divided his holdings among his three sons. Cécile continued to join her sons and daughters in donations until 1147.

76 *HL*, vol. 5, cols. 1171–74.

77 *HL*, vol. 6, 154–57.

78 In 1182 Raimond Aimoin left his wife in charge of his estate and their children. Similarly, in 1215 Raimond Gaucelm de Lunel named his wife guardian of their children. *LIM*, no. 116; Adolphe Auguste Röuet, *Notice sur la ville de Lunel au moyen âge et la vie de Saint-Gérard, seigneur de cette ville au XIIIe siècle* (Montpellier: Leguin, 1878), 401.

role was inclusive of all responsibilities unless otherwise specified.[79] There is little evidence of testamentary practice for the increasingly powerful merchant class of Montpellier during the eleventh or even the twelfth century. One early thirteenth century testament—that of Peter Vesiani—demonstrates that members of the merchant class were observing long practice and custom. His will divided his holdings among his children—specifying that both male and female children were to inherit. His wife received her dowry in full, and a handsome life usufruct with the right to be lady of his house unless she remarried.[80]

5 Conclusion

Practice changed but written law did not. The written laws in the year 1000 were still known, understood, and studied in the year 1200. In the late eleventh century the *Digest* was returned to western Europe, but in this region, it made only the faintest impression. Roman law was already familiar, with a thick veneer of Visigothic interpretation. Legal language changed, but existing forms of behavior remained intact for most of the inhabitants of the region. The exception was the very upper layer of Languedocien society. The magnates of the region systematically changed their practices in the endowment of children, the inclusion of wives in public life, and testamentary disposition. The reason women began to fade from the public record is difficult to explain with legal citations and references to documents. Although integral to dynastic politics and the well-being of the next generation, wives and daughters still began to play a secondary role—or one very much invisible to the harsh reality of document survival. This does not mean that women were without wealth or power—they were without land. The probable answer is simply necessity. Even in a community that was familiar with law in all its regional forms, protecting the patrimony drew the landed elite away from an ideal. Land was in increasingly short supply. Some families did divide and subdivide their property into non-existence.[81] In contrast, the most powerful landed families acquired more and more property and concentrated it into the hands of fewer and fewer family members. Women were excluded and so were cadet sons. The law as a written ideal was no longer uniformly in practice.

---

79 *Le petit thalamus*, Article 7 (1205). Minority was frequently extended. Testaments that specified the age of majority typically chose 17, but sometimes 20 or even 25. *LIM*, nos. 94–96, 99, 116.

80 AM, EE299.

81 Cheyette, *Ermengard of Narbonne*, 133–43.

Bibliography

Manuscripts

Archives Départmentales de l'Hérault: series G, H.

Archives Municipales de Montpellier: series AA, EE.

Liber instrumentorum memorialium ("*Mémorial des nobles*") AA1.

Le petit thalamus AA9; see also http://thalamus.huma-num.fr/.

Arxiu de la Corona d'Aragó (ACA), Cancelleria reial.

Liber feudorum maior, registres, 1; see also https://www.mcu.es/archivos/MC/ACA/Miniaturas/miniaturas/llibre02/000.htm.

Printed Sources

d'Achery, Luc. *Spicilegium: sive Collectio veterum aliquot scriptorum qui in Galliae bibliothecis delituerant.* Edited by Joseph de Barre. 3 vols. Paris: Apud Montalant, 1723.

Bibliotheca legum regni Francorum manuscripta. Edited by Karl Ubl, assisted by Dominik Trump and Daniela Schulz. Cologne, 2012. http://www.leges.uni-koeln.de/en/lex/lex-romana-visigothorum/.

Bullaire de l'église de Maguelone. Edited by Jean Rouquette and André Villemagne. Montpellier: Valat, 1911.

Cartulaires des abbayes d'Aniane et de Gellone. Edited by L. Cassan and E. Meynial. Montpellier: Martel, 1898–1900.

Cartulaire de Maguelone. Edited by Jean Rouquette and André Villemagne. 5 vols. Montpellier: Valat, 1912–1924.

Le cartulaire du chapitre cathédral Saint-Étienne d'Agde. Edited by Raymonde Foreville. Paris: CNRS, 1995.

Cartulaire des Trencavel: analyse détaillée des 617 actes, 957–1214. Edited by Joseph Dovetto. Carcassonne: Centre de recherches et d'information historiques des conférenciers de la Cité, 1997.

Devic, Claude and J-J. Vaissete. *Histoire générale de Languedoc*. New ed. 16 vols. Toulouse: Privat, 1876–1892.

Corpus Juris Civilis. Digesta. The Digest of Justinian. Edited by Theodor Mommsen and Paul Krueger. English translation by Alan Watson. Philadelphia: University of Pennsylvania Press, 1985.

Corpus Iuris Civilis. Edited by Theodor Mommsen and Paul Krueger. Berlin: Weidmann, 1892–1893.

Gallia christiana in provincias distributa; qua series et historia archiepiscoporum, episcoporum et abbatum. 16 vols. Paris: Ex Typographia Regia, 1744–1877.

Layettes du Trésor des Chartes. Edited by Alexandre Teulet et al. 5 vols. Paris: Plon, 1863–1909.

Leges Visigothorum. Edited by Karolus Zeumer. Hanover: Hahn, 1902.

Liber feudorum maior. Cartulario real que se conserva en el Archivo de la Corona de Aragón. Edited by Francisco Miquel Rosell. 2 vols. Barcelona, 1945–1947.

Liber instrumentorum memorialium: Le cartulaire des Guilhems de Montpellier. Edited by Alexandre Germain and Charles Chabaneau. Montpellier: Martel, 1884–1886.

Macé, Laurent. *Catalogues raimondins. Actes des comtes de Toulouse, ducs de Narbonne et marquis de Provence (1112–1229)*. Toulouse: Archives Municipales de Toulouse, 2008.

Thalamus parvus: Le petit thalamus de Montpellier, publié par la première fois d'après les manuscrits originaux. Edited by Ferdinand Pégat, Eugène Thomas, et al. Montpellier: Martel, 1840.

Secondary Sources

Aurell, Martin. "La détérioration de la statut de la femme aristocratique en Provence (xe–xiiie siècles)." *Le Moyen Age* (1985): 5–32.

Aurell, Martin. *Les noces du comte: Mariage et pouvoir en Catalogne (785–1213)*. Histoire ancienne et médiévale, no. 32. Paris: Publications de la Sorbonne, 1995.

Aurell, Martin. *Une famille de la noblesse provençale au Moyen-Âge: Les Porcelet*. Avignon: Aubanel, 1986.

Bisson, Thomas N. *The Medieval Crown of Aragon: A Short History*. Oxford: Oxford University Press, 1986.

Bisson, Thomas N. "Unheroed Pasts: History and Commemoration in South Frankland before the Albigensian Crusades," *Speculum* 65 (1990): 281–308.

Bonnassie, Pierre. *La Catalogne du milieu du Xe à la fin du xie siècle. Croissance et mutations d'une société*. 2 vols. Toulouse: Association des Publications de l'Université de Toulouse-Le Mirai, 1975–1976.

Bourin-Derruau, Monique. *Villages médiévaux en Bas-Languedoc: Genèse d'une sociabilité, xe–xive siècle*. 2 vols. Paris: Harmattan, 1987.

Cheyette, Frederic. *Ermengard of Narbonne and the World of the Troubadours*. Ithaca: Cornell University Press, 2001.

Duhamel-Amado, Claudie. "Femmes entre elles: Filles et épouses languedociennes (xie et xiie siècles)." In *Femmes: Mariages—lignages, xiie–xive. Mélanges offerts à Georges Duby*, 125–55. Brussels: De Boeck, 1992.

Duhamel-Amado, Claudie. *Genèse des lignages méridianaux*. 2 vols. Toulouse: CNRS, 2001, 2007.

Duhamel-Amado, Claudie. "Les Guillems de Montpellier à la fin du xiie siècle, un lignage en péril." *Revue des langues romaneis* 89 (1985): 13–28.

Duhamel-Amado, Claudie. "Poids de l'aristocratie d'origine wisgothique dans la genèse de la noblesse septimanienne." In *L'Europe héritière de lEspagne wisigothique: Colloque international du C.N.R.S, tenu a la Fondation Singer-Polignac (Paris, 14–16 mai, 1990)*, 81–99. Madrid: Collection de la Casa de Velázquez, no. 35, 1990.

Fabre, Ghislaine and Thierry Lochard. *Montpellier: La ville médiévale.* Vol 3 of Montpellier. Etudes du patrimonie. Paris: Imprimerie Nationale, 1992.

Gardner, Jane F. *Women in Roman Law and Society.* Bloomington: Indiana University Press, 1986.

Gouron, André. "Les étapes de la pénétration du droit romain au XIIe siècle dans ancienne Septimanie." *Annals du Midi* 69 (1957): 103–20.

Gouron, André. "*Libertas hominum Montispessulani*: Rédaction et diffusion des coutumes de Montpellier." *Annales du Midi* 90 (1978): 289–318.

Haluska-Rausch, Elizabeth. "Transformations in the Powers of Wives and Widows in Medieval Montpellier, 985–1213." In *The Experience of Power in Medieval Europe 900–1300*, edited by Alan Cooper, Bob Berkhofer, and Adam J. Kosto, 147–62. Aldershot: Ashgate, 2005.

Haluska-Rausch, Elizabeth. "Family, Property, and Power: Women in Medieval Montpellier, 985–1213." Ph.D. diss., Harvard University, 1998.

Haluska-Rausch, Elizabeth. "Unwilling Partners: Conflict and Ambition in the Marriage of Peter II of Aragon and Marie de Montpellier." In *Queenship and Political Power in Medieval and Early Modern Spain*, edited by Theresa Earenfight, 3–20. Women and Gender in Early Modern Europe. Aldershot: Ashgate, 2005.

Herlihy, David. "Land, Family and Women in Continental Europe, 701–1200." *Traditio* 18 (1962): 89–120.

Hilaire, Jean. "Les régimes matrimoniaux aux XIe et XIIe siècles dans la région de Montpellier." *Recueil de mémoires et travaux publiés par la Société d'Histoire du droit et des institutions des anciens pays de droit écrit* 3 (1955): 15–38.

Mayali, Laurent. *Droit savant et coutumes: L'exclusion des filles dotées, XIIe–XVe siècles.* Studien zur Europäischen Rechtsgeschichte, no. 33. Frankfurt am Main: V. Klostermann, 1987.

Mosher Stuard, Susan, ed. *Women in Medieval History and Historiography.* Philadelphia: University of Pennsylvania Press, 1987.

Mundy, John. *Men and Women at Toulouse in the Age of the Cathars.* Toronto: Toronto University Press, 1990.

Ourliac, Paul and Jean-Louis Gazzaniga. *Histoire du droit privé français: De l'an mil au Code civil.* L'evolution de l'humanité. Paris: Albin Michel, 1985.

Poly, Jean-Pierre. *La Provence et la société féodale, 879–1166. Contribution à l'étude des structures dites féodales dans le Midi.* Paris: Bordas, 1976.

Radding, Charles and Antonio Ciaralli. *The* Corpus Iuris Civilis *in the Middle Ages. Manuscripts and Transmission from the Sixth Century to the Juristic Revival.* Leiden: Brill, 2006.

Reyerson, Kathryn. "Women in Business in Medieval Montpellier." In *Women and Work in Preindustrial Europe*, edited by Barbara Hanawalt. Bloomington: Indiana University Press, 1986, 117–44.

Röuet, Adolphe Auguste. *Notice sur la ville de Lunel au moyen âge et la vie de Saint-Gérard, seigneur de cette ville au XIIIe siècle*. Montpellier: Leguin, 1878.
Strayer, Joseph R. *The Albigensian Crusades*. New York: Dial Press, 1971.
Yver, Jean. *Egalité entre héritiers et exclusion des enfants dotés: Essai de géographie coutumière*. Paris: Sirey, 1966.

CHAPTER 8

Sex with Nuns in Medieval France

Sara McDougall

In the spring of 1393 or 1394, a lusty young cleric in his early twenties named Perrin Larchier made his way to the Cordeliers convent on a hilltop outside Provins, a town in the Champagne region of France.[1] He went there, ostensibly, to visit with his kinswoman. Despite their enclosure, these nuns could receive male relations in their parlor, if discreetly on the other side of the grille, and in the company of another nun. It was in these circumstances that Perrin met and fell for a nun called Jeannette la Flamenge. Apparently, the attraction was mutual, as Jeannette agreed to run away with him. One night soon after, Perrin and two companions scaled the convent's walls with the help of a ladder. Inside the enclosure, they found Jeannette waiting, bringing with her some jewelry, clothing, money, and a breviary. The men quickly disguised Jeannette in secular apparel and made off with her on horseback. After a spree of six months travelling to Mont Saint Michel and elsewhere, Perrin returned to Provins with a pregnant Jeannette, whom he left in the care of "family," his or hers, we do not know. Whoever's kin they were, they restored the pregnant nun to her convent, where she gave birth to an infant daughter who died soon after.

We know about all this only because Perrin and one of his accomplices got in a great deal of trouble for this sacrilegious act. This narrative is taken from the royal pardons the two men obtained from King Charles VI.[2] Beyond what was included in these two men's pleas for royal mercy, we know absolutely nothing about Jeannette or her fate. Certainly, her name suggests, but does not guarantee, Flemish origins. We do not know her social status or anything about her family. We do not know when she went to live in the convent and professed as a nun, the specific nature of her religious profession, or what penance she might have been subjected to on her return. We also do not know how much

1 Also known as the Royal Abbey of Ste.-Catherine-lèz-Provins, see further below. The pardon is recorded in Archives nationales, JJ 154 ff. 393v–394r #695; see the appendix for a translation. There is an incomplete edition in Louis Douët-d'Arcq, *Choix de pièces inédites relatives au règne de Charles VI*, vol. 2 (Paris: Jules Renouard, 1864), 15–18, and the pardon is also evoked in Emile Collas, "Enlèvements d'autrefois: moeurs des XIVe et XV siècles," *La Nouvelle Revue* 3, no. 4 (1908): 467–68.

2 Jehan de Remangis, Archives nationales, JJ 147 f. 107r #233, May 1395.

 | DOI:10.1163/9789004710696_010

we can trust the two men's accounts of her temporary removal from the convent, even though they are essentially the same, differing only in the month and year in which the nun's departure from the convent took place.

Moreover, while it is possible that Jeannette was the willing accomplice the two royal pardons made her out to be, we should not be so sure. If Perrin misrepresented her acquiescence to his desires he would not be the first or last man to do such a thing. That both men claimed Jeannette had fallen for Perrin and wanted him to take her from the convent does not mean that it was so. Much as one might like this story to be a romance, it could have instead been a far more brutal or sordid business.

These men had very good reasons to cast their behavior in the best possible light. Execution counted among the possible consequences for the abduction of nuns.[3] This convent's status as under the king's special protection may have made royal officials particularly eager to act against violators of its enclosure. Perrin and his accomplice, therefore, had ample incentive to do what they could to mitigate their culpability. If anything, it is surprising they did not do more to spin the story. Perhaps too many of the facts of the case were known to the royal officials to risk too obvious a falsehood. Other men prosecuted for sex with nuns went to great lengths to diminish the seriousness of their offence, whatever the truth of the matter. Excuses offered by men on trial for this crime in medieval Bologna included, for example, claims that the woman in question had been regularly having sex with other men, or that she was no nun, and was in fact a prostitute.[4] Instead, truthfully or not, Perrin and his accomplice, or their advocates, chose to represent their behavior as a sort of youthful romance. Describing Jeannette as having willfully abandoned her religious enclosure, casting it as a consensual act rather than abduction or rape, could have been part of a strategy to mitigate the men's offence at least to some extent. It could also have been true. Either way, regardless of the nun's wishes, the threat of dire punishment remained for both men: not just for having sex with a nun, but even for the act of removing her from her religious house, with or without her consent.[5]

And what of the nun's own wishes? We do not know, but Jeannette may well have wanted to leave her enclosure, or at least she may have wanted to have sex with Perrin. Either way it was a serious matter for her as well, even aside

3 Gratian, *Corpus Iuris Canonici*, 1: D. 1 de pen. c. 6 and d.p.c. 47; James Brundage, *Law, Sex, and Christian Society in Medieval Europe* (Chicago: University of Chicago Press, 1987), 250.

4 Trevor Dean, "Fornicating with nuns in fifteenth-century Bologna," *Journal of Medieval History*, 34, no. 4 (2008): 374–82.

5 Brundage, *Law, Sex, and Christian Society*, 250.

from the obvious problem of her failure to maintain chastity. An unauthorized departure from the enclosure, and changing into secular attire in particular, would have marked Jeannette as apostate, automatically excommunicate, and as such potentially subject to serious punishment.[6] Other women nonetheless braved these consequences and abandoned religious life, even repeatedly, and for a variety of reasons.[7] Some were taken against their will, or so we are told, though the same problem of knowing if this was true or not remains.[8]

Jeannette la Flamenge's temporary removal from religious life therefore offers an instructive introduction to some of the problems faced by scholars in researching the topic of sex with nuns. For just as is the case with Jeannette, the most difficult question to answer is almost always anything about the nun herself. That we struggle to learn about a medieval woman's wishes hardly surprises, the difficulty of accessing and assessing female agency in medieval sources, is not, unfortunately, surprising. But in fact, there are still more unknowns.

Perhaps most surprising of all is how little we know about the punishment of nuns accused of illicit sex or those "caught in the act" of illicit sex. This is particularly unexpected for readers familiar with the horror stories told from the eighteenth century onward of a nun imprisoned in a convent basement and left to starve and die there, locked away by a powerful priest whose advances she refused, or by a cruel abbess.[9] We know all too well, moreover,

6 Elizabeth Makowski, *Apostate Nuns in the Later Middle Ages* (Woodbridge: Boydell & Brewer, 2019), see esp. ch. 1; F. Donald Logan, *Runaway Religious in Medieval England, c. 1240–1540* (Cambridge: Cambridge University Press, 1996); Christian Knudsen, "Naughty Nuns and Promiscuous Monks: Monastic Sexual Misconduct in Late Medieval England" (Ph.D. diss., University of Toronto, 2012); Knudsen, "Promiscuous Monks and Naughty Nuns: Poverty, Sex and Apostasy in Later Medieval England," in *Poverty and Prosperity: The Rich and the Poor in the Middle Ages and Renaissance*, ed. Anne Scott and Cindy Kosso (Turnhout: Brepols, 2012), 75–91.

7 "Archive shows medieval nun faked her own death to escape convent," The Guardian, accessed August 18, 2022, https://www.theguardian.com/books/2019/feb/11/archive-shows-medieval-nun-faked-her-own-death-to-escape-convent. Also not to be missed is the following discovery: "Joan of Leeds: Her Own Story," The Northern Way, accessed August 18, 2022, https://thenorthernway151149306.wordpress.com/joan-of-leeds-her-own-story/.

8 Eileen Power obviously went too far when she wrote, "It seems quite clear that the nuns who broke their vows were always willing parties to the breach. Few men would have been bold enough to ravish a *Sponsa Dei*. Sometimes a bishop was led to suppose that a nun had been carried away against her will, but he always found out in the end that she had been in the plot; all abductions were in reality elopements." *Medieval English Nunneries c. 1275 to 1535* (Cambridge: Cambridge University Press, 1922), 440.

9 Matthew Lewis, *The Monk: A Romance* (Dublin: J. Bell, 1797); Maria Monk, *Further Disclosures by Maria Monk Concerning the Hotel Dieu Nunnery of Montreal; and Also Her Visit to Nun's Island and Disclosures Concerning that Secret Retreat* (New York: Leavitt, Lord & Co, 1837).

of real horror stories of abuse in postmedieval convents.[10] When we turn to medieval sources, by contrast, we find a good deal of sex, rumored and real, but no evidence that actual nuns caught at this sex received the brutal—and especially the deadly—punishments that later writers would imagine for them.[11]

Do the medieval cloister walls nevertheless conceal among their secrets the untold stories of countless women suffering imprisonment or worse as punishment for sex? None of our evidence comfortably supports this idea. This does not mean, of course, that bad things did not happen to nuns caught at sex. Pregnant nuns may absolutely have suffered enormously. At the same time, we should take stock of what information we do have, and see what we can make of it. As I will argue, we lack evidence for the regular infliction of harsh punishment for women in religious life found pregnant. What we do have a good deal of evidence for is women and children having survived the experience of a nun's pregnancy. We can find not only that, but the reintegration and promotion to higher office of the mothers, as well as efforts to secure the career prospects of the children. In the background, there are at least hints at punishment, and what we can find are largely "medicinal" or restorative efforts.[12] This could include public humiliation, "discipline," and penitential confinement, which could have been terrible for the women concerned. This took place, as far as we can discern, in a broader context of mitigation of punishment, absolution, and even examples of some women escaping punishment entirely. As all this suggests, while some horrible things must have happened, we should hesitate before filling in the silences of our sources with the polemical and often sadomasochistic horror stories produced by another era.

This article offers a new account of what we do know about sex with nuns and its consequences in late medieval France, and in the Champagne in particular. In so doing it seeks to lay out the range of the possible for what could

---

10 "Abused nuns reveal stories of rape, forced abortions," PBS, published June 2011, video, 10:06 https://www.pbs.org/newshour/show/abused-nuns-reveal-stories-of-rape-forced-abortions; Kelly Heyboer, "These 3 N.J. nuns were accused of sex abuse. Here's what we know about them," last modified May 28 2019, https://www.nj.com/news/2019/05/these-3-nj-nuns-were-accused-of-sex-abuse-heres-what-we-know-about-them.html.

11 The one exception is the twelfth century account by Aelred of Riveaulx of the Nun of Watton, recorded in a single surviving manuscript; this example, as I argue elsewhere, is quite exceptional indeed. Moreover, one could certainly argue even with this example it was the man who had sex with the nun who suffered most, as he was castrated. I do not mean to make light of the suffering of the nun in this miracle story, or of any actual nuns who suffered punishment for sexual or any other sins, but I do wish to focus on presenting what sources we have, and to endeavor to avoid making assumptions.

12 Elisabeth Lusset, *Crime, châtiment et grâce dans les monastères au Moyen Âge* (XIIe–XVe *siècle*) (Turnhout: Brepols, 2017), 276.

have happened to Jeannette la Flamenge, in a region that has received little scholarly attention. Benefitting from the recent scholarship of Elisabeth Lusset, Christian Knudsen, and Elizabeth Makowski in particular, who focus largely on England, Germany, and parts of France; and drawing upon a selection of local, royal, and pontifical sources, this article presents a history that is largely one of redemption and reintegration for the nun accused of sexual sin. There could well have been harsh penance, lengthy incarceration, expulsion, or other grave consequences for sex, but our sources do not shed much light on this. Instead, as Lusset explains, "Nuns were threatened with expulsion or remission to secular authority … but this extreme recourse was rarely carried out: redemption and purgation were always possible. Most important above all was for the Church to restore by repentance and penance and to prevent a scandal that would have been provoked by the publicity of a punishment."[13]

Even though pregnancy and especially childbirth could, or even should, have played a probative role, there is nothing to indicate that nuns were punished at a higher rate than monks for illegal sex. In fact, the scholarship that provides statistical analysis of the handling of sexual sin engaged in by both male and female monastics demonstrates that, if anything, we have far more evidence for allegations made against male than against female religious. Priests, in fact, greatly outnumber any other person sworn to religious life in our records of punishment for sexual sin.[14] There are jurisdictional explanations for this to be sure, but it remains the case that our evidence for sex involving nuns, and especially for direct accusations against nuns as opposed to men in religious life, is paltry by comparison.[15]

As to the question of whether there was any greater eagerness to punish the nun caught at sex as a person categorized as the worst kind of sexual sinner, and conceived of as "worst" because female and also because professed religious, once again the evidence points elsewhere. For scholars have most often found that any punishments, when we can find any trace of them, do not appear to have differed greatly for male or female monastics accused of the same sorts of sexual offences.[16] This holds true for Penelope Johnson's work

13 Translation my own. Elisabeth Lusset, "Propriae salutis immemores? Réflexions sur la correction des moniales criminelles en Occident, XIIIe–XVe siècle," in *Figures de femmes criminelles, de l'Antiquité à nos jours*, ed. Loïc Cadiet, Frédéric Chauvaud, Claude Gauvard, Pauline Schmitt-Pantel, and Myriam Tsikounas (Paris: Editions de la Sorbonne, 2010), 265.

14 Deciding how to categorize male religious for statistical purposes is nightmarishly difficult as men could of course be both monks and priests, or canons and priests, and so on.

15 Penelope Johnson, *Equal in Monastic Profession: Religious Women in Medieval France* (Chicago: University of Chicago Press, 1991), 112–33.

16 Knudsen, "Naughty Nuns;" see especially Chapter 4.

on thirteenth century visitation records from Normandy, and also for the more ample—comparatively speaking—sources that scholars have used to study the late Middle Ages. Researching English, French, and German examples from the fourteenth and especially fifteenth centuries, scholars have by and large concluded, as did Johnson before them, that monks and nuns accused of sexual delicts, and other violations of their vows, were for the most part treated the same. As Elizabeth Makowski concludes in her study of apostate nuns in the later Middle Ages, when compared to male religious, nuns were considered "spiritual equals to be dealt with accordingly."[17] That could be a rather optimistic interpretation, it must be said. At the very least, though, we can recognize that there are more similarities than differences in what little we know about the punishments of monks and nuns.

I offer this hesitation because, as already alluded to, it is so difficult to know how ecclesiastical authorities, and especially religious superiors within the convents, handled nuns' engagement in illicit sex. We know much more about the men accused of sex with nuns, and also about the children of nuns, rather than the nuns themselves. This is curious at the very least, as Knudsen has argued, since pregnancy arguably made a nun's participation in illicit sex so much more difficult to deny than accusations against a man. Still, Knudsen was able to find only a few references to pregnant nuns in English visitation records. We know very little about the fate of the mother or the child, but on the whole, we can at least rule out expulsion as a common consequence: "the nuns who had given birth seem to have remained in the monastery as monastics."[18] Just as Lusset found with her analysis of cases of nuns accused of serious crimes, episcopal officials in England seem most concerned with keeping the pregnancy a secret. What, if anything, was done to the nun, as punishment or penance, we know not.[19] Visitation records rarely include any details either.[20] And even these few references are terse in the extreme. What precisely to make of punishment "according to the rule," for example? Lusset lays out the potential consequences for sin, usually a list of possibilities, subject always to the official's discretion, which share general reluctance to expel or even transfer nuns. For the cases studied by Knudsen, he identifies temporary imprisonment and silence as the most common punishments, suggesting as well the likely use of ritual humiliation, and indicating as unlikely the transfer to another monastery or expulsion.

---

17 Makowski, *Apostate Nuns*, 191.

18 Knudsen, "Naughty Nuns," 119–20.

19 See generally Knudsen, "Naughty Nuns;" Makowski, *Apostate Nuns*.

20 Knudsen, "Naughty Nuns," 180–81.

This scholarship also addresses the reasons we have such difficulty finding records of punishment for pregnant nuns. Elisabeth Lusset offers essential guidance on how to study the bad behavior of nuns, making innovative use of both local and pontifical records. As she has written concerning nuns accused of violent crimes, it is doubly difficult to find evidence on this topic.[21] First, because when looking through records of alleged criminal activity, it is always hard to find women among the many more men accused of or prosecuted for crime. Second, religious women accused of crimes are even further obscured from our view than are laywomen. Often, jurisdictional rules shielded them, not just from secular prosecution, but also from a bishop's judicial authority.

Instead, medieval convents appear to have quite successfully kept such affairs secret. The authorities whose oversight convents often had to defend themselves against, in this campaign of concealment, could often prove allies rather than opponents. Some exceptions aside, ecclesiastical authorities would have wanted to hide from the world the sins of nuns, and especially a nun's sexual activity; therefore all church authorities had an obligation to proceed with care in these matters. Punishment of sexually sinful nuns, especially public punishment, had always to be weighed against the imperative of avoiding scandal that might damage the reputation of the church, or of a monastic house.[22] Avoidance of scandal in rendering punishment was a general legal principle in medieval canon law.[23] It was especially important when it concerned scandal that threatened the reputation of the church. This sort of scandal, it was feared, might lead the faithful to question their beliefs, or challenge the authority of religious officials. This held for male clergy also, as their careers could suffer if accusations of sexual impropriety were weaponized against them.[24] Revelations about sexually active nuns, meanwhile,

---

21 Lusset, "Réflexions," 255–65.

22 Arnaud Fossier, "Propter vitandum scandalum. Histoire d'une catégorie juridique (xii–xv siècles)," *Mélanges de l'Ecole française de Rome. Moyen Âge*, 121, no. 2 (2009): 317–48; Richard Helmholz, "Scandalum in Medieval Canon Law and in the English Ecclesiastical Courts," *Zeitschrift der Savigny-Stiftung für Rechtsgeschichte: Kanonistische Abteilung* 96 (2010): 258–74; See also Lindsay Brian, "Periculum animarum: Bishops, Gender, and Scandal," *Florilegium* 19 (2002): 49–73.

23 See especially Helmholz, "Scandalum," 264–65.

24 See, e.g., the episode described by Elizabeth Makowski in *Apostate Nuns*, 137–41, where the cleric who is bringing the runaway nun back to her convent has to be worried about his reputation. See also the allegations of illegal sex studied by Julien Thèry, and the many, many church court prosecutions of clerics caught at illegal sex or accused of it. See, e.g., Julien Thèry, "Judicial Inquiry as an Instrument of Centralized Government: The Papacy's Criminal Proceedings against Prelates in the Age of Theocracy (mid-12th to mid-14th century)," in *Proceedings of the 14th International Congress of Medieval Canon Law*, ed. Joseph

could have serious consequences for the nuns and for their community, as their reputations for sanctity depended so mightily upon maintaining their lifelong commitment to virginity.[25] Inability to restrain female sex indicated not just problems with the holiness of religious women themselves, but a failure of leadership, a serious failing in authorities to control the behavior of the women who owed them obedience.

If in fact no one knew about the sex save the nun, her partner, and a confessor or her religious superior, any punishment ought to be designed to facilitate the salvation of the sinner without revealing the secret to others. Penance and contrition were essential, but ought to be undertaken with care so that the punishment itself not advertise the sin and provoke scandal. If the sin was known, or widely rumored, then punishment in the presence of the other nuns might seem more appropriate, a necessary step towards the preeminent goals of maintaining good order and working towards the salvation of the community as a whole, and also the redemption and reintegration of the sinner into that community. Those charged with discipline may not of course have adhered to these principles, but certainly the existence of these rules helps to explain the possible reasons for the silences of our sources. For all these reasons, we know very little about the consequences of any nun's sexual activities, alleged or real.

Before examining our evidence in detail, we first need to address what precisely we are dealing with when studying the topic of sex involving nuns. There are two problematic terms: that of sex and that of nun. First, often enough with the examples we have, it is not entirely clear if a nun in fact had sex, or even if having had sex is precisely what she is being accused of. For example, with allegations of "frequenting in scandal," or "found in a suspicious place," it is possible that the nun was being accused of scandalous behavior that could have involved sex, but may have been something more innocent—dangerous to her honor and reputation, but less potentially damaging to her salvation. The reputation of her religious house, in fact, might have suffered regardless of the truth. Scandalous rumor could be damaging even if unproven, or if false.

Pregnancy, if obviously evidence of sexual activity, nonetheless offered more nuance than we might realize. For pregnancy, it must be said, while evidence of sex, was not evidence of consensual sex, and whether or not she had consented would have mattered in determining the extent of her sin.[26] We cannot imagine

---

Goering, Stephan Dusil, and Andreas Thier (Vatican City: Biblioteca apostolica vaticana, 2016), 875–89.

25 Johnson, *Monastic Profession*, 112–30.

26 Pregnancy and rape is an enormous topic that cannot be sufficiently addressed here. In brief, there were some medical authorities who wrote that a woman could not become pregnant without emitting "seed" and therefore taking some pleasure in the act, but these

these nuns engaged only in consensual sex. Sexual exploitation, abuse, and rape are all too possible.[27] A great deal more research on this subject is needed. But I cannot resist a speculation that is quite possibly both too pessimistic and too optimistic, assuming widespread sexual exploitation on the one hand, and less horrible than often imagined behavior on the other. To wit: I think that one reason nuns might not have been punished so fiercely for having had sex, even despite the indisputable evidence of pregnancy, reflects a recognition on the part of authorities that the sex may well have happened without the nun necessarily wanting it to happen. Women, after all, were supposed to be subject to male authority. They were not supposed to let men have illicit sex with them, but may have had no choice. It is at least possible that there was some recognition of women's all too real vulnerability, particularly when it came to sex, and that this may have resulted in mitigated punishment for pregnant nuns.

An additional difficulty in studying nuns and their sins is one that also posed problems for the religious officials at the time who sought to assign the appropriate punishments or penances. For those officials, and for modern scholars too, it can be quite difficult to know if a woman was, in fact, a professed nun, or not. Had she formally vowed to live out her life in celibacy along with poverty and obedience, or had she not in fact taken those vows, or not taken those vows willingly? All this could mean that she was not, in fact, bound to live as celibate, or that failing to do so had different consequences. If the woman in question had not in fact taken a formal and permanent vow of celibacy, her having had sex was, if still in all probability sinful, rather less serious. But religious profession, like marital status or legitimate birth, could actually be a matter of some dispute. Many more women spent time in convents than those who swore to live as lifelong celibates, and there were many degrees of profession.

"Full profession" as a nun did lose at least some of its ambiguity beginning in the fourteenth century. As Elizabeth Freeman wrote, "Since 1298, canon law had been very clear on the matter of what constituted formal acceptance into a religious community: candidates were to pronounce the traditional vows of poverty, chastity, and obedience; and they were also to make a formal and public act of profession, which profession was signified by the assumption of

ideas are not present in any French legal theory and practice that I have seen, though the English law discussed pregnancy as proof against an allegation of rape. See Corinne Saunders, *Rape and Ravishment in the Literature of Medieval England* (Woodbridge: Boydell & Brewer, 2001), 73–75.

27 This is a topic that I hope to address in future, but at present, lacking evidence, must reluctantly leave to one side.

the habit."[28] Being of sufficient age to profess, having done so with no sign of constraint, and especially a change in clothing, often exchanging one head covering for another, a switch from white to black veil, for example, could all be taken as evidence of full profession, an unbreakable commitment to religious life in the order and house in which one had professed. But even so, ambiguities and complexities remained, even in the later Middle Ages. For "full profession," free consent to religious life had a primary role, but that meant, too, that claims of coercion could nullify, or at least muddy, any clear sense of a woman's status as nun or not.

Consider the fifteenth century example of Katherine Norfolk, allegedly abducted from her monastic house not once but twice by her kin. As Elizabeth Freeman explains, about forty witnesses deposing before the York consistory courts swore Katherine had professed as nun. For a time this was taken as decisive evidence that she had in fact professed. Nevertheless, she later appears to have abandoned religious life again and married. As Freeman writes concerning the case, "monastic life for some medieval nuns was short-term, and participation in the life of the monastic *familia* by no means ended one's ties with biological families outside the monastery walls."[29] We should probably assume the same for nuns and sexual activity. We cannot know how often nuns left monasteries, had sex, became pregnant, or married, but we should recognize that all these things could and did happen, and that the one thing we are usually furthest from knowing is what the woman in question wanted to happen, and if and when she might have consented.

Having at least recognized the problem that we cannot always be sure who was or was not a nun, or what that even implied in terms of the obligation of celibacy, let us keep that ambiguity in mind as we turn now to address what we can know about consequences for the sexual activity of female religious, broadly conceived.

We can begin with some examples for which we can be certain that sex with nuns took place, with the children of nuns. One of few places to find these children is the records of royal legitimations, provided to correct for at least some of the legal barriers posed by illegitimate birth, as well as records of

---

28 Elizabeth Freeman, "Cistercian Nuns in Medieval England: Unofficial Meets Official," in *Elite and Popular Religion*, ed. Kate Cooper and Jeremy Gregory (Woodbridge: Boydell and Brewer, 2006), 110–19; Makowski, "Pernicious Sort of Woman," xxviii–xxix; Liber Sextus 3:15.1 CIC 2:1053.

29 Freeman, "Cistercian Nuns," 13.

papal dispensation that allowed illegitimate children to advance in ecclesiastical careers.[30]

Let us take from the records of royal legitimation one example from the Champagne region, the place where Perrin Larchier had fallen for the nun Jeannette la Flamenge in the 1390s. As these records of legitimations make clear, Jeannette was not the only woman in religious orders to become pregnant during these troubled times for the Champagne, and for so much of France. When between 1350 and 1370 Bishop Henri of Poitiers had at least four children with nun Jeanne de Chenery of the Paraclete, there was no convent to abscond with her from. The Paraclete had been destroyed, likely in 1358–1359, though the nuns had fled the violence long before.[31] This same Bishop Henri had heartily partaken in that warfare, as a soldier as well as a lover. In 1370, not long after the death of the bishop, Antoine de Chenery—fascinatingly here presented with his mother's rather than father's family name, a most interesting deviation from more usual practice in legitimations—followed by his three sisters Jeanne, Gillette, and Marguerite, all obtained legitimation and the right to inherit their parents' temporal possessions.[32]

We have no sense of when this noble warrior and bishop of Troyes began his relationship with the nun Jeanne, though I am perhaps too bold—or naïve—in venturing the hope that their sex can be characterized as a relationship. Since they had at least four children together it could well be the case that they were already involved before his election to the bishopric, or even her profession, but it seems reasonable to date the beginning of their relations to his arrival in Troyes in 1350 or 1351. There is much to say about this man, his family, and a family penchant for having illegitimate children regardless of episcopal appointments.[33] That said, there are few discernible traces of

30 Romain Chevalier, "Les lettres de légitimation émises par la chancellerie de Charles VII (1430–1461)," 2 vols. (Master's thesis, Université Jean-Moulin Lyon III, 2015). He has also just successfully defended his thesis, "Papes, rois et bâtards: Normes et discours autour de la filiation illégitime (Papauté et royaume de France, XIIIe–XIVe siècles)" (Doctoral thesis, Université d'Avignon, 2023). My thanks to Dr. Chevalier for sharing his unpublished work with me.

31 Henri Deniflé, *La désolation des églises, monastères et hôpitaux en France pendant la guerre de cent ans* (Paris: Picard, 1899), 240–42; Charles Lalore, ed., *Collection des principaux cartulaires du diocèse de Troyes* (Paris: E. Thorin, 1878), 2:154–60.

32 Archives nationales, JJ 100 ff. 183v–84r, #616. http://himanis.huma-num.fr/app//index.php/ui/show/chancery/199/367?feedback=1. Romain Chevalier made a study of 253 letters from between 1307 and 1380 and found only a handful that have the mother's family name.

33 See for example the legitimation of two children of Guillaume of Poitiers, Bishop of Langres, JJ 105 f. 34v #47 (June 1373).

connections between Henri and Jeanne, or Henri and his children, beyond this legitimation. There is no mention of Jeanne or the children in Henri's will, for example.[34] But what about Jeanne? Did she seek and obtain absolution for her sexual relationship with the bishop? Did she return to the Paraclete after its reconstruction? Did she raise her own children? We cannot at present say, as too few sources survived from this tumultuous period. But we can at least allow that all this was possible.

When we turn from royal legitimations to papal dispensations for illegitimate birth we find a good number of petitioners who were born to nuns. They are far from the largest category of illegitimate persons seeking papal help with their status, to be sure. But they existed, and we should think about what their existence means for our efforts to understand the fate of their mothers. All we know is that somehow the children were born, survived, and were provided for.

Kirsi Salonen and Jussi Hanska engaged in extensive research in the records of papal dispensations granted during the pontificate of Pius II (r. 1458–1464). As concerns children of illicit parentage, they found relatively few nuns who sought the benefit of papal grace to advance in their careers. They also found relatively few others who named as mother a woman in religious life. But these relative few are nonetheless important. Among the 3,222 mothers identified as either lay or religious, married, unmarried, and widowed, only 2%, 58 women, were identified as nuns.[35] This could mean many things, some of them grim, for pregnant nuns and their children. But I wish, here and throughout this article, to focus on what we do know.

In this case, we know that at least 58 nuns, and probably more, became pregnant and gave birth to infants who survived. Not only that, but the children of these nuns were given enough nurture and education to be in a position that it seemed worth the time and expense to petition the papacy for dispensation for them. The vast majority of these children were men, since women in religious life only rarely needed such dispensations. Out of these 3,222 petitions only 23 illegitimately conceived nuns sought papal grace.[36] This means that there could have been many more nuns who gave birth to daughters, daughters who may or may not have followed their mothers into religious life, and also still more nuns who gave birth to sons who did not pursue a clerical career, or if they did, did not seek papal dispensation. Their monastic parentage could

34 Charles Lalore, ed., *Collection de Documents inédits relatifs a la Ville de Troyes et a la champagne mèridionale* (Troyes: Dufey-Robert, 1882), 2:154–60.

35 Kirsi Salonen and Jussi Hanska, *Entering a Clerical Career at the Roman Curia, 1458–1471* (Farnham, Surrey: UK Ashgate, 2013), 76.

36 Salonen and Hanska, *Entering a Clerical Career*, 76.

quite possibly have been kept quiet, concealed even from them. Salonen and Hanska, for example, found a priest who had been abandoned as an infant at a church in Siena, who had initially petitioned as the son of unmarried laypersons, but then sought a revised dispensation once he had learned, as he claimed, that he was the son of a priest.[37] Even today there are children who do not know that one or both of their parents were priests or nuns, though DNA testing has begun to seriously challenge the ability of parents or families to keep such matters secret.

We should also recognize that these records are far from complete. There must have been more children, more mothers. Certainly, some petitioners might have concealed the real religious status of their mothers, describing her only as unmarried, "soluta," and with some hope, I imagine, of getting away with it. Moreover, not all illegitimate children who obtained dispensation or legitimation had these acts recorded in papal or princely registers. Ecclesiastical dispensation in particular could happen at a more local level. Monastic orders in some cases could grant dispensations themselves, as could abbots.[38] Also, there could have been many more children of illicit parentage who, whether aware their parents had engaged in illegal sex or not, did not seek legal help with their status. It was not always so necessary.[39]

We cannot assume a happy fate for the child of a nun, or for the nun herself. But at very least what we can assert is that it was possible for a nun to give birth to a child who could obtain nurture. What is less clear is who provided that nurture. There are scattered references to nun's kin taking in their infants, and also references to priests raising nun's children, or fathers more generally taking in children or putting children into the care of their own families, or hiring a wet nurse. Other children, like the priest from Siena who belatedly discovered he was the son of a priest, had been abandoned as an infant and raised by others. Even in this case, enough of a link remained to his parents that he was later able to discover their identity or at least their status. By these or other means, the children of nuns found in these papal petitions had clearly lived long and well enough that it would seem expedient to obtain papal or royal help with legal status.

37 Salonen and Hanska, *Entering a Clerical Career*, 74.

38 Elisabeth Lusset, "Moines et moniales de naissance illégitime: Entrer dans les ordres réguliers et y faire carrière à la fin du Moyen Âge: entre droit général et ius proprium," in *Bâtards et bâtardises dans l'Europe médiévale et moderne,* ed. Carole Avignon (Rennes: Presses universitaires de Rennes, 2016), 129–30.

39 Sara McDougall, "Bastard Priests: Illegitimacy and Ordination in Medieval Europe," *Speculum* 94, no. 1 (2019): 138–72.

On the whole, as Elizabeth Makowski maintains, it seems likely that nuns who became mothers could not keep and raise their children.[40] Certainly if the nun remained in her enclosure, separation of the infant from its mother seems probable. If the pregnant nun left or was removed from the convent, she could perhaps raise her child herself, but at considerable cost to her salvation, and at potential risk of prosecution and punishment by religious or secular authorities. As Makowski writes, "Few apostates would have the sort of charmed existence of Lucretia Buti [mistress of the painter Fra Lippi], who thanks to the patronage enjoyed by her extremely talented lover (a talent shared by their son) lived out her life as mistress and mother in comfort, security, and plain view. Others, however, had a measure of protection that allowed them to hide in plain sight, barring intervention at the highest levels."[41]

But we should juxtapose this with some extremely interesting evidence from Italy, where notarial and other sources document some rather remarkable maternal and matrilineal family involvement in the rearing of an abbess's daughters from Italy, in the work of Roisin Cossar.[42] While we know of no nun given explicit permission to remain in the secular world and care for her children, this does not mean, of course, that mothers did not act in defiance of the law. It is also possible that some mothers could raise their children in their convents, perhaps especially daughters, but again, at present, we do not know.

Cistercian chapter meeting records, and those of the papal penitentiary offer additional means to seek out information as to the fate of nuns caught at sex.[43] These yield at least some evidence of the process of reintegration for nuns who had given birth or at least had been suspected of pregnancy or of sexual sins. These formulaic grants of mercy offered penitent nuns reintegration into their communities with full rights to all offices short of abbess. In 1389, for example, Jacquette de Castillon, nun of l'Amour-Dieu in Troissy-en-Champagne, obtained dispensation from the General Chapter, permitting her access to all offices and honors, regardless of the fact that she had been suspected of pregnancy. In fact, she had neither been formally accused nor convicted of any such offence, so this declaration by the General Chapter served

40 Makowski, *Apostate Nuns*, 194. For a twelfth-century letter written by a nun who missed her child (who may have been in some sense illegitimate) see Alison I. Beach, "Voices from a Distant Land: Fragments of a Twelfth-Century Nuns' Letter Collection," *Speculum* 77, no.1 (2002): 34–54.

41 Makowski, *Apostate Nuns*, 181.

42 Roisin Cossar, "Clerical 'Concubines' in Northern Italy During the Fourteenth Century," *Journal of Women's History* 23, no.1 (2011): 117–18, 110–31; Roisin Cossar, "Defining Roles in the Clerical Household in Trecento Venice," *Viator* 45, no. 2 (2014): 237–45.

43 Here I am once again following the example of Elisabeth Lusset.

to clear her name. In that same year, Jeanne de Prinaco, a nun of the house of Fille-Dieu in Lausanne, obtained mercy for her "carnal lapse and pregnancy."[44] Similarly, in 1401 a nun of the convent of Fontenelle who had given birth obtained absolution and reintegration in her community with all rights to titles save that of abbess, as long as this was agreeable to the abbess and other sisters of the house.[45]

Even examples that seem more extreme in their sinfulness, at least as far as we can tell, could obtain the same treatment by Cistercian officials. In 1409 Sister Marguerite la Coquelette, a nun of the house of Clairmarais,[46] having been found guilty of many sexual acts, with children the result, and apostacy, was granted mercy and access to all offices short of abbess "if her merits sufficed."[47] In another example from Angers, in 1500, we find the same limits in a papal grant of grace. Nun Marie de Chesue, who confessed to incontinence and pregnancy, and who had been imprisoned as a result, sought absolution for "fornication, adultery, *stuprum* and sacrilege," and asked permission to rise to the ranks of prioress and abbess in addition to absolution. She obtained grace, short of the right to be elected abbess.[48] But we should not assume that this would have necessarily been the last word. As we will see, even this last, greatest position of authority and honor might be attained by the repentant nun.

Having failed to find much evidence of punishment, we can at last resort to trying a source that should, in principle, have very little to say. Bishops' church court records are no place to look for the wrongdoing of nuns, real or alleged. Female religious houses normally had exemptions, or at very least the right to be judged in their own houses by a delegated court officer. Nevertheless, there are at least a very few examples that we can consider, and they are certainly revealing.

The alleged wrongful sexual activity handled by the officiality of Troyes that I have found included only heterosexual sex, and so all involved at least one woman. Nevertheless, it was almost always men, and most often male clergy, who were being accused and threatened with punishment, or punished.

44 Canivez, *Statuta*, v.3, 570, #51 (1389).

45 Canivez, *Statuta*, v.4, 15 #33 (1401): "Cum sorore Ioanna de Pirziel moniali monasterii de Fontenellis, quae diabolica versutia castitatis violavit propositum puerperio subsecuto, misericorditer per generale Capitulum dispensatur, ut hoc non obstante ad omnes gradus, status et honores Ordinis legitimos admittatur, citra nihilominus abbatialem dignitatem, dum tamen de beneplacito processerit abbatissae et conventus."

46 Founded in 1140 by St. Bernard in Pas de Calais.

47 Canivez, Statuta, v.4, 104 # 13 (1409).

48 My thanks to Elisabeth Lusset for sharing this reference with me. Archivio della Penitenzieria Apostolica (APA), register 49.

Women are named, or not, as who the man had been having sex with, living with in scandal, or having babies with. In these cases it was the men, male clergy above all, who bore the brunt of the official's efforts to regulate sexual sin. It was male clergy, too, whom this court most often threatened with excommunication and fines as punishment for sexual sins. Among the alleged offenders, nuns are the smallest minority of all. It takes tremendous effort to find them in these registers, for sexual as well as for any other offences.

Analysis of one long fifteenth century register of sentences from Troyes offers ample evidence of this.[49] The register includes 859 allegations of sexual offences. The vast majority of offenders, if we count both the accused and their partner in sin, were male clergy, 523.[50] As for nuns, meanwhile, out of those 859 cases, there are only six allegations of sex either by or with a nun, or nuns, as will be explained in more detail below.[51] And in fact, this actually concerned an even smaller number of women still, only three nuns. With two of those nuns the accusations were that two different men were having inappropriate relationships with them, rather than an accusation against the nuns themselves. So between 1423 and 1471 we know of only three nuns summoned before the bishop's official to address rumors or allegations of sexual scandal.[52]

The rare nun who appeared, not just once but even twice, before the bishop's official clearly deserves our attention, not least because her subsequent career raises some doubts as to the seriousness of any consequences for her as a result of this allegedly bad behavior. To begin where the register first mentions her, if not yet by name, in 1449, Friar Stephan Bonnat, the prior of Vaudes, was accused of causing scandal with the abbess of Bricot-les-Nonnains, and

49 Archives départmentales de l'Aube G.4171. See further Sara McDougall, "The Prosecution of Sex in Late Medieval Troyes," in *History of Sexuality in the Middle Ages and Renaissance*, ed. Albrecht Classen (Berlin: De Gruyter: 2008), 691–713.

50 166 allegations involved priests, 69 friars, 68 curates, 61 chaplains, 57 priors, 16 vicars, and 12 monks. In addition to these there were another 157 clergy identified only as *dominus* or *magister*, who may well have had additional ecclesiastical roles that are not listed in the register.

51 Brother Prior and Sister Agnes, a priest and Abbess Jeanne, the same abbess concerning another priest, two different barbers with Nurse Marie, two different men with Nun Isabelle, and a priest accused of having sex with some unnamed nuns. Archives départmentales de l'Aube G.4180, f. 48r.

52 The first nun accused of sexual impropriety in the sentence register, in 1441, was Sister Agnes, nun of St. Bernard in Troyes. Brother Gerald de Flumine, the prior of St. Bernard in Troyes, was cited before the bishop's official on the grounds that he was keeping Sister Agnes as his concubine. Some question of the official's jurisdictional competence rounds out the session.

the court menaced the friar with excommunication and a fine of ten livres.[53] As for the abbess herself, Sister Jeanne de la Hure (or de la Heuse), we read that she was issued a written warning in which she was ordered not to further consort in scandal with either the prior of Valdieu, Friar Stephan Bonnat, or with another man, Denisot Esglaniter, a layman presumably, from the nearby village of Meix-Saint-Epoing, on penalty of excommunication and 100 sous.[54] If any of these, the abbess, or the two men, did in fact have to pay any fines, or were excommunicated, we are not told. We are also left completely in the dark as to what precisely this could have been about. Was the abbess the victim of false rumors, or was she in fact having some sort of inappropriate or even sexual relationship with at least one of them, or with both men, either at the same time or in succession, by choice or out of some compulsion? Did one man, for example the friar, implicate the other in an effort to detract suspicion from himself? We do not know. What is clear is that this abbess was not long free from suspicions of sexual misbehavior, for once again, in 1458 she was back before the official, and this time warned about her scandalous conduct with yet another man, a priest named Nicholas Vinday.[55]

Most important for our purposes, whatever the truth of all of these allegations, we find this nun still abbess, or at least once again abbess. We never encounter Jeanne de la Hure as anything other than abbess despite the fact that she was accused of scandalous relations with three different men, allegations considered serious enough to result in the exceptional summons of a nun, an abbess even, before the bishop's court, an extreme rarity for late medieval church court records.

What more can we say about this abbess? By lucky coincidence Edouard André, a nineteenth-century scholar, wrote a history of the abbey of Bricot published in 1895. André devoted one chapter to the sorry state of the abbey in

53 Archives départmentales de l'Aube G.4171, f. 68v. "Sabbati ante Bartholomei (Saturday 23 August 1449). Dominus officialis monuit in scriptis fratrem Stephanam Bonnat priorem de Valle Dei ne de cetero frequentet et conversetur cum abbatissa de Bricolio cum qua conversatus est in scandalum sub penis excommunicationis et x livre tournensis."

54 Archives départmentales de l'Aube G.4171, f. 69r. "Veneris post Remegium (Thursday 2 October 1449). Dominus officialis monuit in scriptis sororem Johannam de la Hure abbatissam de Bricolio ne de cetero conversetur in scandalum cum fratre Stephano Bonnot priore de Valle dei nec etiam cum Deniseto Esglaniter de Mazo Sancti Yspani sub penis excommunicationis et centum soldi turonensium." See also Edouard André, *Histoire de l'Abbaye du Bricot en Brie XIIe siècle–1792* (Paris: Picard, 1895), 106.

55 Archives départmentales de l'Aube G.4171, f. 104v. "Mercuris post Cantate (Wednesday, 10 May 1458). Dominus officialis monuit in scriptis dominum Nicolaum Vindey presbiterium et sororem Johannam de la Hense abbissam de Bricolio ne simul conversantur praesumeravit sub penis excommunicationis decem librum et aliis penis iuris."

the fifteenth century, in which he reviewed what woefully few sources survive from mid-century, and noted as well the scandal of an abbess accused of sexual impropriety. Our *érudit* deplored the financial straits into which this house, as with so many of its sister houses, had fallen in the midst of the Hundred Years War. He observed as well that in the midst of all these great troubles, "monastic discipline, in decline since the late thirteenth century" did not spare the abbey the "general contagion."[56] He portrayed Abbess Jeanne de la Hure as "young and professed to the religious life less perhaps by a free choice than by the wishes of her kin and by social necessity, which was not a rarity then," and described how she had "compromised her dignity and the good name of her house by culpable relations with an inhabitant of Meix-Saint-Epoing, Deniset Esglantier, and with a monk, brother Etienne Bonnot, prior of Valdieu."[57] As this suggests, André had some sympathy for what he supposed were Jeanne's circumstances, but gave the abbess no benefit of the doubt. He assumed as well that Abbess Jeanne must have made amends, since 22 years later she was still named as abbess.[58] We, with the interim accusation from 1458 in mind, can maintain some skepticism, but ought to be grateful to André nonetheless for providing a transcription of this document, the last trace of Jeanne's life that I know of. Despite allegations of scandalous conduct with two men in 1449 and again in 1458 with another man, Jeanne was and remained abbess as late as 1471 or 1474.[59]

We can find repeat references to two other nuns as well, both sisters of the convent of Notre-Dame-aux-Nonnains. In April of 1453 the barber Jean Dufour was ordered not to continue his scandalous visits to the convent, and especially to avoid the company of the nurse Sister Marie de Bonsey, unless he had manifest and rational cause for this, on penalty of excommunication and further penalties.[60] About a month later, barber Jean Coquale was also warned to

56 André, *Abbaye*, 105.

57 André, *Abbaye*, 105–6.

58 André, *Abbeye*, 107; see page 109 note 2 for the citation of the document he is referencing.

59 André, *Abbaye*, 109–10, note 2. He gives 1471 in the text and 1474 in the note as the date for the document, taken from AD Marne H "fonds de l'abbaye de Notre-Dame du Bricot, carton IV, liasse 8." I have not been able to verify if this document is still to be found in the AD Marne. See also *Gallia Christiana*, vol. 12 (Paris, 1870), 579.

60 Archives départmentales de l'Aube G.4171, f. 78v. "Lune post Quasimodo (Monday, 9 April 1453) Dominus officialis monuit in scriptis Johannem du Four barbier nec de cetero frequentet in scandalum in Mon Beate Marie ad Mon et maximie cum sorore Maria de Bonsey infirmar dicti mon nisi per manifesti et rationalibi causa sub excommunicationis et al penis jur."

no longer scandalously visit Sister Marie, with the same stipulations.[61] There are certainly many good reasons that a barber would have needed to be in the company of a nurse, but we can only speculate as to why two different men were told to avoid causing further scandal with this woman. Was there a rumor of her having sex with a barber, with suspicion falling first on one man and then the other, because of their shared occupation? Or was Marie in fact involved to some extent with both men? Marie, to my knowledge, never appeared before the official.

Finally, it seems fair to assume that, unless there were two or three women called Isabelle de Rochetaille among the nuns of Notre-Dame-aux-Nonnains in Troyes, she also was able to quite successfully overcome allegations of sexual (and other) misconduct. We find her first, in 1457, in prison. More accurately, we find the record of her release from the bishop's prison in Troyes, under caution, released so that she could go on processions with the other nuns. This temporary release was granted Isabelle until the Thursday after the feast of Saint Bartholomew. After this we lose sight of her for some years. We do not know why she was imprisoned; I will just point out that the few cases of nuns detained in bishops' prisons that I have come across, for which the accusation is known, denote as grounds the nuns' disobedience or defiance of episcopal authority, not allegations of sex or pregnancy.

In May 1466, an Isabelle de Rochetaille, presumably the same person, is named first among the nine nuns admonished in an official summation by the official of Troyes.[62] These nuns, "practically the entire convent," according to the author of the indispensable nineteenth-century inventory for these records, are ordered to stop going out, and not to leave their abbey and enclosure without the permission of their superior.[63] In this case, "superior" likely refers to their unnamed abbess, since the prioress Marguerite de Grevant is among the nuns being admonished. They were not to go out in the streets as they were in the habit of doing, or the bishop would cite them as not exempt from his jurisdiction. They expressed readiness to obey his orders. It was another matter, a scandal involving another nun entirely, whose violence seems to have facilitated this rather irregular inclusion of a scolding of nuns

61 Archives départmentales de l'Aube G.4171, f. 79r. "Dominus officialis monuit in scriptis Johannem Coquile barber ne de cetero frequenet frequentet in scandalum cum sorore Maria de Bonsey infirmar mon beate Marie ad Mon trecen neque in domo mon nisis per manifesta et rationabili causa sub excommunucationis et al penis jur."

62 Archives départmentales de l'Aube G.4180, f. 61r.

63 Henry D'Arbois de Jubainville, ed., *Inventaire sommaire des Archives départementales de l'Aube*, 2 (1873–1896) 384.

in the bishop's registers, as in the preceding pages we read the allegation and depositions concerning an episode of violence and insults engaged in by nuns of the same house.

Also in 1466 as recorded in another register, the sentence register, about a month later, Jean Garre, the parish priest of Verrières, was warned on penalty of excommunication and 10 livres not to further scandalously consort or be seen in a suspicious place with Sister Isabelle de Rochetaille, a nun of Notre-Dame-aux-Nonnains in Troyes, concerning whom he was denounced.[64] This allegation looks rather serious. The words "in concubinage" are there, if crossed out, which in addition to the size of the fine and mention of scandal certainly suggests something more than a brief sexual encounter was alleged.

What more to say concerning Isabelle? We know that previously, in 1451, an Isabelle de Rochetaille, nun of Notre-Dame-aux-Nonnains, was given a bequest of 100 sous in the testament of Robert de Coulaverdey, knight and lord of la Chapelle Saint-Luc, and that he left the lands of Coulaverdey to the knight Jacques de Rouchetaillé. Subsequently, most importantly, in the final trace of this nun, we know that from 1475–1480 an Isabelle de Rochetaillé was Notre-Dame-aux Nonnains' abbess. *Gallia Christiana* records her oath to obey Bishop Louis Raguier in 1475 and her death in 1480.[65]

Before concluding, we can attempt once again to see what we can make of accounts of the pregnant nun Jeannette la Flamenge. We know very little about Jeanette's convent after the thirteenth century, as is too often the case with *champenois* religious houses. The abbey was most likely founded in 1248, and by Thibaut IV of Champagne and Navarre, facing his *palais* at Provins on the hilltop of Mont-Saint-Catherine.[66] Legend has it that Saint Catherine had appeared to Thibaut one evening while he was looking out of the window of his palace where he saw in a divine light a beautiful young woman who showed him that she wished there to be a religious house. It is hopefully true that the

64 Archives départmentales de l'Aube G.4171, f. 145r. "Veneris ante festum Beati Barnabe apostoli (Thursday, 12 June 1466). Dominus officialis monuit in scriptis dominum Johannem Garre presbiterum curatum ecclesie parrochialis de Verreriis (Verrières) sub penis excommunicationis et decem libras tournensis ne de cetero conversari praesumat in scandalum in concubinatu [crossed out in original] nec in loco suspecto cum sororem Isabella de Rochetaille de qua su [crossed out in original] religiosu dotus monasterii beate Marie ad Moniales cum de qua fuit diffamatis."

65 *Gallia Christiana*, vol. 12, 568.

66 There is an edition of the Cartulary of the Abbey of Mont-Sainte-Catherine de Provins in the thesis of Henri Guy, published in 1968 and stored in the National Archives in Paris. See Henri Guy, "Le Cartulaire de l'abbaye du mont-Sainte-Catherine-lès-Provins Ordre de Sainte-Claire" (Ecole des chartes. Positions des theses, 1968), 85–91.

place also had some significance to his son Thibaut v, whose body was laid to rest there, although his heart went to the Jacobins; Thibaut V's wife, Isabelle of France, was also put to rest there.[67] Certainly the house received substantial donations from Thibaut iv and v, and also from Jeanne de Navarre. The sisters of Saint Claire who lived in that convent, which subsequently became a royal abbey, would later have cause to regret its location outside the walls of the city of Provins, for its own walls would serve as insufficient protection on more than one occasion. The 1390s were a moment of relative calm for the Champagne, after the great destruction of religious houses in the 1360s and 1370s.[68] The nuns seem to have returned to their convent in the early or mid-1380s to find their church and their abbey destroyed. Traces of the thirteenth century structure remain today, the gallery of the cloister and the convent walls.[69]

We have no idea how old Jeannette was beyond the fact that she was roughly of childbearing age, and we do not know when she had professed or how much of this history she experienced personally. We do not know anything about her family or social status. We also do not know if her presence during Perrin's meeting with his kinswoman reflects more laxity or prudence on the part of the convent. Was Jeannette there as a sort of duenna, only to turn out herself to be the object of desire? Or were the nuns less strict in their observance of enclosure than some church authorities would have liked, and did Perrin have his choice of nuns to admire as he chatted with his relation? Everything is possible.

To conclude, an allegation of illicit sex, or even pregnancy and childbirth, could cause a nun or her community a great deal of difficulty, and could possibly even prove ruinous for the health or career prospects of the woman in question. At the same time, church officials had obligations beyond correcting individual sin. Scandal had to be avoided and, if possible, reputations protected. The man in question, the religious institution, the nun's family, and the nun herself might therefore find ways to reintegrate the sexual sinner into her community, with or without recourse to "the discipline." We cannot be too optimistic, nor should we always assume the worst. At any rate, we must approach with tremendous care the few surviving sources that help us to address the

67 Art de Vérifier les dates 11 (1818): 383.

68 Deniflé, *La desolation,* 723.

69 "Ancien couvent des Cordelières à Provins," Momentum, accessed August 18, 2022, https://monumentum.fr/ancien-couvent-des-cordelieres-pa00087201.html; "Ancien couvent des Cordelières," Ministère de la Culture, accessed August 18, 2022, http://www2.culture.gouv.fr/public/mistral/merimee_fr?ACTION=CHERCHER&FIELD_1=REF&VALUE_1=PA00087201.

difficult question of what precisely happened when it was said that a nun had sex, or when a nun did have sex, in late medieval France.

Appendix

Archives nationales, JJ154, ff. 393v–394r[70]
1399 Paris February

Charles, by the grace of God King of France. Let it be known to all those present and future … We have received the humble supplication of Perrin Larchier, cleric, of the age of about 27 years, comprising:

In the month of April, the year 1395 or around then, on a certain day that the said Perrin was in the abbey of the Cordelières-lez-Prouvinz, who are enclosed nuns, to see and to speak with one of his kinswomen a nun of that place, to whom he went to speak with at the grille and parlor of the said abbey, and with her there was another nun of the same place, called Jehannette la Flamenge. With the said Jehannette the said Perrin, this day as much as the other days afterwards that followed, by many words beseeched that she became his lady-love, and that she would leave the abbey and go away with him. And to this she agreed. And to accomplish this, one night thereafter, the said Perrin went to the said place, accompanied by two young companions, equipped with a wooden ladder to climb the walls of the enclosure of the said abbey, to take from there the said nun. And when they were there, they set up the ladder and by means of it climbed the wall that made the enclosure, and from that wall descended on an opening joined to this wall. And by means of this, the said nun, of her own free will, without any constraint was taken away with these men outside of the abbey, bringing with her a breviary, a little collection, some cloth, rings and jewelry, that were hers or so she said, and three écus and 10 sous of Paris that were in her purse. And at that moment she was dressed in secular clothing, as they asked her to do, as appropriate for taking her out in the country.

And this accomplished, the said Perrin and his companions or one of them, mounted the nun upon a horse, and in this way they went to Mont-Saint-Michel and elsewhere in many parts of our kingdom and outside it, where they remained for half a year or more. And after the said Perrin returned the said nun, pregnant with an infant, in our city of Provins, near to the said abbey.

---

70 See also Douët-d'Arcq, *Règne de Charles VI*, vol. 2, 15–18, but note that some phrases and words are missing from that edition.

And placed her in the home of relatives living in Provins in order that she be put back in the said abbey; who put her back there, where she gave birth to a daughter, who soon after died. Because of this, the said Perrin was cited to appear before the court by our bailiff of Meaux or his lieutenant of the aforementioned Provins. And out of fear of the rigor of justice he did not dare to appear, and for this he was banished from our kingdom by our bailiff or his lieutenant. And concerning this sentence and judgement of banishment the procurator of the said Perrin appealed, and his appeal is to be raised in the coming days that will be held by us to consider this appeal. This he does not dare to pursue for fear of imprisonment, concerning as a result he abandoned his appeal, and the sentence of banishment given by our bailiff was confirmed. For this the said Perrin is therefore banished from our kingdom and his goods confiscated and he is condemned before our courts in the grand jours, in 60 *livres tournois* of fine because of this appeal. After all this, the said Perrin, to seek before us, if he can, our grace and remission concerning these things, came to our city of Paris. And he was in our domicile of Saint-Pol, where he was seen and recognized by our procureur in the said our city of Provins, who was taken by him or taken on his behalf by the hand the said Perrin, and there was taken with another, to the prisons of Tyron in the said place of Paris. And from there they escaped by subtility and by a ruse, without making any damage or public violence from the said prisons. For this cause for these reasons the said Perrin is in danger of perpetual banishment, foreign to our kingdom, if concerning this he is not given our grace and mercy, as the said carnal friends of the said Perrin say, in humbly seeking this pardon from us. For this reason, we having considered these things, and since the said Perrin, at the time in which he committed the principal offense already stated was a young man, of 22 years or so, and since he restored the said nun to the dwelling of her kin, as is said, regretting and showing contrition for this, and also that the said Perrin, during all the time he had the said nun with him, supported her from his own and her means, and not the goods of the said church, except the said three écus, books and other goods already mentioned, lacking other property, they had together. And he is ready to make restitution of the value of those goods, and that in other cases he was of good life and good renown, born and raised by good people of our said city of Provins. And that, at the time of these things and this banishment, all his goods were confiscated, and also, as far as concerning his person, he is a cleric, not married, and was at the time of this case, because this banishment was by a secular court and could not be binding, as for the corporal punishment we wish in this to prefer equity and mercy to the rigor of justice for the aforementioned Perrin in the cases stated above satisfaction made to the party above all and before any work by us quits remitted and pardoned.

And by those present quit remitted and pardoned the said case brought by the manner that is said and with the banishment, breach of safeguard of prisons and all this that followed and with every financial and corporal penalty criminal and civil in this that could be due us and justice by him and the restitution and his good reputation and name save the law of the confiscation of his goods such as there are given in mandate to our bailiff of Meaux or to his lieutenant at the said place of Provins and to all our other judges and officers who at present are and in the times to come will be or to their lieutenants and to all those of our present grace not constrained in body or goods. And so that this be solid and stable and for always we have affixed our seal and those present save in other things our law and authority in all given at Paris in the month of February the year of our lord 1399 and of our reign the 20th.

By the king in council.

Bibliography

Archival and Primary Source Editions

Archives nationales, 1399, JJ 154 ff. 393v–394r #365.

Archives nationales, 1395, JJ 147 f. 107r #233.

Archives nationales, 1370, JJ 100 ff. 183v–84r #616.

Archives départementales, 1423–1475, 1466; G.4171, G.4180, Aube (Troyes).

Canivez, Joseph Marie, ed. *Statuta capitulorum generalium ordinis Cisterciensis*. 8 vols. Louvain, 1933–1941.

Douët-d'Arcq, Louis. *Choix de pièces inédites relatives au règne de Charles VI*, vol. 2. Paris: Jules Renouard, 1864.

Friedberg, Emil, ed. *Corpus Iuris Canonici.* 2 vols. Leipzig: B. Tauchnitz, 1879. Reprint Graz: Akademische Druck, 1959.

Gallia Christiana, vol. 12. Paris, 1870.

Lalore, Charles, ed. *Collection de Documents inédits relatifs a la Ville de Troyes et a la champagne mèridionale,* vol 2. Troyes: Dufey-Robert, 1882.

Lalore, Charles, ed. *Collection des principaux cartulaires du diocèse de Troyes*. 7 vols. Paris: E. Thorin, 1875–90.

Lewis, Matthew. *The Monk: A Romance*. Dublin: J. Bell, 1797.

Monk, Maria. *Further Disclosures by Maria Monk Concerning the Hotel Dieu Nunnery of Montreal; and Also Her Visit to Nun's Island and Disclosures Concerning that Secret Retreat.* New York: Leavitt, Lord & Co, 1837.

Secondary Sources

André, Edouard. *Histoire de l'Abbaye du Bricot en Brie XIIe siècle–1792*. Paris: Picard, 1895.

Beach, Alison I. "Voices from a Distant Land: Fragments of a Twelfth-Century Nuns' Letter Collection." *Speculum* 77, no. 1 (2002): 34–54. https://doi.org/10.2307/2903785.

Brian, Lindsay. "Periculum animarum: Bishops, Gender, and Scandal." *Florilegium* 19 (2002): 49–73.

Brundage, James. *Law, Sex, and Christian Society in Medieval Europe.* Chicago: University of Chicago Press, 1987.

Chevalier, Romain. "Les lettres de légitimation émises par la chancellerie de Charles VII (1430–1461)," 2 vols. Master's thesis, Université Jean-Moulin Lyon III, 2015.

Chevalier, Romain. "Papes, rois et bâtards: Normes et discours autour de la filiation illégitime (Papauté et royaume de France, XIIIe–XIVe siècles)." Doctoral thesis, Université d'Avignon, 2023.

Collas, Emile. "Enlèvements d'autrefois: moeurs des XIVe et XV siècles." *La Nouvelle Revue* 3, no. 4 (1908): 460–72.

Cossar, Roisin. "Clerical 'Concubines' in Northern Italy during the Fourteenth Century." *Journal of Women's History* 23, no. 1 (2011): 110–31.

Cossar, Roisin. "Defining Roles in the Clerical Household in Trecento Venice." *Viator* 45, no. 2 (2014): 237–45.

Dean, Trevor. "Fornicating with nuns in fifteenth-century Bologna," *Journal of Medieval History* 34, no. 4 (2008): 374–82.

Deniflé, Henri. *La désolation des églises, monastères et hôpitaux en France pendant la guerre de cent ans.* Paris: Picard, 1899.

Fossier, Arnaud. "Propter vitandum scandalum. Histoire d'une catégorie juridique (XII–XV siècles)." *Mélanges de l'Ecole française de Rome. Moyen Âge* 121, no. 2 (2009): 317–48.

Freeman, Elizabeth. "Cistercian Nuns in Medieval England: Unofficial Meets Official." In *Elite and Popular Religion,* edited by Kate Cooper and Jeremy Gregory, 110–19. Woodbridge: Boydell and Brewer, 2006.

Helmholz, Richard. "Scandalum in Medieval Canon Law and in the English Ecclesiastical Courts." *Zeitschrift der Savigny-Stiftung für Rechtsgeschichte: Kanonistische Abteilung* 96 (2010): 258–74. https://doi.org/10.7767/zrgka.2010.96.1.258.

Guy, Henri. "Le Cartulaire de l'abbaye du mont-Sainte-Catherine-lès-Provins Ordre de Sainte-Claire." Ecole des chartes. Positions des theses, 1968.

Johnson, Penelope. *Equal in Monastic Profession: Religious Women in Medieval France.* Chicago: University of Chicago Press, 1991.

Knudsen, Christian. "Naughty Nuns and Promiscuous Monks: Monastic Sexual Misconduct in Late Medieval England." Ph.D. diss., University of Toronto, 2012.

Knudsen, Christian. "Promiscuous Monks and Naughty Nuns: Poverty, Sex and Apostasy in Later Medieval England." In *Poverty and Prosperity: The Rich and the Poor in the Middle Ages and Renaissance,* edited by Anne Scott and Cindy Kosso, 75–91. Turnhout: Brepols, 2012.

Logan, F. Donald. *Runaway Religious in Medieval England, c. 1240–1540.* Cambridge: Cambridge University Press, 1996.

Lusset, Elisabeth. *Crime, châtiment et grâce dans les monastères au Moyen Âge (XIIe–XVe siècle).* Disciplina Monastica 12. Turnhout: Brepols, 2017.

Lusset, Elisabeth. "Moines et moniales de naissance illégitime: Entrer dans les ordres réguliers et y faire carrière à la fin du Moyen Âge: entre droit général et ius proprium." In *Bâtards et bâtardises dans l'Europe médiévale et modern*, edited by Carole Avignon, 125–34. Rennes: Presses universitaires de Rennes, 2016.

Lusset, Elisabeth. "Propriae salutis immemores? Réflexions sur la correction des moniales criminelles en Occident, XIIIe–XVe siècle." In *Figures de femmes criminelles, de l'Antiquité à nos jours*, edited by Loïc Cadiet, Frédéric Chauvaud, Claude Gauvard, Pauline Schmitt-Pantel, and Myriam Tsikounas, 255–65. Paris: Éditions de la Sorbonne, 2010.

Makowski, Elizabeth. *Apostate Nuns in the Later Middle Ages.* Woodbridge: Boydell & Brewer, 2019. https://doi.org/10.1017/9781787445802.

McDougall, Sara. "Bastard Priests: Illegitimacy and Ordination in Medieval Europe." *Speculum* 94, no. 1 (2019): 138–72. https://doi.org/10.1086/700982.

McDougall, Sara. "The Prosecution of Sex in Late Medieval Troyes." In *History of Sexuality in the Middle Ages and Renaissance*, edited by Albrecht Classen, 691–713. Berlin: De Gruyter, 2008. https://doi.org/10.1515/9783110209402.691.

Power, Eileen. *Medieval English Nunneries c. 1275 to 1535.* Cambridge: Cambridge University Press, 1922.

Salonen, Kirsi, and Jussi Hanska. *Entering a Clerical Career at the Roman Curia, 1458–1471.* Farnham, Surrey, UK: Ashgate, 2013. https://doi.org/10.4324/9781315579856.

Saunders, Corinne. *Rape and Ravishment in the Literature of Medieval England.* Woodbridge: Boydell & Brewer, 2001.

Thèry, Julien. "Judicial Inquiry as an Instrument of Centralized Government: The Papacy's Criminal Proceedings against Prelates in the Age of Theocracy (mid-12th to mid-14th century)." In *Proceedings of the 14th International Congress of Medieval Canon Law*, edited by Joseph Goering, Stephan Dusil, and Andreas Their, 875–89. Vatican City: Biblioteca apostolica vaticana, 2016.

CHAPTER 9

Oikos and *Oikonomika*: The Early Modern Family as a Matrix of Modern Economics

John Witte Jr.

Charles Donahue taught me about the vital link between family law and property law in the Western legal tradition. In his course on Roman law, he pointed out how many of the texts on marriage and family law were in fact about marital property and inheritance.[1] In his courses covering medieval legal history, he showed that "marital contracts" were mostly about marital property settlements, and that medieval marital litigation was often about marital property disputes—all of which he documented brilliantly in his *Law, Marriage, and Society in the Later Middle Ages* (2008).[2]

The marital household (the *oikos*) and economics (*oikonomika*) are indeed closely interlinked in the Western legal tradition, and both have depended on each other. The marital household has long been a vital economic unit of its own—especially households with attendant shops, services, and servants which depend on and contribute to stable markets and currencies. The household has also long been a vital source of education, apprenticing, and vocational training central to the success of economic, political, and religious life. It has long provided essential security and provision for parents, children, and other kin; and for caring and sharing, nutrition and nursing, welfare and poor relief when household members became impoverished, injured, incapacitated, sick, elderly, or otherwise dependent—even if these tasks were shared more fully with other social institutions and professions, not least church and state. The formation of a new marital family is often a critical time of property and financial exchange between two families in a prior generation, and it

1 Charles Donahue, "*Ius* in the Subjective Sense in Roman Law: Reflections on Villey and Tierney," in *A Ennio Cortese*, ed. Domenico Maffei et al. (Rome: Il Cigno, 2001), vol. 1, 506–35. See primary texts in Bruce W. Frier and Thomas A. J. McGinn, *A Casebook on Roman Family Law* (Oxford: Oxford University Press, 2004).

2 Charles Donahue, *Law, Marriage, and Society in the Later Middle Ages* (Cambridge: Cambridge University Press, 2008); see further Philip L. Reynolds and John Witte, Jr., eds., *To Have and to Hold: Marrying and its Documentation in Western Christendom, 400–1600* (Cambridge: Cambridge University Press, 2012).

 | DOI:10.1163/9789004710696_011

provides a fundamental conduit for transmitting property to the next generation through gift, trust, donation, inheritance, and more.

In this chapter—dedicated to my great teacher Charlie—I explore the constructive role of the early modern Protestant family in shaping the values of modern economics. One of the hallmarks of early Protestantism was its view of the family as a "little commonwealth"—the most primal school of justice and mercy, morality and virtue, education and welfare in a Godly republic. Martin Luther (1483–1546) called the marital household the "mother of all earthly laws"; John Calvin (1509–1564) called it "the first covenant of a covenant community"; Anglican divines called it "the seminary of the republic."[3] These and other metaphors were designed to underscore the early modern Protestant belief that a well-ordered marital family was an essential foundation of a well-ordered church, state, and society.

Early modern Protestants also believed that the family was an essential foundation for a well-ordered economy. In his famous *Protestant Ethic and the Spirit of Capitalism,*[4] German social scientist Max Weber (1864–1920) traced the rise of the modern economy back to the convergence of new Protestant teachings on vocation, predestination, and asceticism, and he showed how these teachings together helped to catalyze many of the forms and norms of early modern economic life in Europe and North America.

I argue here that it was especially the marital household that served as an incubator of these Protestant teachings and as a laboratory for their application to economic activity. The early modern Protestant family was structured and schooled to cultivate the critical habits of discipline and organization in the economic lives of its members. Protestant catechisms and household manuals set out in detail the moral and religious rules, rights, and responsibilities that husbands and wives, parents and children, masters and servants had to each other and to their neighbors in different stages of life. It is here, in the elementary ethics and intimate experiences of the Protestant household, that many of the basic norms and habits of modern economic life were slowly instilled and cultivated in each new generation.

---

3 See detailed references in John Witte, Jr., *From Sacrament to Contract: Marriage, Religion, and Law in the Western Tradition,* 2nd ed. (Louisville, KY: Westminster John Knox Press, 2012).

4 Max Weber, *The Protestant Ethic and the Spirit of Capitalism* (New York: Scribner, 1958).

1 Max Weber and the Protestant Spirit of Capitalism

It is worth reminding ourselves of Weber's central thesis. He observed that the most highly developed economies in his day were in predominantly Protestant lands; and that the "business leaders and owners of capital, and even more the higher technically and commercially trained personnel of modern enterprises" were "overwhelmingly Protestant."[5] This seemed paradoxical since the capitalist "spirit" of unrepentant utilitarianism and relentless acquisitiveness seemed to contradict the Christian values and virtues that Protestants so strongly emphasized. Yet, to Weber, the correlation between Protestantism and capitalism was no coincidence. It was precisely the ideas, anxieties, and institutional forms of Protestantism that had helped drive and direct the emergence of the modern capitalist order in place of traditional feudal economies and church-dominated monopolies that had held sway over medieval Catholic life.

Three Protestant teachings were particularly important, said Weber. First, Martin Luther's conception of the Christian vocation levelled the professional and spiritual hierarchies of his day and catalyzed greater participation by all in hard work, professionalized labor, and a market economy. Medieval Catholics regarded the clergy as superior to the laity in virtue and spiritual attainment; the lowliest parson was thought to be closer to God than the highest emperor. Luther, by contrast, insisted that priests and monks were no more virtuous or nearer to God than soldiers or maidservants. All were equally slaves to sin, and equally dependent upon divine grace for their salvation. And all were equally entitled and equipped to pursue the Christian vocation that best suited their talents and stations in life. Christians were not called to leave their secular callings of the world for a cloistered life of self-sanctifying religious asceticism and discipline. They were faithfully and dutifully to serve God and neighbor in the ordinary vocations, firm in the knowledge that the work of the butcher, housewife, or soldier was just as spiritual and conducive to salvation as that of the bishop, abbot, or priest. The same devotion and discipline that a cleric directed to spiritual and ecclesiastical ends could be devoted to secular and material ends, with equal assurance of salvation by grace through faith. The broad effect of this teaching, Weber concluded, was that "the moral emphasis on and the religious sanction of, organized worldly labor in a calling was mightily increased."[6]

5 Weber, *The Protestant Ethic*, 35.
6 Weber, *The Protestant Ethic*, 83.

Second, Weber argued, John Calvin's doctrine of predestination engendered religious anxieties that fueled the development of an intense and systematic work ethic among subsequent generations of believers. Lacking the sacramental means of grace that provided Catholics with a reassuring certitude of salvation, Calvinists were anxious to know whether they were among those whom God had elected for eternal salvation rather than damnation. Over time, Weber argued, Calvinists came to view diligent and productive labor and success in one's vocation as both a non-negotiable religious duty and a reliable indicator of one's election. The "systematic self-control" and discipline that Calvinists consequently applied to their lives and work thus served "as the technical means, not of purchasing salvation, but of getting rid of the fear of damnation." "The God of Calvinism demanded of his believers not single good works, but a life of good works combined into a unified system [and] subjected to a consistent method for conduct as a whole."[7]

Third, it was this progressively systematic rationalization of life and work, Weber contended, that drove Protestant societies away from late-medieval feudalism dominated by church monopolies and clergy-dominated guilds toward the highly rationalized and competitive capitalistic economies of Protestant lands. Protestant individuals and communities, spurred on by a sense of vocation and a burning need to prove their state of grace, adopted a feverish and systematic work ethic that subsequently transformed the economic ethos and institutions around them. Even those who did not share the Protestant faith and zeal were forced to embrace the same ethic in order to compete.[8] Feudal traditions and small-scale guilds gave way to the breakneck pace of modern factories and finance. Even as its religious underpinnings and trappings faded from view, the Protestant ethic and the institutions it created remained in place as the basic socio-economic framework into which all were now born. Ironically, where early Protestant reformers sought to elevate the work of ordinary people, emerging economies made the so-called Protestant work ethic all but compulsory. The burgeoning "spirit of capitalism"—ultimately a denatured and perverted caricature of earlier forms of Protestant asceticism—was hollow and mundane: "The Puritan wanted to work in a calling," Weber concluded, whereas now

7 Weber, *The Protestant Ethic*, 115–17.

8 See Max Weber, "The Protestant Sects and the Spirit of Capitalism," in *From Max Weber: Essays in Sociology*, ed. H.H. Geerth and C. Wright Mills (Oxford: Oxford University Press, 1946), 302–22.

> we are forced to do so. For when asceticism was carried out of monastic cells into everyday life, and began to dominate worldly morality, it did its part in building the tremendous cosmos of the modern economic order. This order is now bound to the technical and economic conditions of machine production which to-day determine the lives of all the individuals who are born into this mechanism, not only those directly concerned with economic acquisition, with irresistible force. Perhaps it will so determine them until the last ton of fossilized coal is burnt. In Baxter's view the care for external goods should only lie on the shoulders of the "saint like a light cloak, which can be thrown aside at any moment." But fate decreed that the cloak should become an iron cage.[9]

The "Baxter" whom Weber mentions in this famous "iron cage" passage is Richard Baxter (1615–1691), a distinguished English Puritan theologian who penned exhaustive practical guides for faithful living. If Baxter thought that care for external goods should rest but lightly on the shoulders of God's predestined believers, his writings suggest that the Christians' responsibility to order their daily lives, especially their households, constituted a much weightier responsibility. Baxter is a prime example of the rationalizing and systematizing impulses that Weber attributes to Protestantism generally, and especially to seventeenth-century Calvinism. Yet the title of the 504-page volume in which Baxter discusses most thoroughly the Christian's economic life offers an important clue about the real locus and focus of early Protestants' "economic" reform efforts. Baxter's volume was titled *Christian Economics* (*or, Family Duties*),[10] showing his straightforward equivalence of Christian economics and Christian family life.

Baxter's treatise is only one of scores of extant Protestant household manuals and family directories from the sixteenth to eighteenth centuries.[11] These understudied texts show that, insofar as Protestants did help to shape the "spirit" and institutions of early modern capitalism, they did so first of all by

9 Weber, *The Protestant Ethic*, 181–82.

10 This was one volume in Baxter's much-read set of publications entitled *A Christian Directory: or, A Summ of Practical Theologie, and Cases of Conscience: Directing Christians, How to Use their Knowledge and Faith; How to Improve all Helps and Means, and to Perform all Duties; How to Overcome Temptations, and to Escape or Mortifie Every Sin*, 2nd ed., 4 parts in 5 vols. (London: Robert White, 1678).

11 On household manuals, which also had earlier Catholic and later liberal forms, see John Witte, Jr. and Heather M. Good, "The Duties of Love: The Vocation of the Child in the Household Manual Tradition," in *The Vocation of the Child*, ed. Patrick M. Brennan (Grand Rapids, MI: Eerdmans, 2008), 266–94.

rationalizing the household (the *oikos*) and teaching its members the meanings and measures of vocation, discipline, and hard work. Indeed, the birth of capitalism rested not only on the reorganization of guilds and church monopolies into highly rationalized factories and competitive markets of supply and demand, but also on the radical rationalization of the home—an institution that many Protestants viewed as sociologically, politically, and theologically prior to all other social institutions, including the economy. Household manuals taught the Christian faithful how to manage the interlacing rights and responsibilities of husbands and wives, parents and children, and masters and servants. They offered guidelines for everything from table manners to clothing, diet, work habits, worship, and prayer. They instructed parents on how to instill virtues and combat vices in their children and exhorted children to heed the word (or suffer the rod) of their elders and to tend to them in old age. And they exhorted parents and children, and masters and servants to develop mutual habits of order and discipline that allowed everyone to produce good work in their unique Christian vocations, knowing that hard work was a reflection and affirmation of divine favor.

These household manuals both confirm and qualify some of Weber's key insights. Weber's account was focused on the "public" economy—the productive activities and attitudes of tradesmen and merchants, buyers and sellers, and others who made, exchanged, sold, and purchased goods and services in the marketplace. Early modern Protestants who engaged in such activities may well have been guided, to varying degrees, by the religious motives and beliefs that Weber highlighted. Yet early modern Protestant conceptions of vocation were, emphatically, not limited to a person's public work or career. Fatherhood, motherhood, and childhood were regarded as important vocations for early Protestants, no less than the vocations of blacksmiths or bakers, bankers or barristers. Moreover, a great deal of economic activity in early modern Europe and North America occurred within the household, which often included servants, apprentices, and students along with blood relatives, and which provided a great deal of the nurture, education, social welfare, and moral discipline historically furnished by the medieval Catholic Church. The norms and habits each household member learned in this carefully structured domestic sphere formed an important part of their preparation for public economic life. And the rationalization of the early modern Protestant household was an important step in the gradual rationalization of early modern economies.

2 Illustrations from the Protestant Household Manuals

Let me take four Protestant household manualists as illustrations: Heinrich Bullinger, Robert Cleaver, and William Perkins, as well as Weber's example of Richard Baxter. All four writers built their manuals on biblical, classical, patristic, and humanist learning. All four drew readily from existing manuals, including a few late medieval manuals that went back as early as John Wycliffe's *Of Weddid Men and Wifis and of Here Children Also* (1390). All wrote in highly accessible terms and in the vernacular for all pious persons to understand either by reading or hearing their instruction. All were highly influential writers throughout Great Britain, the European continent, and later, North America; their works were reprinted often, and in multiple languages.

2.1 *Heinrich Bullinger (1504–1575)*

A good example of an early Protestant household manual comes from the pen of Zurich Reformer Heinrich Bullinger, whose work on the family bridged the Lutheran, Reformed, and Anglican worlds. Bullinger's *The Golde Boke of Christen Matrimonye* (1540), written in German but translated into English by the famous Bible translator Miles Coverdale (1488–1569),[12] set out a covenantal model of marriage and family life at the foundation of the covenant community of church, state, and workplace. "Wedlock," he wrote, "is a covenant, a coupling or yoking together" of one man and one woman "by the good consent of the both." "Holy wedlock was ordained of God himself in Paradise." It is thus an "honorable and holy" estate, enjoyed by the "holiest, and most virtuous, the wisest and most noble men" in the Bible, and commended to all persons today—clerical and lay, young and old, single and widowed, rich and poor. For Bullinger, the single adult man or woman living outside a marital household was an aberration.[13]

God created marriage so that a man and a woman "may live together honestly and friendly the one with the other, that they may avoid uncleanness, that they may bring up children in the fear of God, that the one may help and comfort the other." Bullinger followed conventional Protestant arguments regarding the marital purposes of protection from lust and procreation of children, arguing that marriage is God's "remedy and medicine unto our feeble

12 Heinrich Bullinger, *Der christlich Eestand* (Zurich: Christoffel Froschouer, 1540), translated as *The Christen State of Matrimonye* (London: S. L., 1541) (STC 4045) and then as *The Golde Boke of Christen Matrimonye* (London: J. Mayler, 1542) (STC 1723) under Thomas Becon's pseudonym, Theodore Basille.

13 Bullinger, *The Golde Boke*, folios i.b–ii, iii, v, xxi.b, xxiii, xxxvi.b, lxxvii.b–lxxviii.

and weak flesh" and that children are "the greatest treasure" of a marriage. But he placed special emphasis on marital love and friendship, returning to this theme several times. "The love ... in marriage ought to be (next unto God) above all loves," with couples rendering to each other "the most excellent and unpainful service, diligence and earnest labor, ... one doing for another, one longing, depending, helping and forbearing another, suffering, also like joy and like pain one with another." The marital household was the principal social welfare institution for adults, the nerve center for kinship networks that were of vital importance to human flourishing. Bullinger spelled out the mutual duties of husband and wife in detail.[14]

Marital couples blessed with children could find ample instruction in Bullinger's *Golde Boke* on the parental duties of breast-feeding, nurture, protection, discipline, education, and dress of children, and, later, their courtship and contracting of marriage with a suitable partner. Bullinger's comments on discipline and training were typical of the sixteenth-century household manuals. He encouraged parents from the start to engage their children with "godly, honest, grave and fruitful" instruction and example. Parents should teach their children by word and example all the cardinal virtues, lead them in memorizing and reciting the Ten Commandments, Apostle's Creed, and other apt texts from the Gospels and Epistles. They should teach their children to "spend all the time in virtuous uses and never be idle," nor steal, fight, gossip, or harm others or themselves. When children did stray, parents should "correct them duly and discretely for their faults, so that they stand in great fear and awe of them, and if words will not reclaim them, then take the rod or whip of correction discretely used. For the rod of correction ministers wisdom."[15]

Bullinger also encouraged parents to instill industriousness in their children, by helping each child "learn that science or handicraft ... whereunto the child is naturally inclined and unto that occupation let him be put to." It was not good enough just to teach the child literacy and numbers, said Bullinger, or set them up in their own home and marriage in due course, important as all those steps were. A child also needed the preparation, encouragement, and means to thrive in his or her own vocation. Parents who fail to provide and emphasize proper education and vocational training, are, in fact, "ungodly destroyers of themselves, their children, and of all commonwealths and congregations" who need well trained leaders and members to function, conversant not only with

14 Bullinger, *The Golde Boke*, folios iii.b–iiii; iv–v.b; xix; xxi.b; xxii–xxiiii; xxxvi.b–xxxviii; Heinrich Bullinger, *The Decades of Henry Bullinger: The First and Second Decades*, ed. Thomas Harding (Cambridge: Cambridge University Press, 1849), 397–98.

15 Bullinger, *The Golde Boke*, folio lxxii.b.

"God's Law, Prophets, and Gospel" but also the methods and means to succeed in their occupations.[16]

Bullinger connected this new understanding of vocation to broader economic reforms, calling for a system of universal education and vocational training to replace the medieval system of church-based education for principal service in the church's bureaucracy. "In times past, when men saw so many spiritual promotions unto rich bishoprics, benefices, deaneries, abbeys, priories, chancellorships, etc., then they did set fast their children to schools to make them popish priests, idly to live by other men's sweat." But the Protestant Reformation ended this clerical exploitation of the laity, Bullinger argued. Now "the common labor, godliness, and the public profit of all commonwealths and congregations depend upon" all citizens and subjects being trained in proper schools in all manner of vocations, including but going well beyond work within the church. "Now, therefore, O ye Christian parents: seeing that your youth is now by the favor of God endowed with so good wits and inclined unto good letters, let not the graces and gifts of God be offered you in vain, but exercise them" in such a way that your children can "come to be profitable unto the commonwealth, whereunto they be born." Indeed, train them at home and let them be further trained by teachers and masters in "all just and true occupations justly exercised and used" knowing that "God's blessing maketh them to prosper" if they remain "true doers and laborers in their calling."[17]

Thomas Becon (1512–1567), Thomas Cranmer's chaplain, published an English edition of Bullinger's tract in 1542, and it was regularly reprinted thereafter. Becon added his own long foreword to the 1542 edition in which he extolled the marital household not only for the spiritual good of the couple and their children, but also for the civil good of the commonwealth and church. With a properly functioning marital household, Becon wrote with ample bombast, "many noble treasures chance unto us, virtue is maintained, vice is eschewed, houses are replenished, cities are inhabited, the ground is tilled, sciences are practiced, kingdoms flourish, amity is preserved, the public weal is defended, natural succession remaineth, good arts are taught, honest order is kept, Christendom is enlarged, God's word promoted, and the glory of God highly advanced and set further." Indeed, on the strength and stability of "this household's common weal" hangs the security and success of the whole commonwealth of England.[18]

16 Bullinger, *The Golde Boke*, folio lxxii.b.

17 Bullinger, *The Golde Boke*, folios lxxiii–lxxiii.b.

18 Bullinger, *The Golde Boke*, Aiiii.

2.2 *Robert Cleaver (b. ca. 1561)*

This emphasis on the public utility and values of the private marital household was a central theme in Robert Cleaver's hefty tome on *A Godly Form of Householde Gouernment* (1598).[19] Cleaver was a Puritan preacher in Oxfordshire, who wrote popular tracts on the Ten Commandments, Sabbath Day observance, and other aspects of Christian piety. In *A Godly Form of Householde Gouernment,* Cleaver worked hard to systematize and rationalize domestic life, expanding on the themes illustrated by Bullinger. "All government of a family must be directed to two principal ends," Cleaver wrote. "First Christian holiness, and secondly the things of this life." "Religion must be stirring in Christian families, and that good government looketh to bring godly behavior into families, as well as thrift and good husbandry."[20]

The paterfamilias must play the leading role in the "good government" of the family, Cleaver believed. As a husband, he must "live with his wife discreetly." He must "cherish and nourish" her as Christ loves and supports the Church. He must work with her "in all due benevolence, honestly, soberly, and chastely." And he must "govern her in all duties, that properly concern the state of marriage, in knowledge, in wisdom, judgment, and justice." A husband must not be "bitter, fierce, and cruel" to his wife and must "never beat her." Instead, "as a man of knowledge," he must "edify her, both by a good example, and also, by good instructions." As a father, the married man must lead his household in private devotions, daily prayer, catechization, and Bible reading. He must ensure that children and servants are faithful in public worship and Sabbath observance. He must be vigilant in offering his children instruction and admonition with wisdom, and punishment and rebuke with patience.[21]

The duty of the married woman was to be "faithful and loving" to her husband, "wise and prudent" to her family. She must "reverence her husband" and "submit herself unto him," as the Bible enjoins. She must dress and deport herself and her children in accordance with the family's means and station in life. She must avoid sloth and not keep idle, lazy, or untoward company. She must be thrifty, just, charitable, and prudent in her choice of friends. She must keep order and help maintain "the exercise of religion within the household." She

---

19 Robert Cleaver, *A Godly Form of Householde Gouernment* (London: Thomas Creede, 1598).

20 Cleaver, *Householde Gouernment*, 6–7. See further John Dod and Robert Cleaver, *A Plaine and Familiar Exposition of the Ten Commandments, with a Methodicall Short Catechisme, Containing Briefly all the Principall Grounds of Christian Religion* (London: Thomas Creede, 1604), 181 (STC 6968).

21 Dod and Cleaver, *Plaine and Familiar Exposition,* 24, 226–28; Cleaver, *Householde Gouernment*, 92, 114, 159ff., 202ff.

must tend especially to the care of her daughters and maidens, teaching them and exemplifying for them the norms and habits of Christian womanhood.[22]

Husband and wife also have mutual duties to each other and to their children. They "must love one another with a pure heart fervently." They must be "faithful" to each other, constantly "bending their wits, and all their endeavors, to the help each of [the] other, and to the common good of the family." They must pray together, "admonish one another," and serve as "mutual helps to each other in matters concerning their own salvation, and the service of God." Together, they must "instruct and bring up their children even from their cradle, in the fear and nurture of the Lord, … in shame fastness, hatred of vice, and love of all virtue." Such virtues were to be carried out of the home and into the extended economic sphere. As children mature, parents must "bring them up in some profitable and lawful calling, by which they may live honestly and Christianly, and not be fruitless burdens of the earth … or commonwealth." They must also "provide for the disposing of them in marriage," counseling them in their courtship and consenting to their marriage when they come of age and have chosen wisely among available spouses. In response to this, "the duties of the natural child" are very simple: "reverence, obedience, and thankfulness"—exemplified notably in seeking their parents' consent to their own marriage, and in caring for their parents when they become elderly or disabled.[23]

In many households, the man and woman are also the "masters and mistresses" of servants and apprentices, who work and sometimes live within the home or are a daily part of the family business. Cleaver saw the master-servant relationship as a natural and necessary extension of the parent-child relationship. Masters and mistresses must teach their servants diligence and discipline and keep them from idleness and sloth. They must bring up their servants "in honesty, and in comely manners, and in all virtues." They must "instruct their servants and apprentices in the knowledge of their occupations and trades, even as parents would teach their own children, without all guile, fraud, delaying, or concealing." And they must discipline them with "such discretion, pity, and desire of their amendment, as loving parents use to deal with their own dear children." They must maintain order, courtesy, respect and diligence, and

22 Cleaver, *Householde Gouernment*, 52–91, 203–22; Dod and Cleaver, *Plaine and Familiar Exposition*, 221–22.

23 Cleaver, *Householde Gouernment*, 188–91, 243ff.; Dod and Cleaver, *Plaine and Familiar Exposition*, 174–222.

peace among children and servants, and work "to banish sin and corrupt religion out of their dwellings."[24]

The household was to be not only an incubator of Christian morality, but also a model of a good Christian business, said Cleaver. In taking on servants and apprentices, for example, the master must be as sure of "their honest, godly conversation and how they have profited in the knowledge of God" as he is of their skills and strengths and how they have excelled in their craft or profited in their work. For the two are "closely tied": "such servants that take in hand the Lord will much better prosper and give success unto him than otherwise." Once he hired his servants, the master thus was obliged to tend to his servants' souls as much as their bodies. Indeed, he was called to discharge the three-fold office of Christ at home and in business: "rule like a King, teach like a Prophet, and pray like a Priest to show how a godly man should behave himself" at home and at work. Alongside this spiritual leadership, the master must set rules and create conditions of labor that provided servants with adequate food and shelter, rewarded hard work, paid fair wages, maintained reasonable hours, and granted weekly Sabbath rest to all. He must strike a balance between lawful acquisition and proper accumulation of wealth, on the one hand, and "profligacy" and "niggardliness" on the other hand. He must promote collaboration among the workers, and throw himself into the work "so that their necessary affairs and business are dispatched well." Servants, laborers, and apprentices, in turn, must "cheerfully and willingly from their hearts perform the labors and works" they are assigned. Calling to mind Weber's observation that prosperous work eased spiritual anxieties, Cleaver urged workers to "be faithful in all things committed to them" knowing that ultimately "they are serving the Lord, not men; and not only have respect of the earthly reward, but because they know, and are assured, that of the Lord they shall receive the reward of inheritance, in as much as they serve the Lord Christ."[25]

Faithful maintenance of all these household duties and offices was the best guarantee of productive order within the broader commonwealths of church and state, Cleaver insisted, echoing early manualists like Thomas Becon. Indeed, properly functioning households were indispensable to civic flourishing. "[I]f masters of families do not practice at home catechizing, and discipline in their houses and join their helping hands to magistrates and ministers," social order and stability will soon give way to chaos and anarchy.

---

24 For this section on masters and servants see the expanded edition of Robert Cleaver, *A Godlie Forme of Hovseholde Government: For the Ordering of Private Families According to the Direction of God's Word* (London: Felix Kingston, 1600), 363–83.

25 Cleaver, *Householde Gouernment*, 372–73, 378–83.

"[I]t is impossible for a man to understand to govern the commonwealth, that doth not know to rule his own house, or order his own person, so that he that knoweth not to govern, deserveth not to reign."[26]

2.3 *William Perkins* (*1558–1602*)

The "Christian vocation" of the worker was a special focus of another Anglo-Puritan, William Perkins, Fellow of Christ College, Cambridge, and rector of St. Andrew's Church in Cambridge. Perkins wrote a famous *Treatise of the Vocations,* published posthumously in 1605.[27] His description of the well-ordered household was very much like Cleaver's and Bullinger's. "[M]arriage was made and appointed by God himself to be the foundation and seminary of all sorts and kinds of life in the commonwealth and the church," Perkins declared. "[T]hose families wherein the service of God is performed are, as it were, little churches; yea, even a kind of paradise on earth." In a well ordered Christian household, worship of God must come first and undergird all family relationships, duties, and activities: "Common reason and equity showeth it to be a necessary duty: for the happy and prosperous estate of the family, which consisteth in the mutual love and agreement of the man and wife, in the dutiful obedience of children to their parents, and in the faithful service of servants to their Masters, wholly dependeth upon the grace and blessings of God: and this blessing is annexed to his worship." Like Cleaver, Perkins emphasized the parent's and master's responsibilities to children and servants; they were to love, nurture, feed, and clothe them, and protect them against hardship. They were also to "observe both the inclination and the natural gifts of body and mind, that are in the child, and accordingly to bestow it in some honest calling and course of life."[28]

Perkins homed in on the need for an "honest calling" for all members of the community. "Every person of every degree, state, sex, or condition, without exception, must have some personal and particular calling to walk in," Perkins wrote. And he or she must discharge that calling with diligence and zeal, and to the glory and honor of God and neighbor, church and state, family and self. "Sloth and negligence in the duties of our callings, are a *disorder* against that good order which God set in the societies of mankind, in both church

26 Cleaver, *Householde Gouernment*, Preface, A4; 4–5.

27 William Perkins, *Economy, or Household-Government: A Short Survey of the Right Manner of Erecting and Ordering a Family, According to the Scriptures*, in *The Workes of that Famous and Worthy Minister of Christ in the Universitie of Cambridge, M.W. Perkins* (London: John Legatt, 1631).

28 Perkins, *Economy, or Household-Government*, vol. 3, 418–19, 669, 695.

and commonwealth. And indeed, idleness and sloth are the causes of many damnable sins. The idle body, or the idle brain, is the workshop of the devil." Each person must "shake off that spiritual drowsiness" and be constantly ready to answer the question "*What have I done?* Or *How does it stand between God and me?*"[29]

Piling up biblical and classical verses that reflected this vocational ideal, Perkins took sharp aim at those who, in his view, betrayed it. The first were idle beggars and drunks, itinerant vagabonds and mendicants, and others who wrongly exploited the charity of others. These are the classic "undeserving poor," Perkins wrote. They should be put to hard work to restore the charitable and diaconal coffers they emptied so these alms may properly serve the "deserving poor"—widows, orphans, the injured, and the disabled. The second were the "idle rich," who had inherited or earned "great livings and revenues, [and now] spend their days in eating and drinking, in sports and pastimes, not employing themselves in service for church or commonwealth." From those who have been given much, much is expected, Perkins argued, citing Scripture. And those with wealth or time to spare are obliged to "set it in motion" to provide opportunities for others and to enhance the common good. The third and most egregious betrayers of vocational ideals are "monks and friars" and other "popish votaries" who "live apart from the societies of men in fasting and prayer." "This monkish kind of living is damnable," Perkins wrote, for it is sloth and idleness masquerading as a spiritual vocation. In fact, "all monks a[re] thieves and robbers" living on the tithes of others, rather than as "good and profitable member[s] of some society and body."[30]

"Every man must judge that the particular calling in which God has placed him, is the best of all callings for him. I do not say simply *best*, but best *for him*." At minimum this requires each Christian to "join the practice of his personal calling, with the practice of the general calling of Christianity. [I]n his personal calling, he must show himself to be a Christian." Furthermore, a person has to pick a vocation that best suits his inclinations and gifts. Here, Christian parents and masters must play a key role, said Perkins. They must be attentive to their child's inclinations: "some are affected with music more than others; some with merchandise; some with a more liberal kind of learning." Their training must follow these inclinations. The parents must also discern the "natural gifts" of their children. "Those children who excel in the gifts of the body are to be brought up in callings performed by the labor of the body, as in

29 William Perkins, *A Treatise of the Vocations*, in *Workes*, vol. 1, 750–79, using modernized edition of William Gross (2015) (digitalpuritan.net), 9, 13, 17–18, 50.

30 Perkins, *A Treatise*, 13, 16–17.

mechanical arts. And those who excel in the gifts of the mind are to be applied to those sciences that are performed by wit and learning." A parent's failure to encourage and prepare the child for his or her proper vocation "is a great and common sin," Perkins argued:

> For the care of most is that their children may *live*—not regarding at all whether they live *well*, and do service to God in a fit calling or not. And the truth is, parents cannot do greater wrong to their children, and to the society of men, than to apply them to unfit callings—as when a child is fit for learning, to apply him to a trade, or other bodily service; or contrariwise, to apply him to learning when he is fittest for a trade. For this is like a man applying his toes to feeling, and not his fingers; and to go about on his hands and not his feet; and to set the members of the body out of their proper places.[31]

Perkins used this metaphor of the body and its members to argue further that when a person has properly prepared and pursued a vocation most suitable to his talents, that person must "keep himself within the compass, limits, or precincts of it," following the rules of his vocation. Much like a body needs each member to do its own function, or an army needs each soldier to follow his orders, so a properly running society and economy need workers in their places. If a man stays within his calling, he will be blessed, and all society with him. If he strays "outside the compass of his calling, he is out of the way, and by this means he bereaves himself of the protection of the Almighty; and he lies open and naked to all the punishments and plagues of God."[32]

2.4 *Richard Baxter (1615–1691)*

The repeated emphasis on the Christian vocation and the orderly Christian household as an essential foundation for church, state, society, and economy was the starting point for Puritan preacher Richard Baxter, whom Max Weber used to illustrate the early modern Protestant spirit of capitalism. Baxter was a popular preacher in Kidderminster and London and a prolific author, leaving some 168 books. His 500-page tome on *Christian Economics (or Family Duties)*[33] was but one of four huge volumes in Baxter's much-read manual of Puritan moral theology. The position of *Christian Economics* in this collection

31 Perkins, *A Treatise*, 14–19.

32 Perkins, *A Treatise*, 8.

33 Reprinted as Richard Baxter, *A Christian Directory, or, a Body of Practical Divinity and Cases of Conscience*, (London: Richard Edwards, 1825).

is instructive. Baxter placed it second, after a volume on *Christian Ethics* (*or Private Duties*), and before the two volumes on *Christian Ecclesiastics* (*or, Church Duties*) and *Christian Politics* (*or, Duties to Our Rulers and Neighbors*). The very arrangement of the volumes underscored Baxter's perception that the economic duties of the family comprised the critical fulcrum between private and public virtues, the preparation and proving ground for life in church, state, and society.

Max Weber emphasized Baxter's "ascetic" Puritan ethics at work in this and many other tracts. Typical of early modern Puritan manualists, Baxter insisted on discipline over laxness, frugality over sumptuousness, thrift over waste, hard work over idleness, efficiency over sloppiness, the priesthood of all believers pursuing their God-given vocations over the idle clergy luxuriously exploiting the laity to the detriment of economic advancement of all. This Puritan ethic, Weber believed, was conducive to the rise of early modern capitalism. "The worker with a vocational calling will pursue his work in an orderly fashion, while others are stuck in a situation of constant confusion; their businesses fail to operate according to time and place," Weber wrote, quoting Baxter.[34]

Ascetic ethics was clearly part of Baxter's world view, and he laid out his ethical rules in mind-numbingly prolix prose. But it bears emphasis that Baxter saw this ascetic ethic as part and product of the "family duties" that he also outlined at great length in his book on *Christian Economics.* Much like Bullinger, Cleaver, Perkins, and a century of Protestant manualists before him, Baxter believed that these good work habits and economic virtues were cultivated first and foremost in an orderly marital household, where husbands and wives, parents and children, masters and servants all learned to do their Christian duties to each other and to those around them. The "sanctified family" is the foundation of church, state, and economy, Baxter believed—the first school and seminary, the first church and commonwealth, the first workshop and retailer. "The holy government of families is a considerable part of God's own government of the world," he wrote. It "is the preparative to a holy and well-governed church." And it serves "to make a happy state and commonwealth" featuring a humming economy and society. Indeed, the "good education" and vocational training that a child or servant receives within the orderly home "is the first and greatest work to make good magistrates and good subjects, because it tends to make good men." So, Baxter exhorted parents, masters, and mistresses:

34 Weber, *The Protestant Ethic*, 103–09. See further Baxter, *A Christian Directory, vol 1, Christian Ethics* (*or Private Duties*), chap. 3, Grand Directive 10.

> Train up your children in a life of diligence and labour, and use them not to ease and idleness when they are young. Our wandering beggars and too much of the gentry utterly undo their children by this means, especially the female sex. They are taught no calling, nor exercised in any employment, but only such as is meet for nothing but ornament and recreation at the best; and therefore should have but recreation hours, which is but a small proportion of their time. So that by the sin of their parents, they are betimes engaged in a life of idleness.

It is far better to "choose such a calling and course of life for your children, as tendeth most to the saving of their souls, and to the public usefulness for church and state."[35]

Baxter insisted that "the chief part of family care and government consisteth in the right education" not only of one's own children, but also of servants and even slaves. "Servants being integral parts of the family, who contribute much to the holiness or unholiness of it, and to the happiness and misery of it, much concerneth masters to be careful in their choice." Among many other qualifications, Baxter argued, a good servant needs "strength, skill, and willingness," and not "a fleshpleasing, lazy, or sluggish disposition." A good servant needs to have "fear of God, or at least be tractable and willing to be taught," and not be "ungodly, sensual, and profane," for then he will endanger the family, detract from the work, steal from the business, and lead others astray. Indeed, "impious," "fleshly," and "slovenly servants" lack discipline, honor, and order. They will do what pleases them, not what the job needs. They will start their work late and leave early. They will indulge their appetites and not set their sights on productivity and efficiency. And they will follow their own wills, not the will of God, their masters, or even their fellow servants. Such servants must be "cast out" of jobs, homes, and shops, Baxter insisted, and replaced with those more properly disposed, if not already well trained.[36]

Those servants who meet and maintain high moral standards must be treated well and consistently taught the virtues and values of hard work and discipline, Baxter asserted. "Seeing the happiness of a servant, the safety of his soul, and the comfort of his life, depend very much on the family." Masters and mistresses must treat their servants first as fellow Christians, not as beasts of burden. They must give them vigorous and meaningful work commensurate with their vocational skills and reward them and advance them in accordance

35 Baxter, *A Christian Directory, vol. II, Christian Economics (or Family Duties)*, 66–74, 97–105, 186–89.

36 Baxter, *Christian Economics*, 40–44, 155.

with their talents and accomplishments. Masters and mistresses must provide decent food and shelter. They must teach habits of Christian worship, piety, and morality and insist on proper use of Sabbath rest. They must encourage Christian discipline, punish sinful conduct, and separate good servants from bad company. And masters and mistresses must provide models and means of Christian integrity, wisdom, and patience.[37]

3 Summary and Conclusions

The Protestant household manuals that we have sampled mandated a form of rationalization and routinization of the home that would prove critical for the early modern economy. The Protestant home was to be a little church and state that provided much of the nurture, education, social welfare, and moral discipline historically furnished by the medieval Catholic Church and later provided by the modern welfare state. The Protestant home was also to be a little business, with the family farm, shop, estate, or service giving servants and laborers the space and time to learn their craft and earn their keep, ideally under the benign Christian rule of the master. And the Protestant home was to be a little school, where children and apprentices were first taught and disciplined to pursue that vocation that best suited their inclinations and gifts, and learned to excel in that vocation as a form of loving service to God, neighbor, and self.

Like Max Weber's famous thesis in *The Protestant Ethic and the Spirit of Capitalism,* the real impact of these household manuals is difficult to quantify with precision. Numerous scholars have challenged Weber's claim that Protestant ideals and anxieties played a significant role in the emergence of modern economies. If theology affected this transformation at all, they say, its effects were secondary to other innovations in technology, law, and politics. Similarly, sociologists after Weber have shown that the early modern household was one of many new institutions that cultivated the norms and habits of market morality, not least the new public schools that emerged out of the Renaissance and Reformation. And, it is doubtful that every Protestant household lived up to the ideals put forth in these manuals. The sheer prevalence of the manuals may indicate how often Protestants fell short of these norms that thus required constant repetition.

---

37 Baxter, *Christian Economics*, 43, 209–11.

Despite these caveats, household manuals like the ones sampled above clearly illustrate the type of rationalizing impulse that Weber attributed to early modern Protestantism, and they represent one of the means by which this impulse took institutional form. Protestants' elevation of ordinary jobs to divine "callings" transformed the social and religious status of important economic roles and relationships; importantly, this transformation required a thoroughgoing reinterpretation of how ordinary people could fulfill these roles and relationships in practice. The household manuals served this interpretive function. Written for a lay audience, they defined the metes and bounds of household economies. They provided a detailed, scalable model of organizational hierarchy. They furnished a work ethic and value system and a corresponding moral argument for the wellbeing of the individual, the family, and the broader community: industry, discipline, frugality, and mutual care were sacred duties, while idleness and profligacy were unholy vices. The household manuals thus sought to structure domestic life and its constituent economies and values to the finest detail. To the extent that people implemented these instructions, households contributed to the tide of economic transformation that washed over Protestant lands in the early modern period. Protestant households alone do not explain the emergence of modern capitalism. But they are an important part of that story.

Acknowledgements

An earlier version of this chapter was published in Juergen von Hagen et al., eds., *The Impact of Economics on Character Formation in Late Modern Societies* (Leipzig: Evangelische Verlagsanhalt, 2020), 187–210, and is used herein with permission from the publisher.

Bibliography

Baxter, Richard. *A Christian Directory: or, A Summ of Practical Theologie, and Cases of Conscience: Directing Christians, How to Use their Knowledge and Faith; How to Improve all Helps and Means, and to Perform all Duties; How to Overcome Temptations, and to Escape or Mortifie Every Sin.* 2nd ed. 5 vols. London: Robert White, 1678. Reprinted as *A Christian Directory, or, a Body of Practical Divinity and Cases of Conscience.* 5 vols. London: Richard Edwards, 1825.

Bullinger, Heinrich [pseudonym Theodore Basille]. *The Christen State of Matrimonye.* London: s.l., 1541.

Bullinger, Heinrich. *Der christlich Eestand.* Zurich: Christoffel Froschouer, 1540.

Bullinger, Heinrich. *The Decades of Henry Bullinger: The First and Second Decades.* Edited by Thomas Harding. Cambridge: Cambridge University Press, 1849.

Bullinger, Henrich. *The Golde Boke of Christen Matrimonye.* London: J. Mayler, 1542.

Cleaver, Robert. *A Godly Form of Householde Gouernment.* London: Thomas Creede, 1598.

Cleaver, Robert. *A Godlie Forme of Hovseholde Government: For the Ordering of Private Families According to the Direction of God's Word.* London: Felix Kingston, 1600.

Dod, John, and Robert Cleaver. *A Plaine and Familiar Exposition of the Ten Commandments, with a Methodicall Short Catechisme, Containing Briefly all the Principall Grounds of Christian Religion.* London: Thomas Creede, 1604.

Donahue, Charles, Jr. "*Ius* in the Subjective Sense in Roman Law: Reflections on Villey and Tierney." In *A Ennio Cortese*, edited by Domenico Maffei et al., vol. 1, 506–35. Rome: Il Cigno, 2001.

Donahue, Charles, Jr. *Law, Marriage, and Society in the Later Middle Ages.* Cambridge: Cambridge University Press, 2008.

Frier, Bruce W., and Thomas A. J. McGinn. *A Casebook on Roman Family Law.* Oxford: Oxford University Press, 2004.

Perkins, William. *The Workes of that Famous and Worthy Minister of Christ in the Universitie of Cambridge, M.W. Perkins.* London: John Legatt, 1631.

Reynolds, Philip L., and John Witte, Jr., eds. *To Have and to Hold: Marrying and its Documentation in Western Christendom, 400–1600.* Cambridge: Cambridge University Press, 2012.

Weber, Max. *The Protestant Ethic and the Spirit of Capitalism.* New York: Scribner, 1958.

Weber, Max. "The Protestant Sects and the Spirit of Capitalism." In *From Max Weber: Essays in Sociology*, edited by H.H. Geerth and C. Wright Mills, 302–22. Oxford: Oxford University Press, 1946.

Witte, John, Jr. *From Sacrament to Contract: Marriage, Religion, and Law in the Western Tradition.* 2nd ed. Louisville, KY: Westminster John Knox Press, 2012.

Witte, John, Jr., and Heather M. Good. "The Duties of Love: The Vocation of the Child in the Household Manual Tradition." In *The Vocation of the Child*, edited by Patrick M. Brennan, 266–94. Grand Rapids, MI: Eerdmans, 2008.

CHAPTER 10

Legal and Factual Uncertainty in a Seventeenth-Century French Marriage Case

Saskia Lettmaier

The honorand has illuminated the doctrinal and practical past of the law of marriage like no other historian. In his page-turning *Law, Marriage, and Society in the Later Middle Ages*, he brings to life the actual litigation experiences of a selection of couples from late medieval England, France, and Belgium. Working from sources that are often "annoyingly incomplete,"[1] he highlights telltale gaps and inconsistencies, the likely interests of everyone (parties, families, friends and neighbors, social superiors, witnesses, legal actors, etc.) involved, and the strategies of argumentation and manipulation used. On this basis, he offers judicious and measured conclusions as to what probably happened, what the court probably thought happened, and what legal rules the court probably applied.

For this essay honoring Charles Donahue, I have accordingly selected a real-life French marriage case which I thought he might enjoy. The case is reported by François Gayot de Pitaval (1673–1743), a French *ancien régime* jurist and advocate at the *Parlement* (i.e., the supreme court) of Paris.[2] Between 1734 and 1743, Pitaval, partly for commercial reasons, collected and published twenty volumes of what he considered particularly interesting legal cases.[3] His aim, as he explained in the introduction, was to pick notable decisions with broad appeal and to "unlock" the secrets of the judiciary.[4] Based on actual court files, his *Causes célèbres et intéressantes* usually contain quite intricate reproductions of the arguments of counsel and even verbatim extracts from legal briefs,

1 Charles Donahue Jr., *Law, Marriage, and Society in the Later Middle Ages: Arguments About Marriage in Five Courts* (Cambridge: Cambridge University Press, 2007), 46.

2 Although the modern French term *parlement*—like the English *Parliament*—describes the legislature, the *ancien régime parlements* were not legislative bodies, but provincial sovereign courts. Originally, there was only one *parlement*, that of Paris. Others were created later for the provinces, but the *Parlement* of Paris remained the most important one, with a jurisdiction covering nearly half of France.

3 François Gayot de Pitaval, *Causes célèbres et intéressantes, avec les jugemens qui les ont décidées*, 20 vols. (Paris: Guillaume Cavelier, 1734–43).

4 Pitaval, *Causes célèbres*, vol. 1 (1735), v, viij.

 | DOI:10.1163/9789004710696_012

supporting documents, and the sentences of courts, although Pitaval was also anxious not to put off his audience by going into tedious procedural detail or giving what he considered were unnecessary facts.[5] What Pitaval was doing in reporting cases for public consumption was not new. Since the later sixteenth century, French judges and advocates had begun to evade judicial secrecy by publishing their personal notes of court proceedings and selling them to a fast-expanding public, both professional and lay, hungry for legal information. They collectively became known as "arrestographes."[6] While Pitaval was neither the only nor the first writer in that genre, he clearly had a special talent for writing reports that were both instructive and entertaining. His work became immensely popular and went into numerous editions and translations.[7] Given Pitaval's aim to appeal to a broad public and to sell copy, we should not expect his accounts to be either complete or completely faithful records. In fact, Pitaval admitted to sometimes deviating "un peu de l'exactitude, afin de satisfaire l'oreille."[8] Potential incompleteness and inaccuracy are therefore problems we will have to contend with in this chapter. These problems are probably ineradicable from any historical research. As omissions and inaccuracies tend to increase with each new edition and translation, I have decided to base my analysis of the case on Pitaval's original account in the first Paris edition.[9]

1 Pitaval's Mariage declaré abusif après 24 ans

The *arrêt* in our marriage case dates from 1723, but the story that gave rise to it begins much earlier. In 1679, Louis Aymard de Sailly married Adrienne-Elisabeth de Crequy, a relative, and lost her to a fatal illness only forty-three days later. For a second wife, he chose Adrienne's younger sister Charlotte. Because Charlotte and Louis Aymard were related by both blood and marriage,

5 Pitaval, *Causes célèbres*, vol. 1 (1735), viij.

6 As early as the 1540s, Gilles Le Maistre, a judge in the *Parlement* of Paris, kept personal notes on important judicial decisions, which a colleague published after his death. On this development generally, see Sarah Hanley, "'The Jurisprudence of the Arrêts': Marital Union, Civil Society, and State Formation in France, 1550–1650," *Law & History Review* 21, no. 1 (Spring 2003): 461–510.

7 Interestingly, Pitaval's greatest and longest-lasting impact appears to have been in Germany. The French Wikipedia article (unlike the German) is a stub, and the Oxford Reference entry for him draws on the *Oxford Companion to German Literature*.

8 Pitaval, *Causes célèbres*, vol. 1 (1735), xix.

9 Pitaval, "Mariage declaré abusif après 24 ans de cohabitation, & la mort de l'épouse," *Causes célèbres*, vol. 7 (1739), 1–93.

their union required a papal dispensation. In September of 1679 and again in February of 1680, applications for a dispensation from the first degree of affinity and from the third and fourth degree of consanguinity were presented on the couple's behalf by a *banquier-expéditionnaire*, a breed of French public official with the exclusive right to solicit for dispensations and other favors at the Court of Rome.[10] Innocent XI (1676–1689), a pope renowned for his austere piety and moral earnestness,[11] was unmoved by both. When Innocent was succeeded by Alexander VIII (1689–1692), who has been described as "a complete contrast to his severe predecessor,"[12] Louis Aymard launched a third attempt. Another *banquier* presented a new petition in May of 1690, and this time the papal datary did issue a brief commissioning the official of Noyon (i.e., the chief judge of the local bishop) to conduct an investigation into the facts and, if the outcome was favorable, to grant a dispensation on certain terms. A dispensation from the first degree of affinity and from the third and fourth degree of consanguinity was granted by the official of Noyon in January of 1691. The future spouses then signed a *contrat de mariage* that contained mutual gifts of all property in favor of the survivor, and the marriage was eventually celebrated in February of 1691. Fast forward to Charlotte's death (without issue) twenty-four years later: her younger half-brother François Leonor de Crequy by her father's second marriage entered upon her land and—when Louis Aymard invoked the marital gift in his favor—attacked the validity of the marriage. The sentence rendered by the *Grand-Chambre du Parlement* on François Leonor's *appel comme d'abus* ("appeal for abuse [of jurisdiction]") in 1723 found the marriage between Charlotte and Louis Aymard to be "nul, abusif, & non valablement célébré, contracté & exécuté."[13] François Leonor and his progeny[14] got to keep the land.

10 The *banquiers* were originally Italian merchants who transacted business in France and corresponded with Rome. They were given an official title and exclusive status by an edict of March 1673.

11 J. N. D. Kelly, ed., *The Oxford Dictionary of Popes* (Oxford: Oxford University Press, 1986), s.v. "Innocent XI."

12 Alexander VIII was lavish in his personal style and revived the nepotism Innocent XI had sought to stamp out. *See Oxford Dictionary of Popes*, s.v. "Alexander VIII."

13 Pitaval, "Mariage declaré abusif," 61.

14 François Leonor died before the final sentence, but the case was taken over by his widow on behalf of his children.

2 Three Challenges

The above is a succinct and accurate summary of the record, but also one that—to a lawyer and legal historian—is somewhat unsatisfying. As lawyers and legal historians, we do not just want to be told the outcome of a case. We want to understand the factual assumptions, legal propositions, and reasoning processes that led to this outcome. If that is our goal, we are faced with three challenges in dealing with Pitaval's *Mariage declaré abusif*. First, we do not learn much from the *arrêt* itself, although Pitaval reproduces it in full.[15] Other than recapitulating some dates, it does not go very far beyond the pleonastic sentence annihilating the marriage that I have already quoted. This is not unusual. It was the custom of *ancien régime parlements* not to "weaken" the authority of their decisions by providing reasons for them that might be contested.[16] This leaves us with what can be deduced from the parties' arguments in the case. If the court found in favor of one party, it is likely to have followed some or all of that party's factual and/or legal propositions—at least to the extent that this was necessary to decide the case. Pitaval accordingly concentrates on the factual and legal arguments that François Leonor, the Comte de Crequy, and Louis Aymar, the Marquis de Sailly, put forward through a succession of different legal representatives. This is helpful, but it also presents a problem. Arguments are, by definition, tendentious. They do not seek to be accurate statements of fact or law, but to promote a particular cause and to persuade. Therefore, we cannot take either parties' factual or legal assertions at face value. We will have to test how well they stand up against the surviving documentation, our sense of human nature, and our understanding of the social and legal rules governing marriage in late seventeenth-century France. Doing this brings us up against a third challenge. We are approaching this case from a distance of about three hundred years. The documentation we have to go on is rather skimpy. And while human nature may not have changed that much in the intervening period, the legal and social regulation of marriage certainly has.

15 Pitaval, "Mariage declaré abusif," 61–62.

16 Jean-Louis Halpérin, "Les styles judiciares, des traditions nationales?" *Droit et Société* 91 (2015): 496; Serge Dauchy and Véronique Demars-Sion, "La non-motivation des décisions judiciares dans l'ancien droit: principe ou usage," *Revue historique de droit français et étranger* 82, no. 2 (2004): 223.

3 The Institutional and Procedural Background

Before we delve into the finer points of fact and law, a word is in order about the institutional and procedural background to this case. The challenge to the marriage was brought on an *appel comme d'abus* in a *parlement*—which one, we are not told. However, as the story is set in Picardie, a historical territory in the North of France, it is likely to have been the *Parlement* of Paris, which covered the major part of northern and central France and was usually simply referred to as *le Parlement*. The *ancien régime parlements*, as I have said, were superior judicial bodies. They were also *secular* judicial bodies, where justice was dispensed in the king's name. Readers familiar with the history of marriage law might therefore be surprised to find a *parlement* deciding a case where the validity of a marriage was a determinative issue. It is a trite observation that since the High Middle Ages the Church had acquired exclusive legislative and jurisdictional competence over the validity of marriages by claiming marriage as a sacrament of the Church.[17] It is similarly trite to observe that this competence came under severe challenge in Protestant territories as a result of the Reformation.[18] But our case does not come from a Protestant territory; it comes from Catholic France.

Developments in France are in fact a striking illustration that the early modern curtailment of ecclesiastical authority by the state was not an exclusively Protestant phenomenon.[19] As Sarah Hanley has argued, officeholders in the French *parlements*, whose social and political place depended on judicious family formation, and the French kings, who had set their sights set on state building, forged an alliance in the sixteenth and seventeenth centuries, which was designed to end church influence over marriage and to bring the institution

17 There is widespread consensus that the notion of marriage as a sacrament and the Church's legislative and jurisdictional claims are related. See, e.g., Dieter Schwab, *Grundlagen und Gestalt der staatlichen Ehegesetzgebung in der Neuzeit bis zum Beginn des 19. Jahrhunderts* (Bielefeld: Verlag Ernst and Werner Gieseking, 1967), 20–21; John Witte Jr., *From Sacrament to Contract: Marriage, Religion, and Law in the Western Tradition*, 2nd ed. (Louisville, KY: Westminster John Knox Press, 2012), 78–79. For marriage adjudication in the courts of the Roman curia from the seventeenth until the twentieth century, see John T. Noonan Jr., *Power to Dissolve: Lawyers and Marriages in the Courts of the Roman Curia* (Cambridge: Harvard University Press, 1972).

18 For a more nuanced treatment of this trite statement, see Saskia Lettmaier, "Marriage Law and the Reformation," *Law & History Review* 35, no. 2 (May 2017): 461–510.

19 For a summary of the process, see Anne Lefebvre-Taillard, "Marriage in France from the Sixteenth to the Eighteenth Century: Political and Juridical Aspects," in *Marriage in Europe, 1400–1800*, ed. Silvana Seidel Menchi (Toronto: Toronto University Press, 2016), 261–93.

under family and state control.[20] The objective of the attack was to separate the contract from the sacrament of marriage, arguing that the king and his courts had competence over the former because it was the seedbed of the state.[21] The *appel comme d'abus* proved to be a useful tool in this connection.[22] Early modern French legislation in principle retained ecclesiastical jurisdiction in sacramental (including marriage) matters.[23] However, there were two exceptions: the first was where "il s'agit d'une succession, ou autres effets civils, à l'occasion duquel on traiteroit de l'état des personnes décédées." The second was where "il y eut appel comme d'abus interjetté [aux cours seculiers]."[24] An *appel comme d'abus* could be brought against an ecclesiastical decision if it suffered from a procedural mistake, failed to respect royal legislation, and even if it applied the canon law (i.e., "les saincts [*sic*] decrets et canons receuz [*sic*] en ce royaume, droicts [*sic*], franchises, libertés et privilèges de l'Eglise gallicane, concordats")[25] incorrectly.[26] Although the legislative instruments envisaged the *appel comme d'abus* as an extraordinary remedy, which would only be available in cases where the abuse was notorious, the *parlements* routinely ignored this restriction and, once seized, reexamined the matter *au fond*.[27]

---

20 See, e.g., Sarah Hanley, "Family and State in Early Modern France: The Marriage Pact," in *Connecting Spheres: Women in the Western World, 1500 to the present*, ed. Marilyn J. Boxer and Jean H. Quataert (New York/Oxford: Oxford University Press, 1987), 53–63. See also Sarah Hanley, "Engendering the State: Family Formation and State Building in Early Modern France," *French Historical Studies* 16, no. 1 (Spring 1989): 4–27.

21 While the notion of contract as applied to marriage was an old one, Gallican jurists deliberately pursued the distinction between contract and sacrament for the benefit of the state. See Lefebvre-Taillard, "Marriage in France," 268. Robert Joseph Pothier's *Traité du contrat de mariage*, 2 vols. (Paris, 1771) was the coping-stone in this doctrinal edifice.

22 Alain Lottin, *La désunion du couple sous l'ancien régime* (Paris: Ed. universitaires, 1975), 22. On the *appel comme d'abus* generally, see also Robert Génestal, *Les origines de l'appel comme d'abus: notes de cours publiées par les soins de Pierre Timbal* (Paris: Presses Universitaires de France, 1951).

23 See, e.g., *Ordonnance de Henry IV concernant le mariage* of December 1606, art. 12, partially reprinted in Pierre Le Ridant, *Code Matrimonial, ou recueil des édits, ordonnances & déclarations sur le mariage* (Paris: Herissant, 1766), 24–25. Extracts from substantially similar royal legislation of 1610 (art. 4), 1629 (art. 31), 1666 (art. 15), and 1695 (art. 34) can be found in Ignace Moly de Brézolles, *Traité de la jurisdiction ecclésiastique contentieuse*, vol. 1, pt. 2 (Paris: chez Nyon l`ainé & La Porte, 1769), 107–18.

24 Edict of 1695, art. 34, partially reprinted in Brézolles, *Traité*, 1:108.

25 Art. 79 of the *Libertés de l'église gallicane*, cited in Emil Friedberg, *Der Missbrauch der geistlichen Amtsgewalt und der Recurs an den Staat* (Tübingen: Laupp, 1863), 25.

26 Pothier, *Traité*, 2:96.

27 Denis-Auguste Affre, *L'appel comme d'abus, son origine, ses progrès et son état présent* (Paris: A. Le Clerc, 1845), 81–84, 101, 217, 234.

Our case is caught by both exceptions. The validity of Louis Aymard and Charlotte's marriage arose as a preliminary issue in a legal squabble that was really about who got to keep Charlotte's estate. And Charlotte's half-brother François Leonor attacked the marriage on the basis that the papal brief, its execution by the official of Noyon, and the act of celebration of the marriage were abusive and therefore invalid.

4 The Requisite Dispensations

The marriage at the center of the *appel comme d'abus* required dispensations from diriment (i.e., invalidating) marital impediments.[28] But it is in fact unclear which dispensations were required. The first two applications asked for a dispensation from the first degree of affinity and from the third and fourth degree of consanguinity;[29] the third asked for a dispensation from the first degree of public honesty and from the third and fourth degree of consanguinity.[30] Pope Alexander VIII granted a dispensation *in forma commissaria*,[31] that is, by appointing the official of Noyon to act as his delegate in the matter, on the following terms: "*Quod primi publicae honestatis justitia, ex premissis provenientibus,… Ac tertii ex uno & quarti ex altero consanguinitatis, vel affinitatis graduum impedimentis dispensat.*"[32] And the parties eventually obtained a sentence from the official of Noyon, which dispensed them from the first degree of affinity and from the third and fourth degree of consanguinity.[33]

There is consistency as regards the impediment of consanguinity. The parties asked for and were granted a dispensation from the third and fourth degree, and the validity of this dispensation was not put in doubt by anyone in the case. However, the degrees stated do not fit the relationships that

28 Marital impediments were neatly categorized into two kinds: diriment and impedient. Diriment impediments invalidated an attempted marriage. Those who married in the face of an impedient impediment, on the other hand, risked punishment, but their marriage would stand.

29 Pitaval, "Mariage declaré abusif," 5–6.

30 Pitaval, "Mariage declaré abusif," 7.

31 It was common practice for popes to grant marital dispensations *in forma commissaria* rather than *in forma gratiosa* (i.e., as a direct grant to the parties themselves). Johann Friedrich v. Schulte, *Handbuch des katholischen Eherechts* (Gießen: Verlag der Ferber'schen Universiäts-Buchhandlung, 1855), 384; Privat-Joseph Brillaud, *Traité pratique des empêchements et des dispenses de mariage* (Paris: Wattelier, 1884), 193–94.

32 Pitaval, "Mariage declaré abusif," 21 (italics in original).

33 Pitaval, "Mariage declaré abusif," 8.

Pitaval describes in the text. We are told that Louis Aymard is the son ("fils") of Charles de Sailly, who is Charlotte's "oncle."[34] This would mean that the bride and groom are related in the second degree of consanguinity on the canonical computation (counting the generations back to the common ancestor) and in the fourth degree on the civil-law computation (counting the generations back from Louis Aymard to the common ancestor and then down again to Charlotte). The dispensation would make sense if we assume Louis Aymard to be the grandson (*petit-fils*) of Charles, who was Charlotte's *great-great*-uncle. In that case, it would be the fourth degree on Charlotte's side and the third degree on Louis Aymard's, using the canonical computation. This interpretation would also fit the wording of the papal brief, which suggests that the lines on either side were unequal ("*tertii ex uno & quarti ex altero consanguinitatis*"). However, this interpretation requires quite a departure from the kinship designations provided in the text, and it would make Charles quite old. Whatever is going on here, we can conclude that our record is *not* very precise.

There is *no* consistency as regards the second impediment. This is variously described as an impediment of affinity *or* an impediment of public honesty. The question of which of these impediments applied and whether it was validly dispensed from is one of the core issues in the case. The legal difference between the two impediments is easily explained. The basis of affinity in classical canon law was sexual intercourse. It applied if one of the prospective marriage partners had carnally known a blood relative of the other.[35] The impediment arose irrespective of whether the sexual relationship had been licit (i.e., between spouses) or illicit (i.e., outside of marriage),[36] although the Council of Trent (1545–1563) introduced a distinction by limiting the latter kind of affinity (also known as *affinitas per copulam illicitam*) to the second (rather than the fourth) degree.[37] The impediment of public honesty did not arise from sexual intercourse; it arose from a formal engagement or an as yet unconsummated marriage. It was thought indecent for a man to marry his former fiancée's mother, for instance; hence the name.[38] Whether Charlotte

34 Pitaval, "Mariage declaré abusif," 3.

35 Donahue, *Law, Marriage, and Society*, 31; Mathias Schmoeckel, "Vor §§ 1313–1320—Auflösung der Ehe," in *Historisch-kritischer Kommentar zum BGB*, vol. 4, Familienrecht, ed. Mathias Schmoeckel, Joachim Rückert, and Reinhard Zimmermann (Tübingen: Mohr Siebeck, 2018), 379.

36 Donahue, *Law, Marriage, and Society*, 29–30.

37 Sess. XXIV, c. IV, Canones super reformatione circa matrimonium.

38 Donahue, *Law, Marriage, and Society*, 31; Schmoeckel, "Vor §§ 1313–1320—Auflösung der Ehe," 379. The degrees of the impediment of public honesty were radically reduced (from four to one) by the Council of Trent. Donahue, *Law, Marriage, and Society*, 31.

and Louis Aymard's marriage required a dispensation from the first degree of affinity or from the first degree of public honesty therefore hinged on whether the groom's first marriage had been consummated. As far as I can tell, the question of consummation or nonconsummation of the prior marriage is the only factual uncertainty in the case. It is one, however, that has many legal implications.

5 The Plaintiff's Arguments

According to François Leonor and his legal team, the marriage was vitiated by four instances of abuse (*moyens d'abus*). The first two concerned the papal brief, the third the procedure before the official of Noyon, and the fourth the act of celebration of the marriage.

As regarded the papal brief, François Leonor argued, first, that the pope did not have the requisite authority to dispense from the first degree of affinity. The prohibition on marrying one's dead wife's sister, he claimed, was a divine or natural-law precept (rather than a rule of purely ecclesiastical origin) and as such beyond the pope's dispensing power.[39] Further, a papal dispensation would not be recognized in France unless it was confirmed by registered letters patent (which this dispensation had indisputably not been). For the latter proposition, François Leonor relied on article 42 of the *Libertés de l'église gallicane*, a private work by Pierre Pithou of 1594, and on article 22 of Charles IX's Ordonnance of Orléans of 1560.[40] We will take a look at these provisions later. The second flaw of the papal brief, as François Leonor saw it, consisted in the fact that the pope had been tricked. The parties had deliberately provided false information in asserting that Louis Aymard's first marriage had never been consummated. The lie was proved by the fact that their third application had asked for a dispensation from the impediment of public honesty (which implied nonconsummation), when their first two had asked for a dispensation from the impediment of affinity. The effect of this kind of fraud, according to the plaintiff's counsel, was "d'annuller radicalement la Dispense."[41]

Next, François Leonor attacked the procedure before the bishop's official. The papal brief had been issued to the official as the pope's executor (*in forma commissaria*). It had therefore been the official's duty to carry out the pope's commission faithfully, and to stay within the bounds of his delegated power.

39 Pitaval, "Mariage declaré abusif," 14.
40 Pitaval, "Mariage declaré abusif," 15–16.
41 Pitaval, "Mariage declaré abusif," 19.

But instead of examining whether the parties really only needed to be dispensed from the impediment of public honesty, as the brief had required him to do, the official had not heard a single witness on the question of consummation and had granted a dispensation, not from the first degree of public honesty, but from the first degree of affinity.[42] This had been in excess of his power as a delegate.

Finally, the act of celebration was defective. The *curé* who had married Louis Aymard and Charlotte had mentioned neither the papal dispensation nor the publication of banns, and there had been only two witnesses to the ceremony. The Ordonnance of Blois (1579)—the French version of the Tridentine Decree Tametsi (1563)[43]—however, required four, on pains of nullity.[44]

6 The Defense

The Marquis de Sailly's defense consisted in a wholesale refutation of these legal and factual arguments. He claimed, first, that the impediment of affinity was not a divine or natural-law prohibition and that there were in fact numerous examples where even the first degree had been dispensed from, including in the plaintiff's own family.[45] The restriction on the intermarriage of *affines* was mere church-made law, and neither article 42 of the *Libertés* nor article 22 of the Ordonnance of Orléans took away the pope's power to dispense from rules of purely ecclesiastical origin. Second, the pope had not been tricked. The Marquis de Sailly was "ni Jurisconsulte, ni Canoniste, ni Theologien,"[46] and he was therefore quite unfamiliar with the finer points of the law of dispensation. That the parties had initially asked for a dispensation from the first degree of affinity did not prove that they had lied in their third application, which asked for a dispensation from the first degree of public honesty. There was nothing to prevent the parties from asking for more than they needed, and this is what Charlotte and Louis Aymard had done.[47] Third, the procedure before the official of Noyon had been entirely correct. The Marquis de Sailly

42 Pitaval, "Mariage declaré abusif," 23–24.

43 The Decree Tametsi required a priest and at least two witnesses for marriage validity, but not parental consent. This proved so unpopular with the French delegation that they refused to promulgate the decree in their country. Instead, they promulgated their own Ordonnance of Blois, which was similar to Trent but stricter.

44 Pitaval, "Mariage declaré abusif," 24–25.

45 Pitaval, "Mariage declaré abusif," 25–31.

46 Pitaval, "Mariage declaré abusif," 33.

47 Pitaval, "Mariage declaré abusif," 35–36.

had stated that his first marriage had never been consummated. This was credible in light of the fact that the bride had been taken ill only three days after the wedding. Further evidence on the question of consummation was not available. Moreover, the papal brief included an authorization to dispense from the first degree of affinity.[48] The official could therefore dispense from the larger impediment without having to go into the question of whether this dispensation was necessary, strictly speaking.[49] As far as the marriage ceremony was concerned, it was enough that the dispensation had been granted and that a bann of marriage had been published; it was not necessary to mention either fact in the act of celebration. Finally, the shortage of witnesses did not lead to a nullity since the parties had openly lived together as man and wife for twenty-four years.[50]

After countering each of the other side's arguments, Louis Aymard and his legal team had an even more fundamental attack up their sleeve. They argued that the plaintiff had no right to challenge the marriage and that his action should therefore be dismissed without examining the merits of his case. The right to object to a marriage, they contended, was limited to parents and others in power, and even the right of these persons would be lost if they had consented to the marriage at the time of its celebration or thereafter. The plaintiff, in short, was excluded by three *fins de non-recevoir*: because he was a collateral, because he had acquiesced in his sister's marriage during her lifetime,[51] and because his only interest in having the marriage annulled was financial. What the plaintiff was really complaining about was the marital gift. If Charlotte had not made a *donation* in favor of her intended husband, her marriage would never have come under the present attack.[52]

7 What Do We Make of It All?

We know that on the basis of these arguments, the *parlement* rendered sentence for the plaintiff. We also know that the court did not decide the case on the *fins de non-recevoir* because the judgment, which Pitaval reproduces in full, says so.[53] This part of the decision seems in line with the law. The classical

48 Pitaval, "Mariage declaré abusif," 33, 36.
49 Pitaval, "Mariage declaré abusif," 36–37.
50 Pitaval, "Mariage declaré abusif," 37.
51 I am assuming that he was of age at the time of the marriage or subsequently came of age before his sister's death.
52 Pitaval, "Mariage declaré abusif," 38–39, 53–56.
53 Pitaval, "Mariage declaré abusif," 62 ("sans s'arrêter aux fins de non-recevoir").

canon law did not exclude collateral relatives from having a marriage investigated that came within the prohibited degrees.[54] The rights of collaterals might have been more limited in seventeenth-century France. According to Pothier,[55] collaterals could not accuse a marriage during the parties' lifetime. They had to wait until their relative had died, because it was only then that they could show a legitimate (financial) interest in having the marriage invalidated.[56] But even if we accept this restriction, our plaintiff was not disqualified. He raised the invalidity as a preliminary matter in a dispute about Charlotte's estate. The other two alleged *fins de non-recevoir* did not support a dismissal of the plaintiff's action either. It is true that the canon law excluded those who had known of an impediment and said nothing at the time of the marriage, as well as those who could be shown to be motivated by hatred or financial gain.[57] However, these rules do not seem to have applied to an *appel comme d'abus* in seventeenth-century France. Turning to Pothier's treatise again, we learn that signs of approbation during the presumed spouses' lifetime did not disqualify a collateral relative, because his right to attack the marriage did not even arise until one partner had died.[58] And a financial interest, far from putting a collateral accuser out of court, was in fact a necessary precondition for him to be able to bring a case.

As regards the court's other grounds for decision, the *arrêt*—as previously noted—is unfortunately less than explicit. It only finds that "il a été mal, nullement, & abusivement procedé, exécuté" and that the marriage is invalid.[59] Pitaval tells us what he takes the reason for the decision to be: the parties had lied to the pope about the consummation of Louis Aymard's prior marriage.[60] But was that really what motivated the judgment?

The parties' arguments raised a number of questions of both fact and law. The fact-law distinction has been described as "purely a creature of convention,"[61] but there is in fact an analytic difference between fact and law, and

54 A canon of dubious origins held that only relatives could accuse a marriage of invalidity because of consanguinity and affinity, but there was no rule excluding collateral relatives, and even non-relatives were admitted. Donahue, *Law, Marriage, and Society*, 37–38. Adhémar Esmein, *Le mariage en droit canonique* (Paris: Receuil Sirey, 1929), 1:463.

55 His *Traité de mariage* provides a good overview of the marriage law of late *ancien régime* France. See Jean Gaudemet, *Le mariage en Occident* (Paris: Ed. du Cerf, 1987), 332.

56 Pothier, *Contrat de mariage*, 2:81–82.

57 Donahue, *Law, Marriage, and Society*, 38.

58 Pothier, *Contrat de mariage*, 2:84.

59 Pitaval, "Mariage declaré abusif," 62.

60 Pitaval, "Mariage declaré abusif," 62–63.

61 Gary Lawson, "Proving the Law," *Northwestern University Law Review* 86 (1992): 863.

this distinction is important. While statements of law can be rephrased as factual statements (i.e., as descriptions of what legal actors have declared the law to be in a given situation), they are factual statements of a very particular type[62] in that they concern the past conduct of legal officials, which can usually be gleaned from reports, statutes, treatises, etc. Disputed facts, on the other hand—like the question of the consummation of Louis Aymard's first marriage—have a far more ephemeral quality. They usually cannot be determined to a certainty, or a near certainty, at least not by a legal historian trying to do so centuries after the event with nothing to aid her but an old litigation record. We are therefore likely to have an easier time testing the parties' legal propositions. Perhaps the court could even decide the case on purely legal grounds, without having to go into the one factual question of whether Louis Aymard's first marriage was consummated?

The plaintiff's first argument was legal. It was two-pronged. The first prong alleged that the pope could not grant a valid dispensation from the first degree of affinity because this was a divine prohibition. This does not strike me as a very compelling argument, at least not for the early seventeenth century. While there is some support in Leviticus for the proposition that the prohibition of marriage with the dead wife's sister was based on divine law,[63] by the early seventeenth century, when our case was argued, the weight of canonistic opinion was against it. By then it was highly questionable whether even the persons expressly mentioned in Leviticus (and the dead wife's sister was not among them) were excluded as marriage partners as a matter of divine law,[64]

62 Richard D. Friedman, "Standards of Persuasion and the Distinction between Fact and Law," *Northwestern University Law Review* 86 (1992): 917.

63 Leviticus 18:16 prohibits intercourse and hence marriage with a brother's wife. The prohibition might be extended by analogy to cover intercourse and marriage with the wife's sister. Leviticus 18:18 prohibits taking the wife's sister as a rival wife. However, the context makes it clear that the prohibiton is against marrying the sister while the wife is still living.

64 The Council of Trent adopted a canon (J. Waterworth, ed. and trans., *The Council of Trent: The Canons and Decrees of the Sacred and Oecumenical Council of Trent* … [London: Dolman, 1848], Session the Twenty-Fourth, Doctrine on the Sacrament of Matrimony, can. 3, 194) that anathematized anyone who "saith, that those degrees only of consanguinity and affinity, which are set down in Leviticus, can hinder matrimony from being contracted, and dissolve it when contracted; and that the Church cannot dispense in some of those degrees, or establish that others may hinder and dissolve it." The formulation that "some of those degrees" might be dispensed from suggests that the council members continued to regard an unspecified number of degrees as binding moral laws. According to Esmein, however, the Council conclusively rejected the view that *any* of the Levitical degrees were binding. See Esmein, *Le mariage en droit canonique*, 2:391.

and there was in fact ample canon-law precedent for the kind of dispensation that Louis Aymard and Charlotte had received. One particularly notable example, cited by counsel for the defense[65] and mentioned in a number of French treatises on marriage,[66] was a doctor from Beauvais, whose marriage to his dead wife's sister[67] under a papal dispensation had survived an *appel comme d'abus* in 1683.

The second prong of the plaintiff's argument claimed that the papal brief was invalid pursuant to article 22 of the Ordonnance of Orléans and article 42 of the *Libertés de l'église gallicane* because it had not been confirmed by registered letters patent. Once again, I do not think that article 22 of the Ordonnance of Orléans supports the plaintiff's position. This article was entitled "How to Rule on the Possession of Church Benefices."[68] It prohibited judges from paying attention to papal dispensations without the leave of the king, but only "en jugeant le possessoire des Bénéfices," that is, in actions dealing with the possession of benefices. Article 42 of the *Libertés*, however, seems much more on point. In relevant part, it provided that papal bulls and apostolic letters were of no effect ("ne s'executēt") in France "sans pareatis[69] du Roy ou de ses officiers." Unlike the provision in the Ordonnance, this provision was not limited to a certain topic. I think that the wording is general enough to cover papal briefs, which were a simpler and more modern version of bulls,[70] especially since the article goes on to speak of "bulles, rescrits, ou lettres" more generally. If this interpretation is correct—and we have pretty good authority for thinking that it is[71]—then it would not even matter whether the papal brief granted a dispensation from the first degree of affinity or one from the first degree of public honesty; any papal dispensation would require a royal pareatis. While the *Libertés* were only a private work, they were enormously influential (they have even been described as having "force de loi"),[72]

65 Pitaval, "Mariage declaré abusif," 29–30.

66 See, e.g., Michel du Perray, *Traité des dispenses de mariage* (Paris, 1719), 12–13.

67 This was quite a piquant case in that the wife's sister had borne him a child even during the wife's lifetime.

68 The original title read: "Comment on doit statuer sur le possessoire d'un Bénéfice."

69 Letters of Pareatis were documents required for the extension of a legal decision into jurisdictions other than the one in which the decision was originally made.

70 The choice of the precise form of instrument was often arbitrary.

71 The interpretation is borne out by Brézolles, *Traité*, 1:172, Pothier, *Contrat de mariage*, 1:307, and André Marie Jean Jacques Dupin, *Libertés de l'église gallicane: Manuel du droit public ecclésiastique français* (Paris: Henri Plon 1860), 47–48. Dupin's commentary expressly includes "bref ... même ne concernant que les particuliers" (48).

72 Edouard Laboulaye, "Libertés de l'église gallicane," *Revue historique de droit français et étranger* 4 (1858): 480.

and hence any papal dispensation that lacked royal authorization risked being ineffective.[73] The recipient of a papal brief would therefore do well to get it confirmed by registered letters patent just in case. This is what the doctor from Beauvais, whose marriage to his late wife's sister had survived an *appel comme d'abus*, had done.[74]

The plaintiff's second contention was that the dispensation was invalid because the pope had been tricked. The legal part of this statement is sound: If an application for a dispensation asserted false facts or withheld true ones, it would be invalid if the facts concerned were material.[75] The question of consummation—which the parties were alleged to have lied about—was clearly a material fact in that it was much easier to get a dispensation from the first degree of public honesty than it was to get one from the first degree of affinity.[76] And this, finally, brings us up against the one factual uncertainty of the case—the question of consummation. I do not have an answer to this question, but I can offer some speculation. What we do know is that the bride was taken ill within three days of the wedding and that she died forty-three days after.[77] We also know that in the first application, the *banquier* asked for a dispensation from the first degree of affinity, but doubted that the first marriage had been consummated. In the second, he no longer expressed any doubt, but added that the first wife had died "*absque conceptu prolis*," that is, without having conceived any children.[78] And in the third, another *banquier* alleged that the first wife had died "*omninò intacta, & in nullo penitus attentata*;" this *banquier* only asked for a dispensation from the first degree of public honesty.[79]

I do not think that what we know conclusively establishes either consummation or nonconsummation. The mere fact that there was an opportunity to consummate the marriage and that, in a typical case, consummation might be expected to follow quite soon after the wedding did not raise an irrebuttable presumption of consummation. The plaintiff tried to argue this, relying on the maxim "*Solus cum solâ nudus cum nudâ*."[80] While such a *praesumptio*

73 According to Brézolles, *Traité*, 1:179, the matter of nullity was handled differently from *parlement* to *parlement*.

74 Pitaval, "Mariage declaré abusif," 45.

75 Schulte, *Handbuch des katholischen Eherechts*, 368. If the inaccuracy concerned a minor matter, the dispensation might stand if the applicant had been in good faith.

76 Jean-Pierre Gibert, *Consultations canoniques sur le sacrement de mariage* (Paris, 1750), 180, 483; Brillaud, *Traité Pratique*, 62.

77 Pitaval, "Mariage declaré abusif," 3.

78 Pitaval, "Mariage declaré abusif," 6 (original emphasis).

79 Pitaval, "Mariage declaré abusif," 7 (original emphasis).

80 Pitaval, "Mariage declaré abusif," 50 (original emphasis).

violenta did exist,[81] the facts giving rise to it were not made out (Louis Aymard and Adrienne had not been seen in bed together naked), and the presumption seems to have been rebuttable.[82] Morever, this was not a typical case. The marriage was motivated by pecuniary interests (this in itself was not unusual for the period and social class). We are told that Louis Aymard was a younger son, who did not stand to inherit under the *Coutumes de Picardie*, and that it was "l'intérêt qui est le grand mobile des mariages," which made him think of a union with Adrienne, who was evidently an heiress.[83] Moreover, Adrienne was taken ill three days after her wedding. Given the likely absence of sexual ardor on either side and perhaps some early signs of indisposition on Adrienne's part, it is not hard to imagine that consummation was delayed—until it became impossible. The wording of the three applications was also not conclusive. While only the third denied consummation, the first expressed doubt on the matter and even the second did not admit it. The statement that Adrienne died without having conceived any children (*absque conceptu prolis*) did not imply consummation as a logical necessity; only the opposite statement (i.e., that she died having conceived a child by her husband) would. Of course, the plaintiff was perfectly right in contending that Louis Aymard could not possibly have been in any doubt as regards the consummation of his first marriage. So why equivocate? Well, the defense argued that the parties initially tried to get a larger dispensation than they needed (one from the impediment of affinity rather than that of public honesty), and to me this argument seems plausible. The parties (or their legal advisors) probably feared that if they only obtained a dispensation from the impediment of public honesty, their marriage might be impugned later on because someone might think it incredible that the Marquis de Sailly's first marriage had not been consummated. So why not seek a dispensation from the impediment of affinity[84] (even if that cost more)?[85] The equivocation was

81 X 2,23,12. The chapter deals with proof of adultery by a wife. She had been found with another man "solum cum sola, nudum cum nuda, in eodem lecto iacentem." This was said to give rise to a strong ("violenta et certa") suspicion of fornication.

82 Rudolf Brinkmann, *Wissenschaftlich praktische Rechtskunde*, vol. 1 (Schleswig: Taubstummen-Institut, 1831), 33.

83 Pitaval, "Mariage declaré abusif," 3.

84 In fact, J. J. Scarisbrick, *Henry VIII* (London: Eyre & Spottiswoode, 1968), 196, argues that something similar happened in the case of Henry VIII's marriage to Catherine of Aragon. Catherine had previously been married to Henry's late brother, and there is good reason to suppose that this marriage had not been consummated (Catherine consistently denied consummation). The parties still asked for a dispensation from the impediment of affinity.

85 While dispensations themselves were free of charge, the parties had to make a charitable contribution for the breach of ecclesiastical law they were allowed to commit. Brillaud,

necessary because—if we assume nonconsummation—any clear statement by the parties that they wanted a dispensation from the impediment of affinity because of a *consummated* prior marriage with the bride's sister would have involved a direct lie to the pope.

What do we make of the procedure before the bishop's official? It was certainly customary to examine witnesses when fulminating a dispensation as the pope's delegate. The official did not do so in this case; he only interrogated the parties. But it is in fact difficult to see what more the official could have done. The parties' blood relationship as well as Louis Aymard's previous marriage to Charlotte's sister were probably notorious facts in the neighborhood. The only doubtful fact was whether the previous marriage had been consummated. By the time the official came to examine that question, twelve years had passed. One of the marriage partners was dead. The canon law had a procedure for establishing virginity, but that was bound to fail posthumously. It is unlikely that third parties could have thrown much light on the question, although it is of course not impossible that a servant, for instance, might have observed something useful and remembered years after the event. Luckily, we do not have to decide whether the official was remiss in his investigatory duties. For even if this had been the case, the canon law on the question was that the dispensation would still be valid as long as the facts alleged were true[86] (which brings us back to the factual question of nonconsummation once again).

There is, however, a second and more problematic aspect to the official's conduct. He granted a dispensation from the first degree of affinity. The papal brief *in forma comissaria*, which gave him his delegatory powers, was in the following terms: "*Quod primi publicae honestatis justitia, ex premissis provenientibus,… Ac tertii ex uno & quarti ex altero consanguinitatis, vel affinitatis graduum impedimentis dispensat.*"[87] The defense argued that the insertion of the words "*vel affinitatis*" gave the official authority to dispense from the first degree of affinity. While I am not very familiar with the usual style of papal dispensations, the plaintiff's explanation of these words as mere boilerplate strikes me as far more plausible. If the brief was meant to grant authority to dispense from the first degree of affinity, this would have been its most important and far-reaching aspect. So why tack it on—almost as an afterthought—at the

Traité Pratique, 177. Here, the parties paid a *componende* of 24,000 livres. By constrast, the *componende* for a dispensation from the impediment of public honesty would have cost around 500 écus. Pitaval, "Mariage declaré abusif," 46–47.

86 Brillaud, *Traité Pratique*, 214.

87 See supra n. 32.

very end? And why not specify the degrees of affinity that might be dispensed from, like the brief did for the impediments of public honesty and consanguinity? I take "*vel affinitatis*" to be part and parcel of the immediately preceeding phrase "*tertii ex uno & quarti ex altero consanguinitatis.*" Therefore, if these two words gave the official power to dispense from the impediment of affinity (which is doubtful), they only gave that power for the third and fourth degrees.

Finally, there is the act of celebration, which had neglected to mention the dispensation and the publication of banns, and there had been a mere two witnesses. The Ordonnance of Blois (1579) required three banns, of which the last two might be dispensed from, and four witnesses. A succession of seventeenth-century royal enactments reiterated these provisions and stipulated that marriages without the proper formalities would be void ("nuls et non valablement contractez").[88] However, we have it on pretty good authority that seventeenth-century French courts did not take this strict line. They distinguished[89] between the marriages of minors and the marriages of persons over twenty-five. For the latter group, banns were not deemed essential, and two witnesses sufficed for marriage validity.[90] Since Charlotte and Louis Aymard were in their late thirties and early forties, respectively, at the time of their marriage,[91] the ceremony's formal irregularities should not have attracted the sanction of nullity.

8 Conclusion

To sum up: Unlike Pitaval, I do not think that the court relied on the question of consummation to decide the case. If the outcome of the case had depended

88 Ordonnance of December 1606, art. 12. See also Ordonnance of January 1629, art. 29 ("non valablement contractés"); Declaration of 26 November 1639, art. 1. Reprinted in Le Ridant, *Code Matrimonial*, 24–27, 38–39.

89 The distinction was suggested by art. 5 of the Declaration of November 26, 1639, which—rather than expressly invaliding the informal marriages of "majeurs"—prescribed that the children of such marriages should be "incapables de toutes successions." See Le Ridant, *Code Matrimonial*, 44–45.

90 Brézolles, *Traité*, 2:185–6 (on the lack of banns), 209 (two witnesses sufficient for validity). Emil Friedberg, *Das Recht der Eheschliessung* (Leipzig: Verlag von Bernhard Tauchnitz, 1865), 522.

91 The first application for a dispensation mentioned that Charlotte was twenty-five (Pitaval, "Mariage declaré abusif," 5), which would have made her about thirty-seven at the time of her marriage. Louis Aymard was thirty at the time of his first marriage (Pitaval, "Mariage declaré abusif," 46), and approximately forty-two at the time of his second marriage with Charlotte.

on this factual question, I doubt that the court would have reached the result it did: The standard of proof was very high to dissolve a *de facto* marriage of long standing.[92] And the evidence on the question of consummation was not conclusive. Rather, I believe that the court could decide the case on two points of law. The official's dispensation was invalid because he lacked the requisite authority. The papal dispensation *in forma commissaria* did not give him power to dispense from the first degree of affinity. The dispensation the official actually granted was therefore invalid. One might be tempted to argue that the official's (invalid) dispensation from the first degree of affinity included an implicit (and valid) dispensation from the first degree of public honesty. After all, public honesty was the "lesser" impediment. While at first sight this is an attractive argument, I do not think that it withstands closer inspection. The rule was that the parties had to get the *right* dispensation, that is, the one for the impediment that *actually applied* between them. It did not matter whether the dispensation they obtained was larger or harder to get than they one they needed. Their marriage would still have proceeded without the requisite dispensation and hence be invalid.[93] There was a limited exception where an impediment of affinity necessarily implied an impediment of public honesty (as would be the case where one partner had a consummated prior marriage with the other partner's blood relative). In such a case, the dispensation from the impediment of public honesty (which had arisen while the first marriage was yet unconsummated) was implicitly included in the dispensation from the impediment of affinity (which arose when the first marriage was consummated). However, the principle of implicit dispensation could not be invoked where only one *or* the other impediment—rather than both impediments—applied, as in our case.[94] Moreover, the marriage suffered from a second flaw. The dispensation had not been confirmed by registered letters patent, as was required by the *Libertés de l'église gallicane*. While this was only a private work and not a royally sanctioned enactment, we know that at least some French *parlements* disregarded papal documents that lacked royal authorization.[95] It is quite possible that the *parlement* in this case did.

Pitaval's case shows that—as a site of production and reproduction and the connecting point of important intimate, economic, political, and social

92 Donahue, *Law, Marriage, and Society*, 572. While Donahue's statement applies to the attitude of late medieval church courts, *ancien régime parlements* might have been similarly reluctant to invalidate a marriage of long standing where doubts remained.

93 Schulte, *Handbuch des katholischen Eherechts*, 366.

94 Scarisbrick, *Henry VIII*, 184–87.

95 See supra n. 73.

interests—marriage was central to a number of groups in early modern France: to the couples themselves, their families, the church and its officials, as well as to the kings and their *parlaments*. It also shows that by the seventeenth century, family and state power had largely overwhelmed church influence in this area and that this power shift could disadvantage the couple. On my reading of *Mariage declaré abusif*, a state court held that Charlotte's inherited property (rather than being disposed of in accordance with her marital donation) would ascend back to her bloodline of origin because her marriage to Louis Aymard lacked adequate state authorization.

Bibliography

Affre, Denis-Auguste. *L'appel comme d'abus, son origine, ses progrès et son état présent.* Paris: A. Le Clerc, 1845.

Brézolles, Ignace Moly de. *Traité de la jurisdiction ecclésiastique contentieuse*. vol. 1 part 2 and vol. 2 part 4. Paris: Nyon l'ainé & La Porte, 1769.

Brillaud, Privat-Joseph. *Traité pratique des empêchements et des dispenses de mariage*. Paris: Wattelier, 1884.

Brinkmann, Rudolf. *Wissenschaftlich praktische Rechtskunde*, vol. 1. Schleswig: Taubstummen-Institut, 1831.

Dauchy, Serge and Véronique Demars-Sion. "La non-motivation des décisions judiciaries dans l'ancien droit: principe ou usage." *Revue historique de droit français et étranger* 82 no. 2 (2004): 223–39.

Donahue Jr., Charles. *Law, Marriage, and Society in the Later Middle Ages: Arguments About Marriage in Five Courts*. Cambridge: Cambridge University Press, 2007. https://doi.org/10.1017/CBO9780511511776.

Dupin, André Marie Jean Jacques. *Libertés de l'église gallicane: Manuel du droit public ecclésiastique français.* Paris: Henri Plon, 1860.

Esmein, Adhémar. *Le mariage en droit canonique.* 2 volumes. Paris: Receuil Sirey, 1929.

Friedberg, Emil. *Der Missbrauch der geistlichen Amtsgewalt und der Recurs an den Staat.* Tübingen: Laupp, 1863.

Friedberg, Emil. *Das Recht der Eheschliessung in seiner geschichtlichen Entwicklung.* Leipzig: Verlag von Bernhard Tauchnitz, 1865.

Friedman, Richard D. "Standards of Persuasion and the Distinction between Fact and Law." *Northwestern University Law Review* 86, no. 4 (1992): 916–42.

Gaudemet, Jean. *Le mariage en Occident: les mœurs et le droit.* Paris: Ed. du Cerf, 1987.

Génestal, Robert. *Les origines de l'appel comme d'abus: notes de cours publiées par les soins de Pierre Timbal.* Paris: Presses Universitaires de France, 1951.

Gibert, Jean-Pierre. *Consultations canoniques sur le sacrement de mariage.* Paris, 1750.

Halpérin, Jean-Louis. "Les styles judiciares, des traditions nationales?" *Droit et Société* 91, no. 3 (2015): 491–504.

Hanley, Sarah. "Engendering the State: Family Formation and State Building in Early Modern France." *French Historical Studies* 16, no. 1 (Spring 1989): 4–27.

Hanley, Sarah. "Family and State in Early Modern France: The Marriage Pact." In *Connecting Spheres: Women in the Western World, 1500 to the Present*, edited by Marilyn J. Boxer and Jean H. Quataert, 53–63. New York/Oxford: Oxford University Press, 1987.

Hanley, Sarah. "'The Jurisprudence of the Arrêts': Marital Union, Civil Society, and State Formation in France, 1550–1650." *Law & History Review* 21, no. 1 (Spring 2003): 461–510.

Kelly, John N. D. *The Oxford Dictionary of Popes.* Oxford: Oxford University Press, 1986.

Laboulaye, Edouard. "Libertés de l'église gallicane." *Revue historique de droit français et étranger* 4 (1858): 477–503.

Lawson, Gary. "Proving the Law." *Northwestern University Law Review* 86, no. 4 (1992): 859–904.

Le Ridant, Pierre. *Code Matrimonial, ou recueil des édits, ordonnances & déclarations sur le mariage.* Paris: Herissant, 1766.

Lefebvre-Teillard, Anne. "Marriage in France from the Sixteenth to the Eighteenth Century: Political and Juridical Aspects." In *Marriage in Europe, 1400–1800*, edited by Silvana Seidel Menchi, 261–93. Toronto: University of Toronto Press, 2016. https://doi.org/10.3138/9781442625488.

Lettmaier, Saskia. "Marriage Law and the Reformation." *Law and History Review* 35, no. 2 (May 2017): 461–510. https://doi.org/10.1017/S0738248017000104.

Lottin, Alain. *La désunion du couple sous l'ancien régime.* Paris: Ed. Universitaires, 1975.

Noonan, John T., Jr. *Power to Dissolve: Lawyers and Marriages in the Courts of the Roman Curia.* Cambridge: Harvard University Press, 1972.

Perray, Michel du. *Traité des dispenses de mariage.* Paris, 1719.

Pitaval, François Gayot de. *Causes célèbres et intéressantes, avec les jugemens qui les ont décidées.* vol. 1. Paris: Guillaume Cavalier, 1735.

Pitaval, François Gayot de. *Causes célèbres et intéressantes, avec les jugemens qui les ont décidées.* vol. 7. Paris: Guillaume Cavalier, 1739.

Pothier, Robert Joseph. *Traité du contrat de mariage.* 2 vols. Paris: Debure, 1771.

Scarisbrick, J. J. *Henry VIII.* London: Eyre & Spottiswoode, 1968.

Schmoeckel, Mathias. "Vor §§ 1313–1320—Auflösung der Ehe." In *Historisch-kritischer Kommentar zum BGB*, vol. 4, Familienrecht, edited by Mathias Schmoeckel, Joachim Rückert, and Reinhard Zimmermann, 303–455. Tübingen: Mohr Siebeck, 2018.

Schulte, Johann Friedrich von. *Handbuch des katholischen Eherechts.* Gießen: Verlag der Ferber'schen Universitäts-Buchhandlung, 1855.

Schwab, Dieter. *Grundlagen und Gestalt der staatlichen Ehegesetzgebung in der Neuzeit bis zum Beginn des 19. Jahrhunderts*. Bielefeld: Verlag Ernst und Werner Gieseking, 1967.

Waterworth, James. *The Council of Trent: The Canons and Decrees of the Sacred and Oecumenical Council of Trent.* London: Dolman, 1848.

Witte, John, Jr. *From Sacrament to Contract: Marriage, Religion, and Law in the Western Tradition*. 2. ed. Louisville, KY: Westminster John Knox Press, 2012.

CHAPTER 11

Marriage Law between East and West: Charles Maigrot's *Dissertatio de Matrimonio Sinarum*

Stuart M. McManus

From my experience, Charlie's teaching and scholarship always displayed two virtues in particular: philological rigor and interpretative subtlety. Most graduate students probably first encountered the former in his legal history seminar. There, he would sail through page after page of Latin from various periods, pausing only to exhort us to learn other relevant languages in words to this effect: "If you really want to get into the head of someone in another legal system, it really helps to understand the language of that legal system. If that is not possible, then get yourself a teacher who knows it well."

In addition to counsel always to engage with legal sources in the original language, or more frequently *languages*, and to pay constant attention to the problems of transmission in print and manuscript, students were also treated to a masterclass in textual exegesis. Here, Charlie's approach is perhaps best summarized in his aptly-titled essay *Methodus ad facilem historiarum cognitionem*:

> I [...] try to let the text speak to me. What is it saying? Don't assume that the words mean what you think they mean. Why is the author saying this? What is he (or occasionally she) assuming that I may or may not know? Can I figure out from what the text says, what those assumptions might be? Is there other evidence as to what they might be? What is there about the context of the text that might allow me to understand the answers to the previous questions?[1]

As we all know, in Charlie's work this powerful combination of philological rigor and interpretative subtlety was most frequently applied to medieval English law, and in particular cases related to marriage from the ecclesiastical courts. This was a world, he demonstrated, that saw constant interactions

1 Charles Donahue Jr., "*Methodus ad facilem historiarum cognitionem*: Autobiographical and Methodological Reflections," in *Texts and Contexts in Legal History: Essays in Honor of Charles Donahue*, ed. John Witte, Jr., Sara McDougall, and Anna di Robilant (Berkeley: The Robbins Collection, 2016), 12.

 | DOI:10.1163/9789004710696_013

between legal traditions that are often considered separately, such as English common law, Roman law, and canon law, and was shaped by myriad other social, political, and religious factors, as well as the personalities of individual jurists. Together, these considerations created the rich context of Charlie's variety of legal scholarship that ranged from deeply-researched monographs to meticulously-produced editions of unpublished texts.

For those of us interested in other topics and legal traditions, the enduring value of this approach was not necessarily in its particular conclusions, but in the way that it served as a model that could be applied to other times and places. In what follows, therefore, I want to offer my own *actio gratiarum* to Charlie in the form of a study that applies, as best as my humble powers permit, some elements of the method that his work magisterially exemplifies.

In particular, I want to introduce a hitherto unknown early modern manuscript treatise on a topic that Charlie made his own: marriage law. The treatise, entitled *De matrimonio Sinarum dissertatio,* survives among the various extant papers left by the Paris Foreign Missions Society priest, Charles Maigrot (1652–1730), a leading figure in the Chinese Rites Controversy (the debate on the permissibility of certain traditional practices to Chinese Christians that eventually caused an irreparable rift between the papacy and the Qing). In this bilingual Latin-Chinese work of considerable erudition, Maigrot discusses the similarities and differences between Catholic and Chinese marriage with reference to a vast array of classical and contemporary Chinese sources (that he cites at length and in the original language at the foot of each page) with the ultimate aim of creating a model for the sacrament among China's Catholics. In other words, this learned missionary strained every scholarly sinew to build up a comparative framework for understanding marriage in these two distant, but not always so dissimilar, parts of the early modern world. This said, he did not skimp on details of Chinese family formation that would have been rather alien to many of his intended readers. While Chinese men had wives, he noted, they also had concubines and other sorts of subordinate, sexually available women. There were also different sorts of concubines, some of whom were "strictly slaves" (predominately those, he believed, sentenced to penal servitude), and others more akin to secondary wives. Maigrot's treatise is therefore a fascinating forgotten antecedent to modern comparative approaches to the world's diverse legal systems.[2]

2 Charles Donahue Jr., "Comparative Law Before the *Code Napoléon*," in *The Oxford Handbook of Comparative Law*, ed. Mathias Reimann and Reinhard Zimmermann (Oxford: Oxford University Press, 2006), 3–32.

1 The Text and Its Context

Maigrot's *De matrimonio Sinarum dissertatio* is a treatise of around 75,000 words in Latin plus around 40,000 Chinese characters that survives in at least three manuscripts, two in the dazzling Biblioteca Casanatense in Rome and one in the archives of the Paris Foreign Missions Society.[3] It is divided into just four extensive chapters that treat, in turn:

1. On the laws governing Chinese marriage
2. On the impediments to Chinese marriages
3. On Chinese marriage rites
4. On the validity of Chinese marriages for Christian converts

Judging from its structure, style, and location in the archive, it was clearly written as a complement to Maigrot's five-part *De Sinica Religione Dissertationes* that covered Chinese classics (Dissertation 1), whether the Chinese had always been atheists (Dissertation 2), ancestor workshop (Dissertation 3), and the cult of Confucius (Dissertation 4).[4] Both represent essentially massive works of commonplacing, combined with comparative analysis and finally conclusions regarding the validity of Chinese customs from a Christian perspective. However, this is not to say that the bulk of these treatises are just mindless repetitions of Chinese sources. Rather, they represent the careful marshalling of relevant passages from a vast array of texts, from dynastic law codes, to classical texts, and recent Chinese encyclopedias. These are carefully noted in the original language (with no translations) in footnotes that sometimes dwarf the original Latin text and bespeak the careful application of early modern European scholarly practices to Chinese texts.[5] As Maigrot himself described, his method was humanistic and his reading centered on two texts above all, the *Great Qing Code* and the *Book of Rites*:

3 Charles Maigrot, *De matrimonio Sinarum dissertatio*, Rome, Biblioteca Casanatense, ms 1632, fols 1r–89v; ms 2455, fols 397r–532v; Paris, L'Institut de recherche France-Asie, Ancient, ms 467. Throughout this essay, I quote from the first Casanatense manuscript (henceforth *De matrimonio Sinarum*).

4 Rome, Biblioteca Casanatense, mss 2452–2455; Paris, L'Institut de recherche France-Asie, Ancient, mss 456–465. The only real scholarship on these extensive and erudite treatises is: Thierry Meynard 梅謙立, "Shiba shiji chu Bali waifang chuanjiaoshi Yandang 'Zhongguo zongjiao silun' shougao lun fojiao 十八世紀初巴黎外方傳教士顏璫《中國宗教四論》手稿論佛教," *Foguang xuebao* 佛光學報 5.2 (2019): 143–220.

5 Anthony Grafton, *The Footnote: A Curious History* (Cambridge, MA: Harvard University Press, 1997), 150–55.

> Experience has taught me that in individual cases it is necessary to make recourse to original sources to avoid grave errors, unless this is impossible. This is particularly important among the Chinese whose words are less than trustworthy. The chief books are both the *Book of Rites* and the codex of laws, by which China is governed today. In the said code, the ancient laws are to a large degree expounded and validated. There are also the ancient books of rituals, among which is the *ŷ ly* [禮記, *Liji, Book of Rites*]. Whatever is of any value in the books of ritual has been collected in these two [i.e. the law code or the *Book of Rites*.] Therefore, I will relate here in a certain order those things from the books that seemed to me to be of some use. And having laid out these principles, I will consider some of the difficulties related to Chinese marriage.[6]

Here, Maigrot puts forward an expansive understanding of Chinese "law" as including not only dynastic law codes (which contained a mixture of criminal law, administrative law, and ritual instructions), but also canonical Chinese classics that possessed important normative value as well.[7]

It is also worth noting that Maigrot was in a privileged position to undertake this sort of scholarship because of his long (although not uncontroversial) experience in the Qing Empire by the time he came to compose his *De matrimonio Sinarum dissertatio.* After a doctorate in theology from the Sorbonne, he joined the Paris Mission Society and departed for Asia in 1681. Following a short period in Siam, he arrived in Fujian [arch. Fukien] in 1684. There, he quickly rose in the mission hierarchy, being appointed vicar apostolic of Fukien in 1687 and becoming titular bishop of various other provinces, underlining the high esteem in which he was held in Rome. Like non-Jesuits such as the Franciscan Antonio a Santa Maria Caballero (1602–1669), he was opposed to the so-called "Ricci method" championed by the Society of Jesus that permitted the use of

6 *De matrimonio Sinarum,* fol. 1r: "Me enim experientia docuit singulis in rebus, ad fontem esse recurendum; sin minus fieri non potest, ut graviter non erretur; et maxime quidem apud Sinas, quorum dictis fidem habere minus tutum est; praecipui vero libri sunt uterque rituum liber, et legum codex, quibus hodie China regitur. Quo in codice antiquae leges magna ex parte exhibentur et corroborantur; sunt et alii veteres rituum libri; qualis ille est, qui *ŷ ly* apallatur; sed quae in illis alicuius momenti sunt, in duobus memoratis collecta fuere. Itaque illis ex libris, quae alicuius esse utilitatis mihi visa sunt, certo hic ordine referam; iisque positis veluti principiis, nonnullas difficultates expendam, quae ad Sinarum matrimonium spectant."

7 Tomas Duve, "Rechtsgeschichte als Geschichte von Normativitätswissen?," *Rechtsgeschichte—Legal History* 29 (2021): 41–68.

pre-existing Chinese terminology to describe Christian concepts and allowed converts to engage in ancestor worship and the Confucian cult.

In 1693, Maigrot put the cat among the pigeons when he mandated that Christians in his province abstain from participating in ancestor worship, venerating Confucius and reading "superstitious" books, such as the *Book of Changes* (*Yijing*, 易經), a fundamental text in the Chinese canon. He also banned the use of longstanding Chinese religious terms to refer to the Christian God, such as *shangdi* (上帝, "high god") and *tian* (天, "heaven"), favoring instead the recently coined *tianzhu* (天主, "heavenly lord"). This approach would eventually be accepted by the papacy (despite the protestations of the Jesuits at the imperial court) that in 1702 sent the infamous papal legate Charles-Thomas Maillard de Tournon (1668–1710) to Beijing to outline the new rules for Chinese Christians. In 1706, Tournon called Maigrot to Beijing to speak to the Kangxi Emperor. When Maigrot eventually met Kangxi (*r.* 1662–1722) in his Mongolian summer retreat in Chengde in August 1706, his spoken Hokkien (rather than Mandarin, which resulted in a Jesuit having to act as his translator) and embarrassed attempts to explain the rationale behind the Papacy's draconian demands did not impress the Qing emperor. There are also reports that he struggled to read even simple Chinese texts, although this may have been an attempt to discredit him further. In the end, the emperor was so annoyed with Tournon and Maigrot that he banished them from his realm, with particular imperial ire reserved for Maigrot whom Kangxi considered a menace to harmony in the provinces. He also stated clearly that it was Maigrot's lack of flexibility that necessitated the implementation of a registration system for Christian missionaries. After being briefly imprisoned, Maigrot traveled to Rome via Macau and Ireland. He lived out his days in the Eternal City, where he meditated on the lamentable Chinese Rites Controversy that he had inadvertently started, and composed works related to it, including the *De matrimonio Sinarum dissertatio*.[8]

While less famous than the tussles over the name for God and ancestor worship, the validity of Chinese marriage rituals (both before and after conversion) was nonetheless also a thorny issue during this period of the Chinese Rites Controversy. Indeed, long before Maigrot's arrival in the Qing realm missionaries had begun writing treatises in European languages on Chinese marriage customs and parallel works in Chinese explaining Christian marriage to converts. Marriage was an important topic for missionary writers in the Ming

8 Claudia von Collani, "Charles Maigrot's Role in the Chinese Rites Controversy," in *The Chinese Rites Controversy. Its History and Meaning*, ed. David E. Mungello (London: Routledge, 1994). 149–83; Litian Swen, *Jesuit Mission and Submission: Qing Rulership and the Fate of Christianity in China, 1644–1735* (Leiden: Brill, 2021), 130–38.

and Qing empires (as well as in other missionary fields like Japan and India), because Catholics considered it a sacrament—a key outward sign that led the believer to salvation—and one that was expected of the laity. Potential diversions from Catholic orthodoxy among converts in matrimony had significant implications for the ultimate success of the mission. It was therefore far from a peripherical issue.[9]

However, missionaries were divided about the best way to proceed in Qing China. The Jesuits who had dominated the mission for over a century had been keen to be as flexible as possible, often tacitly accepting elements of Chinese marriage that would have raised eyebrows in Rome (e.g. easy divorce, the private nature of the ceremony, etc.). While they outwardly forbade Chinese Christians from using divination to find an auspicious date and from bowing to statues of Chinese deities during the ceremony, in practice they did little to stop it. The Jesuits had also obtained a papal privilege to allow mixed marriages between Christian and non-Christian spouses (*disparitas cultus*). Despite this, their acceptance of the practice was continually criticized by more hardline adherents to the letter of canon law. This included Maigrot, who challenged the status quo and the arguments in favor of the Jesuits' position outlined by the Augustinian friar Álvaro de Benavente (1647–1707), who argued 1) that there were not enough Christians in China to offer Chinese Christians suitable marriages to fellow Christians (i.e. those of the right social class and with a different surname), 2) that mixed marriages were present during the early Church and so should be permitted in young churches as in China, and 3) that the prohibition had not been truly promulgated in China in the first place and so should be given no weight there.[10] This is not to mention the presence of secondary wives and concubines in many elite households, which also caused significant concerns for missionaries. This is not merely because marriage was supposed to be exclusive. Sending them away in the interests of adhering to the Christian ideal of monogamy brought dishonor to the household. If this happened, the women were probably also sold to other men as concubines, again a less than ideal outcome from the perspective of both Christian and elite Chinese observers.[11]

9 On similar issues in Japan, see Jesús López-Gay, *El matrimonio de los japoneses; problema, y soluciones según un ms. inédito de Gil de la Mata, s.j. (1547–1599)* (Rome: Libreria dell'Università gregoriana, 1964).

10 Rome, Biblioteca Casanatense, ms 2455, fols 540r–596r.

11 Claudia von Collani, "Mission and Matrimony," in *Missionary Approaches and Linguistics in Mainland China and Taiwan*, ed. Wei-ying Ku (Leuven: Leuven University Press, 2001), 11–31. In addition, on the unlawful, but apparently rather frequent, practice of

2 Missionary Ethnology and Comparative Law

The first three sections of the *Dissertatio de matrimonio Sinarum* provide a detailed account of Chinese marriage drawn from a variety of works, including dynastic law codes, classical literary-*cum*-philosophical texts, and popular encyclopedias, which are all cited at length in extensive Chinese footnotes. While by the standards of modern scholarship these normative works admittedly fall short of describing the full historical reality, they nonetheless do offer a snapshot of the frameworks privileged by the Qing cultural and administrative elite, who referred to such texts when adjudicating cases.[12] For instance, Maigrot quotes the all-important definition of marriage that is set out in the *Book of Rites* and was widely repeated in later encyclopedic works, such as the Song-era Imperial Reader (太平御覽, *Taiping yulan*):

> Marriage is the harmonious union of two families with different names, with a view, in an upward way, to perform ritual duties to the ancestors and, in a downward way, to secure the continuance of the family line.[13]

To achieve these twin goals, marriages were generally arranged through intermediaries who had a responsibility to determine that there were no impediments to the match.[14] Such stumbling blocks included already being married (and not having divorced), physical disabilities, consanguinity, and having the same surname (sometimes a serious obstacle because of the limited number of Chinese surnames and the clan structure of village societies). All these restrictions and more applied to imperial officials, who were banned from taking a wife from the area where they were posted. The rationale here was to prevent officials becoming too integrated into local society and thereby losing objectivity in administration.[15]

---

wife-selling, see Matthew Harvey Sommer, *Sex, Law, and Society in Late Imperial China* (Stanford: Stanford University Press, 2002), 57–64.

12 Philip C. Huang, *Civil Justice in China: Representation and Practice in the Qing* (Stanford: Stanford University Press, 1996); Yue Du, "Concubinage and Motherhood in Qing China (1644–1911): Ritual, Law, and Custodial Rights of Property," *Journal of Family History* 42, no. 2 (2017): 162–83.

13 *De matrimonio Sinarum*, fol. 7r: n. 10c: 婚禮者，將合二姓之好，上以事宗廟，而下以繼後世也 . See also in "Hunyi 昏義" of *Liji* 禮記 and "Hunyinshang 婚姻上" of *Taiping Yulan* 太平御覽.

14 Huang, *Civil Justice in China*, 56–58.

15 *De matrimonio Sinarum*, fol. 18r.

Of paramount concern to the drafters of the Ming and Qing Codes was transparency on the part of families and matchmakers, with particular attention paid to age, health (especially serious illnesses such as leprosy), natural or adopted status, and the status of the mother (i.e. wife or concubine). Indeed, the punishments for those who deceived the other party (e.g. by hiding certain information or substituting a different child for the one promised) were severe.[16] Provided that all the prerequisites were met, marriages were formalized in either a written contract or an unwritten "private arrangement" (*siyue*, 私約). Unfortunately, the dynastic codes give little sense of the form these marriage contracts and oral agreements should take, with ritual formularies (often of a very local nature) providing the actual models for marriage contracts.[17]

Specific marriage rituals were also mandated, as Maigrot explained in detail in Book 3 of the *Dissertatio*:

> China abounds in marriage rites, as much as in other facets of life. These rites constitute the chief aspect of the duties of human life. Indeed, we have said that the rites of marriage are in great part a means to teach the people what the separation of women from men ought to be. They say that this separation and division of women from men sees to it that a father loves his offspring more as he is sure that it is his own. From this arises the distinction of sons from other relatives; and from the same principle different rites for the diversity of persons have their origin. When this diversity of rites is exactly observed, all things are in order and peace reigns. If on the other hand, the separation between men and women is purposefully undermined, humans (namely because of fear or the presumption of more sex) decline to the condition of beasts.[18]

16 See *Da Ming Lü* [The Great Ming Code] 大明律, Chapter 6 Marriage, Article 1 Marriage (戶律婚姻男女婚姻), https://ctext.org/library.pl?if=gb&res=2671; exact wording used also in *Da Qing Lüli* [*Great Qing Laws and Precedents*] 大清律例, Article 101 Marriage (戶律 婚姻, 一百零一條男女婚姻), https://ctext.org/library.pl?if=gb&res=6315.

17 For examples of such documents, see P. H. Hase, *Custom, Land and Livelihood in Rural South China: The Traditional Land Law of Hong Kong's New Territories, 1750–1950* (Hong Kong: University Press, 2013).

18 *De matrimonio Sinarum*, fol. 33v: "Sinae, cum ceteris in rebus, tum ubi de matrimonio agitur, ritibus abundant; quibus in ritibus praecipuam humanae vitae officiorum rationem constituent: eo vero, magna ex parte matrimonii ritus spectare diximus, ut populi edoceantur quantam faeminarum a viris seiunctionem esse oporteat. Haec enim, inquiunt, faeminarum a viris separatio et sejunctio facit, ut pater prolem eo plus diligat, quo suam esse certior sit. Hinc oritur filiorum ab aliis consanguineis distinctio; eodemque ex principio diversi pro personarum diversitate ritus originem habent. Quae rituum diversitas cum exacte servatur, omnia sibi constant, et in alta pace versantur; si e contrario

Maigrot argued that this separation between the genders was at the core of the ideal Chinese household, and even extended to the use of separate wells for men and women.

One of the rituals that preserved this separation was the reliance on a matchmaker (*internuncius*), with the bride and groom not being allowed to meet before the wedding, when gifts were also exchanged. In addition, the *Book of Rites* mandated six rituals (六禮) to be completed to enact a marriage:

1. Rite of Selection (納采)
2. Asking for the Name (問名)
3. Consulting the Oracle (納吉)
4. Sending the Bride-price (納徵, later known also as 納幣)
5. Choosing the Wedding Day (請期)
6. Receiving the Bride (親迎)[19]

Each of these Maigrot treats in turn in his *Dissertatio de matrimonio Sinarum*, providing a Hokkien Romanization and an extensive description of each ritual and its constituent parts, while noting that in the interests of time these might be reduced to the first, third, and sixth rituals, with the omitted parts effectively folded into these three.

All of the above applied to marriages between Qing subjects. However, in the context of a large-scale and multiethnic empire like that of the Qing, there were of course specific scenarios that had to be dealt with. For instance, Maigrot notes that the family's right to choose a spouse was derogated in the case of marriage of a Chinese person (*Sina*) to a "foreigner" (*alienigena*), which he interprets to mean a Muslim.[20] Here, Maigrot quotes from the chapter in

---

viri et faeminae sedulo ab invicem non sejungantur, homines (propter metum scilicet et praesumptionem concubitus) ad belluarum conditionem redigi necesse est."

19 "Hunyi" of *Liji*.

20 *De matrimonio Sinarum*, fol. 1v: "Derogatur parentum auctoritati duobus in casibus; primus est, si matrimonii pactio fiat cum alienigenis; id est, ut glossa interpretatur, cum Mahumetanis: tunc enim parentibus de matrimonis liberorum non prorsus consentientium pacisci; non licet quippe, inquiunt, cum alienigenarum vivendi ratio, a Sinarum vivendi modo discrepet; aequum est, ut sponte, et prosus quisque arbitrio matrimonium cum illis contrahat. Alius casus est, si pater, aut aliud ad quem id spectat, si modo superior sit in genere consanguinitatis, de filii praefecturae, aut negotiationis causa, domi absentis matrimonio pactus fuerit; ille vero pactionis inscius, uxorem duxerit: valet enim matrimonium: sit tamen nuptiae factae nondum fuerint, pacto quod ille inserat, rescisso, eam in uxorem accipere tenetur, quam parentes aut memorati consanguinei cooptarunt: cui legi qui non paruerit, fuste octogies perentitur, ac nihlo secius cum illa contrahere tenetur, quam illi parentes aut consanguinei, destinarant."

the *Great Qing Code* relating to: "Marriage to foreign barbarians and colored-eyed people" (外番色目人婚姻). This was an updated version of the Ming Code that had spoken of marriage to "Mongolians and colored-eyed people" (戶律蒙古色目人婚姻) and in theory required Mongolians and other outsiders to marry Chinese people.[21] The motivation for mandating interracial marriage between Chinese and Mongols in the Ming Empire (1368–1644) was born out of a desire to create ethnic harmony through assimilation following the Mongol Yuan Dynasty (1271–1368) that had applied different laws to Mongols and Chinese. With the advent of the Qing's new conquest dynasty, centered on a caste of Steppe nomad warriors that overcame the Ming in the 1640s and within a century had tripled the size of their previous empire, the rule was not strictly speaking reversed. Rather, the *Great Qing Code* added an exception that "anyone who cannot find a willing person as a spouse is not within this limitation and they can marry their own kind" (不願為婚姻者，聽從本類自相嫁娶，不在禁限). This allowed the persistence of the Manchus as a ruling ethnic class with separate rights and privileges that endured into the twentieth century.[22]

The final section of the *Dissertatio* then turns to the serious problems with Chinese marriage from a Catholic perspective: its non-consensual nature and the relative ease of divorce. Children seemed to have no freedom to choose their spouses, who were often selected for them before they came of age.[23] Indeed, the Ming and Qing Codes explicitly set out the line of succession if the potential spouse had no surviving parents who could choose their marriage partner for them:

> In the first instance, it is to be observed that the parents decide with regard to the marriage of their children, and especially of their daughters, with almost the highest right. Not only do parents have that right, but in the case of them being absent, those who are superior in the bloodline also have it, i.e. in addition to both parents, the grandfather and grandmother, uncles and their wives, aunts, brothers and sisters elder by birth (those who are blood relatives). They decide on the marriage of inferiors and juniors in the bloodline. But note that only agnatic relatives are

21 *De matrimonio Sinarum*, fol. 20r. See also *Da Ming Lü*, Chapter 6 Marriage, Article 1 Marriage, Article 16 Marriage with Mongolians and Color-Eyed Peoples (戶律蒙古色目人婚姻) and *Da Qing Lü jijie fuli* [Great Qing Code Collection with Explanations and Precedents] 大清律集解附例, Article 119 Marriage with Foreigners and Color-Eyed Peoples (戶律 婚姻，一百一十九條外番色目人婚姻), https://ctext.org/library.pl?if=gb&res=2397.

22 Yonglin Jiang, *The Mandate of Heaven and the Great Ming Code* (Seattle: University of Washington Press, 2011), 126.

23 *De matrimonio Sinarum*, fol. 61r–62r.

> considered to be of the same bloodline, i.e. those from the father's side. Cognatic relatives, i.e. those who are from the mother's side, are considered outsiders when the affairs of the family are discussed, as if they were dealing with the affairs of a different family.[24]

In the footnote, Maigrot quoted the *Great Qing Code*:

> Marriages should all be decided and arranged by grandparents and parents. If one has no grandparents and parents, one should let the remaining relatives arrange the marriage. If a woman's husband has died and wishes to remarry, she should follow her mother's wishes.[25]

Of course, all this is hard to stomach for an orthodox Catholic. Gesturing to natural law (and to Aquinas in particular), Maigrot argues that no one should have an unlimited right to choose another's marriage partner. In addition, no contract could be entered into without the consent of the contracting parties, and marriage was no different in this regard. Indeed, a daughter was not her father's slave to dispose of as he wished, and any marriage entered into unwillingly was invalid. On the other hand, the mere fact that the partner was *chosen* by another was not necessarily a problem if the bride or groom willingly accepted the choice.[26] Here, Maigrot refers to the decretal of Boniface VIII, *si*

---

24 *De matrimonio Sinarum,* fol. 1r: "Observandum in primis est parentes de filiorum, ac praecipue filiarum matrimonio, summo fere jure decernere: neque parentes solum id juris habent, sed in illorum defectu, qui superiores sunt in genere consanguinitatis, quales sunt, praeter utrumque parentem, avus et avia, patrui et illorum uxores amita, fratres et sorores natu [ii in quam consanguinei] majores; de inferiorum juniorumque, consanguinorum, matrimonio decernunt: cum autem consanguinei dicuntur, agnati, qui a patre sunt, vulgo intelliguntur: cognati enim, et qui a matre sunt ubi de familiae rebus agitur, ferre uti extranei habentur; utpote qui ad aliam familiam spectant."

25 See *Da Qing Lüli*, Article 101 Marriage, Precedent 1: 嫁娶皆由祖父母,父母主婚,祖父母父母俱無者,從餘親主婚,其夫亡,攜女適人者,其女從母主婚。.

26 *De matrimonio Sinarum,* fol. 62r: "De illis igitur matrimoniis, idem dicendum est, ac de sponsalibus, quae pro filiis, a parentibus fiunt, quae per accedentem filiorum consensum valida efficiuntur; ut habetur cap. si infantes si infantes ad invicem, vel unus major septennio, et alter minor, sponsalia contraxerint ipsi, vel parentes pro eis; nisi per cohabitationem eorum mutuam, seu alias verbo vel facto, ipsorum liquido appareat eosdem in eadem voluntate factos majores septennio perdurare; sponsalia eiusmodi, quae ab initio nulla erant per lapsum dicti temporis, minime convalescent; et ideo cum sint nulla ratione defectus consensus, publicae honestatis justitiam non inducunt. Porro ex sponsalibus, quae parentes pro filiis puberibus, vel impuberibus plerumque contrahunt ipsi filii si expresse consenserint, vel facile; ut si praesentes fuerint, nec contradixerint, obligantur; et ex eis critur justitia publicae honestatis. Et est idem si filii tempore sponsaliorum absentes, et etiam ignorantes, eadem sponsalia post scientes ratificaverint facile vel

infantes, which states that even if a couple were betrothed as young children, they still have to enter the marriage voluntarily once they reach a more appropriate age, and "such betrothals, which were null from the beginning, are in no way strengthened merely by the passage of time."[27]

At this point, Maigrot changes tack and makes an argument that is highly revealing of his view of some of the excesses of Chinese marriage: the most important thing for Chinese Christians to bear in mind is that parents should be neither "merchants" nor "tyrants." In particular, it was reprehensible to force a child to marry someone for the sake of acquiring wealth through a large brideprice. Rather, the character and virtues of the match should always be of primary concern.[28] Indeed, Maigrot underlines that the most significant difference between Chinese and Catholic marriage was that the husband's family provided a brideprice, and not vice versa. This led the common people to call marriage a "sale" (*emptio*), although the more dignified members of society called the part of the brideprice paid alongside the contract a "pledge" (*arrha*) and the part paid immediately before the marriage a "voluntary contribution" (*honorarium*).[29] Should the woman die before the wedding day, the dynastic codes stated that the first payment need not be returned since profit and loss were of no importance in the matter.[30] Yet, as Matthew Sommer has shown, the profit motive was often the driving force behind marriages in Qing China,

---

expresse: alias ex sponsalibus contractis a parentibus, pro filiis, nec ipsi filii obligantur, nec publicae honestatis justitia inde surgit."

27 Sext. X 4, 2, 1: "Si infantes ad invicem, vel unus maior septennio, et alter minor, sponsalia contraxerint ipsi, vel parentes pro eis, nisi per cohabitationem eorum mutuam, seu alias verbo vel facto ipsorum liquido appareat, eosdem in eadem voluntate factos maiores septennio perdurare: sponsalia huiusmodi, quae ab initio nulla erant, per lapsum dicti temporis minime convalescunt."

28 *De matrimonio Sinarum,* fol. 62r: "monendi tamen Christiani sunt, ut se librorum patres non mercatores, uti ipsi Sinae loquuntur, aut tyrannos esse meminerint; neque illos invitos ad matrimonium adigant: hoc [illis] quoque inculcandum est, quod et ipsi Sinae magnopere commendant, ut ad futuri sponsi vel sponsae indolem et virtutem attendant, non ad diuitios aut ad pecuniam, qua plerumque filias plus offerenti divendunt: mirum itaque incommode inde oriantur."

29 *De matrimonio Sinarum,* fol. 1v–2r.

30 *De matrimonio Sinarum,* fol. 2r: n. 4c: 若已定婚, 未及成親, 而男女或有身故者, 不追財禮 (cf. *Da Ming Lü*, Chapter 6 Marriage, Article 1 Marriage and *Da Qing Lüli*, Article 101 Marriage, Precedent 1).

4d: 財禮, 若娶者知情, 則不論已未成婚, 俱追入官, 不知者, 則追還主 (cf., *Da Ming Lü*, Chapter 6 Marriage, Article 18 Punishment for the arranger of marriage and the matchmaker in illegal marriage 嫁娶違律主婚媒人罪 and *Da Qing Lüli*, Article 117 Punishment for the arranger of marriage and the matchmaker in illegal marriage 戶律婚姻, 一百一十七條嫁娶違律主婚媒人罪).

while concubines and even wives might be sold *in extremis*.[31] Not that Christian observers were the only ones to criticize the transactional nature of some marriages in pre-modern China. Maigrot quotes the Song-dynasty historian Sima Guang (司馬光) who in his *Wengong Shuyi* (溫公書儀) complains that:

> People are greedy nowadays and ask the amount of the dowry when arranging a wife [for their son], or ask how much the brideprice is when marrying off their daughter. And they make a contract requesting a certain sum, as if they were selling their daughter. And there are cases of people breaking the contract and engaging in deception after the daughter is married. This is like selling animals or slaves. How can it be a marriage worthy of a scholar?[32]

While forced marriages violated the canon-law principle of consent, profit-driven marriages violated the norms of Christian virtue and universal human dignity.

The other potential stumbling block with Chinese marriage was the ease of divorce. Indeed, the *Great Qing Code* set out the general principle that "if the couple's relationship is not peaceful and both wish to divorce, they may as it is hard to maintain their relationship when they no longer have any affection; they should not be punished."[33] Such sentiments were entirely lacking in the Christian worldview. However, this is not to say that divorce was loosely regulated in China. Quite the opposite. Instead of merely requiring dispensation from the ecclesiastical authorities, divorce was permitted in a range of specific circumstances that were set out in detail in the *Great Qing Code*, following earlier dynastic codes:

---

31 Beverly Jo Bossler, *Courtesans, Concubines, and the Cult of Female Fidelity: Gender and Social Change in China, 1000–1400* (Cambridge, MA: Harvard University Asia Center, 2012); Matthew Harvey Sommer, *Polyandry and Wife-Selling in Qing Dynasty China: Survival Strategies and Judicial Interventions* (Oakland: University of California Press, 2015); Keith McMahon, *Celestial Women: Imperial Wives and Concubines in China from Song to Qing* (Lanham: Rowman & Littlefield, 2016).

32 *De matrimonio Sinarum*, fol. 4r: 7d: 今世俗之貪鄙者, 將娶婦, 先問資裝之厚薄, 將嫁女, 先問聘財之多少。至于立契約云, 某物若干, 某物若干, 以求售其女者, 亦有既嫁而復欺紿負約者。是乃駔儈賣婢鬻奴之法, 豈得謂士大夫之婚姻哉？See also Sima Guang 司馬光, *Wengong Shuyi* 溫公書儀, juan 3, https://ctext.org/library.pl?if=gb&res=4; Patricia Buckley Ebrey, *The Inner Quarters: Marriage and the Lives of Chinese Women in the Sung Period* (Berkeley: University of California Press, 1993).

33 *De matrimonio Sinarum*, fol. 12r: n. 16a: 若夫妻不相和諧, 而兩願離者, 情既已離, 難強其合, 不坐。Cf. *Da Ming Lü*, Chapter 6 Marriage, Article 17 Divorce the Wife (戶律婚姻出妻) and *Da Qing Lüli*, Article 116 Divorce the Wife (戶律 婚姻, 一百一十六條出妻).

"Seven reasons for divorce" (七出)

1. "cannot bear son" (無子)
2. "adultery" (淫佚)
3. "lack of filial piety to parents-in-law" (不事舅姑)
4. "slander" (多言)
5. "committing theft" (盜竊)
6. "envy" (妬忌)
7. "serious illness" (惡疾)

"Three impediments to divorce" (三不去)

1. "wife mourned for 3 years (for either father- or mother-in-law)" (與更三年喪)
2. "someone was poor before and is now rich" (前貧賤後富貴)
3. "wife has no family to return to" (有所娶無所歸)[34]

The *Great Qing Code* (although not earlier codes) then clarified that the presence of one of the three impediments always trumped a reason to divorce. The only exception to this was the case of adultery.[35] Men who divorced without cause, or those who did not divorce when the situation demanded it were to be punished with 80 strokes of a heavy pole (*zhang*, 杖). If someone divorced his wife for committing one of the "seven reasons for divorce," but there existed one of the "three impediments to divorce," then he was to receive the punishment two classes lower (i.e., 60 strokes) and should remarry his wife.[36] However, there were exceptions to this rule. The old and disabled were allowed to pay a smaller fine, while magistrates had the right to exercise discretion and demand a large fine instead of corporal punishment in other circumstances too.

Given the nature of Chinese divorce as Maigrot understood it, the question then arose whether it was compatible with orthodox Catholicism (*An Sinarum matrimonia, non obstante faciendi certis in casibus divortii licentia, valida sint?*). In the final section of the *Dissertatio*, Maigrot argues that the Decretal

34 *De matrimonio Sinarum,* fol. 12r.

35 *Da Qing Lüli*, Article 116 Divorce the Wife, Precedent 1: 凡妻犯七出之狀, 有三不去之理, 不得輒絕。犯奸者不在此限。.

36 *De matrimonio Sinarum,* fol. 12r: n. 16c: 若犯義絕, 應離而不離者, 亦杖八十。(Cf. *Da Ming Lü*, Chapter 6 Marriage, Article 17 Divorce the Wife and *Da Qing Lüli*, Article 116 Divorce the Wife).

16d: 凡妻于七出無應出之條, 及於夫無義絕之狀, 而擅出之者, 杖八十。雖犯七出, 有三不去, 而出之者, 減二等, 追還完聚。(Cf. *Da Ming Lü*, Chapter 6 Marriage, Article 17 Divorce the Wife and *Da Qing Lüli*, Article 116 Divorce the Wife).

of Innocent III *Gaudemus* solved this problem when it stated that those who had married (or divorced) according to the norms of their previous religion could not simply abandon their existing wives. Baptism washed away sins; it did not dissolve marriages (*baptismus enim abluit peccata, non dirimit matrimonia*). Any divorces and remarriages that predated conversion similarly had to be accepted.[37]

The only exception, provided by a papal privilege for China, was if the wife left her husband because he converted. In this case, he was allowed either to remarry or to be considered married to one of his other wives or concubines. Natural law (*lex naturae*), which bound Chinese and Europeans alike, did not permit polygamy and so the latter was a convenient way to kill two birds with one stone. In other circumstances (or if there were still wives or concubines remaining), a Chinese convert had to send them away once he had settled on a wife. While this was technically divorce, it did not present a problem, Maigrot argued, as every society permitted divorce in some circumstances, from the Romans to the Jews.[38] He did not feel the need to expand on this point, leaving that particular can of worms for later writers.

Second marriages after the death of a husband or wife were also a tricky topic, as they had been in the legal systems of Europe since antiquity.[39] Maigrot judged the situation in China to be as follows:

> As regards men, it is not uncommon for marriages to be repeated after the wife has died. In ancient times, however, after the death of a wife rulers did not assume another wife, lest the records of the two wives of one ruler be placed in the ancestral temples, wherefore in the book *çhūn' çhieu* (*chunqiu*, 春秋, i.e. *Spring and Autumn Annals*) the ruler of the *Lù* (魯) Kingdom is marked by the fact that after the death of his wife who was the legitimate *muńg çhìi* (*mengzi*, 孟子), he elevated one of his concubines, *chuńg çhìi* (*zhongzi*, 仲子) to the rank of wife.
>
> As regards wives, it is forbidden for the wives of high officials to remarry after the death of their husbands. If they do marry, they are to be struck with a club one hundred times, and they are to be cut off from the rank of emperor. The woman is to be separated from her second husband, and the pledge (*arrha*) is given to the treasury, if they have done it

37 *De matrimonio Sinarum*, fol. 62v; Innocent III, X 4.19.8 (*Gaudemus*).

38 *De matrimonio Sinarum*, fol. 62v.

39 Charles Donahue Jr. and Stuart M. McManus, "*Philologia Ancilla Historiae:* An Emendation to *Lex Burgundionum* 42,2," *Zeitschrift der Savigny-Stiftung für Rechtsgeschichte: Romanistische Abteilung*, 131 (2014): 414–23.

knowingly; otherwise, as is the custom, if she is innocent or unconscious of the fact, she is absolved of the crime; and the innocent bridegroom receives the pledge. With permission, the wives and concubines of other men may enter into marriage with another man after the death of a husband. If her or the deceased husband's relatives have any reservations, she cannot marry. And no punishment is allowed to be visited onto the grandfather and grandmother, father or mother, who force the widowed granddaughter or daughter into another marriage; others of the same bloodline as the widow are to be treated the same; in case of their death, there is a mourning period of one year. If they force the widow to marry or become a concubine, they should be beaten with a club eighty times; other inferiors of the same bloodline should be beaten sixty times. Even the grandfather and grandmother of the deceased husband receive this punishment. And others of the same bloodline, in case of their death there is a mourning period of one year, if they force the widow to remarry. The widow herself should return to the husband's house and is allowed to live there unmarried; and he is not subjected to punishment, and his pledges are to be returned to him.[40]

40 *De matrimonio Sinarum,* fol. 14v: "Quo ad viros spectat, nuptias, uxore mortua, repetere nihil frequentius: antiquitus tamen dynastae, mortua uxore, alteram non assumebant, ne duarum unius dynastae uxorum tabellae in progenitorum templis collocarentur: quare in libro *çhūn' çhieu* [*chunqiu,* 春秋], Regni *lù* [魯] dynasta notatur, quod mortua uxore, legitima *muńg çhìi* [*mengzi,* 孟子], unam e concubinis, *chuńg çhìi* [*zhongzi,* 仲子] ad uxoris gradum extulerit. Quod attinet ad uxores, prohibetur ne praefectorum uxores alteri, defuncto marito, nubant: sique nupserint, centies fuste percutiuntur, obtentoque ab imperatore gradu excidunt: mulier a secundo viro separatur: qui matrimonio ex utraque parte praefuerunt, fuste sexagies plectuntur; arrhaeque fisco addicuntur; si modo id illi scienter fecerint: alias, ut moris est, innocens, seu rei inscius paena eximitur; sponsoque innocenti arrhae restituntur. Aliorum viroum uxores et concubinae, pro nutu, alteras, defuncto marito, nuptias ineunt: cogitamen a suis, aut mariti consanguineis non possunt ad nubendum: ac licet lata paena nulla sit in avum et aviam, patrem et matrem, qui neptam aut filiam viduam, ad alteras nuptias adegerint; alii tamen viduae consanguinei; quorum in obitu, uno anno lugetur, si viduam, sive uxor illa fuerit, sive concubina, ad nubendum adigant, fuste octogies; alii inferiores consanguinei sexagies verberantur: qua etiam paena tenentur avus et avia mariti defuncti; aliique eiusdem consanguinei, quorum in obitu, uno anno lugetur; si viduam ad nubendum cogant: ipsi viduae ad mariti domum reverti, et in nuptam vivere licitum est: neque ille cui illa nupsit paenae subiiciur: suaeque illi arrhae restituuntur."

In this section, Maigrot drew largely on the dynastic codes, which had clear instructions regarding remarriage and its implications for filial piety towards family members who forced women to remarry for their own ends.[41]

3 Concubines and Slave Marriage

In contrast to Christian marriage, Chinese customs permitted a husband to take concubines in addition to a wife. According to Maigrot, most of these were effectively low-status wives who were subordinate to the man's one high-status wife. This "wife" in the narrow sense of the word was "the companion of the husband ... and in a certain way equal to him" (*mariti socia ... et quodam modo aequalis*) and also head of the female section of the household. Drawing on a quotation of unknown origin, he also notes that the children of concubines had a different status to those of the main wife:

> The legal wife is *di*, all concubines are *shu*. And thus, the son of the legal wife is called the "*di*-son"; the son by a concubine is called a "*shu*-son."[42]

At the imperial level, this convention of taking concubines, Maigrot explained, developed some time after the reign of the Emperor Yao (帝堯), who is the last emperor who is recorded as having two wives.[43] Despite the appearance of simple monogamy, the emperor nonetheless had an even more complicated domestic arrangement than the rest of the population. In addition to a main wife who was "queen" (*hou*, 后), he had several other tiers of wives. Ritual dictated that this include three secondary wives (*furen*, 夫人) who assisted in imperial rituals, nine tertiary wives (*pin*, 嬪) who were akin to the wives of the highest officials, twenty-seven quartary wives (*shifu*, 世婦) who were equivalent to the wives of middle-rank officials, eighty-one quintary wives (*yuqi*, 御

41 *De matrimonio Sinarum*, fol. 15r: n. 21c 惠公欲以愛妾為夫人, 隱公欲以庶弟為嫡子, 聖人以為諸侯不再娶, 於禮無二適。孟子入惠公之廟, 仲子無祭享之所, 為別立宮以祀之, 非禮也。.
21d: 知係居喪及命婦, 而其為婚姻者, 主婚人各減五等, 財禮入官, 不知者, 不坐, 仍離異, 追財禮。(Cf. *Da Ming Lü*, Chapter 6 Marriage, Article 5 Marriage in the Mourning Period and *Da Qing Lüli*, Article 105 Marriage in the Mourning Period 戶律 婚姻, 一百零五條居喪嫁娶).

42 *De matrimonio Sinarum*, fol. 8r: n. 11d: 嫡, 又嫡庶。庶, 眾也。正妻為嫡, 眾妾為庶也。故正室所生, 為嫡子；眾妾所生, 為庶子也。凡繼統者, 先嫡而後庶。嫡子雖幼, 庶之長者, 不敢與衡。古聖王之貴嫡如此。.

43 *De matrimonio Sinarum*, fol. 9r.

妻) who were equivalent to the wives of commoners and finally a large number of senary wives who were concubines (*qie*, 妾).[44] Except for the queen, all of these women were given the honorific title of "concubine," presumably because to be an imperial concubine was considered a high honor. From the footnotes to *De matrimonio Sinarum*, it is clear that Maigrot sourced all this information directly from the *Book of Rites* or commentaries on the text, such that his description reflected the normative position of the imperial court.[45]

High-ranking officials (*viris aliqua praefectura, aut gradu insignibus*) were also strictly forbidden to have more than one wife, but were permitted to take concubines. Male commoners were in the same situation, although their ability to take concubines was subject to certain restrictions. To have a concubine, commoners had to be over forty years old and lack children. If these conditions were not met, they were to be punished with forty strokes, with similar

44 *De matrimonio Sinarum*, fol. 9v–10r: "Imperator unicam uxorem habet, quae regina vocatur *heu* [后], quasi quae dignitate imperatorem proxime sequitur vel *fȳ* [妃], quasi quae eius socia est. Uxor dynastarum appellatur *fu jiñ* [夫人], quasi quae dynastam in sacrificiis scilicet et rebus domesticis adiuvet. Praefectorum superiorum uxor vocatur *jû jiñ* [孺人], quasi quae illorum ditionis sit. Uxor inferiorum praefectorum dicitur *fú jiñ* [婦人], quasi quae subdita illis est. Uxor aliorum e plebe nuncupatur *çhȳ'* [妻], socia et qualis *çhȳ'* autem nomen generale est, quod uxorem significat, cuius cumque uxor illa sit, atque ut uxor specifice a concubina magis destinguatur, *chińǵ çhȳ'*, quasi quae proprie uxor est, interdum appellatur. Verum imperator alias habet diversique ordinis uxores, aut quasi uxores, quae iisdem pleraeque quibus dynastarum, praefectorum, et pleblaeiorum uxores nominibus appellantur, suntque omnes in summa quinque ordinum. Primi ordinis, uxorem uti diximus, unicam habet, quae ipsa Regina et sola proprie uxor est. Tres habet secondi ordinis, quae vocantur *fú jiñ*. Novem tertii ordinis nuncupatas *pīn* [嬪], quasi hospites; respondentque uxoribus superiorum praefectorum, licet eodem nomine non vocentur. Quarti ordinis uxores habet septem et viginti, vocanturque *xý fú* [世婦]. Quinti denique ordinis sunt una et octoginta; hae vocantur *yú çhȳ'* [御妻], eodem, quo ad litteram *çhȳ'* nomine, quo uxores generatim appellantur licet hanc litteram, ubi de imperatore agitur, alio modo interpretentur; ubi enim de vulgi uxoribus, aequalem et sociam; ubi de imperatoris uxoribus quinti ordinis, subditam significare dicitur. Sexti ordinis uxores dici eae possunt, quae concubinae, *çhiĕ* (妾), quasi adjunctae nuncupantur; harum certus numerus non statuitur, quia sunt sine numero. Dynastae triplicis tantum ordinis uxore habent, eam nimirum, quae unica est, diciturque *fū jin*; aliae quarum numerus non refertur, nuncupantur *xý fú*, et *çhȳ'* praeter concubinas, quas etiam pro nutu dynastae congregant. De dynastis refertur, quod cum nuptiae cum uxore legitima et primi ordinis fiunt, haec duas secum puellas adducit, quas veluti pro munere, marito donat. Eadem et duae quas adducit puellae, duas singulae socias habent, ita ut novem simul dynasta uxores ducat. Atque hae omnes, praeter illam, quam proprie uxorem esse diximus, concubinae etiam appellantur, quo sensu, concubinae nomen honorificum est: idem vero nomen valde demissum et vile reputatur, cum ad eas appellandas adtribetur, quae sponte et ultro se prostituunt."

45 *De matrimonio Sinarum*, fol. 10r: n. b. Cf. "Quli shang 曲禮上" and "Hunyi" of *Liji*.

punishments for treating a wife like a concubine.[46] In reality, however, Maigrot tells us that wealthy commoners frequently had "gaggles of concubines" (*greges concubinarum*). These concubines were bound to their owners/husbands, although not vice versa, with divorce being relatively straightforward.[47] Since dynastic codes contained prohibitions against it, it is also clear that concubines and perhaps even wives were hired out or pawned. This was punishable by sixty strokes for the man. There was no punishment for the commodified woman.[48] Indeed, recent investigation has shown that wife-selling was common, especially among the impoverished during the early Qing period.[49]

In the course of his larger discussion, Maigrot slowly reveals that there was a further type of concubine quite different from the secondary wives to whom he devotes most of his discussion: the so-called "slave concubine" (*concubina serva*). Drawing on the Yuan-era encyclopedia *On the Origins of the Six Types of Character* (*Liuxugu*, 六書故), Maigrot argued that there were both noble (*gui*, 貴) and base (*jian*, 賤) concubines, with slave concubines belonging to the latter category:

> In ancient times, when nobles married a wife from another country, that country would let the *di* (娣) (the woman's sister or in some cases younger relatives) follow her, some others also let *ying* (媵) women (female companions) follow her as well. All those below the wife are concubines, and they are noble concubines. Those recorded as *ping* (聘, a formal invitation to marriage) are wives, and those who are recorded as *ben* (奔, running) are concubines. Base concubines are those confiscated by the

46 *De matrimonio Sinarum,* fol. 11r: n. 14b: 凡以妻為妾者, 杖一百, 妻在以妾為妻者, 杖九十, 並改正。Cf. *Da Ming Lü*, Chapter 6 Marriage, Article 3 Disorder among Wife and Concubines (戶律婚姻妻妾失序) and *Da Qing Lüli*, Article 103 Disorder among Wife and Concubines (戶律 婚姻, 一百零三條妻妾失序).

47 *De matrimonio Sinarum,* fol. 13v: "Concubina pariter strictius marito obligatur, sed non vicissim: quamquam negari nonpossit, quin initus cum concubina contractus aliquam stabilitatem habeat; si quidem a mera mulieris conductione distinguatur: ut enim uxorem sic et concubinam, ad certum tempus, sive breue, sive diuturnum accipere non licet: sed eo non obstante, maritus concubinam pro nutu, aut certe multo, quam uxorem liberius dimittit."

48 *De matrimonio Sinarum,* fol. 11r: n. 15b: 凡將妻妾, 受財立約出典, 驗日暫雇與人為妻妾者, 本夫杖八十, 典雇女者, 父杖六十, 婦女不坐。Cf. *Da Ming Lü*, Chapter 6 Marriage, Article 2 Pawning and Renting of Wife and Women (戶律婚姻典雇妻女) and *Da Qing Lüli*, Article 102 Pawning and Renting of Wife and Women (戶律 婚姻, 一百零二條典雇妻女).

49 Sommer, *Polyandry and Wife-Selling in Qing Dynasty China*, 120–24.

> government due to lawbreaking; they are called *qi* (奚, arch. "slave") or *piqie* (婢妾, "slave concubine").[50]

Such "lawbreaking" was likely not on the part of the woman herself, but on the part of her husband, father, or other male relative, in whose household she resided thereby making her liable for seizure. In addition to such penal concubines, the dynastic codes studied by Maigrot also make clear that such "base" people might also include members of "musical households" (*yuehu,* 樂戶), a hereditary group that it was considered inappropriate for officials to marry or take as concubines, although in practice many men took musician women as concubines as they possessed a range of useful skills.[51]

While Maigrot devotes relatively little space to these slave concubines, he returns to the topic of slavery throughout the *De matrimonio Sinarum dissertatio*, thereby offering us important insights into their plight. Indeed, slavery was a topic of considerable interest to Maigrot, since in Christendom marriage was considered a good that should not be forbidden even to slaves with canonists arguing that the will of a slave's master should be restricted by the need to permit and maintain the bonds of Christian matrimony.[52] In the case of Qing China, Maigrot argued, slavery came into being through various means. This included condemnation for a crime, which Maigrot described as legitimite and typically lasting three years (i.e. not being perpetual slavery). War captives could also be enslaved, although he states that in contrast to Christendom this is almost unheard of in China and those that are sold as such have usually been kidnapped. A legitimate expression of *patria potestas* when a household was suffering from extreme want, sale by parents was also common, he argues, which could either be perpetual or for a period of time. However, parents were always able to buy the child back for the same sum they had sold it for. This issue then elicits a long comparison between Chinese and ancient Jewish slavery, which prescribed freeing a slave after seven years of servitude.

---

50 *De matrimonio Sinarum,* fol. 10r: n. 10i 古者諸侯娶于一國, 其國以娣從, 他國亦以女媵, 自正室而下, 皆妾也, 此貴妾也, 記曰聘則為妻, 奔則為妾。賤妾也, 又有罪沒入官者, 曰奚, 曰婢妾。.

51 *De matrimonio Sinarum,* fol. 19r: n. 28a: 娶樂人為妻妾。28b: 凡文武官并吏, 娶樂人妓者, 杖六十, 並離異。不給于官吏, 亦不還樂工, 斷離歸宗, 財禮入官。Cf. *Da Ming Lü*, Chapter 6 Marriage, Article 13 Marrying Musician as Wife and Concubine (戶律娶樂人為妻妾) and *Da Qing Lüli*, Article 113 Marrying Musician as Wife and Concubine (戶律 婚姻, 一百一十三條娶樂人為妻妾).

52 Stuart M. McManus, "*Partus Sequitur Ventrem* in Theory and Practice: Slavery and Reproduction in Early Modern Portuguese Asia," *Gender & History* 32, no. 3 (2020): 542–61, https://doi.org/10.1111/1468-0424.12499.

The final point of origin for slavery in China was self-sale, which arose because of the unstable nature of Chinese society according to Maigrot:

> While there is scarcely any nobility in China except that which one acquires by one's own efforts or money (for money is the source of great nobility and power in China), if these fail, the other trappings generally disappear, too: China is full of men who, despite the fact that their parents or fathers have been adorned with governorships and dignities, are reduced to the order of the plebeians, and lie in the dust.[53]

Harsh though it was, Maigrot accepted self-sale induced by poverty as legitimate on the authority of Justinian's *Institutes* (1.3.1), as well as Aquinas (*Super sententiis,* lib. 4 d. 36 q. 1 a. 3 co.), who believed that men did not need the permission of their wives to sell themselves into slavery.[54]

Nonetheless, poverty and the slavery that it induced had important implications for penal law that needed to be discussed. According to the dynastic law codes, both male (*nu,* 奴) and female (*bi,* 婢) slaves should receive eighty strokes for running away, while concubines should receive fewer because they had a higher status. If a slave girl got married after having run away, she was to receive 100 strokes.[55] Slavery also impinged directly on marriage, since marriage between people of different statuses was tightly regulated.[56] Officials were not allowed to marry their sons to simple commoners, while a marriage between a commoner and a base person (such as a slave) was punished harshly. Although there were likely multiple possible motivations for such mixed marriages, the Chinese texts available to Maigrot suggested that they were driven primarily by the husband's sexual impulses. As the *Book of Rites* underlined: "Confucius said, 'the love of virtue should be the same to the love of sex.' A landed prince

---

53 *De matrimonio Sinarum,* fol. 16v: "Licet vix ulla proprie apud Sinas nobilitas praeter illam sit, quam sua quasque industria aut pecunia comparat; magna enim in China nobilitas potestasque est pecunia, quae si deficiat, cetera plerumque evanescunt. Plena autem China est hominum, qui cum eorum parentes aut avi prefecturis et dignitatibus ornati fuerint, ad plebaeiorum ordinem redacti iacent in pulvere."

54 *De matrimonio Sinarum,* fol. 88r.

55 *De matrimonio Sinarum,* fol. 13r: n. 18e: 若婢背家長在逃者，杖八十，奴逃者罪亦同。因而改嫁者，杖一百。減妾二等問，給還家長。Cf. *Da Ming Lü,* Chapter 6 Marriage, Article 17 Divorce the Wife and *Da Qing Lüli,* Article 116 Divorce the Wife.

56 *De matrimonio Sinarum,* fol. 16v: "nihilominus in matrimoniis contrahendis, ad quandam conditionum aequalitatem attendant ..." n. 25a: 良賤為婚姻。Cf. *Da Ming Lü,* Chapter 6 Marriage, Article 15 Marriage between Good and Base (戶律婚姻良賤為婚姻) and *Da Qing Lüli,* Article 115 Marriage between Good and Base (戶律 婚姻，一百一十五條良賤為婚姻).

should not lower himself to fish for sex, and a gentleman should distance himself from sex, to be a model for the peasants."[57] Perhaps because modern Christian thought also developed within a hierarchical vision of society and put a premium on abstinence, Confucius's view chimed with Maigrot, who apparently accepted without question the twin premises that marriages should be between social equals and that libido had to be mastered.[58]

4 Conclusion

While the preceding discussion falls far short of the high standards set by Charlie's work, a close reading of Maigrot's bilingual Latin-Chinese treatise nonetheless underlines how a washed-up French missionary to China was able to build up a comparative framework for understanding how Christian marriage should be understood in the Chinese context. This involved careful philological work as he read and commonplaced a variety of legal and literary texts in classical Chinese that are preserved in the treatise's extensive and not unerudite footnotes. From these texts (as well as his long experience in Fujian), Maigrot knew that there were some stubborn sticking points for anyone wishing to harmonize Catholic and Chinese marriage norms, including the lack of a requirement for consent, the relative ease of divorce, and the prevalence of secondary wives and concubines of different statuses. Of course, by the standards of modern scholarship, Maigrot fell short of providing a flawless outline of the laws, customs, and rituals related to marriage in China and their comparative development from antiquity to the early modern period. For instance, his treatise almost entirely lacks an understanding of the fundamental importance of maintaining lineages.[59] Yet, there is little that comes close in its level of detail, even from the Jesuits. The surviving draft of the *De matrimonio Sinensium* of Prospero Introcetta (1626–1696) perhaps comes closest with its extensive marginal quotations from the *Classic of Filial Piety* (*Xiaojing,* 孝經) and other classical Chinese and canon-law texts.[60]

57 "Fangji 坊記" of *Liji*: 子云：好德如好色，諸侯不下漁色，故君子遠色，以為民紀。.

58 Sara F. Matthews-Grieco, "Love, Sex, and Sexuality," in *A Cultural History of Marriage in the Renaissance and Early Modern Age*, ed. Joanne M. Ferraro (New York: Bloomsbury, 2021).

59 David Faure, *Emperor and Ancestor: State and Lineage in South China* (Stanford: Stanford University Press, 2007).

60 Prospero Intorcetta, *De Matrimonio Sinensium*, 24 July 1668, Rome, Archivum Romanum Societatis Jesu, Opp. NN. 147–48, 1r–15v.

While nowadays the importance of comparative law is generally explained as expanding the student's understanding of the possible, for Maigrot and many of his contemporaries the comparative study of marriage in China and in western canon law had almost the opposite purpose. For this missionary recently returned to Europe with his tail between his legs, the application of the humanistic and ethnographic tools of missionary philology to comparative study of Chinese marriage served a higher purpose: the identification of diversions from Catholic orthodoxy and their implications for the China mission and Chinese converts. Given the empire's vast population of around one hundred and fifty million souls (one quarter of the world's population), these were pressing questions indeed.

Acknowledgments

The author would like to acknowledge the assistance of his research assistants, Terence Chan and Alan Ling, as well as the financial support of a United College Endowment Fund Research Grant, Chinese University of Hong Kong.

Bibliography

Manuscripts

Prospero Intorcetta. *De Matrimonio Sinensium*, 24 July 1668. Rome, Archivum Romanum Societatis Jesu, Opp. NN. 147–48, 1r–15v.

Maigrot, Charles. *De matrimonio Sinarum dissertatio*. Rome, Biblioteca Casanatense, ms 1632, fols 1r–89v; ms 2455, fols 397r–532v.

Maigrot, Charles. *De Sinica Religione Dissertationes.* Rome, Biblioteca Casanatense, ms 2452–2455.

Maigrot, Charles. *De Sinica Religione Dissertationes.* Paris, L'Institut de recherche France-Asie, Ancient, mss 456–465, 467.

Printed Primary Sources

Da Ming Lü [The Great Ming Code] 大明律. https://ctext.org/library.pl?if=gb&res=2671.

Da Qing Lüli [The Great Qing Code and Precedents] 大清律例. https://ctext.org/library.pl?if=gb&res=6315.

Da Qing Lü jijie fuli [Great Qing Code Collection with Explanations and Precedents] 大清律集解附例. https://ctext.org/library.pl?if=gb&res=2397.

Sima Guang 司馬光, Wengong Shuyi 溫公書儀. https://ctext.org/library.pl?if=gb&res=4.

Secondary Literature

Amsler, Nadine. *Jesuits and Matriarchs: Domestic Worship in Early Modern China.* Seattle: University of Washington Press, 2018.

Bossler, Beverly Jo. *Courtesans, Concubines, and the Cult of Female Fidelity: Gender and Social Change in China, 1000–1400* (Cambridge, MA: Harvard University Asia Center, 2012).

Collani, Claudia von. "Charles Maigrot's Role in the Chinese Rites Controversy." In *The Chinese Rites Controversy: Its History and Meaning*, edited by David E. Mungello, 149–83. London: Routledge, 1994.

Collani, Claudia von. "Mission and Matrimony." In *Missionary Approaches and Linguistics in Mainland China and Taiwan*, edited by Wei-ying Ku, 11–31. Leuven: Leuven University Press, 2001.

Donahue, Charles, Jr. "*Methodus ad facilem historiarum cognitionem:* Autobiographical and Methodological Reflections." In *Texts and Contexts in Legal History: Essays in Honor of Charles Donahue*, edited by John Witte Jr., Sara McDougall, and Anna di Robilant, 1–21. Berkeley: The Robbins Collection, 2016.

Donahue, Charles, Jr. "Comparative Law Before the Code Napoléon." In *The Oxford Handbook of Comparative Law*, edited by Mathias Reimann and Reinhard Zimmermann, 3–32. Oxford: Oxford University Press, 2006.

Donahue, Charles, Jr. and Stuart M. McManus. "Philologia Ancilla Historiae: An Emendation to Lex Burgundionum 42,2." *Zeitschrift der Savigny-Stiftung für Rechtsgeschichte: Romanistische Abteilung*, 131 (2014): 414–23.

Du, Yue. "Concubinage and Motherhood in Qing China (1644–1911): Ritual, Law, and Custodial Rights of Property." *Journal of Family History* 42, no. 2 (2017): 162–83.

Duve, Tomas. "Rechtsgeschichte als Geschichte von Normativitätswissen?" *Rechtsgeschichte—Legal History* 29 (2021): 41–68.

Ebrey, Patricia Buckley. *The Inner Quarters: Marriage and the Lives of Chinese Women in the Sung Period.* Berkeley: University of California Press, 1993.

Faure, David. *Emperor and Ancestor: State and Lineage in South China.* Stanford: Stanford University Press, 2007.

Grafton, Anthony. *The Footnote: A Curious History*. Cambridge, MA: Harvard University Press, 1997.

Hase, P. H. *Custom, Land and Livelihood in Rural South China: The Traditional Land Law of Hong Kong's New Territories, 1750–1950*. Hong Kong: University Press, 2013.

Huang, Philip C. *Civil Justice in China: Representation and Practice in the Qing*. Stanford: Stanford University Press, 1996.

Jiang, Yonglin. *The Mandate of Heaven and the Great Ming Code*. Seattle: University of Washington Press, 2011.

López-Gay, Jesús. *El matrimonio de los japoneses; problema, y soluciones según un ms. inédito de Gil de la Mata, s.j. (1547–1599)*. Rome: Libreria dell'Università gregoriana, 1964.

Matthews-Grieco, Sara F. "Love, Sex, and Sexuality." In *A Cultural History of Marriage in the Renaissance and Early Modern Age*, edited by Joanne M. Ferraro. New York: Bloomsbury, 2021.

McMahon, Keith. *Celestial Women: Imperial Wives and Concubines in China from Song to Qing* (Lanham: Rowman & Littlefield, 2016).

McManus, Stuart M. "*Partus Sequitur Ventrem* in Theory and Practice: Slavery and Reproduction in Early Modern Portuguese Asia." *Gender & History* 32, no. 3 (2020): 542–61. https://doi.org/10.1111/1468-0424.12499.

Meynard, Thierry 梅謙立. "Shiba shiji chu Bali waifang chuanjiaoshi Yandang 'Zhongguo zongjiao silun' shougao lun fojiao 十八世紀初巴黎外方傳教士顏璫《中國宗教四論》手稿論佛教." Foguang xuebao 佛光學報 5.2 (2019): 143–220.

Sommer, Matthew Harvey. *Sex, Law, and Society in Late Imperial China*. Stanford: Stanford University Press, 2002.

Sommer, Matthew Harvey. *Polyandry and Wife-Selling in Qing Dynasty China: Survival Strategies and Judicial Interventions*. Oakland: University of California Press, 2015.

Swen, Litian. *Jesuit Mission and Submission: Qing Rulership and the Fate of Christianity in China, 1644–1735*. Leiden: Brill, 2021.

PART 3

Medieval and Early Modern Law

CHAPTER 12

Getting Ahead in a Twelfth-Century City: The Ambitious Monks of Saint-Clément, Metz

Samantha Kahn Herrick

The twelfth-century monks of Saint-Clément, Metz, commemorated the translation of their saint, in 1090, with an annual fair. For eight days each May, they hosted markets and provided entertainment. According to the charter detailing the fair's workings in the 1130s, these amusements included horse races:

> so that the memory of this translation may be kept the more joyfully and festively by those gathering at the fair, let a horse worth 15 *solidi* be presented there ... if it should please any of the laypeople amusing themselves with horse races ... to have this particular [horse] exercised against their own horses, let half of its appraised value be left to the victor and the rest assigned to the church. But if on that day this shall not have happened by evening, let the horse be given to the church without any argument.[1]

Although sport often featured in popular celebrations of saints' feasts, this provision seems unusual. Feast-day games elsewhere appear not to have involved money, at least not with the overt sanction of Benedictine monks.[2] Moreover, while 15 *solidi* likely represented the bottom of the equine market, it was a

1 *Privilegium Bischofs Hermann für St. Clemens 1090* (hereafter "Hermann"), ed. Ernst Müsebeck, "Zoll und Markt in Metz in der ersten Hälfte des Mittelalters," *Jahrbuch der Gesellschaft für Lothringische Geschichte und Altertumskunde / Annuaire de la Société d'histoire et d'archéologie lorraine* (hereafter "*ASHAL*") 15 (1903): 1–32 (edition 24–29) at 27. This charter survives in two different versions (discussed below). Müsebeck's edition includes both, designated A and B.

2 For example, Guibert of Nogent, *De vita sua sive monodiarum libri tres*, *PL* 156:837–962 at 845. See also Manfred Zollinger, "*Nundinae ludentes*. Bemerkungen zum Zusammenhang zwischen Ökonomie, Emotion und Glücksspiel auf Messen, Jahrmärkten und Kirchweihfesten vom 15. bis zum 18. Jahrhundert," *Ludica* 11 (2007): 132–50; Elizabeth Tobey, "The *Palio* Banner and the Visual Culture of Horse Racing in Renaissance Italy," *The International Journal of the History of Sport* 28 (2011): 1269–82.

 | DOI:10.1163/9789004710696_014

considerable sum.[3] A horse race orchestrated by monks offering a cash prize seems highly unusual.

It may have been one of the tactics by which the monks of Saint-Clément sought to benefit from their city's growth. From the tenth century, suburban monks developed sophisticated strategies to profit from urban expansion and, conversely, to ward off its dangers.[4] Since there is still much to learn about just how such monks operated, Saint-Clément, an important abbey located outside an important city, offers a valuable case study. Twelfth-century sources show that the monks engaged in commercial, administrative, legal, and hagiographical endeavors. While these efforts have been studied separately, they were in fact closely intertwined—as the horse race illustrates.[5] To understand how the monks of Saint-Clément operated, therefore, we must consider their various pursuits in conjunction.

1 Metz, c. 1050–c. 1130: A City in Flux

Metz was a vibrant city in the early twelfth century. Like many in the medieval West, it was in the midst of long-term economic and social change: between the tenth and the fourteenth centuries, the city's footprint doubled, and its population swelled.[6] As Metz became a thriving center of artisanal production and commerce, new groups (such as merchants and craftsmen) gained wealth and influence. Older elements (such as the local aristocracy and established

3 Evidence for the price of horses in the 1130s is scant, but see Kenneth Hodges, "Medieval Prices," *Internet Medieval Sourcebook*, accessed March 28, 2022, http://faculty.goucher.edu/eng240/medieval_prices.html.

4 To cite just a few studies, mostly relating to Lorraine: Frank G. Hirschmann, *Stadtplanung, Bauprojekte und Großbaustellen im 10. und 11. Jahrhundert. Vergleichende Studien zu den Kathedralstädten westlich des Rheins* (Stuttgart: Hiersemann, 1998); Margit Müller, *Am Schnittpunkt von Stadt und Land. Die Benediktinerabtei St. Arnulf zu Metz im hohen und späten Mittelalter* (Trier: Verlag Trierer historische Forschungen, 1993); Gisela Minn, *Kathedralstadt und Benediktinerkloster: Die Abtei St. Vinzenz und die Stadt Metz im Mittelalter* (Trier: Kliomedia, 2002); Francesca Bocchi, "Monasteri, canoniche e strutture urbane in Italia," in *Istituzioni monastiche e istituzioni canonicali in Occidente (1123–1215)* (Milan: Vita e Pensiero, 1980), 264–313.

5 Jean Schneider, *La ville de Metz aux XIIIe et XIVe siècles* (Nancy: George Thomas, 1950); Mireille Chazan, "Les Vies latines de saint Clément, premier évêque de Metz," *Francia* 31 (2004): 33–34; Eadem, "Les évêques de Metz: Clemens," in *Miracles, Vies et réécritures dans l'Occident médiéval*, ed. Monique Goullet and Martin Heinzelmann (Ostfildern: Thorbecke, 2006), 183–87.

6 Schneider, *Metz*, 27, 55–61.

religious houses) looked askance at this development. Yet they too wished to benefit from the city's rise. The situation bred anxiety and competition.

Such volatility was intensified by the Investiture Contest. Between 1073 and 1122, more than half a dozen bishops of differing allegiances were barred entry to their see, driven from it, or opposed by clerical factions.[7] More than one bishop was accused of alienating episcopal property, while local nobles reportedly seized ecclesiastical rights and possessions.[8] The city's monastic houses thus suffered, while the bishop's power eroded. Other groups, by contrast, gained influence—most notably the cathedral canons and the townspeople. In 1088, Metz's inhabitants expelled an imperial bishop, reportedly for his depredations of church property, and restored the pro-reform Hermann (r. 1073–1090), exiled several years earlier.[9] Upon Hermann's death, a faction of canons successfully rejected the emperor's candidate.[10] In 1097, however, a rival faction united with townsfolk to welcome another imperial bishop, despite a papal interdict. Moreover, they punished the cleric who placed the interdict upon the cathedral's altar by destroying his house.[11] Following the deposition

7 André Dantzer, "La querelle des investitures dans les évêchés de Metz, Toul, et Verdun," *Annales de l'Est* 16 (1902): 85–100; Schneider, *Metz*, 70–71, 77–78; Michel Parisse, "Metz dans l'Église impériale," in *Histoire de Metz*, ed. François-Yves Le Moigne (Toulouse: Privat, 1986), 110–35; Sarah Staats, "Vision of an Augustinian Canon in Lorraine: Echoes of the Investiture Conflict in the Diocese of Metz at the Beginning of the Twelfth Century," *Analecta Bollandiana* 113 (1995): 127–46; Franz-Reiner Erkens, *Die Trierer Kirchenprovinz im Investiturstreit* (Cologne: Böhlau, 1987); Müller, *Schnittpunkt*, 24–39; I. S. Robinson, *Henry IV of Germany, 1056–1106* (Cambridge: Cambridge University Press, 2003), 248, 253; Arnaud Hari, "Écrire l'histoire des évêques de Metz au Moyen Âge: Les *Gesta episcoporum* messins de la fin du VIIIe siècle à la fin du XIVe siècle," 2 vols. (Ph.D. diss., Université Paul Verlaine, Metz, 2010), 1:187–215.

8 Philipp Jaffé, *Regesta pontificum romanorum*, 2nd ed. (Graz: Akademische Druck- und Verlagsanstalt, 1956), 1:627, no. 5084; Bishop Étienne de Bar, "[Charter granted to Abbot Humbert of Saint-Clément, 1130]," (hereafter "Étienne, [1130]"), *Actes des princes lorrains*, ed. Michel Parisse, 2ième série, *Princes ecclésiastiques* 1, *Les évêques de Metz* B, *Étienne de Bar (1120–1162)* (Nancy, [1977]) (hereafter "*Actes*"), 63. See also Parisse, "Metz dans l'église impériale," 120; and the sources listed in the following note.

9 Bernoldus Sancti-Blasii, *Chronicon*, ed. G. H. Pertz, MGH SS 5 (Hannover: Hahn, 1844), 447–48; Erkens, *Trierer Kirchenprovinz*, 45–66; Schneider, *Metz*, 70–71; Hari, "Écrire l'histoire," 1:196–98; Michel Parisse and Arnaud Hari, *Catalogue historique des évêques de Metz: Le moyen âge* (Paris: LAMOP, 2015), 26–27, https://lamop.pantheonsorbonne.fr/sites/default/files/inline-files/Morceaux_choisis_Parisse_Hari_2015.pdf.

10 Bernoldus, *Chronicon*, 456.

11 Balderich, *Gesta Alberonis*, trans. Brian A. Pavlac, *A Warrior Bishop of the Twelfth Century: The* Deeds *of Albero of Trier, by Balderich* (Toronto: Pontifical Institute of Mediaeval Studies, 2008); Jörg R. Müller, Vir religiosus ac strenuus: *Albero von Montreuil, Erzbischof von Trier (1132–1152)* (Trier: Kliomedia, 2006), 90–93; Erkens, *Trierer Kirchenprovinz*,

of that bishop, in 1117 or 1118, the townspeople refused his successor entry to the city.[12] The inhabitants of Metz exhibited their strength in other matters too: they attacked a rival town between 1110–1113 and apparently swore oaths, perhaps in an attempt to form a commune.[13] To some observers, these trends marked a descent into lawlessness.[14]

Nor did the turbulence end with the Investiture Contest. When Bishop Étienne de Bar (r. 1120–1162) finally entered Metz in 1122, over the resistance of both the townspeople and most of the cathedral canons, he sought to reassert episcopal authority. Despite being the pope's nephew and the scion of a local noble family, he faced an uphill battle, for those who had benefited from the tumult sought to preserve their gains.[15] Étienne granted the townspeople a share in the city's governance and consulted them in matters such as the foundation of new religious houses.[16] In other instances, however, he worked to reverse recent trends. He clashed with his cathedral canons, strove to recover episcopal possessions and authority—often by force—and supported religious houses seeking to repair their own losses.[17] This energetic bishop thus labored to restore episcopal authority against a tumultuous backdrop, as numerous groups vied to maintain or improve their positions.

The monks of Saint-Clément were one such group. Their abbey, located about half a mile south of antique Metz, had housed the relics of the city's founding bishop, Clement, since the mid-ninth century.[18] After Bishop Adalbero I (r. 929–1162) installed Benedictine monks, around 945, cathedral

---

185–86, 231–32; Schneider, *Metz*, 71–73; Hari, "Écrire l'histoire," 1:200–203, 209; Parisse and Hari, *Catalogue*, 27–28.

12 *Vita Theogeri abbatis S. Georgii et episcopi Mettensis*, ed. Philipp Jaffé, MGH SS 12 (Hannover: Hahn, 1856), 449–79; Erkens, *Trierer Kirchenprovinz*, 232–39; Hari, "Écrire l'histoire," 1:205–10; Parisse and Hari, *Catalogue*, 28–29.

13 Erkens, *Trierer Kirchenprovinz*, 239–48; Hari, "Écrire l'histoire," 1:208–9. For the oaths, see *Vita Theogeri*, 475 and 478; Schneider, *Metz*, 74.

14 *Satira in Mettenses*, ed. E. Dümmler and H. Boehmer, MGH *Ldl* 3 (Hannover: Hahn, 1897), 618–21.

15 *Gesta episcoporum Mettensium*, ed. Georg Waitz, MGH SS 10 (Hannover: Hahn, 1852), 544 ("Continuatio prima"); Fritz Ruperti, "Bischof Stephan von Metz (1120–1162)," ASHAL 22 (1910): 1–95; Hari, "Écrire l'histoire," 1:211–13 and 216–23.

16 Schneider, *Metz*, 77–88.

17 Ruperti, "Bischof Stephan," 12–15, 41–45; Hari, "Écrire l'histoire," 1:221–35, 345–47; *Gesta episcoporum Mettensium*, 544; Étienne, [1130], 63; Schneider, *Metz*, 82; Müller, *Schnittpunkt*, 39.

18 The abbey was destroyed in 1552. Its exact location is unknown but was likely in the suburb called *ad Basilicas*; see Eugène Voltz, "L'Abbaye S. Clément de Metz: Esquisse de son histoire architecturale," *Mémoires de l'académie de Metz* (1965–66): 37–64 (repr. separately: Metz: Le Lorrain, 1968), at 37–43.

and abbey seem to have remained on good terms.[19] Over the course of the Investiture Contest, however, their relationship appears to have changed. In 1119, the abbot reportedly invited the beleaguered Bishop Theoger (r. 1118–1120) into the abbey and offered to help him enter the city. Although this plan came to naught, it suggests that the bishops' troubles had brought the abbey greater autonomy.[20] The monks had also grown more ambitious. By the early twelfth century, they wished not merely to recover what they had lost during the Investiture Contest, but also to benefit from the city's growth and to fend off potential competitors.

2 The Monks' Ambitions

To judge by the surviving records, many of the monks' ambitions concentrated on their annual fair. The charter that discussed the horse race also outlined other aspects of the fair's operation. It stated that the toll owed to the abbey on trade in livestock and "all things for sale" generally "ought to be known" (and, presumably, paid).[21] The charter pronounced the fair to be *bannal*—that is, subject to the abbey's authority like the territory that constituted its *bannus*.[22] Since the charter elsewhere decreed that justice within the abbey's *bannus* belonged to the abbot of Saint-Clément alone, it implicitly granted him jurisdiction over the fair as well.[23] Nevertheless, the charter stipulated that episcopal officials, the *advocatus* and the three *villici civitatis*, were to help ensure the fair's success.[24] They were expected to see that vendors neither left early nor failed to pay for their stalls. Should a vendor desert his stall, the *villici civitatis* were to help the abbot to recover the rent.[25] To the *advocatus* fell the task of providing a horse, worth 15 *solidi*, against which fairgoers might race their own

19 Samantha Kahn Herrick, "Friend or Foe? The Bishops of Metz in Monastic Historical Narrative, c. 1000–c. 1200," *Journal of Ecclesiastical History* 71 (2020): 253–69.

20 *Vita Theogeri*, 477–78.

21 Hermann, 27.

22 Hermann, 27. The term *bannus* originally signified a collection of abstract powers, but gradually came to designate the territory over which a lord exercised power. In Lorraine, this shift was underway at about the time this charter was produced; see the references listed in n. 38 below. The monks of Saint-Clément, as well as the bishop of Metz, used the term in both senses, even within a single document.

23 Hermann, 27.

24 Three *villici civitatis* (mentioned in version A) took over some of the authority formerly exercised by the *advocatus* (mentioned in version B) in the early twelfth century. For these offices, see Schneider, *Metz*, 77–83.

25 Hermann, 27.

beasts.[26] The charter further instructed the *advocatus* to oversee preparations for the fair "carefully" (*sollicite*) and "in no way to contradict" the abbot.[27] The effort invested in working out all these operational details reflects the fair's scale, complexity, and importance.

Real estate represented another of the monks' prime interests. South of the city, they claimed not only their abbey's suburban *bannus*, in the quarter known as *ad Basilicas*, but also those of five other nearby churches.[28] They dominated this quarter, perhaps not unexpectedly. But they held property elsewhere too, even in one of the city's most vibrant sectors.

Expanding trade was rapidly transforming Metz in the twelfth century. Craftsmen and merchants in search of better living and working conditions flocked to the area outside the ancient wall on the city's eastern side, near its secondary river, the Seille. Here they found open space, which was gradually parceled out for rent.[29] Proximity to the river drew textile workers, who needed water to process hemp into linen, and salt merchants, whose wares came down the Seille from salt fields upstream.[30] Merchants and artisans welcomed the chance to trade somewhere other than the old market and port near the cathedral on the city's main river, the Moselle, and subject to the jurisdiction of episcopal officials.[31] Between the wall and the Seille, where the city's growth was most apparent both in terms of population and economic activity, new markets and neighborhoods sprang up. Perhaps the most important were the contiguous Neufbourg and Champ-à-Seille quarters. The former grew into a thriving settlement, while the latter became the site of the city's largest market and some of its most expensive properties.[32] The development of these quarters led to their being enclosed when the wall was extended in the late twelfth century (or possibly earlier).[33]

---

26 Hermann, 27.

27 Hermann, 27.

28 Hermann, 25–26.

29 Schneider, *Metz*, 31–33, 49, 58; Minn, *Kathedralstadt*, 317–28, 336–38, 349, 265–72.

30 Gaël Brkojewitsch et al., "Nouvelles données sur le quartier Outre-Seille à Metz (Moselle) (époques romaine, médiévale et moderne): la fouille de la place Mazelle," *Revue archéologique de l'Est* 62 (2013): 283–314, http://journals.openedition.org/rae/7831; Julien Trapp and Sébastien Wagner, eds., *Atlas historique de Metz*, 2nd ed. (Metz: Éditions des Paraiges, 2015), 157.

31 Schneider, *Metz*, 29–31, 40–45; Minn, *Kathedralstadt*, 349.

32 Schneider, *Metz*, 47–48.

33 Schneider, *Metz*, 31–35; Brkojewitsch et al., "Nouvelles données."

A little further south stood Metz's ancient amphitheater and, within it, the church of Saint-Pierre-aux-Arènes.[34] In the early twelfth century, the monks of Saint-Clément sought—and received—repeated confirmation that this church belonged to them.[35] They also claimed its *bannus*, which they defined as extending northward "to the old gate, which is named for St Nicholas."[36] Jean Schneider located this gate near the Saint-Nicolas hospital, which stood just east of the city wall—precisely where the Neufbourg and Champ-à-Seille quarters were rising.[37] The claim to Saint-Pierre-aux-Arènes and its *bannus*, therefore, gave the monks a foothold in some of the city's most dynamic new sectors.

All the monks' possessions entailed valuable rights and privileges, many of which stemmed from the *bannus* and *centena* associated with them. Although the meaning and scope of these terms varied—indeed they were very much in flux at precisely this time in Metz, as elsewhere—they generally implied diverse rights over taxation, justice, and the control of economic resources ranging from communal ovens and wine production to weights and measures.[38] In claiming the *bannus* and *centena* of numerous possessions—not only churches, but also a village and agricultural sites—the monks thus

---

34 R. S. Bour and Th. Klauser, "Un document du IXe siècle: Notes sur l'ancienne liturgie de Metz et sur ses églises antérieures à l'an Mil," *ASHAL* 38 (1929): 571; Nancy Gauthier, "Metz," in *Province ecclésiastique de Trèves (Belgica prima)* (Paris: De Boccard, 1986), 35, 42; Trapp and Wagner, *Atlas historique*, 30, 33, 50; INRAP (Institut national de recherches archéologiques préventives), "À Metz, la fouille du quartier de l'amphithéâtre," last modified February 19, 2016, http://www.inrap.fr/metz-la-fouille-du-quartier-de-l-amphitheatre-4940.

35 Calixtus II, *Ex praeteritorum temporum*, ed. G. Wolfram, "Ungedruckte Papsturkunden der Metzer Archive," *ASHAL* 15 (1903): 278–323 (hereafter "Calixtus II, *Ex praet. temp.*"), at 278–80; also Michel Parisse, "Bullaire de la Lorraine (jusqu'à 1198)," *ASHAL* 69 (1969): 5–102, no. 124. This bull may have been forged, but Étienne de Bar referred to it in 1130. Étienne, [1130], 63; Hari, "Écrire l'histoire," 1:421. Étienne's confirmation of 1136 is unedited, but for a brief resumé see *Actes*, 84. Innocent II, *Pie postulatio voluntatis*, ed. Jean François et al., *Histoire de Metz*, 6 vols. (Metz: P. Marchal/Nancy: Lamort, 1769–81; repr. Paris: Éditions du Palais-Royal, 1974), 3:113–15 (hereafter "Innocent II, *Pie post. vol.*").

36 Hermann, 25 (Version B).

37 Schneider, *Metz*, 31–32.

38 Charles-Edmond Perrin, *Sur le sens du mot "centena" dans les chartes lorraines du Moyen Âge* (Paris/Nogent-le-Rotrou: Daupeley-Gouverneur, 1930), 187–90; Perrin, *Recherches sur la seigneurie rurale en Lorraine d'après les plus anciens censiers (IXe–XIe siècles)*, (Paris: [n.p.], 1935; repr. Geneva: Mégariotis, 1978); Jean-Luc Fray, "Recherches sur la seigneurie banale au XIIe siècle d'après le vocabulaire des actes des évêques de Metz (1058–1210)," in *La Seigneurie rurale en Lotharingie: Actes des 3e journées Lotharingiennes*, Publications de la section historique de l'Institut du Grand Duché de Luxembourg 102 (1986), 75–101; Müller, *Schnittpunkt*, 40, 97.

aspired to exercise wide-ranging authority.[39] In some instances they spelled out these prerogatives clearly. The charter that outlined the fair's operation and defined the *bannus* of Saint-Pierre-aux-Arènes also granted the abbey extensive jurisdiction within its holdings. It envisaged annual assemblies in the *bannus* of Saint-Pierre-aux-Arènes to handle disputes and declared the *banni* of the churches in *ad Basilicas* to be "free of any advocate and of all civic justice" and under "the providence and power of the abbot alone." It further stated that revenues arising from these churches should be gathered by monastic agents, while "everything else" pertaining to them should be "under the power and providence of the abbot and his officials."[40] The revenue that such rights could generate meant that a good deal was at stake in delineating the territory in which they applied. The monks' care in defining the *bannus* of Saint-Pierre-aux-Arènes reflected the value that developing sectors held for whoever could claim authority over them, as well as the monks' own aspirations in that regard.[41]

The monks also sought to have churches within their possession recognized as parishes. In confirming that Saint-Pierre-aux-Arènes belonged to Saint-Clément, Pope Innocent II (r. 1130–1143) expressed concern that the clergy serving it provide a worthy model to the "lay folk" (*populo*) who worshipped there. He gave the abbot of Saint-Clément the right to choose its cleric, but urged him to select "a priest, or a monk, or a cleric ... whose life should be an example to, and whose discourse edification for, the lay folk coming together there in the morning for the worship of God."[42] Such concern for the laity reflected the importance of the parish in their spiritual lives. The parish church was where the inhabitants of a particular district worshipped, received the sacraments, baptized their children, offered their tithes, and, most likely, were buried. Urban growth in this period led to the proliferation of urban parishes. In the early twelfth century, distinct urban parishes remained relatively new—Metz, like many cities, may have consisted of a single parish

39 Hermann, 25–26; Étienne, [1130], 62. For similar efforts by a neighboring abbey, see Müller, *Schnittpunkt*, 96–100, 254.

40 Hermann, 25–26. See also Perrin, *Sur le sens*, 186–87; Hari, "Écrire l'histoire," 1:422.

41 Schneider, *Metz*, 82.

42 Innocent II, *Pie post. vol.*, 114. Innocent also referred to Saint-Pierre-aux-Arènes as an *oratorium* and a *parochia*, terms that, while far from unambiguous, could designate a baptismal church and the territory served by it. For expectations of how often the laity would attend church and how often they likely did so, see Norman Tanner and Sethina Watson, "Least of the Laity: The Minimum Requirements for a Medieval Christian," *Journal of Medieval History* 32 (2006): 395–423.

until shortly before that time.[43] By the early fourteenth century, however, the city counted twenty-six parishes.[44] In Metz as elsewhere, this multiplication often resulted from the initiative of regular communities. Monks and canons frequently sought to have churches in their possession, around which new neighborhoods were rising (or were envisaged), recognized as parochial. This step would not only meet the spiritual needs of an expanding population, but would also bring whoever owned the church significant income. Parishes generated revenues from the exercise of spiritual services, such as performance of the sacraments, memorial masses, and—most lucrative of all—burials.[45] Additionally, parishes entailed tithes: parishioners were supposed to give one-tenth of their revenue to support the church and as charity. The clergy serving the parish, however, rarely received all (or even most) of this income. Instead, a large portion of the tithes usually accrued to the patron who owned the church and appointed its clergy.[46] Parishes thus represented extremely valuable assets for those who controlled them, and no doubt this prospect accounted, at least in part, for the monks' determination to see churches within their possession become parishes under their authority. The charter that discussed the fair and

---

43 Christopher Brooke, "The Missionary at Home: The Church in the Towns, 1000–1250," in *The Mission of the Church and the Propagation of the Faith*, ed. C. J. Cuming (Cambridge: Cambridge University Press, 1970), 59–84; Michel Aubrun, *La paroisse en France: des origines au XVe siècle* (Paris: Picard, 1986); F. L. Ganshof, *Étude sur le développement des villes entre Loire et Rhin au moyen âge* (Paris: Presses Universitaires de France, 1943), 47–49; John Hine Mundy, "The Town's Parishes from 1150–1250," in *Studies in the Ecclesiastical and Social History of Toulouse in the Age of the Cathars* (Aldershot: Ashgate, 2006), 13–44; François Comte and Emmanuel Grélois, "La formation des paroisses urbaines: les exemples d'Angers et de Clermont (Xe–XIIIe siècles)," in *La Paroisse: Genèse d'une forme territoriale*, ed. Dominique Iogna-Prat and Elisabeth Zadora-Rio, *Médiévales* 49 (2005): 57–72; Michel Lauwers, "Paroisse, paroissiens et territoire. Remarques sur 'parochia' dans les textes latins du Moyen Age," in *La Paroisse*, ed. Iogna-Prat and Zadora-Rio, 11–32; Hélène Noizet, "De l'église au territoire: les paroisses à Tours (XIe–XIIIe siècles)," in *La Paroisse*, ed. Iogna-Prat and Zadora-Rio, 45–56.

44 Schneider, *Metz*, 27–28 (citing a list of parishes from 1327); for the twenty-six parishes listed in 1360, see "Liste de 1360. Compotus subsidii biennalis civitatis et diocesis Meten.," ed. N. Dorvaux, *Les anciens pouillés du diocèse de Metz*, (Nancy: A. Crépin-Leblond, 1902), 10.

45 Aubrun, *La paroisse*, 128–31; Mundy, "The Town's Parishes;" J.-M. Bienvenue, "Les conflits de sépulture en Anjou aux XIe et XIIe siècles," *Bulletin historique et philologique* (1966): 673–85; Elisabeth Zadora-Rio, "The Making of Churchyards and Parish Territories in the Early-Medieval Landscape of France and England in the 7th–12th Centuries: A Reconsideration," *Medieval Archaeology* 47 (2003): 1–19.

46 Giles Constable, *Monastic Tithes from Their Origins to the Twelfth Century* (Cambridge: Cambridge University Press, 1964), 99–136; Brooke, "Missionary at Home," 72; Aubrun, *La paroisse*, 107–55; Tanner and Watson, "Least of the Laity," esp. 414–15.

the *bannus* of Saint-Pierre-aux-Arènes suggested as much. It reported that one of the five parishes the monks held in *ad Basilicas* had been recognized as such by the bishop to alleviate any trouble the monks might face in gathering tithes or any "impediment" to their "pristine lordship" there.[47] The monks' determination to have churches in their possession recognized as parishes reflects not merely their concern for the spiritual well-being of the city's inhabitants, but also their desire to exercise "lordship."

Indeed, parishes were merely one facet of the monks' lordly aspirations. They not only claimed numerous holdings south of the city, but apparently tried to form them into a territorial lordship stretching for several kilometers along the Seille. The same charter declares: "we decree that the *bannus* of Magny should be united to the *bannus* of Saint-Clément and the *bannus* of Saint-Pierre-aux-Arènes [also], since [these *banni*] belong to this same church."[48] The village of Magny stood on the opposite bank of the Seille, upstream from Saint-Pierre-aux-Arènes. Between these two *banni* lay Saint-Clément and the five parishes the monks claimed, along with their *banni*, in *ad Basilicas*. The charter suggests that the monks aspired to rule a sizeable swathe of territory.[49]

The monks even claimed a stretch of the river itself, roughly five kilometers long, leading up to the city's burgeoning outskirts.[50] There, they established a fishery, which would have provided food and, perhaps, surplus to sell.[51] They may also have charged tolls for crossing or traveling on the river.[52] As the number of merchants and artisans doing business along the Seille rose in the

---

47 Hermann, 25–26.

48 Hermann, 26 (Version B); also Perrin, *Sur le sens*, 186; Hari, "Écrire l'histoire," 1:422.

49 From Magny north to the hospital Saint-Nicolas was about six kilometers. The monks' territory may have included additional *villae* too. See V. Chatelain, "L'amphithéatre gallo-romain de Metz, l'église de Saint-Pierre-aux-Arènes et la légende du Graouly," *Revue historique de Metz et de la Lorraine allemande* 1 (1904): 188–89. The monks of Saint-Arnoul also consolidated their holdings around their abbey from c. 1075; Müller, *Schnittpunkt*, 246, 250.

50 Samantha Kahn Herrick, "'Very Great Strife': The Monks of Saint-Clément as Competitors in Twelfth-Century Metz," *Journal of Medieval History* 46 (2020): 536–51. DOI: 10.1080/03044181.2020.1812423.

51 Étienne de Bar, ["Judgment regarding dispute between Saint-Arnoul and Saint-Clément," 1137–38], *Actes*, 102 (hereafter "Étienne, [1137–38]").

52 There seems to have been a ford along this span. For such assets, see Otto II, ["Charter for Inhabitants of Passau, 976"], ed. Theodor von Sickel, *MGH DD O II* (Hanover: Hahn, 1888), 154–55; Annie Dumont, "Fords of the River Saône," *The International Journal of Nautical Archaeology* 27 (1998): 302–6.

eleventh and twelfth centuries, such ventures could have brought the abbey a nice income.

The monks nurtured bold ambitions for their fair, their parishes, and their lordship south of the city. As Metz grew both in size and economic importance, these projects gave Saint-Clément the opportunity to accrue considerable wealth, status, and power. This outcome was by no means guaranteed, however, for the monks were not alone in trying to capitalize on the city's rise.[53] The success of their plans, therefore, required strategies to shore up their claims and realize their goals.

3 Strategies

One of the monks' more straightforward strategies aimed at securing the goodwill of episcopal officials, the *advocatus* and the three *villici civitatis*. Their cooperation was vital to the smooth operation of the monks' fair. Moreover, justice in the growing city and its suburbs often belonged to them.[54] The abbot agreed to give the *villici civitatis* twelve *denarii* for their help with the fair.[55] The *advocatus* received a fief in return for protecting the abbey's interests more generally.[56] The cooperation of these officials thus came at a price, but one the community of Saint-Clément deemed worthwhile to further their ambitions.

The charter so often cited was the product of another, more audacious, strategy. This document bears the name of Hermann, bishop of Metz in the turbulent 1070s and 1080s, who ostensibly granted it just before his death in 1090.[57] The surviving copies, however, were extensively interpolated by the monks—most likely before 1130 and again between 1134 and 1139.[58] The resulting document accomplished a good deal for Saint-Clément. It outlined the details of the fair's operation, defined the extent of Saint-Pierre-aux-Arènes's

53 Herrick, "'Very Great Strife'."

54 The evolution of these offices at this time involved a redistribution of prerogatives and duties among them, but justice nevertheless remained within their purview; see Schneider, *Metz*, 79; Müller, *Schnittpunkt*, 27, 39–40, 96, 372.

55 Hermann, 27 (Version B); Schneider, *Metz*, 81–82.

56 Hermann, 27 (Version A). This fief belonged not to the *advocatus* personally, but to his office.

57 Hermann was bishop 1073–1090, although he was twice exiled during that time and replaced by imperial bishops. He died in May 1090.

58 Müsebeck, "Zoll und Markt," 29–30; Schneider, *Metz*, 32, 80–81. Schneider proposed various dates for the second interpolation, but seemed to view 1134–1139 as the most likely window, see *Metz*, 81 n. 16.

bannus, asserted control over the Seille and other possessions, and conveyed a host of further claims as well. Moreover, it served as the basis for multiple episcopal and papal confirmations.[59] Simply claiming what they wished to have was thus a strategy that took the monks far.

Judicial action represented another strategy. Sometime before 1130, the monks complained to Bishop Étienne de Bar that a local lord had extorted service from one of their possessions. Étienne appears to have ruled in the monks' favor.[60] Similar attempts did not always yield the desired results, however. In 1137–1138, Étienne interceded in a prolonged and bitter dispute that had caused "great strife" (*grande contention*) between Saint-Clément and another of the city's established religious houses.[61] Although his judgment largely vindicated Saint-Clément, it also demanded some concessions from the monks. Judicial action was a somewhat risky course.

Perhaps for this reason, the monks seem also to have engaged in what looks like intimidation. Bishop Étienne noted that his intervention of 1137–1138 followed the perpetration of "several damages" (*plusieurs domaiges*) by one or both parties.[62] Just who did what to whom is unclear, but it seems that these communities were not above causing their rivals actual harm. The monks of Saint-Clément also sought to intimidate their rivals in other, less tangible, ways. The papal bulls granted to the abbey included standard anathemas designed to intimidate the monks' foes. Thus, Pope Calixtus II (r. 1119–1124) decreed, "let no one at all be permitted to trouble that monastery heedlessly or to take away its possessions, or to diminish them or to trouble them with rash vexations." Instead, those possessions "should be preserved intact for the future benefit of those for whose sustenance and governance they were given."[63] Innocent II repeated the warning almost verbatim.[64] Both popes also threatened dire punishments for those who knowingly violated the abbey's rights and refused to make amends.[65] Reforming popes issued identical warnings frequently in an effort to protect ecclesiastical—and particularly monastic—patrimony.[66]

---

59 The confirmations listed in n. 35 validated many—but not all—of the claims set out in this charter, often citing Hermann's gift.

60 Étienne, [1130], 63; for the lord in question (Folmar), see Hari, "Écrire l'histoire," 1:218.

61 Étienne, [1137–1138], 102 (this judgment survives only in an early-modern French copy); Herrick, "'Very Great Strife'."

62 Étienne, [1137–1138], 102.

63 Calixtus II, *Ex praet. temp.*, 279–80.

64 Innocent II, *Pie post. vol.*, 115.

65 Calixtus II, *Ex praet. temp.*, 280; Innocent II, *Pie post. vol.*, 115. Bishop Étienne de Bar made similar threats when confirming Hermann's concessions; Étienne, [1130].

66 Examples of this language abound. A few early instances include: Pope Stephen VII, *Bulla pro monasterio S. Vincentii Vulturnensis, anno 930*, PL 132:1051–52; Pope John XIX, *Joannes*

Nevertheless, their inclusion betrays genuine anxiety for the security of Saint-Clément's rights and properties. These stern (if standard) warnings were meant to make anyone who might seek to harm the monks' interests think twice.

While bribery, litigation, and intimidation may have had their merits, the monks' most creative strategies drew on the history and reputation of their saint. The story that Clement, a disciple of the Apostle Peter and Metz's first bishop, had consecrated an altar to his mentor in the city's ancient amphitheater went back to the eighth century. This altar ostensibly evolved into Saint-Pierre-aux-Arènes. Perhaps because the earliest account of Clement's life, a short passage in Paul the Deacon's (c. 720–799) *Liber de episcopis Mettensibus*, related little else of Clement's career, this episode became central to his legend.[67] So did Paul's somewhat doubtful observation that, "those who know this place say that ... no serpent can remain [there]."[68] Around the year 1000, the monastic author of the first *Vita Clementis* expanded that remark into a lengthy episode in which Clement purged the amphitheater of myriad deadly serpents or dragons before establishing an altar, or possibly a church, in Peter's name.[69] The story loomed equally large in the third *Vita Clementis*, most likely composed at Saint-Clément in the 1130s: here it takes up nearly half the text.[70] Its length leaves no doubt about the story's importance to this hagiographer and, by extension, to the community of Saint-Clément in the early twelfth century. By playing up Clement's foundation of Saint-Pierre-aux-Arènes, the new *vita* implicitly bound that church to the abbey where the saint lay buried.

So ecclesiastical authorities appear to have reasoned. In confirming that Saint-Pierre-aux-Arènes belonged to Saint-Clément, they repeatedly cited the story that Clement had founded it.[71] If the monks hoped that this legend would

---

XIX ecclesia Silvae Candidae possessiones, petente Petro episcopo, confirmat, anno 1026, PL 141:1125–32; Pope Gregory VII, *Privilegium pro monasterio S. Benigni Divionensis, anno 1078*, PL 148:685–87. The PL database includes five other instances of Calixtus II employing the same language.

67 Paul the Deacon, *Liber de episcopis Mettensibus*, ed. Damien Kempf (Leuven: Peeters, 2013), 48–50, with the foundation at 50.

68 Paul the Deacon, *Liber*, 50.

69 *Vita prima Clementis*, ed. Heinrich Volbert Sauerland, *Sancti Clementis primi Mettensis episcopi vita, translatio, ac miracula* (Trier: Paulinus, 1896), 8–11. The BHL does not clearly distinguish between this *Vita prima* and the *Vita tertia Clementis* (discussed in following note). See Chazan, "Clemens," 154–55, 159–63.

70 *Vita tertia Clementis*. The text has not been edited. For its composition, see Chazan, "Clemens," 183–86. References here are to Montpellier, Bibliothèque Universitaire de Médecine de Montpellier, H 1, tome 1, fols. 163v–168r (hereafter "VC3"), where this episode begins roughly halfway through fol. 164v and ends not far into 166v.

71 Étienne, [1130], 63; Innocent II, *Pie post. vol.*, 114 (repeating nearly verbatim a passage from the bull issued by Calixtus II in 1123).

strengthen their claim to Saint-Pierre-aux-Arènes, therefore, it appears that they succeeded. It is probably no coincidence that the *Vita tertia Clementis*, which retold this episode at such length, was most likely composed at about the same time that the monks were avidly collecting confirmations that Saint-Pierre-aux-Arènes belonged to them.[72]

Hagiography celebrating Clement not only validated his abbey's possession of Saint-Pierre-aux-Arènes, but also supported the campaign to have this church recognized as a parish. Having related the foundation of Saint-Pierre-aux-Arènes, the author of the *Vita tertia Clementis* reported that those who worshipped there twice a week for one year would receive the same spiritual reward "as if they had reached Rome and the thresholds of the holy Apostles with much sweat and labor and, sorrowful, set the prayers and offerings and laments of their needs before the sacred bones of the holy Apostles Peter and Paul."[73] He went on to depict the throngs of faithful Christians who flocked to this church in search of mercy. In so doing, he shifted into the present tense and addressed his reader directly:

> from then until now, so great a crowd of people is produced on the appointed days, so great the spiritual joy in the coming and going of men and women and children and of youths and virgins praising God and confessing their sins, that were you to see it from afar, you would think it the greatest glory to God and his father that might be made.[74]

This startling leap from the first century to the twelfth brings the medieval church of Saint-Pierre-aux-Arènes vividly alive—if not as it actually was, then presumably as the hagiographer and his community wished it to be. The *vita* depicts a church "built for the mercy of its sinners and for obtaining the

72 Chazan, "Clemens," 185.

73 "quicumque aliquibus peccatis aut criminibus irretiti ad dei misericordiam per penitentiam redire. deinceps conarentur; ab itinere romano relaxati. si bis per ebdomadam. scilicet quarta & sexta feria eandem ecclesiam infra arenarium constructam … toto anni curriculo deuotissime adierint; tantundem eis ualere; ac si romam & limina sanctorum apostolorum multo sudore. multoque labore attingerent; & preces oblationesque ac querimonias suarum necessitatum ad sacra sanctorum apostolorum petri & pauli ossa luctuosi deponent," VC3, fol. 166v.

74 "Qua propter hac tam felicis beneficii sanctissima consuetudine. ex tunc usque nunc tantus fit per condictos dies populorum recursus; tanta uirorum ac mulierum infantum etiam iuuenum ac uirginum deum collaudantium et peccata sua confitentium in eundeo & redeundo spiritualis leticia; ut quisquis eminus prospexeris. maximam deo & patri eius gloriam fieri … iudicabis," VC3, fol. 166v.

clemency of God and of saint Peter" and teeming with the lay folk whose spiritual needs it served.[75] This image of Saint-Pierre-aux-Arènes as a thriving center of religious life in Metz, past and present, made its recognition as a parish seem natural, perhaps even inevitable.

This depiction is echoed in the bull Pope Innocent II granted to Saint-Clément in 1139. In describing Saint-Pierre-aux-Arènes, he too mentioned "that habit, by which the people of Metz have become accustomed to frequent that church" and of which he approved "entirely."[76] It seems that the pope not only endorsed Saint-Pierre-aux-Arènes as a parish—as indicated by his concern that the abbot appoint a cleric who would offer a good example to the laity—but even regarded it, more or less, as one already. In his view, it excelled "other parishes" because of having been founded first, "before all other oratories," by the city's first bishop.[77] The pope did not cite the *Vita tertia*, and it is impossible to determine whether he knew this text. Yet the logic implicit in his description of Saint-Pierre-aux-Arènes as something very much like a parish church resembles that of the *vita*—namely, that the church was not only the city's first, but that it had long served the "people of Metz" and should continue to do so.

A more recent episode in Clement's saintly career legitimized the extensive rights and possessions the monks claimed to have received from Bishop Hermann. According to a translation account likely produced at the abbey in the early twelfth century, Hermann reluctantly brought Clement's relics to the cathedral for one night just before his death in May 1090, after having long ignored the saint's demands for greater veneration.[78] The next morning, to atone for his previous disregard, Hermann reportedly made a generous donation of "earthly goods for the use of the brothers serving the saint."[79] The *Translatio* says nothing more specific about this grant. However, the details appear to be enumerated at length in the charter bearing Hermann's name, supposedly issued later the same day, once Clement's relics had returned to the abbey.[80] The two documents thus work together: the *Translatio* provides the backstory for the charter, which begins by briefly recapitulating the translation and ends with Hermann formally confirming his gift before witnesses.

75 "eandem ecclesiam infra arenarium constructam pro peccatorum suorum uenia. & pro clementia dei & sancti petri adipiscenda," VC3, ibid.

76 Innocent II, *Pie post. vol.*, 114.

77 Innocent II, *Pie post. vol.*, 114; the meaning of the term used here (*parochia*) remained imprecise at this time, however.

78 *Hecelini monachi Translatio et Miracula sancti Clementis*, ed. Julius Dieterich, *MGH SS* 30.2 (Leipzig: Hiersmann, 1934), 893–908 (hereafter "*Translatio et miracula*"), 896–99.

79 *Translatio et miracula*, 899.

80 Hermann, 24–25, 27–28.

The story of Clement's brief sojourn in the cathedral, the culmination of much drama and many years' delay, thus lent credence to the claim that Hermann had given the monks numerous gifts.

Like Clement's *vita*, the story of this brief translation and the generous donation that followed it carried some sway. Bishop Étienne de Bar repeatedly cited Hermann's grant when affirming the monks' possessions. In 1130, Étienne singled out for confirmation several gifts that

> The pious pastor, our predecessor of happy memory Hermann gave and ceded to St Clement and the brothers in the hearing of all those who were there in the church of the proto-martyr St Stephen, when by divine admonition he raised the body of blessed Clement.[81]

The monks' fair featured prominently here. Étienne confirmed the abbey's right to hold such an event "for eight continuous days," and also the peace "to be kept by all those coming and going from there." Indeed, he reiterated the charter's threat of excommunication for "anyone who should presume to infringe this institution."[82] Pope Innocent II similarly cited the translation when confirming the monks' right to hold the fair.[83] In 1137–1138, Étienne again echoed the charter nearly verbatim to affirm Saint-Clément's rights on the Seille.[84] The proposition that a dying and penitent bishop made substantial grants to honor a saint he had long ignored was apparently persuasive.

The miracles the monks recorded in the translation's wake reinforced the idea that Clement deserved such honor. The *Translatio* and *Liber secundus miraculorum*, both likely composed in the early twelfth century by the monk Hecelinus, detail twenty such miracles.[85] These texts not only celebrate Clement's power to heal, protect, and punish but also stress the importance

81 Étienne, [1130], 62.

82 Étienne, [1130], 62–63.

83 Innocent II, *Pie post. vol.*, 114.

84 Étienne, [1137–1138], 102.

85 The *Translatio sancti Clementis* (BHL 1862) reports the first ten miracles and the *Liber secundus miraculorum sancti Clementis* (BHL 1863) relates the rest. Most scholars believe that Hecelinus, named as author of the *Liber miraculorum*, wrote both. Since he promoted Saint-Clément's patron, asserted the monks' control over his cult, and supported their claim to the land on which Saint-Nicolas stood, he was probably a monk. He wrote after the translation of 1090, perhaps as late as the 1130s. See Berlin, Staatsbibliothek zu Berlin—Preußischer Kulturbesitz, MS Phillipps 1839 (thirteenth-century), fols. 206r–209v (*Translatio*) and 209v–213r (*Liber secundus*); Dieterich, ["Introduction to *Translatio et miracula*"], 893 and 895–96; Chazan, "Clemens," 174–80; Hari, "Écrire l'histoire," 1:427–30. The texts were also edited by Sauerland, *Sancti Clementis*, 17–41.

of visiting his shrine. One miracle underlines this point clearly. Hecelinus reports that a paralytic man was said to have set out from Cologne in search of aid. Having obtained health while still on his way to Metz, however, he went home—and his ailment promptly returned. Only when he completed his journey to the shrine did he attain full and lasting health.[86] Miracles centered on attempts to steal dust, earth, or bits of wood from Clement's tomb make a similar point. The saint punished these acts and saw that whatever had been taken was returned or, in one case, sent to a church of the saint's choosing (likely Saint-Pierre-aux-Arènes).[87] These miracles thus underline the idea that Clement's power was concentrated at his shrine and encouraged pilgrimage to Saint-Clément.

The monks' annual fair provided the perfect opportunity to make such a pilgrimage. While the fair undoubtedly attracted those eager for commerce, its official purpose was to honor Clement and commemorate his recent translation. Moreover, its timing, in early May, was more conducive to travel than his primary feast in late November.[88] Jean Schneider believed that crowds had already begun streaming to the shrine on this anniversary and that the monks established their fair in order to capitalize on this traffic.[89] Such a plan may well have succeeded, particularly since the fair's scale likely gave it an unusually broad geographic draw: most markets in this region and period lasted a single day.[90] Whatever its other enticements, the fair was officially an opportunity to honor Clement by visiting his tomb, where, the faithful were told, they stood the best chance of experiencing a miracle.

---

86 *Translatio et miracula*, 904–5 (miracle 4 of the *Liber secundus*).

87 *Translatio et miracula*, 899–901 (miracles 1, 2, 3, and 5 of the *Translatio*).

88 The translation took place on the fifth nones of May (May 2), while Clement's feast (like that of the homonymous pope) was the ninth kalends of December (November 23).

89 Schneider, *Metz*, 75.

90 For fairs in Lorraine, see Franz Irsigler, "Jahrmärkte und Messesysteme im westlichen Reichsgebiet bis ca. 1250," in *Europäische Messen und Märktesysteme in Mittelalter und Neuzeit*, ed. P. Johanek and H. Stoob (Cologne: Böhlau, 1996), 11, 26; Jean-Luc Fray, *Villes et bourgs de Lorraine: réseaux urbains et centralité au Moyen Âge* (Clermont-Ferrand: Presses universitaires Blaise Pascal, 2006), esp. 220–24. More generally, see Robert-Henri Bautier, "The Fairs of Champagne," in *Essays in French Economic History*, ed. Rondo Cameron et al. (Homewood, IL: R.D. Irwin, 1970), 42–63; Danny Danziger and John Gillingham, *1215: The Year of Magna Carta* (New York: Simon & Schuster, 2004), 51. For the greater draw of longer markets, see Franz Irsigler, "Anmerkungen zu den Trierer Jahrmärkten vor 1200," in *Liber amicorum necnon et amicarum für Alfred Heit, Beiträge zur mittelalterlichen Geschichte und geschichtlichen Landeskunde*, ed. Friedhelm Burgard et al. (Trier: Trierer historische Forschungen, 1995), 335–42.

4 Conclusion

The suburban monks of Saint-Clément were undoubtedly ambitious. As Metz emerged from the Investiture Contest, they strove not merely to regain rights and resources that (they said) had been taken from them in the turmoil, but to profit from their city's rising fortunes. They sought to exploit resources ranging from the natural (the river Seille), to the spiritual (their shrine and parishes), to the legal (claims to *bannus* and *centena*) and commercial (their fair).

They pursued these goals with a sophisticated web of strategies. Hagiography celebrating their saint, Clement, the city's first apostolic bishop, represented one strand. The monks drew on Clement's *vita*, his more recent translation, and reports of his ongoing miracles to advance their claims. They likewise used more worldly elements: a charter full of contentious legal claims; the practice of facing competitors down with judicial action and intimidation; payments to officials; and an invitation to race horses and, with luck, to win money. These different elements worked together: sacred history legitimized many of the monks' claims and thus helped them to procure (or to pass off as genuine) documents that strengthened their hand when it came to litigation. Payments to episcopal officials were intended to facilitate the smooth operation of the fair, which was in turn designed to draw crowds to the abbey with a blend of commerce, devotion, and entertainment. This traffic both generated income and diffused Clement's renown.

The monks of Saint-Clément actively engaged with the dynamics transforming their city. They deliberately sought to profit from the economic and demographic boom that Metz, like so many cities, experienced in the central Middle Ages. This suburban community saw the opportunities presented by urban growth and developed strategies to seize them. Understanding how they did so—the goals they pursued and the strategies they used—thus illuminates how medieval cities grew and changed.

Bibliography

Primary Sources

Balderich. *Gesta Alberonis*. Translated by Brian A. Pavlac. *A Warrior Bishop of the Twelfth Century: The Deeds of Albero of Trier by Balderich*. Toronto: Pontifical Institute of Mediaeval Studies, 2008.

Bernoldus Sancti-Blasii. *Chronicon*. Edited by G.H. Pertz. *MGH SS5*, 385–467. Hannover: Hahn, 1844.

Calixtus II. *Ex praeteritorum temporum*. Edited by G. Wolfram. "Ungedruckte Papsturkunden der Metzer Archive." Jahrbuch der Gesellschaft für Lothringische Geschichte und Altertumskunde / Annuaire de la Société d'histoire et d'archéologie lorraine (hereafter "*ASHAL*") 15 (1903): 278–323.

Gesta episcoporum Mettensium. Edited by Georg Waitz. *MGH SS* 10, 531–51. Hannover: Hahn, 1852.

Guibert of Nogent. *De vita sua sive monodiarum libri tres*. PL 156:837–962.

Hecelini monachi Translatio et Miracula sancti Clementis. Edited by Julius Dieterich. *MGH SS* 30.2, 893–908. Leipzig: Hiersmann, 1934.

Innocent II. *Pie postulatio voluntatis*. Edited by Jean François et al. *Histoire de Metz*. 6 vols. Metz: P. Marchal/Nancy: Lamort, 1769–1781. Repr. Paris: Éditions du Palais-Royal, 1974. Vol. 3. 113–15.

Jaffé, Philipp, ed. *Regesta pontificum romanorum*. 2nd ed. Graz: Akademische Druck- und. Verlagsanstalt, 1956.

Liber secundus miraculorum sancti Clementis (*BHL* 1863). Berlin, Staatsbibliothek zu Berlin—Preußischer Kulturbesitz. MS Phillipps, 1839. Fols. 209v–213r.

"Liste de 1360. Compotus subsidii biennalis civitatis et diocesis Meten." Edited by N. Dorvaux *Les anciens pouillés du diocese de Metz*, 7–21. Nancy: A. Crépin-Leblond, 1902.

Otto II. ["Charter for Inhabitants of Passau, 976."] Edited by Theodor von Sickel. *MGH DD O II*, 154–55. Hannover: Hahn, 1888.

Parisse, Michel, ed. *Actes des princes lorrains.* 2ième série. *Princes ecclésiastiques*, 1. *Les évêques de Metz* B, *Étienne de Bar* (*1120–1162*). Nancy, [1977].

Parisse, Michel. "Bullaire de la Lorraine (jusqu'à 1198)." *ASHAL* 69 (1969): 5–102.

Paul the Deacon. *Liber de episcopis Mettensibus*. Edited by Damien Kempf. Dallas Medieval Texts & Translations 19. Leuven: Peeters, 2013.

Privilegium Bischofs Hermann für St. Clemens 1090. Edited by Ernst Müsebeck. "Zoll und Markt in Metz in der ersten Hälfte des Mittelalters." *ASHAL* 15 (1903): 1–32 (edition 24–29).

Satira in Mettenses. Edited by E. Dümmler and H. Boehmer. *MGH Ldl* 3, 618–21. Hannover: Hahn, 1897.

Sauerland, Heinrich Volbert. *Sancti Clementis primi Mettensis episcopi vita, translatio, ac miracula.* Trier: Paulinus, 1896.

Translatio sancti Clementis (*BHL* 1862). Berlin, Staatsbibliothek zu Berlin—Preußischer Kulturbesitz, MS Phillipps 1839. Fols. 206r–209v.

Vita tertia Clementis. Montpellier, Bibliothèque Universitaire de Médicine de Montpellier, H 1, tome 1. Fols. 163v–68r.

Vita Theogeri abbatis S. Georgii et episcopi Mettensis. Edited by Philipp Jaffé. *MGH SS* 12, 449–79. Hannover: Hahn, 1856.

Secondary Sources

Aubrun, Michel. *La paroisse en France: des origines au XVe siècle.* Paris: Picard, 1986.

Bautier, Robert-Henri. "The Fairs of Champagne." In *Essays in French Economic History*, edited by Rondo Cameron et al., 42–63. Homewood, IL: R.D. Irwin, 1970.

Bienvenue, J.-M. "Les conflits de sépulture en Anjou aux XIe et XIIe siècles." *Bulletin historique et philiogique* (1966): 673–85.

Bocchi, Francesca. "Monasteri, canoniche e strutture urbane in Italia." In *Istituzioni monastiche e istituzioni canonicali in Occidente (1123–1215)*, 264–313. Milan: *Vita* e Pensiero, 1980.

Bour, R.S. and Th. Klauser. "Un document du IXe siècle: Notes sur l'ancienne liturgie de Metz et sur ses églises antérieures à l'an Mil." *ASHAL* 38 (1929): 497–640.

Brkojewitsch, Gaël, et al. "Nouvelles données sur le quartier Outre-Seille à Metz (Moselle) (époques romaine, médiévale et moderne): la fouille de la place Mazelle." *Revue archéologique de l'Est* 62 (2013): 283–314. https://journals.openedition.org/rae/7831.

Brooke, Christopher. "The Missionary at Home: The Church in the Towns, 1000–1250." In *The Mission of the Church and the Propagation of the Faith*, edited by C.J. Cuming, 59–84. Cambridge: Cambridge University Press, 1970.

Chatelain, V. "L'amphithéatre gallo-romain de Metz, léglise de Saint-Pierre-aux-Arènes et la légende du Graouly." *Revue historique de Metz et de la Lorraine allemande* 1 (1904): 188–89.

Chazan, Mireille. "Les évêques de Metz: Clemens." In *Miracles, Vies et réécritures dans l'Occident medieval*, edited by Monique Goullet and Martin Heinzelmann, 152–90. Ostfildern: Thorbecke, 2006.

Chazan, Mireille. "Les Vies latines de saint Clément, premier êvéque de Metz." *Francia* 31 (2004): 15–43.

Comte, François and Emmaneul Grélois. "La formation des paroisses urbaines: les exemples d'Angers et de Clermont (Xe–XIIIe siècles)." In *La Paroisse: Genèse d'une forme territoriale*, edited by Dominique Iogna-Prat and Elisabeth Zadora-Rio. *Médiévales* 49 (2005): 57–72.

Constable, Giles. *Monastic Tithes from their Origins to the Twelfth Century.* Cambridge: Cambridge University Press, 1964.

Dantzer, André. "La querelle des investitures dans les évêchés de Metz, Toul, et Verdun." *Annales de l'Est* 16 (1902): 85–100.

Danziger, Danny and John Gillingham. *1215: The Year of Magna Carta.* New York: Simon & Schuster, 2004.

Dumont, Annie. "Fords of the River Saône." *The International Journal of Nautical Archaeology* 27 (1988): 302–6.

Erkens, Franz-Reiner. *Die Trierer Kirchenprovinz im Investiturstreit.* Cologne: Böhlau, 1987.

Fray, Jean-Luc. "Recherches sur la seigneurie banale au XIIe siècle d'après le vocabulaire des actes des évêques de Metz (1058–1210)." In *La Seigneurie rurale en*

Lotharingie: Actes des 3e journées Lotharingiennes. Publications de la section historique de l'Institut du Grand Duché de Luxembourg 102 (1986): 75–101.

Fray, Jean-Luc. *Villes et bourgs de Lorraine: réseaux urbains et centralité au Moyen Âge.* Clermont-Ferrand: Presses Universitaires Blaise-Pascal, 2006.

Ganshof, F. L. *Étude sur le développement des villes entre Loire et Rhin au moyen âge.* Paris: Presses Universitaires de France, 1943.

Gauthier, Nancy. "Metz." In *Province ecclésiastique de Trèves (Belgica prima)*, 33–53. Paris: De Boccard, 1986.

Hari, Arnaud. "Écrire l'histoire des évêques de Metz au Moyen Âge: Les *Gesta episcoporum* messins de la fin du VIIIe siècle à la fin du XIVe siècle." 2 vols. Ph.D. diss., Université Paul Verlaine, Metz, 2010.

Herrick, Samantha Kahn. "Friend or Foe? The Bishops of Metz in Monastic Historical Narrative, c. 1000–c. 1200." *Journal of Ecclesiastical History* 71 (2020): 253–69.

Herrick, Samantha Kahn. "'Very Great Strife': The Monks of Saint-Clément as Competitors in Twelfth-Century Metz." *Journal of Medieval History* 46 (2020): 536–51. https://doi.org/10.1080/03044181.2020.1812423.

Hirschmann, Frank G. *Stadtplanung, Bauprojekte und Großbaustellen im 10. und 11. Jahrhundert. Vergleichende Studien zu den Kathedralstädten westlich des Rheins.* Stuttgart: Hiersemann, 1998.

Hodges, Kenneth. "Medieval Prices." *Internet Medieval Sourcebook.* Accessed March 28, 2022. https://faculty.goucher.edu/eng240/medieval_prices.html.

INRAP (Institut national de recherches archéologiques preventives). "À Metz, la fouille du quartier de l'amphithéâtre." Last modified February 19, 2016. https://www.inrap.fr/metz-la-fouille-du-quartier-de-l-amphitheatre-4940.

Irsigler, Franz. "Anmerkungen zu den Trierer Jahrmärkten vor 1200." In *Liber amicorum necnon et amicarum für Alfred Heit, Beiträge zur mittelalterlichen Geschichte und geschichtlichen Landeskunde*, edited by Friedhelm Burgard et al., 335–42. Trier: Trierer historische Forschungen, 1995.

Irsigler, Franz. "Jahrmärkte und Messesysteme im westlichen Reichsgebiet bis ca. 1250." In *Europäische Messen und Märktesysteme in Mittelalter und Neuzeit*, edited by P. Johanek and H. Stoob, 1–33. Cologne: Böhlau, 1996.

Lauwers, Michel. "Paroisse, paroissiens et territoire. Remarques sur 'parochia' dans les textes latins du Moyen Age." In *La Paroisse: genèse d'une forme territoriale*, edited by Dominique Iogna-Prat and Elisabeth Zadora-Rio, 11–32. Saint-Denis: Presses universitaires de Vincennes, 2005.

Minn, Gisela. *Kathedralstadt und Benediktinerkloster: Die Abtei St. Vinzenz und die Stadt Metz im Mittelalter.* Trierer historische Forschungen 45. Trier: Kliomedia, 2002.

Müller, Jörg R. Vir religiosus ac strenuus: *Albero von Montreuil, Erzbischof von Trier (1132–1152).* Trier: Kliomedia, 2006.

Müller, Margit. *Am Schnittpunkt von Stadt und Land. Die Benediktinerabtei St. Arnulf zu Metz im hohen und späten Mittelalter*. Trier: Verlag Trierer historische Forschungen, 1993.

Mundy, John Hine. "The Town's Parishes from 1150–1250." In *Studies in the Ecclesiastical and Social History of Toulouse in the Age of the Cathars*, 13–44. Aldershot: Ashgate, 2006.

Müsebeck, Ernst. "Zoll und Markt in Metz in der ersten Hälfte des Mittelalters," *ASHAL* 15 (1903): 1–32.

Noizet, Hélène. "De l'église au territoire: les paroisses à Tours (XIe–XIIIe siècles.)" In *La Paroisse: genèse d'une forme territoriale*, edited by Dominique Iogna-Prat and Elisabeth Zadora-Rio, 45–56. Presses universitaires de Vincenees, 2005.

Parisse, Michel. "Metz dans l'Église impériale." In *Histoire de Metz*, edited by François-Yves Le Moigne, 110–35. Toulouse: Privat, 1986.

Parisse, Michel and Arnaud Hari. *Catalogue historique des évêques de Metz: Le moyen âge*. Paris: LAMOP, 2015. https://lamop.pantheonsorbonne.fr/sites/default/files/inline-files/Morceaux_choisis_Parisse_Hari_2015.pdf.

Perrin, Charles-Edmond. *Recherches sur la seigneurie rurale en Lorraine d'après les plus anciens censiers (IXe–XIIe siècles)*. Paris: [n.p.], 1935. Repr. Geneva: Mégariotis, 1978.

Perrin, Charles-Edmond. *Sur le sens du mot "centena" dans les chartes lorraines du Moyen Âge*. Paris/Nogent-le-Rotrou: Daupeley-Gouverneur, 1930.

Robinson, I. S. *Henry IV of Germany, 1056–1106*. Cambridge: Cambridge University Press, 2003.

Ruperti, Franz. "Bischof Stephan von Metz (1120–1162)." *ASHAL* 22 (1910): 1–95.

Schneider, Jean. *La ville de Metz aux XIIIe et XIVe siècles*. Nancy: George Thomas, 1950.

Staats, Sarah. "Vision of an Augustinian Canon in Lorraine: Echoes of the Investiture Conflict in the Diocese of Metz at the Beginning of the Twelfth Century." *Analecta Bollandiana* 113 (1995): 127–46.

Tanner, Norman and Sethina Watson. "Least of the Laity: The Minimum Requirements for a Medieval Christian." *Journal of Medieval History* 32 (2006): 395–423.

Tobey, Elizabeth. "The *Palio* Banner and the Visual Culture of Horse Racing in Renaissance Italy." *The International Journal of the History of Sport* 28 (2011): 1269–82.

Trapp, Julien and Sébastien Wagner, eds. *Atlas historique de Metz*. 2nd ed. Metz: Éditions des Paraiges, 2015.

Voltz, Eugène. "L'Abbaye S. Clément de Metz: Esquisse de son histoire architecturale." *Mémoires de l'académie de Metz* (1965–66): 37–64. Repr. separately: Metz: Le Lorrain, 1968.

Zadora-Rio, Elisabeth. "The Making of Churchyards and Parish Territories in the Early-Medieval Landscape of France and England in the 7th–12th Centuries: A Reconsideration." *Medieval Archaeology* 47 (2003): 1–19.

Zollinger, Manfred. "*Nundinae ludentes.* Bemerkungen zum Zusammenhang zwischen Ökonomie, Emotion und Glücksspiel auf Messen, Jahrmärkten und Kirchweihfesten vom 15. bis zum 18. Jahrhundert." *Ludica* 11 (2007): 132–50.

CHAPTER 13

The Papal Constitution *Execrabilis* (1317) and Clerical Justices in the English Royal Courts

Ryan Rowberry

1 Introduction

A recurrent challenge of pastoral administration in the thirteenth and fourteenth century Latin church was pluralism—simultaneous tenure by a cleric of more than one ecclesiastical benefice involving a cure of souls.[1] Pluralism violated the pastoral ideal of a priest living among his congregation and guiding them to God.[2] Instead, pluralist clerics (typically absent from their parishes) could draw substantial revenues from the glebe, tithes, oblations, and altarage of the ecclesiastical benefices they governed while outsourcing salvific duties to resident stipendiary chaplains.[3]

Owing to the fiscal needs of the Holy See, his broader policy of centralizing papal control of benefices, and perhaps genuine disdain for pluralism, Pope John XXII (r. 1316–1334) issued the papal constitution known as *Execrabilis* on November 19, 1317.[4] It contained three stringent and wide-ranging mandates.

1 For the developments of canon law on pluralism prior to *Execrabilis* see John Shinners and William Dohar, eds., *Pastors and the Care of Souls* (Notre Dame: Notre Dame University Press, 1998), 73–75; K. Pennington, "The Canonists and Pluralism in the Thirteenth Century," *Speculum* 51 (1976): 35–48; W. T. Waugh, "Archbishop Peckham and Pluralities," *English Historical Review* 28, no. 112 (1913): 625–35.

2 The bestowal of a benefice "conferred the standing that comes with authority," and benefice holders (rectors) were like secular lords. Michael Burger, *Bishops, Clerks, and Diocesan Governance in Thirteenth-Century England* (Cambridge: Cambridge University Press, 2012), 36.

3 Bishop Oliver Sutton of Lincoln proclaimed that rectors should rule their churches rather than farming them out. See J. W. Ruddock, ed., *The Rolls and Register of Bishop Oliver Sutton (1280–1299)*, vol. VI, (Lincoln: Lincoln Record Society 64, 1969), 63. For evidence of Rothbury farming out Laxfield (Suffolk) and Shillington (Bedfordshire) in 1308–1310, see The National Archives (hereinafter TNA) E 159/82 mss. 29, 60; E 159/81 m. 43; For evidence of Stanton farming out Flixton (Lancashire) in 1317 see TNA E 159/91 m. 92.

4 The Latin text of *Execrabilis* with surrounding glosses may be viewed online at *Corpus Juris Canonici*. Electronic Edition: UCLA Digital Library Program. vol. 3, Constitutiones Joannis Papae XXII, Title 3: De praebendis et dignitatibus (Rome, 1582), 627–39, http://digital.library.ucla.edu/canonlaw.

 | DOI:10.1163/9789004710696_015

First, it revoked all dispensations for plurality granted by previous popes. Second, pluralist clerks, except for cardinals and sons of kings, had to resign all but one benefice with cure of souls gifted by ecclesiastical patrons within one month after notice or all benefices held by that cleric would become vacant *ipso iure*. Benefices in lay patronage and prebends (churches without the cure of souls) were outside the ambit of *Execrabilis*. Finally, all benefices ceded by pluralists were reserved for papal redistribution.[5]

Execrabilis prompted immediate backlash—particularly in England where English clerics had benefitted greatly from Pope Clement V's (1305–1314) generous policies toward granting dispensations for plurality.[6] Alarmed at the fiscal and bureaucratic repercussions of *Execrabilis*, King Edward II (1307–1327) dispatched a letter to Pope John XXII on January 10, 1318. In it he urged the pope not to apply the decretal to England, as many clerics who had received dispensations for plurality would lose their benefices, leading to lax governance in the realm. Edward II also informed the pope that he was directing all English clergy to retain all benefices until he received a reply.[7]

Ultimately Edward's pleas to the pope and commands to his subjects failed to eliminate or even delay the enforcement of *Execrabilis*. Soon after the decretal reached England in January 1318, pluralist clerics began resigning incompatible benefices voluntarily or under episcopal pressure. Bishops compiled lists of resigned benefices for submission directly to the pope, who communicated them to his papal tax collector in England, Rigaud de Asserio, working out of the Dean's Chapter House of St. Paul's in London.[8] The scale of swift benefice

---

5 See J. Robert Wright, *The Church and the English Crown 1305–1334* (Toronto: Pontifical Institute of Mediaeval Studies, 1980), 12–13, 74, 79; William E. Lunt, *Financial Relations of the Papacy with England to 1327* (Cambridge: Medieval Academy of America, 1939), 495–96.

6 Out of 191 dispensations for plurality granted by Pope Clement V from 1311–1314 to clerics in the Latin church, 76 (40%) pertained to England alone. See Wright, *The Church and the English Crown*, 74. One reason for this generosity towards English clerks may be that Clement V (Bertrand de Got) was a Gascon who had formerly been a royal clerk in the service of King Edward I before his elevation. See Barbara Bombi, *Anglo-Papal Relations in the Early Fourteenth Century* (Oxford: Oxford University Press, 2019), 134.

7 Thomas Rymer, ed., *Foedera, Conventiones, Litterae, et cujuscunque generis Acta Publica, inter Reges Angliae et alios quosvis Imperatores, Reges, Pontifices, Principes, vel Communitates ab Ingressu Gulielmi I. in Angliam, A.D. 1066* (London, 1818) vol. II:1, 354.

8 See Wright, *The Church and the English Crown*, 75–76; Lunt, *Financial Relations*, 496; William Lunt and Edgar Graves, eds., *Accounts Rendered by Papal Collectors in England 1317–1378* (Philadelphia: The American Philosophical Society, 1968), xiii–xiv, xxii. For lists of benefices vacated due to *Execrabilis* in the dioceses of London and Winchester, see R. C. Fowler, ed., *Registrum Radulphi Baldock, Gilberti Segrave, Ricardi Newport, et Stephani Gravesend, Episcoporum Londoniensium, A.D. MCCCIV–MCCCXXXVIII* (London: Canterbury

resignations prompted the bishops of the southern province of Canterbury to write a joint letter to the pope on May 30, 1318, claiming the vacancies forced by *Execrabilis* were severely damaging the church in England:[9]

> [T]he service of God is everywhere diminished, the cure of souls is neglected, and no hospitality of any kind is kept up; and the benefices themselves, bereft of the succour of those who should defend them, are in countless ways stripped of their rights and liberties, while the noble buildings raised by the munificence of those now dead, are falling into ruin; and bitterest thought of all, in these our days, the devotion of the lay people to the Church is, in consequence of these evils, growing utterly lukewarm, or rather vanishing altogether.[10]

To alleviate "these evils," the bishops suggested (not devoid of self-interest) that the pope empower them or other clerics in the Canterbury province to confer benefices vacated by *Execrabilis*, or that the pope collate clerks to vacant benefices using an approved list of clerks that would accompany their messenger, Master Andrew de Bruges.[11] Master Andrew's Avignon-bound letter pouch also contained a second letter from Edward II to the pope dated June 7, 1318, that had similar designs. In this letter, the king complained that *Execrabilis* had unduly restricted the benefices available to entice learned men to serve as his Chancery clerks, thereby hampering his ability to provide patronage and rule well.[12] For example, William de Thorntoft, a trusted Chancery clerk and keeper of the hanaper in 1318, resigned four benefices due to *Execrabilis*.[13] Most fourteenth-century English pluralists, however, held fewer than this.[14] To

---

and York Society, 1911) 184–86; F. J. Baignet, ed., *The Registers of John de Sandale and Rigaud de Asserio, Bishops of Winchester 1316–1323* (London: Simpkin, 1897), 94–100.

9 The prelates of the Canterbury province include the Archbishop of Canterbury and the diocesan bishops of London, Lincoln, Coventry and Lichfield, Norwich, Chicester, Bath and Wells, Exeter, Salisbury, Winchester, Ely, Worcester, Hereford, Bangor, and St. Davids. Copies of this May 30, 1318, letter may be found in Fowler, *Registrum Radulphi Baldock*, 182–84 and Baignet, *The Registers of John de Sandale*, 90–93.

10 Baignet, *The Registers of John de Sandale,* xlii–xliii, 183.

11 Fowler, *Registrum Radulphi Baldock*, 82–184; Baignet, *The Registers of John de Sandale*, 90–93.

12 Rymer, *Foedera*, 364; Baignet, *The Registers of John Sandale*, 93, n. 3.

13 Wright, *The Church and the English Crown*, 78, n. 37.

14 Returns of English pluralists in the dioceses of Salisbury and Norwich from 1366 reveal that pluralists held on average "two or three benefices" worth a combined aggregate income of between £20 and £30. See W. A. Pantin, *The English Church in the Fourteenth Century* (Cambridge: Cambridge University Press, 1955), 37.

mitigate this staffing challenge, Edward II advocated that the pope deputize the English Chancellor to confer resigned benefices upon royal clerks throughout the realm or, failing that, that the pope provide resigned benefices to specified Chancery clerks listed upon a second document in Master Andrew's possession.[15] The pope compromised with the bishops and the king: he allowed them to fill a few benefices directly, while the majority of forfeited benefices were filled by papal dispensation at the request of bishops, probably going to clerks on Master Andrew's lists.[16]

While many English parishes and some English Chancery clerks suffered under *Execrabilis*, the effect of this papal constitution on clerical royal justices in England has never been investigated. Gilbert Rothbury (c. 1260–1321), Hervey de Stanton (c. 1260–1327), and John Bacun (c. 1250–1323), well-known to legal scholars, were the only three clerical justices in the royal courts at the time *Execrabilis* was promulgated.[17] Less well known is that each of these men were pluralists. Using extant bishop's registers, Chancery documents, and papal records, this essay will compile or revise the benefice "portfolios" for each of these justices and examine the impact of *Execrabilis* upon them.[18] Such a study offers us a deeper glimpse into judicial finances, judicial patrons, and the relationships among medieval judges, ecclesiastical prelates, and lay leaders in early fourteenth-century England.

---

15 Rymer, *Foedera*, 364; Baignet, *The Registers of John Sandale*, p. 93, n. 3; Wright, *The Church and the English Crown*, 77.

16 Wright, *The Church and the English Crown*, 78–81.

17 For Rothbury, see Ryan Rowberry, "The Social Origins, Education, and Financial Relationships of Gilbert Rothbury, a Clerical Common Law Judge (1295–1321)," in *Proceedings of the Fourteenth International Congress of Medieval Canon Law*, ed. Joseph Goering, Stephan Dusil, and Andreas Thier (Vatican City: Biblioteca Apostolica Vaticana, 2016); Paul Brand, "Rothbury, Gilbert (b. in or before 1260, d. 1321),"*Oxford Dictionary of National Biography*, 2008, https://doi.org/10.1093/ref:odnb/37455. For Stanton, see Andreas Loewe, "Michaelhouse: Hervey de Stanton's Cambridge Foundation," *Church History and Religious Culture* 90, no. 4 (2010): 597–608; Paul Brand, "Stanton [Staunton], Hervey (c. 1260–1327)," *Oxford Dictionary of National Biography*, 2008, https://doi.org/10.1093/ref: odnb/26326.; G. W. Keeton, *Harvey the Hasty: A Medieval Chief Justice* (Chichester: Rose Publishing, 1978). For John Bacun, see Paul Brand, "Bacon [Bacun], John (c. 1250–c. 1323)," *Oxford Dictionary of National Biography*, 2008, https://doi.org/10.1093/ref:odnb/993.

18 Not all bishop's registers survive for the period in question. The earliest extant register for the Bishop of Ely starts in 1337, and that for the Bishop of Chichester remains only from 1396. See David M. Smith, *Guide to Bishops' Registers of England and Wales* (London: Royal Historical Society, 1981) 43–45, 67–68.

2 Creating Benefice Portfolios for Rothbury, Stanton, and Bacun

At the time of *Execrabilis*'s proclamation (November 1317), Gilbert Rothbury, Hervey de Stanton, and John Bacun had already enjoyed long and distinguished careers in royal service, rising from clerks serving in various capacities to justices in one or more of the royal courts. Rothbury served as a junior justice on the King's Bench from 1305 to 1316, when he was transferred to serve as a junior justice on the Common Bench, a post he retained until his death in May 1321.[19] Hervey de Stanton was a junior justice on the Common Bench from 1306 to 1313, after which he served as a Baron of the Exchèquer from 1313 to 1316, and then as Chancellor of the Exchequer from 1316 to 1326. During his chancellorship, Stanton also served as chief justice of the London Eyre in 1321 and as temporary chief justice of the King's Bench in 1323–1324.[20] John Bacun was the keeper of writs and rolls for the Common Bench from 1292 to 1313, at which time he became a junior justice on the Common Bench until his resignation in 1320. He died in October 1323.[21]

The benefice portfolios held by Rothbury, Stanton, and Bacun as clerical justices, however, are relatively opaque compared to their judicial careers. Bacun's benefice portfolio has never been assembled.[22] G. W. Keeton and Andreas Loewe each created a list of benefices for Stanton, but Keeton furnishes no references for his claims, and those of Loewe are incomplete and, in some cases, inaccurate.[23] We do have a benefice portfolio for Rothbury, but it also contains errors.[24] Creating or revising benefice portfolios for these three clerical justices, therefore, is necessary to assess the impact of *Execrabilis* upon clerical justices in the early fourteenth century.

The remainder of this section contains a detailed chronological listing of benefices for Rothbury, Stanton, and Bacun. Each benefice entry contains several items: (1) date of institution/collation to a benefice; (2) patron; (3) papal dispensations to hold a benefice in plurality; (4) annual value of the benefice; (5) date when a benefice was resigned or vacated, and the reason if known. Unless otherwise noted, the value for each benefice is derived from the *Taxatio*

19 Rowberry, "The Social Origins," 454; Brand, "Rothbury, Gilbert."

20 Loewe, "Michaelhouse," 584–86; Brand, "Stanton [Staunton], Hervey."

21 See Brand, "Bacon [Bacun], John."

22 Brand mentions that John Bacun "held a number of ecclesiastical livings" but does not elaborate. See Brand, "Bacon [Bacun], John."

23 Loewe, "Michaelhouse," 582–83; Keeton, *Harvey the Hasty*, 11–14.

24 Rowberry, "The Social Origins," 463–67, 469.

Ecclesiastica Angliae et Walliae, the 1291–1292 ecclesiastical taxation assessments ordered by Pope Nicholas IV (r. 1288–1292) for all English and Welsh parish churches and prebends.[25] These valuations were used to regulate taxation to popes and English kings until the sixteenth century and have been compiled into an online, searchable database—The *Taxatio* Database—hosted by the University of Sheffield.[26]

2.1 *Benefice Portfolio for Justice Gilbert Rothbury*

Swithland, Leicestershire (Diocese of Lincoln)
On December 21, 1286, Rothbury was instituted to Swithland by the Prior of Ware. Rothbury resigned this benefice sometime in the Spring of 1295.[27] Value: £8; 11 marks to rector, 1-mark pension to Prior of Ware.

Carleton Curlieu, Leicestershire (Diocese of Lincoln)
The Prior of Ware instituted Rothbury to Carleton Curlieu on November 28, 1292.[28] Rothbury resigned this benefice through his proctor and probable kinsman, John Rothbury, sometime before March 20, 1298.[29] Value: £20; 26 marks to rector, 4-mark pension to Prior of Ware.

Staindrop, Durham (Diocese of Durham)
Sometime before September 28, 1294, the Bishop of Durham instituted Rothbury to Staindrop. He received dispensation to hold this benefice in plurality on March 20, 1298 and again in February 1306.[30] Episcopal

25 The 1291–1292 valuation was intended to create an "estimated average annual yield" for each benefice, but Lunt has shown that the assessed values "were normally far below the gross actual income." In other words, the benefice values recorded for the *Taxatio*, and thus those used in this paper, probably undervalue benefices. Lunt, *Financial Relations*, 353; J. H. Denton, "The Valuation of the Ecclesiastical Benefices of England and Wales in 1291–2," *Historical Research* LXVI, no. 161 (1993): 240.

26 The Taxatio Database may be found here: Jeff Denton et al., *Taxatio*, 2014, https://www.dhi.ac.uk/taxatio/. For the lasting importance of the 1291–1292 tax, see Lunt, *Financial Relations*, 353–54.

27 Rosalind Hill, ed, T*he Rolls and Register of Bishop Oliver Sutton (1280–1299)*, Vol. VIII (Lincoln: Lincoln Record Society Vol. 76, 1986), 36, 55.

28 Hill, *Bishop Oliver Sutton*, 52.

29 Hill, *Bishop Oliver Sutton*, 68, 122–23. For more information on John Rothbury, see Rowberry, "The Social Origins," 458–59.

30 H. C. Maxwell-Lyte, ed. *Calendar of the Patent Rolls: Edward I, A.D. 1292–1301* (London: Eyre and Spottiswoode, 1895), 93; Hill, *Bishop Oliver Sutton*, 122–23; W. H. Bliss, ed., *Calendar of*

records show Rothbury as rector of Staindrop in 1316,[31] and papal records reveal that Staindrop was vacated due to *Execrabilis* in 1318, suggesting that Rothbury relinquished Staindrop at that time.[32] Value: £93 6s. 8d. to rector.[33]

Christleton, Cheshire (*Diocese of Coventry and Lichfield*)
The Abbot of Chester instituted Rothbury to Christleton sometime before October 18, 1294.[34] In February 1306 Clement v granted Rothbury a dispensation to hold Christleton in plurality.[35] Rothbury resigned Christleton before August 1318 due to *Execrabilis*.[36] Value: £13 3s.; 18 marks to rector, 1-mark 9s. 8d. pension to the Abbot of Chester.

Shillington, Bedfordshire (*Diocese of Lincoln*)
The Abbot of Ramsey instituted Rothbury to Shillington on March 20, 1298.[37] Rothbury received dispensation to hold this benefice in plurality in February 1306, and he held Shillington until he died in May 1321.[38] Value: £47 6s. 8d.; 60 marks to rector, 10-mark pension to the Abbot of Ramsey, 1-mark pension to the Prior of Newnham.

Laxfield, Suffolk (*Diocese of Norwich*)
The Prior of Eye instituted Rothbury to Laxfield sometime before March 20, 1298.[39] He received dispensation to hold this church in plurality in

Papal Registers Relating to Great Britain and Ireland: Volume II, 1305–1342. (London: Her Majesty's Stationery Office, 1895), 19.

31 T. D. Hardy, ed., *The Register of Richard de Kellawe, Lord Palatine and Bishop of Durham* (1314–1316), vol. 2, (London: Her Majesty's Stationery Office, 1874), 832–33. The register states that Rothbury died in 1316, but this is clearly wrong, as he lived until 1321.

32 Hardy, *The Register of Richard de Kellawe*, 832–33; Lunt and Graves, *Accounts Rendered*, 25.

33 Staindrop's value dropped to £60 10s. 4d. in a 1318 reassessment of northern churches due to years of Scottish incursions, see J. Caley, ed., *Taxatio Ecclesiastica Angliae et Walliae, Pope Nicholas IV, Circa 1291* (London: Record Commission, 1802), 330. See also Lunt, *Financial Relations*, 354.

34 Maxwell-Lyte, *Calendar of the Patent Rolls: Edward I, A.D. 1292–1301*, p. 121.

35 Bliss, *Calendar of Papal Registers*, vol. II, 3–4.

36 Bliss, *Calendar of Papal Registers*, vol. II, 175, 182; Lunt and Graves, *Accounts Rendered*, 15.

37 Hill, *Bishop Oliver Sutton*, 122–23.

38 Bliss, *Calendar of Papal Registers*, vol. II, 3–4; Nicholas Bennett, ed., *The Registers of Henry Burghersh 1320–1342*, Vol. III (Lincoln: Lincoln Record Society Vol. 101, 2011), 14.

39 Hill, *Bishop Oliver Sutton*, 122–23.

February 1306.[40] In 1314 Rothbury sued William Maheu and William la Symthesson for arrears of rent and damages to buildings there.[41] Rothbury resigned Laxfield due to *Execrabilis* in July 1318.[42] Value: £39 8s. 8d; 57 marks to rector, 15s. 4d. pension to the Priory of Eye, 1-mark pension to Richard Daneleres.

Hendon, Middlesex (Diocese of London)
The Abbot of Westminster instituted Rothbury to Hendon sometime between August 1303 and February 1306, when he was dispensed to hold this benefice in plurality.[43] Episcopal records show Rothbury as rector of Hendon in 1309, and there are no indications that Rothbury surrendered this benefice due to *Execrabilis*.[44] On May 29, 1321, Hugh de Byford is instituted to Hendon, suggesting that Rothbury retained Hendon until he died in early May 1321.[45] Value: £21 6s. 8d.; 30 marks to rector, 2-mark pension to the Abbot of Westminster.

Rock, Worcester (Diocese of Hereford)
The Prior of Ware instituted Rothbury to Rock sometime before February 1306.[46] Rothbury resigned this benefice due to *Execrabilis* by August 1318.[47] Value: £18; 20 marks to rector, 4-mark pension to the Prior of Ware, 3-mark pension to the Prior of Conches.[48]

40 Bliss, *Calendar of Papal Registers*, vol. II, 3–4.

41 TNA KB 27/215 f. 100d; AALT: http://aalt.law.uh.edu/E2/KB27no215/bKB27no215dorses/IMG_0100.htm.

42 Bliss, *Calendar of Papal Registers*, vol. II, 3–4, 179; Lunt and Graves, *Accounts Rendered*, 19.

43 Peter of Leicester, a royal clerk, was rector of Hendon in August 1303. See W. H. Bliss, ed., *Calendar of Papal Registers Relating to Great Britain and Ireland: Volume I, 1198–1304* (London: Her Majesty's Stationery Office, 1893), 603; Bliss, *Calendar of Papal Registers*, vol. II, 3–4.

44 R. A. Wilson, ed., *The Register of Walter Reynolds, Bishop of Worcester (1308–1313)* (London: Dugdale Society, 1928), 165; Lunt and Graves, *Accounts Rendered*, 2, 11–12.

45 Fowler, *Registrum Radulphi Baldock*, 268.

46 Bliss, *Calendar of Papal Registers*, vol. II, 3–4. In February 1306, these same papal documents state that Rothbury held the church of "Lasyl" in the diocese of Herefordshire. However, I have been unable to find such a church or village, and there is no such church listed in the *Taxatio* database. Perhaps "Lasyl" was a scribal error for one of the "Lacy" churches in Herefordshire (e.g. Ewyas Lacy)? Without further corroborating evidence, I am assuming that Rothbury did not hold "Lasyl."

47 Bliss, *Calendar of Papal Registers*, vol. II, 178; Lunt and Graves, *Accounts Rendered*, 17.

48 As rector of Rock, the *Taxatio* relates that Rothbury also received a 1-mark pension as his portion of Abberly church in Worcestershire a few miles to the south.

Prebend at Bishop's Auckland, Durham (*Diocese of Durham*)
Sometime before February 1306, the Bishop of Durham instituted Rothbury as a canon of St. Andrew's collegiate church in Bishop's Auckland.[49] Episcopal records show Rothbury as a canon in 1316,[50] and papal records list him as a canon in 1318,[51] suggesting he retained this prebend until his death in 1321. Value: £5 to canon.[52]

2.2 *Benefice Portfolio for Justice Hervey de Stanton*

Great Saxham, Suffolk (*Diocese of Norwich*)
The Abbot of St. Edmunds Abbey instituted Stanton to Great Saxham, some five miles south of Bury, on December 18, 1288.[53] He resigned this benefice in 1294 when he was instituted to the church at Thurston in 1294.[54] Value: £14 13s. 2d. to rector.

Thurston, Suffolk (*Diocese of Norwich*)
The Abbot of St. Edmunds Abbey instituted Stanton to Thurston sometime in 1294.[55] He received dispensations to hold Thurston in plurality from Clement v in November 1306, August 1307, and March 1311.[56] Stanton relinquished Thurston due to *Execrabilis* in July 1318.[57] Value: £20 to rector.

49 Bliss, *Calendar of Papal Registers*, vol. II, 3–4.
50 Hardy, *The Register of Richard de Kellawe*, 833. The register states that Rothbury died in 1316, but this is clearly wrong, as he lived until 1321.
51 Caley, *Taxatio Ecclesiastica Angliae et Walliae*, 315, 329–30.
52 The value of this prebend fell to £1 6s. 4d. in a 1318 reassessment of northern churches due to years of Scottish incursions. See Caley, *Taxatio Ecclesiastica Angliae et Walliae*, 329–30.
53 C. T. Martin, ed., *Registrum Epistolarum Fratris Johannis Peckham, Archeiopiscopi Cantuariensis*, vol. III (London: Longman & Co., 1885), 1010, 1049.
54 Bliss, *Calendar of Papal Registers*, vol. II, 19; Elizabeth Gemmill, ed., *The Register of John Salmon Bishop of Norwich* (*1299–1325*) (London: Boydell and Brewer, 2019), 41. Loewe postulates that Stanton held Great Saxham until 1306, but this is certainly wrong. Episcopal records show that on November 24, 1304, Thomas de Pevenseye held custody of Great Saxham, and he is instituted to this benefice on February 17, 1305. See Loewe, "Michaelhouse," 582; Gemmill, *The Register of John Salmon*, 41.
55 Gemmill, *The Register of John Salmon*, 41; Bliss, *Calendar of Papal Registers*, vol. II, 19; Loewe's statement that Stanton acquired Thurston in 1306 is incorrect. See Loewe, "Michaelhouse," 582.
56 Bliss, *Calendar of Papal Registers*, vol. II, 19, 42, 83.
57 Bliss, *Calendar of Papal Registers*, vol. II, 179; Lunt and Graves, *Accounts Rendered*, 19.

Warkton, Northamptonshire (*Diocese of Lincoln*)
The Abbot of St. Edmunds Abbey instituted Stanton to Warkton sometime in 1296.[58] Stanton received dispensation to hold this benefice in plurality in June 1312, but probably resigned the benefice before 1318, as Warkton is not listed in papal records as being forfeit due to *Execrabilis*.[59] This conjecture is bolstered by a report of a new rector, Master Alured de Brok, exchanging Warkton with Nicholas de Meryton on August 8, 1321.[60] Value: £11 6s. 8d. to rector.

East Dereham, Suffolk (*Diocese of Norwich*)
On September 10, 1301, the Abbot of St. Edmunds Abbey instituted Stanton to East Dereham.[61] Stanton received papal dispensations to hold this church in plurality in August 1307 and March 1311.[62] Chancery records reveal that he was still rector of East Dereham on February 11, 1327, suggesting he held this benefice until his death in November 1327.[63] Value: £82 13s. 4d.; 110 marks to rector, 14 marks to vicar.

Custody of the Prebend of St. Crantock, Cornwall (*Diocese of Exeter*)
On November 10, 1309, Bishop Stapeldon granted Stanton custody of one of the prebends of the collegiate church of St. Crantock.[64] Stanton was never collated to this prebend and retained custody for less than a year; William de la Hyde was collated to St. Crantock's by Stapeldon on August 13, 1310.[65] Value: £4 to prebendary.

Thorndon, Suffolk (*Diocese of Norwich*)
On February 1, 1311 the Prior of Eye instituted Stanton to Thorndon.[66] Stanton resigned this benefice sometime before May 11, 1317, when the

58 Bliss, *Calendar of Papal Registers*, vol. II, 19.

59 Bliss, *Calendar of Papal Registers*, vol. II, 100; Lunt and Graves, *Accounts Rendered*, 7–8, 21–24.

60 N. H. Bennett, "The Beneficed Clergy in the Diocese of Lincoln during the Episcopate of Henry Burghersh, 1320–1340," vol. 2 (Ph.D. diss., University of York, 1989), 133.

61 Gemmill, *The Register of John Salmon*, 13; see also Bliss, *Calendar of Papal Registers*, vol. II, 19.

62 Bliss, *Calendar of Papal Registers*, vol. II, 42, 83.

63 H. C. Maxwell-Lyte, *Calendar of Patent Rolls, Edward III, A.D. 1327–1330*, (London: Eyre and Spottiswoode, 1891), 10.

64 F. C. Hingeston-Randolph, ed., *The Register of Walter de Stapledon, Bishop of Exeter, 1307–1326* (London: George Bell & Sons, 1892), 249; Loewe's assertion that Stanton held a prebend of St. Crantock's is erroneous. See Loewe, "Michaelhouse," 583.

65 Hingeston-Randolph, *The Register of Walter de Stapeldon*, 249.

66 Gemmill, *The Register of John Salmon*, 107.

Prior of Eye instituted Master Thomas de Foxtone, professor of Civil Law, to Thorndon.[67] Value: £27 6d. 8d.; 40 marks to rector, 1-mark pension to the Prior of Eye.

Elm, Cambridgeshire (*Diocese of Ely*)
Sometime prior to March 1311 the Bishop of Ely instituted Stanton to Elm, which also contained the dependent chapel of Enmethe.[68] Stanton received papal dispensation under Clement V to hold this benefice in plurality.[69] He remained rector of Elm on December 10, 1317, but appears to have resigned soon thereafter, as papal records indicate that Elm was to be taxed in 1318 due to a new incumbent.[70] While *Execrabilis* was not the direct cause for Stanton's resignation of Elm, it may have been a factor in his decision to relinquish it. Value: £22; 25.5 marks to rector, 7.5-mark pension to Prior of Lewes.

Mellis, Suffolk (*Diocese of Norwich*)
On January 27, 1312, the Prior of Eye instituted Stanton to Mellis, and in June 1312 Stanton received dispensation to hold the church in plurality.[71] Stanton held Mellis for only a few years because Richard de Lughteburgh became rector on December 20, 1315.[72] Value: £10 4s.; 15 marks to rector, 4s. pension to the Prior of Eye.

Prebend of Shaldford, Essex (*Diocese of Bath and Wells*)
In January 1313, Bishop John Drokensford collated Stanton, his erstwhile colleague in the royal courts, to the church of Shaldford, one of the prebends of Wells Cathedral.[73] Stanton likely held this prebend for just over seven years, as Robert de Wamberg was collated to Shaldford in

67 Gemmill, *The Register of John Salmon*, 177.

68 Bliss, *Calendar of Papal Registers*, vol. II, 83. Loewe is incorrect in believing Stanton became "parson of Enmethe" in 1317, see Loewe, "Michaelhouse," 583.

69 Bliss, *Calendar of Papal Registers*, vol. II, 83.

70 H. C. Maxwell-Lyte, ed., *Calendar of Patent Rolls, Edward II, Vol. III, A.D. 1317–1321*, (London: Mackie and Co., 1903), 62, 65; Lunt and Graves, *Accounts Rendered*, 21.

71 Gemmill, *The Register of John Salmon*, 122; Bliss, *Calendar of Papal Registers*, vol. II, 100; Loewe's assertion that Stanton acquired Mellis around 1295 is incorrect, see Loewe, "Michaelhouse," 582.

72 H. C. Maxwell-Lyte, ed., *Calendar of Patent Roll, Edward II, A.D. 1313–1317* (London: Eyre and Spottiswoode, 1898), 377; Gemmill, *The Register of John Salmon*, 171.

73 E. Hobhouse, ed., *Calendar and Register of John de Drokensford, Bishop of Bath and Wells (1309–1329)*, (London: Somerset Record Society, 1887), 151.

June 1321.[74] Value: £17 3s. 4d.; 22 marks to prebendary, 3 marks to Vicar of Shaldford, 10s. to the Abbot of St. Osithe.

North Creake, Norfolk (*Diocese of Norwich*)
On October 17, 1316, Sir Edmund de Packenham, a knight, presented Stanton to North Creake.[75] Stanton still held this benefice as of March 8, 1320, and may have been rector until his death in 1327.[76] Value: £31 4s.; 45 marks to rector, 1 mark 10s. 8d. to the Prior of Norwich cathedral.

Prebend of Flixton, Lancashire (*Diocese of Coventry and Lichfield*)
On October 20, 1316, Bishop Walter Langton collated Stanton to Flixton, a prebend of Lichfield cathedral.[77] On October 25, 1319, Stanton exchanged Flixton with John Husthwaite for his prebend of St. Nicholas, Husthwaite, attached to York Minster. Husthwaite was collated to Flixton on November 11, 1319.[78] Value: £4 13s. 4d. to prebendary.

Prebend of Husthwaite, Yorkshire (*Diocese of York*)
On October 25, 1319, King Edward II presented Stanton to St. Nicholas, Husthwaite, a prebend of York Minster.[79] Stanton held this prebend until his death in November 1327.[80] Value: £26 13s. 4d. to prebendary.

Prebend of Compton Dunden, Somerset (*Diocese of Bath and Wells*)
Sometime before December 1320 Bishop John Drokensford collated Stanton to Compton Dunden, for Stanton presented one of his clerks, John Hunterston,[81] as vicar due to the death of the old vicar, Ralph de Clyvedon.[82] Stanton probably held this prebend until January 1327,

74 *Calendar and Register of John de Drokensford, Bishop of Bath and Wells (1309–1329)*, 202.

75 Gemmill, *The Register of John Salmon*, 170.

76 Maxwell-Lyte, *Calendar of Patent Rolls, Edward II, Vol. III, A.D. 1317–1321*, 446.

77 J. B. Hughes, ed., *The Register of Walter Langton, Bishop of Coventry and Lichfield (1296–1321)*, vol. I (London: Boydell and Brewer, 2001), 100.

78 Hughes, *The Register of Walter Langton*, 166.

79 Maxwell-Lyte, *Calendar of Patent Rolls, Edward II, Vol. III, A.D. 1317–1321*, 393, 403; T. C. B. Timmins, ed., *The Register of William Melton, Archbishop of York, 1317–1340*, vol. V (London: Boydell and Brewer, 2002), 28–29.

80 Timmins, *The Register of William Melton*, 81.

81 Bennett, *The Registers of Henry Burghersh*, 66.

82 Hobhouse, *Calendar and Register of John de Drokensford*, 184. The editors of the *Fasti Ecclesiae Anglicanae* note that Stanton was collated to this benefice in 1313. But this appears to be an error, as their evidence refers to Stanton's collation to Shaldford, not

when Alan de Hothum was collated to Compton Dunden.[83] Value: £10 to prebendary.

2.3 *Benefice Portfolio for Justice John Bacun*

Middleton, Middlesex (*Diocese of London*)
On February 8, 1287, King Edward I presented John Bacun to Middleton.[84] It is unclear how long Bacun held this benefice, but he was probably not rector in 1308, as a papal letter dispensing him for pluralities does not include Middleton.[85] However, a final concord from 1310 has Bacun purchasing John Toucestre's tenement in Middleton for £10, so he did retain some landed interest in the parish.[86] Value: £5 to rector.

Ewelme, Oxford (*Diocese of Lincoln*)
John Bacun acquired the manor and advowson of Ewelme from Adam le Despenser in 1294 and the following year obtained a quitclaim to both from Adam's son, Almaric, for £100.[87] By Trinity term 1295, John Bacun was rector of Ewelme, as Common Pleas records show him bringing a suit of debt against Geoffrey of Kingswell for arrears of payments due on the sale of the fruits of the church.[88] In 1297 John received a royal license to enfeoff his brother, Edmund, with Ewelme manor and its advowson for an annual rent of £20, and by 1311 Edmund had settled the manor on himself and his wife, Joan.[89] John Bacun probably remained rector of Ewelme until around 1317, as papal records show that the church of Ewelme was

---

Compton Dunden. See B. Jones, "Prebendaries: Compton Dundon," in *Fasti Ecclesiae Anglicanae 1300–1541*, Vol. VIII, Bath and Wells Diocese (London: Institute of Historical Research, 1964), 40–41.

83 Hobhouse, *Calendar and Register of John de Drokensford*, 279.

84 H. C. Maxwell-Lyte, ed., *Calendar of Patent Rolls, Edward I, A.D. 1281–1292* (London: Eyre and Spottiswoode, 1893), 263.

85 Bliss, *Calendar of Papal Registers*, vol. II, 39.

86 H. C. Maxwell-Lyte, ed., *A Descriptive Catalogue of Ancient Deeds: Volume 6*, C.6291 (London: His Majesty's Stationery Office, 1915), 324.

87 TNA C143/22/27; TNA E 210/5792; TNA CP 40/110 m. 293. AALT: http://aalt.law.uh.edu/E1/CP40no110/aCP40no110fronts/IMG_1147.htm. I owe this reference to the generosity of Dr. Paul Brand.

88 See TNA CP 40/109, m. 126d. AALT: http://aalt.law.uh.edu/E1/CP40no109/bCP40no109dorses/IMG_0556.htm. I owe this reference to the generosity of Dr. Paul Brand.

89 Maxwell-Lyte, *Calendar of the Patent Rolls: Edward I, A.D. 1292–1301*, 289; H. C. Maxwell-Lyte, *Calendar of Patent Rolls, Edward II, A.D. 1307–1313*, (London: Eyre and Spottiswoode, 1894), 400; H. C. Maxwell-Lyte, ed., *Calendar of the Charter Rolls, Edward I, Edward II, A.D. 1300–1326*, (London: Mackie and Co., 1908), 138.

taxed for first fruits (the installation of a new rector) in 1318.[90] Value: £12 to rector.

Reston, Suffolk (Diocese of Norwich)
Although neither the village nor church of Reston are extant, Reston used to lie somewhere between Southtown and Gorleston in Suffolk.[91] John Bacun owned lands in Reston from at least 1293, and the church in Reston may date from around this time, as we do not find one listed in the *Taxatio* valuations of 1291–1292.[92] By 1306 Bacun was instituted as rector of Reston; he was sued by Robert Rose and eleven others for arrears of payments due on the sale of fruits of the church in Easter term 1307.[93] In June 1308 Bacun received dispensation from Clement V to hold Reston in plurality, and he retained Reston until 1318, when he was forced to resign the benefice due to *Execrabilis*.[94] Value: £40 to rector.[95]

Prebend of Wimborne, Dorset (Diocese of Salisbury)
Prior to July 13, 1310, King Edward II instituted Bacun to a prebend in Wimborne Minster collegiate church.[96] I have been unable to determine how long Bacun held this benefice.[97] Value: £10.

---

90 See Lunt and Graves, *Accounts Rendered*, 22.

91 See Maxwell-Lyte, *Calendar of the Patent Rolls: Edward I, A.D. 1292–1301*, 15. Early in the reign of Edward III the inhabitants of Little Yarmouth (now Southtown), Reston, and Gorleston sent a joint petition to the crown asking to be relieved of a royal tax because sea flooding had damaged their towns. See TNA SC 8/54/2668. Reston may have later been renamed "Bacon's Manor," a subsidiary manor to Gorleston, and a John Bacun (probably a relative) is buried in the chancel of Gorleston church. See Alfred Suckling, "Gorleston," in *The History and Antiquities of the County of Suffolk*, vol. I (Ipswich: W. S. Crowell, 1846), 360–70.

92 On May 18, 1293, Bacun received a royal "license to enclose a way in Reston adjoining his messuage leading from Little Yarmouth to Morford so long as he make another road on his ground leading direct to Morford," Maxwell-Lyte, *Calendar of the Patent Rolls: Edward I, A.D. 1292–1301*, 15. Later, on August 27, 1300, John Bacun received a royal grant of "free warren, in all his demesne lands of Reston." H. C. Maxwell-Lyte, ed., *Calendar of the Charter Rolls, Henry III, Edward I, A.D. 1257–1300* (London: Mackie and Co., 1906), 489.

93 TNA CP 40/163, m. 41. AALT: http://aalt.law.uh.edu/E1/CP40no163/aCP40no163fronts/IMG_0083.htm. I owe this reference to the generosity of Dr. Paul Brand.

94 Bliss, *Calendar of Papal Registers*, vol. II, 214; Lunt and Graves, *Accounts Rendered*, 19.

95 The value of Reston is not listed in the *Taxatio*, but other papal records record its value. See Lunt and Graves, *Accounts Rendered*, 19.

96 Maxwell-Lyte, *Calendar of Patent Rolls, Edward II, A.D. 1307–1313*, 266.

97 In her catalogue of the prebendaries of Wimborne, Patricia Coulstock provides no names for prebendaries between 1300–1320. See Patricia Coulstock, *Collegiate Church of Wimborne Minster* (London: Boydell Press, 1993), 237.

Akenham, Suffolk (*Diocese of Norwich*)
On May 6, 1313, Edmund Bacun granted the custody of Akenham to his brother, John, until November 25, 1313.[98] Soon thereafter, on December 16, 1313, custody of Akenham was transferred to John de Bradewell who became rector on February 3, 1314.[99] Value: £6 13s. 4d. to rector.

Bintree, Norfolk (*Diocese of Norwich*)
On September 26, 1316, Bishop John Salmon presented John Bacun to Bintree.[100] Bacun retained Bintree until early 1318, when he resigned it due to *Execrabilis*.[101] Value: £13 6s. 8d. to rector.

Salle, Norfolk (*Diocese of Norwich*)
On September 26, 1316, Edmund Bacun presented his brother, John, to Salle, which lay adjacent to John's lands in Oulton.[102] John remained rector of Salle until at least late August 1321, and he may have held this benefice until he died in 1323.[103] Value: £26 13s. 4d. to rector.

3 Tabulating the Benefice Information

This section translates the benefice portfolios for Rothbury, Stanton, and Bacun into three separate tables (Tables 13.1–13.3), one for each clerical justice. Each table graphically depicts (1) the location of each benefice; (2) the patron for each benefice; (3) the years each justice held that benefice; (4) the legal position each justice filled during any given year; (5) the annual value for each benefice; and (6) the approximate annual and total income received from benefices. Tables 13.1–13.3, therefore, provide an approximate reconstruction of the income Rothbury, Stanton, and Bacun derived from ecclesiastical livings over the course of their lifetimes.[104] This will allow us to assess the importance

98 Gemmill, *The Register of John Salmon*, 138.
99 Gemmill, *The Register of John Salmon*, 143, 145.
100 Gemmill, *The Register of John Salmon*, 168.
101 Lunt and Graves, *Accounts Rendered*, 19; Gemmill, *The Register of John Salmon*, 187.
102 Gemmill, *The Register of John Salmon*, 18, 26, 168.
103 Bliss, *Calendar of Papal Registers*, vol. II, 198.
104 I use the term "approximate," as the exact dates for all institutions or resignations for each benefice are unknown. Furthermore, clerical justices often farmed out their benefices for certain sums, sometimes the king sequestered the fruits of certain benefices, and other times benefices were taxed at an unknown rate by bishops. See Hill, *Bishop Oliver Sutton*, 122–23.

TABLE 13.1 Patrons and benefices of Gilbert Rothbury

	Year	Prior of Ware			Bishop of Durham		Abbot of Chester	Prior of Eye	Abbot of Ramsey	Westminster Abbey	Approx. annual total
		Swithland (Leic.)	Rock (Heref.)	Carlton Curlieu (Leic.)	Staindrop (Dur.)	Prebend Auckland (Dur.)	Christleton (Ches.)	Laxfield (Suff.)	Shillington (Beds.)	Hendon (Midd.)	
CL Lawyer	1287	£7 6s. 8d.									£7 6s. 8d.
	1288	£7 6s. 8d.									£7 6s. 8d.
	1289	£7 6s. 8d.									£7 6s. 8d.
Clerk of Parl. & Clerk of King's Council	1290	£7 6s. 8d.									£7 6s. 8d.
	1291	£7 6s. 8d.									£7 6s. 8d.
	1292	£7 6s. 8d.									£7 6s. 8d.
	1293	£7 6s. 8d.		£17 6s. 8d.							£24 13s. 4d.
	1294	£7 6s. 8d.		£17 6s. 8d.							£24 13s. 4d.
King's Bench Justice	1295			£17 6s. 8d.	£93 6s. 8d.		£12				£122 13s. 4d.

TABLE 13.1 Patrons and benefices of Gilbert Rothbury (*cont.*)

Year	Prior of Ware			Bishop of Durham		Abbot of Chester	Prior of Eye	Abbot of Ramsey	Westminster Abbey	Approx. annual total
	Swithland (Leic.)	Rock (Heref.)	Carlton Curlieu (Leic.)	Staindrop (Dur.)	Prebend Auckland (Dur.)	Christleton (Ches.)	Laxfield (Suff.)	Shillington (Beds.)	Hendon (Midd.)	
1296			£17 6s. 8d.	£93 6s. 8d.		£12				£122 13s. 4d.
1297			£17 6s. 8d.	£93 6s. 8d.		£12				£122 13s. 4d.
1298				£93 6s. 8d.		£12	£38	£40		£183 6s. 8d.
1299				£93 6s. 8d.		£12	£38	£40		£183 6s. 8d.
1300				£93 6s. 8d.		£12	£38	£40		£183 6s. 8d.
1301				£93 6s. 8d.		£12	£38	£40		£183 6s. 8d.
1302				£93 6s. 8d.		£12	£38	£40		£183 6s. 8d.
1303				£93 6s. 8d.		£12	£38	£40		£183 6s. 8d.

TABLE 13.1 Patrons and benefices of Gilbert Rothbury (*cont.*)

Year	Prior of Ware			Bishop of Durham		Abbot of Chester	Prior of Eye	Abbot of Ramsey	Westminster Abbey	Approx. annual total
	Swithland (Leic.)	Rock (Heref.)	Carlton Curlieu (Leic.)	Staindrop (Dur.)	Prebend Auckland (Dur.)	Christleton (Ches.)	Laxfield (Suff.)	Shillington (Beds.)	Hendon (Midd.)	
1304				£93 6s. 8d.		£12	£38	£40		£183 6s. 8d.
1305				£93 6s. 8d.		£12	£38	£40		£183 6s. 8d.
1306		£13 6s. 8d.		£93 6s. 8d.	£5	£12	£38	£40	£20	£221 13s. 4d.
1307		£13 6s. 8d.		£93 6s. 8d.	£5	£12	£38	£40	£20	£221 13s. 4d.
1308		£13 6s. 8d.		£93 6s. 8d.	£5	£12	£38	£40	£20	£221 13s. 4d.
1309		£13 6s. 8d.		£93 6s. 8d.	£5	£12	£38	£40	£20	£221 13s. 4d.
1310		£13 6s. 8d.		£93 6s. 8d.	£5	£12	£38	£40	£20	£221 13s. 4d.
1311		£13 6s. 8d.		£93 6s. 8d.	£5	£12	£38	£40	£20	£221 13s. 4d.

TABLE 13.1 Patrons and benefices of Gilbert Rothbury (*cont.*)

	Year	Prior of Ware			Bishop of Durham		Abbot of Chester	Prior of Eye	Abbot of Ramsey	Westminster Abbey	Approx. annual total
		Swithland (Leic.)	Rock (Heref.)	Carlton Curlieu (Leic.)	Staindrop (Dur.)	Prebend Auckland (Dur.)	Christleton (Ches.)	Laxfield (Suff.)	Shillington (Beds.)	Hendon (Midd.)	
	1312		£13 6s. 8d.		£93 6s. 8d.	£5	£12	£38	£40	£20	£221 13s. 4d.
	1313		£13 6s. 8d.		£93 6s. 8d.	£5	£12	£38	£40	£20	£221 13s. 4d.
	1314		£13 6s. 8d.		£93 6s. 8d.	£5	£12	£38	£40	£20	£221 13s. 4d.
	1315		£13 6s. 8d.		£93 6s. 8d.	£5	£12	£38	£40	£20	£221 13s. 4d.
Common Bench Justice	1316		£13 6s. 8d.		£93 6s. 8d.	£5	£12	£38	£40	£20	£221. 13s. 4d.
	1317		£13 6s. 8d.		£93 6s. 8d.	£5	£12	£38	£40	£20	£221 13s. 4d.
	EXECRABILIS										
	1318					£1 6s. 4d.			£40	£20	£61 6s. 4d.

TABLE 13.1 Patrons and benefices of Gilbert Rothbury (*cont.*)

Year	Prior of Ware			Bishop of Durham		Abbot of Chester	Prior of Eye	Abbot of Ramsey	Westminster Abbey	Approx. annual total
	Swithland (Leic.)	Rock (Heref.)	Carlton Curlieu (Leic.)	Staindrop (Dur.)	Prebend Auckland (Dur.)	Christleton (Ches.)	Laxfield (Suff.)	Shillington (Beds.)	Hendon (Midd.)	
1319					£1 6s. 4d.			£40	£20	£61 6s. 4d.
1320					£1 6s. 4d.			£40	£20	£61 6s. 4d.
1321										0
Approx. Total	£58 13s. 4d.	£180	£77	£2146 13s. 4d.	£63 13s.	£276	£760	£920	£300	£4575 6s. 4d.

TABLE 13.2 Patrons and benefices of Hervey de Stanton

	Year	Abbot of St. Edmund's				Prior of Eye	
		Great Saxham (Suff.)	Thurston (Suff.)	Warkton (North.)	East Dereham (Suff.)	Thorndon (Suff.)	Mellis (Suff.)
CL Lawyer	1289	£14 13s. 2d.					
	1290	£14 13s. 2d.					
	1291	£14 13s. 2d.					
	1292	£14 13s. 2d.					
Royal Clerk and Assize Justice	1293	£14 13s. 2d.					
	1294		£20				
	1295		£20				
	1296		£20				
	1297		£20	£11 6s. 8d.			
	1298		£20	£11 6s. 8d.			
	1299		£20	£11 6s. 8d.			
	1300		£20	£11 6s. 8d.			
	1301		£20	£11 6s. 8d.			
	1302		£20	£11 6s. 8d.	£73 6s. 8d.		
	1303		£20	£11 6s. 8d.	£73 6s. 8d.		
	1304		£20	£11 6s. 8d.	£73 6s. 8d.		
	1305		£20	£11 6s. 8d.	£73 6s. 8d.		
Common Bench Justice	1306		£20	£11 6s. 8d.	£73 6s. 8d.		
	1307		£20	£11 6s. 8d.	£73 6s. 8d.		
	1308		£20	£11 6s. 8d.	£73 6s. 8d.		
	1309		£20	£11 6s. 8d.	£73 6s. 8d.		
	1310		£20	£11 6s. 8d.	£73 6s. 8d.		
	1311		£20	£11 6s. 8d.	£73 6s. 8d.	£26 13s. 4d.	
	1312		£20	£11 6s. 8d.	£73 6s. 8d.	£26 13s. 4d.	£10
	1313		£20		£73 6s. 8d.	£26 13s. 4d.	£10

ishop of Bath & ells		Bishop of Ely	Bishop of Cov. & Lich.	Arch. of York	Bishop of Exeter	Sir Edmund de Packenham	**Approx. Annual Total**
reb of haldford ss.)	Preb. of Compton Dunden (Som.)	Elm (Camb.)	Preb. of Flixton (Lanc.)	Preb. of Husthwaite (York)	Preb. of St. Crantock (Corn.)	North Creake (Norf.)	
							£14 13s. 2d.
							£14 13s. 2d.
							£14 13s. 2d.
							£14 13s. 2d.
							£14 13s. 2d.
							£20
							£20
							£20
							£31 6s. 8d.
							£31 6s. 8d.
							£31 6s. 8d.
							£31 6s. 8d.
							£31 6s. 8d.
							£104 13s. 4d.
							£104 13s. 4d.
							£104 13s. 4d.
							£104 13s. 4d.
							£104 13s. 4d.
							£104 13s. 4d.
							£104 13s. 4d.
							£104 13s. 4d.
					£2		£106 13s. 4d.
		£17					£148
		£17					£158
14 13s. 4d.		£17					£161 13s. 4d.

TABLE 13.2 Patrons and benefices of Hervey de Stanton (*cont.*)

	Year	Abbot of St. Edmund's				Prior of Eye	
		Great Saxham (Suff.)	Thurston (Suff.)	Warkton (North.)	East Dereham (Suff.)	Thorndon (Suff.)	Mellis (Suff.)
Eyre Justice	1314		£20		£73 6s. 8d.	£26 13s. 4d.	£10
	1315		£20		£73 6s. 8d.	£26 13s. 4d.	£10
Baron and Chancellor of Exchequer	1316		£20		£73 6s. 8d.	£26 13s. 4d.	
	1317		£20		£73 6s. 8d.		
	Execrabilis						
	1318				£73 6s. 8d.		
	1319				£73 6s. 8d.		
	1320				£73 6s. 8d.		
	1321				£73 6s. 8d.		
	1322				£73 6s. 8d.		
	1323				£73 6s. 8d.		
	1324				£73 6s. 8d.		
	1325				£73 6s. 8d.		
	1326				£73 6s. 8d.		
Retired	1327				£73 6s. 8d.		
Approx. Total		£73 5s. 10d.	£480	£77	£1906 13s. 4d.	£160	£40

ishop of Bath & Vells		Bishop of Ely	Bishop of Cov. & Lich.	Arch. of York	Bishop of Exeter	Sir Edmund de Packenham	Approx. Annual Total
reb of haldford Ess.)	Preb. of Compton Dunden (Som.)	Elm (Camb.)	Preb. of Flixton (Lanc.)	Preb. of Husthwaite (York)	Preb. of St. Crantock (Corn.)	North Creake (Norf.)	
14 13s. 4d.		£17					£161 13s. 4d.
14 13s. 4d.		£17					£161 13s. 4d.
14 13s. 4d.		£17					£151 13s. 4d.
14 13s. 4d.		£17	£4 13s. 4d.			£30	£159 13s. 4d.
14 13s. 4d.			£4 13s. 4d.			£30	£122 13s. 4d.
14 13s. 4d.			£4 13s. 4d.			£30	£122 13s. 4d.
14 13s. 4d.				£26 13s.4d.		£30	£144 13s. 4d.
	£10			£26 13s.4d.		£30	£140
	£10			£26 13s.4d.		£30	£140
	£10			£26 13s.4d.		£30	£140
	£10			£26 13s.4d.		£30	£140
	£10			£26 13s.4d.		£30	£140
	£10			£26 13s.4d.		£30	£140
				£26 13s.4d.		£30	£130
117 6s. 8d.	£60	£119	£14	£213 6s. 8d.	£2	£330	£3592 12s. 6d.

TABLE 13.3 Patrons and benefices of John Bacun

	Year	Sir Edmund Bacun		King of England		Unknown	Bishop of Norfolk	Unknown	Approx. Annual Total
		Salle (Norf.)	Akenham (Suff.)	Middleton (Midd.)	Prebend Wimborne (Dor.)	Ewelme (Oxon)	Bintree (Norf.)	Reston (Suff.)	
Royal Clerk	1287			£5					£5
	1288			£5					£5
	1289			£5					£5
	1290			£5					£5
	1291			£5					£5
CB Keeper of Writs and Rolls	1292			£5					£5
	1293			£5					£5
	1294			£5					£5
	1295			£5		£12			£17
	1296			£5		£12			£17
	1297			£5		£12			£17
	1298			£5		£12			£17
	1299			£5		£12			£17

TABLE 13.3 Patrons and benefices of John Bacun (*cont.*)

	Year	Sir Edmund Bacun		King of England		Unknown	Bishop of Norfolk	Unknown	Approx. Annual Total
		Salle (Norf.)	Akenham (Suff.)	Middleton (Midd.)	Prebend Wimborne (Dor.)	Ewelme (Oxon)	Bintree (Norf.)	Reston (Suff.)	
	1300			£5		£12			£17
	1301			£5		£12			£17
	1302			£5		£12			£17
	1303			£5		£12			£17
	1304			£5		£12			£17
	1305			£5		£12			£17
	1306			£5		£12		£40	£57
	1307			£5		£12		£40	£57
	1308					£12		£40	£52
	1309					£12		£40	£52
	1310				£10	£12		£40	£62
	1311				£10	£12		£40	£62
	1312				£10	£12		£40	£62
Common Bench Justice	1313		£3 6s. 8d.		£10	£12		£40	£65 6s. 8d.

TABLE 13.3 Patrons and benefices of John Bacun (*cont.*)

	Year	Sir Edmund Bacun		King of England		Unknown	Bishop of Norfolk	Unknown	Approx. Annual Total
		Salle (Norf.)	Akenham (Suff.)	Middleton (Midd.)	Prebend Wimborne (Dor.)	Ewelme (Oxon)	Bintree (Norf.)	Reston (Suff.)	
	1314				£10	£12		£40	£62
	1315				£10	£12		£40	£62
	1316				£10	£12		£40	£62
	1317	£26 13s. 4d.			£10	£12	£13 6s. 8d.	£40	£102
	EXECRABILIS								
	1318	£26 13s. 4d.			£10				£36 13s. 4d.
	1319	£26 13s. 4d.							£26 13s. 4d.
	1320	£26 13s. 4d.							£26 13s. 4d.
Misc. Jud. Appt.	1321	£26 13s. 4d.							£26 13s. 4d.

TABLE 13.3 Patrons and benefices of John Bacun (*cont.*)

Year	Sir Edmund Bacun		King of England		Unknown	Bishop of Norfolk	Unknown	Approx. Annual Total
	Salle (Norf.)	Akenham (Suff.)	Middleton (Midd.)	Prebend Wimborne (Dor.)	Ewelme (Oxon)	Bintree (Norf.)	Reston (Suff.)	
1322	£26 13s. 4d.							£26 13s. 4d.
1323	£26 13s. 4d.							£26 13s. 4d.
Approx. Total	£186 13s. 4d.	£3 6s. 8d.	£105	£90	£276	£13 6s. 8d.	£480	£1154 6s. 8d.

of ecclesiastical livings to the finances of these clerical justices, determine the pecuniary impact that *Execrabilis* had on the benefice portfolios for each justice, and examine the various relationships that these justices formed with powerful patrons aside from the crown.

Before examining Tables 13.1–13.3, however, some methodological comments are necessary. Annual values for each benefice track contemporary records—either those from the *Taxatio Database* or those from the papal records of Rigaud de Asserio when a *Taxatio* valuation is unavailable. But precisely how and when these clerical justices received the income for each benefice is unknown. Contemporary records suggest that the typical payment arrangement for benefices consisted of two installments annually; one at Easter and a second at Michaelmas.[105] When Rothbury, Stanton, or Bacun held a benefice for only a fraction of a year, I have used a rounding principle: if the justice was instituted before July 1, I have included income from that year; otherwise the income from that benefice begins the following year. Similarly, when a date range exists for when a justice was instituted/collated into a benefice or resigned a benefice, I have assumed the latest year for institutions and the earliest year for resignations.[106] Using this methodology, Tables 13.1–13.3 tend to underestimate rather than overestimate the amount of income these clerical justices received from ecclesiastical livings.

4 Effects of Execrabilis

Much can be said about Tables 13.1–13.3, but two primary conclusions emerge about how *Execrabilis* affected clerical justices serving in the royal courts. The first and most demonstrable effect was financial. Despite their positions at the apex of the English legal system, English bishops swiftly and widely enforced *Execrabilis* against Rothbury, Stanton, and Bacun. Rothbury relinquished four benefices (Staindrop, Christleton, Laxfield, and Rock) worth a combined annual revenue of £157 (over 200 marks) within a year of the papal decree reaching England. Rothbury's revenue from his benefices declined a massive 71% from 1317 to 1318.[107] Bacun also forfeited two of his benefices under

105 The payment to John Bacun for the farm of Ewelme was due half at Easter and half at Michaelmas. See TNA CP 40/109, m. 126d.

106 For example, Rothbury was instituted into Hendon sometime between August 1303 and February 1306. I have assumed that Rothbury's income from Hendon began in 1306.

107 I divided the values of the four benefices Rothbury lost through *Execrabilis* (£157) by his approximate annual total in 1317 (£221).

Execrabilis—those at Reston and Bintree—valued at a total of £53 6s. 8d. (80 marks), losing 58% of his annual benefice revenue.[108] Stanton only lost one benefice (Thurston, £20, or 30 marks), resulting in a 13% decline of his annual benefice revenue; his resignation from Elm in December 1317 might also have been prompted by the papal decree.[109]

The scale of these staggering financial losses due to *Execrabilis* emerges into sharper focus when viewed within the context of contemporary wages. In the late thirteenth and early fourteenth century, a skilled laborer such as a carpenter could be hired at three pennies per day, and the annual wage for many vicars was 5 marks (~£3.5).[110] As junior justices on the Common Bench, Rothbury, Stanton, and Bacun each enjoyed a far greater yearly salary from the crown at £27 (40 marks). When serving as Chancellor of the Exchequer, Stanton would have received even more—£40 (60 marks) per year.[111] Comparing the financial impact of *Execrabilis* to Rothbury's annual royal salary reveals that the papal decretal forced him to forfeit nearly six times his annual judicial salary (£157), enough to hire forty vicars for a year at the standard annual wage of 5 marks. Likewise, under *Execrabilis* Bacun forfeited 80 marks per annum—two times his annual judicial salary—and Stanton lost at least 20 marks, the equivalent of one-half of one year's judicial salary. English clerical justices, therefore, commanded revenue streams through ecclesiastical benefices that routinely dwarfed royal compensation, highlighting the vast reservoirs of wealth available to clerical justices from patrons besides the king.

108 I divided the values of the two benefices Bacun forfeited under *Execrabilis* (£53) by his approximate annual total in 1317 (£92).

109 If we add Stanton's loss of Elm to his loss of Thurston, his benefice revenue losses rise to 23%.

110 Christopher Dyer, *Making a Living in the Middle Ages: The People of Britain 850–1520* (London: Yale University Press, 2002), 240; Shinners and Dohar, *Pastors and the Care of Souls*, xviii.

111 Judicial salaries were standardized in August 1278 following the Parliament at Gloucester. Chief Justices received 60 marks annually in two installments, and junior justices received 40 marks annually in two installments. See H. C. Maxwell-Lyte, ed., *Calendar of Close Rolls, Edward I, A.D. 1272–1279* (London: Eyre and Spottiswoode, 1900), 503–4; G. O. Sayles, ed., *Select Cases in the Court of King's Bench under Edward I*, vol. 1 (London: Bernard Quatrich, 1936), LXXIII–LXXIV. The payment of judicial salaries, however, was often in arrears. Rothbury was paid for four years of judicial service on the King's Bench on December 1, 1299, see TNA C62/79 m. 9. On January 30, 1304, he was paid for the years 1300–1303, see TNA C62/80 m. 4. On February 10, 1309, he was given authorization to receive 200 marks for the royal treasury for the years 1304–1308, see TNA C62/85 m.4. And on October 28, 1317, he was granted 240 marks for his service as a King's Bench justice for the years 1311–1316, see TNA C62/94 m. 3.

Do not grieve too much for Rothbury, Stanton, and Bacun; all three died very rich. Rothbury established two loan chests at Oxford University totaling 250 marks (£167), one of the largest loan-chest endowments in the history of the university.[112] Bacun used his wealth to accrue several manors and lands throughout Norfolk, Suffolk, Essex, and Oxfordshire.[113] In 1326 Stanton had £800 on deposit at St. Edmunds Abbey, which Isabella and Mortimer requisitioned to aid their invasion.[114] Most tellingly, Stanton's great wealth enabled him to found Cambridge's third college, Michaelhouse (subsumed into Trinity College Cambridge).[115] Despite the wealth they accumulated over the course of their legal careers, however, the substantial losses resulting from *Execrabilis* in 1318 must have been jolting.

Financial losses, however, were not the only losses precipitated by *Execrabilis.* Just as important to Rothbury, Stanton, Bacun, and their benefactors was the weakening of relationships founded on the common currency of patronage. Religious houses often had vast landholdings. Access to a clerical judge for legal advice or assistance in litigation to protect their interests was desirable, particularly during the thirteenth and fourteenth centuries when more and more religious houses and secular lords directly managed their demesne lands rather than leasing them out.[116] From the justices' perspective, ecclesiastical patrons were a valuable source of friendship, funding, and influence that could buttress their own positions and desires. We catch a glimpse of this important reciprocal relationship in a few early fourteenth-century letters from John de Sautre, the Abbot of Ramsey (patron of Rothbury's benefice at Shillington worth £40 per year), to the justice. In these letters, the abbot invites Rothbury to stay at Ramsey Abbey, thanks him for procuring specialized Chancery writs, for which he promises to refund him *cum usura*, and requests information about Parliamentary proceedings.[117] The tone of these letters suggests an intimate, comfortable, familiar, and influential relationship between abbot and justice.

---

112 See Rowberry, "The Social Origins," 459–62.

113 See Brand, "Stanton [Staunton], Hervey."

114 William Stubbs, ed., *Chronicles of the Reigns of Edward I and Edward II*, vol. I (London: Longman & Co., 1882), 314; H. C. Maxwell-Lyte, ed., *Calendar of Close Rolls, Edward III, A.D. 1327–1330* (London: Eyre and Spottiswoode, 1896), 189, 249.

115 See Loewe, "Michaelhouse," 588–608. Stanton is buried in the church of St. Michael in Cambridge, and his tomb can still be visited today.

116 J. R. Maddicott, "Law and Lordship: Royal Justices as Retainers in Thirteenth and Fourteenth Century England," *Past & Present*, Supp. 4 (1978): 10, 86.

117 W. D. Macray, ed., *Chronicon Abbatiae Rameseiensis* (London: Longman & Co., 1886), 387, 404.

Tables 13.1–13.3 also tell us something about English bishops at the time. For their part, English bishops appear to have enforced *Execrabilis* strictly, but not entirely. Under *Execrabilis* clerical justices were supposed to resign all but one benefice from ecclesiastical patrons with the cure of souls. By the end of 1318 Rothbury had forfeited four of his six incompatible benefices from ecclesiastical patrons: Staindrop, Rock, Christleton, and Laxfield. Stanton forfeited the church at Thurston, leaving him with one benefice (East Dereham) from an ecclesiastical patron as well as his many prebends. The majority of Bacun's patrons over his lifetime were laymen and thus immune from *Execrabilis*, but he did forfeit benefices at Reston and Bintree.

That Rothbury retained the incompatible benefices of Shillington (Abbot of Ramsey) and Hendon (Abbot of Westminster) until his death in 1321 suggests that not all English bishops were eager to dissolve valuable church-state relationships and embrace the pope's centralizing fiscal policies. In particular, the Abbot of Westminster may have balked at diminishing an important connection with a justice who sat in Westminster Hall. Incomplete episcopal enforcement of *Execrabilis* against clerical justices lends weight to J. Robert Wright and Rowan Dorin's assertions that medieval English bishops were not mere compliant cogs in an ecclesiastical machine, but could mold, reinterpret, circumvent, or ignore papal decrees to solidify their own positions and power.[118]

5 Conclusion

Gilbert Rothbury, Hervey de Stanton, and John Bacun served two masters. Their immediate, secular fealty was to the king. Through patronage as well as legal and administrative acumen, these men rose in prominence in the royal courts, becoming justices and trusted royal counselors. Magnates, prelates, and kin understandably sought to tether themselves to clerical justices who possessed invaluable legal advice and influence at court by awarding them benefices, lubricating the reciprocal wheels of patronage—for a time.

As pluralist clerics, however, Rothbury, Stanton, and Bacun owed obedience to the pope. When John XXII issued *Execrabilis*, choices of how much to comply with this papal constitution had to be made by ecclesiastics throughout Latin Christendom. Our three clerical justices largely heeded the papal constitution, suggesting that Edward II's concerns about the deleterious effect

118 Wright, *The Church and the English Crown*, 87–93; Rowan Dorin, "The Bishop as Lawmaker in Late Medieval Europe," *Past & Present*, vol. 253, no. 1 (2021), 45–47, 80–82.

Execrabilis would have on his ability to employ learned clerics in his Chancery could also extend to clerics and justices in his royal courts. Like the less-exalted Chancery clerks, Rothbury and Bacun suffered substantially under *Execrabilis*, forfeiting revenues far exceeding their annual royal salaries. Stanton, probably the wealthiest of the three, was the least affected, surrendering an amount roughly equivalent to six months of salary. Despite their wealth, however, the immediate financial shock of *Execrabilis* to these clerical justices must have been stinging.

Equally jarring was the loosening of patronage bonds that tethered Rothbury, Stanton, and Bacun to some of the great and powerful of the realm. *Execrabilis* relaxed connections between bishops, priors, and abbots with clerical royal justices who could offer valuable legal advice and serve as critical conduits for their interests at court. Clerical justices meanwhile lost important relationships with ecclesiastical patrons who could offer pecuniary rewards or aid them in their own endeavors. *Execrabilis*'s slackening of ecclesiastical relationships with Rothbury, Stanton, and Bacun likely diminished the influence that English prelates could wield on clerical justices in the common-law courts, aiding a process that was already underway—the complete and irrevocable laicization of the common-law judiciary by the 1330s.[119]

Bibliography

Baignet, F. J., ed. *The Registers of John de Sandale and Rigaud de Asserio, Bishops of Winchester 1316–1323*. London: Simpkin, 1897.

Bennett, N. H. "The Beneficed Clergy in the Diocese of Lincoln during the Episcopate of Henry Burghersh, 1320–1340." vol. II. Ph.D. diss., University of York, 1989.

Bennett, Nicholas., ed. *The Registers of Henry Burghersh 1320–1342*, Vol. III. Lincoln: Lincoln Record Society Vol. 101, 2011.

Bliss, W. H., ed. *Calendar of Papal Registers Relating to Great Britain and Ireland: Volume I, 1198–1304*. London: Her Majesty's Stationery Office, 1893.

Bliss, W. H., ed. *Calendar of Papal Registers Relating to Great Britain and Ireland: Volume II, 1305–1342*. London: Her Majesty's Stationery Office, 1895.

Bombi, Barbara. *Anglo-Papal Relations in the Early Fourteenth Century*. Oxford: Oxford University Press, 2019.

119 For some of the factors leading to the laicization of English common-law judiciary in the first half of the fourteenth century, see Paul Brand, *The Making of the Common Law* (London: The Hambledon Press, 1992), 165–68.

Brand, Paul. "Bacon [Bacun], John (c. 1250–c. 1323)," *Oxford Dictionary of National Biography*, 2008. https://doi.org/10.1093/ref:odnb/993.

Brand, Paul. "Rothbury, Gilbert (b. in or before 1260, d. 1321)," *Oxford Dictionary of National Biography,* 2008. https://doi.org/10.1093/ref:odnb/37455.

Brand, Paul. "Stanton [Staunton], Hervey (c. 1260–1327)," *Oxford Dictionary of National Biography*, 2008. https://doi.org/10.1093/ref:odnb/26326.

Brand, Paul. The Making of the Common Law. London: The Hambledon Press, 1992.

Burger, Michael. *Bishops, Clerks, and Diocesan Governance in Thirteenth-Century England.* Cambridge: Cambridge University Press, 2012.

J. Caley, ed. *Taxatio Ecclesiastica Angliae et Walliae, Pope Nicholas IV, Circa 1291.* London: Record Commission, 1802.

Corpus Juris Canonici. Electronic Edition: UCLA Digital Library Program. Rome 1582. http://digital.library.ucla.edu/canonlaw.

Coulstock, Patricia. *Collegiate Church of Wimborne Minster*. London: Boydell Press, 1993.

Denton, J. H. "The Valuation of the Ecclesiastical Benefices of England and Wales in 1291–2," *Historical Research* LXVI, no. 161 (1993): 231–50.

Denton, Jeff et al. *Taxatio*. 2014. Accessed April 10, 2022. https://www.dhi.ac.uk/taxatio/.

Dorin, Rowan "The Bishop as Lawmaker in Late Medieval Europe," *Past & Present*, vol. 253, no. 1 (2021): 45–82.

Dyer, Christopher. *Making a Living in the Middle Ages: The People of Britain 850–1520.* London: Yale University Press, 2002.

Fowler, R. C., ed. *Registrum Radulphi Baldock, Gilberti Segrave, Ricardi Newport, et Stephani Gravesend, Episcoporum Londoniensium, A.D. MCCCIV–MCCCXXXVIII.* London: Canterbury and York Society, 1911.

Hardy, T. D., ed. *The Register of Richard de Kellawe, Lord Palatine and Bishop of Durham (1314–1316)*. Vol. II. London: Her Majesty's Stationery Office, 1874.

Hill, Rosalind, ed. *The Rolls and Register of Bishop Oliver Sutton (1280–1299)*. Vol. VIII. Lincoln: Lincoln Record Society Vol. 76, 1986.

Hingeston-Randolph, F. C., ed., *The Register of Walter de Stapledon, Bishop of Exeter, 1307–1326*. London: George Bell & Sons, 1892.

Hobhouse, E., ed. *Calendar and Register of John de Drokensford, Bishop of Bath and Wells (1309–1329)*. London: Somerset Record Society, 1887.

Hughes, J. B., ed., *The Register of Walter Langton, Bishop of Coventry and Lichfield (1296–1321)*. Vol. I. London: Boydell and Brewer, 2001.

Jones, B. "Prebendaries: Compton Dundon." In *Fasti Ecclesiae Anglicanae 1300–1541*. Vol. VIII, Bath and Wells Diocese. London: Institute of Historical Research, 1964.

Keeton, G. W. *Harvey the Hasty: A Medieval Chief Justice.* Chichester: Rose Publishing, 1978.

Loewe, Andreas. "Michaelhouse: Hervey de Stanton's Cambridge Foundation." *Church History and Religious Culture* 90, no. 4 (2010): 579–608.

Lunt, William E. *Financial Relations of the Papacy with England to 1327*. Cambridge: Medieval Academy of America, 1939.

Lunt, William E. and Edgar B. Graves, eds. *Accounts Rendered by Papal Collectors in England 1317–1378*. Philadelphia: The American Philosophical Society, 1968.

Macray, W. D., ed. *Chronicon Abbatiae Rameseiensis*. London: Longman & Co., 1886.

Maddicott, J. R. "Law and Lordship: Royal Justices as Retainers in Thirteenth and Fourteenth Century England." *Past & Present*. Supplement 4 (1978): 1–88.

Martin, C. T., ed. *Registrum Epistolarum Fratris Johannis Peckham, Archeiopiscopi Cantuariensis*, Vol. III. London: Longman & Co., 1885.

Maxwell-Lyte, H. C. ed., *A Descriptive Catalogue of Ancient Deeds*. Vol. 6. London: His Majesty's Stationery Office, 1915.

Maxwell-Lyte, H. C., ed. *Calendar of Close Rolls, Edward I, A.D. 1272–1279*. London: Eyre and Spottiswoode, 1900.

Maxwell-Lyte, H. C., ed. *Calendar of Close Rolls, Edward III, A.D. 1327–1330*. London: Eyre and Spottiswoode, 1896.

Maxwell-Lyte, H. C., ed. *Calendar of Patent Rolls: Edward I, A.D. 1281–1292*. London: Eyre and Spottiswoode, 1893.

Maxwell-Lyte, H. C., ed. *Calendar of the Patent Rolls: Edward I, A.D. 1292–1301*. London: Eyre and Spottiswoode, 1895.

Maxwell-Lyte, H. C., ed. *Calendar of Patent Rolls: Edward II, A.D. 1307–1313*. London: Eyre and Spottiswoode, 1894.

Maxwell-Lyte, H. C., ed. *Calendar of Patent Rolls: Edward II, A.D. 1313–1317*. London: Eyre and Spottiswoode, 1898.

Maxwell-Lyte, H. C., ed. *Calendar of Patent Rolls: Edward II, A.D. 1317–1321*. London: Mackie and Co. 1903.

Maxwell-Lyte, H. C., ed. *Calendar of Patent Rolls: Edward III, A.D. 1327–1330*. London: Eyre and Spottiswoode, 1891.

Maxwell-Lyte, H. C., ed. *Calendar of the Charter Rolls, Edward I, Edward II, A.D. 1300–1326*. London: Mackie and Co., 1908.

Maxwell-Lyte, H. C. ed. *Calendar of the Charter Rolls, Henry III, Edward I, A.D. 1257–1300*. London: Mackie and Co., 1906.

Pantin, W.A. *The English Church in the Fourteenth Century*. Cambridge: Cambridge University Press, 1955.

Pennington, K. "The Canonists and Pluralism in the Thirteenth Century." *Speculum* 51 (1976): 35–48.

Rowberry, Ryan. "The Social Origins, Education, and Financial Relationships of Gilbert Rothbury, a Clerical Common Law Judge (1295–1321)." In *Proceedings of the Fourteenth International Congress of Medieval Canon Law*, edited by Joseph Goering, Stephan Dusil, and Andreas Thier, 453–69. Vatican City: Biblioteca Apostolica Vaticana, 2016.

Ruddock, J. W., ed. *The Rolls and Register of Bishop Oliver Sutton (1280–1299)*. Vol. VI. Lincoln: Lincoln Record Society 64, 1969.

Rymer, Thomas, ed. *Foedera, Conventiones, Litterae, et cujuscunque generis Acta Publica, inter Reges Angliae et alios quosvis Imperatores, Reges, Pontifices, Principes, vel Communitates ab Ingressu Gulielmi I. in Angliam, A.D. 1066*. Vol. II:I. London, 1818.

Sayles, G. O., ed. *Select Cases in the Court of King's Bench under Edward I*, vol. I, Selden Society vol. 55. London: Bernard Quatrich, 1936.

Shinners, John and William Dohar, eds. *Pastors and the Care of Souls in Medieval England*. Notre Dame: University of Notre Dame Press, 1998.

Smith, David M. *Guide to Bishops' Registers of England and Wales*. London: Royal Historical Society, 1981.

Stubbs, William, ed. *Chronicles of the Reigns of Edward I and Edward II*. Vol. I. London: Longman & Co., 1882.

Suckling, Alfred. "Gorleston." In *The History and Antiquities of the County of Suffolk*. Vol. I. Ipswich: W. S. Crowell, 1846.

The National Archives, United Kingdom, Series: C 62; C 143; CP 40; E 159; E 210; KB 27; SC 8.

Timmins, T. C. B., ed. *The Register of William Melton, Archbishop of York, 1317–1340*. Vol. V. London: Boydell and Brewer, 2002.

Waugh, W. T. "Archbishop Peckham and Pluralities." *English Historical Review* 28, no. 112 (1913): 625–35.

Wilson, R. A., ed. *The Register of Walter Reynolds, Bishop of Worcester (1308–1313)*. London: Dugdale Society, 1928.

Wright, Robert J. *The Church and the English Crown 1305–1334*. Toronto: Pontifical Institute of Mediaeval Studies, 1980.

CHAPTER 14

Dangerous Dreams: *Le Songe du Vergier* and the Expulsion of Jews from Fourteenth-Century France

Rowan Dorin

In the closing centuries of the Middle Ages, dozens of governing authorities across western Europe—from municipal officials and petty barons to the most powerful kings in Christendom—expelled the Jews living within their jurisdictions. While some authorities proffered little justification for such dramatic acts, many others took pains to publicize the formal reasoning that underpinned their decisions, invoking a variety of supposed dangers and alleged misdeeds. Whatever the rhetorical claims undergirding each successive expulsion, they were formulated against the backdrop of longstanding church teachings emphasizing the Jews' presumptive right to live unmolested within Christian society. Although the strained ambivalence of the Pauline epistles provided the foundations of these teachings, it was from the writings of Augustine and Gregory the Great that later generations derived their most powerful formulations.[1]

Amidst the seeming disjuncture between church doctrine and contemporary realities, late medieval canonists and theologians began reflecting anew on grounds for the continued Jewish presence within Christendom, and by extension, on whether rulers might ever justly drive Jews from their lands. For some thinkers, such reflections served as a vehicle for critiquing the policies of contemporary authorities; others seized them as an opportunity to advocate the further exclusion and expulsion of Jews.[2]

---

1 See generally Kenneth R. Stow, "The Church and the Jews: St. Paul to Pius IX," in *Popes, Church and Jews in the Middle Ages: Confrontation and Response* (Farnham, UK: Ashgate, 2007), art. I, 1–76.

2 For examples of each approach, see William C. Jordan, *Unceasing Strife, Unending Fear: Jacques de Thérines and the Freedom of the Church in the Age of the Last Capetians* (Princeton, NJ: Princeton University Press, 2005), 12–17; Elsa Marmursztejn, "Débats médiévaux sur l'expulsion des juifs des monarchies occidentales," in *Les expulsions de minorités religieuses dans l'Europe des XIIIe–XVIIe siècles*, ed. Isabelle Poutrin and Alain Tallon (Pompignac: Éditions Bière, 2015), 19–44; and Kenneth R. Stow, "Expulsion Italian Style: The Case of Lucio Ferraris," *Jewish History* 3, no. 1 (1988), 51–63.

 | DOI:10.1163/9789004710696_016

Among the latter was the late fourteenth-century French jurist Evrart de Trémaugon (d. 1386). A native of Brittany, Evrart had studied in Bologna in the 1360s before taking up a professorship of canon law at the University of Paris around 1369. His talents evidently drew the attention of King Charles V (r. 1364–80), who appointed Evrart a royal councilor in 1373 and swiftly set him to work on what would become the *Somnium viridarii* ("The Dream of the Orchard").[3] Written in the form of a dialogue between a Cleric and a Knight, this "oneiric disputation" (to borrow Marcia Kupfer's felicitous phrase) aimed above all to affirm the sovereignty of the French Crown against ecclesiastical (especially papal) pretensions, while also digressing into topics as varied as the origins of nobility, the powers of demons, and the merits of astrology.[4]

The first version of Evrart's work, composed in Latin and completed in May 1376, consists largely of lengthy extracts of earlier political writings strung together with varying degrees of coherence. William of Ockham (d. 1347) and Marsilius of Padua (d. ca. 1342) loom large, as does the Italian jurist John of Legnano (d. 1383), who had been among Evrart's teachers in Bologna and whose recently published *Somnium* (a vigorous defense of papal monarchy) inspired the title and framing, though clearly not the political sympathies, of his pupil's work.[5]

Soon after completing the Latin version, Evrart (again probably acting at royal behest) began reworking his text into a new version, this time written in the vernacular. The resulting *Songe du Vergier*, which Evrart presented to his royal patron in 1378, was even longer, due partly to the inclusion of additional topics (ranging from the Immaculate Conception to the disputed status of the duchy of Guyenne), but also to more extensive remarks by the author himself.[6]

3 For biographical details and a summary of the evidence concerning Evrart's authorship of both the *Somnium viridarii* and the *Songe du vergier*, see Marion Schnerb-Lièvre, "Evrart de Trémaugon," *Histoire littéraire de la France* 42, fasc. 2 (Paris: Éditions de Boccard, 2003), 281–96. Schnerb-Lièvre's earlier study ("Evrart de Trémaugon et *Le Songe du Vergier*," *Romania* 101 [1980]: 527–30) definitively established Evrart's authorship of the *Somnium*, confirming a hypothesis first put forth by Alfred Coville in *Evrart de Trémaugon et le Songe du Verger* (Paris: Droz, 1933). For a more detailed discussion of the works' disputed authorship, see the introduction to Evrart de Trémaugon, *Trois leçons sur les Décrétales*, ed. and trans. Marion Schnerb-Lièvre with Gérard Giordanengo (Paris: Éditions du CNRS, 1998), 12–18.

4 Marcia Kupfer, "'Lectres ... plus vrayes': Hebrew Script and Jewish Witness in the 'Mandeville' Manuscript of Charles V," *Speculum* 83 (2008): 90.

5 Evrart refers to John of Legnano as '*dominus meus*' in one of his surviving lectures on the decretals; see his *Trois leçons sur les Décrétales*, 120.

6 Acquired by John of Lancaster (1389–1435) following the death of King Charles VI in 1422, the presentation copy is now London, British Library, MS Royal 19 C IV.

Most of the scholarship on this sprawling—one might even say bloated—treatise has focused either on its disputed authorship (a matter that has at last been conclusively resolved) or on the political theories that it articulates, particularly with regard to the emergence of Gallicanism. Only a handful of scholars have drawn attention to the debate over royal policies toward Jews that appears in *Somnium* and *Songe* alike—notwithstanding the fact that the latter version contains the most thorough discussion of the licitness of expulsion found in any surviving text from the European Middle Ages.[7]

In both the Latin and vernacular versions, the section concerning Jews opens with a consideration of the permissibility of Jewish usury, then shifts somewhat abruptly to the grounds on which Jewish property could be confiscated and the Jews themselves expelled.[8] And while the usual pattern of alternating arguments would lead a reader to expect one of the disputants to oppose expulsion, this is not the case here: in a striking instance of consensus, both the Knight and the Cleric come down firmly in favor of expelling Jews from the kingdom of France.

Given the abundant modern scholarship on medieval Christian attitudes toward Jews, the limited attention to the *Somnium* and *Songe* appears surprising. No doubt it reflects in part the persistent sidelining of the later fourteenth century, at least where the history of France's Jewish population is concerned.[9] It might also result from the editorial history of the texts: although the *Somnium* was printed in 1516 (with this edition then reprinted in 1549, 1611, and 1976) and the *Songe* was printed even earlier (1491, with reprintings in 1731 and 1957; plus two other editions ca. 1500), their sheer length, together with

7 The section concerning Jews in the *Songe* runs to ca. 3200 words, of which 1500 concern the topic of expulsion. It is therefore longer than the two *consilia* on this theme by the early fourteenth-century Avignonese canonist Oldradus de Ponte (which total ca. 800 and ca. 1300 words, respectively); and twice as long as a quodlibet on the same topic by the Cistercian theologian Jacques de Thérines from ca. 1306, which runs to roughly 800 words. For the latter texts, see Oldradus's *Consilia* 87 and 264, in *Jews and Saracens in the Consilia of Oldradus de Ponte*, ed. and trans. Norman Zacour (Toronto: Pontifical Institute of Mediaeval Studies, 1990), 54–58, 62–67 (English translation) and 83–84, 86–89 (Latin); and Jacques de Thérines, *Quodlibets I et II*, ed. Palémon Glorieux (Paris: Vrin, 1958), 157, no. 1.14.

8 *Somnium viridarii*, ed. Marion Schnerb-Lièvre, 2 vols. (Paris: CNRS, 1993), 1.116–20, cc. I.CIII–CIV; *Songe du Vergier*, ed. Marion Schnerb-Lièvre, 2 vols. (Paris: CNRS, 1982), 1.354–62, cc. I.CLXII–CLXIV. Other passing references to Jews are scattered across both versions of the treatise.

9 For an overview (though largely excluding developments in the Midi), see Roger S. Kohn, *Les Juifs de la France du Nord dans la seconde moitié du XIVe siècle* (Louvain: Peeters, 1988). Valuable too are the essays gathered in Gilbert Dahan, ed., *L'expulsion des juifs de France, 1394* (Paris: Cerf, 2004).

their dense intertextuality, cast a forbidding shadow over both works for any reader not already immersed in medieval law and political theory.[10] It is only thanks to Marion Schnerb-Lièvre's patient editorial labors over many decades that the two works have now appeared in critical editions, replete with detailed apparatus and notes, thus facilitating a wider readership. As for the few scholars who have analyzed the discussion of Jews in the *Somnium* and/or *Songe*, they have mostly sought to situate it within the lively intellectual culture of Charles v's court, or else to explicate its relationship to the central political argument of the treatises.[11]

Although Marcia Kupfer has highlighted the Augustinian elements in the Knight's exposition, and Jeannine Quillet (less convincingly) argued for the influence of Nicolas Oresme (d. 1382) on the treatises' handling of usury, it is in fact legal sources that loom largest in the discussion of Jews: Justinian's *Codex* is cited three times as often as Augustine, and references to Gratian's *Decretum* are more numerous still.[12] Moreover, a *consilium* by an early fourteenth-century Avignonese jurist supplied the text for nearly half of the *Somnium*'s discussion of Jews—a verbatim borrowing that eluded the notice of the *Somnium*'s modern editor and has since gone unrecognized by all other scholars of the treatise.[13]

---

10 For the editorial history of the respective works, see *Somnium*, 1.xxiv–xxvii; and *Songe*, 1.xl–xlii.

11 Shulamith Shachar, "The Jews in the Eyes of Court Writers and their Status by Royal Decrees in the Reign of Charles v of France [in Hebrew]," *Zion* 33 (1968), 1–14, offers a detailed paraphrase of the *Songe*'s discussion of Jews (at pp. 2–5). Jean-Pierre Royer's otherwise insightful treatment (*L'Église et le royaume de France au XIVe siècle d'après le "Songe du Vergier" et la jurisprudence du Parlement* [Paris: Pichon et Durand-Auzias, 1969], 202 n. 4) is marred by his strained effort to read the Knight's position as a defense of Charles V's policies. Marcia Kupfer ("Lectres ...," 90–91) has productively situated the *Songe*'s discussion within broader currents of courtly concern with both Jews and Hebrew knowledge. In his recent study *Juden ohne Päpste: Inklusion und Judenfeinlichkeit zwischen Rom und Avignon* (Berlin: De Gruyter, 2021), Davide Liberatoscioli examines the passages on usury from the perspective of late medieval economic ethics (see pp. 110–17), though his analysis (heavily influenced by the work of medievalist Giacomo Todeschini) is not entirely successful in its attempt to harmonize the discordant arguments of the Cleric and Knight into a coherent vision.

12 See Kupfer, "Lectres ...," 91; and Jeannine Quillet, *La philosophie politique du Songe du Vergier (1378): sources doctrinales* (Paris: Vrin, 1977), 147–48. Like Evrart, Nicolas Oresme belonged to the circle of intellectuals surrounding Charles v, but Marion Schnerb-Lièvre's reconstruction of the sources of the *Somnium* and *Songe* has clearly demonstrated Oresme's limited influence on the two works. Moreover, as discussed below, Evrart copied almost the entirety of the section on usury from John of Legnano's *Somnium*.

13 Schnerb-Lièvre marked these passages as "probably original" (*Trois Leçons*, 20). This oversight likely reflects the relative obscurity of Oldradus's consilium prior to Norman

Given that Evrart was a doctor *in utroque iure*, the prominence of law and legal commentaries in his passages on Jews (as in the *Somnium* and *Songe* more generally) is hardly surprising. Indeed, it is precisely Evrart's (mis)use of certain legal *auctoritates* that allowed his authorship of the treatises to be established securely.[14] But in light of the Knight and Cleric's joint espousal of expulsion, Evrart's use of law merits closer attention. After all, deferring to the church's traditional teachings on the matter, no earlier canonist or civilian had proferred such a full-throated argument in favor of the expulsion of Jews. Despite Evrart's heavy reliance on earlier sources for the composition of his treatises, his conclusion—namely, that France's Jewish population should be driven from the kingdom—therefore marked a notable departure from learned tradition.

The *Somnium* and its subsequent vernacular reworking accordingly show how a professional canonist worked to reconcile expulsion with the church's longstanding (and theologically grounded) support for Jewish presence in Christian lands. Even more significantly, they offer a rare glimpse of the reasoning by which a royal councilor might seek to sway the mind of a king against his Jewish subjects. In explaining how Evrart constructed his case, the following analysis of the structure and sources of the *Somnium* and *Songe* therefore aims to reveal the weight of law and legal reasoning in justifying—and even, perhaps, abetting—the final expulsion of Jews from medieval France.

1 A Precarious Presence: Jewish Settlement in Late Fourteenth-Century France

Although Philip the Fair's dramatic expulsion of Jews from his kingdom in the summer of 1306 proved a devastating blow to a once-flourishing community, it did not mark a definitive end to Jewish presence in the kingdom. Over the course of the following two decades, a complicated sequence of recalls and expulsions (both real and threatened) enabled the temporary reestablishment

Zacour's edition and translation (*Jews and Saracens*), published in 1990. In addition, most of the scholarship on this section has focused on the vernacular *Songe* rather than the Latin *Somnium*, making their joint dependence on Oldradus's (Latin) text more difficult to recognize.

14 See the works cited above, n. 1.

of Jewish settlements in various parts of the realm, though these dwindled in size during the 1320s and disappeared altogether after 1327.[15]

Starting in the late 1350s, some Jews living in the neighboring territories evidently began petitioning to return to the kingdom.[16] Desperately short of cash, the future Charles V (then acting as regent for his imprisoned father John II) acquiesced to their requests, granting twenty-year settlement privileges to Jewish newcomers in return for generous up-front payments and the promise of annual contributions thereafter. In 1361, the terms of Jewish residence in the kingdom were formalized still further in a series of royal *ordonnances* that specified both the payments to be made and the broad privileges that the Jews would enjoy in return.[17]

In the eyes of the French Crown, Jewish presence was necessarily dependant on princely consent, as Jews "were of such condition that they had neither a land nor place of their own anywhere in Christendom where they could dwell, visit, or reside, except by the full and personal permission and will of the lord or lords [...] who consented to receive and welcome them."[18] Moreover, in accounting for the newfound royal willingness to welcome and protect returning Jews, the king made no attempt to dissemble his pecuniary motivations. Having first noted the various dangers that the Jews might face from those who sought to do them harm, one of the ordonnances then observed that "the more securely and peacefully they [the Jews] can live in our realm [...], the better they can obey us and pay the contributions that they owe to us."[19]

In order for the Jewish newcomers to satisfy such fiscal demands, it was obviously necessary for them to earn a living, and the ordonnances duly allowed them to engage in all the trades that they were accustomed to perform elsewhere or in the past. Special attention was paid to moneylending, which accounted for seven of the ten economic clauses in the enumeration of privileges granted to Jewish newcomers (and was furthermore the only trade

15 See Elizabeth A. R. Brown, "Philip V, Charles IV, and the Jews of France: the Alleged Expulsion of 1322," *Speculum* 66, no. 2 (1991), 294–329; and the overview in Juliette Sibon, *Chasser les juifs pour régner* (Paris: Perrin, 2016), 129–52.

16 For a discussion of the reestablishment of Jewish settlements, see Kohn, *Juifs de la France du Nord*, 12–54; and Sibon, *Chasser*, 153–69. The acquisition of the Dauphiné in 1349 had also brought its existing Jewish communities within the boundaries of the kingdom, though without any formal acknowledgment of the fact.

17 *Ordonnances des roys de France de la troisième race* ..., ed. Eusèbe Jacob de Laurière et al., 23 vols. (Paris: Imprimerie royale, 1723–1849) [hereafter cited as *Ord.*] 3.467–81.

18 *Ord.* 3.471.

19 *Ord.* 3.474.

to merit specific mention).[20] Although the new settlers no doubt engaged in a variety of economic activities (just as their forebears had done in earlier periods), the surviving documentation from the 1360s and 1370s points clearly to moneylending as the principal source of Jewish wealth within the kingdom.[21]

The royal formalization of the renewed Jewish presence within the realm did not lead to a sudden influx of immigrants. Roger Kohn's meticulous reconstruction of Jewish settlements in northern France in the latter half of the fourteenth century suggests a rather slow increase over the course of the 1360s and into the mid-1370s.[22] Moreover, despite the official assurances of a twenty-year settlement permit, Jewish residence remained at the mercy of royal whims. This was dramatically highlighted in 1367/68, when Charles V ordered the renewed expulsion of Jews from the realm, only to reverse course shortly thereafter. Neither the grounds for the expulsion nor the reasons for the royal volte-face are known, and a few years later the king formally reconfirmed the privileges granted to the Jews in 1361.[23] Moreover, in a seeming gesture of goodwill, Charles even lent to the Parisian Jewish community a large trove of Hebrew manuscripts that had long been held in the royal archives.[24] But the mere threat of expulsion, even if ultimately unenforced, signaled the precarious foundations of the kingdom's newly-reestablished Jewish communities.

---

20 Namely, articles 8, 10–15; see *Ord.* 3.476–78. Article 9 concerned the general permission to engage in customary trades, while articles 16 and 17 concerned the Jews' exemption from various taxes and tolls.

21 Kohn, *Juifs de la France du Nord*, 57–155.

22 Kohn, *Juifs de la France du Nord*, 48–54. For an example from the southern part of the kingdom, see Danièle Iancu-Agou, "Les Juifs à Montpellier à la fin du XIVe siècle," in *L'expulsion des juifs de France*, 51–67.

23 Although the expulsion order itself does not survive, its execution is discussed in a royal letter dated February 1368, and it is mentioned anew in Charles V's 1372 reconfirmation of the 1361 privilege; see *Mandements et actes divers de Charles V (1364–1380)*, ed. Léopold Delisle (Paris: Imprimerie nationale, 1874), 216–17, no. 430; and *Ord.* 5.497. The fullest discussion of this aborted expulsion remains Isidore Loeb, "Les expulsions des Juifs de France au XIVe siècle," in *Jubelschrift zum 70. Geburtstag des Prof. Dr. H. Graetz* (Breslau: Schottlaender, 1887), 52–55.

24 Kupfer, "Lectres ...," 78–80. For the list of manuscripts, see the edition in Siméon Luce, "Les Juifs sous Charles V et le fonds hébraique du Trésor des Chartes, en 1372," *Revue Historique* 7, fasc. 2 (1878): 369–70.

2 Something Borrowed, Something New: Jews and Expulsion in the *Somnium Viridarii*

With its focus on Jewish moneylending, the intertwining of princely grace and Jewish fiscal service, the temporary nature of Jewish settlement, and the legitimacy of expulsion, the discussion of Jews in the *Somnium* and *Songe* maps closely onto the principal themes of royal rhetoric concerning Jews as articulated over the previous two decades. It remains unclear whether Evrart opted to address the topic of the Jews on his own initiative, or whether he did so at the urging of his royal patron. What is clear is that Evrart managed to gather and edit his sources in ways that brought his own hostile attitudes clearly to the fore.

Consider first Evrart's use of the eponymous *Somnium* of his erstwhile teacher, John of Legnano.[25] The Bolognese jurist had completed this work around 1372, only two years before Evrart set to work on his own treatise, and (as its name suggests) framed its somewhat rambling jurisprudential ruminations within the narrative conceit of a dream vision.[26] Evrart drew repeatedly on this work in compiling the Latin version of his own treatise, most notably for his own prologue and epilogue, but also in eighteen of the *Somnium*'s chapters.[27]

Given that John of Legnano's *Somnium* makes only passing reference to Jews, it might have seemed an unpromising springboard for a lengthy discussion thereof—were it not for the fact that it used usury as a case study to defend the superiority of papal to princely statutes. Having dedicated the immediately preceding section to the topic of papal claims to universal dominion, Evrart began chapter 103 of his Latin version with the proposition (lifted verbatim from John of Legnano's *Somnium*, and naturally articulated by the Cleric) that "papal rulings and statutes are of a higher grade and more perfect than the statutes or rulings of earthly princes, for the statutes of the latter ... even allow usury."[28] This is followed by a series of extracts from John

25 Carl Müller, "Über das Somnium Viridarii. Beitrag zur Geschichte der Literatur über Kirche und Staat im 14. Jahrhundert," *Zeitschrift der Kirchenrecht* 14 (1879), 134–205, was the first to show the dependence of the *Somnium* on John of Legnano's eponymous work. G. W. Coopland pursued the connections further in "An unpublished work of John of Legnano: the *Somnium* of 1372," *Nuovi studi medievali* 2, fasc. 1 (1925–26): 65–88, esp. 84–87; while Alfred Coville (*Evrart de Trémaugon*, 31–32) used the borrowings to bolster his case for Evrart's authorshop.

26 For a detailed discussion of the work, see Glynis M. Donovan and Maurice H. Keen, "The 'Somnium' of John of Legnano," *Traditio* 37 (1981): 325–45.

27 See the table in *Somnium*, 2.533–54.

28 *Somnium*, ed. Schnerb-Lièvre, 1.116 (c. I.CIII, §A-1).

of Legnano's text, which first present several traditional objections to usury (drawn from Aristotle, the Bible, and Roman law), then outline three ways in which a particular action may be permitted. Although his source text nowhere mentions Jewish moneylending, Evrart simply interspersed disparaging comments about Jews amidst the borrowed passages. What had been a general condemnation of usury in John of Legnano's *Somnium* thus became a specific attack on Jewish usury in Evrart's reworking.[29]

For John of Legnano, the endpoint of his analysis was straightforward: canon law's strict prohibition on usury rendered it more virtuous than secular law, inasmuch as the latter permitted usurious lending in various ways. In Evrart's adaptation, the emphasis quickly shifts from the superiority of ecclesiastical law to the damage wrought by contemporary French law, with its various permissions and privileges enabling Jews to lend at interest. This reorientation underscores Evrart's instrumental use of his source material, which served less as a source of meaningful argumentation than as a ready-made transition from the main theme of temporal-ecclesiastical relations to the specific topic of usury, and hence (through Evrart's insertions) to the issue of Jews and the royal protections they enjoyed.

Evrart could simply have stopped his initial discussion at this point, leaving the Knight to muster a defense of either secular law or Jewish moneylending. Yet he was clearly determined to address the topic of expulsion, and he had evidently stumbled across a second source—a *consilium* written a half-century earlier by the Avignonese canonist Oldradus de Ponte (d. 1335)—that would allow him to do so without requiring any intellectual spadework of his own.

Oldradus's *consilium* addressed the question of "whether a prince can, without sin, expel Jews and Saracens from his kingdom and confiscate their goods."[30] Following convention, the analysis begins by presenting the negative case ("First, it seems not."). Citing Roman and canon law, the *consilium* first argues that a prince should not confiscate goods from Jews living peacefully under his rule if these goods have been justly acquired. It then lays out the case

29 John of Legnano's only reference to Jews in this part of his *Somnium* appears in the context of the various kinds of permission: "Secundo, aliquid conceditur quia impedimenta, ne adsint, tolluntur, sic lex canonica permittit iudeos in ritibus suis." See his *Somnium*, ed. Maria Consiglia De Matteis and Giulietta Voltolina (Legnano: Banca di Legnano, 2004), 189.

30 Oldradus de Ponte, *Consilium* 87, in *Jews and Saracens*, 54–58 (English translation) and 83–84 (Latin). Given that the text does not seem to have been solicited for an actual legal case, it might more accurately be termed a *quaestio*, but I have adhered to the conventional nomenclature here.

for the general toleration of Jews living in Christian lands, here quoting well-known passages from both Augustine and Gregory the Great.

The *consilium* then proceeds to present the case in favor of expulsion, emphasizing first the servile status of the Jews, then declaring that Christian toleration of Jewish presence should be understood as a matter of piety and grace, rather than necessity. Should the Jews abuse such grace by causing danger or scandal to Christians, Oldradus argued (citing Pope Innocent IV's commentary on the decretal *Quod super his*), they deserved to lose the privileges they enjoyed.[31] The *consilium* then invokes the Biblical account of the servant-woman Hagar, who behaved haughtily toward her mistress Sarah and was duly expelled from her home, together with her son.[32] In Oldradus's reading (here following an exegetical tradition that went all the way back to Paul), the Jews were descendents of Hagar, and her expulsion at the hands of Sarah (i.e. the Church) prefigured the Jews' exclusion from the Christian community.[33]

At this point in the text, Oldradus's *consilium* would seem to be coming down firmly in favor of the licitness of expelling Jews. But it then switches tack, insisting that "where [the Jews] have been living quietly and there has been no scandal, it does not seem right that the pope should require or urge princes [to expel them]." A concluding reference to a letter of Gregory the Great then provides further warrant for tolerating Jews (and indeed, acting benevolently toward them), in the hope that they might be converted.[34] Notwithstanding Oldradus's insistence that rulers could indeed drive Jews from their lands if their presence threatened Christian well-being, his closing lines therefore reaffirmed the general presumption of toleration that had characterized mainstream Christian doctrine for nearly a millennium.

31 For danger or scandal to Christians as grounds for suspending toleration, see Innocent IV, *Apparatus super V libros decretalium* (Venice: Johann Herbort, 1481), *ad* X 3.34.8. On the evolving legal meaning of *scandalum*, see Arnaud Fossier, "'Propter vitandum scandalum': Histoire d'une catégorie juridique (XIIe–XVe siècle)," *Mélanges de l'École française de Rome. Moyen Âge* 121/2 (2009): 317–48. For the quoted maxim ("Privilegium meretur amittere"), see Bruce Brasington, "Power as Privilege: The Maxim Privilegium meretur amittere, qui potestate sibi concessa abutitur," *Zeitschrift der Savigny-Stiftung für Rechtsgeschichte* 109, no. 1 (2023): 53–72.

32 Gen. 21:10; cf. Galatians 4:30.

33 See Deeana Klepper, "Historicizing Allegory: The Jew as Hagar in Medieval Christian Text and Image," *Church History* 84, no. 2 (2015): 308–44.

34 *S. Gregorii Magni registrum epistularum*, ed. Dag Norberg, CCSL 140 (Brepols: Turnhout, 1982), 141, no. 2.50.

Evrart copied nearly every word of Oldradus's *consilium* into the *Somnium*'s discussion of Jews, though (as we shall see) he rearranged the structure of his source to strengthen its case for expulsion.[35] He faced a challenge, however, in that Oldradus's *consilium* said nothing whatsoever about usury. Moreover, since the first part of the Cleric's speech had roundly criticized French secular law for specifically permitting Jews to engage in usury, the mere fact of Jewish moneylending could hardly serve as evidence that the Jews were abusing their privileges (and hence deserved to lose them). How then to segue from a critique of Jewish usury to a demand for Jewish expulsion?

Evrart's solution was to insert a passage alleging that Jews were preying on vulnerable Christian women, who were coerced into having sex with their Jewish creditors in order to satisfy their debts and recover their pawned goods.[36] In the absence of actual evidence for such Jewish wrongdoing, Evrart resorted to the helpfully nebulous authority of *fama publica* and the convenient confidentiality of sacramental confession, claiming that such misdeeds were "well known from public knowledge and from priests who hear the confessions of Christians, wherein things are revealed that cannot be openly revealed to anyone."[37] Acting out of hatred of the Christian faith, the Jews

---

35 The manuscript transmission of Oldradus's *consilia* likely explains two errors found in the Knight's reply in *Somnium* and *Songe* alike, namely, the misquotation of C.16 q.3 c.14 (giving the incipit *Rogo* rather than *Porro*) and the attribution of a text to Jerome (*Jeronimus*) rather than Gregory the Great (*Gregorius*). These same two errors are found in the majority of the manuscripts containing the so-called Vulgate version of Oldradus's *consilia*, including Bordeaux, Bibliothèque municipale, ms. 404, fol. 82v; Paris, BnF, Latin 4276A, fols. 240v–241r (with *Rogo* emended to *Porro* in a later hand); Paris, BnF, Latin 14335, fol. 37r; Tübingen, Universitätsbibliothek, Mc 17, fol. 64v; and Vatican City, Biblioteca apostolica vaticana, Ross. 1096, fol. 54r. For the manuscript tradition of Oldradus's collection, see Brendan McManus, "The *Consilia* and *Quaestiones* of Oldradus de Ponte," *Bulletin of Medieval Canon Law* 23 (1999): 89 n. 10. It also bears noting that the French canonist Pierre Bertrand (1280–1349) silently copied the same *consilium* (together with Oldradus's *Consilium* 264, also on expulsion) into the second recension of his *Apparatus Sexti libri Decretalium cum Clementinis* (completed before 1342), for which I consulted Paris, BnF, Latin 4085, fol. 158rv; and Reims, Bibliothèque municipale, Ms. 737, fol. 194r (*ad* Clem. 5.2.1). Although these manuscripts both contain the same miscitation of *Rogo* for *Porro* (which must therefore have been introduced quite early into the manuscript tradition of Oldradus's *consilium*), they do not reproduce the *Jeronimus/Gregorius* error. This suggests that Evrart was working directly from a copy of Oldradus's *consilia* rather than from Bertrand's *Apparatus* (even as he drew on Bertrand's *Libellus* elsewhere in his treatise).

36 The accusation was a venerable one, featuring for instance in a 1321 petition from the communities of the seneschalsy of Carcassonne to Philip V urging him to expel Jews from the realm; see Clément Compayré, *Études historiques et documents inédits sur l'Albigeois, le Castrais, et l'ancien diocèse de Lavaur* (Albi: Papailhiau, 1841), 255–57, no. 71.

37 *Somnium*, 1.117–18 (c. I.CIII, §9–9 *bis*).

not only perpetrated such wickedness, but even engaged in "many sorceries" (*plurima sortilegia*).

Having observed that the Jews were therefore abusing the royal privileges granted to them, the Cleric goes on to reprise the *consilium*'s hostile passages concerning Jewish servitude and the revocation of Jewish privileges where "danger or scandal" were at play. The Cleric's speech ends with the invocation of Hagar's expulsion, though the argumentative force of the Biblical injunction to "banish (*eice*)" the offending servant and her son was decidedly undermined through a scribal error (*ecce* for *eice*) that resulted instead in a demand to "behold" them instead.[38]

In his reply, the Knight begins by conceding the divine prohibition of Jewish usury, though he impishly adds that if secular lords allowed Jews to exact usury, they were simply following the example of the Roman Church, which both tolerated and profited from Jewish lending. The Knight then segues abruptly to a lengthy defense of Jews, which coincides almost word-for-word with the first part of Oldradus's *consilium*. Having duly quoted Augustine and Gregory the Great in support of the Jews' continued presence in Christian society, the Knight then departs from his source text, stressing that all the foregoing arguments for toleration held true only "where [the Jews] live peacefully and where no scandal is caused to the Christian faith through encounters with them." And in a sudden shift of tone, the Knight continues (still speaking in Evrart's own words):

> Should I find myself in the prince's presence and dare to speak boldly to him, I would counsel him that these days, given their misdeeds and nefarious encounters (*conversacione nephanda*) with Christians, [the Jews] should be expelled far away from the entire realm, following the example of the serving-woman from whom they descend.[39]

Where Oldradus's *consilium* tempers the force of the Hagar narrative by immediately restating the presumption of toleration, the Knight instead doubles

38 Although two early manuscripts of the *Somnium* corrected this error, it evidently featured in Evrart's original text and was carried over into the *Songe*, with the Latin phrase "ecce ancillam et filium eius" rendered as "vecy la chambriere et son filz"; see *Somnium*, 1.118 (c. I.CIII, §16 *suite*); and *Songe*, 1.359 (c. I.CLXIII, §16).

39 *Somnium*, 1.120 (c. I.CIV, §6). In commenting on the corresponding passage in the *Songe*, Marcia Kupfer astutely observed ("Lectres ...," 91) that "the Knight's discourse here changes in tone as if the author himself were breaking into the text to speak in his own voice." And indeed, this marks precisely the point in the Knight's speech where Evrart's borrowing from Oldradus ends and his own original contribution resumes.

down on the necessity of expulsion. Quoting Christ's famous warning, "For what is a man profited, if he shall gain the whole world, and lose his own soul?" (here cited via a decretal in the *Liber extra*), the Knight denounces both the temporal and spiritual damage resulting from the Jews' presence.[40] In his concluding advice to his imagined princely audience, the Knight laments that whatever wealth the prince might draw from harboring Jews, he loses tenfold on account of the impoverishment they cause to his subjects.

Both the Cleric and the Knight therefore conclude their speeches with arguments in favor of expulsion, marking a break from the *Somnium*'s usual disputational structure. Their consensus here is made all the more powerful through the Knight's ventriloquization of Evrart's voice, with the speaker's imagined role as a princely advisor mirroring the author's real-life position at court. Moreover, the new identification of Oldradus's *consilium* as the source for nearly half of the *Somnium*'s discussion of Jews allows Evrart's own voice to be discerned even more clearly: *all* the passages condemning contemporary Jewish misdeeds were penned directly by Evrart himself. Furthermore, he added almost nothing to his source texts *except* these vilifying passages. Whatever ambiguities and ambivalences might have been articulated by John of Legnano or Oldradus de Ponte, Evrart's own attitude—as demonstrated by his edits and additions to their writings—was relentlessly hostile.

3 From the *Somnium* to the *Songe*

Despite Evrart's efforts to smooth the successive transitions from jurisprudence to usury to expulsion, the *Somnium*'s discussion of Jews clearly reads as an awkward excursus from the main thrust of the treatise. The opening claim concerning the superiority of papal statutes to princely ones goes unmentioned in the rest of the Cleric's speech, and the Knight ignores the topic altogether. It resurfaces only in the following chapter (concerning divorce in civil and canon law), in which Evrart simply resumed his verbatim borrowing from John of Legnano's *Somnium*. Evrart seems to have appreciated these structural defects, and in reworking his Latin text into its final vernacular version (the *Songe*), he took pains to smooth over the seams and improve the argumentative structure of the chapters on Jews—while maintaining (and indeed, sharpening) their earlier aggressive conclusions.

---

40 Matthew 16:26, cited from X 5.3.23 (*Matthaeus*).

Gone, for instance, was the awkward introductory framing of papal versus princely statutes. Instead, the discussion of the different forms of permission that had previously featured in the Cleric's speech was moved to the end of the preceding chapter in the *Songe* (on the licitness of trial by battle). At the end of this chapter, the Knight offers the Jews as a case study for the third kind of permission, whereby "a law allows something to be done and eliminates the impediments that would prevent it from being done"—citing a passage from Gratian's *Decretum* insisting that Jews be allowed to observe their festivals unhindered.[41] The Knight then reports the opinion ("as some like to say") that Jews should also be allowed to lend at usury to Christians, since the Biblical prohibition "should be understood in reference to one's brother or neighbor (*prochain*)." Since Jews did not consider Christians to be brothers or neighbors, "it therefore seems to them that they can lend to us at usury without offending God."[42] Unlike the *Somnium*, the *Songe* therefore proffered a notional defense of Jewish lending, relying on a well-worn argument in its favor.

The Knight's concluding lines thus tee up the Cleric's speech, which is nearly double the length of the earlier version.[43] As before, this chapter draws on both John of Legnano's *Somnium* and Oldradus's *consilium*, but where the Latin version featured lengthy unbroken borrowings from these texts (cumulatively representing two-thirds of the Cleric's speech), the vernacular rewriting adopts a much freer approach in which Evrart's own voice predominates.

The first part of the Cleric's speech maps closely onto the thematic organization of the earlier Latin version, with a firm condemnation of usury followed by a criticism of the French king for allowing Jews to lend at interest within the realm. To a much greater degree than in the *Somnium*, however, the remainder of the Cleric's speech focuses on the iniquitous wealth generated by Jewish usury as grounds for the Crown to expropriate Jewish property. Not only were "fifty thousand people in the kingdom of France [...] disinherited and reduced to poverty," but in an inversion of the proper ordering, Jews thus gained power over Christians, since "the debtor is to some degree the slave (*servus*) of the creditor" (a loose quotation of Proverbs 22:7).[44] Moreover, misquoting a Roman

41 D.45 c.3 (*Qui sincera*), taken from a letter of Pope Gregory the Great to the bishop of Naples.

42 *Songe*, 1.354 (c. I.CLXII, §9). For the early interpretative history of this distinction, see Benjamin N. Nelson, *The Idea of Usury* (Princeton, NJ: Princeton University Press, 1949), 3–28.

43 *Songe*, 1.355–59 (c. I.CLXIII).

44 The Biblical phrase ("Qui accepit mutuum, servus est [foenerantis]") is quoted in the Ordinary Gloss to *Cod.* 8.42.3 (*Si delegatio*); see *Accursii Glossa in Codicem* (Venice, 1488; repr. Turin: ex Officina Erasmiana, 1968), fol. 260ra, s.v. *a cliente*. Evrart's formulation

law barring the export of gold outside the empire, the Cleric denounces Jews for using subtle artifice to seize the gold and silver of Christians and then carry it out of the country.[45] While the Cleric repeats the accusation that Jewish moneylenders pressured indebted Christian women for sex in order to recover their pawned goods, the *Somnium*'s accompanying claim that these crimes were known from *fama publica* and sacramental confession disappears in the vernacular reworking—suggesting that either Evrart or his royal patron found its tendentiousness unsatisfactory. As in the *Somnium*, the Cleric concludes by invoking the Biblical account of Hagar's expulsion as a model for contemporary action.

In contrast to the Cleric's speech, much of the Knight's reply adheres closely to the text of the earlier Latin version. After conceding at the outset that usury is forbidden to all, the Knight once again shines a spotlight on ecclesiastical (and specifically papal) complicity with Jewish moneylending. He then reprises the same verbatim restatement of Oldradus's defense of Jews found in the *Somnium*, though with an added reference to the Jews as Christ-killers. At the point where the Knight switches tone to begin advocating expulsion, however, Evrart rewrote his earlier material to pursue a different rhetorical and argumentative approach. First, the imagined dialogue with a princely audience disappears in favor of an extended passage of wishful thinking:

> I believe that if the Most Christian King of Kings, the King of France who is ruling now, was aware of one-tenth of the injuries and wicked things that the Jews inflict on his people, he would not suffer their presence for all the gold and silver in the world. [...] These Jews disinherit the people and hold them in heavy servitude and will hold them a hundred times worse if their mastery persists, since the Jews' riches increase from day to day while the poor people's riches diminish.[46]

more closely echoes the commentary of Bartolus de Saxoferrato (d. 1357) on the same text ("quod debitur videtur quodammodo servus creditoris"); see his *In secundam codicis partem commentaria* (Turin: Bevilacqua, 1577), fol. 112, *ad loc.*

45 *Songe*, 1.357 (c. I.CLXIII, §10): "*Subtyli ingenio, extrahunt aurum a barbaris*; ilz retraient soutifvement l'or et l'argent dez Crestians, et le transportent en aultre contrée." Here the Cleric is reversing the logic of *Cod.* 4.63.2: "Non solum aurum barbaris minime praebeatur, sed etiam si apud eos inventum fuerit, subtili auferatur ingenio" ("*Not only should gold not be offered to barbarians, but also, if it has been discovered among them, it should be removed by careful ingenuity.*"); English translation from *The Codex of Justinian*, ed. Bruce W. Frier et al., 3 vols. (Cambridge: Cambridge University Press, 2016), 2.1054–55.

46 *Songe*, 1.361 (c. I.CLXIV, §7).

Having thus reiterated in even starker terms the earlier fiscal argument in favor of expulsion, the Knight then launches into an extended attack on the Jews' supposed engagement with sorcery and astrology. While the *Somnium*'s Cleric had made only passing reference to the Jews' "many sorceries," the *Songe* develops this allegation in detail, presenting it as yet another way in which the kingdom's Jews "lead many Christians astray" despite the Deuteronomic prohibition on divination and soothsaying.[47]

The Knight's discussion of sorcery and astrology does double duty in the *Songe*: not only does it serve as a further argument for expelling Jews, but it also enables a smooth transition to the next twenty chapters, which are devoted to the topic of astrology (a subject of great interest to Charles V) albeit without further mention of either Jews or expulsion.[48] The discussion of Jews in the *Songe* is therefore much more closely integrated into the preceding and succeeding chapters than in the *Somnium*, though this comes at the cost of a clear peroration in the Knight's remarks.

The extensive organizational reworking, coupled with the fourfold increase in original material, reveals the extent to which Evrart (or perhaps even his royal reader) was dissatisfied with the discussion of Jews in the *Somnium* and sought to improve it in the *Songe*. Yet for all the reordering and elaboration that characterize the vernacular version, the argumentation remains broadly unchanged. In both versions of his treatise, Evrart follows (almost to the letter) Oldradus de Ponte's *consilium* in arguing that secular rulers do have the authority to expel Jews from their lands if they so choose, but per church teachings, Jews should be tolerated so long as they do not pose a threat to Christians. And in both versions, Evrart then departs from his source text in insisting that contemporary Jews (at least in the kingdom of France) *do* pose a threat through the ravages of their usurious lending and other misdeeds, and hence that they should indeed be expelled from the realm. Only with regard to the nature of these other misdeeds do the arguments of the two texts vary significantly: in the *Somnium*, sexual encounters between Jewish men and Christian women loom large, with sorcery mentioned only fleetingly; the reverse is true in the *Songe*. That not all French Jews engaged in moneylending (let alone soothsaying or sex with Christian women) posed little analytical difficuly for Evrart, who—like most other thirteenth- and fourteenth-century Christian writers—took it for granted that entire Jewish communities might be punished collectively for the alleged actions of individual Jews.

47 *Songe*, 1.361–62 (c. I.CLXIV, §8); the reference is to Deuteronomy 18:11.

48 For the royal interest in astrology, see Jeannine Quillet, *Charles V: Le roi lettré* (Paris: Perrin, 1984), 105–14.

4 Subversion, Scandal, and Danger: The Limits of Toleration

In pushing beyond the ambiguity of Oldradus's *consilium* to conclude firmly in favor of expulsion, Evrart's argument notably does not rest on further citations of legal authorities. The few new *allegationes* that Evrart inserted in the *Somnium* either contrast civil and canon law on usury or serve as mere rhetorical flourish.[49] Those added to the *Songe* simply reinforce the condemnation of usury or soothsaying while saying nothing about the expulsion of their practitioners.[50] Notwithstanding Evrart's professional background as a jurist, he bolstered his case for expulsion not by adding more law but rather by invoking political economy, specifically the damaging effects of Jewish usury on the king's subjects and, by extension, on the kingdom as a whole.

The efficacy of this line of argument relies heavily on the presumption (which Evrart lifted directly from Oldradus) that the Christian toleration of Jewish presence was conditional, and hence subject to revocation if Jews caused either "danger or scandal" to their Christian hosts. Only where the Jews were living "quietly" (*quiete*) and without scandal, in Oldradus's formulation, did they merit the church's protection. As noted above, Oldradus drew this argument and its associated language from Innocent IV's commentary to the decretal *Quod super his*. In fact, the passage in question concerned the circumstances under which a pope might suspend the *dominium* of infidel rulers over their Christian subjects; Innocent concluded that this was permitted in cases of "great need" (*magna causa*), but that the pope should refrain from doing so "so long as (*dummodo*) there was no danger (*periculum*) to the Christians, nor serious scandal (*grave scandalum*)."[51]

The linchpin of Evrart's argument for expulsion therefore relied on a tendentious reworking of a brief passage in a decretal commentary. That said, Oldradus and Evrart were hardly alone in framing the church's traditional protection of Jews in conditional terms. Both Pope Innocent III (r. 1198–1216) and

---

49 In the *Somnium*, Evrart's additional citations are to the titles on usury in the *Codex* and *Digest*, to show that civil law permits usury; to X 5.19.4 (*Super eo*), to assert that even the pope cannot dispense from the prohibition on usury; to the Gospel passage (Matthew 16:26) cited above, n. 40; and to the preface of *Nov.* 8 (at §1), for the dictum that "the empire prospers only if its subjects are wealthy."

50 In the *Songe*, the additional citations are to Psalm 14:5 (condemning usury); to *Cod.* 4.63.2, as noted above, n. 45; to D.46 c.10 (*Sicut non suo*), barring the use of Jewish intermediaries for loans between Christians; to the Ordinary gloss on *Cod.* 8.42.3, as noted above, n. 44; and to Deuteronomy 18:11 and C.26 q.5 c.2 (*Qui divinationes*), condemning soothsaying and other dark arts.

51 Innocent IV, *Apparatus, ad* X 3.34.8.

Gregory IX (r. 1227–1241) had similarly emphasized the conditional nature of the church's sufferance, declaring that ecclesiastical protection only extended to Jews "insofar as they did not conspire to the subversion of the Christian faith," a phrase that would become standard in later papal privileges to Jews.[52] Furthermore, in 1253 Innocent IV (r. 1243–1254) had personally approved the archbishop of Vienne's request to expel Jews from his province in light of the "grave dangers" (*gravia pericula*) and "scandal" that they were reportedly causing.[53] But since none of these papal formulations ended up being codified in the *Liber extra* or any subsequent collections, the only formal source that Oldradus could adduce in support was a canonistic commentary (albeit one penned by a pope).

Not all late medieval commentators embraced this emerging conditional paradigm. In a quodlibet on the legitimacy of expelling Jews (composed in the immediate aftermath of Philip the Fair's 1306 expulsion), the Cistercian theologian Jacques de Thérines (d. 1321) argued firmly for the necessity of a Jewish presence within Christendom. His conclusion was straightforward: even if prompted by grave threats to Christians, any expulsion of Jews should be at most temporary. As Elsa Marmursztejn has recently argued, such an approach treated expulsion as a transient exception to a traditional (and ever valid) norm.[54]

By contrast, the conditional framing necessarily raised the question of what threats or misdeeds might justify the forced removal of Jews from Christian lands. For Innocent III and Gregory IX, the appropriate threshold was Jewish scheming to subvert the Christian faith. Innocent IV (perhaps inadvertently) introduced the language of "grave danger" and "scandal" to Christians as

---

52 Compare Innocent III, "Constitutio pro Iudaeis," (15 September 1199), in *Die Register Innocenz' III*, ed. Othmar Hageneder et al., 15 vols. (Graz: Böhlau, 1964–2022), 2.535–36, no. 276/302: "Eos autem dumtaxat hujus protectionis presidio volumus communiri, qui nihil machinari presumpserint in subversionem fidei Christiane"; and Gregory IX, "Etsi judeorum" (6 April 1233), in *Les registres de Grégoire IX*, ed. Lucien Auvray, 4 vols. (Paris: Fontemoing, 1896–1955), 1.691–92, no. 1216: "dummodo nichil machinari presumant in ignominiam fidei Christiane." For the continued appearance of Innocent's phrase, see Rebecca Rist, *Popes and Jews, 1095–1291* (Oxford: Oxford University Press, 2016), 81.

53 Innocent IV, "Sicut tua nobis," (23 July 1253), in *Les registres d'Innocent IV*, ed. Élie Berger, 4 vols. (Paris: Thorin, 1884–1920), 3.314, no. 6980. It is possible that the expulsion was limited to rabbis, as suggested in Cesare Baronio et al., *Annales ecclesiastici*, 37 vols. (Paris: Barri-Ducis, 1864–83), 21.446 (a. 1253, §34).

54 Marmursztejn, "Débats médiévaux," 22. The author suggests that such an approach is characteristic of learned debates over Jewish expulsion in the later Middle Ages, but my reading of Oldradus (as well as the *Somnium/Songe*) suggests otherwise.

grounds for the suspension of ecclesiastical toleration, and Oldradus de Ponte crystallized this formulation in his widely read *consilium*.

Evrart's contribution to this evolving line of reasoning was his energetic insistence that Jewish usury—and the alleged Christian impoverishment that it produced—rose to the level of such danger, while adding in the scandal caused by either sex or sorcery for good measure. While many medieval expulsion orders touted illicit economic or sexual dealings as justification for the ouster of Jewish communities, the concepts of "danger" and "scandal" allowed Evrart to invoke damaging consequences rather than definite crimes—and to overcome thereby the conceptual obstacles posed by ecclesiastical protection and royal privileges alike.[55]

5 The Expulsion of 1394: A Dream Fulfilled?

Given Evrart's powerful position at court, together with King Charles V's apparent role in commissioning the *Somnium* and *Songe*, the treatises' discussion of royal policies toward Jews was more than just a case of abstract theorizing. Indeed, through the Knight's fanciful ventriloquism (in the *Somnium*) and wishful thinking (in the *Songe*), Evrart clearly sought to convey both his personal distress at the damage that Jews were supposedly causing to the kingdom, and his hope that his royal reader would duly take action against them. Such hopes went unrealized during his lifetime: Charles V seems to have paid no heed to Evrart's anti-Jewish demands, even as he otherwise rewarded his councilor handsomely for his services to the Crown.[56]

Evrart was not alone among Charles V's councilors in advocating the expulsion of the kingdom's Jews. So too would his contemporary Philippe de Mézières (d. 1405) in his *Songe du Viel Pelerin,* another sprawling dream vision composed in 1389. There Philippe urged his one-time pupil—now king—Charles VI (r. 1380–1422) to expel Jews chiefly on the grounds of their usurious depredations, as well as other "terrible deeds" they were committing against both the

55 Notable examples include the 1289 expulsion order for Anjou and Maine, and a November 1290 writ defending the recent expulsion of Jews from England; see respectively Pierre Rangeard, *Histoire de l'université d'Angers*, 2 vols. (Angers: Barassé, 1868–77), 2.183–87, no. 24; and *Select Pleas, Starrs, and Other Records from the Rolls of the Exchequer of the Jews, A.D. 1220–1284*, ed. J. M. Rigg (London: Quaritch, 1902), xl–xli.

56 In 1377 (the year preceding the completion of the *Songe*), Evrart was the highest-paid of Charles V's councillors, receiving 600 gold francs per year; see Marion Schnerb-Lièvre, "Les 'gages' d'Evrart de Trémaugon," *Revue du Moyen Âge latin* 43 (1987): 51–52.

Christian faith and the people of the kingdom (notably their "abominable" use of Christian wet nurses).[57] Although Philippe eschewed legal sources almost entirely in his *Songe*, he shared Evrart's desire to show how expulsion was consonant with the church's traditional teachings on Jews, promising his royal reader: "I will teach you an effective and moral means by which … you and your kingdom might be delivered from Jews, without offending either God or the Christian faith."[58]

While Evrart died too early to witness the expulsion of Jews that Charles VI ordered in 1394, Philippe de Mézières surely drew grim satisfaction from the event, which marked—after nearly a century of brutal disruptions and partial reversals—the final expulsion of Jews from the medieval kingdom of France. The formal expulsion order was studiously vague, citing as justification simply the "many crimes, excesses, and offenses" that the Jews had committed, "especially against our faith, as well as against the content of the [privileges] granted to them."[59] Lest anyone suspect that baser motives were at play, the king insisted that "no other causes and considerations" had factored into his decision.[60]

It was left to the official historiographer of Charles's reign, the Saint-Denis monk and chronicler Michel Pintoin, to elaborate on the precise nature of these crimes and offenses. At the top of his litany of supposed Jewish wrongdoing was the "usury that had infected the entire realm and reduced many to terrible poverty," though the king had also been informed of the "many scandals" arising from the presence of Christian wet nurses and servants in Jewish households. Notwithstanding the enormous annual sums that the Jews

57 Philippe de Mézières, *Songe du Viel Pelerin*, ed. Joël Blanchard, 2 vols. (Geneva: Droz, 2015), 1045–57, ch. 69. Among the other "diabolical deeds" of the Jews, Philippe protested the "abomination" of Jewish families hiring Christian wet nurses, as well as the public intermingling of Jews and Christians in the streets of Paris.

58 Mézières, *Songe du Viel Pelerin*, 1047.

59 *Ord.* 7.675–76. The triple invocation of "crimes, excès et deliz" features regularly in contemporary French royal documentation (e.g. *Ord.* 7.21, 197, and 441). I am grateful to Nureet Dermer for her comments on the order's language.

60 Roger Kohn, one of the only scholars to have studied the 1394 expulsion in detail, attributed the royal decision to fiscal concerns, namely the declining revenues gleaned from the kingdom's Jewish communities following a tumultuous period in the early 1380s that saw widespread assaults and a considerable exodus (see Kohn, *Juifs de la France du Nord*, 259–61; and his "Les Juifs en France du Nord dans la seconde moitié du XIVe siècle. Un état de la question," in Dahan, ed., *L'expulsion des juifs de France*, 27). If so, there is a dark irony in the fact that Charles VI's decision was the result not of too much Jewish moneylending, but of too little.

paid into the royal coffers, the king therefore resolved to drive them from his kingdom.[61]

That the Saint-Denis chronicler's account echoed the same concerns of usury and Jewish-Christian intermingling that featured in the *Songes* of both Evrart and Philippe de Mézières is hardly surprising; denunciations of Jewish lending and the Jews' reliance on Christian servants and wet nurses had been staples of anti-Jewish discourse for more than two centuries. It is nevertheless telling that the chronicler cited not only the damage inflicted by Jewish usury, but also the "scandals" arising from cohabitation, thus aligning the royal decision with the very criteria that Evrart (quoting Innocent IV, via Oldradus's rendering) had set forth as sufficient grounds for abrogating the customary protection of Jews.

Moreover, for all the deliberate generality of the expulsion order itself, Charles VI's triple invocation of crimes against the faith, injury to his Christian subjects, and the violation of royal privileges hews closely to the framework articulated by his father's late councilor. Indeed, in Charles's strange insistence that his decision to rid the realm of Jews was motivated by these concerns and no others, perhaps we can even hear the voice of a king anxious to demonstrate that his action was indeed consonant with both the demands of justice and the teachings of the church, as befitting "le très crestian Roy dez roys, le roy de France."[62]

Bibliography

Manuscripts

Bordeaux, Bibliothèque municipale, ms. 404
London, British Library, MS Royal 19 C IV
Paris, Bibliothèque nationale de France, Latin 4085
Paris, Bibliothèque nationale de France, Latin 4276A
Paris, Bibliothèque nationale de France, Latin 14335

61 *Chronique du religieux de Saint-Denys*, ed. Louis Bellaguet, 6 vols. (Paris: Crapelet, 1839–52), 2.118–21 (XIV.17). Another contemporary source (Honorat Bovet's *Apparicion Maistre Jehan de Meun*, completed in 1398) likewise presented Jewish usury as a principal motivation for the expulsion, alongside other unspecified "grans iniquitez"; see *Medieval Muslims, Christians, and Jews in Dialogue: The Apparicion Maistre Jehan de Meun of Honorat Bovet*, ed. and trans. Michael Hanly (Tempe: Arizona Center for Medieval and Renaissance Studies, 2005), 78–80 (ll. 230–35).

62 *Songe*, 1.361 (c. I.CLXIV, §7).

Reims, Bibliothèque municipale, Ms. 737
Tübingen, Universitätsbibliothek, Mc 17
Vatican City, Biblioteca apostolica vaticana, Ross. 1096

Printed Primary Sources

Accursius. *Accursii Glossa in Codicem*. Venice: Battista Torti, 1488; repr. Turin: Bottega d'Erasmo, 1968.

Bartolo da Sassoferrato [Bartolus de Saxoferrato]. *In secundam codicis partem commentaria*. Turin: Bevilacqua, 1577.

Bovet, Honorat. *Medieval Muslims, Christians, and Jews in Dialogue: The Apparicion Maistre Jehan de Meun of Honorat Bovet*. Edited and translated by Michael Hanly. Tempe: Arizona Center for Medieval and Renaissance Studies, 2005.

[Charles V, King of France.] *Mandements et actes divers de Charles V (1364–1380)*. Edited by Léopold Delisle. Paris: Imprimerie nationale, 1874.

Compayré, Clément. *Études historiques et documents inédits sur l'Albigeois, le Castrais, et l'ancien diocèse de Lavaur*. Albi: Papailhiau, 1841.

Evrart de Trémaugon. *Somnium viridarii*. Edited by Marion Schnerb-Lièvre. 2 vols. Paris: CNRS, 1993.

Evrart de Trémaugon. *Songe du Vergier*. Edited by Marion Schnerb-Lièvre. 2 vols. Paris: CNRS, 1982.

Evrart de Trémaugon. *Trois leçons sur les Décrétales*. Edited and translated by Marion Schnerb-Lièvre, with Gérard Giordanengo. Paris: Éditions du CNRS, 1998.

Gregory I, Pope. *S. Gregorii Magni registrum epistularum*. Edited by Dag Norberg. CCSL 140. Brepols: Turnhout, 1982.

Gregory IX, Pope. *Les registres de Grégoire IX*. Edited by Lucien Auvray. 4 vols. Paris: Fontemoing, 1896–1955.

Innocent III, Pope. *Die Register Innocenz' III*. Edited by Othmar Hageneder et al. 15 vols. Graz: Böhlau, 1964–2022.

Innocent IV, Pope. *Apparatus super V libros decretalium*. Venice: Johann Herbort, 1481.

Innocent IV, Pope. *Les registres d'Innocent IV*. Edited by Élie Berger. 4 vols. Paris: Thorin, 1884–1920.

Jacques de Thérines. *Quodlibets I et II*. Edited by Palémon Glorieux. Paris: Vrin, 1958.

John of Legnano [Giovanni da Legnano]. *Somnium*. Edited by Maria Consiglia De Matteis and Giulietta Voltolina. Legnano: Banca di Legnano, 2004.

[Justinian.] *The Codex of Justinian*. Edited by Bruce W. Frier et al. 3 vols. Cambridge: Cambridge University Press, 2016.

Mézières, Philippe de. *Songe du Viel Pelerin*. Edited by Joël Blanchard. 2 vols. Geneva: Droz, 2015.

Oldradus de Ponte. *Jews and Saracens in the Consilia of Oldradus de Ponte.* Edited and translated by Norman Zacour. Toronto: Pontifical Institute of Mediaeval Studies, 1990.

Ordonnances des roys de France de la troisième race.... Edited by Eusèbe Jacob de Laurière et al. 23 vols. Paris: Imprimerie royale, 1723–1849.

[Pintoin, Michel.] *Chronique du religieux de Saint-Denys contenant le règne de Charles VI, de 1380 à 1422.* Edited by Louis Bellaguet. 6 vols. Paris: Crapelet, 1839–56.

Select Pleas, Starrs, and Other Records from the Rolls of the Exchequer of the Jews, A.D. 1220–1284. Edited by J. M. Rigg. London: Quaritch, 1902.

Secondary Sources

Baronio, Cesare, et al. *Annales ecclesiastici.* 37 vols. Paris: Barri-Ducis, 1864–83.

Brasington, Bruce. "Power as Privilege: The Maxim Privilegium meretur amittere, qui potestate sibi concessa abutitur." *Zeitschrift der Savigny-Stiftung für Rechtsgeschichte* 109, no. 1 (2023): 53–72.

Brown, Elizabeth A. R. "Philip V, Charles IV, and the Jews of France: the Alleged Expulsion of 1322." *Speculum* 66, no. 2 (1991): 294–329.

Coopland, G. W. "An unpublished work of John of Legnano: the *Somnium* of 1372." *Nuovi studi medievali* 2, fasc. 1 (1925–26): 65–88.

Coville, Alfred. *Evrart de Trémaugon et le Songe du Verger.* Paris: Droz, 1933.

Dahan, Gilbert, ed. *L'expulsion des juifs de France, 1394.* Paris: Cerf, 2004.

Donovan, Glynis M., and Maurice H. Keen. "The 'Somnium' of John of Legnano." *Traditio* 37 (1981): 325–45.

Fossier, Arnaud. "'Propter vitandum scandalum': Histoire d'une catégorie juridique (XIIe–XVe siècle)." *Mélanges de l'École française de Rome. Moyen Âge* 121/2 (2009): 317–48.

Iancu-Agou, Danièle. "Les Juifs à Montpellier à la fin du XIVe siècle." In *L'expulsion des juifs de France, 1394*, edited by Gilbert Dahan, 51–67. Paris: Cerf, 2004.

Jordan, William C. *Unceasing Strife, Unending Fear: Jacques de Thérines and the Freedom of the Church in the Age of the Last Capetians.* Princeton, NJ: Princeton University Press, 2005.

Klepper, Deeana. "Historicizing Allegory: The Jew as Hagar in Medieval Christian Text and Image." *Church History* 84, no. 2 (2015): 308–44.

Kohn, Roger S. *Les Juifs de la France du Nord dans la seconde moitié du XIVe siècle.* Louvain: Peeters, 1988.

Kohn, Roger S. "Les Juifs en France du Nord dans la seconde moitié du XIVe siècle. Un état de la question." In *L'expulsion des juifs de France, 1394*, edited by Gilbert Dahan, 13–29. Paris: Cerf, 2004.

Kupfer, Marcia. "'... Lectres ... plus vrayes': Hebrew Script and Jewish Witness in the 'Mandeville' Manuscript of Charles V." *Speculum* 83/1 (2008): 58–111.

Liberatoscioli, Davide. *Juden ohne Päpste: Inklusion und Judenfeinlichkeit zwischen Rom und Avignon*. Berlin: De Gruyter, 2021.

Loeb, Isidore. "Les expulsions des Juifs de France au XIVe siècle." In *Jubelschrift zum 70. Geburtstag des Prof. Dr. H. Graetz*, 39–56. Breslau: Schottlaender, 1887.

Luce, Siméon. "Les Juifs sous Charles V et le fonds hébraique du Trésor des Chartes, en 1372." *Revue Historique* 7, fasc. 2 (1878): 362–70.

Marmursztejn, Elsa. "Débats médiévaux sur l'expulsion des juifs des monarchies occidentales." In *Les expulsions de minorités religieuses dans l'Europe des XIIIe–XVIIe siècles,* edited by Isabelle Poutrin and Alain Tallon, 19–44. Pompignac: Éditions Bière, 2015.

McManus, Brendan. "The *Consilia* and *Quaestiones* of Oldradus de Ponte." *Bulletin of Medieval Canon Law* 23 (1999): 85–113.

Müller, Carl. "Über das Somnium Viridarii. Beitrag zur Geschichte der Literatur über Kirche und Staat im 14. Jahrhundert." *Zeitschrift der Kirchenrecht* 14 (1879): 134–205.

Nelson, Benjamin N. *The Idea of Usury*. Princeton, NJ: Princeton University Press, 1949.

Quillet, Jeannine. *La philosophie politique du Songe du Vergier (1378). Sources doctrinales*. Paris: J. Vrin, 1977.

Quillet, Jeannine. *Charles V: Le roi lettré.* Paris: Perrin, 1984.

Rangeard, Pierre. *Histoire de l'université d'Angers*. 2 vols. Angers: Barassé, 1868–77.

Rist, Rebecca. *Popes and Jews, 1095–1291*. Oxford: Oxford University Press, 2016.

Royer, Jean-Pierre. *L'Église et le royaume de France au XIVe siècle d'après le "Songe du Vergier" et la jurisprudence du Parlement.* Paris: Pichon, 1969.

Schnerb-Lièvre, Marion. "Evrart de Trémaugon et *Le Songe du Vergier.*" *Romania* 101 (1980): 527–30.

Schnerb-Lièvre, Marion. "Les 'gages' d'Evrart de Trémaugon." *Revue du Moyen Âge latin* 43 (1987): 51–52.

Schnerb-Lièvre, Marion. "Evrart de Trémaugon." *Histoire littéraire de la France* 42, fasc. 2, 281–296. Paris: Éditions de Boccard, 2003.

Shachar, Shulamith. "The Jews in the Eyes of Court Writers and their Status by Royal Decrees in the Reign of Charles V of France [in Hebrew]." *Zion* 33 (1968): 1–14.

Sibon, Juliette. *Chasser les juifs pour régner*. Paris: Perrin, 2016.

Stow, Kenneth R. "Expulsion Italian Style: The Case of Lucio Ferraris." *Jewish History* 3, no. 1 (1988): 51–63.

Stow, Kenneth R. "The Church and the Jews: St. Paul to Pius IX." In *Popes, Church and Jews in the Middle Ages: Confrontation and Response*, art. I, 1–76. Farnham, UK: Ashgate, 2007.

CHAPTER 15

Suicide in Early Modern Italy

Elizabeth W. Mellyn

We begin with a brief letter from the voluminous archives of Santa Dorotea, Florence's first hospital dedicated to the care of the severely mentally ill. It is March 1761. A farm laborer from the eastern outskirts of Florence named Migliore petitions the hospital.[1] With the help of a scribe, he claims that his fiftyish-year-old son Michel Angelo has long suffered with melancholy from "fixations of the head." "From time to time," Migliore explains, his son "becomes raving mad." Three times he threw himself into a well. Had people not been there to fish him out, Michel Angelo would have died.[2]

The season is significant. March was the month Tuscany began to wake from its winter slumber. A wet chill still cut the air, but, as Migliore pointed out, the heat of summer, which "made similar sicknesses worse," drew near. In his mind, disaster loomed; climatic conditions were ripening for Michel Angelo to attempt suicide again. Migliore asked that Santa Dorotea intervene by admitting his son to "cure him from his sickness."[3]

The hospital dispatched Antonio Lulli, one of its salaried physicians, to conduct an examination. Lulli agreed that Michel Angelo was an appropriate candidate for treatment in hospital. Yet, his reasons departed somewhat from Migliore's. Michel Angelo's suicide attempts deserved consideration, but Lulli uncovered more alarming behavior. When he met with the prospective patient, he did not find that his insanity immediately threatened to "disturb public peace or harm public morality [*onestà*]," as the letter of the law required.[4] Yet,

1 *ASF*, SD 4: no. 17. The petition is signed, "Io Giuseppe Mongozzi a nome del supplicante mano propria." ("I Giuseppe Mongozzi in the name of the supplicant, [in my] own hand.")

2 *ASF*, SD 4, no. 17, "come si ritrova in casa un suo figliolo, chiamato Michel Arcangelo in età di circa anni 50, quale patisce di pazzia malinconica per fissazioni di capo, per cui di tempo in tempo diventa furioso, e per la terza volta si è gettato nel pozzo ove sarebbe rimasto estinto se non vi fossero stati pronti gli aiuti per ripescarlo."

3 *ASF*, SD 4, no. 17, "e temendo il supplicante che una volta si ammazzi da se, tanto più che s'avvicina l'estate in cui simili malattie diventano peggiori. Supplica perciò [...] a volersi degnare di comandare che sia ricevuto nello spedale di S. Dorotea per esser ivi curato di detta infermità".

4 A government decree issued on November 12, 1750, after months of revision, identified those Santa Dorotea was established to house as "abandoned furiosi, wandering the public streets." From the government's perspective the hospital was a useful instrument for maintaining

 | DOI:10.1163/9789004710696_017

Lulli reported, "at various times, [Michel Angelo] raged against the people in his house and especially against the children." What that "rage" looked like, the physician left undefined, but use of similar language in other cases suggests violence. Lulli was startled enough to probe further. When he asked Michel Angelo "the reason he did such things," the allegedly insane man replied that "he felt transported [by] *fantasia* without knowing what he was doing."[5] In Lulli's mind, it was these "rages" that were the problem. Michel Angelo's condition threatened the physical safety of the entire household and particularly the safety of the children. On May 6 of that year, he was formally admitted.[6] Two and a half years later, on November 25, 1763, he died there. His body was taken to San Jacopo where the hospital gave him a Christian burial. This was a sad outcome, but perhaps the best the family could have hoped for.

The case of Migliore and his son Michel Angelo offers a rare, documented glimpse of how families in pre-modern Europe dealt with the suicidality of their relatives. In Tuscany, they could and did petition to have people like Migliore's son certified as mentally ill and committed for care and treatment to a hospital. Had Michel Angelo been born before 1647, the year Santa Dorotea started accepting patients, his behavior would have landed him in criminal court rather than in a hospital room. In the Middle Ages and for most of the early modern period, religious and secular authorities proclaimed suicide a crime and a sin. They considered it an affront to self, to community, and, above all, to God.[7] Suicide flouted the fifth commandment against murder, denied God the power he alone possessed over life and death, suggested capitulation to demonic temptation, and renounced the ties of mutual obligation that bound families, communities, and polities together.[8] Throughout Europe, suicide initiated criminal proceedings that could end in the confiscation of property and the defilement of the suicide's corpse. By dramatic contrast, between

public order. But, as this and many other cases demonstrate, Santa Dorotea's physicians used their discretion in determining whether a prospective patient qualified for admission, regardless of whether they might pose a risk to public safety. Paraphrase of *ASF*, SD 4, 17, "Antonio Lulli sarebbe [...] di sentiment che dovesse mandarsi nel detto spedale per esservi curato per impedire maggiori disgrazia, dacchè sebbene nel tempo della visita da esso fattali non lo abbia trovato offeso dal male della pazzia in quell'ecceso per cui gl'infermi di tal genere rendendosi a furiosi o scandalosi e perciò turbatori della pubblica quiete sono."

5 Paraphrase of SD 4, 17, "in vari tempi si è infuriato contro le persone di casa e particolarmente contro I ragazzi ed interrogatolo per qual motive faceva tale cose, ha risposto che si senta trasportare la fantasia senza saper quello si faccia."

6 *ASF*, SD 35, 93; SD 36, 16.

7 Thomas Aquinas, *Summa Theologiae*, II, II, q. 64, a. 5.

8 See, Augustine, *The City of God*, Book I, chs. 17, 19, 20, 22, 23, 24, 27, and Aquinas, *Summa Theologiae*, II, II, q. 64, a. 5.

the sixteenth and eighteenth centuries, voluntary death was increasingly decriminalized, medicalized, and secularized.

All of Europe trod a historical path that led from "sin to insanity." Yet, we should be wary of seeing that path as a straight line moving from hostility to acceptance or intolerance to tolerance. The route was littered with discontinuities and reversals borne of the profound ambivalence the act of suicide engendered at home, in court, in the pulpit, in a neighborhood, and in a polity throughout this transitional period. At times, prescriptions laid down in normative treatises or legislation aligned with practice; at other times a great gap yawned between them. Local or regional factors tended to shape prevailing views and how they were expressed in practice.[9] English historians who have uncovered the richest evidence have employed an oceanographic metaphor to describe the shift in English attitudes. "Tides of change," drifted first toward greater severity, before gradually ebbing and flowing back toward greater tolerance. In England, where revolutions in government and religion intensified hostility to self-killing in the sixteenth and early seventeenth centuries, profound changes in legal institutions, local government, and religious and intellectual culture mitigated attitudes to suicide after 1660.[10]

But "undertows of opposition and eddies of ambivalence" always accompanied "the main currents of opinion."[11] These discontinuities better capture what took shape in other parts of Europe. Electoral Saxony, for example, represents a "powerful countercurrent" within the "rising tide of secularization." In the seventeenth century, Saxon jurists and city councilors secularized the burial of suicides, based on theories of church subordination to state authority. In the early eighteenth century, extraordinary political tension between the Electors of Saxony, the Lutheran state church, and Saxon nobles combined to reverse this process, thereby "desecularizing" the burial of the suicide's corpse. The suicide's post-mortem body became a highly contested symbol of jurisdictional conflict between church and state. Despite muscular civil attempts and intellectual justifications for secular control of the burial of suicides, the church won out, putting the post-mortem bodies of suicides entirely in the

9 I borrow the term "from sin to insanity" from the title of the superb collection of essays edited by Jeffrey Watt, *From Sin to Insanity: Suicide in Early Modern Europe* (Ithaca: Cornell University Press, 2004). See also the key studies of Georges Minois, *History of Suicide: Voluntary Death in Western Culture*, trans. Lydia Cochrane (Baltimore: Johns Hopkins University Press, 1998).

10 Michael MacDonald and Terrence R. Murphy, *Sleepless Souls: Suicide in Early Modern England* (Oxford: Clarendon Press, 1990).

11 MacDonald and Murphy, *Sleepless Souls*.

hands of church authorities who had the sole right to decide where and how to bury them.[12]

Golden Age Spain furnishes another context in which religious conflicts and anxieties were expressed on and through the bodies of suicides. In Spain, attitudes to self-murder were forged within a militantly Catholic Christian culture bent on repressing religious pluralism by stomping out remnants of Judaism and Islam. Church and state spoke with one draconian voice against suicide by connecting it to heresy and apostasy, even as social and cultural attitudes were increasingly exploring ways in which suicide could be considered an act of religious martyrdom or heroic valor.[13]

Attitudes to suicide in Italy also shifted from sin to insanity from the medieval to the early modern period, yet their trajectory remains a blind spot in this larger history.[14] Extant case law, admittedly less complete than for other parts of Europe, reveals a complex picture. Despite heavy-handed legal and ecclesiastical prohibitions against voluntary death, Italian justice remained restitutive, tending toward mercy in cases of suicide from the fourteenth through the eighteenth century.[15] Italian jurists condemned suicide as a sin while simultaneously remaining skeptical that judges and magistrates could prove suicide dispositively in court. In the face of such uncertainty, Italian civil authorities and legal scholars gave judges and magistrates discretion to adjudicate suicide cases as they saw fit. These judges and magistrates, in turn, used their discretion to depart from the severity of normative law in favor of returning verdicts that restored social order or avoided further disorder to what an act like suicide could bring to families and communities.[16]

---

12 Craig Koslofsky, "Controlling the Body of the Suicide in Saxony," in *From Sin to Insanity*, 48–63. He uses the tidal metaphor on 63.

13 Elizabeth G. Dickenson and James M. Boyden, "Ambivalence Toward Suicide in Golden Age Spain," in *From Sin to Insanity*, 100–115.

14 Two articles on suicide in medieval and early modern Italy shed light on Italy's distinct legal, religious, and cultural history. See Trevor Dean, "Getting out of Jail: Suicide, Escape, and Release in Late Medieval and Renaissance Bologna," *Historical Research*, 90:249 (August 2017): 449–64 and Sharon Strocchia, "Women on the Edge: Madness, Possession, and Suicide in Early Modern Convents," *Journal of Medieval and Early Modern Studies* 45:1 (January 2015): 53–77.

15 The present study does not see evidence in Tuscan courts for the shift from restitutive to retributive justice that Riikka Meittinen has found for Sweden beginning in the latter half of the seventeenth century in her superb book *Suicide, Law, and Community in Early Modern Sweden* (London: Palgrave MacMillan, 2019).

16 In his superb book, *Abortion in Early Modern Europe* (Cambridge, MA: Harvard University Press, 2021), John Christopoulos observed a similar reliance on the discretion of judges and their preference for maintaining order in communities over strict adherence to normative law in abortion cases. See chapter 3.

An important part of this story remains unknown. The history of voluntary death in Europe has typically been told through criminal and civil case law and literary or artistic representation. But histories of hospitals like Santa Dorotea offer another index of Europe's changing attitudes to voluntary death. The suicidal men and women who came to reside in Santa Dorotea had repeatedly and publicly sought death at their own hand. They had submitted their private desire to public gaze, making it nearly impossible for families to represent the event as anything other than suicide in criminal proceedings. Santa Dorotea and its European counterparts offered an extra-judicial, institutional refuge for families and communities that had no hope of concealing the suicidal intentions and actions of their troubled members.

Great variety in structure, governance, and mission distinguished these hospitals from one another. Yet they remain unique and underappreciated lenses onto the history of suicide. Santa Dorotea's founding in the seventeenth century is a powerful indicator of Tuscany's ongoing medicalization and decriminalization of suicide in the early modern period. The hospital's administrators and salaried physicians readily acknowledged that severe forms of mental illness could induce suicidal behavior, tragically causing some men and women to bring about their own deaths. The hospital was founded to provide medical and spiritual care to such people with the express aim of curing them so that they could return to their lives, their families, and their communities. We can doubt the institution's rate of success; we can focus on its shortcomings and failures. But that does not change the fact that it held out to families the possibility of relief for the care of deeply troubled and troubling people. It even held out hope for their cure. For a relatively brief space of time, families unburdened themselves of the tremendous time, energy, and financial resources they had to expend in the constant surveillance of suicidal relatives. For a relatively brief space of time, they were able to pass the terrible responsibility for a suicidal relative's safety onto an institution that claimed to specialize in his or her treatment. And, for a relatively brief space of time, they were able to entertain the hope that their kin would return home, "better."

We can imagine that Santa Dorotea's services appealed to families who harbored a suicidal relative in their households. Especially in the eighteenth century, the hospital's increasing visibility in the public health landscape made it possible to treat suicidal men and women not as criminals, but as worthy objects of charity and medical care. In this context, their behavior did not invite the wrath of a criminal judge, but treatment by a medical practitioner. Their proper place was not prison, but a pious house dedicated to physical and spiritual healing. When Migliore's suicidal son died in Santa Dorotea, the hospital ensured he had a Christian burial. The records say nothing of whether his family was present when his soul was entrusted to God, but to God, through holy ground, he was sent.

1 "A Wicked and Detestable Outrage and a Damnable Sin"

We enter the complex cultural history of suicide in medieval and early modern Italy through a formal treatise on criminal law by the Roman jurist Prospero Farinacci (1544–1618). Farinacci was one of the most important criminal lawyers of the early modern period. Between 1581 and 1601, he sought to collect and address criminal questions in one immense "thesaurus of all criminal matters," for the practical use of lawyers and judges.[17] In question 128, he lays bare the tortured legal and cultural history of suicide from the ancient world to his own time.[18] In so doing, he shows the contradictions and tensions inherent in European legal culture, which drew both from ancient Roman law—generally tolerant of suicide—and medieval Christian theology—dead set against it.

Farinacci opened question 128 from the medieval Christian perspective, suffused as it was with religious abhorrence of voluntary death. "How detestable and horrendous his crime is," Farinacci begins, "who brings about his own demise."[19] He then extensively rehearsed hundreds of years of jurisprudence that labelled suicide a crime and a sin: Multiple sources argued that the person who took his or her own life "injured the republic and community." Others claimed that the man who murdered himself committed a greater crime than the man who murdered another, since the one who kills another is said only to kill a body, "while the suicide, like Judas Iscariot impiously loses both his body and his own soul." "The Christian religion," he further related, "considers this crime as a wicked and detestable outrage and a damnable sin," and so on.[20] In sum, legal language surrounding suicide was unequivocal. As a sin and a crime, it led only to condemnation in life and damnation in death.

---

17 Prospero Farinacci, *Praxis et theoricae criminalis* (Palthenius: Frankfurt, 1604), Quaestio CIV.

18 Kenneth Pennington, "Torture and Fear: Enemies of Justice," *Rivista internazionale di diritto comune,* 19 (2008): 27.

19 Farinacci, *Praxis et theoricae criminalis* (Palthenius: Frankfurt, 1610), 395, "Quam detestabile et horrendum sit crimen eius, qui sibi ipsi mortem conscivit".

20 Farinacci, *Praxis et theoricae criminalis* (1610), 395, "Ubi quod iniuriam facit repilublicae et communitati." "Ubi bene docet, quanto magis delnquatis, qui se ipsum occidit, quam qui alium occidit ... et corpus et animam propriam nefande perdit et point exemplum de Iuda Iscariote. ... Ubi quod Christiana religio habet hoc crimen pro impio facinore detestabilique et famndabili scelere."

Despite strong religious prohibitions against it, Farinacci noted that ancient and "modern" history was full of examples of people who had taken their own lives. The reasons were many: some killed themselves because they had committed crimes and feared punishment, while others committed suicide because they could not endure the weariness of life or physical pain; still others acted out of desperation, madness (*furore*), drunkenness, shame, or because of debt. Some committed suicide for love, while others did so out of arrogance or because they misguidedly believed they might win immortality. Some committed suicide so as not to betray secrets entrusted to them or to consent to a crime, or for many other pretexts or passions of the soul and body.[21] Yet, Farinacci argued, the general rule held: "killing oneself is prohibited by every law, civil, canonical, natural, and divine."[22] He further acknowledged both the judge's right to hang "the cadaver of the man who kills himself as punishment if that judge thought it appropriate" and the cleric's right to deny a suicide burial in consecrated ground or to exhume and profane a suicide's body that had been accidentally or wrongly buried there.[23]

The Bible, which did not condemn suicide outright, was not the soil from which these attitudes sprung. Christianity's "founding event" was Jesus's sacrifice of his own life for the sins of mankind. His disciples glorified his voluntary self-sacrifice and invited his followers to emulate it.[24] "There is no greater

21 Farinacci, *Praxis et theoricae criminalis* (1610). I have paraphrased the following paragraph: "Plura autem et antiquorum et modernorum recensentur exempla, eorum scilicet qui sibi ipsis aut manus inferendo aut se praecipites dando, aut se in puteum vel flumen proiiciendo, aut se venenando, aut se etiam suspendendo mortem consciverunt, cum nonnulli conscientia patrati criminis, metuve subiturae poenae, nonnulli autem taedio vitae, aut doloris impatientia, ac etiam nonnulli ex desperatione, furore, ebrietate, pudore, contracti aeris alieni (prout quandoque Florentinis contigisse testantur Doctores) aut ob aliam caussam, vel etiam amore, ac nonnulli etiam ex iactatione, immortalitatisve consequendae (ut credebant) caussa, nonnulli ne secreta sibi commissa panderent, ne peccato consentirent, variisque aliis praetextibus, animique et corporis passionibus se ipso occiderunt".

22 Farinacci, *Praxis et theoricae criminalis* (1610), 395, "Regulam: Itaque in proposita materia constituo, quod occidere se ipsum, omni iure prohibitum est, non solum civili et canonico. ... sed etiam naturali." He argues why it is against natural law for a few paragraphs before then stating that it is also an affront to divine law in Amplia I. On 396, Amplia III, "Ut propterea cadaver illius se ipsum occidit, pro poena suspendi possit, si ita iudici visum fuit," and on 397, Amplia IV, "Quia seipsum occidens sepultura caret ... Ubi refert, quod alias quidam Canonicus, qui seipsum laqueo suspendit, cum fuisset in Ecclesia sepultus a canonicis ignorantibus mortis genus, fuit postea detecta mortis forma, exhumantus, et profanae sepulturae traditus."

23 Farinacci, *Praxis et theoricae criminalis* (1610), 396.

24 Minois, *History of Suicide*, 26.

love than this," the Gospel of John declared, "to lay down one's life for one's friends."[25] Early Christian martyrs were similarly celebrated in the Christian hagiographical tradition for their willingness to die for their faith. The early church fathers distinguished sharply however between being killed for one's faith and killing oneself, which they vociferously opposed. Augustine of Hippo, the most influential among them, wrote at some length against suicide in *The City of God*. His position was ancient by Farinacci's lifetime, and yet it was still the dominant cultural refrain.

Augustine placed suicide in the domain of the fifth commandment. As he saw it, the injunction against the murder of others applied also to murder of the self.[26] This was an absolute rule that admitted no exceptions.[27] Augustine acknowledged that life's challenges might make voluntary death appear reasonable or even appealing to avoid shame, pain, grief, torture, oppression, or violence. One might even feel compassion for those who took their own lives to avoid terrible crimes being visited on their bodies.[28] Yet, he remained firm that suicide was not permissible under any circumstance. "Whatever anyone does with or to the body, provided that it cannot be avoided without committing sin," Augustine told his Christian audience, "involves no blame to the sufferer."[29] Let violators do what they may to the flesh, so long as the will remained steadfast in its suffering, the soul remained inviolate.

Augustine was particularly tough on famous Romans whose honor-bound suicides would come to resonate with Europe's intellectual elite beginning in the fourteenth century. Take the Roman matron Lucretia who killed herself after being raped by the son of the last Roman king, Sextus Tarquinius. In Augustine's mind, she destroyed herself because she "could not endure the horror of the foul indignity." But the crime was not hers to repent; the guilt attached not to Lucretia, but to her ravisher. Sextus Tarquinius's violation of her body could not in any way imperil her virtuous will. By killing herself she committed her own murder, adding one crime to another. It was for this reason that Augustine chastened the Roman historian Livy for "heap[ing] the highest praises for modesty upon [her]."[30] Augustine was similarly dismissive of the Roman statesman Marcus Portius Cato, who had sided with Pompey against

25 John 15:13. Cited in Minois, *History of Suicide*, 24.

26 Augustine, *The City of God*, trans. Henry Bettenson (London: Penguin Books, 1972), Book I, ch. 20.

27 Eltjo Schrage, "Suicide in Canon Law," *The Journal of Legal History*, 57 (2000): 59.

28 Augustine, *City of God*, Book I, ch. 17.

29 Augustine, *City of God*, Book I, ch. 16.

30 Augustine, *City of God*, Book I. ch. 19.

Julius Caesar during the Roman civil war. After defeat at Pharsalus, Cato killed himself at Utica in 46 BCE rather than submit to Caesar. For Augustine, Cato's act was not one of valor, but cowardice.

Early compilers of canon law followed Augustine in arguing that suicide was a mortal sin because it denied God the power he alone possessed over life and death.[31] Where penance remained an outlet for the person who attempted suicide, completed suicide led to excommunication and burial in unconsecrated ground. This precept laid the groundwork for punishment of the suicide's body in death by exhibiting the cadaver on gallows or exhuming the suicide's body from consecrated ground if it had already been buried there.[32]

These acts of ritual exclusion and bodily debasement that made suicides outlaws unto eternity enjoyed incredible theoretical staying power throughout Europe. Regional customary laws universally expressed religious abhorrence of the act by subjecting a suicide's dead body to ghoulish rituals of desecration. In England, it was customary to bury suicides near highways or crossroads with a stake thrust through their bodies.[33] In parts of Germany and France, the suicide's corpse was put on a hurdle and dragged to a gallows place, where it was hanged and left on display. In the Low Countries, the suicide's body was "hanged 'to feed the ravens.'"[34] In theory at least, Italians also hanged their suicides like criminals. The seventeenth-century Tuscan jurist Marc'Antonio Savelli (1624–1695) noted that the cadavers of suicides "were brought to the gibbet and, once there, although they were already dead, [their bodies were] hanged and quartered."[35]

Like the ritual punishment of criminal bodies, the post-mortem defilement of a suicide's physical remains was not necessarily designed to punish the dead, but to deter the living from emulating criminal behavior. Citing numerous jurists on this point, Savelli remarked that the Italian practice of hanging and quartering the suicide's body served as "an example and a terror to

31 *Corpus Juris Canonici, Inst.* Ill, x, "Nouissime sciendum est pro his, qui quocunque praetextu voluntarie ferro, vel veneno, vel suspendio, vel quolibet modo sibi mortem inferunt, nullam in Oblatione faciendum esse commemorationem, & Ecclesiastica eos debere carere sepultura, non aliter atque Ulos, qui pro suis sceleribus impoenitentes moriuntur."

32 Schrage, "Suicide in Canon Law," 61.

33 MacDonald and Murphy, *Sleepless Souls*, 19–20. Regional practices are cited in nearly every essay in *From Sin to Insanity*, edited by Jeffrey Watt.

34 Machiel Bosman, "The Judicial Treatment of Suicide in Amsterdam," in *From Sin to Insanity*, 11.

35 Marc'Antonio Savelli, *Practica universal* (Parma, 1733), "Omicidiari," 225, "Quando li medesimi cadaveri si possino far condurre alle force, et ivi benché già estinti sospenderli, et anco squartarli."

others."[36] An older English contemporary of Savelli's similarly argued that the English practice was meant to "terrify all passengers, by that so infamous and reproachful burial, not to make their final passage out of this present world."[37] The deterrent effect of these sanctions is impossible to measure, but the moral message remains clear.

Secular and ecclesiastical authorities could be yet more vindictive in cases of suicide by confiscating the suicide's goods and property, potentially visiting impoverishment on the relatives left behind.[38] In England, for example, the moveable goods of suicides, "including tools, household items, money, debts owed to them, and even leases on the land that they had worked were forfeited to the crown or to the holder of a royal patent."[39] The French crown or territorial lords could similarly confiscate the property of subjects who took their own lives.[40]

These laws lived not merely in books. In many parts of Europe, they were exercised on the bodies and estates of men and women. But the manner of their execution was wholly contingent on social and political context. In 1513, for example, when an alleged Jewish sympathizer, Isabel de los Olivos y López, committed suicide by throwing herself into a well, the Spanish ecclesiastical authorities of the Inquisition "pronounced Isabel excommunicate and damned her memory." They ordered that her bones be exhumed and "broken in pieces" before being handed over to the secular authorities. The public executioner then burned Isabel's bony fragments to expunge utterly any trace of her existence from the earth. The inquisitors further "deprived her heirs in the male and female lines of their rights to her property and barred her descendants in perpetuity from holding any ecclesiastical or public office."[41] In Isabel's case, her connection to Judaism seems to have activated the severest execution of the law. Similarly, in 1595, after Elizabeth Wickham, a poor widow from St. Botolph's Aldgate parish in London, "hanged herself upon a garden pale by her apron strings," the coroner's jury determined that she was *felo de se*, a self-murderer. She was then buried "'in the alley where she hanged herself, according to her deserts, having a stake driven through her in remembrance of

36 Savelli, *Practica universal*, 225, "per esempio, e terrore de gli altri."

37 Cited in Paul S. Seaver, "Suicide and the Vicar General in London," in *From Sin to Insanity*, 27.

38 Alexander Murray, *Suicide in the Middle Ages*, vol. 2, *Curse on Self Murder* (Oxford: Oxford University Press, 1998–2000), 63–77.

39 MacDonald and Murphy, *Sleepless Souls*, 15.

40 See Minois, *History of Suicide*, 36 and Jeffrey Merrick, "Suicide in Paris, 1775," in *From Sin to Insanity*, 159.

41 Dickenson and Boyden, "Ambivalence Toward Suicide," in *From Sin to Insanity*, 103.

her wicked [act?]'."[42] Where Isabel's suicide became a cudgel in the hands of ecclesiastical authorities opposed to religious pluralism, Elizabeth Wickham's sentence seems to reveal a community unsympathetic to the plight of an unattached woman known to be "an incontinent person."

Despite heavy-handed laws, Italians tended to show mercy in cases of suicide from the fourteenth through the eighteenth century. Farinacci's treatise, which toed the Augustinian moral line, insists that judges and magistrates enjoyed total discretion when it came to adjudicating cases of suicide. That discretion was shaped as much by social and cultural factors as it was by statutes or normative law. The revival of Roman law beginning in the late eleventh century first in Italy gave judges and magistrates a powerful exculpatory legal fiction that could abrogate the perceived need to humiliate a suicide's cadaver while opening the possibility of Christian burial if they chose to employ it. Religious or cultural abhorrence may have adhered to the act of taking one's life, causing the family and friends of suicides or suicidal people shame, embarrassment, horror, or despair. But the law in practice also opened the possibility of mitigating consequences of the act in the criminal arena. The admittedly meager case law that exists tends to show that Italians worried less about following the letter of the law than about maintaining order and stability in families and communities.

2 The Roman Law Legacy

Roman law was tolerant of voluntary death except in cases where a suspect had been charged with a crime before laying violent hands on him- or herself. The property of criminals who committed suicide to avoid facing future penalties was confiscated to the Roman treasury.[43] By contrast, non-criminals who killed themselves because of bodily suffering, weariness of life, or illness suffered no penalties and their property devolved to their heirs.[44] Roman law framed the acceptable legal justification for suicide in several ways: weariness of life or unendurable pain (*taedio vitae vel impatientia doloris*); or unbearable pain, sickness, or grief (*impatientia doloris aut morbi luctusve*) or, in later

42 Cited in Seaver, "Suicide and the Vicar General in London," in *From Sin to Insanity*, 26.

43 C.9.50.1, "Eorum demum bona fisco vindicantur, qui conscientia delati admissique criminis metuque futurae sententiae manus sibi intulerint."

44 C.9.50.1, "Ea propter fratrem vel patrem tuum si nullo delato crimine, dolore aliquo corporis aut taedio vitae aut furore aut insania aut aliquo casu suspendio vitam finisse constiterit, bona eorum tam ex testamento quam ab intestato ad successores pertinebunt."

Roman law, weariness of life or raving madness or insanity (*taedio vitae aut furore aut insania*).[45]

Medieval and early modern jurists used this language even if they did not readily adopt the ancient Stoic view of suicide, which acknowledged the natural right of men to choose death when sickness made participation in an ethical life unbearable or impossible.[46] Christians could not rationally choose death. As Augustine argued, to choose death was to choose sin, no matter the pain or suffering enduring life entailed. Christian jurists sidestepped the problem by using Roman law to ponder questions of intent. Read from a Christian point of view, Roman law identified conditions under which physical or mental suffering conquered one's ability to understand the consequences of one's actions or made a sufferer vulnerable to demonic temptation. If the suicide's will had been materially compromised by unbearable physical suffering or mental illness, the person could not have been seen to have exercised will or intent and so not knowingly committed a sin or a crime.

Much like in criminal cases of homicide of which suicide was a particular variety, Farinacci pointed out that determining a person's intent was central. At the same time, he admitted the difficulty of establishing a person's state of mind in cases of suicide. Where criminals might exploit statutes to justify their crimes, he maintained, others might try to dress self-harm in more noble raiment to avoid reproof in life or death. A condemned criminal, for example, was not permitted to wound or kill himself under the cover of a statute that allowed condemned criminals to be killed by others with impunity.[47] "Since it is prohibited to kill oneself immediately and directly," Farinacci pithily observed, "it is also prohibited to kill oneself mediately and indirectly."[48] A person, for example, could not disclose false crimes about himself and then admit to them so

45 D.48.19.38.12, "Miles, qui sibi manus intulit nec factum peregit, nisi impatientia doloris aut morbi luctusve alicuius vel alia causa fecerit, capite puniendus est: alias cum ignominia mittendus est." 48.21.3.4, "Si quis autem taedio vitae vel impatientia doloris alicuius vel alio modo vitam finierit, successorem habere divus Antoninus rescripsit," and 48.21.3.6, "Nam omnimodo puniendus est, nisi taedio vitae vel impatientia alicuius doloris coactus est hoc facere." 49.14.45.2, "Eius bona, qui sibi ob aliquod admissum flagitium mortem conscivit et manus intulit, fisco vindicantur: quod si id taedio vitae aut pudore aeris alieni vel valetudinis alicuius impatientia admisit, non inquietabuntur, sed suae successioni relinquuntur." C.9.50.1.

46 Schrage, "Suicide in Canon Law," in *From Sin to Insanity*, 58.

47 Farinacci, *Praxis et theoricae criminalis* (1610), 398, Amplia IX, "In bannito, qui seipsum vulnerans aut occidens, non excusatur virtute statuti volentis bannitum posse impune occidi."

48 Farinacci, *Praxis et theoricae criminalis* (1610), 398, Amplia X, "Quia non solum prohibitum est seipsum occiderere immediate et directe, sed etiam indirecte et immediate."

that he might die.[49] Farinacci's example suggests that he was thinking of heresy cases in which an accused was innocent but, after seeing witnesses speak against him, accepted guilt and death over fear of torture.[50] He thought also of soldiers who might camouflage suicide in acts of diplomacy or courage.[51] But Farinacci called them out: "it is not even permitted to put oneself in the hands of the enemy, and, as is commonly said, at [the enemy's] discretion, to seek peace or for some other reason."[52] Those languishing in prison were similarly prohibited from inviting their own death by starvation though they might be suffering.[53] Even the belief that one was "doing the just thing to achieve salvation" was not allowed. "For something evil must not be done," Farinacci claimed, "for us to advance to eternal life."[54] On this point, he took Augustine's position against suicide even to avoid participating in sinful behavior, as in the case of forced sex. Without mentioning her explicitly, Farinacci condemned the oft-cited Lucretia by claiming that a woman could not kill herself to protect her chastity. "Christian piety," Farinacci stated, "admits no reason for someone licitly to be able to bring death by his own hand on himself."[55]

---

49 Farinacci, *Praxis et theoricae criminalis* (1610), 398, "ut moriatur falsa sibi crimina obiicit et fatetur."

50 Farinacci, *Praxis et theoricae criminalis* (1610), 398, "ubi de confitente crimen falsum metu tormentorum, ac etiam de eo, qui in crimine haeresis videns se a testibus convictum, illud fatetur, licet vere non sit culpabilis, ut ab Ecclesia ad poenitentiam recipiatur, effugiatque Curiae seculari tradit."

51 Farinacci's discussion of "indirect suicide," or what Kathy Stuart has called "suicide by proxy," does not touch on a pattern she has observed in German lands around 1700 in which suicidal women murdered children so that they would be tried and executed by criminal courts. This strategy was intended to avoid the damnation attendant on direct suicide. See, Kathy Stuart, *Suicide by Proxy in Early Modern Germany: Crime, Sin, and Salvation* (Palgrave MacMillan, 2023).

52 Farinacci, *Praxis et theoricae criminalis* (1610), 398, Amplia XI, "Ut nec etiam licitum sit pro habenda pace, vel alia de caussa ponere se in manibus inimici, et, ut vulgo dicitur, ad eius discretionem."

53 Farinacci, *Praxis et theoricae criminalis* (1610), 399, Amplia XII, "Etiam in eo, qui nolens comedere et vivere, seipsum, ut fame pereat, interimit, prout saepe contigit incarceratis, qui aut desperatione, aut ex criminis conscientia se Ipsos sic occidere volunt."

54 Farinacci, *Praxis et theoricae criminalis* (1610), 399, Amplia XIV, "Ut seipsum occidere non liceat, etiam credendo se rem iustam facere, ut aeternam consequatur gloriam. Non enim malum aliquod agendum est, ut ad vitam aeternam eamus."

55 Farinacci, *Praxis et theoricae criminalis* (1610), 399, Amplia XIV, "Ubi quod nec etiam licet sibi mortem inferre ad effugiendum stuprum, vel ad evitandum quodcunque peccatum. … Ubi quod Christiana pietas nullam caussam admittit, qua quis possit licite sibi manus inferre, etiam ex caussa assequendae aeternae gloriae … ne ob timorem peccato consentirent."

Yet, in accord with the jurists who came before him, Farinacci cautioned those in the position to judge against making assumptions about the cause of suspicious death given suicide's grave legal consequences. "It should not be presumed," Farinacci argued, "that a person found suspended from a noose hanged himself." "And moreover," he added, "should anyone be found suffocated in a well, it should not be presumed that he cast himself into that well, but rather that he could have been thrown there by someone else."[56] Windows, rivers, and wells were dangerous places. They were also ambiguous places. They invited accidents and foul play as much as opportunities for self-harm. Trying to recreate what happened at one of these perilous sites required "clearer proofs" and not reliance on "common gossip" to determine what series of events ended in someone's untimely death.[57] Influenced by Roman law, Italian jurists like Farinacci latched onto doubts about intent to complicate the adjudication of alleged suicide. In the main, they left the interpretation of hearsay evidence and statute law in the hands of judges. Often, Italian judges and magistrates erred on the side of mercy.

Laws pertaining to suicide appeared in the early statutes of some Italian cities. As in other parts of Europe, it *could* be punished as a crime with postmortem hanging, denial of Christian burial, and the confiscation of goods and property. Yet, as Farinacci pointed out, judges and magistrates had discretion to hew close to the letter of normative law or to express compassion as they saw fit on an ad hoc basis. Italian case law for suicide is thin on the ground relative to the case law that historians have uncovered for England, inviting future comparative study of the prosecution of suicide in medieval and early modern Italy's civil and criminal courts. The evidence that does exist suggests that judges and magistrates tended to mete out mitigated punishments in cases of both attempted and completed suicide. In 1379, for example, Florence's main criminal court issued a sentence against one Stefano who tried to kill himself, "studiously with both knowledge and intent," by drawing a sharp knife from his own bag and sticking it into his throat. The judge fined him 200 lire but softened the penalty by a quarter because Stefano was said to have repented through confession.[58] In Bologna thirty-six years earlier, a man

56 Farinacci, *Praxis et theoricae criminalis* (1610), 400, Limita 1, "ubi quod laqueo repertus suspensus, non praesumitur, quod se ipsum suspenderit. Et propterea si quis in puteo suffocatus reperiatur non praesumetur, quod ex seipso praecipitem dederit in puteum, sed potius quod ab alio fuerit illuc praecipitatus."

57 Farinacci, *Praxis et theoricae criminalis* (1610).

58 Cited in Umberto Dorini, *Il Diritto Penale e la Delinquenza in Firenze nel secolo XIV* (Lucca: Domenico Corsi, 1916), 135.

named Brandelisio admitted after he had been in a fight with two men that he had tried to kill himself in despair, calling on the devil to take him. His father appealed on his son's behalf, arguing that Brandelisio's self-harm was not a crime because it "'did not cause any damage or shame to anyone else but only to himself.'" In 1459 at Mantua, the judge demanded that the memory of a man who took his own life "be damned and half of his goods confiscated," while "the other half [be] assigned to his heirs," in accord with the city's statutes. The city confiscated half the property of another Mantuan man who drowned himself in a ditch the same year. No further penalties were recorded in any of these cases, suggesting though not proving that defilement of the body did not take place.[59]

By the fourteenth century, Florentines officially gained recourse to the insanity defense via Roman law. Florentine statutes from this period did not hold severely mentally ill men and women liable for criminal offenses, no matter the crime. These statutes allowed petitioners from the fourteenth through the eighteenth centuries to justify or excuse strange, eccentric, and even violent or homicidal behavior in criminal courts without depriving someone of his or her legal rights or privileges. As I have argued elsewhere, the dilemma in cases of criminal insanity was not how to punish the severely mentally ill, but what do to with them.[60] Santa Dorotea, as we shall see, offered another custodial option that held out the possibility of cure. Although the goals of families sometimes clashed with those of the state, for the most part judges and magistrates worked together with petitioners to bring order to households, streets, and communities in ways that served public and private interests. Farinacci's analysis suggests that the same principle held for suicide. If raving madness released a criminal offender from liability for an offense, as Roman law established and medieval Italian law recognized, then it also released a suicide from liability for self-murder. This legal fiction could not remove the social or cultural stain suicide might set into the reputation or memory of a family, but it did protect that family from suffering the indignities of seeing the body of their relative treated like a criminal in death, denied Christian burial and, with it, hope of divine forgiveness or salvation.

These cases show that prior to the seventeenth century, although suicide was typically prosecuted in criminal courts and could end in fines, sentences were often mitigated when it came to property confiscation and denial of burial in consecrated ground, effectively protecting the deceased's family. The tendency

59 The Bolognese and Mantuan examples are cited by Dean, "Getting out of Jail," 457.
60 Dean, "Getting out of Jail," 457.

to restitutive justice in these cases reflects broader trends in Italian civil and criminal law that show the willingness of judges and magistrates to negotiate criminal sentences with family members and communities.[61] Suicide led to the eternal damnation of an individual's soul—no judge or magistrate had any say on that count—but it need not lead to the ruination of a family or the desecration of a corpse. On that score, a judge or magistrate played a critical role in the containment of further social or economic instability.

3 From Sin to Insanity

In the autumn of 1629, a little over a decade before Santa Dorotea's founders began building what would become Florence's first mental hospital, Galileo was putting the final touches on his *Dialogues on the Two Chief World Systems*. As he wrote from his airy hillside perch overlooking Florence, he received a dreadful letter from one of his daughters in residence at a nearby convent. In it, she described the "tempest" of "torments" that shook her community when one of the fellow nuns violently attempted suicide. Sister Maria Celeste, as she was called, begged that her father excuse her last cursory letters. "For truly, I was half beside myself," she explained, "shaken by the terror aroused in me and in all of us by our novice mistress, who, overpowered by those [humors] or [ravings] of hers, tried twice in recent days to kill herself." In the first attempt, the woman bashed her head and face on the ground "with such force that she became monstrously deformed." When that failed, she stabbed herself thirteen times in the throat and abdomen. "I leave you to imagine, Sire," Maria Celeste continued, "the horror that gripped us when we found her body all bloody and battered."[62] The nuns were more astonished still when the severely injured nun drew them to her cell with a noise to ask for her confessor. When he arrived, she confessed, surrendering the small knife she had used to harm herself. Maria Celeste marveled at the strangeness of the situation that made it seem like her sister in religion was at once sane (*savia*) and insane (*pazza*). To imperil one's immortal soul was an act of madness; to try at the last minute to save it through confession showed soundness of mind. As Maria Celeste saw it, that the woman would grievously harm herself yet still have the presence of mind and power of body to beg forgiveness at the last moment smacked

61 See Elizabeth W. Mellyn, *Mad Tuscans and Their Families: A History of Mental Disorder in Early Modern Italy* (Philadelphia: University of Pennsylvania Press, 2014), chapters 1 and 2.

62 Sister Maria Celeste Galilei, *Letters to Father: Suor Maria Celeste to Galileo, 1623–1633*, trans. Dava Sobel (New York: Penguin Books, 2001), 92–93.

of the divine. With no way to explain it, she chalked it up to the "mysterious judgments of the Lord."

The nightmare at Maria Celeste's convent did not end with the nun's near deathbed confession. After the trauma of her suicide attempts came the trauma of trying to keep the woman alive. "In the wake of these events," Maria Celeste told her father, "we have guarded her continually day and night. Now that the rest of us are recovered, by the grace of blessed God, and she is tied in her bed, albeit with the same delirium, we continue to live in fear of some new outburst."[63] The nun's suicide attempts evoked shock and horror among her convent sisters. When her first attempt failed, those around her were enveloped in fear that she would do it again but remained unsure of what to do about it. The visceral violence of the second attempt led the community to tie her up, since constant surveillance seemed inadequate to prevent further escalation. Even bound, she filled her compatriots with dread of what she might do next.

Maria Celeste's letter begins to close the distance that separates authoritative pronouncements on the question of suicide from the ways in which ordinary men and women experienced it in their private lives. Galileo's daughter drew on two important explanatory frameworks for interpreting the suicidal nun's behavior, one naturalistic, the other religious. First, she assumed that the woman was driven to her desperate acts because of a physical illness that affected her capacity for rational thought and behavior. In short, the nun was recognizably mentally ill and had been for some time. Maria Celeste described this disturbed nun in an earlier letter as suffering from "humors" that induced distressing (*travaglioso*) behavior under the best of circumstances.[64] By the seventeenth century, the idea that madness could be caused by a physical illness adversely affecting brain function was commonplace throughout Europe and, in Italy, had been for centuries.[65]

Second, Maria Celeste acknowledged that, however confusing the young nun's behavior was, God was present throughout the terrible ordeal. She even seems to have found some comfort in the possibility that it was God's mercy that drove the nun to confess, thereby potentially saving her soul. In Maria Celeste's interpretation, where madness stripped the nun of her will, God returned it to her at that critical moment when she stood at death's doorway. We see here how the medicalization of mental illness helped soften the religious abhorrence that still clung to the act. And I would argue that we must

63 Galilei, *Letters to Father*, 92–93. I learned of this example from Strocchia, "Women on the Edge," 53–54.

64 Galilei, *Letters to Father*, 85.

65 Mellyn, *Mad Tuscans*, 135.

take seriously the *terrore* she spoke of in her letter that she said possessed her and, as she put it, transported her almost outside of herself (*fuori di me*)—a phrase that was often used of people who had been seized by madness. We must take seriously also the dread she and her convent sisters experienced at what lay in store for the suicidal nun in death if she died flouting God's will.

One way of protecting oneself from the horror of suicide lay in the act of forgetting it. In the space of a few weeks after the nun's suicide attempt, fear and horror dissipated. Maria Celeste turned to speaking in the same letter of other things on her mind. Namely that she was desperate to improve her living arrangements. For several months she had been asking her father for money to purchase a private cell and had entered negotiations with several convent sisters to that end. Now that the "air was slightly more serene," she asked her father to give her money to buy the room that represented, "all I could ever want in the way of comfort and satisfaction." Before ending the letter, she thought back to the "sick nun," who, Maria Celeste reported, was likely "on the verge of death." The point was not to mourn the poor woman, but to encourage her father to give money for the room expeditiously since the abbess would likely use it to cover funerary costs.[66]

4 Suicide and the Hospital

Maria Celeste's account—a mix of the monstrous, the mercenary, and the mundane—helps give voice to the silences that exist between the lines in petitions like the one Migliore sent Santa Dorotea to admit his suicidal son to the hospital in 1761. There's something of the monstrous, the mercenary, and mundane in many of these letters. Although it is not explicitly mentioned in the brief, formulaic letters seeking admission to Santa Dorotea, we can imagine that a similar sense of religious anxiety hung heavily in the air around suicidal people and yet one that might dissipate quickly were they to disappear from daily life. While present, they put people around them on edge. They imbued mundane places that posed ordinary risks with a sense of menace. Windows, doors, wells—everyday architectural structures—took on new significance as dangerous portals to damnation. What power did family and friends have to pull these sick men and women back from such perilous brinks?

In the 1620s, when Maria Celeste wrote those letters to her father, Tuscany had no definitive institutional answer to this question. The primary custodial

66 Galilei, *Letters to Father*, 94–97.

institution for the mentally ill was and always had been the family. Petitions for admission to the hospital show that disturbed men and women sometimes cycled in and out of other pious houses in Florence's charitable landscape, including the hospitals of Santa Maria Nuova, Bonifazio, and San Giovanni di Dio, as well as the home for beggars (the *Mendicanti*), the home for abandoned girls and boys (the *Innocenti*), and the home for poor girls and widows (the *Orbatello*). These troubled men and women had sometimes ended up in prison.[67] In 1642, a Carmelite monk and twelve of Florence's elite convinced the grand ducal regime to build a dedicated space both to cure men and women of the mental illnesses that compelled them to self-harm and to relieve families of the burden of their constant surveillance and care. The founding of Santa Dorotea marked a new chapter in the history of suicide in Tuscany. The hospital institutionalized the link between suicide and mental illness, thereby further decriminalizing and secularizing the act. By admitting men and women who had repeatedly attempted suicide, the hospital gave families a strategy for potentially avoiding the criminal courts altogether. Suicidal men and women were insane, not criminal. They were sick, not sinful.

Petitions seeking care for suicidal men and women reflect the medicalization, decriminalization, and, to a less clear extent, the secularization of suicide. First, petitioners explicitly linked suicide to mental illness, a physical disease that adversely affected one's ability to think and act in appropriate or reasonable ways. Where lay petitioners often used more generic terms denoting mental illness to describe a relative's condition, certifying physicians often applied the more technical language current in medical schools to classify the specific disease driving a person to self-harm. Second, petitioners tended to argue that care at home or in a community setting was not possible because adequate supervision could not be found or paid for. Finally, several cases refer to the "disorder" the suicidality of mentally ill men and women unleashed in households and communities. Santa Dorotea helped resolve this disorder by removing it, even if only temporarily, from households and streets.

A case brought to Santa Dorotea in 1757 illustrates the clear link Tuscans made between mental illness and suicidal behavior. Sometime in May,

67 ASF, SD, *Memorie* 23/14, n.p.; 42, fol. 1r; SD, Regio Diritto (RD) 341, fols. 508r–509r. See Graziella Magherini and Vittorio Biotti, *L'isola delle Stinche et i percorsi della follia a Firenze nei secoli XIV–XVIII* (Florence: Ponte alle Grazie, 1992); Graziella Magherini and Vittorio Biotti, eds., *"Un luogo della città per custodia de' pazzi": Santa Dorotea dei Pazzerelli di Firenze nelle delibere della sua congregazione (1642–1754)* (Florence: Casa Editrice Le Lettere, 1997); and Lisa Rocscioni, *Il governo della follia: Ospedali, medici e pazzi nell'età moderna* (Milan: Bruno Mondadori, 2003).

Pier Anton Bocci wrote in his own hand to the grand duke in the sparest of terms about his unmarried, twenty-six-year-old daughter. Maria Caterina, he claimed, had become so crazy (*pazza*) that she threw herself from a high window. He says nothing about whether she sustained injuries in the fall. We can imagine though that it was this drastic act that brought the seriousness of her illness to the attention of local authorities. Pier Anton reported that he could not find accommodation for her in their hometown of Fauglia, a tiny hamlet rising amidst the Pisan hills in the valley extending along the left bank of the Era River. He asked that Santa Dorotea grant her a space where she could be cared for.

The governor of the district's regional seat at nearby Lari confirmed her condition. He said that when the nature of the young woman's insanity (*pazzia*) had been investigated, it quickly became clear that she was widely considered to be raving mad (*pazza furiosa*). After reporting that Pier Anton had sufficient resources to cover the cost of her stay in hospital, the governor himself argued that the grand duke should indeed instruct Santa Dorotea to accept "the raving maniac" (*maniaca furiosa*).[68] The language used to describe Maria Caterina was generic but revealing. *Pazza* generally denoted insanity while *furiosa* described its severity. *Pazza furiosa* suggested insanity with a high degree of agitation indicating the likelihood of harm to self or others. *Mania* was a well-worn term that indicated a physical illness, causing uncontrollable rage and anger. It had appeared regularly in medical literature in the Middle Ages and had entered Tuscan courts of law by the sixteenth century.[69] Over a quarter of the petitions sent to Santa Dorotea in its last thirty years of operation used the phrase *pazza furiosa* while nearly 60% used the more overtly medical phrase *maniaca furiosa* to describe violent or self-harming men and women who warranted admission.

Fauglia's salaried physician, Domenico Fontanelli, submitted a more detailed report, elaborating further on the medical nature of Maria Caterina's condition and its need for special treatment in hospital. He swore to the authorities that he had visited Maria Caterina "several different times." On these visits "he

68 *ASF*, SD 2, no. 65, "come ritrovandosi l'oratore una sorella [later investigation by the Nove confirmed that Maria Caterina was Pier Anton's daughter, not his sister] per nome Maria Caterina Bocci fanciulla d'anni 26 ed essendo la medesima a sequo tale divenuta pazza che è giunta sua a gettarsi a terra da una ben alta fenestra; e non avendo l'oratore il commodo di poterla far curare in questa città." A summary report from the Lari official revealed: "la Maria Caterina Bocci ... è figlia e non sorella del supplicante e iguardo alla qualità della sua pazzia si rileva ... ella pazza furiosa ... Onde essendo la detta fanciulla maniaca furiosa."

69 Mellyn, *Mad Tuscans*, 148–49.

found her almost always raving without a fever." The lack of fever is significant because it ruled out the presence of other diseases that were known temporarily to induce frenzied or delirious behavior. After seriously considering "the nature and type of her ravings or delirium," he concluded, "with a high level of certainty," that she suffered a type of insanity that "was called by its Latin name *furor eroticus* or *furor vesanus* in medical schools." In simpler terms, Maria Caterina exhibited a pathological form of romantic love characterized by, "melancholic delirium." In this state, sufferers experienced an "obsessive fixation" and the "constant summoning to mind of the beloved object." Upon the realization that one could not obtain that beloved object, "the delirious [sufferer] cries bitterly one moment [only to] regret it deeply the next," and then becomes enraged, descending into "ravings and furies" as had happened in the case of Maria Caterina.[70] Fontanelli clarified that it was in this state that she threw herself from a window, falling over fifteen feet (8 *braccia*) before hitting the ground. Like Maria Caterina's father, Fontanelli says nothing about the injuries she surely sustained in this fall. His purpose was only to identify the specific nature of the mental illness that caused her to attempt suicide, thereby making her an appropriate candidate for admission into Santa Dorotea.

Local secular authorities went to the aid of the young woman's father, Pier Anton. Two of them submitted their testimony along with Fontanelli's, confirming Maria Caterina's insanity and her need for care in hospital. Ambrogio Maria del Corda, one of Fauglia's governors, stated that Maria Caterina "had done some crazy things." "One day," he continued, "she had thrown herself from one of her windows just as it had been explained by Fontanelli in his testimony." The other governor, in turn, confirmed his co-governor's testimony without adding anything further. These statements convinced grand ducal authorities, and she was admitted.

If families and communities found the supervision of suicidal people a challenge, apparently it was not an easy task for the care staff at Santa Dorotea either. On June 5, 1757, Maria Caterina crossed the hospital's entry threshold.

---

70 *ASF*, SD, 2: no. 65, "Io infrascritto medico fisico condotto in comune di Fauglia per a verità ricercato atestato a chiunque qualemente avendo visitator più e diverse volte la Maria Caterina Bocci di detto luogo, l'ho ritrovata quasi sempre vaneggiante senza febbre ed avendo seriamente considerate l'indole e la natura di tal vanegiamento o sia delirio sicuramente concluso … ridurre a quella spezie che nelle scuole mediche chiamasi col nome latino uror eroticus sive furor vasanus, il quale alla preteso di ridurlo al delirio melanconico in cui mediante la fissa oppinione e costante immaginazione della cosa amata sulla reflessione di non poterla ottenere … il delierante ora amaramente piange ora fortemente dolersi ed ora incollerita … in vesanie e furori come il tutto e accaduto nella sopradetta Maria Caterina Bocci."

A month later, the patient register announced her departure by a very different route. On July 10, it was reported, "she plummeted into the Arno from the first-floor terrace from which fall she died." It was not her family but the Company of the Misericordia, a voluntary lay religious group responsible for organizing the transport and burial of the sick and dead, that collected her body and had her buried.[71] There is no mention of whether she was interred in sacred ground.

The language used in Maria Caterina's case is representative of the language used in all patient admission letters whether they involved suicide or not. The key point here is that families, neighbors, civil and ecclesiastical authorities, and, of course, hospital administrators and salaried physicians associated suicide with insanity, understood insanity in medical terms, and thought the proper course of action was medical treatment in a hospital not criminal prosecution in court.

Other cases explicitly state rather than imply that care was beyond a family or community's capacity. In May of 1761, for example, the Auditore Fiscale received a letter from the Orbatello, Florence's house for girls and widows, that bore an eerie resemblance to the situation Maria Celeste had described to her father Galileo a century before. But with Santa Dorotea on the scene, the outcome was different. In May on that year, Senator Filippo Maria Guadagni, the director of the confraternity that oversaw the Orbatello, informed the grand duke that a thirteen-year-old resident named Maria Teresa Cassigoli from Pontassieve had "for several months lost her senses." The term Guadagni used to describe the young girl's condition was that she had "left herself" (*uscita fuori di sè*), language like that Maria Celeste used to describe her shock at seeing her convent sister bloodied by her own hand. Maria Teresa, he continued, was showing "several clear signs of raving madness (*pazza furiosa*), striking and trying to harm anyone who came near her." Her violence induced her co-residents "to deprive her of knives." No one at the Orbatello, Guadagni insisted, was able to watch her, look after her needs, or manage her behavior.[72]

Antonio Lulli, the physician who certified the case that opened the chapter, was quickly dispatched across town to examine the young girl. During his

71 *ASF*, SD, 35, 50, "@ di 19 Luglio a ore 10 = d.m.n. la di contro Maria Caterina Bocci si precipito in Arno dalla terrazza di mezzo, della qual' caduta se ne morì, e fù presa dalla Compagnia della Misericordia per seppellirla."

72 *ASF*, SD 4, 23, "Essendo da qualche mese uscita fuori di sè la fanciulla Maria Teresa Cassigoli dal Pontassieve, e commorante da tredici anni in qua in una delle stanze del Conservatorio d'Orbatello in Firenze, presentemente da I più chiari segni di pazzia fuoriosa, percuotendo, e tentando di ferire chiunque le va d'intorno; onde è stata private di cultelli … e non avendo nesuno de' suoi da poter esser guardata, curate, e mantenua, essendo essa fin qui vissuta con filare il cotone alla Congregazione de' Poveri."

interview, he found that Maria Teresa “was *demente* and in such conditions of frenzy (*frenesia*),” that she warranted immediate admission to Santa Dorotea where she could be supervised and cured of her illness. Lulli also learned on his visit that in addition to being a threat to her neighbors, she was a threat to herself. “She gave signs,” he noted, “of wanting to take her own life by bashing her head against walls.”[73] The institution was simply not equipped to watch over a young girl bent on the destruction of self and others. Members of the community might be able to prevent her from obtaining dangerous objects she could turn against herself, but they could not prevent her from using the building itself as a weapon of opportunity.

The hospital director wrote to the chancellor of Pontassieve, her town of origin, to see whether she had relatives who could pay her maintenance fees. When none could be found, Santa Dorotea admitted Maria Teresa with a community subsidy so that “she would be cured there of her disease.”[74] She died four months later. Whether the injuries she sustained during her violent episodes caused her death in hospital, the record does not say.[75]

Where Maria Teresa’s case implies the practical challenges families and communities faced in trying to thwart a suicidal person’s tendency to self-harm, other admission documents use the terms “disordine” or “inconveniente” to capture these struggles. In 1758, for example, a Bolognese cleric asked the Tuscan grand duke to grant his cleric brother Domenico Fabbri admission to Santa Dorotea. Domenico, he claimed, had suffered “hypochondriac mania” for quite some time. One of the manifestations of this long-recognized gastro-intestinal ailment was severe mental disturbance.[76] Domenico’s condition had grown serious enough that he had tried “to take his own life.” The family’s problem was not a lack of money; they could draw on vast resources to pay the bill. His brother Clemente, in fact, agreed to pay the institution’s highest recorded maintenance fees at seventy lire (10 scudi) a month. The family’s reason for confinement was rather the challenge of caring for a person who caused “disorder.” Five physicians—a professor of medicine at the University of Bologna, a Bolognese medical doctor, and three of Santa Dorotea’s salaried

73 *ASF*, SD 4, 23, “ci asserisce d’averla trovata demente ed in tali condizioni di frenesia, che la costituiscono in grado di esser prontamente rinchiusa nello spedale di Santa Dorotea, poichè oltre all’esser inquieta a tutto il vicinato, nell’atto ancora di visitarla diede segni di volersi toglier la vita con battere il capo nella muraglia.”

74 *ASF*, SD 4, 23, “sia ricevuta nello spedale di Santa Dorotea la Fanciulla Maria Teresa Cassigoli pazza furosa per esservi curate della sua malattia.”

75 *ASF*, SD, 35, 94.

76 Paolo Zacchia, *De’ Mali Hipochondriaci* (Roma, 1639), Lib. I, cap. IV “Delle differentie e specie di questi mali,” 20–23.

physicians—certified Domenico's "melancholic delirium," applying a different diagnostic category while still confirming the medical appropriateness of the admission.[77] Hospital administrators explicitly stated too that Santa Dorotea "was built for the relief of the subjects of the most honorable duke"—a frank reminder that the hospital was cognizant of the challenges families faced caring for severely mentally ill men and women at home even when money was no object. The problem in Domenico's case was that he was not a Tuscan subject, a point hospital governors discussed at some length before finally admitting him.[78] Domenico's guardian who wrote the petition on Clemente's behalf used a telling phrase to describe what Clemente was after, namely, "to remedy whatever disorder [arose from] getting him supervision." The desire to remedy "disorder" or a "problem" (*inconveniente*) appears in other petitions to express the broader challenges posed by caring for a severely disturbed and suicidal relative.[79] The wealthy Fabbri would have had no trouble paying someone to supervise their suicidal brother. It would seem then that these generic terms contained the social, cultural, and religious ambivalence that adhered to the act for most people through the eighteenth century regardless of wealth or status. In the case of Domenico, Santa Dorotea would resolve that "disorder" for a mere month before he was released into the care of his guardian.

Few people were as well-resourced as the affluent Fabbri of Bologna. By the eighteenth century, it was more common to hear petitioners claiming they could not pay maintenance fees in or out of the hospital and so needed charitable aid. This was true in the case of Maria Rosa Cianchi, a "poor and

77 *ASF*, SD, 3, 28, "Affermiamo noi infrascritti, che il Signore Dottore Domenico Fabbri sacerdote, e Cittadino Bolognese è da più mesi soggetto a continuo deliro melanconico. In fede ci sottoscritti di proprio pugno. Pietro-Paolo Molinelli, pubblico Professor dei Medicina nell'università di Bologna, Joseph Verati, Philosophus et Medicus et Doctor." The following page: "Noi infrascriti medici attestiamo d'aver visitator Domenico Fabbri di Bologna, e d'averlo trovato in stato di dovere esser ammesso e curato nello spedale di Santa Dorotea atteso un delirio melanconico che soffre da qualche tempo e che alcune volte l'ha trasportato in eccessidi privarsi di vita in fede di che, Giovanni Targioni-Tozzetti, Medico fisico, mano propria, Lodovico Scutellari, medico fisico fiscale, Antonio Lullu, medico fisico."

78 *ASF*, SD, 3, 28, "detto spedale sia stato fabbricato per sollievo dei suddito della Cesarea Maestà Vostra."

79 *ASF*, SD, 3, 28, "Clemente Fabri della città di Bologna ... rappresenta come ritrovandosi un fratello sacerdote per nome Domenico, Lettor Pubblico di questo studio, che ha dato in una mania ipocondria fino al segno di togliersi la vita, e desiderando il medesimo di riparare a qualunque disordine con farlo custodire." See also, *ASF*, SD 3, 34, another iteration of the Fabbri case. See also, *ASF*, SD 9, 117. In a petition of 1773, several brothers used the phrase "to remedy each inconvenience" (*per remediare ag ogni inconveniente*) as justification for the admission of their suicidal sister Teresa Taddei who had descended into *pazzia maniaca*.

wretched agricultural laborer," from the outskirts of Fiesole who worked on the lands of Florence's foundling hospital, the *Innocenti*.[80] In July of 1770, her parish priest, who served the double role of scribe and witness, wrote a petition on her behalf explaining how, for several months, her sixty-four-year-old husband Anton Maria Cianchi had suffered from the illness of *demenza* and "was rather *furioso*." He reported that Anton Maria had "tried several times to throw himself in the Arno river and also wished to kill [his wife]."[81] Because of her poverty, Maria Rosa argued through her priest that "she could not provide her husband with supervision nor could she keep him confined."[82] The hospital's physician, Antonio Lulli, certified Anton Maria's "stato furioso," which caused suicidal "frenzies," and a financial investigation confirmed that Maria Rosa could not pay her husband's maintenance fees. The hospital approved the petition, but, because Maria Rosa did not live in Florence, her community would have to agree to cover those costs, a process that dragged on for the greater part of the year.

Eight months after Maria Rosa sent her first petition, a local official wrote to the grand duke in Florence, describing more recent developments. While the community was deciding Maria Rosa's request, her husband "gave signs of improvement in such a way that, hoping for his total recovery, it was no longer considered necessary to request money for him to be admitted and treated in Santa Dorotea."[83] These improvements were not to last; his condition deteriorated again. Anton Maria "had returned to trying to take his own life by throwing himself into a well, from which, by good fortune, he was dragged unharmed."[84] The local official now "believed it expedient" that Anton Maria be provisionally admitted to the hospital in advance of receiving the maintenance fees committed by his community with the understanding that the community would eventually pay. Invoking the freighted idea of "disorder," the local official remarked that the purpose of admitting Anton Maria as soon as

80 *ASF*, SD, 2, n. 43, "Maria Rosa Cianchi dei subborghi di Fiesole … povera e miserabile lavoratora di terre dello spedale degl' Innocenti."

81 *ASF*, SD, 2, n. 43. "si ritrova Anton Maria Cianchi suo marito di anni sessanta quattro colla malatti della demenza ed assai furioso avendo il medesimo tentato per più volte di gettarsi in Arno e di volersi ancor dar la morte."

82 *ASF*, SD, 2, n. 43, "non potendo l'oratrice attesa la sua miserabilità tenerlo guardato nè respettivamente mantenerlo riserrato."

83 *ASF*, SD, 8, 85, "In questo tempo di mezzo il prefate Anton Maria Cianchi diede segni di miglioramento, in guise che sperandosene la total guarigione, non fù altrimenti creduto venisse ricevuto et curato nello spedale suddetto."

84 *ASF*, SD, 8, 85, "esser detto Dianchi ricaduto di privarsi di vita con essersi gettato in un pozzo, da cui per buona sorte è stato tratto illeso."

possible was "to remedy those greater disorders that could occur."[85] Again, the term "disorder" connoted the burden Maria Rosa's household and community faced in caring for Anton Maria, the financial and psychological devastation that care could bring, the possibility of his death at his own hand, and all the cultural ambivalence attached to the act of suicide itself.

There is no systematic study of case law that would allow the kind of granular analysis of suicide that historians have done for other parts of Europe, especially England. Nevertheless, Tuscan evidence suggests that by the eighteenth century, hearsay evidence indicating mental illness in pretrial proceedings could preclude criminal prosecution altogether. By that time the Auditore Fiscale (minister of criminal justice), had developed a form of extrajudicial inquiry in some cases to ascertain whether they warranted a full criminal trial.[86] Cases of completed suicide tended not to progress to trial when hearsay evidence strongly indicated that severe mental illness had compromised a person's intent. In early December of 1754, the minister of Florence's Jesuit college of San Giovannino informed the Auditore of a tragedy only a few hours after it had taken place. On December 6, one of the brothers, "weighed down by a *furore* of madness," threw himself from one of the College's terraces to his death.[87] The Auditore interviewed members of the community to assess what to do next. He learned from the minister that this brother, Antinucci, had suffered under a "similar furor" when he was serving previously at a Jesuit college in Prato, but "had returned to health" shortly thereafter.[88] He was sent to Rome where he fared well and remained until he came to Florence as a companion to Padre Niccolai, a senior cleric. Antinucci gave no further "sign of a disturbance of mind" until a few days prior to the incident when he "had shown melancholy." While "doing his service" in the cell of father Niccolai that morning, "he suddenly threw himself to his knees, asking [Father Niccolai] forgiveness for his shortcomings." This episode "confirmed the suspicion of some

85 *ASF*, SD, 8, 85, "one per riparare a quei maggiori disordini che potrebbero succedere."

86 See Mariana Labarca, *Itineraries and Languages of Madness in the Early Modern World: Family Experience, Legal Practice, and Medical Knowledge in Eighteenth-Century Tuscany* (New York: Routledge, 2021), 139.

87 Cited in Labarca, *Itineraries*. I am grateful to Mariana for sharing her transcription of this case with me.

88 Cited in Labarca, *Itineraries*. *ASF*, Consiglio di Reggenza, Fiscale F, 758, no. 61, "Mi raccontò detto Padre Ministro, che servendo questo religioso Antinucci gli anni adietro nel Collegio di Prato, fu sorpreso da altro simile furore, ma che inappresso risanò, e che fu mandato a Roma, dove stiede bene, e si trattenne fin che il Padre Niccolai lo ricondusse seco in questa capitale per suo compagno."

new disturbance."[89] In response, the college leadership immediately wrote to their rector in hopes of making some arrangement for Antinucci's supervision. But Antinucci's sickness would progress quickly.

One of the servants of the College church would go before the tribunal together with his nephew to relate Antinucci's last tortured moments before falling to his death. It was a dramatic account, but especially important for the Auditore in determining Antinucci's intent. Around the hour of afternoon prayer, the servant claimed that he saw Antinucci standing precariously on a terrace cornice with his feet projecting outward. The servant's nephew interrupted the testimony at this point claiming that "in that act he was yelling, saying that Father Niccolai and Father Himenes were the cause of his [Antinucci's] illness."[90] After this outburst, the servant continued. He was so terrified at the sight of Antinucci tottering on the terrace's edge at that height that he ran to the stairs. He got onto all fours and crawled out onto the terrace to see if he could restrain Antinucci. As he inched closer, Antinucci grabbed a stone and threatened him with it. The servant pretended to retreat, but then hid. Satisfied that the servant had left, Antinucci put the stone down, giving the servant the opportunity to sneak up behind him and grab him. But it was too late. The servant claimed that just as he got closer, Antinucci, "extending his hands as if in the act of prayer [and] naming Father Niccolai and Father Himenes, rushed to the edge of the cornice and, standing upright, went over."[91] He died

89 Cited in Labarca, *Itineraries*. ASF, Consiglio di Reggenza, Fiscale F, 758, no. 61, "Che non aveva dato altro segno di sconcerto di mente; ma che pochi giorni prima del seguito accidente aveva dimostrata della malinconia, e che in quella stessa mattina, facendo il suo servizio nella stanza del padre Niccolai, a un tratto se gli era gettato a piedi, chiedendoli perdono de suoi mancamenti, e che questa cosa aveva confermato il sospetto di qualche sua nuova turbazione."

90 Cited in Labarca, *Itineraries*. ASF, Consiglio di Reggenza, Fiscale F, 758, no. 61, "Avendo ricavato dalle di lui risposte, che un certo Gaetano Martini, che fa il servo della Chiesa di San Giovannino, aveva veduto tutto il seguito, e che secolui l'aveva ancora veduto Vincenzo Martini suo nipote, stimai di dover fare rilevare il loro deposto al Tribunale, da cui in sostanza si ricava, che al secondo tocco di Vespro, che potevano essere circa le ore trè dopo il mezzo giorno, fu osservato dai predetti Martini il Converso Antinucci suo Cornicione più alto corrispondente nel cortiel con i piedi più fuori che dentro di detto cornicione, con manifesto pericolo di precipitarsi, aggiungendo il Martini nipote, che in tal'atto gridava dicendo che il Padre Niccolai e il Padre Himenes erano la causa del suo male."

91 Cited in Labarca, *Itineraries*. ASF, Consiglio di Reggenza, Fiscale F, 758, no. 61, "Che sopreso, e spaventato da tale spettacolo il servo, corse su per le scale, e andiede carponi nel terrazzo, per vedere d'impedirlo e trattenerlo, e che arrivato vicino a detto Antinucci, il medesimo diede di piglio a un mezzo mattone, di cui si era provvisto, minacciando di scagliarglielo contro, se si accostava. Che finse allora il servo di partirsi, ma che si nascose dietro a un vaso, e che l'Antinucci credendolo partito, riposò il sasso dietro al vaso, che

from the fall. The servant's telling coupled with his nephew's impassioned outburst suggest conflict in the relationship between Antinucci and his superiors. But it was not the Collegio's inner workings that interested the Auditore. He focused rather on the state of Antinucci's mind when he cast himself nearly thirty feet to his death. On that point, he concluded from the testimonies he heard that Antinucci, "overcome by an attack of *frenesia* ... exposed himself to the danger in which he perished."[92] In other words, gripped by madness that deprived him of his will, Antinucci could not be held responsible for his self-murder. Without the presence of clear intent, the Auditore did not think the case should proceed to trial; it ended there.

Cultural, political, and social histories of suicide in medieval and early modern Europe tend not to reveal how voluntary death affected individual families and communities. Letters exchanged between families, hospital administrators and doctors at Santa Dorotea give us rare glimpses of the practical struggles people faced in finding time and money to care for suicidal people. They show that whatever social or cultural concerns may have fueled anxieties about suicide, the immediate concerns of families and communities tended to be pragmatic. How to prevent someone from jumping from a window, into a well or river to their death, how to stop someone from stabbing or hanging himself or hitting her head against a wall, these were problems of surveillance and the resources available to provide it before anyone considered the repercussions of a person's suicide. Even families with abundant resources had to contend with the kind of social disorder a suicidal mentally ill relative brought to a family, neighborhood, or a small town. Italian judges and magistrates understood these struggles. From the fourteenth century, they used the discretion granted them in law to mitigate the criminal punishments a relative's suicide could inflict on a family's social and material well-being.

The foundation of Santa Dorotea in the mid-seventeenth century shifted the temporal focus of suicide from its legal aftermath and the focus on a suicide's corpse in death to treatment and prevention of a mentally ill suicidal man or women in life. As early as the twelfth century, the revival of Roman law had helped Italians connect suicide to insanity rather than to sin. This

riuscì al Martini di guadagnarglielo senza che se ne accorgesse. Allora procurò il servo di accostarsi, ma in quell'istante gestendo colle mani, come atto di predicare, nominando il Padre Niccolai, e il Padre Himenes, si precipitò rasente al cornicione, e cadde ritto."

92 Cited in Labarca, *Itineraries*, Consiglio di Reggenza, Fiscale F, 758, no. 61, "A me non sembra che sia luogo a far di vantaggio in questo disgraziato accidente, vedendosi manifestamente che sorpreso da un'assalto di frenesia il povero religioso si espose al pericolo, in cui perì."

gave them a legal way of mitigating or circumventing draconian laws against suicide, which cultural abhorrence of the act had shaped. The roughly contemporaneous revival of Greek medicine in Italy helped link insanity more specifically to bodily illness. By the 1620s, when Galileo's daughter was writing to him in Florence, the link between suicide and mental illness was commonplace in secular and religious settings. By institutionalizing the connection between suicide and mental illness, the foundation of Santa Dorotea in the mid-seventeenth century helped shift Tuscany's reaction to suicide more firmly from the legal to the medical realm.

Bibliography

Archival Sources in the Archivio di Stato of Florence (ASF)
Ospedale di Santa Dorotea (SD)
Auditore dei benefici ecclesiastici poi segreteria del regio diritto (RD)
Consiglio di Reggenza (CR)

Printed Primary Sources

Aquinas, Thomas. *Summa Theologiae*. Milan: Edizioni San Paolo, 1988.

Augustine. *The City of God*. Translated by Henry Bettenson. London: Penguin Books, 1972.

Sister Maria Celeste Galilei. *Letters to Father: Suor Maria Celeste to Galileo, 1623–1633*. Translated by Dava Sobel. New York: Penguin Books, 2001.

Farinacci, Prospero. *Praxis et theoricae criminalis*. Palthenius: Frankfurt, 1604 and 1610.

Savelli, Marc'Antonio. *Practica universale*. Parma: Paolo Monti, 1733.

Zacchia, Paolo. *De' Mali Hipochondriaci*. Rome, 1639.

Secondary Sources

Bosman, Machiel. "The Judicial Treatment of Suicide in Amsterdam." In *From Sin to Insanity: Suicide in Early Modern Europe*, edited by Jeffrey Watt, 9–24. Ithaca: Cornell University Press, 2004.

Christopoulos, John. *Abortion in Early Modern Europe*. Cambridge, MA: Harvard University Press, 2021.

Dean, Trevor. "Getting out of Jail: Suicide, Escape, and Release in Late Medieval and Renaissance Bologna." *Historical Research*, 90:249 (August, 2017): 449–64.

Dickenson, Elizabeth G. and James M. Boyden. "Ambivalence Toward Suicide in Golden Age Spain." In *From Sin to Insanity: Suicide in Early Modern Europe*, edited by Jeffrey Watt, 100–15. Ithaca: Cornell University Press, 2004.

Dorini, Umberto. *Il Diritto Penale e la Delinquenza in Firenze nel secolo XIV.* Lucca: Domenico Corsi, 1916.

Koslofsky, Craig. "Controlling the Body of the Suicide in Saxony." In *From Sin to Insanity: Suicide in Early Modern Europe*, edited by Jeffrey Watt, 48–63. Ithaca: Cornell University Press, 2004.

Labarca, Mariana. *Itineraries and Languages of Madness in the Early Modern World: Family Experience, Legal Practice, and Medical Knowledge in Eighteenth-Century Tuscany*. New York: Routledge, 2021.

MacDonald, Michael and Terrence R. Murphy. *Sleepless Souls: Suicide in Early Modern England.* Oxford: Clarendon Press, 1990.

Magherini, Graziella and Vittorio Biotti. *L'isola delle Stinche et i percorsi della follia a Firenze nei secoli XIV–XVIII*. Florence: Ponte alle Grazie, 1992.

Magherini, Graziella and Vittorio Biotti, eds. *"Un luogo della città per custodia de' pazzi": Santa Dorotea dei Pazzerelli di Firenze nelle delibere della sua congregazione (1642–1754)*. Florence: Casa Editrice Le Lettere, 1997.

Mellyn, Elizabeth W. *Mad Tuscans and Their Families: A History of Mental Disorder in Early Modern Italy*. Philadelphia: University of Pennsylvania Press, 2014.

Meittinen, Riikka. *Suicide, Law, and Community in Early Modern Sweden.* London: Palgrave MacMillan, 2019.

Merrick, Jeffrey. "Suicide in Paris, 1775." In *From Sin to Insanity*, edited by Jeffrey Watt, 158–74. Ithaca: Cornell University Press, 2004.

Minois, Georges. *History of Suicide: Voluntary Death in Western Culture*. Translated by Lydia Cochrane. Baltimore: Johns Hopkins University Press, 1998.

Murray, Alexander. *Curse on Self Murder.* Volume 2 of *Suicide in the Middle Ages*. Oxford: Oxford University Press, 1998–2000.

Pennington, Kenneth. "Torture and Fear: Enemies of Justice." *Rivista internazionale di diritto commune*. 19 (2008): 1–39.

Roscioni, Lisa. *Il governo della follia: Ospedali, medici e pazzi nell'età moderna.* Milan: Bruno Mondadori, 2003.

Schrage, Eltjo. "Suicide in Canon Law." *The Journal of Legal History*. 57 (2000): 57–62.

Seaver, Paul S. "Suicide and the Vicar General in London." In *From Sin to Insanity*, edited by Jeffrey Watt, 25–47. Ithaca: Cornell University Press, 2004.

Strocchia, Sharon. "Women on the Edge: Madness, Possession, and Suicide in Early Modern Convents." *Journal of Medieval and Early Modern Studies* 45:1 (January, 2015): 53–77.

Stuart, Kathy. *Suicide by Proxy in Early Modern Germany: Crime, Sin, and Salvation.* Palgrave MacMillan, 2023.

Watt, Jeffrey. *From Sin to Insanity: Suicide in Early Modern Europe.* Ithaca: Cornell University Press, 2004.

CHAPTER 16

The "Desire of Deeds": On Cherishing Medieval English Charters

Carol Symes

One August day in 1477, a Devonshire gentleman named Robert Spurway was asked to sit for a written deposition about an incident that had clearly remained strong in his memory for eighteen years (Figure 16.1a).[1] Spurway testified that, in the autumn of 1459, he had intervened in a dispute between his neighbor, Thomas Worth of Washfield, and a certain Squire John Wenard from the neighboring county of Cornwall. This altercation had occurred at the quarter session held in Exeter after Michaelmas, and it was still notorious in public memory a generation later.[2] The story behind it, and the trove of medieval charters that witness and preserve this story, among many others, are material memorials to the lived experience of the Common Law in later medieval and early modern England. Now housed in the Harvard Law School Library, they remain of enduring value to those studying the learned law as well as its everyday applications.

1 HSC Deeds 117 (dated 17 Edward IV) [18 August 1477], https://nrs.lib.harvard.edu/urn-3:hls.libr:10159819.

2 The feast of St. Michael (Michaelmas) falls on September 29. This deposition was taken down at Spurway's manor "Gormondishaies" in Tiverton, a name that I have not been able to locate in any of the standard topographical surveys of Devon. However, the Worth estate at Washfield would have been less than six miles away from Spurway's home. In this document, and in HSC Deeds 116 (see below), the name "Wenard" is given as "Wynard," whereas the spelling "Wenard" is given in a grant of 1453 (HSC Deeds 165) made in the name of this same individual. I have decided on the latter spelling here, but note that both spellings seem to have been in local use and do not necessarily designate different families. On the one hand, a certain "Wenard, of Cornwall" is mentioned as the father-in-law of Sir John de Stonore (d. 1361) of Stonor manor in Oxfordshire in John Burke, *A Genealogical and Heraldic History of the Landed Gentry; Or, Commoners of Great Britain and Ireland, etc.* (London: Henry Colburn, 1837–1838), 441. On the other hand, a William Wynard is named as a public official in Exeter during the reigns of Henry V and VI, the founder of an almshouse in his name, and the owner of extensive lands in Devon. See George Alexander Cooke, *Topographical Survey of the County of Devon, Historical, Statistical, and Descriptive, etc.* (London: Printed for C. Cook by Brimmer and Co., 1817), 88.

 DOI:10.1163/9789004710696_018

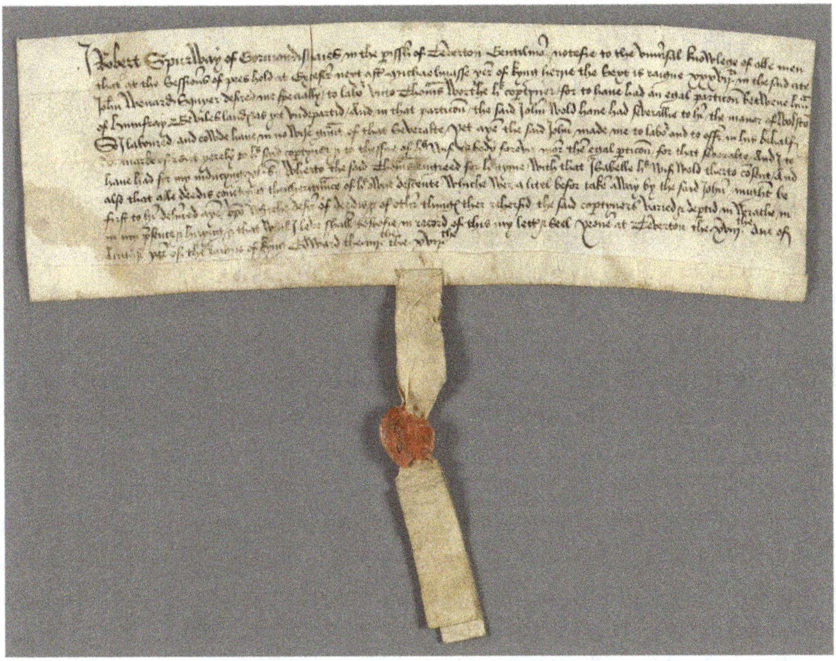

FIGURE 16.1A Deposition by Robert Spurway of Tiverton (Devon), testifying to the "desire of deeds," HSC Deeds 117.

According to a rare paper draft, drawn up in Latin and preserved in the same archive as the deposition, the trouble began when Wenard and Worth had met at Worth's home about six weeks before the Michaelmas quarter, on August 11, to make an agreement regarding the division of certain lands.[3] Spurway's deposition describes the men as "copartyners," and the draft reveals that they were joint claimants to a network of properties that had been amassed in Cornwall by Humphrey Beville, the father of Isabella Worth, Thomas Worth's wife. (Wenard's connection with the Beville family is unclear.) One of the properties in question was the substantial manor of Woolston, named as "Wolveston" in the draft, which records that, in return for Worth's grant of a clear title to it, Wenard would give Worth three other named manors in Cornwall and a dozen specified holdings in that vicinity. A similar paper draft would have presumably been made at the same time in Wenard's name, making a corroborating

3 HSC Deeds 116, dated at "Worth" (i.e. Washfield, Devon), 37 Henry VI [11 August 1453], https://nrs.lib.harvard.edu/urn-3:hls.libr:101159798.

grant to Worth and his wife. This draft does not survive, and was presumably destroyed when the deal fell through.

This was the falling-out that Spurway witnessed in Exeter that September. Normally, Worth and Wenard would have attended the court to have their respective drafts transferred to parchment, publicly notarized, and properly sealed. Yet something had clearly occurred, in the intervening weeks, to scupper the arrangement—something so egregious that, as Spurway reported, Wenard "desired me specially to labor unto Thomas Worthe his copartyner for to have had an equal particion between them." And when "yet agen the said John made me to labor and to offer in his behalf," Wenard felt obliged to offer Worth an additional yearly rent of five marks, payable to himself and his wife's heirs forever, if he would agree to the new arrangement.[4] According to Spurway, Worth had retorted that he would only agree if "all deedis containing the heritance of his owne descent whyche were a litel befor taken away by the said John might be first to him be delivered agen." As Spurway recalled, that was the end of the negotiation: for "upon which desir of deedis & of other thinges ther rehersid" the men "varied & departed in wrathe in my presence & hiryng & that whil I leve shall testefie."

The "desire of deeds": Spurway's testimony reveals that, at some point—probably when Wenard had been a visitor at Washfield in August—he had made off with Worth's extensive family archive, or at least a portion of it. Recall that their projected transaction had involved at least four manors and multiple adjacent properties in Cornwall, each of which would have generated its own archive, all which may have been on hand during the negotiation of the paper drafts. As Tom Johnson has shown, these litigants were working in "a world awash with humdrum legal writings" that included "great hordes of private legal instruments," most of which do not survive.[5] Maybe Wenard thought that he was justified in rummaging through his host's muniments and removing deeds that pertained to the manor he had been granted on paper; and perhaps he could not read well enough to tell the difference between those deeds and the other parchments stored there. Or perhaps he intended to hold some or all of Worth's deeds hostage, as a guarantee of his acquiescence to the final deal. Either way, Wenard had obviously gone too far, as evinced by Spurway's vivid memory of the scene and its evident public notoriety.

4 In medieval England, the mark was not a coin but a unit of account, worth 13*s* 4*d* (two-thirds of a pound sterling).

5 Tom Johnson, *Law in Common: Legal Cultures in Late-Medieval England* (Oxford: Oxford University Press, 2020), 241.

Worth's injury was one that would be felt by anyone with a family cache of documents that could all too easily succumb to fire, loss, or theft—and by 1459, that was any family in England with claims to any property at all. Just a few years later, immediately after her husband's death in 1466, the Norfolk matriarch Margaret Paston would warn her eldest son John to guard against just such a calamity as had befallen Worth: "& in alwyse I avyse you for to be ware that ye kepe wysly youre wrytyngys that ben of charge, that it come not in here handys that may hurt you heraftere." Recalling the multiple imprisonments her husband had endured, and the family's ongoing litigations, she reminded him that "Youre fadere ... In hys trobyll seson set more by hys wrytyngys & evydens that he dede by any of his moveabell godys. Remembere that yf tho were had from you ye kowd neuer gyte no moo."[6] Although unable to write letters on her own behalf, Margaret well understood that legal "writings and evidence" counted alongside "moveable goods" as very valuable material possessions.[7]

Especially for families whose fortunes had recently risen, like the Worths and the Pastons, deeds were not merely essential legal instruments; they were carefully curated heirlooms treasured for their own sake as part of the family patrimony. According to Spurway's testimony, Thomas Worth called them "deeds containing the heritage of his own descent": *containers* of a heritage that could be traced back two hundred years. They were vessels conveying the remains of his distant Worth ancestors and of the much more powerful Abbe/Abbot-Beauchamp family, whose lands had since come down to him via his own father's strategic marriage. They also bound him to another local family, the Hawkyns or Hawkes, whose progenitor Robert de Hobekyn had been a serf. The very fact that the documents making up Worth's archive in 1459 had been so carefully kept for at least seven generations by three different families of such varying socio-economic status—lords of the manor, local gentry, and small farmers descended from an unfree laborer—indicates that the "desire of deeds" was yet another thing that families passed down. On

6 Norman Davis et al., eds., *Paston Letters and Papers of the Fifteenth Century*, 3 vols. (Oxford and New York: Oxford University Press, 2004), 1:333–334 (No. 198).

7 See Rebecca Krug, *Reading Families: Women's Literate Practice in Late Medieval England* (Ithaca: Cornell University Press, 2002), 17–64; Johnson, *Law in Common*, 254–61. On the meanings attached to writing and its material manifestations in late-medieval England, see, e.g., Susan Crane, "The Writing Lesson of 1381," in *Chaucer's England: Literature in Historical Context*, ed. Barbara A. Hanawalt (Minneapolis: University of Minnesota Press, 1992), 201–21; and Steven Justice, *Writing and Rebellion: England in 1381* (Berkeley: University of California Press, 1994).

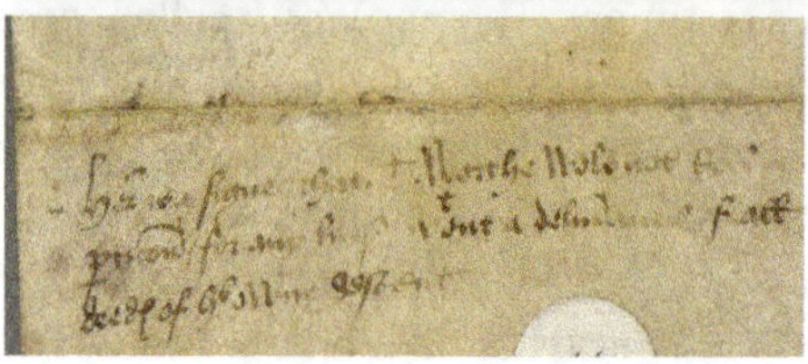

FIGURES 16.1B AND 16.1C Dorsal inscription (and detail) by Thomas Worth the younger: "Herein so sign[ifi]e that T Worthe wold not [seal to] a partition for any thing without a deliverance of all deeds of his owne descent."

the dorse of the document that recorded Robert Spurway's testimony to his father's quarrel with Wenard, Thomas Worth the younger (Thomas Worth II) has written: "Herein so sign[ifi]e that T Worthe wold not [seal to] a partition for any thing without a deliverance of all deeds of his owne descent" (Figures 16.1b and 16.1c [detail]).[8]

Among other precious items, the archive of the Worth family's "descent" contained the fragment of parchment (7.5 × 18 cm.), the size of man's hand,

8 Even if Thomas the younger did not write the endorsement himself, his intervention is still important.

attesting that Robert de Hobekyn had been made a free man during the 55th year of Henry III's long reign (1270–1271), in a ceremony witnessed by Thomas's distant ancestor Richard de la Worthe (Figures 16.2a and 16.2b).[9] Carefully folded into a tiny packet, as in Figure 16.3, it could have been secreted in a pocket or even worn as an amulet protected by a leather or metal casing. Indeed, dorsal discoloration and a dark stain on the worn exterior folds shows that it was frequently handled and displayed, making it an extremely early and unusual example of the personal identification documents that proliferated in England after the Black Death, in the later fourteenth century.[10]

Worth's archive also contained an undated *inspeximus* declaring that Henry Abbe had, in the 18th year of Edward I (1289–1290), ceremoniously viewed an earlier undated charter made by his grandfather, William le Abbe, granting a furlong of land to that same Robert de Hobekyn: a grant then confirmed to Robert's son, with Thomas Worth's ancestor Alexander as a witness.[11] A dark stain, similar to that marking the original manumission, may indicate that they were kept together (Figures 16.4a and 16.4b). The archive further contained the deed that Thomas Worth had himself obtained in 1429, and by which he acquired the land named in that *inspeximus*, as well as the *inspeximus* itself.[12] And when Worth's desired deeds were finally recovered from John Wenard, as they evidently were, this archive would contain the nullified paper deed he had drawn up in 1459, as well as Robert Spurway's sworn deposition bearing witness to Wenard's perfidy.

But why was that deposition taken down in 1477, so many years after Wenard's theft of the family archive? Perhaps Spurway was ill or dying ("and that while I live I shall testify," he had declared) and young Thomas needed a sworn affidavit to strengthen the retaliatory legal actions he was taking against Wenard (or his heirs).[13] He may also have been moved to make this record for reasons more nostalgic, as a testament to his late father's tenacity in regaining family heirlooms. As Thomas II's dorsal inscription had put it, his father would not take "any thing" from Wenard except the return of his documents, and there may even have been more in the Worth archive than deeds. As Spurway had recollected, it was "desire of deeds and other things there rehearsed" that

9 HSC Deeds 8, https://nrs.lib.harvard.edu/urn-3:hls.libr:36828856.

10 Johnson, *Law in Common*, 248–254.

11 HSC Deed 10, https://nrs.lib.harvard.edu/urn-3:hls.libr:36828872.

12 HSC Deeds 37, dated 8 Henry VI, https://nrs.lib.harvard.edu/urn-3:hls.libr:36828765.

13 Later deeds in the archive suggest that Worth was still pressing a claim to the disputed manor of Woolston into the sixteenth century: see below.

FIGURES 16.2A AND 16.2B Manumission of Robert Hobekyn (measuring 7.5 × 18 cm.), dated to the 55th year of Henry IV (1270–1271), HSC deeds 8.

FIGURE 16.3 Reconstructed folding of the manumission (Figure 16.2), showing its actual size. AUTHOR'S PHOTOGRAPH

had caused the breach with Wenard in 1459. He could have meant that "other things" were said: invective was exchanged. But he could also have meant that "other things" were missing and enumerated by Worth in the "presence and hearing" of witnesses.

The medieval archive was a trove of keepsakes, in which documents were preserved alongside articles of clothing, relics, and many other artifacts that had accrued value or evidentiary status.[14] In the archive of the cathedral treasury at Exeter, for example—just a short walk from the place where Worth and Wenard had "varied and departed in wrath" (the quarter sessions were held either at the castle or in the cathedral's chapter house nearby)[15]—a spearhead

14 See, e.g., Karl Josef Heidecker, ed., *Charters and the Use of the Written Word in Medieval Society* (Turnhout: Brepols, 2000); Esther Cohen and Mayke De Jong, eds., *Medieval Transformations: Texts, Power, and Gifts in Context* (Leiden: Brill, 2001); Marco Mostert and P. S. Barnwell, eds. *Medieval Legal Process: Physical, Spoken, and Written Performance in the Middle Ages* (Turnhout: Brepols, 2011).

15 See A. H. A. Hamilton, *Quarter Sessions from Queen Elizabeth to Queen Anne: Illustrations of Local Government and History, Drawn from Original Records (chiefly of the County of Devon)* (London: Low, Marston, Searle, & Rivington, 1878), 29.

FIGURES 16.4A AND 16.4B Undated *inspeximus* of Henry Abbe, made in the 18th year of Edward I (1289–1290), testifying to an earlier undated charter made by his grandfather, William le Abbe, granting a furlong of land to Robert de Hobekyn, HSC Deeds 10. The dark stains, similar to those marking the original manumission (Figure 16.2), may indicate that they were kept together.

was lying on an unbound booklet made during the Domesday inquest of 1086, and was leaving an indelible mark on the parchment.[16] During King Edward's

16 This booklet (now Q[uire] 85, fols. 436v and 430r) forms part of the corpus known as the "Exeter Domesday" (Exeter Cathedral Library MS 3500). It was bound with companion gatherings into a codex sometime around 1500. The components were later rebound and reorganized after the edition prepared by Abraham Farley and Henry Ellis, *Libri censualis*

(in)famous *Quo warranto* proceedings, in the 1280s, one earl's indignant response to the novel demand that all barons show "by what warrant" (*quo warranto*) they held their lands and titles was to brandish another such rusty sword in the judges' faces: "'Here, my lords, here is my warrant. For my ancestors came with William the Bastard and these lands were conquered by the sword, and by the sword I will defend them.'" His meaning was plain: the deed that guaranteed his rights was not a sealed charter; it was the blood shed by his forefather when he had used that very sword to advance the cause of Edward's ancestor in 1066.[17] Thomas Worth's ancestor Henry Abbe had probably been preparing for these same proceedings in 1289–1290, when he inspected and authenticated—so he claimed—his own grandfather's charter, which had probably never existed in written form. This was not an uncommon problem at the time, especially for those who had no weapons dating back to the Conquest; in this case, the missing deed pertained to a humble grant of land to the manumitted serf Robert de Hobekyn, made around 1270, when the only "proof" of the transaction might have been a pebble or a little pouch of earth.

The *Quo warranto* inquest prompted a rash of retrospective record-making along these lines, invoking the "dead voice" (*vox mortua*) of legal codification through affective writing techniques.[18] Yet objects and actions could still be both more authoritative and more potent than documents—even at a time when, according to M. T. Clanchy's paradigm, legal transactions in England had allegedly moved "from memory to written record."[19] Just because

---

vocati Domesday-book, additamenta ex codic. antiquiss. Exon' domesday. Inquisitio eliensis. Liber Winton. Boldon book (London: Printed by G. Eyre and A. Strahan, 1816). For a clear account of this process, see Colin Flight, *The Survey of the Whole of England: Studies of the Documentation Resulting from the Survey Conducted in 1086* (Oxford: Archaeopress, 2006), 38–39. This modern codex was unbound in 2014 and the medieval components are currently being digitized. I examined these booklets and their implications for understanding the processes undergirding the royal survey and its documentation in my article "Doing Things beside Domesday Book," *Speculum* 93 (2018): 1048–1101.

17 *The Chronicle of Walter of Guisborough, Previously Edited as the Chronicle of Walter of Hemingford or Hemingburgh*, ed. Harry Rothwell; 89 (London: Offices of the Society, 1957), 216, "'Ecce domini mei ecce Warentum meum. Antecessores enim mei cum Willelmo bastardo uenientes conquesti sunt terras suas gladio et easdem gladio defendam.'" This story, famous in its own time, appears in three related manuscript chronicles known as the "Osney-Abingdon compilations."

18 On this potent medieval legal concept, see Jésus R. Velasco, *Dead Voice: Law, Philosophy, and Fiction in the Iberian Middle Ages* (Philadelphia: University of Pennsylvania Press, 2020). For English manifestations, see Tom Johnson, "Byland Revisited, or Spectres of Inheritance," *Journal of Medieval History* 48 (2022): 439–56.

19 M. T. Clanchy, *From Memory to Written Record: England, 1066–1307*, 3rd ed. (Chichester, 2013). The larger narrative of writing's scarcity prior to the eleventh century—and hence

documentation becomes more prevalent, it does not follow that the written artifact is always narrowly practical, kept solely for the value of the words transcribed upon it. It would be very hard to account for the existence of lavishly illuminated manuscripts or jeweled and gilded bindings if that were the case. To be sure, charters like the ones in Thomas Worth's archive are not lovely, and some are not very skillfully written; indeed, according to Clanchy, these features should be construed as evidence of the degree to which record-making had become habitual and starkly utilitarian by the end of the thirteenth century. But as more recent scholarship shows, medieval documents also conveyed meaning through their physical features, the marks of handling and human contact, display, ritual, and their relationship with other things. They were, in the words of Matthew Innes, "material actors within the societies they purported to define."[20] Even the formulaic language of a deed could be personalized in the performance that accompanied its making, and enlivened again through occasional readings, whether familiar or public.[21] Deeds' individual

the arguments for its increased importance later on—has been definitively challenged by the work of Warren Brown, Mario Costambeys, Matthew Innes, and Adam Kosto, eds., *Documentary Culture and the Laity in the Early Middle Ages* (Cambridge: Cambridge University Press, 2013). For a model study of pragmatic literacy, see Simon Franklin, *Writing, Society and Culture in Early Rus, c. 950–1300* (Cambridge: Cambridge University Press, 2002). Other studies include Olivier Guyotjeannin, Laurent Morelle, and Michel Parisse, eds., *Pratiques de l'écrit documentaire au XIe siècle* (Paris: Librairie Droz, 1997); R. H. Britnell, ed., *Pragmatic Literacy, East and West, 1200–1330* (Woodbridge, Suffolk and Rochester, NY: Boydell Press, 1997); Elke Goez, *Pragmatische Schriftlichkeit und Archivpflege der Zisterzienser: Ordenszentralismus und regionale Vielfalt, namentlich in Franken und Altbayern (1098–1525)* (Münster: LIT, 2003); Mary Garrison, A. P. Orbán, and Marco Mostert, eds., *Spoken and Written Language: Relations between Latin and the Vernacular Languages in the Earlier Middles Ages* (Turnhout: Brepols, 2013).

20 Matthew Innes, "Archives, Documents, and Landowners in Carolingian Francia," in *Documentary Culture and the Laity*, ed. Brown et al., 186. See also Johnson, *Law in Common*, 241–68.

21 For an exemplary analysis of affective documentation and the personalization of formulaic language, see Geoffrey Koziol, "A Father, His Son, Memory, and Hope: The Joint Diploma of Lothar and Louis V (Pentecost Monday, 979) and the Limits of Performativity," in *Geschichtswissenschaft und "performative turn": Ritual, Inszenierung und Performanz vom Mittelalter bis zur Neuzeit*, ed. Jürgen Martschukat and Steffen Patzold (Köln: Böhlau, 2003), 83–103. See also M. B. Parkes, *Scribes, Scripts, and Readers: Studies in the Communication, Presentation, and Dissemination of Medieval Texts* (London: Hambledon Press, 1991); Petra Schulte, Marco Mostert, and Irene van Renswoude, eds., *Strategies of Writing: Studies on Text and Trust in the Middle Ages* (Turnhout: Brepols, 2008); Jonathan Wilcox, ed., *Scraped, Stroked, and Bound: Materially Engaged Readings of Medieval Manuscripts* (Turnhout: Brepols, 2013); Carol Symes, "Liturgical Texts and Performance Practices," in *Understanding Medieval Liturgy: Essays in Interpretation*, ed. Helen Gittos and Sarah Hamilton (Aldershot: Ashgate, 2016), 239–67.

idiosyncrasies—scripts and seals, but also smudges and signs of use—were part of what made them objects of desire.

As warrant for this claim, I reference an archive that I once knew intimately. The more than fifty documents that attest to the changing fortunes of Thomas Worth's extended lineage—what I have called "The Washfield Saga"—are now among some 820 parchment deeds in the Historical and Special Collections of the Harvard Law School Library.[22] The items in this composite archive were haphazardly assembled by Frederick Arthur Crisp (1851–1922), an English antiquarian and genealogist. In 1922, they were purchased by another English antiquarian, Alfred Butler, who sold them to Harvard College in 1923, after which they were moved to the Law Library in 1925. At each stage in this process, Thomas Worth's "deeds of his own descent" came to serve as proofs of a different kind. For Crisp, acquiring ancient family archives was a means of safeguarding a collective English patrimony while certifying his own intellectual credentials. For Butler, conversely, maintaining the coherence of these collections was irrelevant, so he disarticulated and rearranged all of their components to form a single chronological sequence, presumably to attract a buyer interested in acquiring a set of historical specimens.

For an American university, these decontextualized deeds accordingly constituted a ready-made archive that could help to ground a modern (formerly colonial) foundation in medieval English precedent. The Worth archive thus joined a large number of manuscript purchases facilitated by the chaos and cash-strapped postwar economy of Europe, to enhance the prestige of Harvard College. In the library of the Law School, specifically, they augmented a growing aggregation of medieval English statute-books and legal treatises, in order to create the impression that Harvard had inherited the mantle and matériel of the English Common Law. To ratify this tacit claim, a young English legal historian on the Law School's faculty, Theodore F. T. Plucknett (1897–1965), reorganized the collection of deeds according to a classification of his own devising, so that his students and colleagues could view its contents through their modern jurisprudential lenses.[23] The notes he made on each deed, between the

22 Carol Symes, *HISTORY IN DEED: Medieval Society and the Law in England, 1100–1600, An Exhibition of Deeds & Charters from the Harvard Law Library*, with an introduction by Charles Donahue, Jr. (Cambridge, MA: President and Fellows of Harvard College, 1993), 40–47. The catalogue is now available at https://iiif.lib.harvard.edu/manifests/view/drs:49950868o$1i.

23 My reconstruction of the provenance is based on the brief account by Seymour de Ricci et al., *Census of Medieval and Renaissance Manuscripts in the United States and Canada*, 3 vols. (New York: Hon. W. Wilson, 1935), 1:1042–44.

years 1923 and 1931, also became part of this new archive and were still interleaved with their medieval counterparts when Clanchy conducted research on the Harvard collection in 1972.[24] Otherwise, all of these deeds remained largely forgotten until a newly appointed Curator of Manuscripts and Archives found ten dusty black boxes in a dark corner of the stacks in 1988. Plucknett's notes are now enclosed in the same archival folders as the deeds. I know, because I put them there.[25]

Severally and collectively, these charters tell stories of land tenure and legal rivalries; they also tell other stories about documents as talismans of identity, status, and intergenerational affect. While I cannot know what fed Thomas Worth's "desire of deeds," I know what it means to develop an attachment to pieces of parchment for reasons that have little to do with their written content. Like Worth's, "my" archive subsumed many smaller collections of deeds, chancily preserved over time. Like his, too, it was treasured because its ownership conferred legitimacy, an instant heritage. I have also witnessed the degree of these charters' material attractions at first hand. Most of the visitors to the Law Library who are shown a careful selection—kept ready for the perusal of prominent alumni and eminent jurists—cannot read them, but they are still powerfully moved by a desire to make contact. "Can I touch them?" they invariably ask.

And no wonder: medieval charters are tantalizing. They are tactile, haptic. In fact, they have to be touched in order to be read and, in many cases, have to be *wrestled,* because most have been folded so tightly for so long that they will spring back and withdraw into themselves, like turtles, if they are not carefully splayed open and gently weighted down. This is another quality that makes them animate: they move. They move, and they make noise. They can also be hefty, heavy with the burdens of wax and (in some cases) twisted silk cords or protective metal skippets, or encumbered with tangled bunches of pendant seals that knock together with a sound like dried chestnuts: seals of delicate beauty or proud heraldry or crude design, mostly green or brown or red, but sometimes a sullied white. Occasionally, a thumb has imprinted itself on the

24 HSC MS 180 (a copy of the *Tractatus de legibus* attributed to Glanville, made in 1327) includes notes by Clanchy (then at the University of Glasgow) dated March of 1972. A number of deeds from this collection were used in *From Memory to Written Record*, first published by Harvard University Press in 1979 and now in its third edition: see above, n. 19.

25 I was fortunate to be hired by David de Lorenzo in 1992, during my second year in the Ph.D. program at Harvard, and so to become the first (and only) Curator of Medieval Deeds and Charters at the Harvard Law School Library, a part-time post I held until 1995.

bulbous swell of a seal's back. Occasionally, the wax is impressed with a circlet of braided rushes, still remarkably yellow.[26] One example of royal letters patent measures nearly half a meter across and is freighted with the plate-sized equestrian seal of Henry IV; it must have cost so much—the waste of parchment alone was expensive—that the recipients dispensed with having the document decorated, so that the H of the king's name is just a grid of ruled lines (Figure 16.5).[27]

How did the people of the past feel about these deeds? There are clues. A scruffy, undated and unsealed charter concerning Dunster Priory (Somerset) hardly seems like it could be important, since it mentions just a few acres of land. However, it also notes that the prior of Dunster is a free tenant on this land—which mattered because, when the deed was made, the prior was attempting to achieve independence from the cathedral of Bath and needed to prove his autonomy. Hence the scrap of parchment that has been inserted into the slot for the missing tab and seal, declaring that "this charter is the best charter of all the other charters in the monastery" (*ista carta meliora carta est ab omnibus aliis cartis monasterie*)—something that would not be at all discernable from its appearance (Figures 16.6a and 16.6b [detail]).[28]

In another case, a note added to a deed aimed to transform it into a different kind of legal instrument and keepsake. On New Year's Day in 1483, Thomas Staunton made a grant to John Wilne, Thomas Peg, and Robert Barker. At some later time, on the fold at the bottom of the Latin text, a shaky hand wrote, "I wille that Pegg & Robert Barker make / a lauful astate to John Wilne & Margaret his | wife of Þe place & to þe here[s] of Marg[ar]et" (Figures 16.7a and 16.7b [detail]).[29] The original grant was a type of conveyance known as a "feoffment to uses," making the three men tenants of a property; but with the additional note—which may not have been legally probative—the grantor is willing at least a portion of it to his daughter Margaret and his new son-in-law, the tenant John Wilne. The fact that Thomas Staunton did not simply preside

26 As in HSC Deeds 508, from Sandwich (Kent), http://id.lib.harvard.edu/alma/990058314090203941/catalog.

27 HSC Deeds 744, https://nrs.lib.harvard.edu/urn-3:hls.libr:8654805.

28 HSC Deeds 124, https://nrs.lib.harvard.edu/urn-3:hls.libr:10159663. Two other deeds (122 and 123) in this collection relate to the priory and the former, dated 1301, claims to be a transcript of an earlier missing grant. The priory achieved independence in 1332: see William Page, ed., *A History of the County of Somerset: Volume 2* (London: Victoria County History, 1911), 81–82.

29 HSC Deeds 439 (22 Edward IV), author's photograph.

FIGURE 16.5 Letters patent (measuring 37 × 44 cm.) to John Norys and others, with the great seal of Henry IV (12 cm. circumference); the "H" of the king's name is left unilluminated, HSC Deeds 744.

over the formal documentation of this new arrangement suggests that he was dying and did not have time to do that. The preservation of this charter was thus an act of filial piety as well as a routine archival decision.

FIGURES 16.6A AND 16.6B "This charter is the best charter of all the other charters in the monastery"—note (detail) appended to a charter from Dunster Priory (Somerset), HSC Deeds 124.

In still another case, the people of Woolston—the Cornwall estate in dispute between Wenard and Worth—assisted in the production of a document testifying vociferously as to the name of their village, "swearing me with oon vois … how thay never herd it callid or knowen in court or out of court by the name of Wolneston a name feyned & new altered as ferre as any of ham can remember" (Figure 16.8). Thomas Worth II had come to their parish on the Sunday before Whitsun, May 23, 1501, precisely to have their voices recorded on parchment and so to capture their collective historical memory in his

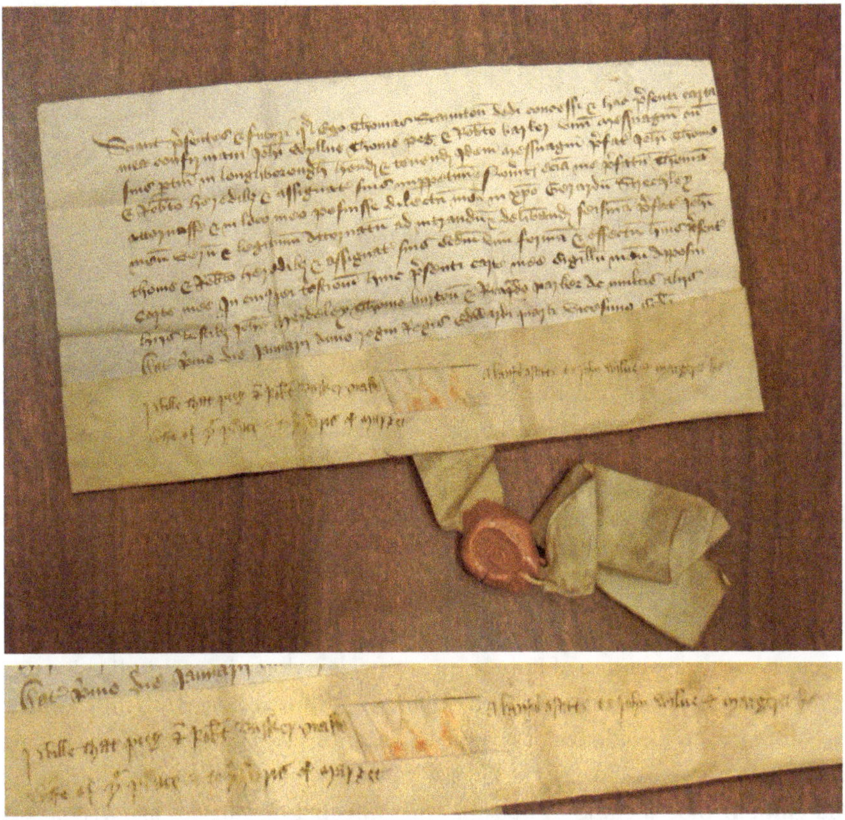

FIGURES 16.7A AND 16.7B "I wille that Pegg & Robert Barker make / a lauful astate to John Wilne & Margaret his | wife of Þe place & to þe here[s] of Marg[ar]et," HSC deeds 439.
AUTHOR'S PHOTOGRAPH

archive.[30] Worth seems to have been trying to disprove any rival title to the manor on the grounds that it had been named as "Wolneston" or "Wolveston" in previous Latin deeds—including the paper draft granting "Wolveston" to Wenard in 1459. Certifying their collective affidavit was John Brode, curate of Minster, the parish that included Woolston manor. His hand is also that

30 HSC Deeds 118, dated 17 Henry VII [23 May 1501], https://nrs.lib.harvard.edu/urn-3:hls.libr:101159837.

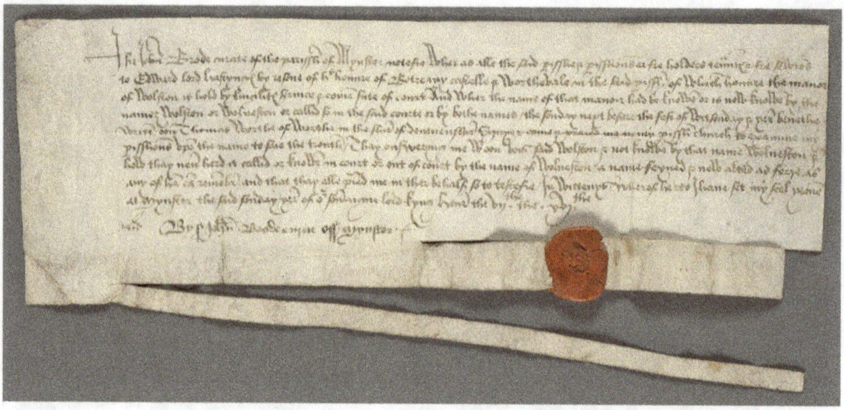

FIGURE 16.8 Certificate by Sir John Brode, curate of Minster (Cornwall), testifying that the people of Wooston told "me with oon vois" that they had "never herd it callid or knowen in court or out of court by the name of Wolneston a name feyned & new altered as ferre as any of ham can remember," HSC Deeds 118. Compare the hand to that of the deposition in Figure 16.1.

recording the deposition of Robert Spurway, taken down in 1477, indicating that Brode had been working as a Worth family scribe for at least a quarter century.

If the material evidence of bygone transactions was as meaningful as I have articulated here, when did the "desire of deeds" abate? How did all of these parchment pieces come to be sold and collected and resold again? For one thing, the evidence required to prove title in England was already changing in the seventeenth century, after the end of the English Civil War, as were family fortunes. At the same time, the value of family archives as heirlooms was also being eroded. The Paston family's "wrytyngys & evydens," so carefully curated for nearly four centuries, were evidently considered worthless compared to the "moveabell godys" which William Paston, the second earl of Yarmouth (1654–1732), began to liquidate in the first decade of the eighteenth century, in a vain effort to pay off his enormous debts. When he died without heirs, his ancestors' voluminous correspondence—the source of their fame today—was still stored, apparently untouched for decades, in the family house at Oxnead, a manor which the first William Paston had bought around 1420. There, they were examined by the Reverend Francis Blomefield, a local historian who described a room full of boxes, chests, and sacks containing "court-rolls, surveys, extent-books, deeds and other things" a well as "innumerable letters, of good consequence in history, still lying among the loose papers, all which I laid up in a corner of the room on a heap." He informed the earl's executors that the letters "seem to have some family affairs of one nature or other intermixed in them" and asked whether he should "preserve them, or whether you will have them burnt"—especially "those (of which there are many) that relate to nothing but family affairs only … a great number [of which] have perished entirely."[31] Happily, some eventually found their way into the hands of influencers like Horace Walpole (1717–1797), who recognized them as "invaluable" and advocated for their publication.[32]

By the end of the nineteenth century, then, when Crisp was assembling the composite collection that would form the core of the Harvard Law School archive, the contents of many old muniments chests had been on the market, or in the hands of antiquaries, for a century and a half. This makes the longevity of the Worth family's collection at Washfield even more remarkable, since it appears to have descended intact from Robert de Hobekyn, manumitted in 1270 during the reign of Henry IV, to John Worth III, esquire, the great-great-great-great-great-grandson of Thomas, who was still keeping the archive in 1800, the 40th year of George III. Even though these deeds were no longer legally potent, they appear to have been treasured nonetheless. In fact, John Worth III occasionally added new items to this old family treasure. The last addition is simply a letter, written to him by his paternal uncle, Charles Worth, on March 27, 1800 (Figure 16.9).[33]

> My Dear Sir:
>
> The time draws near for my departure, therefor I am to beg your Aſsistance in conveying me in your Chair tomorrow to Twiston. I should wish if it perfectly suits you to leave Washfield about 5 o'Clock to avoid the cool of the evening.
>
> Will thank you for any cuttings of Geraniums or anything that you think will be Gay for my garden Pots, and an Honey-Suckle.
>
> Yesterday brought me the melancholy account of the death of My Deer Childe Henry *last Sunday*.
>
> I have known nothing but trouble these 5 Years but we must submit. My love to Mrs. Worth & the Children.
>
> I remain Your Affte. Uncle
>
> *Charles Worth*

31 Cited by Davis in *Paston Letters and Papers*, 1: xxv–xxvi.

32 Cited by Davis in *Paston Letters and Papers*, 1: xxiv.

33 HSC Deeds 64, https://nrs.lib.harvard.edu/urn-3:hls.libr:101010085.

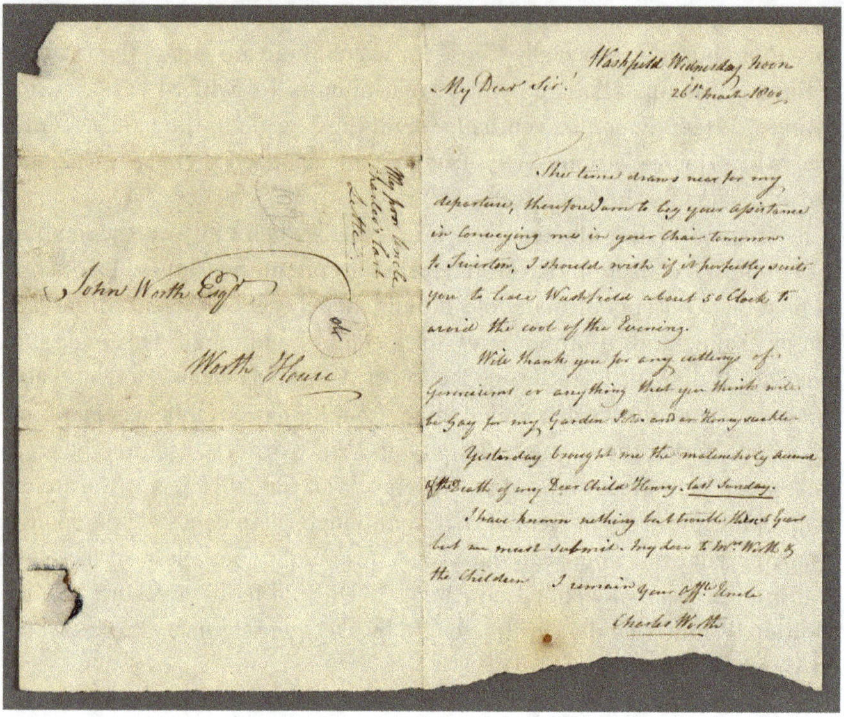

Washfield Wednesday Noon
26th March 1800.

My Dear Sir!

The time draws near for my departure, therefore I am to beg your assistance in conveying me in your Chair tomorrow to Tiverton, I should wish if it perfectly suits you to leave Washfield about 5 o'Clock to avoid the cool of the Evening.

Will thank you for any cuttings of Geraniums or anything that you think will be gay for my Garden [illegible] and or Honeysuckle.

Yesterday brought me the melancholy account of the Death of my Dear Child Henry. last Sunday.

I have known nothing but trouble [illegible] but we must submit. My love to Mrs. Worth & the Children I remain your Affte. Uncle

Charles Worth

John Worth Esqr.

Worth House

My poor Uncle Charles's last Letter

FIGURE 16.9 Letter from Charles Worth to John Worth III, dated March 26, 1800, HSC Deeds 64. The recipient has endorsed this last "deed" in the Worth family archive, "my poor uncle Charles's last letter."

Charles Worth appears to have been staying in a house near or on his nephew's entailed estate. Almost in passing, amid the request for seedlings and transportation, he announces the news of his own son's death. The shock and grief may have been what killed him. At the bottom of the page, John Worth added his own inscription: *My poor Uncle Charles's last letter.* It must have seemed fitting to place this artifact, with its sad notice of an heir's untimely demise, among the family's cherished medieval charters.

Acknowledgments

An early version of this essay was published as Carol Symes, "The 'Desire of Deeds': On Cherishing Medieval Charters," in *English Language Notes* vol. 53, no. 2, pp. 149–159. Copyright 2015, Carol Symes. Reprinted by permission of the copyright holder. All rights reserved. www.dukeupress.edu. It has since been revised and expanded. Images are provided by the Harvard Law School Library Historical & Special Collections (HSC), except where otherwise specified. I am warmly grateful to the Library's staff, with whom I worked so happily during the 1990s and occasionally since. I am especially grateful to Charles Donahue, on whose expertise I constantly relied at that time, and whose influence has endured in so many aspects of my scholarship and teaching. Thanks are also due to Elizabeth Papp Kamali, who was my own undergraduate student during the years when I became familiar with this collection.

Bibliography

Manuscripts

Harvard Law School Library Historical & Special Collections, Cambridge, MA:
Deeds 8, 10, 37, 64, 116–18, 122–24, 439, 508, 439, 744
MS 180 (copy of the *Tractatus de legibus* attributed to Glanville)
Exeter Cathedral Library MS 3500 ("Exeter Domesday"), Exeter, UK: Quire 85

Printed Primary Sources

The Chronicle of Walter of Guisborough, Previously Edited as the Chronicle of Walter of Hemingford or Hemingburgh. Edited by Harry Rothwell. London: Offices of the Society, 1957.

Davis, Norman et al., eds. *Paston Letters and Papers of the Fifteenth Century*. 3 vols. Oxford and New York: Oxford University Press, 2004.

Farley, Abraham and Henry Ellis, eds. *Libri censualis vocati Domesday-book, additamenta ex codic. antiquiss. Exon' domesday. Inquisitio eliensis. Liber Winton. Boldon book*. London: Printed by G. Eyre and A. Strahan, 1816.

Secondary Sources

Britnell, R. H., ed. *Pragmatic Literacy, East and West, 1200–1330*, Woodbridge, Suffolk and Rochester, NY: Boydell Press, 1997.

Brown, Warren C., Mario Costambeys, Matthew Innes, and Adam Kosto, eds. *Documentary Culture and the Laity in the Early Middle Ages*. Cambridge: Cambridge University Press, 2013.

Burke, John. *A Genealogical and Heraldic History of the Landed Gentry; Or, Commoners of Great Britain and Ireland, etc*. London: Henry Colburn, 1837–1838.

Clanchy, M. T. *From Memory to Written Record: England, 1066–1307*, 3rd ed. Chichester: Wiley-Blackwell, 2013.

Cohen, Esther and Mayke De Jong, eds. *Medieval Transformations: Texts, Power, and Gifts in Context*. Leiden: Brill, 2001.

Cooke, George Alexander. *Topographical Survey of the County of Devon, Historical, Statistical, and Descriptive, etc.* London: Printed for C. Cook by Brimmer and Co., 1817.

Crane, Susan. "The Writing Lesson of 1381." In *Chaucer's England: Literature in Historical Context,* edited by Barbara A. Hanawalt, 201–22. Minneapolis: University of Minnesota Press, 1992.

Flight, Colin. *The Survey of the Whole of England: Studies of the Documentation Resulting from the Survey Conducted in 1086.* Oxford: Archaeopress, 2006.

Franklin, Simon. *Writing, Society and Culture in Early Rus,* c. *950–1300*. Cambridge: Cambridge University Press, 2002.

Garrison, Mary, A. P. Orbán, and Marco Mostert, eds. *Spoken and Written Language: Relations between Latin and the Vernacular Languages in the Earlier Middles Ages.* Turnhout: Brepols, 2013.

Goez, Elke. *Pragmatische Schriftlichkeit und Archivpflege der Zisterzienser: Ordenszentralismus und regionale Vielfalt, namentlich in Franken und Altbayern* (*1098–1525*). Münster: LIT, 2003.

Guyotjeannin, Olivier, Laurent Morelle, and Michel Parisse, eds. *Pratiques de l'écrit documentaire au XIe siècle.* Paris: Librairie Droz, 1997.

Hamilton, A. H. A. *Quarter Sessions from Queen Elizabeth to Queen Anne: Illustrations of Local Government and History, Drawn from Original Records* (*chiefly of the County of Devon*). London: Low, Marston, Searle, & Rivington, 1878.

Heidecker, Karl Josef, ed. *Charters and the Use of the Written Word in Medieval Society.* Utrecht Turnhout: Brepols, 2000.

Innes, Matthew. "Archives, Documents, and Landowners in Carolingian Francia." In *Documentary Culture and the Laity,* edited by Warren Brown et al., 152–88. Cambridge: Cambridge University Press, 2013.

Johnson, Tom. "Byland Revisited, or Spectres of Inheritance." *Journal of Medieval History* 48 (2022): 439–56.

Johnson, Tom. *Law in Common: Legal Cultures in Late-Medieval England.* Oxford: Oxford University Press, 2020.

Justice, Steven. *Writing and Rebellion: England in 1381.* Berkeley: University of California Press, 1994.

Koziol, Geoffrey. "A Father, His Son, Memory, and Hope: The Joint Diploma of Lothar and Louis V (Pentecost Monday, 979) and the Limits of Performativity." In *Geschichtswissenschaft und "performative turn": Ritual, Inszenierung und Performanz vom Mittelalter bis zur Neuzeit,* edited by Jürgen Martschukat and Steffen Patzold, 83–103. Köln: Böhlau, 2003.

Krug, Rebecca. *Reading Families: Women's Literate Practice in Late Medieval England.* Ithaca: Cornell University Press, 2002.

Mostert, Marco and P. S. Barnwell, eds. *Medieval Legal Process: Physical, Spoken, and Written Performance in the Middle Ages.* Turnhout: Brepols, 2011.

Page, William, ed. *A History of the County of Somerset: Volume 2*. London: Victoria County History, 1911.

Parkes, M. B. *Scribes, Scripts, and Readers: Studies in the Communication, Presentation, and Dissemination of Medieval Texts*. London: Hambledon Press, 1991.

de Ricci, Seymour et al. *Census of Medieval and Renaissance Manuscripts in the United States and Canada.* 3 vols. New York: Hon. W. Wilson, 1935.

Schulte, Petra, Marco Mostert, and Irene van Renswoude, eds. *Strategies of Writing: Studies on Text and Trust in the Middle Ages*. Turnhout: Brepols, 2008.

Symes, Carol. "Doing Things beside Domesday Book." *Speculum* 93 (2018): 1048–1101.

Symes, Carol. *HISTORY IN DEED: Medieval Society and the Law in England, 1100–1600, An Exhibition of Deeds & Charters from the Harvard Law Library*. With an introduction by Charles Donahue, Jr. Cambridge, MA: President and Fellows of Harvard College, 1993. https://iiif.lib.harvard.edu/manifests/view/drs:49950868o$1i.

Symes, Carol. "Liturgical Texts and Performance Practices." In *Understanding Medieval Liturgy: Essays in Interpretation,* edited by Helen Gittos and Sarah Hamilton, 239–67. Aldershot: Ashgate, 2016.

Velasco, Jésus R. *Dead Voice*: *Law, Philosophy, and Fiction in the Iberian Middle Ages.* Philadelphia: University of Pennsylvania Press, 2020.

Wilcox, Jonathan, ed. *Scraped, Stroked, and Bound: Materially Engaged Readings of Medieval Manuscripts*. Turnhout: Brepols, 2013.

PART 4

American Legal History

CHAPTER 17

Lawyers and Their Book Collections: Notes from the Eighteenth Century

Sally E. Hadden

> Anyone who has ever visited Charlie Donahue's office knows that the man treasures books.

∵

Despite their logically companionable fields, legal historians and historians of the book have shown a remarkable disinterest in getting together. With some notable exceptions, American legal historians have largely ignored what might be learned from studying legal texts through the medium of bibliographic history.[1] This situation drew the attention of historian Chris Tomlins, who wrote that "the [legal] treatise … was a neglected *source* for the writing of legal history [but] not itself a subject *in* legal history."[2] Meanwhile historians of the book have mostly considered the book collections of lawyers to be much the same as all the others accumulated by curious readers, tending to downplay the important role attorneys filled in early America as book importers and library builders. And this is a shame—analyses of law books and the collectors

1 W. Hamilton Bryson, *Census of Law Books in Colonial Virginia* (Charlottesville: University Press of Virginia, 1978); Michael Hoeflich, "Legal History and the History of the Book: Variations on a Theme," *University of Kansas Law Review* 46, no. 3 (1988): 415–31; John D. Gordan III, "John Nutt: Publisher and Printer 'In the Savoy,'" *The Library, Transactions of the Bibliographical Society*, 7th ser., 15, no. 3 (2014): 243–60; Angela Fernandez and Markus D. Dubber, eds., *Law Books in Action: Essays on the Anglo-American Legal Treatise* (Oxford: Hart Publishing, 2012); Warren M. Billings, "'Send Us … What Other Lawe Books You Shall Thinke Fitt': Books That Shaped the Law in Virginia, 1600–1860," *Virginia Magazine of History and Biography* 120, no. 4 (2012): 314–39; Warren M. Billings and Brent Tarter, eds., *"Esteemed Bookes of Lawe" and the Legal Culture of Early Virginia* (Charlottesville: University of Virginia Press, 2017).

2 Christopher Tomlins, "Commentary: Effects of Scale: Toward a History of the Literature of Law," in *Law Books in Action*, ed. Angela Fernandez and Markus D. Dubber, 221.

 | DOI:10.1163/9789004710696_019

who purchased and read them could enhance what historians of the book have learned thus far about early modern collecting habits.[3]

For historians of the book—whose subject encompasses a variety of topics including book creation, acquisition, circulation, readership, collection building, and library formation—lawyers should be a natural occupational group to investigate. Lawyers of the past, particularly in America's colonial period, typically amassed collections of law books in order to commence practice. Attorneys usually kept their assembled volumes together and added to them as their careers continued, and not infrequently bequeathed their accumulated editions to younger family members upon retiring. Also, lawyers viewed law books as a good investment in one's career—after all, one could only argue in court using the precedents that one knew about. Of course, the cost of amassing such book collections represented a barrier to entry for men without sufficient funds; book acquisition was a virtual requirement to become a lawyer, ensuring that the early American legal ranks recruited new members largely from families of means.

Discovery and analysis of law book collections from the colonial era has, for some time, focused upon probate inventories of lawyers or collectors of law books.[4] A smaller law book collection might contain thirty to forty books, while larger inventories could encompass more than 200 legal volumes.[5] But another set of little-used primary sources can provide information about law book availability, perceived demand, and resale on the used market: newspapers printed in seaport cities such as Boston, Philadelphia, and Charleston. Advertisements run by booksellers listing new law books for sale provide a method to learn about book availability and merchant perceptions of the demand for legal texts in colonial North America. Ads placed by executors or resellers likewise shed interesting light upon the circulation of legal texts on the secondary market.

---

3 Billings attributes this to a fixation upon literary genres. Billings, "'Send Us ... What Other Lawe Books,'" 314. I'm using "legal book" for its broader definition to include law books produced for mass consumption, not just those used by attorneys. Michael Widener, "From Law Book to Legal Book: The Origin of a Species," *Rechtsgeschichte-Legal History* 29 (2021): 431.

4 See, e.g., Walter B. Edgar, "Notable Libraries of Colonial South Carolina," *South Carolina Historical Magazine* 72, no. 2 (1971): 105–10; Bryson, *Census of Law Books in Colonial Virginia*; Edwin Wolf 2nd, *Book Culture of a Colonial American City: Philadelphia Books, Bookmen, and Booksellers* (Oxford: Clarendon Press, 1988).

5 An exemplary version of this type of study is W. Hamilton Bryson, "Private Law Libraries Before 1776," in *Virginia Law Books: Essays and Bibliographies*, ed. W. Hamilton Bryson (Philadelphia: American Philosophical Society, 2000), 479–99; and Edgar, "Notable Libraries."

Copies of individual laws had been sold in colonial cities as early as the seventeenth century, but compilations of provincial laws were probably the first law books marketed anywhere on the mainland of North America.[6] The earliest advertisement indicating collected laws for sale appeared in March 1713. Benjamin Eliot (1665–1741), a Boston book dealer, advertised for sale the Massachusetts Bay charter as well as "the Laws of the said Province compleat, with a new Table." The charter and digested laws sold for 18 shillings 6 pence, putting them well beyond the reach of an average book purchaser.[7] This collection of Massachusetts colonial laws appears not to have survived to the present day: no entry exists for it within the Early American Imprints database (Evans) nor is it referenced within Morris Cohen's comprehensive *Bibliography of Early American Law*.[8] The following year, Eliot offered for sale a copy of the colonial charter, but this time without the digested laws.[9] Bookmen like Eliot regularly sold editions of the colony's charter; many new residents wanted a copy of the legal rights they possessed, and the influx of immigrants ensured Eliot and his competitors steady sales.[10] This pattern held true in other colonies as well: individual laws and copies of royal or proprietary charters sold several years before printers marketed digests of local law.

Digests of colonial laws remained a relative rarity. Individual session laws continued to sell in the early 1700s, but compilations were slower to appear. One possible reason: if an individual law was amended or repealed, the collection containing it might appear flawed. Far simpler to throw away a broadsheet containing the text of a single invalid law than to discard an entire book. More

---

6 One limitation to using advertisements is that advertisements could be misleading about the stock a printer held for sale or had highest demand for. David Hall of Philadelphia left behind records indicating he advertised (in rank order by subject area) religion, history, medicine, law, and literature books for sale, but that literature texts outsold all other types. Elizabeth Reilly and David D. Hall, "Customers and the Market for Books," in *The Colonial Book in the Atlantic World*, ed. Hugh Amory and David D. Hall (Cambridge: Cambridge University Press, 2000), 390.

7 "The Charter Granted to the Province of the Massachusetts-Bay and the Laws of the Said Province Compleat," *Boston News-Letter*, March 30, 1713, 467 edition.

8 The Early American Imprints database is marketed by Readex. A description may be found here: https://www.readex.com/products/early-american-imprints-series-i-evans-1639-1800. Morris L. Cohen, ed., *Bibliography of Early American Law*, 6 vols. (Buffalo NY: William S. Hein, 1998).

9 *The Charter Granted by Their Majesties King William and Queen Mary, to the Inhabitants of the Province of the Massachusetts-Bay in New-England* (Boston: Benjamin Eliot, 1714).

10 Morris L. Cohen, "Legal Literature in Colonial Massachusetts," in *Law in Colonial Massachusetts*, ed. Daniel Coquillette (Boston: Colonial Society of Massachusetts, 1984), 253–54.

importantly, digests had price tags beyond the means of many individuals. Digests, however, appeared as laws proliferated: collections of Massachusetts laws were printed roughly once every decade, in 1699, 1714, 1726, 1742, and 1759.[11] Despite requests starting in the 1690s from the Board of Trade to every provincial legislature to provide digested copies of colonial laws, few assemblies produced them regularly. Some legislatures, like those of Rhode Island and Connecticut, seem to have deliberately not printed compilations to make repeal of their laws by the Privy Council more difficult.[12]

Following Eliot's 1713 advertisement, nearly twenty years passed before a similar digest appeared in a Philadelphia newspaper. The New Jersey "Book of the Laws" was marketed in 1730 as a subscription project. Printers William Bradford (1663–1752) and Andrew Bradford (1686–1742) sensed a digest might attract subscribers, so they tested the proposition: "Those private Gentlemen who are willing to have and subscribe for the same" had to pay a five-shilling deposit.[13] The Bradfords may have been inspired by William Parks (1699–1750), who brought out a Maryland legal digest, *A Compleat Collection of the Laws of Maryland*, by subscription in 1727. Parks advertised his book through the legislature's session laws that he printed, rather than newspapers.[14] Not every subscription project for legal texts found subscribers, however.[15]

In the colonies, the most famous subscription printing project was Robert Bell's (1732–1784) American printing of Blackstone's *Commentaries*, which was publicized in the early 1770s.[16] In 1773, *Rivington's New York Gazetteer* carried an advertisement for Bell's American edition, promising subscribers the

11 Cohen, "Legal Literature," 254. The earliest digest of colonial laws printed was *The Lawes of Virginia Now in Force*, in 1662 (London: E. Cotes).

12 Mary Sarah Bilder, *The Transatlantic Constitution: Colonial Legal Culture and the Empire* (Cambridge, MA: Harvard University Press, 2004), 66–67; Sally E. Hadden, "Early American Governors' Councils, Their Judicial Functions, and Changing Constitutional Perceptions of Their Duties" (presentation, American Society for Legal History annual meeting, New Orleans, 2021).

13 "Proposals for Re-Printing the Laws of the Province of New-Jersey," *American Weekly Mercury*, December 22, 1730.

14 No extant newspaper advertisement has been located for Parks's digest. Calhoun Winton, "The Southern Book Trade in the Eighteenth Century," in *The Colonial Book in the Atlantic World*, ed. Hugh Amory and David D. Hall (Cambridge: American Antiquarian Society, Cambridge University Press, 2000), 226.

15 Three lawyers attempted to publish a handbook for courtroom practice, based upon colonial laws, which never appeared. "Advertisement, 'To Be Published, When There Shall Appear, a Sufficient Number of Subscribers,'" *Connecticut Gazette*, February 6, 1762.

16 Jenni Parrish, "Law Books and Legal Publishing in America, 1760–1840," *Law Library Journal* 72 (1979): 360.

complete set of four volumes, since the fourth volume was "now ready to be delivered." The individual names of over 800 subscribers were included in the volumes, giving their location and occupation—a veritable who's who of colonial lawyers.[17]

Subscription projects for digests or treatises were rare compared to the sale of ordinary law books in colonial America. The first imported law books advertised were those with widest appeal. In Charleston, Edward Wigg (1715–c. 1755) advertised 32 distinct titles for sale in 1732, including the "Law concerning Masters & Servants," the sole legal text.[18] Presumably he thought he would find a customer in a province of slave owners.

Making guesses of this kind shaped the legal book trade. Dealers predicted which imported books would sell best, choosing titles in which the largest number of purchasers might be interested.[19] So the earliest colonial book advertisements listed legal guidebooks and manuals that might be used by nearly anyone. In the early modern period, handbooks and instruction manuals were perennial bestsellers. Such guidebooks on every legal topic had a steady market among eighteenth-century London law students: the quality of teaching at the Inns of Court had declined so badly that many would-be lawyers had to teach themselves the rudiments of law.[20] The foremost handbook creator in the eighteenth century was Giles Jacob (1686–1744) and his law guides sold well on both sides of the Atlantic.

Jacob's Law Dictionary (first published in 1729) and Jacob's *Every Man His Own Lawyer* (first published in 1736) were the first law books sold in many British colonies. Philadelphia printer and book seller Benjamin Franklin (1705–1790) advertised *Every Man His Own Lawyer* for sale in January 1742.[21] Later that year, Franklin added *Jacob's Law Dictionary*. He did not stock many law books. An August 1742 advertisement sandwiched four legal titles among 80 others on geography, history, religion, and fiction: *Jacob's Law Dictionary*, plus *Wood's Institutes* on both common law and civil law and Cooke's *Reports*.[22]

---

17 "Advertisement, 'The Sons of Science in America,'" *Rivington's New York Gazetteer*, May 27, 1773.

18 "Book Advertisement Listing for Sale Law Concerning Masters & Servants," *South Carolina Gazette*, April 15, 1732.

19 Such early merchants might not be book dealers exclusively, which might explain their great caution when investing too much cash into titles of works they did not know well.

20 Julia Rudolph, "That 'Blunderbuss' of Law: Giles Jacob, Abridgment, and Print Culture," *Studies in Eighteenth-Century Culture* 37 (2008): 200.

21 Benjamin Franklin, "Advertisement, 'Books Sold by Benjamin Franklin, near the Market, in Philadelphia,'" *Pennsylvania Gazette*, January 7, 1742.

22 Benjamin Franklin, "Book Advertisement, 'Books Sold by B. Franklin,'" *Pennsylvania Gazette*, August 12, 1742.

Jacob's Law Dictionary remained a successful moneymaker from its first printing to the end of the eighteenth century, reaching a tenth edition by 1782.[23] In part, this was due to Jacob's incessant publication of law-related books; he was without doubt the most prolific London publisher of legal manuals and handbooks, churning out nearly 30 titles in roughly the same number of years, and his self-help volume *Every Man His Own Lawyer* reportedly outsold his very popular law dictionary. Alexander Pope (1688–1744) snidely dubbed Jacob the "Blunderbus of law."[24]

With *Every Man His Own Lawyer,* Jacob created a work for readers of "every Capacity" and "those who are Ignorant in the Practice of the Law," not specialists.[25] His work touched upon marriage, wills and the division of estates, property transfers, and even the basics of legal process. *Every Man His Own Lawyer* gained a wide readership due to its portable size and ease of use by non-specialists. Published in octavo, the book could be carried anywhere easily, unlike large format folio editions—nearly double the size—that rarely left a home or law office.[26] Little wonder, then, that *Every Man His Own Lawyer* sold widely in early America throughout the eighteenth century.

Newspaper advertisements demonstrate the handbook's nearly ubiquitous availability. *Every Man His Own Lawyer* appeared in advertisements all over North America: newspapers from Georgia (1764) and Rhode Island (1767) to as far north as New Hampshire (1792) carried the handbook.[27] In Hartford, Connecticut, the Lathrop and Smith "Druggist and Apothecary" shop stocked *Every Man* intermixed with books on surgery, fevers, and smallpox.[28] German speakers saw ads for *Every Man* in the Lancaster, Pennsylvania, *Der Wahre Amerikaner* as late as 1806.[29] A pirated American version of the text appeared

23 A. H. Bullen, "Jacob, Giles," in *Dictionary of National Biography*, ed. Leslie Stephen and Sidney Lee, 22 vols. (New York: Macmillan, 1917), vol. 10, 553.

24 Alexander Pope, *The Dunciad* (Dublin, 1728), 44.

25 Giles Jacob, *Every Man His Own Lawyer: Or, A Summary of the Laws of England in a New and Instructive Method* ..., 4th ed. (London: Henry Lintot, 1750), v. For further consideration of legal manuals as created and used in the European context, as compared to nineteenth-century America, see Annamaria Monti, "Popular Legal Manuals as Sources and Mechanisms of Acquiring Legal Literacy," in *Legal Literacy in Premodern European Societies,* ed. Mia Korpiola (Switzerland: Palgrave Macmillan, 2019), 191–210.

26 Rudolph, "That 'Blunderbuss' of Law," 205.

27 "Advertisement, 'Just Imported, and to Be Sold by James Johnston,'" *Georgia Gazette,* June 21, 1764; "Advertisement, 'Just Imported from London, via Boston, and to Be Sold,'" *Providence Gazette,* September 12, 1767; "Advertisement, 'Books and Stationary for Sale by J. Melcher,'" *New-Hampshire Gazette,* July 19, 1792.

28 "Advertisement, 'Lathrop and Smith, Druggist and Apothecary,'" *Hartford Courant,* August 10, 1767.

29 "Advertisement, 'For Sale at This Office,'" *Der Wahre Amerikaner,* November 1, 1806.

in New York in 1768, printed by Hugh Gaine, who retained Giles Jacob as the (unpaid) author on the front cover.[30] Jacob's name sold law books.

While law students and a fair number of legal practitioners owned handbooks like Jacob's, they needed more advanced, technical resources to assist their clients, such as law reports, treatises, and abridgments. Law reports contained the precedents lawyers used when presenting a case to judge or jury; the books included court decisions and, in some instances, the legal arguments employed by counsel on both sides.

Among the earliest colonial advertisements offering law reports for sale was a March 3, 1733, *South Carolina Gazette* notice about goods to be auctioned at the Charleston public market. The ad listed thirty-four discrete legal titles, including abridgments or law reporters in abundance: "Lutwich [Lutwyche], Lenard [Leonard], Rolls [Rolle], Modem [Modern], Levinz, Lord Cook [Coke], Pollixsen [Pollexfen], Bulstrode, Hardres, Showers, Sanders [Saunders], Noy, Dyer, and Anderson's Reports."[31] Named for the judges and lawyers who compiled them, the volumes covered the sixteenth to the eighteenth centuries.[32] This set of editions may have originally comprised the working library of a Charleston lawyer who had recently died, as the auction notice did not indicate whether the books were new or used.

English law reporters continued to be sold in North America throughout the eighteenth century. Although there were no advertisements for Burrell's (1584–1674), Dickens's (1559–1798), Tothill's (1559–1646), Barnardiston's (1726–1735) or Wilmot's (1757–1770) reports in early American newspapers, every other law reporter printed in England between 1600 and 1775 was advertised. Of the eighty-eight distinctly titled reporters printed in London covering that time span, eighty-three appeared in advertisements in early American newspapers.

In addition to case reports, legal practitioners needed treatises, monographs that offered one author's interpretation of a legal subject. Students of the law might commence their training with treatises rather than law reports, starting with Sir Edward Coke's *Institutes of the Lawes of England*. Published beginning in 1628, *Coke's Institutes* consisted of four volumes, sometimes referred to

---

30 Giles Jacob, *Every Man His Own Lawyer: Or, A Summary of the Laws of England, in a New and Instructive Method, under the Following Heads …* (New York: Hugh Gaine, 1768); for more on Gaine's background, see Parrish, "Law Books and Legal Publishing in America," 361.

31 "Advertisement, 'On Wednesday next, under the New Market House, Is to Be Sold,'" *South Carolina Gazette*, March 3, 1733.

32 Bulstrode (1603–1639), Rolle (1614–1625), Hardres (1654–1669), Levinz (1660–1697), Saunders (1666–1673), Modern (1669–1732), Pollexfen (1669–1685), Lutwyche (1682–1704), and Shower (1678–1695).

as *Coke upon Littleton* because Coke's work glossed an earlier book, Thomas Littleton's *Tenures*.[33] Less well-organized than the later *Wood's Institutes* (1720), *Coke's Institutes* nonetheless provided many budding attorneys with their first taste of legal knowledge. *Coke's Institutes* continued to be popular through the eighteenth century, in addition to *Wood's Institutes* published in 1720. *Coke's* and *Wood's Institutes* would eventually give way to Blackstone's *Commentaries*, published in the 1760s. Virtually every practitioner in early America owned a copy of *Coke upon Littleton, Wood's Institutes*, or Blackstone's *Commentaries* and many owned more than one: treatises provided structure to the common law's complexities. Small wonder, then, that all three titles appeared repeatedly in newspaper advertisements.

The earliest Philadelphia ad for *Coke upon Littleton* appeared in 1747, soon followed by another ad in New York City, where printer James Parker (1714–1770) sold the volumes at his office on Beaver Street.[34] *Coke upon Littleton* (or versions of it) continued to be offered for sale via newspapers for many decades, ultimately giving rise to an American edition in 1853.[35]

Advertisements for *Wood's Institutes*, like those for *Coke's Institutes* or *Every Man His Own Lawyer*, proliferated across virtually every colony. The earliest ads featuring the treatise appeared in Philadelphia in 1738, 1739, and 1742.[36] In the 1742 advertisement, Benjamin Franklin included *Wood's Institutes* among the dozens of volumes he had for sale, but placed the title near the very bottom, suggesting he did not think it would be very popular.[37] Perhaps Franklin sensed that his predominantly Quaker customers would be put off by books

33 J. H. Baker, *An Introduction to English Legal History*, 4th ed. (Oxford: Oxford University Press, 2002), 189.

34 "Advertisement, 'To Be Sold by Peter Robertson, in Front-Street, Philadelphia,'" *Pennsylvania Gazette*, March 16, 1747; "Advertisement, 'Books for Sale, Imported from London, in the Last Ships,'" *New-York Gazette, or Weekly Post-Boy*, September 12, 1748.

35 Charles Butler, ed., *The First Part of the Institutes of the Laws of England, or, A Commentary upon Littleton: Not the Name of the Author Only, but of the Law Itself: … Authore Edwardo Coke, Milite. Revised and Corrected, with Further Additions of Notes, References, and Proper Tables, by Francis Hargrave and Charles Butler, Esqrs. of Lincoln's Inn, Including Also the Notes of Lord Chief Justice Hale and Lord Chancellor Nottingham; and an Analysis of Littleton*, 1st American ed., from the 19th London ed., 2 vols. (Philadelphia: Robert Small, 1853).

36 "Advertisement, 'Just Imported and To Be Sold by B. Franklin,'" *Pennsylvania Gazette*, May 25, 1738; "Advertisement, 'Benj. Franklin, Printer, Is Just Removed,'" *Pennsylvania Gazette*, January 18, 1739. An advertisement in the Pennsylvania Gazette from February 7, 1740, included no law titles except *Jacob's Law Dictionary*.

37 Franklin, "Advertisement, 'Books Sold by Benjamin Franklin, near the Market, in Philadelphia,'" *Pennsylvania Gazette*, January 7, 1742.

that discussed litigation; the Society of Friends threatened members with discipline or expulsion who did not mediate differences rather than litigate them.[38] Boston booksellers John (1728–1777) and Thomas Leverett (1730–1778) took a different approach: *Wood's Institutes* was the third title in their long advertisement in June 1752, preceded by Pufendorf's *Of the Law of Nature and Nations* and Hale's *Pleas of the Crown*.[39] Similar advertisements appeared from New Hampshire (1756) to Georgia (1763) with most placing *Wood's Institutes* near the top each time.[40]

Accessing information contained in thousands of English cases required compilations that cross-indexed the reporters: abridgments. Abridgment editors grouped information by subject area, pulling together case citations scattered in different reporters. Fitzherbert's or Brooke's abridgments (from the sixteenth century) or Sheppard's, Hughes's, or Rolle's abridgments (from the seventeenth century) could help a lawyer master the wealth of material contained in dozens of volumes. Abridgments brought order out of chaos by, as legal historian J. H. Baker put it, "systematizing the confused mass of ideas in the reports," which by the eighteenth century had madly proliferated.[41] An indexing tool such as Sheppard's, Hughes's, or Rolle's abridgments permitted a colonial attorney to find legal precedents to support his argument, even ones contained in reporters he did not possess. Given the uneven quality of some reporters published from 1650 to 1750 and the expense of purchasing law books from England, an abridgment might be a superior investment compared to individual reporters churned out in the period. Advertisements indicate that older abridgments continued to be sold alongside newer ones: Sir Anthony Fitzherbert's *Le Graunde Abridgment* from 1514 appeared in a Boston advertisement from 1738.[42] Strangely, when Viner's new *General Abridgment of Law and Equity* began publication in 1741, it did not immediately attract purchasers. Its massive size—running eventually to 23 volumes—made the set a pricey acquisition, despite the fact that it incorporated 200 years of new case information.[43]

---

38 F. Peter Phillips, "Ancient and Comely Order: The Use and Disuse of Arbitration by New York Quakers," *Journal of Dispute Resolution* 2016 (2016): 81–114.

39 "Advertisement, 'Just Imported, and Sold by John and Thomas Leverett,'" *Boston Gazette*, June 30, 1752.

40 "Advertisement, 'Catalogue of Books Continued, Sold by the Printer of This Paper,'" *New-Hampshire Gazette*, October 28, 1756; "Advertisement, 'Catalogue of Books to Be Sold at the Printing-Office,'" *Georgia Gazette*, November 10, 1763.

41 Baker, *Introduction to English Legal History*, 186.

42 "Advertisement, 'To Be Sold by Publick Venue or Auction,'" *Boston Evening-Post*, March 6, 1738.

43 Charles Viner, *A General Abridgment of Law and Equity*, 23 vols. (Aldershot: Viner, 1741).

Once complete, a few booksellers did stock the Viner set: New Yorkers James Rivington (1724–1803) and Samuel Brown (active 1755) advertised Viner's *Abridgment* for sale in 1762.[44] Printers such as Daniel Henchman (Boston, 1689–1761), Benjamin Franklin and David Hall (Philadelphia, 1714–1772), or James Rivington (Philadelphia and New York City) tried to keep law books on hand for their faithful customers.[45]

Once they accumulated some legal books, printers and bookmen advertised their law book stock through catalogues distributed locally or via the mail; this provided customers with a shopping list to fill up their law libraries. Catalogues might be advertised in newspapers instead of specific book titles. Following the practice of London publisher John Worrall (d. 1771) with his *Bibliotheca Legum: or a New and Compleat List of All the Common and Statute Law Books of this Realm*, Franklin produced a law book catalog in 1744 and Rivington generated his own (of 90 pages) in 1762.[46] An additional catalog of law books appeared in his own newspaper, *Rivington's New York Gazetteer*, in 1773 and should be considered an essential supplement to the 1762 pamphlet.[47] Rivington even invited orders from purchasers outside of New York: "The Orders of Gentlemen living at a distance, shall be supplied by the first opportunities after they are received."[48]

While booksellers like Rivington offered law reports, treatises, and abridgments for sale, another sort of advertisement reveals the "second life" of legal books: used book sales and estate auctions. Law books were sufficiently expensive that they might comprise a significant portion of a dead man's property. Should he have a son or nephew trained in the law, that individual might inherit and put the books to use. But law books belonging to dead men with

44 "Rivington and Brown, Booksellers and Stationers," *New-York Gazette*, November 8, 1762.

45 On Rivington, see Parrish, "Law Books and Legal Publishing in America," 361–62.

46 T. H. Howard-Hill, *The British Book Trade 1475–1890: A Bibliography* (London: British Library and Oak Knoll Press, 2008), vol. 2, 1609–12; Benjamin Franklin, *A catalogue of choice and valuable books, consisting of near 600 volumes, in most faculties and sciences, viz. divinity, history, law, mathematics, philosophy, physic, poetry, &c. Which will begin to be sold for ready money, only, by Benj. Franklin, at the Post-Office in Philadelphia, on Wednesday, the 11th of April 1744* (Philadelphia: Franklin, 1744), Evans 5396. At 4, he listed for sale copies of Leonard's, Ventris's, and Modern Reports. James Rivington and Samuel Brown, *A catalogue of books, sold by Rivington and Brown, booksellers and stationers from London, at their stores, over against the Golden Key, in Hanover-Square, New-York: and over against the London Coffee-House, in Philadelphia* (Philadelphia: Heinrich Miller, 1762), Evans 9259.

47 "Advertisement, 'Addition to J. Rivington's First Published List of Law Books,'" *Rivington's New York Gazetteer*, October 14, 1773.

48 "Advertisement, 'To the Gentlemen of the Law, A Large Library of Second Hand Reports,'" *Rivington's New York Gazetteer*, August 19, 1773.

no male heirs, or no heir practicing law, were an exotic treasure to be liquidated for cash. Grieving widows or other legatees might attempt to sell the books themselves (a difficult proposition) or place the books in the hands of auctioneers to resell. Both options provided other lawyers with opportunities to expand their law libraries without having to purchase new books from overseas. Used law books sold for a fraction of the original price.

In 1738, John Roberts placed an ad in the *New York Gazette* offering more than 300 volumes for sale, a significantly sized collection and probably used. His catalog of a "Choice and Valuable Collection of Law-Books, consisting of Reports of all the chief and eminent Lawyers" included a full set of the *Statutes at Large* and Domat's *Civil Law Institutes* that likely belonged to a deceased lawyer's estate. Roberts's use of the word "Collection" suggests as much. Copies of the catalog could be had from his office near "Long Bridge" in the city, but sadly, no catalog survives.[49]

Like Roberts, Tench Francis Jr. (1730–1800) of Philadelphia offered a law library for sale at his store on Front Street in 1755, listing 146 distinct law titles for sale, many in multi-volume sets. The used books had been his late father's collection, and included a complete run of all Common Pleas and King's Bench cases heard in London going back more than 100 years, plus three different abridgments: Fitzherbert's, Rolle's, and Viner's.[50] Francis already sold new and used books in his shop, but his usual advertisements featured barely a dozen law books crammed between titles such as *Archbishop Sharpe's Sermons* and *Taylor's Life of Christ*, which explains the special 1755 advertisement.[51] Another Philadelphia book merchant, William Laplain (active 1772), listed more than thirty different legal titles for sale in a 1772 advertisement and seemed eager to unload them—unlike his poetry, novels, sermons, and songbooks—as a group. "Gentlemen of the law who are inclined to purchase a quantity of scarce old law books, shall, for the sake of ready cash, have a reasonable allowance."[52] Given the large Quaker population in Philadelphia, Francis and Laplain may have been wise to stock more religious literature than law for their customers.

49 "Advertisement, 'To Be Sold, a Choice and Valuable Collection,'" *New York Gazette*, May 8, 1738.

50 "Tench Francis, Jun. at His Store in Front Street," *Pennsylvania Journal and Weekly Advertiser*, November 20, 1755.

51 "Advertisement, 'Just Imported from London, and to Be Sold by Tench Francis, Jun.,'" *Pennsylvania Gazette*, July 18, 1754.

52 "Advertisement, 'William Laplain, at His Book-Store in Market-Street, Opposite the London Coffee-House, Has for Sale, An Assortment of Useful and Scarce Books, in Most Sciences, among Which Are,'" *Pennsylvania Packet*, November 30, 1772.

In smaller towns, the books of dead lawyers sold even more slowly. An advertisement like Laplain's appeared in the *Pennsylvania Gazette*, describing seventy-five unsold law books of "the late Joseph Scattergood." Scattergood's library was in Burlington, Delaware, twenty-five miles away from Philadelphia. With no local newspaper, his Burlington executor used the Philadelphia-based *Gazette* to drum up purchasers interested in Giles Jacob's *Lex Mercatoria*, Saunders's *Reports*, or a nearly complete set of Viner's *Abridgment*.[53] In North Carolina, which had no newspaper until 1787, executors for an Edenton lawyer's estate resorted to advertising in the Williamsburg-based *Virginia Gazette*, published over 100 miles away.[54] The February 1777 Virginia paper doubtless filtered into the hands of northeastern North Carolina readers, who might be close enough to Edenton to attend the auction the following month.[55]

Occasionally, the accoutrements of a law office appeared alongside law books at an auction. If Virginians did attend the 1777 Edenton North Carolina sale of Thomas Jones's effects, the auctioneer promised much finery: in addition to Jones's law books, auctioneers would sell "Mohogany Chairs and Tables," a "single RIDING CHAIR and HARNESS," various furnishings including a pair of gilt-edged "Looking-glasses," plus multiple houses and land tracts spread across two counties.[56] A Charleston newspaper advertisement for a 1768 auction listed the "collection of law books, comprehending almost all the reports" plus a "neat convenient mahogany writing Table" and "four large glazed Book Cases" made with joints, such that they could be disassembled for transportation.[57] Peter Manigault's Charleston estate sale featured not only his law book collection (complete with his Middle Temple bookplates) but "three large Mahogany Book Cases," a quantity of "excellent Old Madeira Wine" plus his coach and "quite genteel chariot."[58] Auctioned property might include human beings. Following the 1758 death of Abraham Lodge in New York City,

53 "Advertisement, 'A List of the Late Joseph Scattergood's Books Remaining Unsold at Burlington,'" *Pennsylvania Gazette*, March 18, 1755; "Advertisement, 'A List of the Late Joseph Scattergood's Books Remaining Unsold at Burlington,'" *Pennsylvania Gazette*, March 25, 1755.

54 Edward C. Lathem, *Chronological Tables of American Newspapers, 1690–1820* (Worcester: American Antiquarian Society, 1972), 19.

55 "Advertisement, 'Edenton, North Carolina, February 15, 1777, To Be Sold,'" *Virginia Gazette*, March 7, 1777.

56 "Advertisement, 'Edenton, North Carolina, February 15, 1777, To Be Sold,'" *Virginia Gazette*, March 7, 1777.

57 "Advertisement, 'To Be Sold at Auction, by Charles Crouch,'" *South Carolina Gazette*, June 14, 1768.

58 "Advertisement, 'To Be Sold at Publick Vendue, on Wednesday the 18th Day of May,'" *South Carolina Gazette*, April 22, 1774.

the newspaper advertisement listed his law books, riding chair, and "Negroes, &c." to be sold to the highest bidder.[59]

Smart estate executors understood that the fastest way to sell law books was to go where lawyers could be found: the courthouse. Following the death of Virginian George Davenport in 1766, executors advertised two methods by which a "choice collection of law books" would be sold. Purchasers could approach his widow Katherine to make a private sale, but they should hurry; any books still in her hands after three months would be auctioned at the October 30 assembly of the General Court, when lawyers from across Virginia would gather in Williamsburg. In colonies with few large urban areas, savvy executors took advantage of assemblies to draw additional bidders together and get the highest prices. New Jersey native V. Pearse Ashfield (b. 1738), executor for the late Lewis Morris Ashfield (c. 1723/4–1769), adopted the same strategy: the law books would be auctioned off at the next sitting of the New Jersey Supreme Court, in Perth-Amboy.[60]

Auction catalogs from the colonial period remain relatively rare. Those that have survived to the modern period primarily include religious texts, such as those from Boston in 1717 and 1718, describing libraries owned by Ebenezer Pemberton, George Curwin, and Joshua Moodey.[61] Individuals who intended to bid at an auction would acquire a catalog prior to the sale. That allowed them to gauge their interest in spending money early or late at the event, which might stretch over several days. They might also decide whether attending was worth their time or not based on the catalog contents. Typically, catalogs were available where the auction would happen, or at the home or store of a person related to the original collector. Peter Robertson, attempting to sell his father-in-law Peter Evans's (d. 1745) collection of law books, made catalogs of the

59 "Advertisement, 'New-York, July 17, 1758. To Be Sold at Publick-Vendue,'" *New-York Gazette, or Weekly Post-Boy*, July 17, 1758, 17.

60 "Advertisement, 'To Be Sold at Public Vendue, at Perth-Amboy,'" *New-York Gazette and Weekly Mercury*, August 27, 1770.

61 *A catalogue of curious and valuable books, belonging to the late reverend & learned, Mr. Ebenezer Pemberton, consisting of divinity, philosophy, history, poetry, &c. Generally well bound, to be sold by auction, at the Crown Coffee-House in Boston, the second day of July 1717* (Boston: B. Green, 1717), Evans 1921; *A catalogue of curious and valuable books, (which mostly belonged to the Reverend Mr. George Curwin, late of Salem, deceased) consisting of divinity, philosophy, history, poetry, &c.* (Boston: J. Franklin, 1717), Evans 1953; *A catalogue of rare and valuable books, being the greatest part of the library of the late Reverend and learned, Mr. Joshua Moodey, and part of the library of the Reverend & learned, Mr. Daniel Gookin, late of Sherbourn, deceas'd* (Boston: Samuel Kneeland, 1718), Evans 1984.

Evans books available at his Philadelphia store.[62] A Providence Rhode Island sheriff, selling law books at public auction in 1773 to satisfy a debt, indicated that he had only one catalog, which could be seen at his home by interested parties.[63]

Auctions (with or without catalogs) merited repeated coverage in colonial newspapers for good reason. So long as the arrival of new law books remained uncertain (given the vagaries of trans-Atlantic shipping), customers paid attention to advertisements for used goods. Ads for auctions that mentioned law books—without any titles given—appeared first in the *Boston News-Letter* in 1718, following the death of merchant Grove Hirst. His collection of "Divinity, History, Law, [and] Poetry" books was auctioned off by bookseller Samuel Gerrish (c. 1680–1741), following a week on display to the public.[64] A far larger collection of law books went under the auctioneer's gavel three years later when Thomas Newton (1660–1721), legal practitioner in Massachusetts and New York, died in 1721. Newton studied law in England and became New York attorney general during the brief Dominion of New England regime (1686–1689). A September newspaper advertisement offered details about Newton's Boston legal collection. Interested customers could either collect a catalog or personally examine the law books, "being the greatest and best Collection of Law Books that ever was exposed to Sale in the Country," for two weeks prior to the sale. Individuals wishing to purchase books from Newton's library were informed that "Catalogs may be had gratis at the said House."[65] The auction was held at his widow's downtown Boston home on Queen Street "opposite to the Prison."[66]

In Charleston, auction catalogs described two extremely large legal libraries auctioned off in 1757 and 1761. The *South-Carolina Gazette* carried advertisements from printer and bookseller Robert Wells (1728–1794) that he would auction the "entire library of that learned and able lawyer, the late honourable Andrew Rutledge, Esq." (1709–1755) from 6 to 8 p.m., complete with a catalog of the available books.[67] Four years later, the "very complete collection of Law,

62 "Advertisement, 'To Be Sold by Publick Vendue, on Friday the 31st Day of This Inst. July,'" *Pennsylvania Gazette*, July 16, 1747.

63 "Advertisement, 'Notice Is Hereby Given,'" *Providence Gazette*, August 28, 1773.

64 "Advertisement, 'A Valuable Collection of Books,'" *Boston News-Letter*, May 26, 1718.

65 "Advertisement, 'To Be Sold by Auction upon the Third Tuesday of October Next,'" *Boston News-Letter*, September 18, 1721.

66 "Advertisement, 'To Be Sold by Auction upon the Third Tuesday of October Next,'" *Boston News-Letter*, September 18, 1721.

67 "Advertisement, 'To Be Sold at Auction, at the Usual Place in Eliott Street, by Robert Wells,'" *South-Carolina Gazette*, March 3, 1757.

civil, statute, and common" belonging to the deceased Chief Justice James Michie (d. 1760) went under the gavel. Again, Wells offered bidders a catalog and a late afternoon sale between 4 and 7 p.m. Among lawyers whose estates were inventoried, Michie's law library was the second largest in South Carolina's colonial era, valued at £1120; Rutledge's was the sixth largest, at £340.[68] In other colonies, book auctions including law texts remained relatively rare until the 1760s, then flourished in the second half of the century.

Notices of library auctions in colonial America might give the name of the deceased individual, like Newton, Rutledge, or Michie, along with some details about the library and other property to be sold. The advertisement typically indicated the time, date, and location of the sale and the terms of sale (e.g., cash only), but might not include how many volumes would be available or list specific titles. Following Jeremiah Gridley's (1702–1767) death, J. Russell (active 1760s–1770s) placed an advertisement in the *Boston Evening-Post* notifying the public when Gridley's books would be sold. In Gridley's case, the contents of his library merited a separate advertisement from the sale of his home and land in Brookline. Auctioneer Russell sold the books in February 1768, while Gridley's land was sold later that year.[69] An auction of John Bassnett's (1683–1761) estate in May 1761 prompted Charleston auctioneer Thomas Legare (active 1760–1774) to list *Wood's Institutes* specifically, in between Bassnett's two houses and "30 valuable slaves." It is one of the very few estate sale notices to include a specific book title.[70]

On occasion, an auction of law books might be prompted by reasons other than insolvency or a lawyer's death. In 1753, Charles Pinckney (1699–1758) advertised that he intended to leave Charleston for a trip to London in a month's time. Prior to his departure, he offered to rent his town house and his country plantation, rent many of his enslaved men and women who had particular skills, and completely dispose of his library which consisted chiefly of "law and history."[71] Pinckney, whom some consider the first native-born lawyer to practice in South Carolina, had been appointed as colonial agent by

68 Edgar, "Notable Libraries," 107.

69 "Advertisement, 'On Thursday the 2d of February Next,'" *Boston Evening-Post*, January 25, 1768; "Advertisement, 'To Be Sold, A House in Good Repair,'" *Boston Evening-Post*, February 22, 1768; "Advertisement, 'To Be Sold, by Order of the Superior Court, the Real Estate in Brookline,'" *Boston Evening-Post*, April 25, 1768.

70 "Advertisement, 'To Be Sold on Wednesday the 27th of May, at the House Where Mr. John Bassnett, Diseased, Lately Lived in King Street,'" *South Carolina Gazette*, April 25, 1761.

71 "Advertisement, 'The Subscriber Intending to Embark for Great-Britain, Sometime in April Next,'" *South-Carolina Gazette*, January 29, 1753.

the governor and council and would be leaving Charleston for some time.[72] His original intention was to remain in London for three years, after which he would return to Charleston. Already in his mid-fifties, Pinckney likely realized that he would not practice law upon returning to Carolina. Moreover, he had amassed significant wealth through nearly twenty years of legal practice and two fortunate marriages, so he did not need to resume practice, whenever he returned. His decision to sell the law books seems prescient: his three-year absence in London kept getting extended, and when Pinckney returned five years later, he soon died from malaria.[73]

Auctioneers acted in concert with others to restore large libraries prior to selling them off, even for men still alive. When the *Boston News-Letter* advertised the library of lawyer William Bollan (c. 1710–1776) for sale in 1765, auctioneer J. Russell described the "great number of BOOKS wrote by the best Authors in Law" that would be included. In 1765, Bollan had lived in England for twenty years but was out of work, having been replaced as colonial agent (1745–1762) for the Massachusetts government three years earlier. Needing funds to sustain him in London and not having practiced law since the 1740s, Bollan had concluded his law library constituted a disposable asset. Below Russell's ad, Bollan's friend pleaded that "If any gentleman has borrowed any of Mr. Bollan's books, he is desired to return them to Nathaniel Hatch, Esq." Recapturing loaned books would raise the largest amount of money at an auction.[74] Law books also went under the auctioneer's gavel when early American merchants who sold them went out of business, died, or decided to recoup some capital through a sale. After Boston bookseller Thomas Leverett died in 1778, the contents of his store were auctioned, including a "valuable collection of Books." Law, divinity, and history were invariably mentioned in ads such as these.[75] Nicholas Langford's (d. 1778) 1770 advertisement in Charleston was quite precise about what books he was selling off at reduced prices: expensive sets that had been gathering dust. The "Modern Universal History" at

72 Edward McCrady, *The History of South Carolina under the Royal Government, 1719–1776* (New York: Macmillan, 1899), 279, 281.

73 Walter B. Edgar and N. Louise Bailey, eds., *Biographical Directory of the South Carolina House of Representatives. Volume II: The Commons House of Assembly 1692–1775* (Columbia: University of South Carolina Press, 1977), 521.

74 "Advertisement, 'Boston, August 15, 1765, To Be Sold by Auction,'" *Boston News-Letter*, August 15, 1765; "Advertisement, 'New-York, July 17, 1758. To Be Sold at Publick-Vendue.'"

75 "Advertisement, 'To Be Sold by Public Auction, on Wednesday the 20th Current,'" *Boston Gazette*, May 18, 1778.

thirty-five volumes clearly needed to go, as did Blackstone's "*Commentaries on the Law*, 4 vols., *new*."[76]

Who purchased books at colonial auctions can only be surmised, but bidders were likely individuals with disposable wealth, a professional interest in the subject matter—such as lawyers buying law books—or an emotional attachment to the deceased or the deceased's books. When Jeremiah Gridley died, John Adams (1735–1826) purchased several of Gridley's law books at auction, among them the first law book that Gridley lent him, a copy of Johannes van Muyden's abridgment of Justinian's *Institutes*. The flyleaf of the book reveals that Adams was at least the third owner of the book; before Gridley, a "Jo: Campbell" had owned the abridgment.[77] Previously owned books were often advertised for sale by condition, as in a Charleston auction that mentioned "some second-hand law books."[78] Advertising that books had had more than one owner served as a warning that bindings might be worn or pages dog-eared.

Auctioneers sometimes grouped together law books from multiple sources into a single sale. Philadelphian William Dunlap (c. 1730–1779) not only sold books when an estate was to be liquidated; Dunlap actively advertised for used books that he could auction by putting books together from various sellers. "Those who have any second-hand books to dispose of, are desired to send them as soon as possible to said DUNLAP, that they may be properly numbered and disposed for the said Auction."[79] Philadelphian Robert Bell, printer of the American edition of Blackstone's *Commentaries*, followed the same practice. Bell sought out collections, drawing in libraries like William Byrd's from Virginia, for sale in Philadelphia. He turned book auctions into spectacles, cracking jokes, drinking beer, and bidding up sales, sometimes to higher prices than he regularly charged for the same items in his bookstore. As unorthodox as his methods seemed, Bell rarely sold at a loss and he made Philadelphia a hub for book auctions before and during the American Revolution.[80]

---

76 "Advertisement, 'To Be Sold, by Auction, on Wednesday the 19th,'" *South Carolina Gazette; and Country Journal*, December 4, 1770 (emphasis in the original).

77 John Adams, *The Adams Papers: The Earliest Diary of John Adams, June 1753–April 1754, September 1758–January 1759* (Cambridge, MA: Belknap Press of Harvard University Press, 1966), xii.

78 "Advertisement, 'To Be Sold, by Auction, on Friday the 18th,'" *South-Carolina Gazette*, November 14, 1768.

79 "Advertisement, 'William Dunlap and Co. Proposes to Open an Auction of Books,'" *Pennsylvania Journal and Weekly Advertiser*, November 3, 1763.

80 Carl Bridenbaugh, "The Press and the Book in Eighteenth Century Philadelphia," *Pennsylvania Magazine of History and Biography* 65, no. 1 (1941): 16.

The demand for English law books was nearly unquenchable in eighteenth-century British America: Edmund Burke (1729–1797) reportedly remarked in 1775 that he had been told "by an eminent Bookseller, that in no branch of his business, after tracts of popular devotion, were so many books as those on law exported to the Plantations."[81] Yet that wealth of law books was spread unevenly: the absence of legal texts that impoverished law student and novice practitioner John Adams experienced in the late 1750s and early 1760s[82] only became worse in wartime.[83] During the War for Independence, auctions of law books continued, driven by the need for hard cash as well as the scarcity of law texts. The situation deteriorated in Boston, Philadelphia, and Charleston when those seaports experienced military occupation. British soldiers burned or looted private libraries, but worse was yet to come. As loyalists decamped, whether legislators, judges, or lawyers, they packed up their law libraries and took the books with them. The impact of loyalist flight was devastating for those who relied upon borrowing legal texts, another means by which lawyers gleaned knowledge from books they did not personally own.

The study of newspaper advertisements about law books provides insights into how much law attorneys might actually know when they entered a courtroom, as well as the movement of books and book reselling. Presumptions about the amateurish quality of legal arguments in the colonies have pervaded many analyses of this period, not reckoning with the presence, use, and availability of such texts. It becomes clear from examining newspaper ads that many lawyers had ready access to new and used English legal texts, including abridgments, treatises, and law reporters. A vibrant resale market existed, driven—somewhat morbidly—by auctions of dead lawyers' libraries. Advertisements for law books might draw individuals from near and far to booksellers, auction rooms, or sites as odd as an apothecary shop. Further exploration of these advertisements, in conjunction with records maintained by booksellers in London and booksellers in North America, will continue to expand what we know about the availability and marketing of law books in early America.

---

81 Wolf, *Book Culture of a Colonial American City*, 131.

82 John Adams autobiography, 1758–1761, part 1, sheet 7 of 53 [electronic edition], via *Adams Family Papers: An Electronic Archive*, Massachusetts Historical Society (accessed January 11, 2014), https://www.masshist.org/digitaladams/archive/autobio/.

83 "I suffered very much for Want of Books, which determined me to furnish myself, at any Sacrifice, with a proper Library: and Accordingly by degrees I procured the best [*illegible*] Library of Law in the State." John Adams autobiography, 1758, part 1, available via *Adams Family Papers: An Electronic Archive*, Massachusetts Historical Society (accessed December 9, 2021), https://www.masshist.org/digitaladams/archive/autobio/.

Acknowledgments

I am delighted to thank Jeffrey Mark Joslin (M.A., 2019) and Nora Hafez (M.A., 2022), graduate students of the History Department at Western Michigan University, whose research efforts made this essay easier to complete. Thanks also to John D. Gordan III, who read and commented upon it. References to specific newspapers were drawn from the following databases: Accessible Archives (https://www.accessible-archives.com/) for all Charleston newspapers and *Pennsylvania Gazette*; America's Historical Newspapers for all others (https://www.readex.com/products/americas-historical-newspapers).

Bibliography

Adams, John. *The Adams Papers: The Earliest Diary of John Adams, June 1753–April 1754, September 1758–January 1759*. Cambridge, MA: Belknap Press of Harvard University, 1966.

Adams, John. The Autobiography, 1758–1761, part 1, sheet 7 of 53 [electronic edition]. via *Adams Family Papers: An Electronic Archive.* Massachusetts Historical Society. Accessed January 11, 2014. https://www.masshist.org/digitaladams/archive/autobio/.

American Weekly Mercury. "Proposals for Re-Printing the Laws of the Province of New-Jersey." December 22, 1730.

Baker, J. H. *An Introduction to English Legal History*. 4th ed. Oxford: Oxford University Press, 2002.

Bilder, Mary Sarah. *The Transatlantic Constitution: Colonial Legal Culture and the Empire*. Cambridge, MA: Harvard University Press, 2004.

Billings, Warren M. "'Send Us ... What Other Lawe Books You Shall Thinke Fitt': Books That Shaped the Law in Virginia, 1600–1860." *Virginia Magazine of History and Biography* 120, no. 4 (2012): 314–39.

Billings, Warren M., and Brent Tarter, eds. *"Esteemed Bookes of Lawe" and the Legal Culture of Early Virginia*. Charlottesville: University of Virginia Press, 2017.

Boston Evening-Post. "Advertisement, 'On Thursday the 2d of February Next.'" January 25, 1768.

Boston Evening-Post. "Advertisement, 'To Be Sold, A House in Good Repair.'" February 22, 1768.

Boston Evening-Post. "Advertisement, 'To Be Sold, by Order of the Superior Court, the Real Estate in Brookline.'" April 25, 1768.

Boston Evening-Post. "Advertisement, 'To Be Sold by Publick Venue or Auction.'" March 6, 1738.

Boston Gazette. "Advertisement, 'Just Imported, and Sold by John and Thomas Leverett.'" June 30, 1752.

Boston Gazette. "Advertisement, 'To Be Sold by Public Auction, on Wednesday the 20th Current.'" May 18, 1778.

Boston News-Letter. "Advertisement, 'A Valuable Collection of Books.'" May 26, 1718.

Boston News-Letter. "Advertisement, 'Boston, August 15, 1765, To Be Sold by Auction.'" August 15, 1765.

Boston News-Letter. "Advertisement, 'To Be Sold by Auction upon the Third Tuesday of October Next.'" September 18, 1721.

Boston News-Letter. "The Charter Granted to the Province of the Massachusetts-Bay and the Laws of the Said Province Compleat." March 30, 1713, 467 edition.

Bridenbaugh, Carl. "The Press and the Book in Eighteenth Century Philadelphia." *Pennsylvania Magazine of History and Biography* 65, no. 1 (1941): 1–30.

Bryson, W. Hamilton. *Census of Law Books in Colonial Virginia*. Charlottesville: University Press of Virginia, 1978.

Bryson, W. Hamilton. "Private Law Libraries Before 1776." In *Virginia Law Books: Essays and Bibliographies*, edited by W. Hamilton Bryson, 479–99. Philadelphia: American Philosophical Society, 2000.

Bullen, A. H. "Jacob, Giles." In *Dictionary of National Biography*, edited by Leslie Stephen and Sidney Lee, vol. 10, 553. New York: Macmillan, 1892.

Butler, Charles, ed. *The First Part of the Institutes of the Laws of England, or, A Commentary upon Littleton: Not the Name of the Author Only, but of the Law Itself: … Authore Edwardo Coke, Milite. Revised and Corrected, with Further Additions of Notes, References, and Proper Tables, by Francis Hargrave and Charles Butler, Esqrs. of Lincoln's Inn, Including Also the Notes of Lord Chief Justice Hale and Lord Chancellor Nottingham; and an Analysis of Littleton*. 1st American ed., from The 19th London ed. 2 vols. Philadelphia: Robert Small, 1853.

A catalogue of curious and valuable books, belonging to the late reverend & learned, Mr. Ebenezer Pemberton, consisting of divinity, philosophy, history, poetry, &c. Generally well bound, to be sold by auction, at the Crown Coffee-House in Boston, the second day of July 1717. Boston: B. Green, 1717. Evans 1921.

A catalogue of curious and valuable books, (which mostly belonged to the Reverend Mr. George Curwin, late of Salem, deceased) consisting of divinity, philosophy, history, poetry, &c. Boston: J. Franklin, 1717. Evans 1953.

A catalogue of rare and valuable books, being the greatest part of the library of the late Reverend and learned, Mr. Joshua Moodey, and part of the library of the Reverend & learned, Mr. Daniel Gookin, late of Sherbourn, deceas'd. Boston: Samuel Kneeland, 1718. Evans 1984.

The Charter Granted by Their Majesties King William and Queen Mary, to the Inhabitants of the Province of the Massachusetts-Bay in New-England. Boston: Benjamin Eliot, 1714.

Cohen, Morris L., ed. *Bibliography of Early American Law*. 6 vols. Buffalo NY: William S. Hein, 1998.

Cohen, Morris L. "Legal Literature in Colonial Massachusetts." In *Law in Colonial Massachusetts*, edited by Daniel R. Coquillette, 243–72. Boston: Colonial Society of Massachusetts, 1984.

Connecticut Gazette. "Advertisement, 'To Be Published, When There Shall Appear, a Sufficient Number of Subscribers.'" February 6, 1762.

Edgar, Walter B. "Notable Libraries of Colonial South Carolina." *South Carolina Historical Magazine* 72, no. 2 (1971): 105–10.

Edgar, Walter B., and N. Louise Bailey, eds. *Biographical Directory of the South Carolina House of Representatives. Volume II: The Commons House of Assembly 1692–1775*. Columbia: University of South Carolina Press, 1977.

Fernandez, Angela, and Markus D. Dubber, eds. *Law Books in Action: Essays on the Anglo-American Legal Treatise*. Oxford: Hart Publishing, 2012.

Franklin, Benjamin. "Advertisement, 'Books Sold by Benjamin Franklin, near the Market, in Philadelphia.'" *Pennsylvania Gazette*, January 7, 1742.

Franklin, Benjamin. "Book Advertisement, 'Books Sold by B. Franklin.'" *Pennsylvania Gazette*, August 12, 1742.

Franklin, Benjamin. *A catalogue of choice and valuable books, consisting of near 600 volumes, in most faculties and sciences, viz. divinity, history, law, mathematics, philosophy, physic, poetry, &c. Which will begin to be sold for ready money, only, by Benj. Franklin, at the Post-Office in Philadelphia, on Wednesday, the 11th of April 1744*. Philadelphia: Franklin, 1744. Evans 5396.

Georgia Gazette. "Advertisement, 'Catalogue of Books to Be Sold at the Printing-Office.'" November 10, 1763.

Georgia Gazette. "Advertisement, 'Just Imported, and to Be Sold by James Johnston.'" June 21, 1764.

Gordan III, John D. "John Nutt: Publisher and Printer 'In the Savoy.'" *The Library, Transactions of the Bibliographical Society*, 7th ser., 15, no. 3 (2014): 243–60.

Hadden, Sally E. "Early American Governors' Councils, Their Judicial Functions, and Changing Constitutional Perceptions of Their Duties." Paper presented at the American Society for Legal History annual meeting, New Orleans, 2021.

Hartford Courant. "Advertisement, 'Lathrop and Smith, Druggist and Apothecary.'" August 10, 1767.

Hoeflich, Michael. "Legal History and the History of the Book: Variations on a Theme." *University of Kansas Law Review* 46, no. 3 (1988): 415–31.

Howard-Hill, T. H. *The British Book Trade, 1475–1890: A Bibliography*. 2 vols. London: British Library and Oak Knoll Press, 2008.

Jacob, Giles. *Every Man His Own Lawyer: Or, A Summary of the Laws of England in a New and Instructive Method ...* . 4th ed. London: Henry Lintot, 1750.

Jacob, Giles. *Every Man His Own Lawyer: Or, A Summary of the Laws of England, in a New and Instructive Method, under the Following Heads ….* New York: Hugh Gaine, 1768.

Lathem, Edward C. *Chronological Tables of American Newspapers, 1690–1820.* Worcester: American Antiquarian Society, 1972.

McCrady, Edward. *The History of South Carolina under the Royal Government, 1719–1776.* New York: Macmillan, 1899.

Monti, Annamaria. "Popular Legal Manuals as Sources and Mechanisms of Acquiring Legal Literacy." In *Legal Literacy in Premodern European Societies,* edited by Mia Korpiola, 191–210. Switzerland: Palgrave MacMillan, 2019.

New York Gazette. "Advertisement, 'To Be Sold, a Choice and Valuable Collection.'" May 8, 1738.

New-Hampshire Gazette. "Advertisement, 'Books and Stationary for Sale by J. Melcher.'" July 19, 1792.

New-Hampshire Gazette. "Advertisement, 'Catalogue of Books Continued, Sold by the Printer of This Paper.'" October 28, 1756.

New-York Gazette. "Rivington and Brown, Booksellers and Stationers." November 8, 1762.

New-York Gazette and Weekly Mercury. "Advertisement, 'To Be Sold at Public Vendue, at Perth-Amboy.'" August 27, 1770.

New-York Gazette, or Weekly Post-Boy. "Advertisement, 'Books for Sale, Imported from London, in the Last Ships.'" September 12, 1748.

New-York Gazette, or Weekly Post-Boy. "Advertisement, 'New-York, July 17, 1758. To Be Sold at Publick-Vendue.'" July 17, 1758.

Parrish, Jenni. "Law Books and Legal Publishing in America, 1760–1840." *Law Library Journal* 72 (1979): 355–452.

Pennsylvania Gazette. "Advertisement, 'A List of the Late Joseph Scattergood's Books Remaining Unsold at Burlington.'" March 18, 1755.

Pennsylvania Gazette. "Advertisement, 'A List of the Late Joseph Scattergood's Books Remaining Unsold at Burlington.'" March 25, 1755.

Pennsylvania Gazette. "Advertisement, 'Benj. Franklin, Printer, Is Just Removed.'" January 18, 1739.

Pennsylvania Gazette. "Advertisement, 'Just Imported and To Be Sold by B. Franklin.'" May 25, 1738.

Pennsylvania Gazette. "Advertisement, 'Just Imported from London, and to Be Sold by Tench Francis, Jun.'" July 18, 1754.

Pennsylvania Gazette. "Advertisement, 'To Be Sold by Peter Robertson, in Front-Street, Philadelphia.'" March 16, 1747.

Pennsylvania Gazette. "Advertisement, 'To Be Sold by Publick Vendue, on Friday the 31st Day of This Inst. July.'" July 16, 1747.

Pennsylvania Journal and Weekly Advertiser. "Advertisement, 'William Dunlap and Co. Proposes to Open an Auction of Books.'" November 3, 1763.

Pennsylvania Journal and Weekly Advertiser. "Tench Francis, Jun. at His Store in Front Street." November 20, 1755.

Pennsylvania Packet. "Advertisement, 'William Laplain, at His Book-Store in Market-Street, Opposite the London Coffee-House, Has for Sale, An Assortment of Useful and Scarce Books, in Most Sciences, among Which Are.'" November 30, 1772.

Phillips, F. Peter. "Ancient and Comely Order: The Use and Disuse of Arbitration by New York Quakers." *Journal of Dispute Resolution* 2016 (2016): 81–114.

Pope, Alexander. *The Dunciad*. Dublin, 1728.

Providence Gazette. "Advertisement, 'Just Imported from London, via Boston, and to Be Sold.'" September 12, 1767.

Providence Gazette. "Advertisement, 'Notice Is Hereby Given.'" August 28, 1773.

Reilly, Elizabeth, and David D. Hall. "Customers and the Market for Books." In *The Colonial Book in the Atlantic World*, edited by Hugh Amory and David D. Hall, 387–99. Cambridge: Cambridge University Press, 2000.

Rivington, James, and Samuel Brown. *A catalogue of books, sold by Rivington and Brown, booksellers and stationers from London, at their stores, over against the Golden Key, in Hanover-Square, New-York: and over against the London Coffee-House, in Philadelphia*. Philadelphia: Heinrich Miller, 1762. Evans 9259.

Rivington's New York Gazetteer. "Advertisement, 'Addition to J. Rivington's First Published List of Law Books.'" October 14, 1773.

Rivington's New York Gazetteer. "Advertisement, 'The Sons of Science in America.'" May 27, 1773.

Rivington's New York Gazetteer. "Advertisement, 'To the Gentlemen of the Law, A Large Library of Second Hand Reports.'" August 19, 1773.

Rudolph, Julia. "That 'Blunderbuss' of Law: Giles Jacob, Abridgment, and Print Culture." *Studies in Eighteenth-Century Culture* 37 (2008): 197–215.

South Carolina Gazette. "Advertisement, 'On Wednesday next, under the New Market House, Is to Be Sold.'" March 3, 1733.

South Carolina Gazette. "Advertisement, 'To Be Sold at Auction, by Charles Crouch.'" June 14, 1768.

South Carolina Gazette. "Advertisement, 'To Be Sold at Publick Vendue, on Wednesday the 18th Day of May.'" April 22, 1774.

South Carolina Gazette. "Advertisement, 'To Be Sold on Wednesday the 27th of May, at the House Where Mr. John Bassnett, Diseased, Lately Lived in King Street.'" April 25, 1761.

South Carolina Gazette. "Book Advertisement Listing for Sale Law Concerning Masters & Servants." April 15, 1732.

South Carolina Gazette; and Country Journal. "Advertisement, 'To Be Sold, by Auction, on Wednesday the 19th.'" December 4, 1770.

South-Carolina Gazette. "Advertisement, 'The Subscriber Intending to Embark for Great-Britain, Sometime in April Next.'" January 29, 1753.

South-Carolina Gazette. "Advertisement, 'To Be Sold at Auction, at the Usual Place in Eliott Street, by Robert Wells.'" March 3, 1757.

South-Carolina Gazette. "Advertisement, 'To Be Sold, by Auction, on Friday the 18th.'" November 14, 1768.

Tomlins, Christopher. "Commentary: Effects of Scale: Toward a History of the Literature of Law." In *Law Books in Action: Essays on the Anglo-American Legal Treatise*, edited by Angela Fernandez and Markus D. Dubber, 220–42. Oxford: Hart Publishing, 2012.

Viner, Charles. *A General Abridgment of Law and Equity*. 23 vols. Aldershot: Viner, 1741.

Virginia. *The Lawes of Virginia Now in Force*. London: E. Cotes, 1662.

Virginia Gazette. "Advertisement, 'Edenton, North Carolina, February 15, 1777, To Be Sold.'" March 7, 1777.

Der Wahre Amerikaner. "Advertisement, 'For Sale at This Office.'" November 1, 1806.

Widener, Michael. "From Law Book to Legal Book: The Origin of a Species." *Rechtsgeschichte-Legal History* 29 (2021): 431–44.

Winton, Calhoun. "The Southern Book Trade in the Eighteenth Century." In *The Colonial Book in the Atlantic World*, edited by Hugh Amory and David D. Hall, 224–46. Cambridge: American Antiquarian Society, Cambridge University Press, 2000.

Wolf, Edwin, 2nd. *Book Culture of a Colonial American City: Philadelphia Books, Bookmen, and Booksellers*. Oxford: Clarendon Press, 1988.

CHAPTER 18

The American Importation of the Comparative Accusatorial/Inquisitorial Divide: Francis Lieber's Failed Transplant and Its Early Twentieth-Century Resurgence

Amalia D. Kessler

When and why did American lawyers and jurists begin to deploy the terms "adversarial" (or as those in the civil law world prefer, "accusatorial") and "inquisitorial" to compare across procedural systems? As I have explored elsewhere, the use of the accusatorial/inquisitorial terminology for purposes of comparative procedural analysis first emerged in continental Europe—in Italy and Germany, and soon thereafter in France—during the 1830s.[1] But how did it come to be absorbed within the American legal lexicon? And how did its usage relate to the longstanding Anglo-American discourse distinguishing between the English common law and the Roman-canon civil law traditions?

It was in the wake of the 1815 restoration that the accusatorial/inquisitorial divide first developed in Europe as a comparative framing device. After the final French defeat, emerging nation-states—especially Italy and Germany—debated the extent to which to retain French law (including criminal procedure) and whether to return to the old regime order or instead pursue some degree of liberalization. In this context, contemporary debates over constitutional politics and criminal procedure became intertwined in the struggle to define national identity. More particularly, the contrast between accusatorial and inquisitorial modes of procedure became a shorthand for distinguishing between liberty-promoting (possibly democratic) procedures and constitutional structures, on the one hand, and monarchical (possibly authoritarian) procedures and constitutional structures, on the other.[2]

That the terms "accusatorial" and "inquisitorial" were not previously deployed for comparative purposes does not, of course, mean that they were

1 Amalia D. Kessler, "Toward an Account of the Nineteenth-Century Emergence of the Comparative Accusatorial/Inquisitorial Divide," *American Journal of Comparative Law* 71 (2023): 296–327. All translations in this chapter are my own, unless otherwise noted.

2 Kessler, "Toward an Account," 296–327.

 DOI:10.1163/9789004710696_020

theretofore unknown. The distinction between the two terms first arose around the twelfth and thirteenth centuries, on the heels of the rediscovery of Roman law, as a means of differentiating between two types of criminal procedure that might be applied within a given legal system. While accusatorial proceedings were initiated through the accusation of a private complainant, inquisitorial proceedings were commenced on the basis of a judicial investigation and prosecution.[3] It was, however, only in the nineteenth century that these terms came to be deployed as a means of comparing across legal systems, including especially those of the continental European Roman-canon law, on the one hand, and the English common law, on the other.[4]

Since it developed in Europe in the 1830s, we might imagine that this comparative framework was quickly embraced by American lawyers. After all, this was a period of U.S. history that was marked by extensive debates over procedure. Moreover, as I have argued elsewhere, these debates were framed around the question of the purported virtues and vices of lawyer-driven, oral and public procedures—precisely the kind that would come to be characterized as "accusatorial." As the United States struggled to address the challenges posed by radical economic transformations and embarked on postbellum Reconstruction, those who sought to deploy state power to temper perceived market excesses and to promote racial justice embraced various forms of judge-controlled, written and secret procedure, of the type that would later be termed (more or less) "inquisitorial." But ultimately, by the close of Reconstruction, those insisting on the merits of the common law's lawyer-controlled, oral and public procedures proved triumphant, successfully depicting these as a necessary foundation of an exceptionalist American identity, defined by a distinctive commitment to liberty and laissez-faire—one that placed significant limits on the uses of state power.[5]

As this brief overview suggests, there were important parallels between nineteenth-century procedural debates in Europe and the United States, including not least a shared tendency to frame key questions of national political identity in terms of the choice between lawyer- and judge-controlled

3 Kenneth Pennington, "The Jurisprudence of Procedure," in *The History of Courts and Procedure in Medieval Canon Law*, ed. Wilfried Hartmann and Kenneth Pennington (Washington, DC: The Catholic University of America Press, 2016), 125–59; Richard Vogler, *A World View of Criminal Justice* (Aldershot: Ashgate, 2005), 23–32.

4 Kessler, "Toward an Account," 299–300; Máximo Langer, "The Long Shadow of the Adversarial and Inquisitorial Categories," in *The Oxford Handbook of Criminal Law*, ed. Markus D. Dubber and Tajana Hörnle (Oxford: Oxford University Press, 2014), 889–92.

5 Amalia D. Kessler, *Inventing American Exceptionalism: The Origins of American Adversarial Legal Culture, 1800–1877* (New Haven: Yale University Press, 2017).

procedural forms. We might thus expect that nineteenth-century Americans would readily embrace the comparative distinction between accusatorial and inquisitorial procedure as a means of framing their own debates. But with the exception of Francis Lieber, whose work I discuss below, this was not, in fact, the case. American procedural debates were framed instead in terms of the distinction between the English common law and the Roman-canon civil law.[6]

As Máximo Langer observes, a discourse extolling the unique virtues of the common law vis-à-vis the civil law dates back at least as far as the writings of the fifteenth-century jurist John Fortescue.[7] It then came to flourish during the seventeenth-century English Revolution, when it was further developed and refined so as to highlight the liberty-promoting nature of the common law, in contrast to the supposedly monarchical tendencies of the Roman-canon civil law. In this period, parliamentarians joined with the common-law courts to lambast the monarchy and its courts of equity, asserting that the latter were rooted in the alien (and "papist") tradition of the civil law. Thereafter, this rhetoric of common-law exceptionalism reemerged during the American Revolution, as the new country sought to distance itself from the British monarchy. Accordingly, when nineteenth-century American lawyers and jurists engaged in procedural debate—including, not least, over whether to preserve and expand courts of equity—it was to this readily available rhetoric that they turned.[8]

That nineteenth-century Americans continued to rely on the common law/civil law divide, rather than embracing the distinction between accusatorial and inquisitorial procedure, may have been due, at least in part, to the fact that these American debates were focused on civil procedure, whereas the emerging accusatorial/inquisitorial divide was framed around criminal procedure. Indeed, as discussed below, when Americans did at last adopt the accusatorial/inquisitorial terminology in the early twentieth century, they applied it to debates over criminal procedure as well as administrative procedure (a much-contested category whose boundaries did not seem to fall neatly within

6 Kessler, *Inventing American Exceptionalism*, 40–47, 116–18, 216–21.

7 Máximo Langer, "In the Beginning Was Fortescue: On the Intellectual Origins of the Adversarial and Inquisitorial Systems and Common and Civil Law in Comparative Criminal Procedure," in *Visions of Justice: Liber Amicorum Mirjan Damaška*, ed. Bruce Ackerman, Kai Ambos, and Hrvoje Sikirić (Berlin: Duncker & Humblot, 2016), 280–96.

8 Kessler, *Inventing*, 19, 24–25, 40–43; D. E. C. Yale, introduction to *Lord Nottingham's Manual of Chancery Practice and Prolegomena of Chancery and Equity*, ed. D. E. C. Yale (Cambridge: Cambridge University Press, 1965), 7–8; Louis A. Knafla, *Law and Politics in Jacobean England: The Tracts of Lord Chancellor Ellesmere* (Cambridge: Cambridge University Press, 1977), 162–63.

the traditional civil/criminal divide). But as noted, there was one nineteenth-century American jurist who did make use of this terminology: the German-born Francis Lieber (1798–1872). The accusatorial/inquisitorial framework made an initial, though very limited appearance in the second volume of his *Manual of Political Ethics*, published in 1839.[9] Lieber fully introduced the concept to his American readers in his highly influential 1853 publication, *On Civil Liberty and Self-Government*.[10] There, he used the framework in ways very much in line with American lawyers' contemporary efforts to expound an exceptionalist, liberty-oriented national identity—namely, as a means of asserting a distinctively American, liberty-promoting approach to criminal procedure (and, relatedly, to politics). But while Lieber's book proved to be enormously successful and was in fact adopted for generations as a leading college textbook, the accusatorial/inquisitorial terminology would not enter the American legal lexicon until the close of the first decade of the twentieth century.[11]

In the following pages, I examine Lieber's attempted transplant of the comparative accusatorial/inquisitorial framework and inquire into the interrelation between this imported terminology, on the one hand, and the native and deep-rooted common law/civil law distinction, on the other. Although Lieber's effort to import the European terminology did not bear fruit during his own lifetime, his melding of these two modes of comparative discourse would prove prescient, foreshadowing the writings of the early twentieth-century American lawyers who ultimately succeeded where he had failed. The end result was subtly, but significantly, to reframe the meaning of accusatorialism (or as it would later be called, adversarialism), presenting it as all but synonymous with Anglo-American modes of procedure (or indeed, American procedure tout court), rather than as a broader procedural type encompassing, but not limited to, its Anglo-American sub-types.

Given the brief span of these pages, the history that I sketch below is necessarily of limited scope, such that I must leave a number of questions unaddressed. These include when the accusatorial/inquisitorial terminology first began to be deployed within England, as well as how the English and American receptions of this terminology interrelate. So too, there remains the question

9 Francis Lieber, *Manual of Political Ethics*, vol. 2, *Political Ethics Proper* (Boston: Little and Brown, 1839).

10 Francis Lieber, *On Civil Liberty and Self-Government*, vol. 1 (Philadelphia: Lippincott, Grambo and Co., 1853).

11 For details concerning the publication of *On Civil Liberty and Self-Government*, see "Dr. Francis Lieber," Library of Congress, accessed March 5, 2021, https://www.loc.gov/item/n50050452/dr-francis-lieber/.

of precisely when and why the Anglo-American world later opted to abandon the term "accusatorial" in favor of "adversarial." But, however incomplete, the comparative procedural history recounted here strikes me as a fitting tribute in a festschrift for Charles Donahue Jr. A scholar of wide-ranging comparative interests and deep erudition, Charlie has written extensively about a great many topics. But a key, abiding interest of his has been the history of courts and their procedure, including the initial rise of the Roman-canon procedure that replaced the ordeals and that came to be divided into distinctive accusatorial and inquisitorial forms.[12] Such research is vital, he has argued, for understanding how the law works in practice, since rights are operationalized only to the extent that courts are willing to enforce them. Yet, as he laments, despite the importance of procedure, "legal discourse, particularly in the academy, frequently focuses on substantive rights and duties and ignores procedure."[13] My hope is that the following account may play at least some small role in addressing the gap in the literature whose existence Charlie has identified and bemoaned.

1 The German-American Connection: Carl Joseph Anton Mittermaier and Francis Lieber

Giovanni Carmignani (1768–1847), a professor of criminal law at the University of Pisa, was one of the first jurists to deploy the accusatorial/inquisitorial divide for purposes of comparative procedural analysis. In his 1832 treatise, *Teoria delle leggi della sicurezza sociale*, Carmignani developed two arguments that would continue to inform scholarly usage of this terminology for many decades to come (and arguably, into the present). First, all systems of criminal procedure can be understood as falling more or less within an accusatorial (party-controlled) or inquisitorial (judge-controlled) mold. Second, there is an

12 Charles Donahue Jr., *Law, Marriage, and Society in the Later Middle Ages: Arguments about Marriage in Five Courts* (Cambridge: Cambridge University Press, 2007), 33–41; Charles Donahue Jr., "Procedure in the Courts of the Ius Commune," in *The History of Courts and Procedure*, 74–124; Charles Donahue Jr., "'The Hypostasis of a Prophecy': Legal Realism and Legal History," in *Law and Legal Process: Substantive Law and Procedure in English Legal History*, ed. Matthew Dyson and David Ibbetson (Cambridge: Cambridge University Press, 2013), 1–16.

13 Donahue, "Procedure in the Courts," 77; Donahue, "The Hypostasis of a Prophecy," 6.

important linkage between a state's procedural system (accusatorial or inquisitorial) and its broader political values and structures.[14]

These ideas were further developed and propagated through the influential writings of the contemporary German jurist Carl Joseph Anton Mittermaier (1787–1867). A professor at the University of Heidelberg, Mittermaier published a review of Carmignani's treatise that appeared in both German and French legal journals, while also discussing it extensively in his own 1834 treatise, *Die Lehre vom Beweise im deutschen Strafprozesse*.[15] In so doing, Mittermaier reinforced Carmignani's claims that procedural systems ought to be compared according to the extent to which they are accusatorial or inquisitorial and that "the political organization of society" has an important influence on the choice of procedural form.[16]

In thus asserting a necessary interrelation between procedure and politics, Mittermaier argued that it was accusatorial procedure that was best suited to promote the liberal nation-building he aimed to foster—a goal that would thereafter lead him to serve as president of the Frankfurt pre-parliament, which helped to launch the 1848 Revolution.[17] As a Germanist, Mittermaier was eager to free Germany from its reception of Roman law, which he viewed as suited to authoritarian rule, and to restore in its place the country's native, purportedly liberty-promoting Germanic traditions.[18] In line with his politics,

14 Kessler, "Toward an Account," 302–03; Giovanni Carmignani, *Teoria delle leggi della sicurezza sociale*, vol. 4 (Pisa: I Fratelli Nistri, 1832), 33, 67; "Carmignani, Giovanni" in *Enciclopedia Trecanni*, accessed January 5, 2021, https://www.treccani.it/enciclopedia/giovanni-carmignani_(Dizionario-Biografico)/.

15 Kessler, "Toward an Account," 303–04; Carl Joseph Anton Mittermaier, "Beurtheilung der neuesten criminalistischen schriften: Teoria delle leggi della sicurezza sociale di G. Carmignani, Vol. I–IV," *Neues Archiv des Criminalrechts* 13 (1833): 612; Carl Joseph Anton Mittermaier, "Teoria delle leggi della sicurezza sociale: par G. Carmignani, Vol. I–IV," *Revue étrangère de legislation et d'économie politique* 1 (1834): 147–56; Carl Joseph Anton Mittermaier, *Die Lehre vom Beweise im deutschen Strafprozesse nach der Fortbildung durch Gerichtsgebrauch und deutsche Gesetzbücher in Vergleichung mit den Ansichten des englischen und französischen Strafverfahrens* (Darmstadt, Johann Wilhelm Heyer 1834); Brian Vick, "Liberalism, Nationalism, and Gender Dichotomy in Mid-Nineteenth-Century Germany: The Contested Case of German Civil Law," *The Journal of Modern History* 82 (2010): 546.

16 Mittermaier, *Die Lehre vom Beweise*, 30 and n. 3.

17 Vick, "Liberalism, Nationalism, and Gender," 546; Markus Dirk Dubber, "The German Jury and the Metaphysical Folk: From Romantic Idealism to Nazi Ideology," *American Journal of Comparative Law* 43 (1995): 241–42.

18 James Q. Whitman, *The Legacy of Roman Law in the German Romantic Era: Historical Vision and Legal Change* (Princeton: Princeton University Press, 1990), 122–23, 133–34, 200–09.

Mittermaier insisted on a linkage between accusatorial procedure and the "democratic principle," on the one hand, and inquisitorial procedure and the "monarchical form," on the other.[19] As he observed, "in antiquity, and especially in the periods of republics, we see the accusatorial form predominate, as we also see it in force in the ancient German law."[20] Indeed, he remarked, given contemporary trends toward liberalism in Europe, "one is not surprised ... to find in various European statutes and recent legislative attempts certain tendencies toward the accusatorial form."[21]

According to Mittermaier, it was "English procedure" that came closest to adopting accusatorial methods "in their purity."[22] But properly contextualized, it was clear, he insisted, that English procedure was of a kind with a broader model of accusatorial, party-controlled procedure that could be found in many different times and places (in the West), including not least, in medieval Germany prior to the reception of Roman law.[23] Seeking to assimilate English procedure to a broader accusatorial model that encompassed native German traditions as well, Mittermaier thus presented the jury as a pan-Germanic institution of which the Anglo-American type was merely one variant.[24] In so doing, he espoused the embrace of a mixed procedural system that would temper Roman-law inquisitorialism and facilitate a restoration of what he viewed as Germany's suppressed accusatorial legacy.[25]

Mittermaier's development of the accusatorial/inquisitorial divide as a means of framing comparative procedural analysis would find its way into the American legal literature through the pen of Francis Lieber. Born in Berlin in 1800, Lieber fought as a teenager to free Germany from hated French rule, only then to find himself within the crosshairs of a reactionary Prussian regime unwilling to tolerate his widely known liberal sympathies.[26] After repeated arrests, he chose exile, eventually moving to the United States in 1827.[27] As a new immigrant on American shores, he quickly managed to establish himself as a leading intellectual, in part through his remarkable talent for cultivating connections with prominent political and intellectual figures on both sides of

19 Mittermaier, *Die Lehre vom Beweise*, 30, 41–44.

20 Mittermaier, *Die Lehre vom Beweise*, 34.

21 Mittermaier, *Die Lehre vom Beweise*, 40.

22 Mittermaier, *Die Lehre vom Beweise*, 40.

23 Mittermaier, *Die Lehre vom Beweise*, 30–31.

24 Dubber, "The German Jury," 233–34, 253, n. 182.

25 Mittermaier, *Die Lehre vom Beweise*, 50.

26 Thomas Sergeant Perry, ed., *The Life and Letters of Francis Lieber* (Boston: James R. Osgood and Co., 1882), 2, 7, 29, 56–64.

27 Perry, *Life and Letters*, 69.

the Atlantic.[28] He thus secured professorships in history and political science, first at South Carolina College and then at Columbia College, where he would remain until his death in 1872.[29]

As M. H. Hoeflich has shown, Mittermaier was among the closest of the many connections that Lieber cultivated throughout his long life. Lieber's acquaintance with Mittermaier began soon after he arrived in the United States. In drafting a report on American prisons, Lieber read and came to admire greatly Mittermaier's writing on prisons. This, in turn, led him to initiate a correspondence with Mittermaier in 1831 that would continue until the latter's death almost forty years later.[30] Forged over decades, this relationship played a role in shaping both men's scholarly activities. For example, when Mittermaier started a new academic journal, he turned to Lieber for help in identifying American jurists willing to contribute articles regarding U.S. law.[31] Lieber, in turn, sought Mittermaier's guidance and approval in undertaking his own scholarly pursuits. In a February 1837 letter to the lawyer Charles Sumner, Lieber in fact complained that he was torn between the conflicting advice of Joseph Story and Mittermaier, both of whom he eagerly sought to impress in his quest to "*force* the political and legal world to quote me."[32] More particularly, Lieber lamented, "Story continually asks me to finish my 'Political Ethics.' Mittermaier says: 'Let the Ethics rest, and write your 'Penology.' We want it exceedingly.'"[33] Although these comments were clearly intended to impress Sumner with the stature of his interlocutors, they also suggest that Lieber's longing for Mittermaier's esteem and endorsement ran deep.

Lieber published his *Political Ethics* soon thereafter, making a very brief mention of the accusatorial/inquisitorial framework in a footnote that appears in the second volume, issued in 1839.[34] Although he published an extended "Essay on Subjects of Penal Law," he never wrote a monograph on penology—a choice that perhaps followed from his decision to remain in the United States, where Story's good opinion was ultimately more important than that

28 M. H. Hoeflich, "Transatlantic Friendships & the German Influence on American Law in the First Half of the Nineteenth Century," *American Journal of Comparative Law* 35 (1987): 599–611.

29 John Fabian Witt, *Lincoln's Code: The Laws of War in American History* (New York: Free Press, 2012), 103, 105, 183; Perry, *Life and Letters*, 104, 294, 430.

30 Hoeflich, "Transatlantic Friendships," 603 and n. 25.

31 Hoeflich, "Transatlantic Friendships," 603.

32 Perry, *Life and Letters*, 114 (italics in original).

33 Perry, *Life and Letters*, 115.

34 Lieber, *Manual*, 2:622–23.

of Mittermaier.[35] Nonetheless, Lieber continued to cultivate his relationship with Mittermaier actively over the ensuing decades and, in so doing, reflected on matters of criminal law and procedure.[36] Indeed, *On Civil Liberty and Self-Government*, the book in which he first fully developed his account of the accusatorial/inquisitorial divide, devotes a number of chapters to these themes and cites Mittermaier several times, commenting favorably on the latter's scholarly contributions.[37]

As this suggests, there is good reason to conclude that it was from Mittermaier that Lieber first absorbed the accusatorial/inquisitorial comparative framework. But while embracing core features of Mittermaier's Germanist account of accusatorial and inquisitorial procedure, Lieber did not merely parrot his predecessor. Instead, he grafted the language of accusatorialism and inquisitorialism onto a longstanding Anglo-American account of the distinctively liberty-promoting nature of the common law, as contrasted with the supposedly slavish tendencies of the civil law. In so doing, he drew on a burgeoning American discourse that linked public, lawyer-controlled proceedings—and the powerful lawyers who enabled these—to an exceptionalist American identity, defined first and foremost by its distinctive commitment to liberty.

2 Lieber's Account of the Accusatorial/Inquisitorial Divide

Lieber's comparative discussion of accusatorial and inquisitorial procedure appears within a broader account of the ways in which "civil liberty" hinges on what he called "the freedom of the law."[38] In referring to the "freedom of the law," Lieber drew on the Germanist argument, developed by Mittermaier and his ilk, that the effort to liberalize Germany hinged on the revivification of native Germanic legal traditions and the rooting out of received Roman law. On this view, Germanic law had the potential to become a living law, rising up freely from the customary norms of the community, in contrast to Roman law, perceived as the rules of a dead civilization imposed from above. Whereas

35 Francis Lieber, *A Popular Essay on Subjects of Penal Law, and on Uninterrupted Solitary Confinement at Labor, as Contradistinguished to Solitary Confinement at Night and Joint Labor by Day* (Philadelphia: Philadelphia Society for Alleviating the Miseries of Public Prisons, 1838).

36 See, for example, a letter from Lieber to Mittermaier (March 30, 1846), in *The Life and Letters of Francis Lieber*, 200–04 (discussing "the German Criminal Trial and Procedure").

37 Lieber, *On Civil Liberty*, 1:88 and n. 3, 259 n. 8, 321 n. 1.

38 Lieber, *On Civil Liberty*, 1:220.

the Roman civil law was autocratically "la[id] down" by the "government or a 'minister of justice,'" the common law was "decided in court" and therefore "by the whole organism established to give reality and practical life to justice, and in the natural course of things."[39] In short,

> the civil law, where it now exists, has been introduced as a dead and foreign law; it is a matter of learned study, of antiquity; while common law is a living, vigorous law of a living people. It is this that constitutes more than half its excellence; and though we should have brought from England all else, our liberty, had we adopted the civil law, would have had a very precarious existence.[40]

As suggested by this reference to the United States and England, Lieber not only insisted on the superiority of Germanic law vis-à-vis the Roman civil law, but also embraced a discourse of common-law exceptionalism. He argued that it was the English common law alone—a product of what he called "the Anglican tribe"—that was fully free and alive.[41] As he explained, the common law, which formed "the broad basis of all our own [American] constitutions," was "a body of law and 'practice,' in the administration of justice which has never been deadened by the superinduction of a foreign and closed law, as was the case with the common law of those [other, Germanic] nations that received the civil law."[42] In thus substituting the English common law for the broader category of Germanic law, Lieber's account in some ways anticipated the large body of late nineteenth-century scholarship that would insist on the allegedly Teutonic roots of Anglo-American law.[43] Unlike these later scholars, however, he was not interested in the question of origins. His goal was instead simply to draw parallels between these two forms of non-Roman law—and in so doing, to highlight the common law's superiority.

Lieber identified several distinctive features of the common law that, he claimed, undergirded its unique capacity to promote civil liberty. One key feature within this broader catalog was the law-finding and law-refining role played by the courts—an institution uniquely able to channel the community's

39 Lieber, *On Civil Liberty*, 1:230.

40 Lieber, *On Civil Liberty*, 1:230.

41 Lieber, *On Civil Liberty*, 1:230.

42 Lieber, *On Civil Liberty*, 1:221.

43 David M. Rabban, *Law's History: American Legal Thought and the Transatlantic Turn to History* (Cambridge: Cambridge University Press, 2012) (discussing the late nineteenth-century scholars who embraced "Teutonic germ-theory").

customary traditions. Lieber emphasized, however, that courts could serve this function only to the extent that they themselves remained free from domination. Accordingly, "[t]he independence of the law ... requires ... a clear division of the judiciary from other powers ... [and] the independence of the judge."[44] Yet, judicial independence alone was also not enough. In order for independent courts to produce a free and living law, they had to employ accusatorial, or party-controlled, criminal procedures.

Like Mittermaier and other contemporary continental European jurists, Lieber defined the accusatorial model as consisting first and foremost of party-controlled proceedings (including investigation), such that the judge's role was simply to supervise and oversee the dispute.[45] In Lieber's words, "accusatorial process is ... that penal trial which places the court wholly above the two parties in criminal matters."[46] As such, accusatorial procedure was defined in antithesis to its court-controlled, inquisitorial counterpart: "The accusatorial trial is ... contradistinguished from the inquisitorial trial, [in] which ... the judge inquires, investigates, in one word, is the prosecuting party as well as the judging, and in some cases he is even expected to be likewise the protecting party of the indicted prisoner."[47]

In line with Mittermaier's views, Lieber argued that accusatorial procedure went hand in glove with political liberty, such that it could be found among all free peoples through time. As he explained, "[i]t may be said that the public accusatorial trial has prevailed or been aimed at by all free nations, modern and ancient. We, the English, the Netherlanders, the Norwegians, the Swedes, the French, since the first revolution, the Germans, in the earlier times the Greeks and Romans—all have had it."[48] But even while suggesting that accusatorialism was widespread among free peoples, Lieber continued to insist on common-law exceptionalism, arguing that the public accusatorial trial "has nowhere been carried out with that consistency which we find in the Anglican penal trial."[49] Indeed, England owed the fact that it was "the freest nation of Europe" in large part to the excellence of its accusatorial procedure.[50]

44 Lieber, *On Civil Liberty*, 1:222.

45 Kessler, "Toward an Account," 325 (discussing how European jurists defined accusatorialism).

46 Lieber, *On Civil Liberty*, 1:238.

47 Lieber, *On Civil Liberty*, 1:238.

48 Lieber, *On Civil Liberty*, 1:239.

49 Lieber, *On Civil Liberty*, 1:239.

50 Lieber, *On Civil Liberty*, 1:239.

While claiming that the degree of party versus judicial control was the defining element of the distinction between accusatorial and inquisitorial procedure, Lieber—like Mittermaier and other contemporary European jurists—also suggested that the jury was intimately connected with the accusatorial model.[51] Trial by jury is "necessary," he asserted "for a complete accusatorial procedure."[52] That the jury was so essential to accusatorial procedure stemmed from the fact that the jury enabled the judge to occupy the "independent position between the parties" required by the accusatorial model.[53] By taking responsibility for "the finding of guilt or innocence, or of the facts," the jury protected the judge from being "exposed to taking sides in the trial."[54] Lieber claimed, moreover, that just as accusatorial procedure was necessary for promoting and preserving a living and free common law, so too "[i]t is hardly possible to imagine a living, vigorous, and expanding common law without [the jury]."[55] Serving as the voice of the community, the jury ensured that the courts, engaged in accusatorial, lawyer-controlled proceedings, channeled law in a bottom-up fashion, reflecting historically rooted, yet ever evolving, customary norms.

In addition to the jury, Lieber identified the existence of a strong and independent bar as yet another institutional feature that undergirded the common law's distinctively accusatorial tradition. It was possible, he argued, to find a powerful, independent legal profession emerging, alongside accusatorial procedure, in every country that pursued freedom:

> Nearly in all free countries, but especially in all modern free countries, has the advocate assumed a prominent position. He is an important person as advocate, and as belonging to that profession from which the people necessarily must always take many of their most efficient law-makers, from which arise many of the greatest statesmen ... and which has formed in every free people many of their immortal orators.[56]

In contrast, "[w]here the inquisitorial trial exists, where the judiciary in general is not independent..., it is in vain to look for independent advocates, as a

51 Kessler, "Toward an Account," 304, 316–18 (discussing European jurists' account of the jury as a core component of the accusatorial model).

52 Lieber, *On Civil Liberty*, 1:254.

53 Lieber, *On Civil Liberty*, 1:250.

54 Lieber, *On Civil Liberty*, 1:250.

55 Lieber, *On Civil Liberty*, 1:256.

56 Lieber, *On Civil Liberty*, 1:262–63.

class of men."[57] As always, however, Lieber combined the transcultural generalization implicit in the accusatorial model with an emphasis on the common law's superiority. He thus insisted on the distinctive "position of the advocate in the Anglican accusatorial trial."[58]

For Lieber's contemporary American readers, this assertion that lawyers, wielding accusatorial procedures, played an essential role in promoting freedom would have been familiar, as it resonated with a then burgeoning discourse pursuant to which lawyer-empowering procedure was identified as a defining feature of a uniquely liberty-oriented national identity. Like many Americans (and especially American lawyers), Lieber claimed that it was in the United States that the lawyer-controlled, liberty-promoting procedures of the common law were most fully perfected. As he explained, the structural underpinnings of liberty developed by the "Anglican tribe" had found unique and distinctively powerful expression within the United States: "All the broad Anglican principles, as they have been stated, are necessary to us, but there is, nevertheless, that which we can call American liberty—a development of Anglican liberty peculiar to ourselves."[59] Key among the features that made "American liberty" unique was the fact that the nation was a republic, such that "republicanism has thoroughly infused itself into all ... [American] institutions and views."[60] It was precisely by appealing to classical republican ideals that nineteenth-century American lawyers claimed a distinctive role for themselves in helping to govern the polity. According to this prevalent, contemporary discourse, lawyers—by deploying both legislative oratory and accusatorial, lawyer-empowering courtroom procedures—served to promote the civic virtue required for liberty to survive and to thrive.[61] In line with these widely held views, Lieber dedicated *On Civil Liberty and Self-Government* "To My Former Pupils"—young men, he proudly remarked, whom he had helped to prepare for "the citizenship of a great republic" and who were now serving as the "law-makers of a vast and growing commonwealth."[62]

---

57 Lieber, *On Civil Liberty*, 1:258.

58 Lieber, *On Civil Liberty*, 1:262.

59 Lieber, *On Civil Liberty*, 1:276.

60 Lieber, *On Civil Liberty*, 1:277–78.

61 Kessler, *Inventing American Exceptionalism*, 151–99.

62 Lieber, *On Civil Liberty*, 1:v.

3 Americans' Early-Twentieth-Century Embrace of the Accusatorial/ Inquisitorial Divide

Despite the great success enjoyed by *On Civil Liberty and Self-Government*, Lieber's introduction of the accusatorial/inquisitorial terminology into the American legal discourse failed to stick. A search of HeinOnline's Law-Journal Library, which includes "more than 2,800 law and law-related periodicals"—many dating to the early nineteenth century—reveals that the first article containing these terms that appeared in an American journal was published in 1867 by none other than Lieber himself.[63] The next such article, discussed below, did not appear until 1908, after which many pieces referring to accusatorial and inquisitorial procedure began to be published regularly and in close succession. A review of all federal and state cases on Westlaw suggests, not surprisingly, that courts were even slower to embrace the accusatorial/inquisitorial terminology, likely absorbing it from juristic writings. With the exception of one outlier opinion also dated to 1867, no cases including these terms were issued until 1927, after which many others soon followed.[64]

Why did American lawyers suddenly begin to make use of the accusatorial/ inquisitorial distinction in the early twentieth century, after neglecting it for several decades? The answer is not that they had previously lacked interest in comparative procedural questions as such. To the contrary, as noted, a robust, comparative discourse regarding American procedural exceptionalism persisted throughout much of the nineteenth century—at least through the end of Reconstruction. But these debates continued to be framed by reference to the traditional distinction between the Anglo-American common law and the Roman-canon, civil law. Moreover, in the final decades of the nineteenth century and continuing into the early twentieth, the U.S. Supreme Court wrote several opinions alluding to important distinctions between the common law and the civil law approaches to justice.[65]

So what had changed by 1908? The complexity of this history is such that there is no way to do full justice to it within the limited scope of these pages.

---

63 Francis Lieber, "The Unanimity of Juries," *The American Law Register* 6 (1867): 727–32.

64 *Blair v. Ridgely*, 41 Mo. 63 (1867) concerned the Missouri test oath and is a striking example of how, as I have argued elsewhere, Southern whites rejected Reconstruction by depicting it as an unlawful and alien imposition of inquisitorialism. Kessler, *Inventing American Exceptionalism*, 263–322. See also *Reed v. State*, 94 Fla. 32 (1927).

65 Andrew Kent, "The Jury and Empire: The Insular Cases and the Anti-Jury Movement in the Gilded Age and Progressive Era," *Southern California Law Review* 91 (2018): 414; Máximo Langer and David S. Tanenhaus, "What Are Children Due? American Juvenile Justice, Due Process and the Problem of Adversarial Power" (under contract, Oxford University Press).

That said, two developments seem especially relevant in accounting for the sudden interest in the accusatorial/inquisitorial divide in this period. The first was the growing predominance of German universities and German legal science, as a result of which many elite American lawyers began to follow the German (and more generally, European) legal literature and also to study abroad.[66] A second set of developments that contributed to the American embrace of the accusatorial/inquisitorial terminology at this time stemmed from the new challenges posed by the rise of modern industrial society, combined with those following from the country's recent imperialist adventures. Amidst growing frustration that courts and their procedures were becoming increasingly outdated, Progressive-era reformers urged the need to remake procedural systems and to develop new administrative agencies. In so doing, many looked to Europe for inspiration.[67] Among these, some advocated the adoption of aspects of the civil-law approach to criminal procedure and others called for the transplantation of administrative mechanisms that were gaining ground abroad. In the ensuing debates, references to the distinctions between accusatorial and inquisitorial procedure were weaponized in service of pleas for reform, as well as pleas to preserve the status quo. So too, such comparative discussion was given a boost by the country's imperialist ambitions, which led newly appointed territorial administrators to confront the civil law modes of procedure previously in force in places like Puerto Rico and the Philippines.

The 1908 article that was the first, post-Lieber, to discuss accusatorial and inquisitorial procedure was a printed version of a speech by American Bar Association (ABA) president Jacob M. Dickinson (1851–1928).[68] Dickinson was at the forefront of a new generation of American lawyers who had become increasingly interested in European, and especially German legal science. After attending Columbia Law School, he spent a year studying law in Leipzig (and briefly Paris), where he focused on learning Roman law and improving his German. Upon returning to the United States, he embarked on what would

66 Rabban, *Law's History*, 86–87; Ugo Mattei, "Why the Winds Changed: Intellectual Leadership in Western Law," *American Journal of Comparative Law* 42 (1994): 202–03; Mathias Reimann, "Nineteenth Century German Legal Science," *Boston College Law Review* 31 (1990): 896–97.

67 Daniel T. Rogers, *Atlantic Crossings: Social Politics in a Progressive Age* (Cambridge: Belknap Press of Harvard University Press, 1998); Langer and Tanenhaus, "What Are Children Due?"

68 Jacob M. Dickinson, "Address of the President," *Report of the Thirty-First Annual Meeting of the American Bar Association*, vol. 33 (Aug. 1908), 341–419.

prove to be a highly successful legal and political career, including a 1909 appointment as Secretary of War.[69]

Dickinson devoted much of his ABA speech to criticizing the emergence of new administrative agencies that threatened to displace the courts as the foundation of American governance—a development widely bemoaned by contemporary lawyers, not least because they feared that it would lead to non-lawyer bureaucrats assuming the positions of power once reserved for the legal profession.[70] He thus lamented that "[f]rom the least governed people in the world, we are rapidly becoming the most governed people in the world," as "[o]ur increasing commissions for almost every department of public affairs are making our government, state and national, the most comprehensive system of bureaucracy ever known."[71] It was in criticizing the displacement of courts by administrative agencies that Dickinson drew on the comparative discourse of accusatorial and inquisitorial procedure. Administrative agencies, he complained, embraced a form of inquisitorial procedure that empowered state bureaucrats, serving as decision-makers, to investigate and decide the facts in accordance with their own lawless preferences. In so arguing, Dickinson—like Lieber before him—melded the accusatorial/inquisitorial distinction with the longstanding rhetoric of Anglo-American common-law exceptionalism. He thus asserted that these developments served to undermine "Anglican civil liberty"—a point he made by quoting Lieber, though not by name:

> The administration of justice should be by the courts alone. It is subversive of every idea of Anglican civil liberty for the judge to commit himself in any way to an opinion until the cause shall have been presented according to law. This is the distinguishing feature between the accusatorial and the inquisitorial trial, in which the judge inquires, becomes the prosecutor, and at the same time is theoretically the protector of the arraigned, 'thus uniting a triad of functions within himself which amounts to a psychological incongruity.'[72]

---

69 "Dickinson, Jacob McGavock," in *The National Cyclopaedia of American Biography*, vol. 14 (New York: James T. White and Co., 1917), 410–11.

70 Amalia D. Kessler, "Arbitration and Americanization: The Paternalism of Progressive Procedural Reform," *Yale Law Journal* 124 (2015): 2951–55; Wayne K. Hobson, *The American Legal Profession and the Organizational Society, 1890–1930* (New York: Garland, 1986); Michael J. Powell, *From Patrician Elite to Professional Elite: The Transformation of the New York City Bar Association* (New York: Russell Sage Foundation, 1988).

71 Dickinson, "Address of the President," 345.

72 Dickinson, "Address of the President," 345 (quoting Lieber, *On Civil Liberty*, 1:238–39).

In Dickinson's view, the inquisitorial administrative state was in such fundamental tension with the accusatorial underpinnings of Anglo-American liberty—including, not least, the extraordinary power of the American legal profession—that it simply could not persist. As he concluded, "[t]he American people will not perpetuate a system so foreign to the principles which have been the foundation and safeguard of their prosperity, property rights and civil liberty."[73]

While critics of the administrative state turned to the accusatorial/inquisitorial divide to decry new agencies as lawless and alien inquisitorial imports, some advocates of criminal procedure reform sought instead to valorize aspects of the civil law's ostensibly inquisitorial approach. This was the case, for example, of Frederic R. Coudert II (1871–1955), who published a 1910 article on "French Criminal Procedure."[74] The grandchild of a French immigrant who had established a prominent law firm in New York, Coudert grew up with a father, Frederic R. Coudert Sr., who was fluent in multiple European languages, including French, and who became famous for his contributions to the field of international law.[75] Although we know considerably less about the younger Coudert than about his famous father, it is clear that he joined the family firm and appears to have made a career in his father's shadow.[76]

Coudert's article on "French Criminal Procedure" was representative of a growing American interest in civilian criminal procedure, as reflected in the 1913 publication by Boston-based Little Brown of an English translation of Adhémar Esmein's magisterial *A History of Continental Criminal Procedure*.[77] But while Coudert's account was focused on French procedure, his article opened by referring to the recent American conquest of Puerto Rico and the

73 Dickinson, "Address of the President," 346.

74 Frederic R. Coudert, "French Criminal Procedure," *Yale Law Journal* 19 (1910): 326–40. There is some confusion as to which Frederic R. Coudert actually published this article—Frederic R. Coudert Sr. (1832–1903) or his son by the same name, Frederic R. Coudert II (1871–1955). The piece is signed simply Frederic R. Coudert, suggesting that it is the father who wrote it. But if this were the case, the piece was published posthumously. Since no mention is made of posthumous publication, it seems probable that the son was the author.

75 Frederic R. Coudert, "Introductory Note," in *Frederic R. Coudert: Addresses, Historical—Political—Sociological* (New York: G. P. Putnam's Sons, 1905), ix–xvii.

76 "Frederic René Coudert Jr.," in *Official Congressional Directory for the Use of the United States Congress* (Washington, DC: Government Printing Office, 1949), 85–86 (mentioning Frederic R. Coudert II in a discussion of his son, also Frederic R. Coudert, who served as a New York Representative to the U.S. Congress).

77 Adhémar Esmein, *A History of Continental Criminal Procedure: with Special Reference to France*, trans. John Simpson (Boston: Little, Brown and Co., 1913).

Philippines, which was forcing his compatriots, he observed, to grapple with important comparative questions. As he noted, "[t]he annexation of twelve millions of people living under the civil law has brought under the American flag institutions which we had formerly scarcely known, save by caricature."[78] Reflexively equating all civil law systems with one another and that of France, Coudert remarked that Americans were inclined to "thunder [...] away at the monstrous medievalism of the French legal procedure" that they observed in these annexed islands.[79] Especially shocking to many was the discovery that the defendant was required to take the stand, "a thing unknown to our common law procedure."[80] But careful reflection, he asserted, revealed that there were aspects of the civil law approach—including the choice to make the defendant testify—that might productively be incorporated into American law.

It was in the context of calling for more nuanced comparative reflection on the differences between the common law and civil law approaches to criminal procedure that Coudert made reference to the accusatorial/inquisitorial divide—though he preferred the terms "controversial" and "litigious" to accusatorial. The choice to have the defendant testify was representative, he suggested, of the fundamental differences between the civil law and common law approaches—differences, he explained, that were best encapsulated by the distinction between accusatorial and inquisitorial modes of procedures. As this suggests, Coudert, like Lieber and Dickinson, melded the accusatorial/inquisitorial framework with a longstanding discourse of common-law exceptionalism. While Mittermaier (and even Lieber) stated that accusatorial modes had appeared in different times and places throughout history, Coudert indicated that such procedure was all but synonymous with the Anglo-American common law:

> The popular instinct in thus seizing upon the point [that the defendant is made to testify], which appeared to it so anomalous, hit upon the really fundamental distinction between the two great systems of criminal procedure which divide the civilized world—one a lineal descendant of the Imperial Roman procedure, the other purely English in its origin and development. In the domain of criminal law the world-wide antithesis is between the Roman or inquisitorial system and the English or controversial system.[81]

78 Coudert, "French Criminal Procedure," 326.
79 Coudert, "French Criminal Procedure," 326.
80 Coudert, "French Criminal Procedure," 327.
81 Coudert, "French Criminal Procedure," 327.

Having thus equated accusatorial procedure with that of the common law, Coudert observed that there were many aspects of this procedural approach that were "valuable acquisitions which American law should not lightly surrender."[82] But it was possible, he suggested, to preserve the core liberty-promoting features of accusatorialism—including, "the jury system, the public nature of all trials ... and the litigious [lawyer-controlled] as distinguished from inquisitorial [judge-controlled] method of procedure"—while also importing particular features of the civil law's broader inquisitorial system, recognized to be superior.[83] On this view, the American "rule against compelling examination of parties in criminal cases" should be recognized "to have outlived ... its usefulness," such that it ought to be jettisoned and replaced by procedures designed to induce the defendant's testimony.[84]

In so arguing, Coudert drew on the longstanding association between accusatorial procedure and liberty, on the one hand, and inquisitorial procedure and subjugation, on the other—but in ways that challenged the usual insistence that the United States, as a distinctively liberty-oriented nation, was irrevocably wedded to accusatorialism. It was precisely because the country needed more authoritative governance, he suggested, that it ought to import aspects of inquisitorial procedure. Like many Progressive-era reformers, Coudert was convinced that the United States was facing an unprecedented threat of criminal activity—one that followed in significant measure from the recent growth of large urban populations, consisting in no small part of seemingly alien immigrants from Southern and Eastern Europe.[85] Coudert thus bemoaned the era's purported "[i]ncrease in crimes of violence, epidemics of commercial fraud and general disregard for law."[86] From this perspective, some inquisitorial procedural muscle was desperately needed. Indeed, as he recognized, much the same point was then being made by those appointed to govern the United States' newly conquered island territories. Eager to preserve order, these men were suddenly discovering the virtues of the civilian inquisitorial procedures they encountered in their new posts. Coudert thus remarked that in "recent addresses and review articles," William Taft—named the chief

82 Coudert, "French Criminal Procedure," 339.

83 Coudert, "French Criminal Procedure," 339.

84 Coudert, "French Criminal Procedure," 339.

85 Kent, "The Jury and Empire," 394–96; John Higham, *Strangers in the Land: Patterns of American Nativism, 1860–1925*, rev. ed. (New Brunswick, NJ: Rutgers University Press, 2002), 160, 267–68; Michael Willrich, *City of Courts: Socializing Justice in Progressive Era Chicago* (Cambridge; Cambridge University Press, 2003), 138, 281–90.

86 Coudert, "French Criminal Procedure," 340.

civil administrator of the Philippines in 1900—praised the inquisitorial criminal procedure that "he had found and studied" there.[87] As Coudert reported, Taft had concluded that "there is much in our criminal procedure that may well have outlived its usefulness, and that some of the elements of the Latin procedure … were not without advantage."[88]

4 Conclusion

Although Lieber's attempt to import the comparative accusatorial/inquisitorial framework into the American legal lexicon failed, his efforts proved prescient. The early twentieth-century American jurists who ultimately succeeded in domesticating this framework did so, in part, by melding it with the long-standing rhetoric of common-law exceptionalism, much as Lieber had done a half-century earlier. As a result, the term "accusatorial"—initially defined by European jurists as a procedural type that appeared in many different times and places (even if with particular force in England)—became equated with Anglo-American (common-law) procedure, and indeed, to some extent, with American procedure tout court.

In later decades, lawyers and jurists in the Anglo-American world would come to prefer the term "adversarial." An exploration of the reasons for this development lies well beyond this text. Nonetheless, it bears emphasis that these jurists' choice to characterize their own procedure as "adversarial," even as their civilian counterparts continued to refer to the "accusatorial" model, is very much in line with the broader story recounted here. It suggests, in short, a distinctively Anglo-American gloss to the accusatorial model—one that implicitly reinforces a claim of Anglo-American procedural exceptionalism.

For Lieber himself, the insistence on Anglo-American, and especially American, procedural exceptionalism went hand in glove with an account of American superiority—an account by means of which he sought, in part, to demonstrate his devotion to the country he had adopted as his own. But in many ways, Lieber was not unique. As I have detailed elsewhere, the initial emergence in Europe of the accusatorial/inquisitorial divide as a comparative framing device was tied to nation-building, such that the terminology was regularly deployed to advance what Frédéric Audren and Jean-Louis Halpérin have described as a broader post-restoration project of drawing on history to reveal

87 Coudert, "French Criminal Procedure," 327.
88 Coudert, "French Criminal Procedure," 327.

the "native national genius."[89] Similarly, as we have seen, Lieber's American successors included those, like Dickinson, who claimed that American procedure is distinctively accusatorial in order to laud the nation's inherited legal system—in his case, as a means of resisting new forms of administrative procedure.

That the terms accusatorial (or adversarial) and inquisitorial are so readily imbued with a nationalist valence and, in turn, deployed to reinforce the status quo is an argument that scholars have raised against their continued use.[90] That said, long before these terms were successfully imported into American law, Anglo-American lawyers made extensive use of the common law/civil law distinction for similarly nationalistic (or proto-nationalistic) ends. As this suggests, the danger would seem to lie not in the accusatorial/inquisitorial framework as such, but rather in any comparative typology—at least those structured as a dichotomy between two opposing types. There are thus good reasons for caution.

But these dangers are not inevitable. By the early twentieth century, jurists like Coudert had begun to deploy the accusatorial/inquisitorial framework toward very different ends—in service of national critique and reform. Of course, the particular ends that Coudert sought to promote are hardly attractive, stemming as they did from anxieties about a crumbling social order that were deeply tinged by racism and xenophobia. Moreover, his efforts to augment penal authority seem especially troubling from the retrospective vantage point of today's carceral state. But we need not embrace Coudert's policy goals to recognize the critical, reformist potential inherent in thoughtful, comparative uses of the accusatorial/inquisitorial framework. This now deep-rooted framework invites us to explore the broader political—and even social—entailments of our procedural legacies and choices with an eye toward fostering productive change.[91] Although not all proposed reforms are likely to be in service of liberal, democratic ideals, this should hardly surprise us. As so often in matters of legal analysis, we are left with the question of political will.

---

89 Kessler, "Toward an Account," 307–11; Frédéric Audren and Jean-Louis Halpérin, *La culture juridique française: entre mythes et réalités, XIXe–XXe siècles* (Paris: CNRS, 2013), 105.

90 Sarah J. Summers, *Fair Trials: The European Criminal Procedural Tradition and the European Court of Human Rights* (Oxford: Hart Publishing, 2007), 9, 11; Langer, "The Long Shadow," 906.

91 Kessler, "Toward an Account," 324–37; Kessler, *Inventing American Exceptionalism*, 323–54.

Acknowledgments

My deepest thanks to Máximo Langer for his very helpful comments.

Bibliography

Audren, Frédéric, and Jean-Louis Halpérin. *La culture juridique française: entre mythes et réalités, XIXe–XXe siècles*. Paris: CNRS, 2013.

Blair v. Ridgely, 41 Mo. 63 (1867).

Carmignani, Giovanni. *Teoria delle leggi della sicurezza sociale*, vol. 4. Pisa: I Fratelli Nistri, 1832.

Coudert, Frederic R. *Frederic R. Coudert: Addresses, Historical—Political—Sociological*. New York: G. P. Putnam's Sons, 1905.

Coudert, Frederic R. "French Criminal Procedure." *Yale Law Journal* 19 (1910): 326–40.

Dickinson, Jacob M. "Address of the President," *Report of the Thirty-First Annual Meeting of the American Bar Association*, vol. 33 (Aug. 1908), 341–419.

Donahue, Charles, Jr. *Law, Marriage, and Society in the Later Middle Ages: Arguments about Marriage in Five Courts*. Cambridge: Cambridge University Press, 2007.

Donahue, Charles, Jr. "Procedure in the Courts of the Ius Commune." In *The History of Courts and Procedure in Medieval Canon Law*, edited by Wilfried Hartmann and Kenneth Pennington, 74–124. Washington, DC: The Catholic University of America Press, 2016.

Donahue, Charles, Jr. "The Hypostasis of a Prophecy: Legal Realism and Legal History." In *Law and Legal Process: Substantive Law and Procedure in English Legal History*, edited by Matthew Dyson and David Ibbetson, 1–16. Cambridge: Cambridge University Press, 2013.

Dubber, Markus Dirk. "The German Jury and the Metaphysical Folk: From Romantic Idealism to Nazi Ideology." *American Journal of Comparative Law* 43 (1995): 227–71.

Esmein, Adhémar. *A History of Continental Criminal Procedure: with Special Reference to France*. Translated by John Simpson. Boston: Little, Brown and Co., 1913.

Official Congressional Directory for the Use of the United States Congress. Washington, DC: Government Printing Office, 1949.

Higham, John. *Strangers in the Land: Patterns of American Nativism, 1860–1925*. Rev. ed. New Brunswick: Rutgers University Press, 2002.

Hobson, Wayne K. *The American Legal Profession and the Organizational Society, 1890–1930*. New York: Garland, 1986.

Hoeflich, M. H. "Transatlantic Friendships & the German Influence on American Law in the First Half of the Nineteenth Century." *American Journal of Comparative Law* 35 (1987): 599–611.

Kent, Andrew. "The Jury and Empire: The Insular Cases and the Anti-Jury Movement in the Gilded Age and Progressive Era." *Southern California Law Review* 91 (2018): 375–466.

Kessler, Amalia D. "Arbitration and Americanization: The Paternalism of Progressive Procedural Reform." *Yale Law Journal* 124 (2015): 2940–93.

Kessler, Amalia D. *Inventing American Exceptionalism: The Origins of American Adversarial Legal Culture, 1800–1877*. New Haven: Yale University Press, 2017.

Kessler, Amalia D. "Toward an Account of the Nineteenth-Century Emergence of the Comparative Accusatorial/Inquisitorial Divide." *American Journal of Comparative Law* 71 (2023): 296–327.

Knafla, Louis A. *Law and Politics in Jacobean England: The Tracts of Lord Chancellor Ellesmere*. Cambridge: Cambridge University Press, 1977.

Langer, Máximo. "In the Beginning Was Fortescue: On the Intellectual Origins of the Adversarial and Inquisitorial Systems and Common and Civil Law in Comparative Criminal Procedure." In *Visions of Justice: Liber Amicorum Mirjan Damaška*, edited by Bruce Ackerman, Kai Ambos, and Hrvoje Sikirić, 280–96. Berlin: Duncker & Humblot, 2016.

Langer, Máximo. "The Long Shadow of the Adversarial and Inquisitorial Categories." In *The Oxford Handbook of Criminal Law*, edited by Markus D. Dubber and Tajana Hörnle, 887–912. Oxford: Oxford University Press, 2014.

Langer, Máximo, and David S. Tanenhaus. "What Are Children Due? American Juvenile Justice, Due Process and the Problem of Adversarial Power." Under contract, Oxford University Press.

Lieber, Francis. *A Popular Essay on Subjects of Penal Law, and on Uninterrupted Solitary Confinement at Labor, as Contradistinguished to Solitary Confinement at Night and Joint Labor by Day*. Philadelphia: Philadelphia Society for Alleviating the Miseries of Public Prisons, 1838.

Lieber, Francis. *Manual of Political Ethics*. Vol. 2, *Political Ethics Proper*. Boston: Little and Brown, 1839.

Lieber, Francis. *On Civil Liberty and Self-Government*. 2 volumes. Philadelphia: Lippincott, Grambo and Co., 1853.

Lieber, Francis. "The Unanimity of Juries." *The American Law Register* 6 (1867): 727–32.

The Life and Letters of Francis Lieber, edited by Thomas Sergeant Perry. Boston: James R. Osgood and Co., 1882.

Mattei, Ugo. "Why the Winds Changed: Intellectual Leadership in Western Law." *American Journal of Comparative Law* 42 (1994): 195–218.

Mittermaier, Carl Joseph Anton. "Beurtheilung der neuesten criminalistischen schriften: Teoria delle leggi della sicurezza sociale di G. Carmignani, Vol. I–IV." *Neues Archiv des Criminalrechts* 13 (1833): 610–28.

Mittermaier, Carl Joseph Anton. *Die Lehre vom Beweise im deutschen Strafprozesse nach der Fortbildung durch Gerichtsgebrauch und deutsche Gesetzbücher in Vergleichung mit den Ansichten des englischen und französischen Strafverfahrens.* Darmstadt: Johann Wilhelm Heyer, 1834.

Mittermaier, Carl Joseph Anton. "Teoria delle leggi della sicurezza sociale: par G. Carmignani, Vol. I–IV," *Revue étrangère de legislation et d'économie politique* 1 (1834): 147–56.

The National Cyclopaedia of American Biography. New York: James T. White and Co., 1917.

Pennington, Kenneth. "The Jurisprudence of Procedure." In *The History of Courts and Procedure in Medieval Canon Law*, edited by Wilfried Hartmann and Kenneth Pennington, 125–59. Washington, DC: The Catholic University of America Press, 2016.

Powell, Michael J. *From Patrician Elite to Professional Elite: The Transformation of the New York City Bar Association*. New York: Russell Sage Foundation, 1988.

Rabban, David M. *Law's History: American Legal Thought and the Transatlantic Turn to History*. Cambridge: Cambridge University Press, 2012.

Reed v. State, 94 Fla. 32 (1927).

Reimann, Mathias. "Nineteenth Century German Legal Science." *Boston College Law Review* 31 (1990): 837–900.

Rogers, Daniel T. *Atlantic Crossings: Social Politics in a Progressive Age*. Cambridge: Belknap Press of Harvard University Press, 1998.

Summers, Sarah J. *Fair Trials: The European Criminal Procedural Tradition and the European Court of Human Rights*. Oxford: Hart Publishing, 2007.

Vick, Brian. "Liberalism, Nationalism, and Gender Dichotomy in Mid-Nineteenth-Century Germany: The Contested Case of German Civil Law." *The Journal of Modern History* 82 (2010): 546–84.

Vogler, Richard. *A World View of Criminal Justice*. Aldershot: Ashgate, 2005.

Whitman, James Q. *The Legacy of Roman Law in the German Romantic Era: Historical Vision and Legal Change*. Princeton: Princeton University Press, 1990.

Willrich, Michael. *City of Courts: Socializing Justice in Progressive Era Chicago*. Cambridge: Cambridge University Press, 2003.

Witt, John Fabian. *Lincoln's Code: The Laws of War in American History*. New York: Free Press, 2012.

Yale, D. E. C. Introduction to *Lord Nottingham's Manual of Chancery Practice and Prolegomena of Chancery and Equity*, edited by D. E. C. Yale. Cambridge: Cambridge University Press, 1965.

PART 5

Literature and Legal Theory

CHAPTER 19

Faust: Goethe's Guide to Legal Progress

Anton Chaevitch

1 Introduction

Goethe studied law, practiced it, and, for fifty-six years, served as a statesman in the Duchy of Saxony-Weimar-Eisenach, including as Privy Counselor and Minister of Finance. And yet the interaction between Goethe's literary works and the law has garnered relatively little scholarly attention.[1] This article seeks to show two key interactions between the law and Goethe's literary works, focusing on *Faust*. First, reading *Faust* as a lawyer opens it up to new understandings. Second, reading this literary work reveals Goethe's views on what drives legal progress. The starting points for this article are three questions. They are simple from a lawyer's perspective, and yet have not (or have hardly) been asked. First, did Margarete (Gretchen) kill her child? Second, why does Faust believe that Lynceus, the watchman who failed to detect Helena's arrival, must be executed without being heard? Third, why does Goethe not provide the actual text of the pact between Faust and Mephistopheles, pursuant to which Mephistopheles seeks to claim Faust's soul?

Each of these three questions focuses on a key aspect of *Faust*, namely the resolution of the Gretchen Tragedy, the role of Helena (around whom Faust's desires center), and the pact between Faust and Mephistopheles. Each of these aspects has distinctly legal elements: Gretchen is sentenced to death, presumably for killing her infant child (but is saved after being judged, presumably by God); Helena acts as a judge and acquits Lynceus, who is accused of a capital crime; and Mephistopheles invokes the pact as a legal document to claim Faust's soul.

The answer to the first question is that the reader cannot know if Margarete killed her child, because Goethe does not provide enough evidence. However,

1 See generally Peter Schneider, *Der Elefant: Goethe über Recht, Staat und Gesellschaft in Faust II* (Freiburg i.Br.: Rombach Verlag, 2009); Klaus Lüderssen, ed., *Die wahre Liberalität ist Anerkennung: Goethe und die Jurisprudenz* (Baden-Baden: Nomos, 2002); Alfons Pausch and Jutta Pausch, *Goethes Juristenlaufbahn: Rechtsstudent, Advokat, Staatsdiener—eine Fachbiographie* (Köln: O. Schmidt, 1996); Johannes Meissner, *Goethe als Jurist* (Berlin: Kortkampf, 1885).

 | DOI:10.1163/9789004710696_021

it has almost universally been assumed that Margarete did kill her child. This raises a further question: how is it possible that Margarete is so widely considered to have killed her child? Margarete herself offers the key to the answer: "Ein altes Mährchen endigt so" (4448).[2] She is judged to have killed her child because a narrative so dictates. This may seem strange, but in Goethe's time, infanticide was one of the most pervasive topics—and yet from plays to actual court cases, the narrative was invariably that the mother killed the child.

The answer to the second question is that Faust has taken the system that deemed Margarete to have killed her child yet further. Where Margarete was still heard—at least in that she was allowed to speak, if only to deaf ears—Lynceus is not heard by Faust at all. With Mephistopheles's help, Faust has been building a system where the law within fixed borders emanates from a center, where it is formalistic and inflexibly wedded to the written word. Helena is the opposite of this legal order. To borrow a word from Faust, she is "gränzunbewußt" (9363)—"unconscious of borders." She crosses in and out of the borders of Faust's realm with ease, actually hears Lynceus, the accused—"So üb' ich nun des Richters erste Pflicht, / Beschuldigte zu hören. Rede denn" (9216–17)[3]—and recognizes the narrative he recounts in the various narratives about her, and then acquits him. This simple act of narrative justice so astonishes Faust that he questions the world he has been building and begins to build a different one.

The answer to the third question is that the explanation for Faust's victory over Mephistopheles—Mephistopheles fails to claim Faust's soul in the end—does not lie in the text of the pact, but in the changes to the legal order that Helena set in motion. It has been commonly assumed that some part of the discussion between Faust and Mephistopheles is the text of the pact, especially the words "Werd' ich zum Augenblicke sagen: / Verweile doch! du bist so schön! / Dann magst du mich in Fesseln schlagen, / Dann will ich gern zu Grunde gehn!" (1699–1702).[4] However, the discussion between Faust and

2 "An old (fairy) tale ends thus." References to Goethe's *Faust* use line numbers for the text in verse and page numbers for the text in prose, and rely on the Weimar Edition, which preserves the original spelling to which Goethe attached considerable significance. See Eric Albert Blackall, *The Emergence of German as a Literary Language, 1770–1775* (Cambridge: Cambridge University Press, 1959). The Weimar Edition was published between 1887 and 1919 by the Böhlau Verlag under the supervision of the Grandduchess Sophie von Sachsen-Weimar-Eisenach, and is hence also known as the "Sophienausgabe" ("Sophie's edition"). Faust, Part I was published in the Wiemar Edition in 1887; Faust, Part II was published in 1888. Translations are my own.

3 "Thus I now exercise the judge's first duty, to hear the accused. So speak."

4 "If I [Faust] will say to the moment: Just linger, you are so beautiful, then you [Mephistopheles] can put me in chains, then I will gladly perish."

Mephistopheles is just that—a discussion of the pact, not the actual text of the written document. As such, we cannot analyze Mephistopheles's defeat with reference to this unknown text. What we do know is that Faust has been building a very different system after Helena shook him to his core: a *gränzunbewußte* system (one "unconscious of borders") in which Mephistopheles's written pact signed in blood for a man's soul is not enforceable.

If *Faust* is thus a story of legal progress, then the question arises of how such progress was achieved. Faust starts with a legal system in which a woman is sentenced to death without meaningfully having been heard, a man is about to be executed without being heard at all, and a pact with the Devil for a man's soul is enforceable. But it ends with a system in which both that woman and that man are saved, and the Devil is left empty-handed. The question thus arises, what changed in this legal system, and how?

The answer of Goethe's *Faust* to this question is simple and unusual: it comes down to narratives and a *gränzunbewußte* legal order. Narratives are key, because when there is only one narrative to explain a given set of facts, then there is no need to hear what the accused has to say—as was the case with Gretchen and Lynceus—for all he can do is repeat that narrative. And a *gränzunbewußte* order is key, because it allows narratives to travel—for instance, Helena brings narratives about herself with her and applies them, and these allow her to acquit Lynceus. If a legal order were closed off, then it would not allow a Helena to enter and act as a judge, and introduce new narratives.

Goethe's answer to what drives legal progress is at once against the grain of his time and a product of it. Goethe does not endorse the major attempts at legal progress of this time: revolutions, empire-building, and the first legal codifications. He associates these attempts with the legal order that Faust is building until Helena astonishes him, one that is centralized and tied to state borders, expansionist through force, inflexibly wedded to the written word, and formalistic. At the same time, Goethe's views are a product of his time. It was a time that saw the gradual disappearance of a legal order made up of a complex patchwork of courts, such as the courts of the Holy Roman Empire, the *Schöffenstuhl* (local courts with lay judges), and ecclesiastical courts;[5] local rulers; and of authorities, such as Roman law, ecclesiastical law, the *Constitutio Criminalis Carolina* of 1532, and local laws and customs. It was also a time in which legal progress was taking place, and Goethe, as a statesman, was involved

5 Charles Donahue Jr., "The Ecclesiastical Courts," in *The History of Courts and Procedure in Medieval Canon Law*, ed. Wilfried Hartmann and Kenneth Pennington (Washington, DC: The Catholic University of America Press, 2016).

in much of it. For instance, in German lands in the eighteenth century, and even into the nineteenth century, torture was still a legitimate method of obtaining evidence in legal proceedings. In Saxony-Weimar-Eisenach, torture was only finally abolished in 1819.[6] *Kirchenbuße,* an ecclesiastical punishment involving public humiliation, was still legal—and women sentenced for fornication could be seen paraded through town on a donkey. *Kirchenbuße* was abolished in Saxony-Weimar-Eisenach in 1786.[7]

One may well wonder what a *gränzunbewußte* legal order looks like, and if it can even work. *Faust* does not offer practical specifics. But a useful analogy is international commercial arbitration today. International commercial arbitration today is *gränzunbewußt* in that, on the one hand, state borders continue to exist and to be important, but, on the other hand, the role of those borders is diminished to the extent that many actors in international arbitration do not need to be conscious of them most of the time.[8] This is not to say that international commercial arbitration today equals the *gränzunbewußte* order that Goethe envisioned. One obvious difference is that international commercial arbitration does not cover criminal matters, whereas Gretchen and Lynceus were accused of capital crimes. Still, the comparison to international commercial arbitration lends some concreteness to the meaning of *gränzunbewußt,* and also helps to distinguish it from another way of approaching global law, namely public international law. Public international law exists between bordered entities—defined borders is a crucial part of the definition of a state under public international law[9]—and is significantly more centralized and formal than international arbitration.

6 Volker Wahl, ed., *"Das Kind in meinem Leib": Sittlichkeitsdelikte und Kindsmord in Sachsen-Weimar-Eisenach unter Carl August: eine Quellenedition, 1777–1786* (Weimar: Böhlaus Nachfolger, 2004), 45.

7 Wahl, *Das Kind in meinem Leib*, 124.

8 See George A. Bermann, *International Arbitration and Private International Law* (Leiden: Brill, 2017), 247–56, and footnotes. In the interests of full disclosure, I note that I was involved in drafting the lectures that formed the basis for this book. See also Jan Paulsson, *The Idea of Arbitration* (Oxford: Oxford University Press, 2013), 35; Bermann, *International Arbitration*, 241.

9 Montevideo Convention on Rights and Duties of States (1933), 165 LNTS 19, Art. 1: "The State as a person of international law should possess the following qualifications: (a) a permanent population; (*b*) *a defined territory*; (c) government; and (d) capacity to enter into relations with the other States" (emphasis added).

2 Question 1. Did Gretchen Kill Her Child—and Why Has It Been Assumed that She Did?

2.1 *Did Gretchen Kill Her Child?*

Gretchen is almost universally assumed to have killed her child.[10] Scholars and commentators who write about Faust[11] or about Goethe more generally;[12] those who condemn Goethe's attitude towards infanticide[13] and those who defend him;[14] those who write about infanticide in the literature of Goethe's time,[15] or in the literature of other periods;[16] legal historians[17] and political scientists[18]—all labor under the same flawed assumption. Although some do argue that Gretchen does not carry the moral guilt for her child's death, the simple question of whether she actually killed her child is not asked. She has become one of literature's most infamous child-murderesses.[19]

However, the evidence against Gretchen is very scant. In its entirety, the evidence is a statement by Faust—"Als Missethäterin im Kerker zu entsetzlichen

10 The sole exception, to the best of my knowledge, is Arnd Bohm. See Arnd Bohm, "Margarete's Innocence and the Guilt of Faust," *Deutsche Vierteljahrsschrift für Literaturwissenschaft und Geistesgeschichte* 75, no. 2:220. ("Literary critics have analyzed *Faust* on the unquestioned premise that Margarete committed infanticide. Indeed, the assumption has gone so without challenge that the secondary literature does not even know the question of her guilt or innocence as a topic.... Unanimously, the critics are convinced that Margarete/Gretchen is guilty of infanticide.")

11 See, e.g., Albrecht Schöne, *Johann Wolfgang Goethe—Faust: Kommentare*, 5th ed. (Frankfurt: Deutscher Klassiker Verlag, 2003).

12 See, e.g., Fritz Breithaupt, "Goethe's Conscience," *MLN* 129, no. 3 (2014): 549–62.

13 See, e.g., Susanne Kord, *Murderesses in German Writing, 1720–1860: Heroines of Horror* (New York: Cambridge University Press, 2009), 146 and n. 96.

14 See, e.g., Wolfgang Wittkowski, "Hexenjagd auf Goethe. November 1783: Hinrichtung einer Kindsmörderin und 'Das Göttliche,'" *Oxford German Studies* 31, no. 1 (2002): 63–102.

15 See, e.g., Jan Matthias Rameckers, "Der Kindesmord in der Literatur der Sturm-und-Drang-Periode: ein Beitrag zur Kultur-und Literaturgeschichte des 18. Jahrhunderts" (Doctoral diss., Rotterdam: Nijgh & van Ditmar, 1927).

16 See, e.g., Matthias Luserke-Jaqui, *Medea: Studien zur Kulturgeschichte der Literatur* (Tübingen: A. Francke, 2002).

17 See, e.g., Wilhelm Wächtershäuser, *Das Verbrechen des Kindesmordes in Zeitalter der Aufklärung: eine rechtsgeschichtliche Untersuchung der dogmatischen, prozessualen und rechtssoziologischen Aspekte* (Berlin: Erich Schmidt, 1973).

18 See, e.g., Ekkehart Krippendorff, *Goethe: Politik gegen den Zeitgeist* (Frankfurt: Insel, 1999). For a further list of commentators who have assumed that Gretchen committed infanticide, *see* Bohm, "Margarete's Innocence," 220 and nn. 12–13.

19 At least one work on child-murderesses is even named after her: Marita Metz-Becker, *Gretchentragödien: Kindsmörderinnen im 19. Jahrhundert (1770–1870)* (Sulzbach am Taunus: U. Helmer, 2016).

Qualen eingesperrt" (226)[20]—and Gretchen's confession in the final scene of *Faust I*, *Kerker* (Dungeon). Faust's statement is mere hearsay. He does not explain the source of his information, does not tell us what crime she is locked up for, and does not even say that she committed the crime—only that she is locked up as a criminal. Both Faust and Mephistopheles then call into question the objectivity of those who sentenced Margarete: Faust refers to her as "Bösen Geistern übergeben und der richtenden gefühllosen Menschheit!" (226),[21] and Mephistopheles refers to "Bande des Rächers" (227).[22] Gretchen's confession is contradicted by her own earlier claim that "Sie nahmen mir's [das Kind] um mich zu kränken / Und sagen nun, ich hätt' es umgebracht" (4445–46)[23] and her later claim that the child is still alive[24]—all in the same scene. In addition, confessions are hardly reliable, especially in a world where torture could be used to secure them, and the confessor is a very young woman (possibly still a child)[25] who has, in a short amount of time, lost her mother, brother, lover, and likely her child, is living with the shame and the stigma of having given birth out of wedlock, and is facing imminent execution.

Thus, there is very little basis on which to conclude with any certainty that Margarete killed her child, and one may even wonder if her child is dead.

2.2 *Why Has It Been Assumed that Gretchen Killed Her Child?*

Then why, if Goethe provides insufficient evidence of Margarete having killed her child, has it been assumed that she did? The answer lies in the narrative of infanticide that prevailed in Goethe's time: first, an unmarried woman is seduced, then she conceals (or attempts to conceal) her pregnancy and the birth of her child, and then she kills her child. For *infanticide*, this was *the only* narrative. That is, if an infant was *killed*, then the only narrative that explained the killing was this narrative, with the mother as the culprit.[26]

20 "Imprisoned in the dungeon as a criminal and subjected to terrible torments."

21 "Handed over to evil minds and to judgmental, unfeeling humanity!"

22 "Bonds of the avengers."

23 "They took it [the child] from me to hurt me / And now they say that I killed it."

24 "Es zappelt noch!" (4561). "It [the child] is still moving!"

25 Faust's claim that Gretchen "[i]st über vierzehn Jahr doch alt" (2627), coupled with the numerous references to her as a *Kind* (e.g. 2609, 2655, 2713) strongly suggest that she is very young, even if her exact age remains unclear.

26 There were related narratives, but they did not include the killing of the child, such as stillbirth or instances where the woman kept the child. See, e.g., Susanne Ude-Koeller, "'Straff der weiber so jre kinder tödten' Zur sagenhaften Geschichte des Kindsmordes," *Fabula: Zeitschrift fur Erzahlforschung/Journal of Folktale Studies/Revue d'Etudes sur le Conte Populair* 32, no. 1–3 (1991): 270.

The existence of only one narrative of infanticide is all the more striking because infanticide dominated discourse in Germany for decades starting in about 1770. This crime was not merely a topic of discussion among jurists or policymakers, but rather a hotly discussed topic by people from various walks of life: philosophers, physicians, clergymen, writers, and many others. For instance, a study of the works of the *Sturm und Drang* reveals the following about infanticide: "Kein Stürmer and Dranger, der sich nicht daran versucht hätte."[27] A *Preisfrage* in 1780 on the question "Welches sind die am besten ausführbaren Mittel, dem Kindermorde Einhalt zu thun?"[28] drew a record 400 responses. By comparison, in the same year, a *Preisfrage* by none less than Frederick the Great drew forty-two responses, already considered a large number.[29] In a different context, Immanuel Kant (generally a proponent of the death penalty) singled out maternal infanticide and killing in a duel as two crimes for which the death penalty would be problematic (he makes no mention of the possibility of other perpetrators of infanticide).[30]

Infanticide trials also drew great attention from the public, and Goethe was no stranger to some of these trials. For instance, in 1771, just months after Goethe returned to his hometown of Frankfurt upon completing his legal studies (one of the theses he defended to graduate was "An fœmina partum recenter editum trucidans capite plectenda sit? quæstio est inter Doctores controversa"),[31] the talk of the town was the case of Susanna Margaretha Brandt, who was accused of infanticide. Goethe showed enormous interest in the case and even obtained the full court records, which he appears to have read thoroughly, though no records of his thoughts on the case survive. Brandt

---

27 Rameckers, "Der Kindesmord," 4–5 (original emphasis). Cf. Kirsten Peters, *Der Kindsmord als schöne Kunst betrachtet: eine motivgeschichtliche Untersuchung der Literatur des 18. Jahrhunderts* (Würzburg: Königshausen & Neumann, 2001), 63–64. "There wasn't an author of the Storm and Stress who didn't try his hand at it."

28 "[Preisfrage]," *Rheinische Beiträge zur Gelehrsamkeit* 2 (1780): 84–86. "What are the most feasible means of stopping infanticide?"

29 Otto Ulbricht, *Kindsmord und Aufklärung in Deutschland* (München: R. Oldenbourg, 1990), 217–18.

30 "Es gibt indessen zwei todeswürdige Verbrechen, in Ansehung deren, ob die *Gesetzgebung* auch die Befugnis habe, sie mit der Todesstrafe zu belegen, noch zweifelhaft bleibt. Zu beiden verleitet das Ehrgefühl. Das eine ist das der *Geschlechtsehre*, das andere der *Kriegsehre*, und zwar der wahren Ehre, welche jeder dieser zwei Menschenklassen als Pflicht obliegt. Das eine Verbrechen ist der mütterliche *Kindesmord* (infanticidium maternale); das andere der *Kriegsgesellenmord* (commilitonicidium), der Duell." Immanuel Kant, *Werkausgabe in zwölf Bänden*, ed. Wilhelm Weischedel, vol. 8 (Frankfurt: Suhrkamp 1977), 457–58. (Original emphasis).

31 Wahl, *Das Kind in meinem Leib*, 455.

was put to death on January 14, 1772.[32] Goethe's next major involvements with infanticide cases came in the duchy of Saxony-Weimar-Eisenach, where he joined the *Geheimes Consilium* (Privy Council) as a *Legionsrat* in June of 1776, and was promoted to a *Geheimer Rat* (Privy Counselor) in September of 1779.[33] In 1781, Dorothea Altwein was accused of killing her child; in 1783, Johanna Catharina Höhn faced the same charge. The Altwein case prompted the Duke of Saxony-Weimar and Saxony-Eisenach, Karl August (1757–1828) to ask his Privy Counselors to vote on the abolition of *Kirchenbuße*[34] (they unanimously voted in favor) and also to commute her death sentence to a life sentence.[35] In the Höhn case, the Duke discussed with his *Geheimräte* a different legislative proposal: to replace the death penalty for infanticide with incarceration coupled with repeated humiliation and painful procedures for the mothers, which the Duke thought would be a stronger deterrent.[36] The *Geheimräte* unanimously rejected the idea; Goethe took about two weeks to do so, and indicated that he considered this an issue of such importance that he would submit an essay on it to the Duke, rather than explain himself in a vote.[37] This essay does not survive.[38]

In all these instances, the narrative of infanticide dictated that the mother killed her child, not anyone else. Against this backdrop, *Kerker*, the final scene of *Faust I*, stands out in that it offers alternative narratives for the death (or disappearance) of Gretchen's child, and thus leaves open the question of whether she killed her child. When Faust arrives in the *Kerker*, he is greeted by the sound of Margarete singing the *Märchen von Machandelbaum*, in which a mother kills her child and then feeds it to the father. But Margarete soon offers an alternative narrative—and suggests that the reason she is deemed to have killed her child is an old *Märchen*.[39]

32 Rebekka Habermas and Tanja Hommen, *Das Frankfurter Gretchen: der Prozess gegen die Kindsmörderin Susanna Margaretha Brandt* (Munich: C.H. Beck, 1999).

33 Willy Flach, "Goethes amtliche Schriften. Zur Begründung ihrer Voröffentlichung," *Viermonatsschrift der Goethe-Gesellschaft* 12 (1951): 129.

34 Wahl, *Das Kind in meinem Leib*, 45, 124.

35 Wahl, *Das Kind in meinem Leib*, 28.

36 Wahl, *Das Kind in meinem Leib*, 33.

37 The vote is reprinted in full in Wahl, *Das Kind in meinem Leib*, 106.

38 Lothar Frede, "Kindesmord und Kirchenbuße bei Goethe," *Zeitschrift für die gesamte Strafrechtswissenschaft* 78, no. 3 (1966): 425.

39 Gretchen is likely referring to the *Märchen von Machandelbaum*, but she could be referring to any one of the many other *Märchen* wherein a mother kills her child. See below, n. 56.

> Sie nahmen mir's [das Kind] um mich zu kränken
> Und sagen nun, ich hätt' es umgebracht.
> Und niemals werd' ich wieder froh.
> Sie singen Lieder auf mich!
> Es ist bös von den Leuten!
> Ein altes Mährchen endigt so,
> Wer heißt sie's deuten? (4444–49)[40]

Such vigilantism is plausible, especially if we recall that Gretchen's neighbor Liesschen discussed how the townspeople would take justice into their own hands in Gretchen's case in an earlier scene,[41] and how both Faust and Mephistopheles described Gretchen facing revenge rather than justice.[42]

After Faust loudly calls her by her name, Margarete recognizes him, and seeks his caresses. She does not receive them. To her "weile" (4479), he (changing one crucial letter), retorts "eile" (4481).[43] His kiss does not convince her: "Wie? du kannst nicht mehr küssen?" (4484).[44] Believing that Faust no longer loves her, she resorts to the standard version: "Mein Kind hab' ich ertränkt."[45] However, there is no good reason to suppose that her current version is closer to the truth than the previous one. Indeed, Faust's coldness may be the final straw that makes her accept society's verdict.

But before Faust leaves, Gretchen tells him another story still—the third version of what happened to their child.[46] The child, she claims, is still alive, and she tells Faust how to find it:

> Rette dein armes Kind.
> Fort! Immer den Weg
> Am Bach hinauf,
> Über den Steg,
> In den Wald hinein,

40 "They took it [the child] from me to hurt me. And now they say that I killed it. And never again will I be happy. They sing songs at me! It is evil of the people. An old (fairy) tale ends thus. Who told them to interpret it?"

41 "Kriegt sie ihn, soll's ihr übel gehn. / Das Kränzel reißen die Buben ihr, / Und Häckerling streuen wir vor die Thür!" (3574–76).

42 See nn. 21 and 22 above.

43 "Linger" / "hurry."

44 "What? You can no longer kiss?"

45 "My child I drowned."

46 Bohm, "Margarete's Innocence," 228–29. ("Even though the language [of lines 4551–62] is so powerful, critics have found almost nothing to say about these lines, relegating them to the background noise of dramatic atmosphere.")

Links wo die Planke steht,
Im Teich.[47]
Faß es nur gleich!
Es will sich heben,
Es zappelt noch!
Rette! rette!" (4552–4562)[48]

Again, we have no good reason to believe this version any more or less than the other ones. It is perfectly plausible that a young woman in a desperate situation would abandon her child (indeed, abandoned infants were found from time to time in Goethe's days).[49] However, Faust does not appear to believe her, for he does not seek his child. Rather, he attempts to carry her off by force, but she refuses. She stays for her impending death and surrenders herself to God's court. Mephistopheles exclaims that she is judged—a voice from above (presumably God's) says she is saved.

One other thing about the power of narratives bears mentioning. Gretchen is not only sentenced because of a narrative, but she also refuses to fight on for her life because of narratives. For instance, she believes that life for a woman who has had an extramarital child is pure misery: "Es ist so elend betteln zu müssen" (4546)[50] and will result in her being caught "Und sie werden mich doch ergreifen!"(4549)[51]—both beliefs recall her brother's story of the life of women who have extramarital children: "Unter Bettler und Krüppel dich verstecken" (3761)[52] and "Auf Erden sein vermaledeit!" (3763).[53] Gretchen's beliefs run contrary to the reality of the play, however. Faust and Mephistopheles have magical black horses on which to take her away, and in *Faust II* they will soon be in the *Saal des Thrones* of a *Kaiserliche Pfalz* (throne room of an imperial palace)—where norms and values generally permitted unmarried people to

47 "Teich" can be rendered as "dike" or "pond." *Teich* commonly referred to the kind of pond from which the water could be let out, meaning that Gretchen's child could be alive in a drained pond. Johann Christoph Adelung, *Grammatisch-kritisches Wörterbuch der hochdeutschen Mundart, mit beständiger Vergleichung der übrigen Mundarten, besonders aber der Oberdeutschen*, rev. ed., vol. 4 (Leipzig: Georg Olms, 1801), 550.

48 "Save your poor child. Away! Stay on the path up the stream, across the bridge, into the woods, left where the plank stands, in the pond."

49 Ulbricht, *Kindsmord und Aufklärung in Deutschland*, 140.

50 "It is so miserable to have to beg."

51 "And they will catch me anyway."

52 "Hide yourself among beggars and cripples."

53 "Being damned on earth!"

live together.[54] However, it is not reality that determines Gretchen's decision, but rather the narratives she believes.

Still, *Faust I* ends on a hopeful note, for Margarete is saved. It also offers a glimpse of the way to legal progress: multiple narratives have to be considered to explain a given set of facts and a *gränzunbewußte* adjudicator is needed for that to happen. Margarete presented alternative narratives for her child's fate, but they have not been taken seriously, and it took God (the ultimate *gränzunbewußte* actor) to save her.

3 Question 2. Why Does Faust Fail to Hear the Accused—and Why Has He Forgotten the Basics of Due Process?

If Faust fails to hear Margarete in that he does not believe her, then by the time of Act III of *Faust II*, Faust simply fails to hear the accused at all. But Helena, who finally appears before Faust in Act III, does hear the accused, and thus has a profound effect on Faust.

Act III is generally regarded as central to all of *Faust*, and Helena as one of Goethe's most important characters,[55] whom Faust described as "mein einziges Begehren!" (7412).[56] In this central act, the first (and arguably only) real action Helena performs is to judge. In the second scene of Act III, Helena arrives in the *Innerer Burghof* (inner courtyard) of Faust's palace, a walled and constrained space. She is met by an impressive procession of marching men. Faust then appears "oben an der Treppe in ritterlicher Hofkleidung des Mittelalters und kommt langsam würdig herunter" (9181).[57] He is displeased, for he was unable to prepare what he would consider an adequate reception.

Faust blames Lynceus for this failure, and he brings him onto the stage in chains. Lynceus's duties as a watchman included to report "[w]as etwa da und dort sich melden mag" (9202).[58] But "[h]eute, welch Versäumniß! / Du

54 Goethe himself enjoyed a similarly privileged position that effectively placed him above the laws and the stigma that Gretchen fears so much. He had lived with Christiane Vulpius for many years—and they had many children—before they legalized their marriage in 1806. Heinz Müller-Dietz, "Die Strafjustiz in der Sicht Goethes," *Jahrbuch der Juristischen Zeitgeschichte* (2010): 297–98.

55 Jochen Schmidt, *Goethes Faust: erster und zweiter Teil: Grundlagen, Werk, Wirkung*, 2nd ed. (Munich: Beck, 2001), 234–35.

56 "My only desire!"

57 "At the top of the stairs in knightly court attire of the Middle Ages and slowly descends in a dignified manner."

58 "What may come forward here or there."

[Helena] kommst heran, er meldet's nicht, verfehlt / Ist ehrenvoller, schuldigster Empfang / So hohen Gastes" (9206–09).[59] For this failure, Faust explains, Lynceus deserves death—had it been up to Faust, Lynceus would be dead already, but he leaves the decision to Helena.

Helena takes the task of judging most seriously: "So hohe Würde wie du sie vergönnst, / Als Richterin, als Herrscherin, und wär's / Versuchend nur, wie ich vermuthen darf" (9213–15).[60] She promptly announces: "So üb' ich nun des Richters erste Pflicht, / Beschuldigte zu hören. Rede denn" (9216–17).[61] She is the first character in the law-laden work that is *Faust* who actually listens to the accused. After praising (or perhaps flattering) Helena, Lynceus tells his story: the sun miraculously rose in the south, rather than the east. He sought the sun with his eyes, but when this dazzling goddess appeared, he was blinded by her beauty, and forgot his duties as a watchman.

Helena acquits Lynceus: "Entferne diesen Guten, laß ihn frei" (9256).[62] She recognizes that "[d]as Übel das ich brachte darf ich nicht / Bestrafen" (9246–47).[63] In other words, she recognizes Lynceus's narrative, for it has been familiar to her all her life, namely that she has a strange effect on men and even gods:

> Welch streng Geschick
> Verfolgt mich, überall der Männer Busen
> So zu bethören, daß sie weder sich
> Noch sonst ein Würdiges verschonten. Raubend jetzt,
> Verführend, fechtend, hin und her entrückend,
> Halbgötter, Helden, Götter, ja Dämonen,
> Sie führten mich im Irren her und hin.
> Einfach die Welt verwirrt' ich, doppelt mehr,
> Nun dreifach, vierfach bring' ich Noth auf Noth. (9247–55)[64]

---

59 "Today, what oversight! You [Helena] come up, he doesn't report it, missed is the most honorable, obliged reception of such a distinguished guest."

60 "As high a dignity as you grant, as a judge, as a ruler, even if it were only trying, as I may suspect."

61 "Thus I now exercise the judge's first duty, to hear the accused. So speak."

62 "Remove this good man, set him free."

63 "The evil that I brought I may not punish."

64 "What severe fate pursues me, everywhere so to beguile men's bosoms, that they spare neither themselves nor other worthy men. Now robbing, seducing, fencing, rapturing back and forth, demigods, heroes, gods, demons even, they lead me astray here and there. Simply I confuse the world, doubly more, only threefold, fourfold I bring trouble upon trouble."

This simple act of narrative justice leaves Faust "Erstaunt, o Königin" (9258).[65] His entire world, even his sense of self, is collapsing:

> Was bin ich nun? Auf einmal machst du mir
> Rebellisch die Getreusten, meine Mauern
> Unsicher. Also fürcht' ich schon, mein Heer
> Gehorcht der siegend unbesiegten Frau.
> Was bleibt mir übrig als mich selbst und alles,
> Im Wahn das Meine, dir anheim zu geben?
> Zu deinen Füßen laß mich, frei und treu,
> Dich Herrin anerkennen, die sogleich
> Auftretend sich Besitz und Thron erwarb. (9264–72)[66]

Faust's mighty walls no longer provide security. Faust now believes that all his property, which he only mistakenly thought was his, should belong to Helena, as should he. Lynceus is similarly struck. He brings Helena all his possessions, which involve significant treasures, which he now believes are worth less than a look from Helena.

This scene borders on the grotesquely absurd. Faust, who studied "Juristerei ... mit heissem bemühn" (355–57),[67] did not see fit to hear a man before executing him. Helena then hears Lynceus—the first character in all of *Faust* to do so—and acquits him because of a narrative that Faust knew as well. For not only is Faust learned enough to know of the effect Helena has had on men, but he experienced it first-hand, when, after seeing Helena (or a phantom of her) at the end of *Faust II*, Act I, he was then paralyzed for the first two scenes of Act II.

How is it possible, then, that Faust fails to hear Lynceus, and is so shocked that Helena does? The answer lies in the fact that Faust has been building out even further the world of *Faust I*, the world of formal and centralized law constrained by strict borders. The Faust of Act III is building an empire that he rules from his walled castle, divided into fiefdoms run by vassals. In this world, the law is very clear that Lynceus must die and there is no point in hearing him

65 "Amazed, o queen."

66 "What am I now? Right away, you make rebellious to me my most loyal ones, my walls. And so I fear, my army obeys the defeatingly undefeated woman. What remains to me, but to give myself and all that I imagine mine own, to give to you? At your feet let me, free and loyal, recognize you as mistress, who, immediately appearing, acquired property and throne."

67 "Law ... with hot engagement."

first. The Faust of *Faust I* ignored Gretchen's narrative that his own child could still be alive, and the Faust of *Faust II* ignores even the need to hear Lynceus's narrative at all. For in *Faust I* there was only one narrative of infanticide, and in *Faust II* there is only one narrative for Lynceus's failure—until Helena changes that by bringing her own narrative to bear on the case.

In fact, she herself is made up of multiple narratives, from those of Homer to Euripides and beyond. Many of these narratives are referenced in Faust. Helena first calls Tindareos her father (8497), but later calls herself a daughter of Zeus (8647). In the *Classical Walpurgisnight*, Faust had to go to the underworld to obtain her release, yet here she is alive and well, returned to Sparta in one piece, not killed or sacrificed. Phorkyas—that is, Mephistopheles in disguise—brings up that she in fact stayed in Egypt rather than in Troy (8872–73).[68] Helena herself is confused by all these versions: "Verwirre wüsten Sinnes Aberwitz nicht gar. / Selbst jetzo, welche denn ich sei, ich weiß es nicht" (8874–75).[69] For instance, she recalls the narrative that Achilles followed her out of Hades,[70] but does not know if it actually happened: "Ich als Idol, ihm dem Idol [Achill] verband ich mich. / Es war ein Traum, so sagen ja die Worte selbst. / Ich schwinde hin und werde selbst mir ein Idol" (8879–81).[71]

Helena is not merely one who brings multiple narratives. She is also someone from outside Faust's centralized and bordered system, and is not constrained by it. She comes into his world from the boundless seas at the beginning of Act III, and simply vanishes into thin air at the end of Act III, leaving Faust holding only her clothes. She is *gränzunbewußt*.

If it seems strange that Faust is so shaken by Helena's act of judging; consider how shaken he would be if Helena had been the one to judge Gretchen, had listened to her, and found Faust's child alive, hidden away as Gretchen said, or else found that the child had been murdered by others. Consider also how such a judgment could shake a legal system that had considered that only mothers could be guilty of infanticide—for that system would have to

68 The first known recording of this version of the Helena myth can be found in Stesichorus's *Palinode*. Euripides incorporated it into his plays *Elektra* and *Helena*. In this version, Helena stayed in Egypt until Menelaus fetched her from there, while Paris had only brought an idol, a phantom to Troy. Johann Wolfgang von Goethe, *Sämtliche Werke. Briefe, Tagebücher und Gespräche*, ed. Rose Unterberger (Frankfurt: Deutscher Klassiker Verlag, 1994), vol. 7/2, 600; Johann Wolfgang von Goethe, *Sämtliche Werke nach Epochen seines Schaffens*, ed. Karl Richter (Munich: Hanser, 1998), vol. 18/1, 952.

69 "Confuse not readily yourself with wild absurdity. Even so, which one I am, I do not know."

70 This myth can be traced back to Pausanias. Goethe, *Sämtliche Werke. Briefe*, vol. 7/2, 600.

71 "As an idol, I joined myself to him, the idol [Achilles]. It was a dream, so say the words themselves. I fade away and become an idol to myself."

confront its major and tragic blind spot. That is why such a seemingly simple act on Helena's part—hearing Lynceus's narrative and entertaining multiple narratives to explain the situation—so deeply shakes Faust.

4 Question 3. Why Is the Text of the Pact Concealed and Why Does Mephistopheles Fail to Claim Faust's Soul?

Mephistopheles's defeat—his failure to claim Faust's soul—is frequently analyzed in terms of the text of the pact between Faust and Mephistopheles. However, Goethe does not provide the text of the pact, but only a discussion of it, an omission that has, to the best of my knowledge, been overlooked. This raises the question of why Goethe obscures this crucial text from his readers, and how to analyze Mephistopheles's defeat without recourse to the unknown text of the pact.

In the second *Studirzimmer* scene of *Faust I*, Faust and Mephistopheles conclude the pact. Before Faust signs this pact in blood, however, he has a lengthy conversation with Mephistopheles. First, Mephistopheles offers himself as a companion to Faust, even as a servant:

> Ich bin dein Geselle
> Und, mach' ich dir's recht,
> Bin ich dein Diener, bin dein Knecht! (1646–48)[72]

Mephistopheles's price is that Faust shall serve him *drüben*[73] (presumably in the world to come), a price Faust seems to value at zero:

> *Mephistopheles.*
> Ich will mich *hier* zu deinem Dienst verbinden,
> Auf deinen Wink nicht rasten und nicht ruhn;
> Wenn wir uns *drüben* wieder finden,
> So sollst du mir das Gleiche thun.
> *Faust.*
> Das Drüben kann mich wenig kümmern; (1656–70)[74]

---

72 "I am your companion, and if I do right by you, I am your servant, am your knave!"

73 "Above."

74 "Mephistopheles: *Here* I want to bind myself to your service, at your behest neither pause nor rest; if we find each other *over there* again, then you should do the same for me. Faust: Over there concerns me little." Original emphasis.

After some further back-and-forth, Faust and Mephistopheles shake hands on a bet:

> *Faust.*
> Werd' ich beruhigt je mich auf ein Faulbett legen,
> So sei es gleich um mich gethan!
> Kannst du mich schmeichelnd je belügen
> Daß ich mir selbst gefallen mag,
> Kannst du mich mit Genuß betrügen;
> Das sei für mich der letzte Tag!
> Die Wette biet' ich!
> *Mephistopheles.*
> Top!
> *Faust.*
> Und Schlag auf Schlag! (1692–98)[75]

A handshake was a way of sealing an agreement under medieval *Faustrecht*, and Faust is under the impression that the pact has been concluded.[76] He restates his understanding of the pact:

> Werd' ich zum Augenblicke sagen:
> Verweile doch! du bist so schön!
> Dann magst du mich in Fesseln schlagen,
> Dann will ich gern zu Grunde gehn!
> Dann mag die Todtenglocke schallen,
> Dann bist du deines Dienstes frei,
> Die Uhr mag stehn, der Zeiger fallen,
> Es sei die Zeit für mich vorbei! (1699–1706)[77]

---

75 "Faust: If I ever lie down, calmed down, on a lazy bed, so let it be done for me at once! Can you ever flatteringly deceive me into liking myself, can you cheat me with pleasure; that will be the last day for me! This bet I offer! Mephistopheles: Top! Faust: And handshake on handshake!"

76 Georg Müller, *Das Recht in Goethes Faust* (Berlin: C. Heymann, 1912).

77 "Were I to say to the moment: Stay a while! You are so beautiful! Then you can put me in chains, then I would like to perish! Then may the death knell sound, then you are free of your service, then may the clock stop, may the hand fall, the time for me will be over!"

Mephistopheles immediately stresses that this pact will not be forgotten, to which Faust readily acquiesces verbally. But Mephistopheles insists on putting the pact in writing:

> *Mephistopheles.*
> Bedenk' es wohl, wir werden's nicht vergessen.
> [...]
> Nur eins!—Um Lebens oder Sterbens willen,
> Bitt' ich mir ein paar Zeilen aus. (1707–15)[78]

Faust is frustrated by this request, for he would rather that his word alone sufficed. He knows that only a parchment, with writing and sealed, is feared by all. He also understands that the written word is immutable in a way that the spoken word is not. But Mephistopheles insists that Faust sign in blood, which Faust reluctantly does, seemingly without paying attention to the contents of the written document. The pact is concluded, and it will not be explicitly invoked again until Mephistopheles pulls out this "blutgeschriebnen Titel"[79] (11613) towards the end of *Faust II*.

Before we return to *Faust II*, it is worth noting a few further indications in the *Studirzimmer* scene that the text of the written document is hidden from the reader. First, previous versions of *Faust*—including the *Faustbuch* and Marlowe's *Dr. Faustus*—do provide the text of the pact.[80] Second, Faust's understanding of the pact (and the discussion about it) are not based on the text of the pact—Mephistopheles does not produce the written document until *after* the two have discussed their agreement. Faust then signs in blood, apparently without reading the document carefully, if at all. Third, Mephistopheles only asks Faust to sign "ein paar Zeilen"[81]—but their discussion was significantly longer than that, and the reader is not told which two lines from their extensive conversation Mephistopheles has chosen, or if those lines are even verbatim from their conversation.

When Mephistopheles invokes the pact in the scene *Grablegung* (Entombment) towards the end of *Faust II* (again without providing its text), he believes it gives him a right to Faust's soul—but he also knows, *before*

78 "Mephistopheles: Think about it, we won't forget it. [...] Only one!—For the sake of living or dying, I ask for myself a few lines."

79 "Blood-written title."

80 For an overview of the Devil's Pacts in the various versions of *Faust*, see Schmidt, *Goethes Faust*, 22–24.

81 "A few lines."

Faust's soul escapes, that he will not be able to claim it. For after Faust has died—after famously uttering "Zum Augenblicke dürft' ich sagen: / Verweile doch, du bist so schön!" (11581–82)[82]—but before Faust's soul has left his body, Mephistopheles pulls out their pact, the "blutgeschriebnen Titel" (11613),[83] but laments: "[d]och leider hat man jetzt so viele Mittel / Dem Teufel Seelen zu entziehn" (11614–15).[84] The temporal "jetzt" (now) suggests that something has changed. This is underlined by the words that follow: "Auf altem Wege stößt man an, / Auf neuem sind wir nicht empfohlen" (11616–17)[85] and "[u]ns geht's in allen Dingen schlecht!" (11620).[86] Mephistopheles then explains that this change has a legal aspect: "Herkömmliche Gewohnheit, altes Recht, / Man kann auf gar nichts mehr vertrauen" (11620–22).[87] He continues to dwell on that theme after Faust's soul is carried away by the angels to the heavens: "Bei wem soll ich mich nun beklagen? / Wer schafft mir mein erworbenes Recht?" (11832–33)[88]

Mephistopheles has lost not because of the text of the pact, but because something has changed. This legal change has at least two parts: the *altes Recht* (old law) no longer governs, and there are no courts to enforce ("Bei wem soll ich mich nun beklagen?"—"To whom should I complain now") a contract ("erworbenes Recht"—"acquired right"). Understanding this change—this progress away from a system that enforces contracts for men's souls—not the text of the pact, is the key to understanding Mephistopheles's defeat. Just like Gretchen and Lynceus, Faust is ultimately judged by a *gränzunbewußte* judge. This judge is an angel "schwebend in der höheren Atmosphäre, Faustens Unsterbliches tragend":[89]

> Gerettet ist das edle Glied
> Der Geisterwelt vom Vösen,
> "Wer immer strebend sich bemüht
> Den können wir erlösen." (11934–37)[90]

---

82 "To the moment, I could have said: Linger, you are so beautiful."
83 "Blood-written title."
84 "Unfortunately, there are now so many ways to pull away souls from the devil."
85 "On old ways one bangs one's head, one new one is not recommended."
86 "It goes poorly for us in all things!"
87 "Conventional custom, old law, one can't trust anything anymore."
88 "To whom should I complain now? Who furnishes me my acquired rights?"
89 "Hovering in the higher atmosphere, carrying Faust's immortal soul."
90 "Rescued is the noble member, from the spirit world of evil, 'Whoever always strivingly applies himself, him we can redeem.'"

This different judging is made possible by the world Faust built due to the effect Helena had on him. This world is radically different from the bordered and centralized realm Faust had constructed by the beginning of Act III or the realm of the *Kaiser*. Indeed, when Mephistopheles tells Faust that he need only speak to complete that realm ("So sprich daß hier, hier vom Palast / Dein Arm die ganze Welt umfaßt") (11225–26),[91] Faust interrupts him: "Das verfluchte *hier*!" (11233).[92]

Faust rejects Mephistopheles's vision of a centralized, bordered empire spanning the whole world, and curses the very center of his realm where his palace stands. And when Faust no longer has much time left to live, he finally exits his palace, the seat of centralized power, and explains what he has built. Faust has created a world of perpetual striving and activity, a "paradiesisch Land."[93] His description of it contains no centers, internal or external borders (except to keep water out), vassals, or formal and rigid laws.

5 Conclusion

Two simple words are at the core of this article: narrative and *gränzunbewußt* (unconscious of borders). Yet understanding Goethe's *Faust* in their terms has yielded new insights. For instance, Gretchen may not have killed her child, but is deemed to have done so because of narratives, not evidence, and is saved because of a *gränzunbewußte* interference by the Lord. Mephistopheles' defeat despite the blood-signed pact is due to the emergence of a *gränzunbewußte* legal order, precipitated by Helena through the narratives that she brought with her and applied in Lynceus's case.

The focus on narratives and borders does not mean that other aspects connected to legal progress are irrelevant. For instance, one could likely establish that sexism is part of the reason that only mothers were held responsible for infanticide. But what Goethe contributes is a way to tackle such sexism through the introduction of narratives and a change in the legal importance of borders and centers.

One may well wonder why narratives require adjudicators such as Helena to spread them, and do not enter the legal realm effectively through, for instance, literature. It appears that even the greatest literature still needs people to apply it to the law. This is confirmed by the fact that many narratives in which

91 "So speak that here, here from the palace, your arm will embrace the whole world."

92 "The cursed *here*!" Original emphasis.

93 "Paradisiacal country."

someone other than the mother kills the child predate Goethe's time, but had somehow faded from consciousness. For instance, in the Bible Abraham almost sacrificed Isaac, the Pharaoh killed many Israelite children, the Lord killed the firstborn of Egypt, Psalm 137 ("By the Waters of Babylon") ends with the verse "Happy shall *he* be, that taketh and dasheth thy little ones against the stone" (emphasis added), and in the Massacre of the Innocents, King Herod attempted to kill the infant Jesus by slaughtering the children of Bethlehem. In addition, the killing of Christ has been portrayed as an infanticide in the Christian tradition—but naturally not by the Virgin Mary.[94] Folktales have no shortage of infanticide stories in which someone other than the mother is the perpetrator.[95] Legal scholars as late as the first half of the eighteenth century still took it for granted that the father can also be guilty of infanticide.[96] But this did not prevent only one narrative from dominating in Goethe's time: the mother killed her child.

This article has focused on only a few scenes in *Faust*, but the framework applied here can be used for *Faust* as a whole and for other works by Goethe. In *Faust*, one may think of Mephistopheles's repeated efforts to prevent change through written and rigid law within a centralized, bordered realm, such as the paper money he conjures to preserve the *Kaiser*'s empire. In Goethe's other works, one may also think of the English Lord who appears in *Die Wahlverwandtschaften* (Elective Affinities) and, by recounting a novella, has such an impact on Charlotte that she becomes willing to grant a divorce—he appears only briefly, has no fixed abode, and travels ceaselessly. It may also be possible to understand why Goethe so often wove infanticide into his works—to present counternarratives to the dominant narrative of infanticide, for instance, *Die Wahlverwandtschaften* (Charlotte's child dies while in Ottilie's care), *Iphigenie auf Tauris* (Tantalus offers his son to the gods as a meal), *Vor Gericht* (a pregnant woman refuses to tell the court who the father is), *Erlkönig* (mysterious cause of death in spite of father's attempts to protect the child), and *Die Ersticker in London* (criminal gangs kill children to sell their bodies to hospitals for teaching purposes).

---

94 See Bohm, "Margarete's Innocence," 217–18.

95 Ude-Koeller, "Straff der weiber so jre kinder tödten," 269–72.

96 See, e.g., Joh. Jodocus Beck, *Tractatus de eo, quod justum est circa stuprum: von Schwäch- u. Schwängerung der Jungfern und ehrlichen Wittwen. Worrinnen von der Obligation dess Stupratoris, der demselben bey fälschlicher Beschuldigung gebührenden Satisfaction, der Straffe dess Stupratoris und der Geschwächten … gehandelt wird aus denen allgemeinen Reichs-Rechten, und denen bewährtesten Scriptoribus zusammen getragen* (Nürnberg: Johann Georg Lochners, 1743), 852–53.

My hope is that this framework can be useful in legal historical work as well, especially because this is a contribution to a *Festschrift* for a legal historian. If Goethe was correct that legal progress is achieved through narrative and *Gränzunbewußtheit*, then the question arises of whether it can be shown that historical legal progress occurred in this way. I leave that to the historians.

Acknowledgments

This essay would not have been possible without Charlie Donahue. Charlie generously shared his immense knowledge of legal history with me—and patiently taught me his thorough approach to it—when I was working on my dissertation. He kindly attended my dissertation defense and shared his thoughts on it. This article is based on that dissertation. I am also profoundly grateful to Peter Burgard, Gordon Teskey, and Katharina Pistor for supervising the dissertation, and to Luis Girón-Negrón for his invaluable input. Any views expressed here, and any mistakes, are my own and in no way represent the views of Three Crowns or its clients.

Bibliography

Adelung, Johann Christoph. *Grammatisch-kritisches Wörterbuch der Hochdeutschen Mundart, mit beständiger Vergleichung der übrigen Mundarten, besonders aber der Oberdeutschen.* 2nd ed. Leipzig: Georg Olms, 1793–1801.

Beck, Joh. Jodocus. *Tractatus de eo, quod justum est circa stuprum: von Schwäch- u. Schwängerung der Jungfern und ehrlichen Wittwen. Worrinnen von der Obligation dess Stupratoris, der demselben bey fälschlicher Beschuldigung gebührenden Satisfaction, der Straffe dess Stupratoris und der Geschwächten ... gehandelt wird aus denen allgemeinen Reichs-Rechten, und denen bewährtesten Scriptoribus zusammen getragen.* Nürnberg: Johann Georg Lochners, 1743.

Bermann, George A. *International Arbitration and Private International Law.* Leiden: Brill, 2017.

Blackall, Eric Albert. *The Emergence of German as a Literary Language, 1770–1775.* Cambridge: Cambridge University Press, 1959.

Bohm, Arnd. "Margarete's Innocence and the Guilt of Faust." *Deutsche Vierteljahrsschrift für Literaturwissenschaft und Geistesgeschichte* 75, no. 2 (2001): 216–50.

Breithaupt, Fritz. "Goethe's Conscience." *MLN* 129, no. 3 (2014): 549–62.

Donahue, Charles, Jr. “The Ecclesiastical Courts.” In *The History of Courts and Procedure in Medieval Canon Law*, edited by Wilfried Hartmann and Kenneth Pennington. Washington, D.C.: The Catholic University of America Press, 2016.

Flach, Willy. “Goethes Amtliche Schriften. Zur Begründung Ihrer Voröffentlichung.” *Viermonatsschrift der Goethe-Gesellschaft* 12 (1951): 126–43.

Frede, Lothar. “Kindesmord Und Kirchenbuße Bei Goethe.” *Zeitschrift für die gesamte Strafrechtswissenschaft* 78, no. 3 (1966): 420–31.

Goethe, Johann Wolfgang von, *Faust. Eine Tragödie.* [*Erster Theil.*] I, 14 S. Weimar: Hermann Böhlau, 1887.

Goethe, Faust. *Eine Tragödie.* [*Zweiter Theil.*] I, 15 C1. Weimar: Hermann Böhlau, 1888.

Goethe, Johann Wolfgang von, *Sämtliche Werke. Briefe, Tagebücher und Gespräche.* Edited by Rose Unterberger. Frankfurt: Deutscher Klassiker Verlag, 1994.

Goethe, Johann Wolfgang von, *Sämtliche Werke nach Epochen seines Schaffens*. Edited by Karl Richter. Munich: Hanser, 1998.

Habermas, Rebekka, and Tanja Hommen. *Das Frankfurter Gretchen: Der Prozess Gegen Die Kindsmörderin Susanna Margaretha Brandt.* Munich: C.H. Beck, 1999.

Kant, Immanuel. *Werkausgabe in Zwölf Bänden.* Edited by Wilhelm Weischedel. Vol. 8, Frankfurt: Suhrkamp, 1977.

Kord, Susanne. *Murderesses in German Writing, 1720–1860: Heroines of Horror.* Cambridge Studies in German. New York: Cambridge University Press, 2009.

Krippendorff, Ekkehart. *Goethe: Politik Gegen Den Zeitgeist.* Frankfurt: Insel, 1999.

Lüderssen, Klaus, ed. *Die wahre Liberalität ist Anerkennung: Goethe und die Jurisprudenz.* Baden-Baden: Nomos, 2002.

Luserke-Jaqui, Matthias. *Medea: Studien Zur Kulturgeschichte Der Literatur.* Tübingen: A. Francke, 2002.

Meissner, Johannes. *Goethe als Jurist*. Berlin: Kortkampf, 1885.

Metz-Becker, Marita. *Gretchentragödien: Kindsmörderinnen im 19. Jahrhundert (1770–1870)*. Sulzbach am Taunus: U. Helmer, 2016.

Müller-Dietz, Heinz. “Die Strafjustiz in Der Sicht Goethes.” *Jahrbuch der Juristischen Zeitgeschichte* 11 (2010): 277–306.

Müller, Georg. *Das Recht in Goethes Faust.* Berlin: C. Heyman, 1912.

Paulsson, Jan. *The Idea of Arbitration.* Oxford: Oxford University Press, 2013.

Pausch, Alfons, and Jutta Pausch. *Goethes Juristenlaufbahn: Rechtsstudent, Advokat, Staatsdiener—eine Fachbiographie*. Köln: O. Schmidt, 1996.

Peters, Kirsten. *Der Kindsmord als schöne Kunst betrachtet: Eine Motivgeschichtliche Untersuchung der Literatur des 18. Jahrhunderts.* Würzburg: Königshausen & Neumann, 2001.

“[Preisfrage].” *Rheinische Beiträge zur Gelehrsamkeit* 2 (1780): 84–86.

Rameckers, Jan Matthias. "Der Kindesmord in der Literatur der Sturm-und-Drang-Periode: Ein Beitrag zur Kultur- und Literaturgeschichte des 18. Jahrhunderts." Doctoral diss., Rotterdam: Nijgh & van Ditmar, 1927.

Schmidt, Jochen. *Goethes Faust: Erster und Zweiter Teil: Grundlagen, Werk, Wirkung.* 2nd ed. Munich: Beck, 2001.

Schneider, Peter. *Der Elefant: Goethe über Recht, Staat und Gesellschaft in Faust II.* Freiburg i.Br.: Rombach Verlag, 2009.

Schöne, Albrecht. *Johann Wolfgang Goethe—Faust: Kommentare.* 5th ed. Frankfurt: Deutscher Klassiker Verlag, 2003.

Ude-Koeller, Susanne. "'Straff der Weiber so ire Kinder tödten' Zur sagenhaften Geschichte des Kindsmordes." *Fabula: Zeitschrift fur Erzählforschung/Journal of Folktale Studies/Revue d'Etudes sur le Conte Populair* 32, no. 1–3 (1991): 258–74.

Ulbricht, Otto. *Kindsmord und AufkläRung in Deutschland.* Munich: R. Oldenbourg, 1990.

Wächtershäuser, Wilhelm. *Das Verbrechen des Kindesmordes im Zeitalter der Aufklärung: Eine rechtsgeschichtliche Untersuchung der dogmatischen, prozessualen und rechtssoziologischen Aspekte.* Berlin: Erich Schmidt, 1973.

Wahl, Volker, ed. *"Das Kind in Meinem Leib": Sittlichkeitsdelikte nd Kindsmord in Sachsen-Weimar-Eisenach unter Carl August: Eine Quellenedition, 1777–1786.* Weimar: Böhlaus Nachfolger, 2004.

Wittkowski, Wolfgang. "Hexenjagd auf Goethe. November 1783: Hinrichtung einer Kindsmörderin und 'Das Göttliche.'" *Oxford German Studies* 31, no. 1 (2002): 63–102.

CHAPTER 20

Wesley Hohfeld's Modernist Imagination

Bharath Palle

1 Introduction: The Obscure Object of Analysis

There is a passage in one of Wesley Newcomb Hohfeld's (1879–1918) more neglected articles that places his philosophical concerns in an unusual light. "[I]t is a serious obstacle," he wrote shortly before his death, "to close analysis and clear thinking that [lawyers] habitually deal with the [concept of an] easement … as if it were a simple unity to be adequately described by a few loose and ambiguous terms[.]" Rather, he continued, those terms, "such as 'property,' 'title,' 'ownership,' '*right* of ownership,' 'right,' 'privilege,' 'incorporeal(!) right,' etc., [are] utterly insufficient to indicate the precise elements involved [in an easement]."[1] Throughout his corpus, Hohfeld often passionately attacked the use of certain ordinary categories in legal analysis. This passage, however, suggests that Hohfeld's radicalism may have been more thoroughgoing, and that he firmly rejected some common-sense assumptions within legal theory at the time.

Hohfeld is among the most important and influential legal philosophers of the twentieth century. Born in Oakland, California, Hohfeld obtained his philosophy degree at the University of California at Berkeley in 1901, where he was the most brilliant undergraduate in a quarter century. Hohfeld went on to complete his law degree at Harvard and later taught law at Stanford and Yale. Hohfeld is famous primarily for two articles that he published in the *Yale Law Journal* in 1913 and 1917.[2] In these articles, Hohfeld developed a system of interlinked logical concepts for analyzing important legal categories, such as "rights" and "property ownership," within common-law theory. In the century since, Hohfeld's conceptual innovations have informed a great deal of work within Anglophone moral, political, and legal theory. In the United States, law

1 Wesley Newcomb Hohfeld, "Faulty Analysis in Easement and License Cases," *Yale Law Journal* 27, no. 1 (November 1917): 70.

2 Wesley Newcomb Hohfeld, "Some Fundamental Legal Conceptions as Applied in Judicial Reasoning," *Yale Law Journal* 23, no. 1 (November 1913): 16; Wesley Newcomb Hohfeld, "Fundamental Legal Conceptions as Applied in Judicial Reasoning," *Yale Law Journal* 26, no. 8 (June 1917): 710.

 | DOI:10.1163/9789004710696_022

students are most likely to encounter Hohfeld's work in their first-year property course.

Despite Hohfeld's pre-eminent stature among legal philosophers, his work remains widely misunderstood. The familiar summary of his life and work does not accurately depict Hohfeld's broader philosophical concerns. The bulk of his corpus is concerned with the problems of shareholder liability for corporate debts, equitable trusts, and conflict of laws.[3] This would doubtless surprise students who have only encountered his work in their first-year property law course. Although Hohfeld's interests ranged widely, he was convinced that the central task of jurisprudence was in analyzing what he called "complex legal interests," such as property ownership, easements, and most of all, trusts and corporations.[4] Hohfeld's famous logical scheme emerged directly from his analysis of these complex legal forms.

Hohfeld's project had a negative side and a positive side. On the positive side, Hohfeld developed some exacting logical schemes to capture the "precise elements" involved in complex legal interests. It is the negative side, however, that marks him as truly radical. Hohfeld insisted that ordinary legal language could not adequately describe these complex legal forms or usefully structure legal analysis. Using the concept of "title" or "ownership" within legal analysis is akin to using the concept of a "chair" within theoretical physics. Those categories are perfectly adequate in ordinary discourse; but they have no useful place within careful legal analyses or scientific explanations. Lawyers, Hohfeld insists throughout his work, must abandon using ordinary legal language and instead rely on a more precise and scientific system of logical concepts. Developing those concepts preoccupied Hohfeld for much of his life.

I argue that this concern with ordinary language categories marks Hohfeld as a modernist figure. In this short essay, I juxtapose Hohfeld's work with a key text in literary modernism to reveal a surprising set of affinities. We can observe curious similarities and continuities between Hohfeld and the Viennese writer Hugo von Hofmannsthal on using ordinary language categories. More generally, we can explain a great deal about Hohfeld's work when we perceive how he was drawn by the "lure of heresy" like so many other modernist figures.[5]

3 See, for example, Wesley Newcomb Hohfeld, "Nature of Stockholders' Individual Liability for Corporation Debts," *Columbia Law Review* 9, no. 4 (April 1909): 285; Wesley Newcomb Hohfeld, "Individual Liability of Stockholders and the Conflict of Laws," *Columbia Law Review* 9, no. 6 (June 1909): 492; Wesley Newcomb Hohfeld, "The Relations between Equity and Law," *Michigan Law Review* 11, no. 8 (June 1913): 537.

4 Hohfeld, "Some Fundamental," 28.

5 Peter Gay, *Modernism: The Lure of Heresy* (New York: W. W. Norton, 2008), 3–10.

This rather unusual juxtaposition is necessary because there is much about Hohfeld that remains obscure. Due to persistent scholarly neglect, we know little about the immediate context in which he produced his philosophical works. No surviving archives chronicle Hohfeld's intellectual development. We do not know how and when he arrived at his mature positions, nor do we have a clear sense of the primary intellectual influences on his famous logical system of legal concepts. We do not therefore know what might illuminate the dense, difficult, and sometimes strange texts of this major twentieth-century legal philosopher. In what follows, I will point to one possible source of illumination, as distant and unexpected though it may appear.

But before we can talk of logical systems any further, we must first discuss an intellectual crisis.

2 Philipp's Intellectual Crisis

The intellectual crisis is fictional, or at least partly so. It is described at considerable length in one of the central texts of early twentieth-century literary modernism: Hugo von Hofmannsthal's (1874–1929) *Ein Brief* published in 1902. The text purports to be a letter written in 1603 by Philipp, Lord Chandos (a wealthy English aristocrat whom Hofmannsthal invented) to Francis Bacon (a real historical figure who was England's Chancellor of the Exchequer in the early seventeenth century). Philipp was a precocious poet who had published a series of highly acclaimed poetic works in his teens. By his twenties, he abruptly ceased publishing poetry and retreated from public life. Bacon had evidently expressed concern that Philipp had ceased his literary activity. Philipp responds with his letter explaining that he had given up writing poetry because of a painful and extended intellectual crisis. The letter describes the crisis at considerable length and examines how it affects nearly every aspect of Philipp's life.

The letter is fictional, but some have speculated that the intellectual crisis was partly real. There are some striking similarities between Hofmannsthal and Philipp. Like Philipp, Hofmannsthal was born to considerable wealth: in this case, a prominent Viennese banking family. Hofmannsthal was also a precocious poet, whose work was greeted with rapturous acclaim. He was polylingual, and his work drew heavily from the ancients. This too might describe Philipp. The most striking similarity is that Hofmannsthal gave up writing poetry shortly after publishing *Ein Brief*. Hofmannsthal continued to write and publish for the remainder of his life, but he mostly produced libretti (some of them for Richard Strauss) and a few plays. He never published poetry after

1902. Some therefore conclude that the crisis that Philipp describes so elaborately was quite similar to something that Hofmannsthal himself experienced during this period.[6]

The precise nature of the crisis is not easy to capture using a familiar label. Philipp instead describes certain consequences of the crisis in a series of lovely, disconcerting images. The text repeatedly returns to how Philipp experiences the relationship between his language and his world. As Philipp explains to Bacon, he composed his early poetry without perceiving any divide between the world of language and the material world in which he lived. Both his language and his world were bound up in a harmonious unity.

> [There was] no difference between drinking warm foaming milk which a tousled rustic at my hunting lodge had squeezed into a wooden bucket from the udder of a fine, mild-eyed cow, and drinking in sweet and frothy spiritual nourishment from an old book as I sat in the window seat of my study. The one was like the other … And so it went throughout the entire sweep of life all around me.[7]

The subsequent intellectual crisis interrupts this perception of unity. Philipp ceases to believe that his linguistic resources can be so effortlessly integrated into his experience of the world. He discovers instead that linguistic and conceptual structures obscure, conceal, and elide important aspects of the natural and social worlds. Formulaic expressions, he sensed, caricature, or simplify, a world that is at once vaster and more strange.

> Once I saw through a magnifying glass that an area of skin on my little finger looked like an open field with furrows and hollows. That was how it was for me now with people and their affairs. I could no longer grasp them with the simplifying gaze of habit.[8]

---

6 Steven C. Schaber, "Hofmannsthal's Lord Chandos Letter," *Germanic Review* 45, no. 1 (January 1970): 52–53; H. Stefan Schultz, "Hofmannsthal and Bacon: The Sources of the Chandos Letter," *Comparative Literature* 13, no. 1 (Winter 1961): 2–3; J. D. McClatchy, "Introduction," in *The Whole Difference: Selected Writings of Hugo von Hofmannsthal*, ed. J. D. McClatchy (Princeton: Princeton University Press, 2008), 7–8.

7 Hugo von Hofmannsthal, *The Lord Chandos Letter*, trans. Joel Rotenberg (New York: NYRB Classics, 2005), 120.

8 Hofmannsthal, *Lord Chandos*, 122.

As a result, Philipp says, he has "completely lost the ability to think or speak coherently about anything at all."[9] Those "abstract words which the tongue must enlist as a matter of course in order to bring out an opinion disintegrated in my mouth like rotten mushrooms." Using words such as "'spirit,' 'soul,' or 'body'" filled him with such "inexplicable uneasiness," and offering up opinions became so "fraught with difficulties" that he found he was unable to participate in even the most ordinary conversations.[10] Hearing others prattle on without appreciating those difficulties "filled [him] with inexplicable fury."[11] He suggests that the many familiar language categories are akin to fictions or elaborate rhetorical devices that are simply the product of longstanding conventions. Those devices fail to describe anything or accurately explain any set of processes in the world.

Ordinary language does not transparently afford access to the world of experience. This insight casts doubt on some of the basic assumptions that structured Philipp's life. As he comes to distrust those familiar linguistic and conceptual categories, Philipp finds it impossible not only to write poetry, but also to participate meaningfully in the familiar rituals of everyday life. He finds that he is unable to read the ancients; unable to express his opinions or converse with his peers about the affairs of court; reprimand his young daughter for lying; express his opinion about commonplace matters; or provide simple instructions to his workers.[12] Philipp then stops writing poetry and even retreats from public life. He goes through the motions of his life—a life that he now regards as trivial and uninteresting—concealing his true interests and concerns. Or he feigns interest in those matters that, as a matter of social hierarchy, ought to engage a member of the landed gentry such as himself.[13]

Hofmannsthal's dreamlike fable has an important moral dimension. This is evident from Philipp's account of the incident with rat poison. As Philipp tells Bacon, he spread some rat poison in a milk cellar in his dairy farm to exterminate rodents. This was such an ordinary event during his day that he did not think anything about it. Afterwards, as he goes riding, Philipp suddenly has a vision of that same cellar—from the perspective of the rats that have been exposed to the poison. He imagines the fury and the fright of those rats as they realize that they are going to die; how those rats desperately and vainly attempt to escape from the cellar only to be thwarted; how they might perceive the

9 Hofmannsthal, *Lord Chandos*, 121.
10 Hofmannsthal, *Lord Chandos*, 121.
11 Hofmannsthal, *Lord Chandos*, 122.
12 Hofmannsthal, *Lord Chandos*, 121–22.
13 Hofmannsthal, *Lord Chandos*, 125–26.

confusion and calamity that unfolds around them. Philipp likens placing poison in the milk cellar to the Roman sack of Carthage during the Punic wars—he imagines that the rats react to the inevitability of their impending deaths the same way that the Carthaginians reacted to their Roman adversaries.[14]

Disenchantment with ordinary language categories places certain habitual actions and practices in a new light. Philipp suddenly feels "a vast empathy" for those creatures that he had poisoned.[15] The world is, he realizes, much more continually surprising and more alien than he suspected; it is just that habitual use of ordinary linguistic categories, through excessive simplification or rhetorical maneuvers, conceals that strange and wondrous world. There are significant moral and aesthetic elements in everyday situations that remain hidden so long as he uses ordinary linguistic categories to think through those situations.

In the same way that Philipp becomes aware of the moral features hidden behind everyday actions, he also becomes aware of the captivating beauty of the pastoral scenes that he encounters every day. By extricating himself from the traps laid by familiar structures of thought, Philipp catches fleeting glimpses into an unfamiliar new world that he can neither describe nor explain. The discovery leaves him convulsed with experiences of love and joy.

> At [certain] moments an insignificant creature, a dog, a rat, a beetle, a stunted apple tree, a cart path winding over the hill, a moss-covered stone ... rise up before me with such a plenitude, such a presence of love that my joyful eye finds nothing dead anywhere.[16]

Philipp does not abandon his conception of the life around him as a harmonious unity. The world of experience continues to remain coherent and integrated; and Philipp maintains that he stands in some harmony with the world. It is just that assertions, descriptions, and explanations using familiar linguistic terms and categories seem alien to that larger world. Those categories do not figure into Philipp's sense of the unity of that world of experience.

Philipp is convinced that his experiences will remain elusive, so long as he has access to the limited set of resources that ordinary language affords him. The world in all its moral and aesthetic complexity, he thinks, is fundamentally resistant to being described in those ordinary linguistic and conceptual categories. To fully describe his experiences, Philipp needs to develop an entirely

14 Hofmannsthal, *Lord Chandos*, 123–24.

15 Hofmannsthal, *Lord Chandos*, 124.

16 Hofmannsthal, *Lord Chandos*, 125.

new vocabulary and set of conceptual resources. He is convinced, however, that he does not have access to those resources. This is what finally condemns him to a solitary existence. He wanders through life alone, unable to communicate his experiences to anyone else. He concludes,

> [T]he language in which I might have been granted the opportunity not only to write but also to think is not Latin or English, or Italian, or Spanish, but a language of which I know not one word, a language in which mute things speak to me.[17]

3 Hohfeld's Philosophical Motivations

> Are we forced to recognize that mere words–especially if they are Latin words–have such a surprisingly potent tendency to control thought?[18]

At this point, one might well be tempted to ask, what does all of this have to do with Hohfeld? Hohfeld briefly mentions Francis Bacon at the start of one of his papers; Hofmannsthal for a time studied law at Vienna. These coincidences aside, there seems no further connection between the son of a German piano teacher in 1870s Oakland and the scion of a prominent banking family in *fin-de-siecle* Vienna. Hohfeld does not seem to have had any literary interests or inclinations whatsoever; his prose is renowned for being exceptionally dreary. He hardly mentions any figure from a field outside of legal theory in his corpus. There is however an interesting exception. In a footnote to one of his papers, Hohfeld quotes from Lewis Carroll's *Through the Looking Glass*.[19] Carroll or Charles Dodgson as he was known when he was not publishing children's books, also worked in mathematics and symbolic logic. It is not clear if Hohfeld knew that he shared some of those interests with Dodgson. In any event, that passage has since become a staple in legal literature quoted by many others who have no literary inclinations whatsoever.

My claim is not that Hofmannsthal directly influenced Hohfeld. Rather, viewing Hohfeld's corpus as among the key texts of modernism is exegetically fruitful. Hofmannsthal explicitly articulates a set of themes and ideas about the unreliability of ordinary language categories to describe or explain

17 Hofmannsthal, *Lord Chandos*, 127–28.

18 Hohfeld, "Fundamental," 759–60.

19 Hohfeld, "Fundamental," 750. The famous passage concerns an exchange between Alice and Humpty Dumpty about whether words can mean different things.

complex features of the world. Ordinary language categories either fail to capture or fundamentally misrepresent important aspects of the world of experience. Such categories occlude the moral and aesthetic qualities of familiar thoughts, practices, beliefs, and the other objects of everyday life. As Philipp realizes this, he suffers a crisis that upends his world. He is forced to reject the premises on which he had conducted his former life. It has been hinted that Hofmannsthal himself may have suffered a similar crisis. Could we say something similar about Hohfeld? And what would it say about his motivations for developing a new conceptual vocabulary in legal theory?

Hohfeld was deeply concerned with the vagaries of ordinary legal language. He often quotes from judicial decisions and commentaries at considerable length. One can hardly be blamed for reading these lengthy extracts with increasing bewilderment and boredom. Why Hohfeld sets out those passages at such length is less clear. No legal philosopher either before or after Hohfeld has adopted this practice of block quoting from judicial decisions. Hohfeld's idiosyncratic scholarly practice is better explained when viewed through the lens of the modernist concern with ordinary language. Hohfeld first carefully assembles different passages that establish certain prominent accounts of supposedly basic legal concepts, such as legal right, duty, power, ownership, equity, contract, etc. Hohfeld then sets about refining, clarifying, and criticizing those accounts. He offers alternative accounts, and sometimes even develops neologisms to designate more familiar concepts. Ordinary legal language then furnishes Hohfeld with the raw materials for his philosophical interventions.

Hohfeld rejected most familiar legal concepts to structure legal analysis. Mental habits, or what he describes in another context as "the modes of thought and language involved in working out the various [legal] problems," are effectively traps.[20] Those traps lead language users to make a series of logical missteps in working through legal problems. So what were Hohfeld's objections to ordinary legal categories?

4 Hohfeld's Criticisms of Ordinary Legal Language—I

Hohfeld's most well-known objection to using ordinary legal language is not a distinctly modernist objection. Familiar terms, he claims, are often ambiguous since they are used to express several distinct ideas in different contexts. The term "property" is used to refer to duties, powers, and other legal relations that

20 Hohfeld, "Relations," 557.

obtain between a set of individuals, namely the owner of a given resource and the non-owners. The term also is used to refer to the resource in question—land, jewelry, or trademarks and goodwill—to which those relations pertain. Such ambiguity makes this term treacherous for legal analysis.

By itself, there is nothing objectionable about this ambiguity. Rather, it is a problem when lawyers fail to see that there are two distinct ideas involved here. Such failures often result in logical missteps in legal analysis. Hohfeld also demonstrates that many such ordinary legal terms are similarly ambiguous. He is highly critical of the terms "rights *in rem*" and "rights *in personam*" to describe how the owner of a particular resource stands in relation to non-owners. Lawyers usually take "[t]he phrases *in personam* and *in rem* ... to be of unvarying meaning and free of ambiguities calculated to mislead the unwary [although the] exact opposite is, however, true."[21] We can set this objection aside: one need not be a modernist to see that ordinary legal terms can be ambiguous.

Hohfeld's other objections are more unusual. He claims that ordinary legal terms are abbreviated ways of representing a complex social reality. Existing conceptual categories and discursive patterns represent "as simple that which is really complex." Hohfeld argues that this causes "serious obstacle[s] to the clear understanding ... of legal problems."[22] Many ordinary legal terms present unduly simple pictures of legal institutions by abbreviating a complex set of processes and facts. Talk about "corporations" or "corporate bodies," for instance, are simply compressed ways of referring to an immensely complex network of social relations between individuals. If one says that a corporation owns a particular piece of land, then one relies on a convention to refer, in a highly simplified manner, to the complex range of social facts that obtain in this situation.

Such abbreviations are sometimes useful. Lawyers go awry, however, when they fail to appreciate that these terms simplify complex facts and instead take those facts as adequately describing the social world. There is a danger that lawyers might take these fictions too literally. Even if there was no such danger, those concepts would still lack the theoretical resources for working through some important problems in corporate law. Those terms often obscure or elide important facts about the social world that are necessary for adequate legal analysis. Hohfeld insists that terms such as "corporation" or "corporate person," because they are so unduly simple, cannot usefully structure legal analysis.

21 Hohfeld, "Fundamental," 713.

22 Hohfeld, "Some Fundamental,"19.

Using common sense categories, such as "a corporate person," to solve legal problems is "like looking at things through smoked glass and then holding a candle on the other side in order to see them[.]"[23]

Rather, Hohfeld continues,

> [A]ll corporate transactions and all propositions relating to the corporations can be stated in terms of ultimate realities rather [than] in terms of the fictions more commonly employed … [A]n attempt must be made to describe these liabilities without employing the descriptive formula of corporate personality.[24]

It is here that Hohfeld develops the notorious idea of the "complex aggregate of jural relations"[25] or, as it has since come to be known, as a "bundle of rights." Ordinary legal discourse presents certain legal institutions as simple or straightforward; Hohfeld represents them instead as complex, intricate, and strange. He claims that many ordinary legal concepts that previously seemed analytically simple or basic, such as property, title, ownership, right of ownership, or right, turn out to refer to complex networks of legal relationships among an indefinitely large class of individuals.[26]

> [T]he tendency—and the fallacy—has been to treat the specific problem as if it were far less complex than it really is; and this commendable effort to treat as simple that which is really complex has … furnished a serious obstacle to the clear understanding, the orderly statement, and the correct solution of legal problems.[27]

Hohfeld develops his conceptual structures to access those hidden aspects of the social world. He argues that all talk about "ownership" or "corporate liability" can be restated without remainder into legal relations among individuals. Restating in this way would better guide judicial reasoning and explain social processes. To this end, Hohfeld develops elaborate formal structures to solve different legal problems and capture some previously unappreciated aspects of the social world.

---

23 Hohfeld, "Nature," 291.

24 Hohfeld, "Nature," 292.

25 Hohfeld, "Fundamental," 746–47.

26 Hohfeld, "Faulty Analysis," 70–71.

27 Hohfeld, "Some Fundamental," 19.

5 Hohfeld's Criticisms of Ordinary Legal Language—II

There are often no terms or words in ordinary legal language to refer to some extremely important legal relations or positions. For this reason, lawyers often fail to appreciate that certain common social positions are *legal* positions. To rectify these omissions, Hohfeld introduces a series of neologisms to identify and analyze those legal positions.

Consider the conceptual distinction that Hohfeld is most famous for: the distinction between a claim and a privilege. Hohfeld invents the term "no-right" because there exists no term in ordinary legal language to describe the specific legal position that he is trying to capture. Hohfeld argues that the ordinary use of the term "right" refers to two sets of legal relationships. First, a right is used to identify the right-holder's protection from certain kinds of interferences with respect to some activity or object. Under common law, for instance, landowners usually enjoy claims that others not trespass on their land. Second, one uses the term "right" to refer to a legal permission, or privilege, that the right-holder enjoys to carry on a certain activity. Landowners often have the privilege of hosting a party or pitching a tent on their land. Sometimes, a right-holder may enjoy both of these relationships, i.e., protection from non-interference and permission to act in various ways. However, one may well have permission to carry on an activity that is not protected from interference. For example, you are permitted to park your car along a public road, but you are not protected from others also engaging in that activity, because someone can cut you off and beat you to a parking space. Most modern economic competition is similarly structured by legal permissions: even if you are permitted to carry on your enterprise, a competitor may still drive you out of business. Such ambiguity surrounding the term "right" often results in significant logical errors in many prominent legal texts and judicial decisions.

Ordinary legal language occludes the aspect of social reality in which the legal system grants permissions to actors for doing or refraining from doing various things. Such background permissions are pervasive and as important a feature of social reality as the more prominent claims against non-interference.[28] It follows from this that our lives are more systematically regulated than we may have previously appreciated. But there is no term in ordinary legal language to designate how one stands in relation to someone who has the legal privilege of doing something. This requires Hohfeld to invent the term *no-right*.

28 Hohfeld, "Some Fundamental," 42.

Hohfeld also invents a series of related terms—*unital*, *paucital*, and *multital*—for somewhat different reasons. He claims that there are several distinct extensions of the term "right *in rem*." Again, the ambiguity of the term causes lawyers to make logical errors in their analysis. Hohfeld introduces his neologisms to identify a distinct set of legal relationships that the term right *in rem* obscures or conflates with other sets of relationships. The neologism *multital* is useful because Hohfeld finds that important aspects of the social world,

> [have] been greatly obscured not only by the habitual tendency to treat a multiplicity of fundamentally similar rights ... as if they were only one, but also by the equally strong tendency to include under the hazy blanket term, right *in rem*, especially in the case of tangible objects, the multiplicity of privileges and other jural relations that the holder of the multital right ... may have.[29]

The final objection is perhaps most characteristically modernist. Hohfeld claims that ordinary legal terms conceal a set of important moral features in common legal situations. This is the express implication of Hohfeld's analysis of the distinction between claims and privileges. There are legal positions that are not recognized as such by ordinary language users. Legal privileges can and do often exist without any supporting claims against non-interference. So when should claims of noninterference accompany legal privileges? Should such claims accompany certain kinds of actors engaged in certain forms of economic competition? The ambiguity of "rights-talk," as well as some key missing terms and concepts, prevent lawyers from appreciating that there are such choices involved in quotidian situations.

Hohfeld argues that those choices should be confronted as ethical or policy decisions. Such questions cannot be resolved by legal concepts or materials alone. As Hohfeld puts it,

> such a privilege or liberty to deal with others at will might very conceivably exist without any peculiar concomitant rights against "third parties" as regards certain kinds of interference. Whether there should be such concomitant rights (or claims) is ultimately a question of justice and policy; and it should be considered, as such, on its merits.[30]

29 Hohfeld, "Fundamental," 745–46.

30 Hohfeld, "Some Fundamental," 36.

Hohfeld similarly argues that many ordinary concepts and linguistic categories—e.g., property, ownership, corporations, easements, rights, etc.—not only lack the theoretical resources to work through legal problems, but also obscure important normative considerations within various situations.

Taken jointly, the upshot of these various objections is clear. Many ordinary legal terms present a misleading picture of the social world, either by concealing important moral features of the social world or by occluding the social relationships within that world. Hohfeld had a dismissive term of such ordinary terms—"fictions"—and he usually mentions those fictions with a mixture of anger and contempt.

> [C]an there be any doubt that the notions of "knowledge," "intention," and "agreement to be bound" are ... worthless fictions, impossible of application and calculated merely to befog serious legal questions that ... are, despite the *language* of the judges, decided according to objective and substantial considerations of justice and policy?[31]

Such Hohfeldian fictions neither guide legal analysis nor explain social outcomes. Judges who purport to reason using those fictions merely present a misleading picture of the cognitive and ethical processes underlying their decisions. Those fictions, which are merely rhetorical devices or products of convention and ritual, should be ignored for any serious scientific study of the social world. Hohfeld is furious that those fictions are instead used so prominently within common-law reasoning. That attitude seems oddly reminiscent of Philipp's fury at hearing notions like "'spirit,' 'soul,' or 'body.'"[32]

6 Some Modernist Heresies

Hohfeld is in many ways the paradigmatic modernist legal philosopher. He begins analyzing ordinary legal institutions and shows them to be stranger, more complex, and teeming with difficult ethical problems. If you think that the world is not quite like that, then Hohfeld's logical system might appear puzzling, even peculiar. Over forty years ago, Duncan Kennedy and Frank Michelman wrote that, "Hohfeld is often envisaged as a chap with a scholastic passion for terminological nicety—at worst a carping bore, at best an

31 Wesley Newcomb Hohfeld, "Individual Liability of Stockholders and the Conflict of Laws," *Columbia Law Review* 10, no. 6 (June 1910): 530–31 (emphasis in original).

32 Hofmannsthal, *Lord Chandos*, 122.

authentic, if pedantic exemplar of the academic virtue of precision."[33] This puzzlement is not merely characteristic of the later reception of Hohfeld's ideas. Arthur Corbin recounts several episodes from the 1920s illustrating how his colleagues reacted to Hohfeld's work with a sense of bewildered amusement.[34] If we understand Hohfeld to be mounting a radical challenge to conventional ways of thinking about the social world, this sense of puzzlement starts to make sense.

Useful and important conceptual distinctions, for Hohfeld, frequently do not track linguistic usage. First, he defines ordinary legal concepts in counterintuitive ways. One can, according to Hohfeld, exercise a legal power through any action that changes one's (or another's) legal relations. We can thus exercise a legal power even by committing a crime or a tort. This is because by committing the crime or tort, we place ourselves in a different legal position, straddled with new burdens that we did not previously have. Again, for Hohfeld, someone has a legal liability if they are susceptible to having their legal relations changed by another person. The capacity to inherit land, receive monetary gifts, or enter binding contracts is the susceptibility of having one's legal position changed (from non-owner to owner of the land or money, or into newly possessing contractual powers and duties) through the acts of another person (the testator, donor, or other contractual party). Such abilities to inherit, receive gifts, and enter contracts therefore count for Hohfeld as legal liabilities. Just as powers can sometimes be disadvantageous to the holder, so liabilities can be advantageous.[35] Hohfeld deliberately goes against the grain of ordinary linguistic usage here. This gleeful revisionism inevitably disconcerts conservative legal philosophers, who assume that their pre-existing intuitions largely present a useful and accurate picture of the social world.[36]

Second, Hohfeld's analysis of a legal privilege is fundamentally at odds with prevailing assumptions within modern political philosophy about the importance of the distinction between positive and negative liberty. As the philosopher N. E. Simmonds argues, by "locat[ing action] within a complex field of consequences wherein choice is never excluded, but is equally never without

33 Duncan Kennedy and Frank Michelman, "Are Property and Contract Efficient?," 8 *Hofstra Law Review* (1980): 752.

34 Arthur Corbin, "Foreword," in *Fundamental Legal Conceptions as Applied in Judicial Reasoning*, ed. Walter Wheeler Cook (New Haven: Yale University Press, 1964), xi–xii.

35 Hohfeld, "Some Fundamental," 44–55. See also Visa A. J. Kurki, *A Theory of Legal Personhood* (Oxford: Oxford University Press, 2019), 114–15.

36 Joseph Raz, "Voluntary Obligations and Normative Powers," in *Normativity and Norms: Critical Perspectives on Kelsenian Themes*, ed. Stanley L. Paulson and Bonnie Litschewski Paulson (Oxford: Clarendon Press, 1998), 452–53.

cost," Hohfeld establishes that "freedom as the pure absence of constraint is … a chimera."[37] Someone's freedom is in short always at the expense of another's unfreedom. Thus, Hohfeld's departures from common-sense definitions and assumptions are intended to present a radically different picture of the social world than what more familiar legal concepts permit.

There is one final interesting convergence between Hohfeld and modernists like Hofmannsthal. Concluding his most famous article, Hohfeld claims that there are deeper analogies and similarities between distinct subjects of the common law that are obscured by ordinary legal-language categories. By relinquishing those familiar modes of thought and by using a novel logical system, Hohfeld argues, one might be able to perceive the "fundamental unity and harmony in the law."[38] Through this process of looking at the world with a new conceptual apparatus,

> it becomes possible not only to discover essential similarities and illuminating analogies in the midst of what appears superficially to be infinite and hopeless variety, but also to discern common principles of justice and policy underlying the various jural problems involved. [39]

Ordinary legal categories prevent lawyers from perceiving the order underlying the seemingly chaotic growth of the common law. Beneath the "infinite and hopeless variety" of legal doctrines, there are recurring patterns and analogies. It is to bring out the "unity and harmony" of the common law that Hohfeld develops his new philosophical vocabulary.

7 Some Historiographical Observations

By situating Hohfeld among other modernists, we can appreciate that there is a single motivational structure that underlies his corpus. Hohfeld's broad aim was in developing a philosophical vocabulary—shorn of ordinary legal categories—that could describe precisely certain facts about the social world.[40] Apart from understanding Hohfeld better, this juxtaposition has some interesting implications.

37 Matthew H. Kramer, Nigel E. Simmonds, and Hillel Steiner, *A Debate Over Rights: Philosophical Enquiries* (Oxford: Oxford University Press, 1998), 167–68.

38 Hohfeld, "Some Fundamental," 59.

39 Hohfeld, "Some Fundamental," 59.

40 I explain why Hohfeld embarked on a specific line of inquiry that eventually led him to develop his logical system. I do not explain why Hohfeld drew four distinctions for his

First, the traditional understanding of American Legal Realism is mistaken. As one might suspect from the discussion about "fictions," Hohfeld thought that judicial opinions were generally useless for explaining why judges decided the way that they did, or for guiding legal analyses. The legal realists of the following decades take their cues from Hohfeld. Notably, Hohfeld does not characterize judges as canny politicians who artfully conceal the explanations and justifications for their decisions. Common law terms and concepts, for someone like Jeremy Bentham (1748–1832), were a secret language accessible only to a cabal of insiders. Technical legal terms were completely opaque and mysterious to those who were not instructed in the codes and formulas of the common law. Judges wielding considerable political power deliberately made common-law reasoning arcane. Because the common law was so complicated and technical, Bentham argued, judges were often able to perpetuate injustice while escaping accountability from the general public.[41]

Hohfeld's position was different. He argued that judges lack the theoretical resources to work through certain common problems. Due to certain habits of the mind, judges fail to appreciate that certain ordinary legal terms are either ambiguous or are simplified abbreviations of a complex set of relations. Unwittingly trapped by these categories, judges fail to appreciate that certain common situations involve ethical problems that can only be solved using the resources of moral philosophy or economic thought. As judges lack the relevant theoretical resources, they are forced to rely on what Karl Llewellyn and Herman Oliphant would later call "intuitions of experience" or "situation-types" to decide disputes.[42] But judges might not be able to articulate those intuitions even if they tried. *That* makes the content of judicial opinions weak explanations or justifications for judicial decisions. The widespread fallacies in judicial opinions are not by design; those fallacies are simply the consequence of the fact that lawyers do not have access to the proper tools or resources for conducting precise legal analysis.

---

logical system—between rights, privileges, powers, and immunities—rather than, say, three or ten. Hohfeld's motivations alone do not determine the contents of his logical apparatus. That outcome is shaped as much by the raw materials with which Hohfeld was working as by his orientation, assumptions, and methods. Having a sense of Hohfeld's broad goals, as well as contexts for the analysis, provides the basis for evaluating whether Hohfeld's logical distinctions are appropriate.

41 Gerald Postema, *Bentham and the Common Law Tradition* (Oxford: Oxford University Press, 1986), 265–67.

42 Herman Oliphant, "A Return to Stare Decisis," *The American Law School Review* 6, no. 5 (March 1928): 225; K. N. Llewellyn, "Through Title to Contract and a Bit Beyond," *New York University Law Quarterly Review* 15, no. 2 (January 1938): 171–72.

Second, existing intellectual histories of U.S. legal theory might be unduly narrow. One can discover broad convergences in modes of analysis and thought if one locates legal theory within the broader context of the period's intellectual developments. Since American Legal Realism directly grows out of Hohfeld's work, the history of that movement might well be closely bound up with the features of modernist thought.

There is finally no invariant set of problems that constitutes the tradition of analytic legal philosophy. The assumptions, methodologies, and concerns at any particular historical moment shape even abstract objects such as logical systems. As those problems, goals, and motivations gradually change over time, this tradition comes to have a history. Intellectual historians would have to examine not only how analytic legal philosophers proceeded to respond to certain questions, but also why they asked specific questions at certain moments in time, how those questions changed over time, and how their philosophical endeavors related to the political and intellectual ferment in the world outside of philosophy.

8 Modernism and Philosophical Pragmatism

The bridge that spans the work of Hohfeld and Hofmannsthal was developed by philosophical pragmatism. We can do no more than sketch those philosophical developments here. The Harvard psychologist William James (1842–1910), whose ideas profoundly influenced Hohfeld, devotes an entire chapter in *Pragmatism* to arguing that common-sense categories, such as space, time, bodies, minds, kinds, things, and causation "are constructions as patently artificial as any that science can show."[43] Common-sense categories, for James, were simply instruments with which human beings successfully navigated the world of experience. Those categories, because they were so useful, insinuated themselves into the "very structure of language," leaving human begins "incapable of thinking naturally in any other terms." James stressed that those categories were themselves revisable. Following the scientific revolutions of the early modern period in Europe, James argued, human beings began to exert a more powerful control over the natural world than what could be squared with common sense. As scientific knowledge "burst the bounds of common sense,"

43 William James, *Writings, 1902–1910*, ed. Bruce Kuklick (New York: Literary Classics of the United States, 1987), 564.

common-sense categories in turn became less useful in navigating the modern world.[44]

Philosophical pragmatism was an international movement; disenchantment with common-sense categories owed much to a broader set of philosophical developments that took place across the transatlantic world at the turn of the twentieth century.[45] James developed his ideas in concert with many European thinkers. The figure who perhaps most powerfully influenced both James and European modernism was the Viennese professor Ernst Mach (1838–1916).[46]

Mach argued that even the most successful scientific laws, such as the laws of mechanics, were simply working hypotheses that required further revision and adjustment.[47] One of Mach's most influential works showed how historical conditions profoundly shaped the production of the scientific knowledge of mechanics. Mach had also argued that common-sense categories were vulnerable to future scientific developments. As modern scientific understandings overthrew common-sense notions, this fundamentally transformed the kinds of questions that were integral to philosophy. The kinds of questions previously canonical to philosophy—questions connected with "body and soul, the seat of the soul, immortality, the world in the mind, a priori intuition … panpsychism, God and the world, free will, responsibility and sin"—were swept away by modern science, bringing forth new kinds of questions in their place.[48]

A young Hofmannsthal attended Mach's lectures at the University of Vienna. It is likely not an accident that Philipp expresses discomfort with similar ideas in his letter. Nor is it likely a coincidence that Philipp addresses his letter to Francis Bacon, to whom much of modern scientific thinking is (wrongly) traced.

---

44 James, *Writings*, 566–71. For useful commentaries of James's views on common sense, see Bruce Kuklick, *A History of Philosophy in America, 1720–2000* (New York: Oxford University Press, 2001), 159–60; Cheryl Misak, *Cambridge Pragmatism: From Peirce and James to Ramsey and Wittgenstein,* (Oxford: Oxford University Press, 2016),73–74.

45 Duncan Bell, *Dreamworlds of Race* (Princeton: Princeton University Press, 2020).

46 Catherine Wilson, "Mach, Musil, and Modernism," *The Monist* 97, no. 1 (January 2014): 139; Gerald Holton, "Ernst Mach and the Fortunes of Positivism in America," *Isis* 83, no. 1 (March 1992): 33–36.

47 Ernst Mach, *The Science of Mechanics*, trans. Thomas J. MacCormack (Chicago: The Open Court Publishing Co., 1919).

48 Wilson, "Mach, Musil" 152.

9 Conclusion

This piece has been about logical systems and intellectual crises. I have suggested that Hohfeld, in his own dogged way, pursued the modernist project in legal theory. By discussing Hohfeld in the context of an author that he was (probably) not aware of, this piece has deliberately staked out a radical position. I have played up the broad affinities between Hohfeld's philosophical orientation and that of literary modernists. This has been necessary because few commentators have tried explaining Hohfeld's motivations; fewer still have paused to examine whether any consistent thread runs across his corpus.

Hohfeld's project was one of intellectual emancipation. Like Philipp, Hohfeld realized that impugning common-sense modes of thought brought forth some radical implications. Any pedagogy or social theory founded on ordinary legal concepts was bound to be worthless for studying social institutions. To design a law school curriculum properly attentive to complex social realities required drastically changing existing pedagogical frameworks. Only by completely revising the law school structure and curriculum could lawyers be instructed in new ways of perceiving and analyzing the world. Lawyers and social scientists, emancipated from the profound confusions brought on by common-sense modes of thought, would be able to develop a new science of society to explain, predict, and alter social institutions. Hohfeld wanted to develop new conceptual frameworks and modes of analysis as the basis for more scientific forms of pedagogy and social theory.[49] Hohfeld's project had some wide-ranging moral and political consequences, whose implications he was starting to explore when he suddenly died in 1918.

Hohfeld devoted his life to attacking certain common-sense ideas within legal analysis and judicial opinions. But as austere and rigorous as Hohfeld's conceptual model was, it could not entirely displace common-sense notions about rights or property ownership that were firmly entrenched in lay and legal discourse in the common-law world. William James had appreciated, in a way that Hohfeld perhaps could not, this staying power of common sense.

> When you begin a piece of music in a certain key, you must keep the key to the end. You may alter your house ad libitum, but the ground-plan of the first architect persists—you can make great changes, but you cannot

---

49 Wesley Newcomb Hohfeld, "A Vital School of Jurisprudence and Law: Have American Universities Awakened to the Enlarged Opportunities and Responsibilities of the Present Day?," *Association of American Law Schools. Proceedings of the Annual Meeting 1914* (December 1914): 76–140.

change a Gothic church into a Doric temple. You may rinse and rinse the bottle, but you can't get the taste of the medicine or whiskey that first filled it wholly out.[50]

Bibliography

Bell, Duncan. *Dreamworlds of Race*. Princeton: Princeton University Press, 2020.

Corbin, Arthur. "Foreword." In *Fundamental Legal Conceptions as Applied in Judicial Reasoning*, edited by Walter Wheeler Cook, vii–xv. New Haven: Yale University Press, 1964.

Gay, Peter. *Modernism: The Lure of Heresy*. New York: W. W. Norton, 2008.

Hofmannsthal, Hugo von. *The Lord Chandos Letter*. Translated by Joel Rotenberg. New York: NYRB Classics, 2005.

Hohfeld, Wesley Newcomb. "Faulty Analysis in Easement and License Cases." *Yale Law Journal* 27, no. 1 (November 1917): 66–101.

Hohfeld, Wesley Newcomb. "Fundamental Legal Conceptions as Applied in Judicial Reasoning." *Yale Law Journal* 26, no. 8 (June 1917): 710–70.

Hohfeld, Wesley Newcomb. "Individual Liability of Stockholders and the Conflict of Laws." *Columbia Law Review* 9, no. 6 (June 1909): 492–522.

Hohfeld, Wesley Newcomb. "Individual Liability of Stockholders and the Conflict of Laws." *Columbia Law Review* 10, no. 6 (June 1910): 520–49.

Hohfeld, Wesley Newcomb. "Nature of Stockholders' Individual Liability for Corporation Debts." *Columbia Law Review* 9, no. 4 (April 1909): 285–320.

Hohfeld, Wesley Newcomb. "The Relations between Equity and Law." *Michigan Law Review* 11, no. 8 (June 1913): 537–71.

Hohfeld, Wesley Newcomb. "Some Fundamental Legal Conceptions as Applied in Judicial Reasoning." *Yale Law Journal* 23, no. 1 (November 1913): 16–59.

Hohfeld, Wesley Newcomb. "A Vital School of Jurisprudence and Law: Have American Universities Awakened to the Enlarged Opportunities and Responsibilities of the Present Day?" *Association of American Law Schools. Proceedings of the Annual Meeting 1914* (December 1914): 76–140.

Holton, Gerald. "Ernst Mach and the Fortunes of Positivism in America." *Isis* 83, no. 1 (March 1992): 27–60.

James, William. *Writings, 1902–1910*. Edited by Bruce Kuklick. New York: Literary Classics of the United States, 1987.

50 James, *Writings*, 560.

Kennedy, Duncan, and Frank Michelman. "Are Property and Contract Efficient?" *Hofstra Law Review* 8, no. 3 (1980): 711–70.

Kramer, Matthew H., N. E. Simmonds, and Hillel Steiner. *A Debate Over Rights: Philosophical Enquiries*. Oxford: Oxford University Press, 1998.

Kuklick, Bruce. *A History of Philosophy in America, 1720–2000*. New York: Oxford University Press, 2001.

Kurki, Visa A. J. *A Theory of Legal Personhood*. Oxford: Oxford University Press, 2019.

Llewellyn, K. N. "Through Title to Contract and a Bit Beyond." *New York University Law Quarterly Review* 15, no. 2 (January 1938): 159–209.

Mach, Ernst. *The Science of Mechanics*. Translated by Thomas J. MacCormack. Chicago: The Open Court Publishing Co., 1919.

McClatchy, J. D. "Introduction." In *The Whole Difference: Selected Writings of Hugo von Hofmannsthal*, edited by J. D. McClatchy, 1–19. Princeton: Princeton University Press, 2008.

Misak, Cheryl. *Cambridge Pragmatism: From Peirce and James to Ramsey and Wittgenstein*. Oxford: Oxford University Press, 2016.

Oliphant, Herman. "A Return to Stare Decisis." *The American Law School Review* 6, no. 5 (March 1928): 215–30.

Postema, Gerald. *Bentham and the Common Law Tradition*. Oxford: Oxford University Press, 1986.

Raz, Joseph. "Voluntary Obligations and Normative Powers." In *Normativity and Norms: Critical Perspectives on Kelsenian Themes*, edited by Stanley L. Paulson and Bonnie Litschewski Paulson, 451–70. Oxford: Clarendon Press, 1998.

Schaber, Steven C. "Hofmannsthal's Lord Chandos Letter." *Germanic Review* 45, no. 1 (January 1970): 52–58.

Schultz, H. Stefan. "Hofmannsthal and Bacon: The Sources of the Chandos Letter." *Comparative Literature* 13, no. 1 (Winter 1961): 1–15.

Wilson, Catherine. "Mach, Musil, and Modernism." *The Monist* 97, no. 1 (January 2014): 138–55.

APPENDIX

Reflections from Former Students

APPENDIX 1

When Giants Roamed: A Reflection

Thomas S. Burns

Charles Donahue (aka Charlie) and I first met back in the day when at universities "Giants Roamed," at least we graduate students knew that to be true. I had recently reenrolled in the Ph.D. program of the Department of History at the University of Michigan after serving two years in the US Army. My Ph.D. advisor, Sylvia Thrupp, founder and editor of *Comparative Studies in Society and History*, while I was in the service, had invited Charlie to be on her editorial committee. When Miss Thrupp [as she wished to be called] "encouraged" me to look into Donahue's seminar on Roman Law, I made an appointment to see him forthwith. When I met with Charlie, I explained that I wanted to sit in, would complete all assignments, participate fully in discussions but did not wish to undertake written examination since I already had a full class load. Charlie was only four years older than I, and we both looked much younger than our age. He did have more hair on his face, however.

My recollections of that first seminar center around the differences that I witnessed between the rest of the students, all lawyers-to-be, and myself in what we sought from having an acquaintance with Roman Law. Their passion was for "process" with minimal interest in what lay behind the legal texts, whereas mine was the reverse. We all profited greatly from the fact that our professor was passionate about both. Charlie has always manifested an old dictum about teaching. Teaching is passion for the subject combined with well-organized presentation. I carried on his dual approach throughout my own 35-year academic career and now into teaching ancient and medieval history and archaeology to fellow seniors.

The following spring he offered a seminar on Canon Law, which I also actively audited. Soon after that seminar Charlie asked me if I would like to be his research assistant. He even paid me! When he took a sabbatical leave the following year, I continued as his research assistant with the added bonus that before his departure he gave me a key to his office for my use. I cleared a modest space on his desk to work and was careful not to disturb elsewhere, although the temptation was high. I vividly recall an occasion when I was confronted by the circulation staff of the law library over checking a folio volume out to his office. The scene might have become confrontational had I not quickly produced Charlie's note on his official stationery attesting that I was his proxy and

 | DOI:10.1163/9789004710696_023

had his permission to check out materials in his name. To me this underscored the fact that "giants did roam" and that, although young, Charlie was already in tutelage to share their lofty domain.

Two aspects drawn from my own experiences must suffice as concrete illustrations of how his teaching and engagement with the primary sources influenced my later work and reflect Charlie's imprint. The first example concerns my doctoral thesis on the Ostrogoths, who ended up in Italy at the invitation of the Roman Emperor in Constantinople, then struggling against the remnants of the Roman army in Italy. I gave Charlie a copy of my thesis to read about a month before the formal defense, as I did all four members of my committee. All needed time to read and consider 380 pages of text and notes. When it was his turn for cross-examination, we went over various legal texts that I had used, as was expected. Then he asked whether I was aware that recently an Italian scholar had raised significant questions as to whether a basic text used in my thesis [the *Edictum Theodorici Regis*, ed. 1875–1889] should be attributed to Theodoric the Great, a sixth-century king of the Ostrogoths—as I and everybody else had always assumed—or, as this author proposed, to a Visigothic king by the same name who had reigned in southern France a century before. I was not.

The committee accepted my thesis with the provision that I look at the relevant publications by the Italian scholar. I did so immediately and, like all historians, added a paragraph and a rather lengthy footnote. The lesson learned was to be even more careful staying abreast of the secondary literature in my field, but not to the point of accepting the latest argument over an older interpretation simply because the former is more recent. In the ensuing years and later publications, I continued to wrestle with the conflicting opinions concerning the author of this particular text, at first almost agreeing, but ultimately rejecting the new for the old, an argument from the nineteenth century over that of 1967.

The other example that I would like to share with regard to Charlie's long-lasting influence on my career concerns what is arguably the most important Roman law for understanding the creation and evolution of medieval Europe: the Law of Welcoming [*hospitalitas*, the *Codex Theodosianus*, 7.8.5, ed. 1923–1926, issued from Constantinople in 398 CE]. Succinctly, the law of *hospitalitas* was initially intended to underpin an official system of compulsory quartering of troops on the land and in the houses of landowners, but within two decades the law was being used to facilitate the settlement of barbarians inside the Empire. The law stipulated that landowners were to "share" their estates with their "guests" and that the degree of this sharing was to be in accordance with the wealth of the landowner. The law also ordered landowners to make available the supplies needed to take up farming. The wealthiest owners were to share up to half of their estate, not including any equipment used in industrial production; lesser owners, a third.

What came to be regarded as the traditional understanding of this system was first proposed in the middle of the nineteenth century and had experienced only fine tuning to its basic feature of land transfer. That unanimity ended around 1980, when a series of publications challenged that basic design. The new interpretation argued that rather than actually getting land for farming, the barbarian guests received the tax paid on the land by the traditional owner. Therefore, according to the new theory the barbarians were soldiers—mercenaries rather than farmers—and money, not land, was exchanged.

The Latin primary sources for these events in the fifth and sixth centuries are torturous in their ambiguity. Neither archaeology nor epigraphy offers greater clarity. I was but one of many scholars expressing doubt as to the validity of the new theory of monetary settlement rather than actual land, but, as we labored towards reaching a resolution, we all agreed that the intense discussions of the new ideas were producing a much better understanding of the late Roman tax system and had raised a crucial issue regarding when that system had ceased to exist. Charlie had always stressed thoroughness in investigation; take your time and look under every rock. Truly, his admonition haunted me then and now. So I looked again at the same old sources and at the oft-cited opinions of the great historians of the last century. One in particular stood out, A. H. M. Jones, surely one of the foremost historical minds in the first few decades following World War II.

Concerning the barbarian settlement, Jones had accepted the traditional interpretation that land and supplies were given to barbarians to farm or subdivide into farms for their followers. Jones had also said of a contemporary chronicle written in the mid-fifth century by Philostrogios writing in the East, in Greek, that it had nothing to add to the discussion. "Be thorough, be careful," thank you, Charlie. I read Philostrogios on the settlement and came to the realization that Jones's insight declaring Philostrogios had nothing to add concerning the settlements was quite important to the current debate: nothing new, if you took for granted the traditional interpretation, but a contemporary writing about the same events in a different language offered a new component to the present debate. Whereas in Latin the terms used are indeed somewhat ambiguous, the Greek is crystal clear, the barbarian being settled on Roman soil was called a "Georgos" [as a verb meaning to till the soil] and hence the English personal name George, a farmer. As farmer/soldiers, barbarians were much more readily integrated into Roman rural society than had they become merely absentee landlords. One tends to overlook that at least 90% of Roman society were always farmers. The new settlers contributed their own farming and military skills to the mix that became medieval.

Charles Donahue is the last remaining member of my thesis committee, and I am honored to be a contributor to this volume and hope that in a small way, I assisted with a few paragraphs of his *magnum opus* on the law of medieval marriage. My debt to Charles (aka Charlie) Donahue will never be marked, "paid."

APPENDIX 2

De magistro eruditissimo et beneficentissimo: A Reflection

Mary Elizabeth Basile Chopas

In 1995 I was introduced to Professor Charles Donahue by Professor Daniel Coquillette who had asked me to retranslate the late thirteenth-century treatise *Lex Mercatoria*, the earliest known treatment of the law merchant, for a publication of the Ames Foundation. I was honored to be asked to be involved in this project, but worried that my college studies in medieval Latin literature were insufficient preparation for translating a manuscript on commercial law. Dan Coquillette told me there was no need to worry because I would be guided by Charlie Donahue, and "no one knows Latin better than he does." I soon found out that Dan was not exaggerating.

Since I was a practicing attorney in Boston at the time, Charlie generously offered to meet me on Saturday mornings in his office in Hauser Hall at Harvard Law School. I remember feeling intimidated by an office with books piled high on every chair and taking up every inch of floor space. I had never met anyone more fluent in the Latin language, and I felt humbled by his willingness to guide someone with a solid Latin background in literary verse, but unfamiliar with the complexity of legal Latin, to tackle the translation of such a challenging manuscript. In many three-hour sessions, Charlie patiently explained the special syntactical oddities of legal medieval Latin and how to smooth out the dense language describing mercantile law for our readership. Using a microfilm copy of the original manuscript, we also had to deal with issues of paleography in deciphering the ancient handwriting—the oddly shaped letters and cryptic symbols such as those to indicate dropped endings on words. During these meetings, Charlie not only instructed me in how to translate the treatise, but spent considerable time explaining the social, political, and economic influences upon the marketplace and the transaction of business in medieval Europe so that I understood the context in which this treatise was written. I was the beneficiary of a private lecture in medieval mercantile law in addition to a lesson in medieval Latin. Our work also involved a bit of sleuthing in determining who might have written the treatise and how well that person knew Latin.

 | DOI:10.1163/9789004710696_024

The most important result of our meetings was the determination that the Latin manuscript did not make sense. Although the treatise had been written by someone knowledgeable in Latin, the text apparently had become corrupt in the multiple times it was copied by hand. This meant that Charlie, along with Jane Bestor, another researcher at HLS, had the daunting task of reconstructing what the Latin might originally have said. Only then could the Latin text be cleanly translated into a readable text in English. Charlie's patience, good humor, irresistible laughter at the absurdity of the language at times, and his practical sense made my contribution to this project very enjoyable. I have always appreciated that while his expectations are high and he is frank when something is inaccurate, he is also quick to praise when something is done well and to share credit for the work. I understood early on that his criticism is always constructive and indicates that he deeply cares about my growth as a scholar. I have tried to pattern my own teaching and mentoring of students according to that same level of intellectual integrity. After not seeing Charlie for about ten years since moving to North Carolina, I had the pleasure of being seated next to him at a constitutional law conference at UNC School of Law in the fall of 2015. We had a great time catching up on professional and personal matters. In typical Charlie Donahue fashion, he was interested in learning the Greek derivation of my married surname. Not knowing it myself, I asked him to suggest what he thought it might be, and sure enough, when I checked with my husband's family, he was correct about the spelling of the original name. Of course, Charlie is not just a Latinist, but equally fluent in Greek—a classicist in the purist sense.

When I returned to the Boston area, Charlie contacted me about translating the biographies of Italian jurists who contributed to the *Tractatus Universi Iuris* for a digital history project of the Ames Foundation. I was thrilled to work with him again. Our meetings have been very similar to what they were like back in 1995—lively discussions about the historical context of the work and lessons in the nuances of the language, this time Italian. With the advancements of digital history, we are utilizing a more widely accessible environment for sharing scholarship. Not surprisingly, Charlie has approached the digital platform with his usual sense of pragmatism and has even taught me some word processing tricks to make translating easier. He aims to provide translations that are easily understood and can be appreciated by a wide audience.

It has been a real privilege to collaborate with Charlie on two of his many labors of love for future generations of legal historians.

APPENDIX 3

The Teachings of Charles Donahue on the Middle Ages from the Perspective of a Student of Mexican Legal History: A Reflection

William Suárez-Potts

Charles Donahue, Jr., is a renowned legal historian of Europe's Middle Ages and a remarkable and beloved teacher at Harvard Law School. I am neither a medievalist nor an alumnus of HLS, but a historian of modern Latin America and Mexico. My planned historical specialization was surely far from Donahue's. Harvard's history department, however, had a requirement that its graduate students prepare an examination field in a premodern era. Many students specializing in Latin America prepared one in early African history to avoid the European Middle Ages, and this path was recommended to me. I was definitely interested in legal history, and schemed to circumvent reading about Vikings and others dating from the mists of time with an alternate route, by reading a little European legal history during its formative period. But the history department caught on to the scheme and invoked a rule (the text of which I never saw), requiring preparation in the premodern field with a professor within the department. The outcome was that I read in two medieval fields and more than a smattering of early legal history. From a modernist perspective, I came to realize the value of medieval history, and medieval legal history in particular, thanks to Charlie (and the belief of the history department that its students gain depth and breadth in their education for the doctorate).

My encounters with Professor Donahue thus began as a first-year graduate student in 1996. It was one late afternoon in the fall when I dropped by his office: a large, dimly lit chamber in Hauser, with columns of books stacked across the floor. Whatever it vaguely resembled—a room in a manor, maybe a Hogwarts set—it was far from being a law office. (Later another student told me of a secret passage, a staircase, in the back of the room.) In any event, Professor Donahue, after patiently listening to my interests and vague dissertation plans, offered how he could guide me through a field in legal history. That field, and the syllabus he drafted, have continued to guide me in my turn to studying the transition from the legal order of New Spain to a liberal system that formed in Mexico in the nineteenth century.

 | DOI:10.1163/9789004710696_025

The study of the legal history of Latin America, in the U.S. at least, normally has had to deal preliminarily with the question of what kind of law could exist if it was weakly enforced by the state. What does law mean there, if there is no "rule of law"? It was Charlie's gift to me to show, not so much abstractly but historically, how the Western legal tradition had evolved, without necessarily a strong state (or even the state in any modern sense). Latin America's normative systems and institutions, of course, constitute part of the Western legal tradition, as do those of the United States. And there is a rich history of law and juridical activity that forms part of the region's social and political relations, which have changed over time since the end of the fifteenth century. But if one insists, as do many contemporaries in the twenty-first century (like those in the nineteenth and twentieth centuries), that weak enforcement efforts or deviations from formal application of the stated rules indicate how law is largely irrelevant to social relations, then its study becomes more difficult to justify. Viewing the trajectory of legal change and continuity over centuries, from a perspective informed by knowledge of European legal history, however, opens the possibility of asking more interesting historical questions. Indeed, these questions are posed by legal historians writing in the Iberian world, and more than one has mentioned to me that broad knowledge of continental Europe's legal development since Roman times is essential for comprehending law reform and practice since the late nineteenth century. They are correct, and fortunately I had the benefit of being Charlie's student.

In the classes on English and continental European legal history that Donahue taught around the turn of the century, when I had the pleasure of assisting him as teaching fellow for discussion sections of undergraduate students, questions about the relationship between law and the state arose regularly.[1] At the beginning of the course, students typically imagined the ahistorical existence of a transcendent state and assumed that law meant constitutional or criminal law, and civil rights and liberties. Courses that emphasized the fashioning of property rules, civil obligations, and marriage law, while considering the modern state as an abstraction that was meaningful in modern times, or perhaps by the end of the period of study, could be bewildering.

1 In connection with the relationship between HLS and FAS (Harvard's Faculty of Arts and Sciences) it probably would be interesting to reminisce about how Donahue long ago organized these classes to obtain their cross-listing, and then lecture to a packed hall of both law students and undergraduates. I never quite understood how he had managed to secure FAS and history department approval for the law courses, other than to gather that one condition was the presence of an affiliate of FAS in the class (hence, a teaching fellow from the history department), regardless of the number of undergraduate students enrolled.

But the undergraduate students who enrolled in Donahue's classes loved them, were in awe of him, and worked through the redacted primary sources that comprised the reading assignments diligently—in part because they were motivated by the teacher's manifest enthusiasm and originality.[2] And what they came to realize was that in Europe's Middle Ages and early modern period, political authority and struggles over the power to control people and resources certainly came to have legal sides, but that it was anachronistic to speak of the state (or the church) as simple, eternal entities in a direct relationship with law. Students learned that much of the story about the evolution of law and society did not involve what is called public law now (and maybe also in the times of Gaius and Justinian): indeed, that the process of categorization of law as either private or public was part of the historical story of the Western legal tradition. People lived largely according to laws and customs concerning marriage, property, and civil obligations—what we call private law. If they litigated in fora that were at least partially constituted by political authorities (including those of the Church), the doctrines and modes of argumentation and procedure nonetheless were products of intellectuals who in tribunals or early centers of higher learning made and remade the law.

I had already left Cambridge and regular contact with Charlie when I read his article, "Private Law without the State and during Its Formation."[3] As the author wrote in his first footnote, it was based on a lecture given at a conference. Maybe partly for this reason the essay evoked nostalgic memories of Donahue's classes: his voice seemed to resonate throughout the text. The points he made were helpful to a historian insistent that legal doctrine and practice had mattered in Mexico during a century or more when most assumed there had been little state enforcement (and this latter observation was what needed to be recounted). The first point Donahue posited was that, "it is possible to have private law without the state"—"a proposition" that he thought was "non-controversial."[4] For many, of course, this proposition is not self-evident. I assume that Donahue made this move, which he substantiates

2 One should also acknowledge Charlie's sometimes self-deprecating sense of humor, which made him more approachable to undergraduate students. For more than one, the thought of approaching him, or knocking on the door of the office of an HLS professor, was intimidating. All of those who ventured across Cambridge Street to the law school and reported to me later were immensely grateful for having had the opportunity to meet with him; a few commented about the chamber in the modern brick castle.

3 Charles Donahue, Jr., "Private Law without the State and during Its Formation," *The American Journal of Comparative Law* 56, no. 3 (2008): 541–65. The article was a contribution to a special symposium issue: "Beyond the State: Rethinking Private Law."

4 Donahue, "Private Law without the State," 562.

with examples drawn from Jewish, Islamic, and Roman legal traditions, partly in order to limit one line of discussion and turn to a more illuminating one, which could be sketched to explain historically the complicated and at times tenuous relationships between what was becoming "the state" and the domain of "private law." For Donahue, as he sums up in his conclusion, "the basic developmental mechanisms of private law" were not the result of early modern state dictates but, in England, judicial decision-making and lawyers' advocacy, or, on the European continent, "juristic discussion" predominantly situated in universities.[5] As noted, this was a point that he had made in his classes, and which he summarized for students somewhat schematically in tables illustrating in different columns successive legal, intellectual, and political events over several hundred years. At the time, I was not completely persuaded by his tables, if only because they were schematic. Yet the tables like the article reflect an understated command of the relevant sources and scholarship, and demonstrate that private law as a historical phenomenon is not reducible to a function of governments that legislate.

I recommend Charlie's article and (at least) the introduction of his magisterial book, *Law, Marriage, and Society in the Later Middle Ages*, to historians, including, in particular, anybody interested in the legal history of Latin America. I do so not only because, as mentioned, Latin America's legal history is part of the Western legal tradition, of which another part is continental Europe's, or because there are comparable patterns in the political, economic, and social structures of the distant regions. Donahue's approach to interpreting history is a fruitful model for students specializing in fields other than the European Middle Ages. It avoids the temptation of centering an analysis on the single case, which can have its place but also detract from comprehension of the whole. Donahue with much subdued wit in a few pages (out of an opus numbering more than 600 pages) explains the value of the quantitative approach against an exclusive focus on the singular.[6] One might note that he is a classicist and (the term is no longer used, I realize) philologist, as well as a lawyer, so that his arguments for sampling and quantifying (along with other methods; he is not a cliometrician) are worth reading and sharing with humanists who have been disinterested in approaches outside of close readings of texts. In reference to Latin America, I suspect partly due to the tremendous amount of labor entailed in collecting, as a preliminary endeavor,

5 Donahue, "Private Law without the State," 563.

6 Charles Donahue, Jr., *Law, Marriage, and Society in the Later Middle Ages: Arguments About Marriage in Five Courts* (Cambridge: Cambridge University Press, 2007), 6–12.

large numbers of cases, in widely dispersed archives, quantitative analysis of judicial decisions is rarely undertaken, at least by North Americans.

The potential benefits of the approaches signaled by Donahue certainly exist for legal and historical scholarship. Probably because he has taught at large law schools, and not been cabined in a history department, he does ably reach larger audiences; his work definitely has broader significance without compromising the standards of medieval historical scholarship. It was incredibly good fortune to have been a student of Charlie's, not least, ultimately, because of how he expressed himself, often humorously, and almost always with genuine, near-Socratic humility, some of which comes through in his writing. The undergraduate students whose papers he graded could not get over how he wrote for them detailed comments, sometimes about as long as their essays; no other Harvard professor had accorded them such respect. The attention and kindness he afforded these students were just instances of the truly generous scholar and humane *magister*, which Charles Donahue has always embodied and which anybody who knows him can only appreciate.

APPENDIX 4

Chi Squares, Chant, and Charlie: A Reflection

Claire Valente

My memories of Charlie probably conform to that of all of his students: the Wolfman hair and beard, the pipe, the long pause looking at the sky and audible intake of breath as he thought of what to say next, the labyrinthine location of his office in the library, made more labyrinthine by the piles of books one had to navigate to find a chair. And the kindness, and the personal interest, and the keen intellectual back and forth, and the refusal to accept second-best work. Charlie created a general exam field for me and a handful of similarly legally-inclined medievalists, and kept me sane during my anguished thesis-writing. He laboriously checked chi squares and backed my insistence on doing the thesis my way, even though the book would have to be rearranged. Moreover, his willingness to let me avoid my thesis at times by focusing on the bizarrely difficult timeline of Edward II's deposition led to what is still my most read publication. But for me, Charlie provided something else, something far more critical than intellectual mentorship and knowledge and love of medieval case law. For Charlie was almost unique among my professors in being, like me, a believing, practicing Catholic.

Never one to take things lying down, at Harvard I fought with bigoted, often ex-Catholic, professors for years, ones who made off-handed anti-Catholic remarks and expressed their disdain for those of us who believed in a higher power, assuming there were no Catholics in the room (they found out otherwise). I was lucky as an undergraduate and graduate student to work with Tom Bisson, the son of missionaries, who maintained a quiet Episcopalian faith in the midst of increasingly agnostic and atheistic Harvard, and also with James Hankins, who fervently embraced the intellectual heritage of Catholicism. But Charlie was different, because for me Charlie became a spiritual as well as an intellectual friend. I frequently saw Charlie at Mass, singing as part of the men's schola at St. Paul parish. Charlie recommended me for the liturgy committee for the parish, at that point (and still today?) known as the Church of the Tasteful Redeemer. And Charlie invited me to sing Vespers twice a week with a small group in the downstairs chapel. Those Vespers not only provided me with an essential oasis of spiritual calm in the difficulties of early graduate school, but gave me an appreciation for the Liturgy of the Hours and a familiarity with psalmody that has lasted me my entire life.

 | DOI:10.1163/9789004710696_026

Today as a wife and mother who teaches part-time, but rarely on the topic of medieval law, I still use the chant skills Charlie modeled and helped me cultivate. For several years, I directed the choir for the local Latin mass, the introits and anthems hearkening back if imperfectly to the halcyon days of the music at St. Paul. I founded a children's choir and passed on to at least two dozen children the knowledge of psalm tones and chant modes that friendship with Charlie had led me to study. And still almost every week, I lead chant and psalm-singing with a small schola of my students at DeSales High, and at my parish, St. Francis of Assisi, with (when she is home) the help of my beautiful daughter Mary Elizabeth, who has come to love chant and traditional Latin hymns as much as I do, and who now sings them at Notre Dame. Since Charlie, having used his God-given talents to the fullest and achieved laudable worldly success, nevertheless values the path to heaven even higher, I hope he won't be too disappointed at my career trajectory, which has left depositions behind for chants sung for the glory of God. Happy Birthday, Charlie. Thank you for all you taught me. Ad multos annos, et conveniemus in caelum.

Bibliography

Charles Donahue

1964

"An Historical Argument for the Right to Counsel During Police Interrogation." *Yale Law Journal* 73: 1000–57.

1967

Review of John Honnold, *The Life of the Law*. *Columbia Law Review* 67: 1353–60.

1968

"The Alaska Purchase: For a Private Communications System." *Public Utilities Fortnightly* 82: 40–51.

1970

"The Supreme Court vs. Section 10(b)3 of the Selective Service Act: A Study in Ducking Constitutional Issues." *UCLA Law Review* 17: 908–74.

1971

"Lawyers, Economics, and the Regulated Industries: Thoughts on Professional Roles Inspired by Some Recent Economic Literature." *Michigan Law Review* 70: 195–220. Reprinted in *Corporate Practice Commentator*, 14 (1973): App. II, 1–33.

1972

With Jeanne P. Gordus, co-author of "A Case from Archbishop Stratford's Audience Act Book and Some Comments on the Book and its Value." *Bulletin of Medieval Canon Law* 2 (n.s.): 45–59.

"Some Thoughts on Michigan's Copy of the Argentoratene Gratian." *Law Quadrangle Notes* 17: 8–11.

1973

Review of Arthur Schiller, *An American Experience in Roman Law*. *Michigan Law Review* 71: 1275–85.

Review of John Noonan, *Power to Dissolve*. *Quis Custodiet?*: 59–64.

1974

"Change in the American Law of Landlord and Tenant." *Modern Law Review* 37: 242–63.

"Roman Canon Law in the Medieval English Church: Stubbs vs. Maitland Re-Examined after Seventy-Five Years in the Light of Some Records from the Church Courts." *Michigan Law Review* 72: 647–716.

"The Civil Law in England [review article on Brian Levack, *The Civil Lawyers in England*]." *Yale Law Journal* 84: 167–181.

With Thomas E. Kauper and Peter W. Martin, co-author and co-editor of *Cases and Materials on Property: An Introduction to the Concept and the Institution*. St. Paul: West Publishing Co.

1975

With Peter W. Martin, co-author of *A Course in Basic Property*. St. Paul: West Publishing Co.

1976

"The Policy of Alexander the Third's Consent Theory of Marriage." In *Proceedings of the Fourth International Congress of Medieval Canon Law*, edited by Stephan Kuttner, 251–81. Città del Vaticano: Biblioteca Apostolica Vaticana.

Review of Anne Lefebvre-Teillard, *Les officialités à la veille du Concile de Trente*. *Michigan Law Review* 74: 644–53.

1977

"Comparative Reflections on the 'New Matrimonial Jurisprudence' of the Roman Catholic Church." *Michigan Law Review* 75: 994–1020.

"Scandal and the Church's New Matrimonial Jurisprudence." *Law and Justice* 52/53: 34–51.

1978

"The Case of the Man Who Fell Into the Tiber: The Roman Law of Marriage at the Time of the Glossators." *American Journal of Legal History* 22: 1–53.

1979

"Comparative Family Law: Law and Social Change? [review article on Mary Ann Glendon, *State, Law and Family*]." *Michigan Law Review* 77: 350–62.

Review of John Barton and T. F. T. Plucknett (ed.), *Doctor and Student*. *Tijdschrift voor Rechtsgeschiedenis* 47: 182–86.

"What Causes Fundamental Legal Ideas? Marital Property in England and France in the Thirteenth Century." *Michigan Law Review* 78: 59–88.

1980

"Foreword" to Bruce W. Frier, *Landlords and Tenants in Imperial Rome*, xi–xv. Princeton: Princeton University Press.

"The Future of the Concept of Property Predicted from its Past." In *Property*, Nomos 22, edited by J. Roland Pennock and John W. Chapman, 28–68. New York: New York University Press.

"The Interaction of Law and Religion in the Middle Ages." *Mercer Law Review* 31: 466–76.

1981

"Proof by Witnesses in the Church Courts of Medieval England: An Imperfect Reception of the Learned Law." In *On the Laws and Customs of England: Essays in Honor of Samuel E. Thorne*, edited by Morris S. Arnold, Thomas A. Green, Sally Scully, and Stephen White, 127–58. Chapel Hill: North Carolina University Press.

With Norma Adams, co-editor of *Select Cases from the Ecclesiastical Courts of the Province of Canterbury, c. 1200–1301*. London: Selden Society.

1982

"The Dating of Alexander the Third's Marriage Decretals: Dauvillier Revisited after Fifty Years." *Zeitschrift der Savigny-Stiftung für Rechtsgeschichte* 99: 70–124.

"Lyndwood's Gloss *propriarum uxorum*: Marital Property and the *ius commune* in Fifteenth Century England." In *Europäisches Rechtsdenken in Geschichte und Gegenwart: Festschrift für Helmut Coing*, edited by Norbert Horn, Klaus Luig, and Alfred Söllner, 1: 19–37. München: C. H. Beck.

Review of Ralph Houlbrooke, *Church Courts and the People during the English Reformation, 1520–1570*. *Journal of Modern History* 54: 550–52.

1983

"The Canon Law on the Formation of Marriage and Social Practice in the Later Middle Ages." *Journal of Family History* 8: 144–58.

With Thomas E. Kauper and Peter W. Martin, co-authors and co-editors of *Cases and Materials on Property: An Introduction to the Concept and the Institution*. 2nd ed. St. Paul: West Publishing Co.

With Thomas E. Kauper and Peter W. Martin, co-author of *A Course in Basic Property*. 2nd ed. St. Paul: West Publishing Co.

Review of Alan Watson, *The Making of the Civil Law*. *Michigan Law Review* 81: 972–76.

1985

"Church Court Records on the Continent and in England." In *Englische und kontinentale Rechtsgeschichte: ein Forschungsprojekt*, edited by Helmut Coing und Knut Wolfgang Nörr, 63–71. Berlin: Duncker & Humblot.

"Noodt, Titius, and the Natural Law School: The Occupation of Wild Animals and the Intersection of Property and Tort." In *Satura Roberto Feenstra*, edited by J. A. Ankum, J. E. Spruit, and F. B. J. Wubbe, 609–29. Fribourg [CH]: Presses Universitaires de Fribourg.

"Prophecy and Politics: Reflections on a Recent Campaign (Mother Elizabeth Seton Lecture, January 17, 1985)." *Winter Bulletin, 1985* (Portsmouth [RI]: Portsmouth Abbey School), 4–10.

1986

"*Animalia Ferae Naturae*: Rome, Bologna, Leyden, Oxford and Queen's County, N.Y." In *Studies in Roman Law in Memory of A. Arthur Schiller*, edited by Roger S. Bagnall and William V. Harris, 39–63. Leiden: E. J. Brill.

Review of Christopher R. Cheney, *The English Church and its Laws*. *Zeitschrift der Savigny-Stiftung für Rechtsgeschichte* 103: 434–35.

Review of Antonio García y García (ed.), *Constitutiones Concilii Quarti Lateranensis*. *Speculum* 61: 149–50.

Review of Kenneth Pennington (ed.), *Johannis Teutonici Apparatus glossarum in Compilationem tertiam*. *American Journal of Legal History* 30: 79–85.

Review of Louis Théo Maes, *Recht heeft vele significatie*. *Law and History Review* 4: 473–74.

Why the History of Canon Law Is Not Written (Selden Lecture, July 3, 1984). London: Selden Society.

1987

"Introduction" to *Henry Fielding, An Institute of the Pleas of the Crown: An Exhibition of the Hyde Collection at the Houghton Library, 1987*, edited by Hugh Amory. Cambridge, MA: Houghton Library.

"Law, Civil—*Corpus Juris*, Revival and Spread." In *Dictionary of the Middle Ages*, edited by Joseph R. Strayer, 7: 418–25. New York: Charles Scribner's Sons.

"On Translating the *Digest* [review essay of *The Digest of Justinian*, edited by Alan Watson]." *Stanford Law Review* 39: 1057–77.

"Preface" and "Introduction" to *Year Books of Richard II: 8–10 Richard II, 1385–1387*, edited by L. C. Hector and Michael E. Hager, v–xii. N. p. Cambridge, MA: The Ames Foundation.

Review of Brian Tierney, *Religion, Law, and the Growth of Constitutional Thought, 1150–1650*. *Journal of Legal Education* 37: 444–48.

1988

"Institutional History from Archival History: The Court of Canterbury Rolls." In *The Weightier Matters of the Law: Essays in Law and Religion, A Tribute to Harold J. Berman*, edited by John Witte Jr. and Frank S. Alexander, 33–55. Atlanta, GA: Scholars Press.

1989

Editor of *The Records of the Medieval Ecclesiastical Courts: Reports of the Working Group on Church Courts Records, 1: The Continent*. Berlin: Duncker & Humblot.

1990

Review of R. H. Helmholz (ed.), *Select Cases on Defamation to 1600*. *Speculum* 65: 419–23.

1991

"Comment on R. H. Helmholz, 'Conflicts Between Religious Law and Secular Law.'" *Cardozo Law Review* 12: 729–35.

"A Legal Historian Looks at the Case Method." *Northern Kentucky Law Journal* 19: 17–47.

1992

"'Clandestine' Marriage in the Later Middle Ages: A Reply." *Law and History Review* 10: 315–22.

"English and French Marriage Cases: Might the Differences Be Explained by Differences in the Property Systems?" In *Marriage, Property, and Succession*, edited by Lloyd Bonfield, 339–66. Berlin: Duncker & Humblot. Reprinted in *Miscellanea Domenico Maffei Dicata: Historia-Ius-Studium*, edited by Antonio García y García and Peter Weimar, 4: 283–310. Goldach: Keip, 1995.

"*Ius commune*, Canon Law, and Common Law in England." *Tulane Law Review* 66: 1745–80.

"Property Law." In *Encyclopaedia Britannica: Macropaedia*, vol. 26, 180–205.

1993

"Introduction" to *History in Deed: Medieval Society & the Law in England, 1100–1600: An Exhibition of Deeds & Charters from the Harvard Law School Library, November-December 1993*, edited by Carol Symes. Cambridge, MA: The President and Fellows of Harvard College.

Review of R. H. Helmholz, *Roman Canon Law in Reformation England*. *Law and History Review* 11: 442–8.

With Thomas E. Kauper and Peter W. Martin, co-author of *A Course in Basic Property*. 3rd ed. St. Paul: West Publishing Co.

With Thomas E. Kauper and Peter W. Martin, co-author and co-editor of *Cases and Materials on Property: An Introduction to the Concept and the Institution*. 3rd ed. St. Paul: West Publishing Co.

"Women Plaintiffs in Marriage Cases in the Court of York in the Later Middle Ages: What Can We Learn From the Numbers?" In *Wife and Widow in Medieval England*, edited by Sue Sheridan Walker, 183–213. Ann Arbor: University of Michigan Press.

1994

Editor of *The Records of the Medieval Ecclesiastical Courts: Reports of the Working Group on Church Courts Records, 2: England*. Berlin: Duncker & Humblot.

1995

Editor of *Samuel Edmund Thorne: 1907–1994*. Cambridge, MA: Harvard Law School.

Review of Gratian, *The Treatise on Laws* (*Decretum* DD. *1–20*) *with the Ordinary Gloss*, translated by Augustine Thompson and James Gordley. *Catholic Historical Review* 81: 427–9.

"Was There a Change in Marriage Law in the Late Middle Ages?" *Rivista internazionale di diritto commune* 6: 49–80.

With T. N. Bisson and Giles Constable, co-author of "Samuel Edmund Thorne." *Speculum* 70: 732–4.

"Theology, Law & Women's Ordination: *Ordinatio sacerdotalis* One Year Later." *Commonweal* 122 (June 2): 11–16.

1996

With Samuel E. Thorne, Michael E. Hager, and Margaret M. Thorne, co-editors of *Year Books of Richard II: 6 Richard II, 1382–1383*. N. p. Cambridge, MA: The Ames Foundation.

"The Monastic Judge: Social Practice, Formal Rule and the Medieval Canon Law of Incest." In *De Iure Canonico Medii Aevi: Festschrift für Rudolf Weigand*, edited by Peter Landau and Martin Petzolt, 49–69. Romae: LAS.

1997

"Comparative Legal History in North America." *Tijdschrift voor Rechtsgeschiedenis* 65: 1–17.

1998

With Mary Elizabeth Basile, Daniel R. Coquillette, and Jane Fair Bestor, co-editor of *Lex Mercatoria and Legal Pluralism: A Late Thirteenth-Century Treatise and its Afterlife*. Cambridge, MA: The Ames Foundation.

Review of R. B. Outhwaite, *Clandestine Marriage in England*. *Journal of Modern History* 70: 453–55.

1999

"Biology and the Origins of the English Jury." *Law and History Review* 17: 591–96.

Review of J. H. Baker, *A Catalogue of English Legal Manuscripts in Cambridge University Library*. *Manuscripta* 43/44: 193–94.

2000

"Gerard Pucelle as a Canon Lawyer: Life and the Battle Abbey Case." In *Grundlagen des Rechts: Festschrift für Peter Landau zum 65. Geburtstag*, edited by R. H. Helmholz, Paul Mikat, Jörg Müller, and Michael Stolleis, 333–48. Paderborn: Schöningh.

"Malchus's Ear: Reflections on Classical Canon Law as a Religious Legal System." In *Lex et Romanitas: Essays for Alan Watson*, edited by Michael Hoeflich, 91–120. Berkeley, CA: The Robbins Collection.

"An Upbeat View of Fourteenth-Century English Justice [review article on Anthony Musson and W. M. Ormrod, *The Evolution of English Justice: Law, Politics and Society in the Fourteenth Century*]." *Michigan Law Review* 98: 1725–37.

2001

"*Ius* in the Subjective Sense in Roman Law: Reflections on Villey and Tierney." In *A Ennio Cortese*, edited by Domenico Maffei, Italo Birocchi, Mario Caravale, Emanuele Conte, and Ugo Petronio, 1: 506–35. Rome: Il Cigno Edizioni.

Review of Michael M. Sheehan, *Marriage, Family, and Law in Medieval Europe: Collected Studies*. *Catholic Historical Review* 87: 97.

2003

"Bassianus, That Is to Say, Bazianus?—Bazianus and Johannes Bassianus on Marriage." *Rivista internazionale di diritto commune* 14: 41–82.

"The Emergence of the Crime-Tort Distinction in England." In *Conflict in Medieval Europe: Changing Perspectives on Society and Culture*, edited by Warren C. Brown and Piotr Górecki, 219–28. Ashgate: Aldershot.

"P 265 = JL 16635?: A Mild Heresy Stated and Defended." In *"Ins Wasser geworfen und Ozeane durchquert": Festschrift für Knut Wolfgang Nörr*, edited by Mario Ascheri et. al., 165–87. Köln: Böhlau.

2004

"Bassianus, That Is to Say, Bazianus?—Johannes Bassianus on Marriage." In *"Panta rei": Studi dedicati a Manlio Bellomo*, edited by Orazio Condorelli, 2: 179–204. Roma: Il Cigno Edizione.

"Equity in the Courts of Merchants." *Tijdschrift voor Rechtsgeschiedenis* 72: 1–35.

"Medieval and Early Modern *Lex mercatoria*: An Attempt at the *probatio diabolica*." *Chicago Journal of International Law* 5: 21–36.

"Pucelle, Gerard (*d.* 1184)." In *Oxford Dictionary of National Biography*. Oxford: Oxford University Press.

2005

"A Crisis of Law? Reflections on the Church and the Law over the Centuries." *The Jurist* 65: 1–30.

"Benvenuto Stracca's *De mercatura*: Was There a *Lex mercatoria* in Sixteenth Century Italy?" In *From* lex mercatoria *to Commercial Law*, edited by Vito Piergiovanni, 69–120. Berlin: Duncker & Humblot.

Review of Paul Brand, *Kings, Barons and Justices: The Making and Enforcement of Legislation in Thirteenth-Century England*. *Speculum* 80: 782.

2006

"Comparative Law Before the *Code Napoléon.*" In *The Oxford Handbook of Comparative Law*, edited by Mathias Reimann and Reinhard Zimmermann, 3–32. Oxford: Oxford University Press. Reprinted with light revisions in *id.* 2nd ed., 2019.

"Genesis in Western Canon Law." *The Jewish Law Annual* 16: 155–84.

"Johannes Faventinus on Marriage (With an Appendix Revisiting the Question of the Dating of Alexander III's Marriage Decretals)." In *Medieval Church Law and the Origins of the Western Legal Tradition: A Tribute to Kenneth Pennington*, edited by Wolfgang P. Müller and Mary E. Sommar, 179–97. Washington, DC: Catholic University of America Press.

2007

"Aggadic Stories About Medieval Western Jurists?" *Diné Israel: Studies in* Halakhah *and Jewish Law* 24: 209–15.

Law, Marriage, and Society in the Later Middle Ages: Arguments About Marriage in Five Courts. New York: Cambridge University Press (with an additional 304 pages online at https://www-cambridge-org.ezp-prod1.hul.harvard.edu/resources/0521877288/5363_9780521877282tc_p673-976.pdf).

Review of Anders Winroth, *The Making of Gratian's Decretum*. *Law and History Review* 25: 401–3.

Review of R. H. Helmholz, *The Canon Law and Ecclesiastical Jurisdiction from 597 to the 1640s*. *Law and History Review* 25: 217–19.

2008

"Private Law Without the State and During its Formation." *American Journal of Comparative Law* 56: 541–66. Reprinted in *Beyond the State: Rethinking Private Law*, edited by Nils Jansen and Ralf Michaels, 121–43. Tübingen: Mohr Siebeck, 2008.

"Reflections on the Editing of Medieval Church Court Records." In *Iuris Historia: Liber Amicorum Gero Dolazalek*, edited by Vincenzo Colli and Emanuele Conte, 345–53. Berkeley, CA: The Robbins Collection.

"Reform, Renewal, Religion and Social Discipline: Reflections of a Medievalist." In *The Law Applied: Contextualizing the Islamic Shari'a: A Volume in Honor of Frank E. Vogel*, edited by Peri Bearman, Wolfhart Heinrichs, and Bernard G. Weiss, 1–21. London: I. B. Tauris.

"The Western Canon Law of Marriage: A Doctrinal Introduction." In *The Islamic Marriage Contract: Case Studies in Islamic Family Law*, edited by Asifa Quraishi and Frank E. Vogel, 46–56. Cambridge, MA: Harvard University Press.

2009

"*Ex officio* Cases in the Officiality of Paris, 1384–1387" In *Mélanges en l'honneur d'Anne Lefebvre-Teillard*, edited by Bernard d'Alteroche et. al., 393–412. Paris: Éditions Panthéon-Assas.

"Papyrology and 3 Canes 175." *Law and History Review* 27: 179–84.

Review of Jan K. Bulman, *The Court Book of Mende and the Secular Lordship of the Bishop*. *Catholic Historical Review* 95: 601–2.

"Whither Legal History." In *Transformations in American Legal History: Essays in Honor of Professor Morton J. Horwitz*, edited by Daniel W. Hamilton and Alfred L. Brophy, 327–43. Cambridge, MA: Harvard Law School.

2010

"Law, Marriage, and Society in the Later Middle Ages: A Look at the English and 'Franco-Belgian' Regions." In *Proceedings of the Thirteenth International Congress of Medieval Canon Law (Esztergom-Budapest, August 3–9, 2008)*, edited by Peter Erdö and Sz. Anzelm Szuromi, 17–39. Città del Vaticano: Biblioteca Apostolica Vaticana.

"Malchus's Ear Revisited." *Law & Justice* 165: 144–58.

"A New Synthesis of the History of Canon Law in the Classical Period [review article on *The History of Medieval Canon Law in the Classical Period, 1140–1234: From Gratian to the Decretals of Pope Gregory IX*, edited by Wilfried Hartmann and Kenneth Pennington]." *Zeitschrift der Savigny-Stiftung für Rechtsgeschichte* 96: 609–15.

Review of Anne Lefebvre-Teillard, *Autour de l'enfant: Du droit canonique et romain médiéval au Code Civil de 1804*. *Law and History Review* 28: 260–62.

Review of Giuliano Marchetto, *Il divorzio imperfetto: I giuristi medievali e la separazione dei coniugi*. *American Historical Review* 115: 270–71.

"What Difference Does It Make If Marriage Is a Sacrament? An Historical Approach." In *Jurisprudence of Marriage and Other Intimate Relationships*, edited by Scott FitzGibbon, Lynne D. Wardle and A. Scott Loveless, 15–35. Buffalo: William S. Hein & Co., Inc.

"What Happened in the English Legal System in the Fourteenth Century and Why Would Anyone Want to Know?" *Southern Methodist University Law Review* 63: 949–66.

2011

"Comparative Approaches to Marriage in the Later Middle Ages." In *Regional Variations in Matrimonial Law and Custom in Europe, 1150–1600*, edited by Mia Korpiola, 289–316. Leiden: Brill.

"Diritto, matrimonio e società nel tardo medioevo: Considerazioni sull'area inglese e area «franco-belga»." *Rivista storica italiana* 123: 1129–79.

"*Ius* in Roman law." In *Christianity and Human Rights: An Introduction*, edited by John Witte Jr. and Frank S. Alexander, 64–80. New York: Cambridge University Press.

"The Mysterious Canonist Bazianus on Marriage." In *Law as Profession and Practice in Medieval Europe: Essays in Honor of James Brundage*, edited by Kenneth Pennington and Melodie Harris Eichbauer, 263–92. Farnham, Surrey: Ashgate.

Review of Patrick Nold, *Marriage Advice for a Pope: John XXII and the Power to Dissolve*. *Catholic Historical Review* 97: 782.

2012

"The Legal Professions of Fourteenth-Century England." In *Lawyers and Texts: Studies in Medieval Legal History in Honour of Paul Brand*, edited by Susanne Jenks, Jonathan Rose and Christopher Whittick, 227–51. Leiden: Brill.

"Thoughts on Diocesan Statutes: England and France, 1200–1500." In *Canon Law, Religion, and Politics: Liber Amicorum Robert Somerville*, edited by Uta-Renate Blumenthal, Anders Winroth, and Peter Landau, 253–71. Washington, DC: Catholic University of America Press.

2013

"'The Hypostasis of a Prophecy': Legal Realism and Legal History." In *Law and Legal Process: Substantive Law and Procedure in English Legal History*, edited by Matthew Dyson and David Ibbetson, 1–16. Cambridge: Cambridge University Press.

2014

Appeals to the Privy Council from the American Colonies: An Annotated Digital Catalogue. Compiled by Sharon Hamby O'Connor and Mary Sarah Bilder with the assistance of Charles Donahue Jr. Cambridge, MA: The Ames Foundation.

"By Way of a Conclusion." In *Les officialités dans l'Europe médievale et moderne: Des tribunaux pour une société chrétienne*, edited by Véronique Beaulande-Barraud and Martine Charageat, 325–38. Turnhout: Brepols.

"The Role of the Humanists and the Second Scholastic in the Development of European Marriage Law from the Sixteenth to the Nineteenth Centuries." In *Law and Religion: The Legal Teachings of the Protestant and Catholic Reformations*, edited by Jordan Ballor, Wim Decock, Michael Germann, and Laurent Waelkens, 45–62. Göttingen: Vandenhoeck & Ruprecht.

With Stuart McManus, co-author of "Philologia ancilla historiae: An Emendation to lex Burgundionum, 42,2." *Zeitschrift der Savigny-Stiftung für Rechtsgeschichte* (*Romanistische Abteilung*) 113: 414–23.

2015

"Ethical Standards for Advocates and Proctors of the Court of Ely (1374–1382) Revisited." In *Studies in Canon Law and Common Law in Honor of R. H. Helmholz*, edited by Troy L. Harris, 41–60. Berkeley, CA: The Robbins Collection.

2016

"The Ecclesiastical Courts: Introduction." In *The History of Courts and Procedure in Medieval Canon Law*, edited by Wilfried Hartmann and Kenneth Pennington, 247–99. Washington, DC: Catholic University of America Press.

"The Legal Background: European Marriage Law from the Sixteenth to the Nineteenth Century." In *Marriage in Europe 1400–1800*, edited by Silvana Seidel Menchi, 33–60. Toronto: Toronto University Press.

"Magna Carta in the Fourteenth Century: From Law to Symbol?: Reflections on the 'Six Statutes.'" *William & Mary Bill of Rights Journal* 25: 591–628.

"*Methodus ad facilem historiarum cognitionem*: Autobiographical and Methodological Reflections." In *Texts and Contexts in Legal History: Essays in Honor of Charles Donahue*, edited by John Witte Jr., Sara McDougall, and Ana di Robillant, 1–21. Berkeley, CA: The Robbins Collection.

"Procedure in the Courts of the *Ius commune*." In *The History of Courts and Procedure in Medieval Canon Law*, edited by Wilfried Hartmann and Kenneth Pennington, 74–124. Washington, DC: Catholic University of America Press.

With Sara McDougall, co-author of "France and Adjoining Areas." In *The History of Courts and Procedure in Medieval Canon Law*, edited by Wilfried Hartmann and Kenneth Pennington, 300–343. Washington, DC: Catholic University of America Press.

"'The Whole of the Constitutional History of England is a Commentary on This Charter.'" *North Carolina Law Review* 94: 1521–44.

2017

"'Delictum est vobis quod judicia habebitis inter vos' (1 Cor. 6:7): Defamation Cases in Ely Diocese, 1374–1382." In *From Learning to Love: Schools, Law, and Pastoral Care in the Middle Ages: Essays in Honour of Joseph W. Goering*, edited by Tristan Sharp et al., 492–514. Toronto: PIMS.

"The Modern Laws of Both Tort and Contract: Fourteenth Century Beginnings?" *Manitoba Law Journal* 40: 9–40.

"Popes Alexander III and Innocent III." In *Christianity and Family Law*, edited by John Witte Jr. and Gary S. Hauk, 161–78. Cambridge: Cambridge University Press.

Review of Bruce C. Brasington, *Order in the Court: Medieval Procedural Treatises in Translation*. *Bulletin of Medieval Canon Law* 34: 281–97.

Review of D. L. D'Avray, *Papacy, monarchy and marriage, 860–1600*. *Journal of Ecclesiastical History* 68: 398–99.

2019

"Another Way of Doing Manuscript Catalogues?" In *English Legal History and its Sources: Essays in Honour of Sir John Baker*, edited by David Ibbetson, Neil Jones, and Nigel Ramsay, 282–99. Cambridge: Cambridge University Press.

"The Status of Women in the Laws of Athelberht." In *Languages of the Law in Early Medieval England: Essays in Memory of Lisi Oliver*, edited by Stefan Jurasinski and Andrew Rabin, 3–24. Peeters: Leuven.

"What Could You Do With a Law Degree in Fourteenth-Century England? Archbishop Winchelsey's Statutes and the Advocates of the Court of Arches." *Bulletin of Medieval Canon Law* 36: 315–29.

2020

The Right of Spoil of the Popes of Avignon 1316–1415. 2nd ed. Revised and augmented by Daniel Williman and Karen Corsano. Edited by Charles Donahue Jr. Cambridge, MA: The Ames Foundation.

Review of Elisabeth van Houts, *Married Life in the Middle Ages, 900–1300*. *Journal of Ecclesiastical History* 71: 630–32.

2021

With Richard H. Helmholz, Kenneth Pennington, and Robert Somerville, co-author of "Peter Landau." *Speculum* 96: 945–47.

Review of Tom Johnson, *Law in Common: Legal Cultures in Late-Medieval England. Renaissance Quarterly* 74: 1349–50.

2023

Review of Wolfgang P. Müller, *Marriage Litigation in the Western Church, 1215-1517. Law and History Review* 41: 229–31.

Forthcoming

"Once More Alexander III on the Consent Theory of Marriage." In *Proceedings of the Fourteenth International Congress of Medieval Canon Law*, edited by Franck Roumy. Città del Vaticano: Biblioteca Vaticana.

"*Cherchez le seigneur. Et la femme?*," forthcoming in a volume of essays in honor of Professor F. Donald Logan.

"What Difference Did Roman Law Make?," forthcoming in a volume of essays in honor of Professor Anne Josephine Duggan.

Index

Abbe, Henry 429, 432–433, 434
Abbe, William le 429, 432–433
abbey 231–232, 234–235, 236–237, 342–343, 349–353
  See also Saint-Clément, abbey of
abduction 174*n*65, 216, 217*n*8, 224
  See also rape
Abelard, Peter 168–169, 171, 174, 176
  See also Heloise
abjuration 174, 185
Abraham 520
accomplice liability 161, 174, 175–177, 185, 187, 215–216
Accursius 10, 63, 65–66, 73, 74, 80–83
  Glossa ordinaria 10, 66, 80–82, 172*n*33
accusatorial procedure 13, 475–481, 483, 485–487, 488–493, 494–495
Adalais de Conas 205
Adalbero I, bishop 314
Adams, John 467, 468
Adelais de Toulouse 209
administrative agencies 13, 477–478, 489–491, 495
Adorno, Antoniotto 104
Adriatic Sea 105–106
adultery 35, 151, 229, 276*n*81, 296
  and witnessing 35, 47, 51
  as grounds for divorce 296
  See also Lex Iulia de adulteriis
adversarial procedure
  See accusatorial procedure
Aelius Gallus 48
affidavit 42, 429, 441
affinity
  See marital impediment
Aiswy, William and Alice 182
Alaric II 194
  See also Lex Romana Visigothorum
Albigensian crusades 192*n*1, 193, 194
Aldricus 10, 65, 71–73, 75, 77
Alexander III, pope 6, 96, 162–163, 167
Alexander, Severus 43
Alexander VIII, pope 263, 267
Aleyn, John and Catherine 182
Altwein, Dorothea 508
American Revolution 8, 467, 468, 477
Ames Foundation XIV, 9, 551, 552
André, Edouard 231–232
anger
  See ire
Anglican Church 242, 247
animal
  capture of 117–119, 123, 128, 131, 137
  domesticated 125, 128, 131, 134
  pig 11, 118, 123–124, 125–128, 131–132, 135, 136
  wild 11, 90*n*, 92, 116*n*2, 117–120, 123–124, 125–131, 134, 136
  wolf 11, 123–124, 125–128, 131–132, 133, 135, 136
  See also fox
animus
  See intention
animus revertendi 125
Ankere, John le 165
annulment
  See marriage
Antias, Valerius 56, 57
Antinucci 419–421
Antoninus Pius 39
apparatus 66, 77, 81
appel comme d'abus 263, 265–266, 267, 272, 274
Aquinas, Thomas 108–109, 293, 303, 395*n*7
arbiter 49*n*125, 146–147
arbitration XV, 12, 14, 141, 146–147, 459*n*38, 490*n*70, 504
  See also compromissum
arbitration agreement
  See compromissum
arbitrator 147
Arcadius Charisius 45, 51, 53*n*144, 56*n*163
aristocratic 7, 109, 148, 194, 197*n*19, 205, 207, 209, 312
Aristotle 109–110, 378
arrestographe 262
arson 177–178
artisans 194*n*4, 205, 312, 316, 320–321
asceticism 9, 242, 243, 244–245, 256
Ashfield, Lewis Morris 463

Ashfield, V. Pearse 463
Asketel, Walter and Catherine 182
Asserio, Rigaud de 335, 362
Audren, Frédéric 494–495
Augustine of Hippo 169, 370, 373, 379, 381
  City of God 395*n*8, 401
  on suicide 395, 401–402, 405, 406
Augustinian Order 288, 313*n*7
August, Karl 508
Austin, J. L. 166
Austria
  Vienna 530, 541
Ayenbite of Inwyt 171–172
Azo 71*n*32, 77, 79*n*57, 80, 81, 83
Azpilcueta, Martín de 150, 153

Bacon, Francis 526–528, 530, 541
Bacun, John 337, 338, 346–348, 358–361, 362–366
Baker, J. H. 459
Balduinus, Jacobus 74–75
Baldus de Ubaldis 10, 67, 68*n*25, 70, 87, 89, 98–102, 103–104, 106, 110, 111
bannus 315–318, 320, 322, 328, 405*n*47
banquier-expéditionnaire 263, 275
Barbaro, Francesco 110
Barbarossa, Frederick, emperor 96
Barbeyrac, Jean 117
Barker, Robert 438, 441
Barnardiston's *Reports* 457
Bartolus de Sassoferrato 63, 68*n*25, 70*n*28, 73, 74, 76*n*, 79, 82, 83, 84*n*75, 154*n*58, 383*n*44
Barton, Engelram of 176
Barton, Simon of 176
Barwick, Margaret wife of Simon of 184
Bassnett, John 465
bastardy 82, 228–229, 506, 510
  legitimation 224–227
Batinus 161, 179
Baxter, Richard 245, 255–258
Beatrice, countess of Melgueil 205
Becon, Thomas 247*n*12, 249, 252
Bell, Robert 454–455, 467
Benavente, Álvaro de 288
Benedictine Order 16, 311, 314
benefice 16, 149–150, 249, 274, 334–339
  See also Bacun, John; pluralism; Rothbury, Gilbert; Stanton, Hervey de
Bentham, Jeremy 539
Bernard, Robert 176–177
Bernard-Aton IV, viscount of Béziers 204, 209
Bernard-Aton V, viscount of Nîmes and Agde 204, 209
Bernard-Aton VI 204
Bernard IV, count of Melgueil 200, 204
Bestor, Jane 552
betrothal 165, 192*n*2, 293–294
  See also marriage
Beville, Humphrey 425
Biblioteca Casanatense 285
Bisson, Thomas 192*n*2, 196*n*14, 558
Black Death 1, 429
Blackstone's *Commentaries* 454, 458, 467
Blomefield, Francis 442–443
Blythe, James M. 109
Bocci, Maria Caterina 413–415
Bocci, Pier Anton 413–414
Bollan, William 466
Boniface VIII, pope 293–294
Bonnassie, Pierre 197*n*19, 202
Bonnat, Stephan 230–231
Bonsey, Marie de 232–233
Book of Rites 285–286, 289–291, 300, 303–304
  See also marriage
books, law
  abridgments 8, 457, 459–460, 461, 462, 467
  collecting 451–452, 460–468
  digests of laws 453–455
  law reports 8, 176, 181, 182, 457, 460, 468
  market for 8, 452–468
  treatises 8, 454–455, 457–459, 460, 468
  See also tractatus
Bouwsma, William J. 96–97, 103
Bracton 166*n*32, 175, 178, 181–182, 183–184, 186
Bradford, Andrew 454
Bradford, William 454
Brandelisio 407–408
Brandt, Susanna Margaretha 507–508
Breviary of Alaric
  See Lex Romana Visigothorum
Brode, John 441–442
Brooke's *Abridgment* 459
Brown, Samuel 460

Bruges, Andrew de 336–337
Bryn, Margery 185
Bugge, Nicholas 177
Bulgarus 66–67, 71, 73
 See also Four Doctors
Bullinger, Heinrich 247–249, 250, 253, 256
Burckhardt, Jacob 107
Burke, Edmund 468
Burrell's *Reports* 457
Buti, Lucretia 228
Butler, Alfred 436
Byrd, William 467
Byzantine Empire 95–96

Caccialupi, Giovanni Battista 142, 143, 155
Caesar, Julius 402
Caines, George 116
Calixtus II, pope 317*n*35, 322, 323*n*71
Callistratus 23*n*11, 41*n*93, 46, 47*n*116, 49
Calvin, John 242, 244
Calvinism 244, 245
Canning, Joseph 67*n*18, 89*n*, 102, 103*n*, 106*n*51
canon law
 canonists 12, 140–147, 149–151, 153–154, 302, 370–371, 372*n*7, 374, 378, 380*n*35, 387
 Corpus Iuris Canonici 150, 151
 instruction in 547
 of marriage 5, 162–168, 266, 268, 272–274, 277, 288, 295, 305
 of settlements 140–147, 149–154
 of slavery 302
 of usury 378, 386
 on expulsion of Jews 378–379
 on profession to religious life 223–224
 on suicide 400–402, 405
 See also pluralism; Roman-canon law; scandal
capture
 See animal
Carmelite Order 412
Carmignani, Giovanni 479–480
Carolus de Tocco 10, 65, 73, 77–81
Carroll, Lewis 530
Cassigoli, Maria Teresa 415–416
Cassius Longinus 51
Castillon, Jacquette de 228
Catherine, saint 234
Cato, Marcus Portius 401–402
Cécile de Provence 204
centena 317, 328
Champlin, Edward 36*n*65, 37, 50*n*133
Chancery 336–337, 364, 366, 477*n*8
 See also equity
Charles IX, king of France 269
Charles V, king of France 15, 371, 373, 375, 376, 385, 388
Charles VI, king of France 215, 388–389, 390
charter 196, 204, 311, 313*n*8, 315–316, 318, 319–320, 321–322, 325–326, 328, 346*n*89, 347*n*92, 424, 429, 431*n*14, 433–440, 453
 See also deed
Chaucer, Geoffrey 172, 185
Chenery, Antoine de 225
Chenery, Jeanne de 225–226
Chesue, Marie de 229
China 14–15, 284–305
Chinese Rites Controversy 284, 287
Chobham, Thomas 164
Christ
 See Jesus
Cianchi, Anton Maria 418–419
Cianchi, Maria Rosa 417–419
Cicero 21, 23, 26, 29, 33–34, 36–37, 38*n*74, 40–41, 42–43, 45–46, 50*n*133, 55
Cistercian Order 224*n*28, 228–229, 372*n*7, 387
civil law 13, 455, 475, 477, 483, 484, 488–489, 491–492
 on inheritance 36, 37*n*71, 39–40
 on marriage 150, 278
 on usury 386*n*49
 See also Roman law
civitas Venetorum 100–101
Clanchy, M. T. 434–435, 437
Classic of Filial Piety 304
Cleaver, Robert 250–253
clergy 15, 16, 83, 84, 155, 215, 221, 225–226, 228*n*42, 229–230, 236–237, 243, 244, 249, 256, 313, 318–319, 325, 334–338, 343*n*60, 362–366, 371–374, 377, 380–385, 400, 416, 419
 priests 14–15, 149, 163, 165*n*27, 167, 171, 217, 219, 227, 230*n*50, 231, 234, 243, 249, 270*n*43, 280, 318, 334, 380, 418
 See also monks; nuns

Clement, saint 312*n*5, 314, 323–324, 325–327, 328
Vita Clementis 323
Vita tertia Clementis 323–325
Clement v, pope 335, 340, 342, 344, 347
Code 10, 15, 67, 87*n*1, 195, 373
apparatus 77
on custom 70–71
on inheritance 206
on legal certainty 78
on marital property 199*n*26, 203
on Nicene Christianity 69
on settlement 141–142, 143, 144, 151, 153
on usury 386*n*49
on witnesses 23*n*10, 40*n*87, 43, 45*n*108, 46
See also Corpus Iuris Civilis
Codex Gregorianus 194
Codex Hermogenianus 194
coercion
See duress
Cohen, Morris 453
Coke, Edward 457–458
Colden, Cadwallader David 11, 117–118, 137
Columbia College 482
Columbia Law School 489
commentators
See Roman law
Common Bench 338, 346, 352, 354, 359, 363, 461
common law, English 13, 424, 426*n*5, 436, 475–478, 483–487, 488, 490, 492, 494–495
and women 181*n*89
literature of 454–461, 465, 468
of crime 173–186
of property 135*n*50, 534
presumptions 179*n*83
theory of 484–486, 524, 536, 538–539
See also books, law
Comnena, Eudocia 195
Company of the Misericordia 415
A Compleat Collection of the Laws of Maryland 454
complicity
See accomplice liability
compositio 12, 144, 150–151
amicabilis 12, 144, 146–147, 151, 152
compromissum 12, 146–147
concubines 163
base 301–302
in China 15, 284, 288, 289*n*12, 290, 295, 297–298, 299–303, 304
in England 182–183
in France 230*n*52, 234
in Italy 228*n*42
noble 301
confession 163, 169*n*47, 222, 229, 324, 380, 384, 407, 409–410
confessors' manuals 150
of crime 152, 161, 174, 185, 506
conflict of laws 10, 63–65, 67–68, 71–85, 525, 536*n*31
consanguinity
See marital impediment
consent 137*n*
future 162–163
of feudal lord 149
of parents 251, 270*n*43, 292–293
of religious superior 148
of witnesses 57
present 162, 164, 187
proof of 167–168, 187
tacit 131
to crime 6, 161–162, 173–186, 400
to custom 70, 79
to Jewish presence 375
to jury trial 174
to marriage 5*n*7, 6, 162–168, 187, 247, 251, 271, 291*n*20, 292–295, 304
to religious life 224
to settlement 145, 153
to sex 216, 222–223
to sin 168–173, 406*n*55
consilium 68, 79*n*61, 98–99, 101–102, 104, 105, 372*n*7, 373, 378–382, 383, 385, 386, 388
Constantine 33*n*54, 46
Constitutio Criminalis Carolina 503
contempt 168, 170–171, 173
contract 45*n*108, 74, 133, 136, 518, 531, 537, 539*n*42
and concubinage 301*n*47
and conflict of laws 76–77, 79
and coverture 186
and insanity 178
innominate 145
of debt 400*n*21
of dowry 76, 79

contract (*Cont.*)
of marriage 75, 151, 164–166, 198–200, 203, 241, 242*n*3, 248, 263, 266, 273*n*64, 278, 290, 293–295
of partnership 132*n*43
of sale 41, 150
of settlement 141–143, 145, 146, 153, 154
sealed 41
unenforceable 14
void 278
written 40–41, 199–200, 290
See also stipulatio
contrectatio 121, 127–128, 132
Cooke's *Reports* 455
Coquale, Jean 232–233
Coquillette, Daniel 551
Corbin, Arthur 537
Corda, Ambrogio Maria del 414
Cordelières-lez-Prouvinz, abbey 235*n*69, 236
coroner 174, 175, 177, 403
corporate personhood 90, 100–101, 102, 103–107, 110, 111, 532–533
Corpus Iuris Civilis 10, 21, 69, 71, 77, 87, 89, 95, 98, 111, 118, 194–195
See also Code; *Digest*; *Institutes*; *Novels*
Cossar, Roisin 228
Coudert, Frederic R., II 491–494, 495
Coudert, Frederic R., Sr. 491
Coulaverdey, Robert de 234
Courson, Robert 169–171
court
See Chancery; Common Bench; ecclesiastical court; Exchequer; eyre; King's Bench; *parlement*; quarter session; royal court; York consistory court
coutumes
See custom
Coverdale, Miles 247
Cranmer, Thomas 249
crepundia 128*n*, 129, 130
Crequy, Adrienne-Elisabeth de 262, 276
Crequy, Charlotte de 262–263, 267, 268, 270, 271, 272, 278
Crequy, François Leonor de 263, 264, 267, 269
crime 6, 7, 161–162, 173–186, 221, 388, 389, 390, 493, 501, 504, 506, 537
and settlement 151–152
enslavement as punishment for 302
false confession of 405–406
forgery 37, 152
sexual crimes 46*n*109, 216, 384
treason 46*n*109
See also accomplice liability; arson; *furtum*; homicide; infanticide; rape; suicide; theft
Crisp, Frederick Arthur 436, 443
Crok, Agnes 182
Cunctos populos
See Edict of Thessalonica
Curwin, George 463
custom 7, 15, 193, 194, 195, 206, 207, 210, 264, 390, 402, 483, 486, 503, 518*n*87
and Roman law 48, 51, 66–67, 70–74, 77–79, 82, 84, 100, 133, 147
of Bologna 66–67, 71, 81
of Chartres 75–76
of China 285, 287, 290*n*17, 299, 304
of Genoa 100, 105
of Modena 81
of Montpellier 195, 199, 200, 201–202, 203, 204, 205, 206, 207, 209
of Paris 75–76
of Picardie 276
of Venice 100, 105
See also pays de droit coutumier

Dandolo, Andrea 96*n*19, 97
Davenport, George 463
Davenport, Katherine 463
deafness
and consent 166*n*32
and *ius disponendi* 148
and witnessing 49
debt
as motivation for suicide 400
in canon law 144
in colonial America 464
in English common law 186*n*120, 346, 403, 442
in Roman law 27, 41
of corporations 525
owed to Jewish creditors 380, 383–384
deceit 153
decretal 98*n*32, 150, 163*n*15, 164*n*21, 293–294, 296–297, 335, 363, 371*n*3, 379, 382, 386

Decretum
See Gratian's *Decretum*
deed 8–9, 426–428, 429, 435–437, 442–443
See also charter
defamation 53
democratic 475, 481, 495
Deuteronomy 118, 134, 385, 386*n*50
Diacono, Giovanni 97
Dickens's *Reports* 457
Dickinson, Jacob M. 489–491, 495
Diet of Roncaglia 67
Digest 67, 111, 195, 210
on conflict of laws 75*n*48
on custom 70
on inheritance 206*n*58
on jurisdiction 71, 79
on marital property 199*n*26
on property 10–11, 95, 100, 118, 119, 121–122, 123–124, 125–126, 127, 131–133, 136
on *res communes omnium* 87–89, 91–93, 102, 105
on settlement 141–142, 143
on suicide 404–405
on theft 121–122
on treatment of slaves 44*n*103
on usury 386*n*49
on witnesses 13, 21, 22, 23*n*11, 26*n*22, 32*n*52, 33*n*53, 34*n*58, 35–41, 44–51, 54–56
on women's legal agency 203
See also *Corpus Iuris Civilis*
diocese 165
of Bath and Wells 344–346
of Coventry and Lichfield 340, 345
of Durham 339–340, 342
of Ely 344
of Exeter 343
of Hereford 341
of Lincoln 339, 340, 343, 346–347
of London 341, 346
of Norwich 340–341, 342, 343–344, 345, 347, 348
of Salisbury 347
of Winchester 165
of York 224, 345
dispensation 227, 228, 229*n*45, 295
papal 225, 226, 263, 267–271, 273–278, 279, 335, 337, 338–344, 346–347, 386*n*49
divorce 382, 520
in China 15, 288, 292, 295–297, 301, 304
See also marriage
Dodgson, Charles
See Carroll, Lewis
doge (Italian) 94–97, 101, 104, 108–109
Dolling, Alice 165
dolus
See deceit
Domat's *Civil Law Institutes* 461
dominion
See ownership
Donahue, Charles IV, 451
as steward of manuscripts 9
as teacher and mentor XIII–XVIII, 1–3, 4–5, 11, 12, 17, 63–64, 90*n*, 116, 241–242, 283, 445, 521, 547–550, 551–552, 553–557, 558–559
bibliography 560–574
Law, Marriage, and Society 5, 14, 241, 261, 479, 556
on archives and manuscripts 8n, 436*n*22
on comparative law 284*n*
on ecclesiastical courts 503*n*
on law and religion 15*n*
on legal procedure 12*n*13, 479
on *lex mercatoria* 10
on marital property 7*n*
on marriage 5–6, 16*n*, 163–165, 167, 261, 268, 272, 279*n*92, 283–284, 297*n*39
on property 11–12, 92*n*12, 116, 118
on Roman law 63–64
on witnesses 12*n*14
scholarly method 2–4, 14–15, 16, 17–18, 58, 261, 283–284, 479, 556–557
dowry
See marital property
Dufour, Jean 232
Dunchirche, Henry of 176
Dunlap, William 467
duress 153, 164, 178, 179, 181, 186, 201, 224

ecclesiastical court 2, 8*n*, 12*n*14, 73, 165, 167, 231, 279*n*92, 283, 503
ecclesiastical law
See canon law
economics
and Jews in medieval France 375–376

economics (*Cont.*)
  and Protestantism 9, 241–242, 243–246, 249, 251, 255–257, 258–259
  and usury 373*n*11
  in Hohfeld 534, 535
  in medieval Metz 312, 316–317, 321
  See also benefice
Edict of Thessalonica 10, 69, 77–78, 80, 83, 84
Edward I, king of England 346, 429, 433–434
Edward II, king of England 335, 336–337, 345, 347, 365–366, 558
Edward III, king of England 347*n*91
Eleanor of Aquitaine 147
Eliot, Benjamin 453
emptio venditio 41
encomienda 149
England
  Cambridge 253, 364
  Canterbury 164, 165*n*27, 336
  Cornwall 343, 424–426, 440, 442
  Devonshire 424
  Exeter 343, 424, 426, 431, 433*n*
  London 38*n*76, 41, 164*n*18, 177*n*77, 182, 185, 255, 335, 338, 341, 346, 403, 455, 456, 457, 460, 461, 465–466, 468, 520
  Norfolk 177*n*76, 345, 348, 358–361, 364, 427
  Northamptonshire 176*n*72, 180–181, 185, 343
  Norwich 177, 180, 184, 185, 336, 340, 342–345, 347–348
  Oxfordshire 250, 364, 424*n*2
  Somerset 161, 345–346, 438, 440
  Surrey 180
  Warwickshire 176
  Wiltshire 161–162, 179–180, 182, 185
  Winterbourne Stoke 165
  Yorkshire 180, 224, 345, 355, 357
  See also Anglican Church; English Civil War; eyre
English Civil War 442, 477
Epitome regularum Ulpiani 47*n*114, 49, 55
equity 71–72, 147, 253, 459, 477, 525*n*3
  See also Chancery
Ermessende de Castries 205, 208
Esglaniter, Denisot 231, 232
Esmein, Adhémar 272*n*54, 273*n*64, 491
Étienne de Bar, bishop of Metz 313*n*8, 314, 317*n*35, 320*n*51, 322, 326
Evans, Peter 463–464
Exchequer 338, 356, 363, 526
Execrabilis 16, 334–338, 340–344, 347–348, 352, 356, 360, 362–366
Exodus 134
eyre 356
  Bedford Eyre of 1202 184*n*108
  Devon Eyre of 1238 180*n*86
  Kent Eyre of 1313–1314 186*n*120
  London Eyre of 1276 185*n*114
  London Eyre of 1321 338
  Northamptonshire Eyre of 1329–1330 176*n*72, 178*n*79, 180–181, 182*n*95, 185
  Surrey Eyre of 1255 180
  Warwickshire Eyre of 1221 176
  Wiltshire Eyre of 1249 161–162, 179–180, 182, 185
  Yorkshire Eyre of 1257 180

Fabbri, Clemente 416–417
Fabbri, Domenico 416–417
fair 311, 315–316, 318, 321, 326–327, 328
fama publica 380, 384
family archive 8, 426, 429, 436, 442
family law 241
Farinacci, Prospero 7, 399–400, 404, 405–408
Faust 13–14, 501, 503–504, 508, 510–514, 515, 517, 519–520
  Faust 14, 501–503, 505–506, 508–519
  Helena 14, 501–503, 511–515, 519
  Liesschen 509
  Lynceus 14, 501–504, 511–515
  Margarete (Gretchen) 13–14, 501–504, 505–506, 508–511, 514, 519
  Mephistopheles 14, 501–503, 506, 509–510, 514, 515–520
  Tindareos 514
  See also Goethe, Johann Wolfgang von
Faustbuch 517
Fedele, Dante 98*n*32, 99–100
Feenstra, Robert 133–134
felony
  See crime

Festus, Pompeius 29*n*34, 30, 31, 48*n*122
feudalism 82, 149, 209, 243, 244
fides 22–23, 25, 31, 33, 38*n*78, 39, 41–43, 44–47, 57, 58
fin de non-recevoir 271–272
finder 118, 121–123, 127, 128, 132–135, 136
Fiorentini, Mario 93*n*14
Fitzherbert, Anthony 459, 461
fitz John Byyondethebrok, Richard and Alice 180–181
fitz Walter, Thomas 176
Fleta 182–185, 186
Fole, John 177
Folur, Agnes and Robert le 161–162, 179, 186
Fontanelli, Domenico 413–414
Fonte, Roger and Joan de 185
Fortescue, John 477
Four Doctors 67, 71
  See Bulgarus; Hugo de Porta Ravennate; Jacobus de Boragine; Martinus Gosia
fox IV, 11, 116–117
France
  Champagne 215, 218, 225, 228, 234, 235, 327*n*90
  Chartres 75
  Languedoc 7, 192–210
  Montpellier 192, 193, 195, 196, 197, 198–201, 203–210, 323*n*70, 376*n*22
  Normandy 220
  Paris 14, 21, 75–77, 168, 169, 236–238, 261–262, 265, 284–286, 371, 376, 389*n*57, 403*n*40, 489
  Picardie 265, 276
  Toulouse 192–193, 194, 197*n*19, 209, 319*n*43
  Troyes 225, 226*n*34, 229–230, 233–234
  See also Metz
Francis, Jr., Tench 461
Franklin, Benjamin 455, 458, 460
Frederick the Great 507
Fredona, Robert 105
Freeman, Elizabeth 223, 224
Frier, Bruce 93*n*14
furtum 121, 125*n*25, 127, 133*n*44
  furtum conceptum 34–35
  See also theft

Gaine, Hugh 457
Gaius 29*n*34, 30*n*42, 31*n*44, 34–36, 44, 49*n*128, 51*n*135, 56, 88*n*4, 125, 555
  Institutes 29*n*34, 32, 34–36, 37*n*71, 38, 40, 44, 48*n*119, 50, 194
  Res cottidianae 90*n*, 119
Galileo Galilei 409
  Maria Celeste, daughter of 409–411, 415
Gallia Christiana 196, 234
Gallicanism 266, 269, 274, 279, 372
  See also Libertés de l'église gallicane
Garburgis 201
Garre, Jean 234
Garriga, Carlos 155
Gaunter, John and Agnes le 185
Geheimes Consilium 508
Gellius, Aulus 28, 29, 31, 56–57
George III, king of England 443
Germanic law 483–484
Germany 262*n*7, 402, 406*n*51, 475, 480–481, 483–484, 489, 502*n*2, 504, 507
  Berlin 481
  Frankfurt 480, 507
  Heidelberg 480
  Leipzig 489
  Saxony-Weimar-Eisenach 501, 504, 508
Gerrish, Samuel 464
Gilbert, Felix 94*n*, 107–108, 109–110
Glossa ordinaria
  See Accursius
glossators
  See Roman law
Goethe, Johann Wolfgang von 13–14, 501, 503, 505, 507–508, 511*n*54, 515, 519–520
  See also Faust
Golden Bull 96
Gouron, André 194, 195*n*10
grace 218*n*12, 226, 229, 237–238, 243–244, 377, 379
  See also pardon
Granesete, Robert of 185
gränzunbewußt/Gränzunbewußtheit 13, 502–504, 511, 514, 518, 519
Gratian's *Decretum* 8*n*9, 15, 162, 216*n*3, 373, 383
Great Qing Code 285–286, 290*n*16, 292–293, 295–296
Gregory I, pope 370, 379, 380*n*35, 381, 383*n*41
Gregory IX, pope 98*n*32, 386–387

Gregory the Great
  See Gregory I, pope
Gregory XIII, pope 144
Grevant, Marguerite de 233
Gridley, Jeremiah 465, 467
Grotius, Hugo 11, 105*n*46, 117, 118, 128–134, 135, 136–137
  De iure belli ac pacis 11, 118, 128*n*, 132–133, 134
Grubb, James S. 94*n*, 98
Guadagni, Filippo Maria 415
Guang, Sima 295
Guérin, Charles 25*n*13, 26
Guillem d'Aumelas 205
Guillem III of Montpellier 208
Guillem IV of Montpellier 208
Guillem V of Montpellier 200, 208
Guillem VI of Montpellier 200, 208
Guillem VII of Montpellier 200, 204
Guillem VIII of Montpellier 195, 200, 208–209
Guillemette, daughter of Guillem V 200, 204
Guillemette, daughter of Guillem VII 204
Gutzwiller, Max 64, 73*n*43

Hackl, Karl 28*n*31, 32
Hadrian, emperor of Rome 38*n*74, 91
Hagar 379, 381, 384
Hale, Matthew 458*n*35
  Pleas of the Crown 459
Hall, David 453*n*6, 460
Halpérin, Jean-Louis 264*n*16, 494–495
Hampton, William de 177
Hanawalt, Barbara 177*n*76, 179–180, 184*n*109
Hankins, James 103n, 558, 108*n*60, 110*n*68
Hanley, Sarah 262*n*6, 265–266
Hanska, Jussi 226, 227
Harvard College XIII, XV, 4, 436, 540
Harvard Graduate School of Arts and Sciences XIII–XVIII, 553, 558
Harvard Law School XIII–XVII, 1, 4, 64, 524, 551, 552, 553
Harvard Law School Library 8–9, 18, 187, 424, 443
  Historical and Special Collections XV, 436, 437, 445
Hatch, Nathaniel 466
Hawysa wife of Robert 180
Hay, Denys 109
Heloise 168
  See also Abelard, Peter
Henchman, Daniel 460
Henri of Poitiers, bishop 225–226
Henry III, king of England 429
Henry IV, king of England 438, 439, 443
Henry V, emperor 66
Henry VII, emperor 97
heresy 69–70, 166, 397, 406
Hermann, bishop of Metz 311*n*1, 313, 315–316, 321–322, 325–326
Herod, king 520
Hevia Bolaño, Juan de 146, 152
Himenes, Father 420
Hirst, Grove 464
Histoire générale de Languedoc 196
Hobbes, Thomas 117
Hobekyn, Robert de 9, 427, 429–433, 434, 443
Hobelot, Christiana 161, 179
Hoeflich, H. M. 451*n*1, 482
Hofmannsthal, Hugo von 17, 525–531, 538, 540–542
  Ein Brief 526
  See also Lord Chandos Letter; Philipp, Lord Chandos
Hohfeld, Wesley Newcomb 17, 524–526, 530–541
Höhn, Johanna Catharina 508
Holy Roman Empire 66–67, 96–97, 99–100, 143, 503
homicide
  and intention 405
  in England 169–171, 175–176, 177, 179–180, 185
  in Italy 405, 418
  in Roman law 33–35
  See also infanticide; suicide
Horace 37*n*71, 57
Horwitz, Morton 17
hospital 7–8
  Bonifazio 412
  Saint-Nicolas 317
  San Giovanni di Dio 412
  Santa Dorotea 394–395, 398, 408, 411–418, 421–422
  Santa Maria Nuova 412

Hughes's *Abridgment* 459
Hugo de Porta Ravennate 71
  See also Four Doctors
Hugolinus 77, 80
humanism 108–110, 154*n*62, 247, 285, 305, 556
Humbert, Michel 25*n*17, 52*n*143, 54–56
Hundred Years War 232
Hure, Jeanne de la 231–232

imprisonment
  escape from 237, 238
  fear of 237
  for rape 174*n*65
  in China 287
  in *Faust* 506*n*20
  in the United States 482
  of mentally ill persons 398, 406, 412
  of nuns 217–218, 220, 229, 233
independence
  of judiciary 485, 486–487
  of the bar 486–487
  sovereign 89, 94–95, 98–101, 103–105, 108–109, 111
indicia 130, 131–132, 136
infamia 49*n*124, 53*n*145, 69*n*27, 152
infancy
  as excuse for crime 186
infanticide 13, 501–502, 505–511, 514
  narratives of 506, 519–520
  by men 520
inheritance
  See testamentary disposition
iniuria 53*n*144, 93*n*14, 399*n*20
Innes, Matthew 435
Innocent II, pope 317*n*35, 318, 322, 323*n*71, 325, 326
Innocent III, pope 164*n*21, 296–297, 386–387
Innocent IV, pope 90, 111, 379, 386, 387–388, 390
Innocent XI, pope 263
Inns of Court 455, 462
inquisitorial procedure 13, 403, 475–481, 483, 485–487, 488–495
insanity 69–70, 394–395, 413, 415–417
  and *ius disponendi* 148
  and suicide 7–8, 394, 398, 400, 405, 408, 409–410, 412–413, 415, 419
  and testamentary disposition 49
  and witnessing 49
  as bodily illness 410, 413–415, 416, 419, 422
  as excuse for crime 175, 177–178, 186
  as impediment to marriage 164
inspeximus 429, 433
Institutes
  abridgment of 467
  on custom 70
  on property 92, 119–120, 123, 128–129
  on *res communes omnium* 10, 87–88, 95
  on slavery 303
  on witnesses 37*n*71, 40*n*87, 50*n*130, 51*n*134, 52, 55*n*155
  See also Corpus Iuris Civilis
intention 6, 118, 120–123, 124, 130, 131–132, 135, 136–137, 169–171, 174–175
  and dowry 79
  and suicide 405, 407, 420–421
  animus furandi 121–122, 127, 135
  See also consent
international law 10, 63, 95*n*, 504
  See also conflict of laws, *lex mercatoria*
intestacy 36, 39, 53*n*149, 201, 206, 207, 404*n*44
intoxication 165–166, 254, 400
Introcetta, Prospero 304
Investiture Controversy 313–315, 328
ire 69, 172, 395, 413, 414, 426, 431
Irnerius 71
Isabel de los Olivos y López 403–404
Isabelle of France 235
island, legal status of 99, 101
Italy
  Bologna 63, 65, 66–67, 71, 77–79, 80–83, 216, 371, 397*n*14, 407, 416–417
  Florence 74*n*44, 79, 90, 94*n*, 98*n*29, 103, 107–110, 394, 407–408, 409, 411–412, 415, 418–419
  Genoa 90, 100, 103–107
  Lombardy 72–73
  Mantua 408
  Modena 77–83
  Padua 105
  Perugia 79
  Piacenza 77
  Pisa 413, 479
  Rome 29*n*36, 47, 56, 70, 79, 96, 142, 263, 285, 286, 287, 324, 419

Italy (*Cont.*)
  Salerno 77
  San Severino Marche 155
  Siena 142, 227
  See also Venice
iudex
  See judges
iura propria 80, 84
ius civile
  See civil law; Roman law
ius commune 63, 66, 71, 73, 74, 80, 82, 84, 142–143, 146, 147, 151
  See also canon law; civil law; Roman law
ius disponendi 147–148
ius gentium 88*n*3, 89, 99–100, 105, 106

Jacob, Giles 455–457
  Every Man His Own Lawyer 455, 456–457, 458
  Jacob's Law Dictionary 455, 456
  Lex Mercatoria 462
Jacobus de Boragine 71
  See also Four Doctors
James, William 540–541, 542–543
Jeanne de Navarre 235
Jeannette la Flamenge 215–217, 219, 225, 234–235, 236–237
Jesuit Order 141, 145, 286–288, 304, 419
Jesus 250, 252, 382, 384, 461, 520
jettison 121–123, 127, 136–137
Jewish law 134–136, 302
Jews
  and moneylending 375–376, 377, 378, 380, 384, 385, 389*n*60
  expulsion of 15, 370, 372, 374–376, 377–382, 384–385, 386–390
  toleration of 378–379, 381, 385, 386–388
John, gospel of 401
John II, king of France 375
John son of William 177–178
Johnson, Penelope 219–220
Johnson, Tom 426, 434*n*18
John XXII, pope 16, 334–336, 365
Jolowicz, Herbert Felix 121*n*13, 122
Jones, A. H. M. 549
Jones, Thomas 462
Judas Iscariot 399
judges
  and conflict of laws 71–73, 79
  and fictions 536
  and law reporting 262, 457
  and settlement 155
  appointment of 32
  clerical 16–17, 263, 337–338, 362–366
  common-law 337*n*17, 539
  enslaved persons as 48
  finances of 339–362
  in benefice cases 274
  in formulary procedure 33
  in matrimonial cases 150, 263
  in suicide cases 397, 400, 404, 407–409, 421
  in testamentary cases 151
  laicization of 16–17, 366
  patronage of/by 362–366
  witnesses as 30*n*38, 34
  women as 48, 501, 503*n*3, 503, 511–515
  See also accusatorial procedure; inquisitorial procedure
jury, trial by 161, 174, 177–178, 179–180, 182, 480*n*17, 481, 486, 488*n*65, 493
Justinian, emperor 79, 87*n*1, 194–195
  See also Corpus Iuris Civilis

Kangxi, emperor 287
Kant, Immanuel 507
Kaser, Max 25*n*14, 28*n*31, 32, 105*n*45, 120*n*11
Keeton, G. W. 337*n*17, 338
Kennedy, Duncan 536–537
King's Bench 338, 349, 363*n*111, 461
Kirchenbuße 504, 508
Knudsen, Christian 217*n*6, 219, 220
Kohn, Roger 372*n*9, 375*n*16, 376, 389*n*60
Kokener, Geoffrey and Catherine le 180
Kupfer, Marcia 371, 373, 376*n*24, 381*n*39

Labeo 39, 125
laesio 154
  enormis 153–155
  enormissima 154
lagoon 95, 97
  See also Venice
Langer, Máximo 476*n*4, 477, 488*n*65
Langford, Nicholas 466
Laplain, William 461–462
Larchier, Perrin 215–216, 236–238
Lateran Council, Fourth 163
Latin America 554–556

legal fiction 404, 408, 532–533, 536, 539
legal realism 2, 479*n*12, 539–540
Legare, Thomas 465
Leges Henrici Primi 175–176
Leges Visigothorum 194, 199, 202, 206
 See also Lex Romana Visigothorum; Visigothic law
Legnano, John of 371, 373*n*12, 377–379, 382–383
Le petit thalamus 195, 196, 206
Leverett, John 459
Leverett, Thomas 459, 466
Leviticus 273
Lévy-Bruhl, Henri 24*n*, 25–31, 32*n*51, 54*n*152
Lex Cornelia de falsis 37
Lex Horatia 56–57
Lex Iulia de adulteriis 35, 46*n*109, 47, 51
Lex Iulia de vi 47*n*116, 49
Lex Iulia repetendarum 51
Lex mercatoria 10, 98, 462, 551
Lex Romana Visigothorum 194
 See also Leges Visigothorum; Visigothic law
Liber extra 98, 100, 111, 141–142, 149, 150, 382, 387
Liber feudorum maior 196
Liber instrumentorum memorialium 195, 196, 204–205
Liber iudiciorum 194
Libertés de l'église gallicane 266, 269, 274, 279
 See also Gallicanism
liberty 87, 90, 96–99, 101, 103, 108–109, 117, 119, 125, 128–131, 477–478, 483–487, 490–491, 493, 537
Lieber, Francis 13, 478, 481–487, 488, 490, 494
 Manual of Political Ethics 478, 482
 On Civil Liberty 13, 478, 483–487, 488
Lippi, Fra 228
litis contestatio 30*n*38, 31–32, 53, 57*n*168
Littleton's *Tenures* 458
Livy 52*n*143, 401
Llewellyn, Karl 539
Locke, John 11, 118, 137
Lodge, Abraham 462–463
Loewe, Andreas 337*n*17, 338, 342–244, 364*n*115
Lollardy 166
 See also heresy
Lombard law 72–73, 77
Lombard, Peter 162
López, Gregorio 154
Lord Chandos Letter 17, 526–530, 541
 See also Hofmannsthal, Hugo von; Philipp, Lord Chandos
Lucretia 401, 406
Lulli, Antonio 394–395, 415–416, 418
Lusset, Elisabeth 218*n*12, 219, 220, 221, 227*n*38, 228*n*43
Luther, Martin 242, 243
Lutheran Church 143, 247, 396

MacCormack, Geoffrey 25*n*17, 27–28, 32*n*50, 34*n*59
Mach, Ernst 541
Maigrot, Charles 14–15, 284, 286–288, 304–305
 Dissertatio de Matrimonio Sinarum 14–15, 284, 285, 289–304
Maimonides, Moses 134–135
Maitland, Frederic 167, 180*n*86
Makowski, Elizabeth 217*n*6, 219, 220, 221*n*24, 228
mancipatio 27–28, 33*n*53, 35–40, 47*n*114, 53, 54*n*152, 57*n*168
Manigault, Peter 462
Mannyng, Robert 164–165, 167
manucaption 11, 117–118, 137
manuum consertio 29–31
Marcian 45, 46, 87–88, 91
Mareschal, Henry 176
Marguerite la Coquelette 229
Maria, widow of Raimund de Oliveto 201–202
Marie de Montpellier 195, 201, 205
marital household 7, 181–183, 241–242, 245–246, 248–249, 250–252, 253, 256
marital impediment 164, 272, 289–290
 affinity 268, 269–271, 273–278, 279
 consanguinity 262–263, 267–268, 273, 277–278
 diriment 267
 impediment 267*n*28
 public honesty 268, 269–270, 274–276, 278, 279
 See also insanity

marital property 7, 197, 198–199, 207, 241, 263
 brideprice 294–295
 donatio propter nuptias 75–76, 198–200
 dowry 74*n*44, 75–76, 79, 197, 199–202, 205, 206, 210, 295
 prestation 198–201
Markaunt, Willliam and Emma of 185
Marlowe, Christopher 517
Marmursztejn, Elsa 370*n*2, 387
marriage 75–76, 247, 263
 and childrearing 248–249, 250–251, 253, 254–255, 257
 annulment 150
 arranged 292–294
 banns 270, 271, 278
 Catholic 265, 284
 clandestine 164
 consummation 162–163, 268–271, 272, 275–277, 278–279
 duties of spouses 248, 250–251, 253
 forced 293
 in China 14–15, 284, 287–288, 289–299
 mixed 288, 291–292, 303
 sacramental 265–266, 287–288
 second 297–298
 validity 14, 263, 265, 267, 272
 See also betrothal; consent; contract; divorce; marital household; marital impediment; marital property
Marsilius of Padua 371
Martinus Gosia 71
 See also Four Doctors
Mary, mother of Jesus 520
master-servant relationship 246, 251–252, 253, 256–258
mayorazgo 148–149
Mazzacane, Aldo 105
McLeod, Grant 125
McSheffrey, Shannon 164*n*18, 166
Meijers, E. M. 64, 71*n*32, 75*n*49, 77*n*52, 78*n*, 79*n*57, 81
mens rea
 See intention
merchants 98*n*30, 105, 195, 205, 246, 263*n*10, 294, 312, 316, 320, 452, 455*n*19, 461, 464, 466
 See also Lex mercatoria
metus
 See duress
Metz 16, 311–315, 316–321, 325, 328
Mézières, Philippe de 388–390
Michelman, Frank 536–537
Michie, James 465
Michigan, University of 547
 Law School 1, 4
Migliore, Michel Angelo 394–395, 398
Minnis, Alastair 166
miracle 326–327, 328
missionary 15, 284, 287–288, 304
Mittermaier, Carl Josef Anton 479–485, 492
modernism 17, 525, 526, 530–531, 535–542
Modestinus 23*n*11, 44*n*103, 45
Molina, Luis de 12, 140–141, 144–145, 149, 154
monastery 202, 220, 224, 322, 438
Mongols 292
monks 16, 176, 217*n*6, 219–220, 230*n*50, 232, 243, 254, 311–312, 314–328, 389, 412
monogamy 288, 299
Moodey, Joshua 463
Murillo Velarde, Pedro 12, 140–141, 143–144, 145–146, 148, 151–152, 154, 155
muteness
 and consent 166*n*32
 and *ius disponendi* 148
 and witnessing 49
Muyden, Johannes van 467

natural law 11, 88*n*3, 98, 103, 104, 105
 and marriage 269, 270, 293, 297
 and property 87–88, 89, 116, 117–118, 128, 133–134
 and sovereignty 90, 94–95, 100, 111
 and suicide 400*n*22
 See also res communes omnium
Necton, Alexander of 185
Netter, Thomas 166
Neumeyer, Karl 64, 78*n*55
Newton, Thomas 464
Niccolai, Father 419, 420
Nicene Christianity 69
Nicholas IV, pope 339
Norfolk, Katherine 224
no-right 534
 See also Hohfeld, Wesley Newcomb

North America, colonial
Boston 452, 453, 459, 460, 463, 464, 465, 466, 468
Charleston 452, 455, 457, 462, 464, 465–466, 467, 468
Connecticut 454, 456
Delaware 462
Georgia 456, 459
Maryland 454
New Hampshire 456, 459
New Jersey 454, 463
New York City 457, 458, 460, 461, 462–463
North Carolina 462
Pennsylvania 456
Philadelphia 452, 454, 458, 460, 461, 464, 467, 468
Rhode Island 454, 456, 464
South Carolina 465
Virginia 462, 463, 467
notary 152
Notre-Dame-aux-Nonnains, convent of 232–234
Novels 87*n*1, 195
See also Corpus Iuris Civilis
nuns
and pregnancy 215, 218, 220, 222–223, 225–226, 228–229, 235
and suicidality 409–411
children of 16, 215, 218, 220, 224–228
profession of 219*n*14, 223–224
punishment of 217–223, 229, 233
sexual activity of 15–16, 215–218, 221–222, 225–226, 228–234
See also Bonsey, Marie de; Castillon, Jacquette de; Chenery, Jeanne de; Chesue, Marie de; Grevant, Marguerite de; Hure, Jeanne de la; Jeannette la Flamenge; Marguerite la Coquelette; Norfolk, Katherine; Prinaco, Jeanne de; Rochetaille, Isabelle de

oath 314
by a nun 234
compurgation 73
in marriage 164
in the *legis actio sacramento* 32
jury 178
of witnesses 23, 440
occupatio 116
See also ownership; possession
Ockham, William of 371
Odofredus 75*n*48, 83
oikonomika
See economics
oikos
See marital household
Oldradus de Ponte 372*n*7, 373*n*13, 378–382, 383, 384, 385, 386–388
Oliphant, Herman 539
Oñate, Pedro de 12, 140–141, 142, 146–147, 156
On the Origins of the Six Types of Character 301
Orbatello 412, 415
ordeal, trial by 173, 479
Ordonnance of Blois 270, 278
Ordonnance of Orléans 269, 270, 274
Oresme, Nicolas 373
ownership 10, 27–29, 37*n*72, 44, 50, 88–89, 91–92, 100, 102, 106, 117–118, 119–124, 128, 129–132, 134–137, 202, 524–525, 532, 533, 534, 537, 548–549
See also occupatio; possession

Padilla y Meneses, Antonio de 12, 140–141, 143–144, 145*n*17, 150*n*37, 152, 153*n*52, 155
Panormitanus 147
papal datary 263
Papinian 46*n*109, 51, 55*n*155, 93*n*14
pardon 177, 178, 215–216, 237–238
Paris Foreign Missions Society 14, 284, 285
parish 318–321, 324, 325, 334, 337, 339
Parker, James 458
Parks, William 454
parlement (French court) 261, 262*n*6, 263, 264, 265–266, 271, 275*n*73, 279
Paston, John 427
Paston, Margaret 427
Paston, William 442
pater familias 56
patria potestas 50, 56, 302
Paul the Deacon 30*n*41, 31, 32*n*50, 323
Paul, jurist 38*n*78, 39, 41, 43, 45, 46*n*109, 47–48, 49, 51–52, 55*n*155, 93*n*14
Paul, saint 324, 370, 379
pays de droit coutumier 193

pays de droit écrit 193, 195
Peg, Thomas 438, 441
peine forte et dure 174
Pemberton, Ebenezer 463
penance 169–171, 218, 219, 220, 222, 228, 402
Pennington, Kenneth 67*n*16, 98*n*30, 102, 334*n*1, 399*n*18, 476*n*3
per aes et libram 27, 28, 35, 36, 48*n*122, 57
Perkins, William 253–255
Peter II, count of Barcelona and king of Aragon 199*n*29, 201, 205
Peter, saint 69, 323, 324–325
  See also Saint-Pierre-aux-Arènes
Petrarch 108
Petrus Bellaperticus 84
Philip IV, king of France 374, 387
Philippines 141*n*3, 489, 491–492, 494
Philipp, Lord Chandos 526–530, 541
  See also Hofmannsthal, Hugo von; *Lord Chandos Letter*
Philostrogios 549
Pierre de Belleperche
  See Petrus Bellaperticus
Pierson, Jesse 116–117
Pierson v. Post 11, 116–117
pilgrimage 172, 327
Pinckney, Charles 465–466
Piñel, Arias 154–155
Pintoin, Michel 389–390
Pirhing, Heinrich 145–146, 151*n*45, 152*n*47
Pitaval, François Gayot de 14, 261–262, 264, 267–268, 271–272, 278–279
Pithou, Pierre 269
Pius II, pope 226
Plato 110, 111
Plautus 30*n*43, 53–54
Pliny the Elder 125
Pliny the Younger 21, 46
Plucknett, Theodore F. T. 436–437
pluralism 16, 334–337, 339–344, 346–347, 365
  See also benefice
political thought 10, 66–67, 89–90, 94–95, 98–102, 103–112, 480–481, 484–487, 489–491, 493
Pompey 401
Pomponius, jurist 36*n*66, 37*n*68, 50*n*132, 93, 123–124, 126, 127–128, 132
Pope, Alexander 456
Poret, Adam and Agnes 177
Porphyrio, Pomponius 57
possession 11, 105, 117–120, 128–131, 274
  bonorum possessio 33*n*55, 37–40, 47*n*114
  See also occupatio; ownership; prescription
Post, Lodowick 116–117
postglossators
  See Roman law
Pothier, Robert Joseph 266*n*21, 272, 274*n*71
poverty 217*n*6, 223, 303, 383, 389, 418
  deserving poor 254
praetor 29–30, 37–40, 42, 44, 49*n*125, 121*n*14
  urban 93
pragmatism 540–541
Praxis et theoricae criminalis
  See Farinacci, Prospero
predestination 9, 242, 244, 245
prescription 79
  longi temporis praescriptio 105–106
presumption 39, 41, 118, 135, 136–137, 152*n*47, 166, 179, 181, 183–184, 186, 187, 275–276, 407
priests
  See clergy
Prick of Conscience
  See Ayenbite of Inwyt
Prinaco, Jeanne de 229
Pringsheim, Fritz 21, 25*n*16, 34*n*59
Priscian 48
Priscus, Neratius 91–92
prison
  See imprisonment
private law 10, 11–12, 45*n*107, 65*n*11, 83, 89, 90, 95, 102, 103, 106, 151, 555–556
  See also contract; property
privilege
  Hohfeldian 524, 534–535, 537
  imperial 66, 96, 104
  papal 288, 297, 387
  royal 375, 376, 378–379, 380–381, 388, 389, 390
Proculians 120
proof 12*n*14, 26, 35–36, 39–41, 43, 45–46, 53, 73, 167–168, 171, 174–175, 222*n*26, 276*n*81, 279, 407, 434
  written 43, 427

property 7–9, 11, 27, 50, 74*n*44, 87–89, 91–93, 102, 116, 118–120, 123–124, 125–137, 241, 524, 531–532
  abandonment of 11, 119–123, 128–130, 132, 133–137
  See also marital property; *occupatio*; ownership; possession; *res communes omnium*
Protestantism
  and capitalism 9, 243, 244, 246, 249, 256, 259
  and catechism 242
  and family 242
  and household manuals 9, 242, 245–246, 247–259
  See also Anglican Church, Lutheran Church
Puerto Rico 489, 491–492
Pufendorf, Samuel 2, 117, 130*n*38, 136, 459

Qing Empire 286–296, 301–302
quaestio 68, 72, 77, 78, 122*n*17, 378*n*30, 380*n*35, 399*n*17, 507
Quakers 458–459, 461
quarter session 424, 431
Quillet, Jeannine 373, 385*n*48
Quintilian 23, 24–25, 26
quo warranto 433–434

Rabel, Ernst 85
Raguier, Louis, bishop 234
Raimond II, count of Melgueil 204
Raimond Trencavel 200, 209
Ralph son of Ralph 177
rape 161, 174*n*65, 216, 218*n*10, 222–223, 401
  See also abduction
Recceswinth, king 194
repetitio 68, 82
res communes omnium 10, 87–89, 91–93, 94–95, 98, 99, 102, 104, 106, 111–112
  See also natural law; property
res judicata 144, 145, 152
res manicipi
  See mancipatio
responsum 76
restitution 76, 133*n*45, 144, 153, 237–238, 397
"Ricci method" 286–287
right 524, 531, 532, 533, 534–536, 542
  See also Hohfeld, Wesley Newcomb
Rivington, James 454, 460
Roberts, John 461
Robertson, Peter 458*n*34, 463–464
Rochetaille, Isabelle de 233, 234
Roger II Trencavel 209
Rolle's *Abridgement* 459, 461
Roman-canon law 13, 476–477, 479
Roman law 193–195, 198, 199, 200–201, 202–203, 206, 208, 210, 483–484
  commentators 64, 65, 66, 67, 68, 73, 74, 78
  glossators 10, 63–64, 65–66, 67–68, 71–83
  of adultery 35, 46*n*109, 47, 51, 151
  on gifts between spouses 76
  on *hospitalitas* 548–550
  on suicide 399, 404–409, 421
  on witnesses 12–13, 21–58
  postglossators 65
  reception of 12*n*14, 480, 481, 483
  revival of 63, 66, 476
  See also conflict of laws; property; *res communes omnium*; *transactio*; Twelve Tables
Rothbury, Gilbert 337, 338, 339–342, 349–353, 362–366
Rouchetaillé, Jacques de 234
royal court
  See also Chancery; Common Bench; Exchequer; eyre; King's Bench
Russell, J. 465, 466
Rutledge, Andrew 464–465

Sabinians 120
Sachier, Isabel widow of Geoffrey le 185
Sailly, Charles de 268
Sailly, Louis Aymard de 262–263, 264, 268, 269–271, 272–273, 276–278
Saint-Clément, abbey of 16, 311–312, 314–327
Saint Paul Church, Harvard Square 4, 558–559
Saint-Pierre-aux-Arènes 317–318, 320, 321–322, 323–325, 327
Salamanca, School of 12, 141, 150, 154
Salic law 194
Sallust 52
Salonen, Kirsi 226, 227
Salutati, Coluccio 108*n*57, 109

sanctuary 174
San Giovannino, college of 419
Santa Dorotea
  See hospital
Sanuto, Marino 108
Saunders's *Reports* 457, 462
Savelli, Marc'Antonio 402–403
scandal 221, 222, 379, 381, 386–388, 389–390
Scattergood, Joseph 462
Schneider, Jean 312*n*5, 315*n*24, 317, 321*n*54, 327
Schnerb-Lièvre, Marion 371*n*3, 373, 388*n*56
seal 33, 37–42, 96, 238, 426, 428, 437–439, 517
Selden, John 11, 134
self-defense 33*n*57, 175, 178, 185
Seneca the Younger 40*n*88, 41
Sententiae Pauli 43
Servius 52
servus
  See slavery
settlement agreement
  See transactio
Sheppard's *Abridgment* 459
Siete Partidas 154
Sima Guang 295
Simmonds, N. E. 537–538
simony 149–150, 151
sin 168–173, 219, 221–223, 230, 297
  See also confession; consent; suicide
slavery
  enslaved persons 44–48, 257, 284, 295, 383, 463, 465
  fugitive 128–129
  in China 301–303
  in colonial America 455
Sleghe, Alicia and William le 180
Smith, William 165
Society of Jesus
  See Jesuit Order
Solórzano Pereira, Juan de 149
Sommer, Matthew 288*n*11, 294–295, 301*n*49
Somnium viridarii
  See Trémaugon, Evrart de
Songe du Vergier
  See Trémaugon, Evrart de
Songe du Viel Pelerin
  See Mézières, Philippe de
sorcery 381, 385, 388
Soto, Domingo de 150, 151
sovereignty
  See independence; natural law
Spain
  Barcelona 192–193, 196, 201, 202
  Coimbra 154
  Cuenca 141
  Salamanca 12, 141, 150, 154
Speculum Christiani 171, 173
Sperwe, Nicholas 177
Sprot, Christiana 179–180
Spurway, Robert 424, 425, 426, 427–428, 429, 431, 442
Standard Gloss
  See Accursius
Stanford Law School 524
Stanton, Hervey de 337, 338, 342–346, 354–357, 363–366
statutes 33*n*56, 66–67, 70, 73–74, 78, 79, 80–83, 84, 377, 382–383, 407–408
Statutes at Large 461
Staunton, Thomas 438–439
stipulatio 40–41, 45*n*106, 142, 145
Story, Joseph 482
Strauss, Richard 526
Sturm und Drang 505*n*15, 507
suicide and suicidality
  ancient Rome 401
  as crime 7, 395, 399, 403, 407–409
  as illness 398, 412–415, 416, 418
  as sin 7, 395, 397, 399, 401, 402, 406
  Electoral Saxony 396
  England 396, 402, 403
  France 402, 403
  Germany 402
  Italy 7, 394–395, 397, 402, 404, 407–408, 409–410
  Low Countries 402
  reasons for 400–401, 404–405
  Spain 397, 403
  See also insanity
Sumner, Charles 482
superstites 29–32
Sybille d'Aumelas 205

Taft, William 493–494
Tametsi 270
Taracia, Gaia 26*n*23, 56–57

Tarquinius, Sextus 401
Taxatio Ecclesiastica Angliae et Walliae 338–342, 347, 362
Tebbe, Henry 185
testamentary disposition 151, 200, 201, 205, 206, 207–210, 234
  partition 197, 206, 207–208
  primogeniture 207
  wills 35–40, 47, 50, 54–55, 194*n*4, 210, 226
  See also intestacy
testis
  See witnesses
theft 33–34, 120–122, 124, 127, 132, 179–181, 182, 183–184, 185
  burglary 182, 184, 185
  larceny 182
  robbery 181
  See also furtum
Theodosian Code 194, 548
Theodosius I 69
Theoger, bishop 314*n*12, 315
theologian 12, 140–142, 145*n*19, 153, 155, 164, 168–169, 245, 370, 387
Thérines, Jacques de 370*n*2, 372*n*7, 387
Thibaut IV of Champagne and Navarre 234–235
Thibaut V 235
Thirneby, Peter of 176
Thorne, Samuel E. 64, 85
Thorntoft, William de 336
Thrupp, Sylvia 547
Tiburge d'Aumelas 205
Tiburge d'Orange 205
Tiburgette, daughter of Tiburge d'Orange 205
Tomlins, Christopher 451
torture 45, 46*n*109, 47, 399*n*18, 406, 504, 506
Tothill's *Reports* 457
Tournon, Charles-Thomas Maillard de 287
tractatus 68, 143*n*10, 155, 437*n*24, 520*n*96
  See also books, law
Tractatus Universi Iuris 552
Trajan 46
transactio 12, 140–156
  and benefices 149–150
  and crime 151–152
  and inheritance 151
  and marriage 150–151
  nuda 142, 145
translatio 311, 323*n*69, 325–328
treatise
  See books, law
Treaty of Turin 106
Trebizond, George of 110
Trémaugon, Evrart de 15, 371, 374, 377–378, 380–382, 384, 388
  Somnium viridarii 15, 371–374, 377–378, 380–382
  Songe du Vergier 15, 371–374, 382–385
Trent, Council of 167*n*39, 268, 270*n*43, 273*n*64
trespass 116
Twelve Tables
  on false testimony 23*n*10
  on *fraus* 23
  on theft 33, 34
  on witnessing 13, 21, 24, 25*n*17, 27, 28, 29, 30, 34–35, 36, 52–53, 56, 57
Tyrrhenian Sea 106

Ubaldis, Angelus de 105–106
Ubaldis, Baldus de
  See Baldus de Ubaldis
Ulpian 71*n*33, 93*n*14
  De furtis 121
  on natural law 88*n*3
  on property 123–128, 131–133, 136
  on torture 45
  on treatment of slaves 44*n*103
  on witnessing 33*n*53, 35, 36–37, 38*n*78, 39, 40*n*87, 43*n*100, 44, 45–47, 48, 49, 50–51, 54, 55, 56
  on written evidence 41*n*92
ultramontani 64–66
United States 475–478, 481, 484, 487, 488–494
  Reconstruction 476, 488
  Supreme Court 488
  See also Puerto Rico
usury 70, 364, 372, 373, 377–378, 380, 381, 383, 384, 385, 386, 388, 389–390

Varro 125
Velleian decree 203, 206
Venice 10, 87, 89, 90, 94–102, 103–106, 107–110, 111–112
  topography of 97, 101, 102*n*42, 106
Venuleius 21, 36*n*65, 49
Vesiani, Peter 210
Vinday, Nicholas 231

Viner's *General Abridgement of Law and Equity* 459–460, 461, 462
Visigothic law 193, 194, 198, 199, 200, 201, 202, 203, 204, 206, 207, 208, 210
See also Leges Visigothorum; *Lex Romana Visigothorum*
Vita Clementis
See Clement, saint
vocation 9, 243, 244, 245*n*11, 246, 248–249, 253–259
voluntas 120*n*10, 169, 175

Walpole, Horace 443
war 107, 225, 302, 482*n*29
of Chioggia 106
Punic 529
Roman civil 401
Third Genoese 106
World War I 436
World War II 549
See also American Revolution; English Civil War; Hundred Years War
Warenne, John de 434
"Washfield Saga" 436
See also Worth, Thomas
Watson, Alan 29*n*36, 30*n*38, 31–32, 37*n*71, 38*n*74, 45*n*107, 46, 121*n*15
Weber, Max 9, 242, 243–246, 252, 255–256, 258–259
Wells, Robert 464–465
Wenard, John 424–426, 428–429, 431, 440–441
Wesenbeck, Matthew 143, 144*n*12, 151*n*45, 154
Wickham, Elizabeth 403–404
Wigg, Edward 455
will
See testamentary disposition; *voluntas*
William I, king of England 434
Wilmot's *Reports* 457
Wilne, John and Margaret 438, 441
witnesses 12–13, 21–58
and adultery 35, 47, 51
and criminality 51–52
and deafness 49
and family relations 49–50, 55–56
and mental illness 49
and muteness 49
heirs as 50–51
humiliores 47
improbus 28, 52
instrumental 24, 26–28, 33, 41, 44–45, 47–48, 50, 51–52
intestabilis 28, 52–57
judicial 24–25, 26–28, 33, 35, 41, 44–45, 47, 48, 50, 51–52, 57
Junian Latins 47*n*114, 55
minors as 48–49
to marriage 167, 270, 271, 278
women as 26*n*23, 47–48, 51, 55, 56–57
wives
and administrative responsibilities 197, 202–204, 207, 209
and crime 6, 161–162, 179–186
quartary 299
quintary 299
secondary 288, 299, 301
selling of 301
senary 300
tertiary 299
See also concubines; marital household; marital property; marriage; women
women
and crime 161–162, 177, 178–179
as guardians 197, 205, 206, 207, 208, 209
as widows 197, 199, 201, 203, 204, 205, 206, 207, 208, 209, 293, 297–298
See also nuns; wives
Wood's Institutes 455, 458, 459, 465
Woolchurch Haw, Henry of 177
Worrall, John 460
Worth, Charles 443–444
Worthe, Richard de la 429
Worth III, John 443–444
Worth II, Thomas 428, 429, 440–442
Worth, Isabella 425–426
Worth, Thomas 424–426, 427, 429, 431, 434, 435, 436
Wroxham, Adam of 182
Wulward, Roger of 176
Wycliffe, John 166, 247
Wydewesone, William and Alice 185

Yao, emperor 299
Yale Law School 2, 524
York consistory courts 224

Ziani, Sebastiano 96
Ziegler, Caspar 130–131
Zurich 247

www.ingramcontent.com/pod-product-compliance
Lightning Source LLC
LaVergne TN
LVHW010657300926
849161LV00005B/1157